Shakespeare's Legal Language

STUDENT SHAKESPEARE LIBRARY

Series Editor

Sandra Clark (Birkbeck College, University of London)

Shakespeare's Legal Language	B. J. Sokol & Mary Sokol
Military Language in Shakespeare	Charles Edelman
Shakespeare's Theatre	Hugh Richmond
Literature in Shakespeare	Stuart Gillespie

STUDENT SHAKESPEARE LIBRARY

Shakespeare's Legal Language

A Dictionary

B. J. SOKOL & MARY SOKOL

continuum
LONDON • NEW YORK

Continuum
The Tower Building   15 East 26th Street
11 York Road   Suite 1703
London SE1 7NX   New York 10010

First published in 2000 by
THE ATHLONE PRESS

This edition 2004

British Library Cataloguing in Publication Data
*A catalogue record for this book is available
from the British Library*
ISBN 0 8264 7778 X

Library of Congress Cataloging in Publication Data
Sokol, B. J.
    Shakespeare's legal language / B.J. Sokol & Mary Sokol.
      p. cm. — (Athlone Shakespeare dictionary series)
    Includes bibliographical references (p.   ) and index.
    ISBN 0–485–11549–2 (cloth : alk. paper)
      1. Shakespeare, William, 1564–1616—Knowledge—Law—Dictionaries. 2. English
language—Early modern, 1500–1700—Dictionaries. 3. Law—England—History—16th
century—Dictionaries. 4. Law—England—History—17th century—Dictionaries. 5. Law in
literature—Dictionaries. I. Sokol, Mary, 1945– II. Title, III. Series.
PR3028 .S65 2000
822.3'3—dc21
                                                                        99–043014

Distributed in The United States, Canada and South America by
Transaction Publishers
390 Campus Drive
Somerset, New Jersey 08873

Previously published in hardback in the
Athlone Shakespeare Dictionary series

Typeset by RefineCatch Limited, Bungay, Suffolk
Printed and bound in Great Britain by
Antony Rowe Ltd, Chippenham, Wiltshire

for Mark, Kate and Anna

Contents

Series Editor's Preface

The Athlone Shakespeare Dictionaries aim to provide the student of Shakespeare with a series of authoritative guides to the principal subject-areas covered by the plays and poems. They are produced by scholars who are experts both on Shakespeare and on the topic of the individual dictionary, based on the most recent scholarship, succinctly written and accessibly presented. They offer readers a self-contained body of information on the topic under discussion, its occurrence and significance in Shakepeare's works, and its contemporary meanings.

The topics are all vital ones for understanding the plays and poems; they have been selected for their importance in illuminating aspects of Shakespeare's writings where an informed understanding of the range of Shakespeare's usage, and of the contemporary literary, historical and cultural issues involved, will add to the reader's appreciation of his work. Because of the diversity of the topics covered in the series, individual dictionaries may vary in emphasis and approach, but the aim and basic format of the entries remain the same from volume to volume.

Sandra Clark
Birkbeck College
University of London

Acknowledgements

We thank the Universities and schools that have supported us in this project with grants of leave: the School for Legal Studies at the University of Sussex, and Goldsmiths College University of London and its English Department. We have received help, kindness and invaluable assistance from many individuals. We wish to thank in particular Ann Aldrich, Connor Carville, Steve Clews, James Harner, David Ibbetson, Andrew Lewis, Dr C. M. Rider of the Inner Temple, the staff of the British Library and its Lending Division, the Institute of Advanced Legal Studies, the Institute of Historical Research, Harvard University Law School Library, The Senate House Library of The University of London, The Shakespeare Institute Library, The University of Sussex Library. Any errors are ours alone.

Abbreviations

1H4	1 Henry IV
1H6	1 Henry VI
2H4	2 Henry IV
ADO	Much Ado About Nothing
AIT	All Is True (Henry VIII)
ANT	Antony and Cleopatra
AWW	All's Well That Ends Well
AYL	As You Like It
COR	Coriolanus
CYL	The First Part of the Contention (2 Henry VI)
CYM	Cymbeline
ERR	The Comedy of Errors
H5	Henry V
HAM	Hamlet
JC	Julius Caesar
JN	King John
LC	'A Lover's Complaint'
LLL	Love's Labour's Lost
LRF	The Tragedy of King Lear (Folio)
LRQ	The History of King Lear (Quarto)
LUC	The Rape of Lucrece
MAC	Macbeth
MM	Measure for Measure
MND	Midsummer Night's Dream
MV	The Merchant of Venice
OTH	Othello
PER	Pericles, Prince of Tyre
R2	Richard II
R3	Richard III
RDY	Richard, Duke of York (3 Henry VI)
ROM	Romeo and Juliet
SHR	The Taming of the Shrew

SON	Sonnets
STM	Sir Thomas More
TGV	The Two Gentlemen of Verona
TIM	Timon of Athens
TIT	Titus Andronicus
TMP	The Tempest
TN	Twelfth Night, or What You Will
TNK	Two Noble Kinsmen
TRO	Troilus and Cressida
VEN	Venus and Adonis
WIV	The Merry Wives of Windsor
WT	The Winter's Tale

B & M   J. H. Baker and S. F. C. Milsom, *Sources of English Legal History: Private Law to 1750*, (London, 1986) (Baker & Milsom, 1986)

Introduction

The law is much more than a collection of technical terms or phrases, and Shakespeare's familiarity with these terms does not suggest that he was limited by them in his dramatic treatment of legal issues. Nevertheless, of the thirty-seven Shakespeare plays considered in this Dictionary, thirty-five contain the word 'judge', and thirty-five the word 'justice'. *The Tempest* is one of the plays lacking the word 'judge', but it twice contains a metaphor of a 'trial', and indeed has judgement and pardon at its core. It also treats directly and indirectly legally vexed issues of 'plantation', slavery and servitude. Reference to a trial appears one or more times in twenty-five of Shakespeare's plays, and many contain or describe trial scenes. The sole Shakespearian playtext that contains neither the words 'judge' nor 'trial' is *The Taming of the Shrew* (other than the dramatic fragment *Sir Thomas More*, which concerns the early career of a great Lord Chancellor). But *The Taming of the Shrew* has marriage and marriage settlements at its core; in fact terms related to the legalities of marriage constitute the largest thematic cluster in this Dictionary.

Thus on bare statistics it is possible to argue that Shakespeare was law-obsessed. But in this he was not unique; other contemporary dramatists used proportionately even more law-terminology than he did, and some among of them were indeed trained as lawyers (see Clarkson and Warren, 1942, pp 285–6). Such a statistical effort attaches to a school of commentators bent on denying nineteenth century speculations made most famously in Campbell, J., 1859 that Shakespeare was formerly a lawyer or law clerk. We are not concerned with questions of Shakespeare's biography; yet, authorial history aside, matters of social history cannot be ignored in discussions of either theatre or law.

Shakespeare and the Lawyers
The language of the law was common currency in Shakespeare's litigious age for several reasons. As J. H. Baker has pointed out, it is

1

anachronistic to assume that only lawyers were learned in the law (Baker, 1985). Elizabethan landowners were well versed in land law, merchants were concerned with enforcing debt, and in the absence of legislated forms private legal arrangements were needed by many to agree marriage portions, to draft wills, or to convey land.

Also, there appear to have been special links between Elizabethan drama and the contemporary culture of the law; London audiences probably included lawyers and students from the Inns of Court, and plays were performed at the Inns. Perhaps accordingly, some of Shakespeare's most common themes confronted the same political and philosophical issues that are also reflected in the conflicts and exuberant inventiveness which characterise the great developments in the common law in Shakespeare's time. For instance, the degree to which the state should control personal conduct or beliefs, or the justifiable extent of community or parental influence over marriage choices, fascinated Shakespeare and vexed lawmakers and litigants.

More prosaically, Keeton, 1967, p 41, suggests that inspiration gained in tavern meetings between lawyers and laymen may have supplemented visits to Westminster Hall's (very) public law courts as a source of playwrights' legal terminology. He cites Dekker's 1609 *Gull's Handbook* on lawyers' gregarious chatter:

> if they chance to discourse, it is of nothing but of statutes, bonds, recognizance, fines, recoveries, audits, rents . . . of such horrible matter.

Here we have a fair sample of precisely the terms of law used by Shakespeare.

Shakespeare's use of legal language was not always very serious, and certainly not always straightforward. He frequently employed legal ideas and terminology metaphorically or in symbolic contexts, especially in his lyric or narrative poems. For instance in *The Rape of Lucrece* the rule that allowed judges summary jurisdiction over offences that were actually committed in court (despite Magna Carta) informs a complex metaphor. Having been herself blamed for inspiring the lust of her rapist, Lucrece laments:

> My bloody judge forbade my tongue to speak;
> No rightful plea might plead for justice there.

His scarlet lust came evidence to swear
That my poor beauty had purloined his eyes;
And when the judge is robbed, the prisoner dies.
(LUC 1648–52)

To understand this fully we have to note also that robbery was a capital felony, that defendants could not offer sworn evidence but the prosecution could, that assize judges wore scarlet. All of these points are covered in our glossary.

Because of his complex usages, sheer legal word-spotting is not a wholly reliable indication that Shakespeare took a precise or detailed account of substantive English law. Yet, the overall impression given by this Dictionary may well contradict frequently reiterated claims that Shakespeare's interest in law was at best superficial, and that Shakespeare exploited legal ideas, circumstances, and language with no regard for any factor aside from 'poetic' effect. It is our view, derived from cumulative evidence, that on the contrary Shakespeare shows a quite precise and mainly serious interest in the capacity of legal language to convey matters of social, moral, and intellectual substance.

Sources of Legal History

The law implied in most of Shakespeare's plays, even those with classical, fantastical, or continental settings, is the English law of his time, most often derived from common law, and sometimes from canon law. This was the law familiar to him and to his audiences, and its assumptions were integral to their outlook. The history of English law is therefore a valuable resource for understanding Shakespeare.

The history of law can be a history of the development of legal doctrines (for example the unity of persons in marriage), or of institutions (the system of courts), or of procedures (the system of writs and bills). Therefore, law can seem to have its own independent history which need take little note of any wider context. However our aim has not been to look at either law or literature in isolation, but to place both in historical and cultural contexts. Interdisciplinary work requires some awareness of both the differing norms of relevance and the inter-relatedness of distinct fields. With this caveat, some understanding of legal institutions and doctrines may illuminate early modern social, political and literary history, and vice versa.

Knowledge of 'black-letter' law (statutes, law reports), will not reveal

3

whether that law was accepted or met with opposition, whether it was vigorously applied or a dead letter, or what social purpose it may have served. But it can be equally misleading to write about substantive law without some understanding of its structure and aims. An example important to medieval and early modern England would be the way in which structures constituting land law provided the framework for relations between people and between the state and an individual. Literalism may also lead to the pitfalls of overlooking the use made of legal fictions and formulae (e.g. see under **battery** on the formulaic wording of writs for trespass against the person).

For the purposes of our historical investigations we take the common law in early modern England to include enacted law (legislation), judicial law, and customary law. English common law tradition held that the authoritative source of law was found in the common learning of judges and lawyers of the royal courts, but if we seek it in texts we find that these were various, and formed no fixed hierarchy. One form of documentary source is the legal treatise. The treatises mentioned in this Dictionary, from Glanvill in the late twelfth century, Bracton and Britton in the thirteenth century, Littleton in the fifteenth century, St German in the sixteenth century, to Swinburne and Lambard in the seventeenth century, provide evidence of accepted legal opinion and practice at the time written, but subject to certain qualifications. They did not provide a summation or ordered view of contemporary English law, but might consist of collections of miscellaneous writs, or even descriptions of theory or practice which is not wholly English, like Swinburne's work. Although not authoritative, legal learning is evidenced also in the moots and teaching exercises of the Inns of Court.

Another form of documentary source is statute law. Early modern England saw the transition from medieval legislation as the royal response to petitions and complaints to an increasing tide of Tudor parliamentary legislation. In addition to statutes, customary law (which may be discovered in the records of local borough and manor courts) remained important despite the extended role of royal justice.

Lastly, the arguments and opinions of judges and lawyers given in cases were collected into anonymous manuscript Year Books from about the mid thirteenth century, written in Anglo-French. Many were abridged and printed in the sixteenth century. After the printed Year Books came to an end in 1535, and before the later sixteenth century when the first of the named Reports appeared in print, there was a lack of contemporary printed law reports. Between 1600 and 1648 only the reports of Coke and Hobart were printed (Bryson, 1995, p 114; these were collected together with some others in the English Reports in the early twentieth century). Coke's Reports although sometimes faulty, remain authoritative because of Coke's personal standing. The paucity of Reports, together with the limitations of the treatises, has led legal historians to describe Shakespeare's age as one of crisis in legal literature (Ibbetson, 1995, p 73; Bryson, 1995).

The investigation of early modern English law, not to mention its social setting, is of course incomplete, contains controversies, and no doubt will offer surprises as it is being actively pursued. In the early 1970s John Baker called Shakespeare's age the 'dark age of English legal history' (Baker, 1986c); the great English legal historian, Maitland, had concentrated his investigations on medieval law. But a great deal has since been done (much by Baker himself) to illuminate the darkness. Continuing work on law reports (Baker, 1978, Bryson, 1995), and on ecclesiastical courts (Helmholz, 1990 and many others), for instance, enlarges knowledge.

Organization and Structure of the Dictionary
This Dictionary or Encyclopaedia-style book is arranged alphabetically by terms, an arrangement which may be most convenient for seekers both after ideas and textual explication. The terms glossed are those actually found in Shakespeare's texts. We found that glossing this range of terms, using cross referencing, in effect produced an outline of English law and its institutions in Shakespeare's age: the courts; law officers; the laws of property, inheritance, marriage and status; contract and debt, crime, misdemeanour, and regulation of morals.

Extensive cross-referencing of legal terms, using **bold** type, is used to display the clusterings and inter-relatedness of many legal issues and ideas. To avoid repetition, sometimes there will be 'main' discussions of legal concepts that apply in common to groups of legal terms. For instance, as noted above, issues concerning the valid creation of a marriage were very important for Shakespeare; these matters are discussed at length under **pre-contract**. There are cross references back to this main discussion from a number of other entries concerning the law of marriage, for instance, **impediments**. These related entries are arranged so that each is self-sufficient, yet each can be more fully explored by means of backward tracing through cross references to the discussion of marriage formation under **pre-contract**.

Another sort of cross connection arises because one Shakespearian passage can contain a number of diverse legal terms. We treat the conceptual and historical aspects of each legal term in separate entries, but the single Shakespeare passage in which they all arise will have only one main discussion. That discussion will appear under the alphabetical entry that seems to us best suited to it, although briefer discussions of the passage may appear elsewhere. For instance in treating Hamlet's mention of 'recognizances' we will direct the reader to 'see under **fine and recovery**' for the main discussion of the context in the play.

The alphabetical entries are of three types. Most are long entries in three sections, the first on law and legal history, the second on Shakespearian contexts, and the third a bibliography. According to circumstance, the bibliographies may be more or less extended and descriptive, or greatly truncated by uses of cross-referencing to other entries' bibliographies. A second briefer type of entry is presented in a single section; in these most of the relevant material is usually indicated by cross-referencing. The third type of entry contains only, or nearly only, a cross reference. Its purpose is to alphabetise small differences in spelling or usage (such as with **prentice** and **apprentice**) or to tie alphabetically non-adjacent entries into composite entries, such as in the entry under **clemency** which contains merely 'See **pardon/clemency**'.

(Deliberate and Regretted) Omissions

We apologise if we have unintentionally overlooked work on Shakespeare's legal language or on early modern law, and can only hope that these omissions are not too extensive. Where we follow our own perceptions, we apologise if similar insights are published in places that we have not traced.

Some of the material we did trace has not been cited; in particular we have not noted discussions focused mainly on Shakespearian biography or the authorship question. There is a long tradition of lawyers' interests in Shakespeare, some of it profound; one aspect of this culminated in a 1988 mock trial on the Shakespearian authorship question argued by eminent counsel before three American Supreme Court justices (see Armstrong, 1991). Citations of some lay work on literature by lawyers which is insensitive to literary content, or vice versa, seemed best omitted.

Not all instances of Shakespeare's legal language are glossed, because of the impracticality where there are excessively many instances. Also not all possible terms are glossed. For example, the word 'process' lacks an entry because in the few places where its use suggests a legal process (as in ANT 1.1.30, and WT 2.2.63, 4.3.94–5) it carries only a well-known meaning. Yet a single usage possibly obliquely suggestive of a legal 'process' may once convey a peculiar force. This is Othello's 'Such was my process' (*Othello* 1.3.141), which may insinuate a complaint that he in effect stood trial (for being an exotic) at Brabantio's house preliminary to being tried on Brabantio's charges before the Venetian Senate, for erotic witchcraft. This oblique possibility, suggested by Cheadle, 1994, is discussed under **witchcraft**.

The extensive legal language used in Shakespeare's poems is only occasionally, and briefly, discussed. This is largely because, in the contexts of the poems, legal language is most often used in a highly figurative manner. Most if not absolutely all of this language is discussed at length and illustrated with instances chosen from the plays.

Legal maxims and legally inclined set phrases echoed by Shakespeare are infrequently mentioned. These are perhaps too inventively searched out in works such as Rushton, 1869, 1907, as is complained of in Barton, S. D. P., 1929, pp 121–7.

Shakespeare's reflections of the mainly international laws of warfare are well treated in works such as: Ranald, 1987; Rauchut, 1991, 1994; Meron, 1992, 1993; Spencer, 1996. The laws of war are not discussed here except passingly; they would otherwise complicate an already bewildering array of English jurisdictions. Similarly the purported *jus gentium* of international law merchant is only touched upon; this is discussed (sceptically) in Baker, 1986f, and in Sokol, 1992.

Highly politicized issues of the age, such as of the royal prerogative, were treated by Shakespeare with extreme circumspection. As a result, and also because these matters have been extensively treated in political histories, they will be met here only obliquely, as can be seen under **chief justice**, **civil doctor**, **equity**, **jurisdiction**, **letters patents**, and even **audit/account**. For interest, an excellent article on the mysteries of prerogative in Shakespeare's time and just after is Morgan, 1984.

The Shakespeare Texts

For the Shakespeare canon and for texts of plays and poems we have used the electronic version of the modernised Oxford Shakespeare edition, Wells and Taylor, 1989. We have modified this only in the substitution of familiar spellings for certain characters' names. From the electronic edition of this text we take also title abbreviations, and lineation. An exception is made where we specify First Folio texts; then the cited through-line-numbers (tln) derive from Hinman, 1968. Following the practice of the Oxford Shakespeare, we have not included *Edward III*, but we have referred to the dramatic fragment Sir Thomas More, the content of which is, of course, highly relevant to the subject-matter of our dictionary.

The Oxford Shakespeare electronic edition also sometimes supplies textual variants bearing strange looking line and scene numbers (such as HAM A.P. 3). Where such lines are cited their origins and positions in the texts are noted, and where appropriate the Hinmon Folio tln as well.

We append a table of the Oxford Electronic Shakespeare edition title abbreviations. A few of these do need explanation. The Oxford electronic edition's CYL stands for *The First Part of the Contention of the Two Famous Houses of York and Lancaster*, which derives from the title of the 1594 quarto of the play called in the First Folio *The second Part of Henry the Sixt*. RDY stands for *The True Tragedy of Richard Duke of York and the Good King Henry the Sixth*, and this derives from the title of the quarto (c. 1594) of the play called in the First Folio *The third Part of Henry the Sixt*. AIT stands for *All Is True*, which is a possible earlier title of the play that is called in the First Folio *The Famous History of the Life of King Henry the Eight*.

To be consistent with the Oxford electronic edition, we use CYL throughout (and never 2H6), RDY (and never 3H6), and AIT (and never H8). We have retained and use the separate Oxford text abbreviations (and texts) LRF and LRQ: these are the 1623 First Folio and 1608 Quarto texts respectively of *King Lear*. Where we need to refer to this play in general we will diverge from our use of Oxford abbreviations, and write *King Lear*.

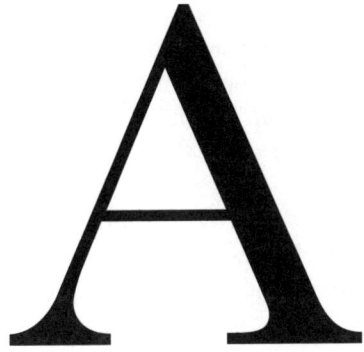

A

account See **audit/account**.

appeal (A) The term 'appeal', when used in legal contexts in early modern England, usually had a meaning quite different from its meaning today.

In Shakespearian contexts an 'appeal' could be a call for aid or relief; heaven, kings or heads of state were appealed to by the condemned for mercy or **pardon**, as in H5 2.2.75, or MM 1.2.162. But in Shakespeare's England there was no system of appellate courts nor of legal review of cases. The higher courts at Westminster, by issuing writs or prohibitions, were able to correct only technical errors in the indictments or procedures of lower courts. (However it is possible that higher courts may have searched with zeal to find such technical faults in some individual cases which particularly merited mitigation; on traces of this practice see under **pardon**.)

An early medieval exception was an appeal from the judgment of an English Church court to the Papal courts in Rome. But long before Shakespeare's time making such an appeal was prohibited by statutes against **praemunire** and was severely punished by forfeiture of land and goods.

In Shakespeare's England, in legal uses, an 'appeal' was not usually a call for an appellate review, but instead commonly referred to the now unfamiliar 'appeal of felony', which was a form of private criminal prosecution brought by the victim of a crime or their next of kin. The appeal of felony was one of the two ways in which wrongdoers could be brought to justice, the other being indictment by a 'presenting' (pre-trial) **jury**. So by Shakespeare's time accusations of wrongdoing were brought either by the community through the jury of presentment, or by appeal.

Baker, 1986b, p 262, says that although in 1550 prosecution by appeal was common, it was nearly non-existent by 1660. Baker also notes a particular instance of judicial hostility to an appeal in 1610. The appeal is said to have declined because of the success of the indictment system, the unpopularity of trial by battle as a method of proof on appeal, and the heavy fines and imprisonment imposed on unsuccessful appellors (see Holdsworth, 1903, vol 2, pp 256–7, 360–5). However Whittick, 1984, p 57 argues that the decline was temporary and that prosecution by indictment and appeal were not in competition but rather complimented each other, while Ernst, 1984, p 168 claims that private prosecutions continued to play a part in the criminal process throughout the sixteenth and seventeenth centuries.

By Shakespeare's time only serious criminal accusations could be made by appeal, in appeals of **felony** for treason, homicide, rape, assault, theft, false imprisonment and arson among others. The appel-lor would either make an oral complaint in the County Court, or after the fifteenth century could alternately issue a writ in the king's courts at Westminster. If the litigant lived outside London the case would almost certainly be heard locally at trial by *nisi prius* (see under **lawyers**), when the King's justices visited on assize. Trial could could be by petty **jury**, or alternatively the appellee (the defendant) could demand trial by judicial combat, to wage battle (see **lists**). In the middle ages most battles actually fought were following appeals of **treason**, but few appeals did end in judicial combat, and almost certainly none did in Tudor times (Baker, 1978, p 116). If an appellor was successful, the appellee was treated as a convicted **felon**, so he was punished with execution or **outlawry** and all his personal property was forfeit.

Judicial dislike for the appeal is indicated by the early modern restric-tion of judicial combat to appeals of **homicide** where no other evidence existed apart from the appellor's accusation. Also, a 'presumption of malice' automatically applied in every appeal of **felony**. Every appellor was presumed to have malicious intent and as a result defendants were allowed legal counsel after 1488 in appeals of death (where the accusation was for a capital crime). The court indeed offered all assistance to defendants in notorious cases of malice, but evidence also exists of judicial sympathy and assistance to the appellor (for example see Whittick, 1984, pp 58–9, where both appellors cited were women).

In law, a woman was allowed to bring an appeal for **rape**, or for the **murder** of her husband, and sometimes was allowed by the **justices** to bring appeals for the killing of a son or brother, or even for **robbery**. Here possibly the ancient belief that it was the duty of the victim or their family to pursue the wrongdoer was still relevant. Women were not allowed to fight in judicial combat but in any event their appeals were usually non-suited (abandoned before that stage) probably because most of these were cases which were settled after financial compensation necessary for her support was paid to a **widow**, following arbitration. To bring an appeal of murder was an accepted, popular and effective method of obtaining compensation. Publicity was given to the wrong, and the appellee was attached (arrested) which caused discomfort and notoriety. Also the appeal process was more flexible than indictment (for instance it was not necessary to distinguish between the principal and accessory to a homicide). Appeals of murder could also be used by next of kin when presentment juries failed to indict. **Pardon** was not available to convicted appellees.

The continuing numbers of appeals that were brought for **theft** underlines the importance of the appeal process to obtaining restitution and compensation from the offender. Although from 1529 compensation was allowed on conviction for theft following indictment, an appeal still remained popular because whereas indictment must be brought in the place where the goods had been lost, appeal could be brought anywhere at all, which allowed the appellee to be more effectively pursued.

An appeal could also be brought by a confessed **felon** who would receive partial immunity for his own crimes upon the conviction of others against whom he had informed (this practice and its possible Shakespearian echoes is discussed under **approve**). Briefly, a successful appeal could be the means for an 'approver' to obtain the conviction or convictions need for his own salvation from hanging; most cases of criminal trial by battle (see **lists**) were between an approver and his accused, and some approvers appealed large numbers of people.

(B) Refusing to accept Cardinal Wolsey for her judge, Henry VIII's Queen Katherine wishes to 'appeal unto the Pope, / To bring my whole cause 'fore his holiness, / And to be judged by him' (AIT 2.4.117–19). She leaves the court, and Cardinal Campeius hopes she may be induced to 'call back her appeal / She intends unto his holiness' (2.4.231–2). In the light of this perhaps unique Shakespearian mention of a legal appeal in our modern sense, King Henry thinks of a radical alternative to 'This dilatory sloth and tricks of Rome' (2.4.234), and begins the English Reformation.

An 'appeal' as an accusation is much more often mentioned by Shakespeare. In MM 5.1.298 Isabella's charges against Angelo are called her 'manifest appeal'. She is not addressing an official 'higher' court of appeal, and of course does not seek trial by battle.

In ANT 3.5.10 we are told that Lepidus has been seized by Caesar 'upon his own appeal', meaning accusation. Posthumus's dream vision provides a context in which his brothers' phrase 'we appeal' is replied to by Jupiter's 'How dare you ghosts / Accuse the thunderer' (CYM 5.5.185 and 188–9).

Mentions of an 'appeal' connect with repeated challenges to trial by combat on charges of high **treason** in R2 1.1.4, 1.1.9, 1.1.27, 1.1.142, 1.3.21, 4.1.44, and 4.1.70. The first inquiry made by King Richard following his mention of Bolingbroke's 'boist'rous late appeal' (1.1.4) against Mowbray is 'If he appeal the Duke on ancient malice / Or worthily, as a good subject should, / On some known ground of treachery in him?' (1.1.9–11), which reflects the presumption of malice in appeals mentioned above. During the dissension leading to Richard II's deposition later in R2, several appeals of felony calling for trials by battle are also heard. For instance, immediately after Norfolk's claim 'Aumerle is guilty of my true appeal' Aumerle says 'Some honest Christian trust me with a gage', and throws it down (R2 4.1.70 and 4.1.74).

(C) See **lists** on trials by battle in Shakespeare following appeals of treason. See: Bellamy, 1973, pp 125–34; Whittick, 1984; Ernst, 1984; Russell, 1980b; Baker, 1986b, Baker, 1990b, pp 574–6. On the actual problems of frequent appeals of treason in the times of Richard II and Henry IV see Bellamy, 1970, pp 115–16 and 143–6.

apprenticehood On laws applicable to apprenticehood see under Shakespeare's ususal spelling of apprentice, **prentice**. 'Apprentice' appears in a passage included only in the quarto of R2, positioned following folio 1.3.256:

> Must I not serve a long apprenticehood
> To foreign passages, and in the end,
> Having my freedom, boast of nothing else
> But that I was a journeyman to grief?
> (R2 A.C.4–7)

The stages of training from 'apprenticehood' to gaining the 'freedom' of a 'journeyman' of a trade are named by the socially proud Bolingbroke perhaps to indicate to his father that he feels he has been degraded by his **exile**.

approve (A) An approver was someone indicted for a crime but not yet convicted who, in return for life or liberty, confessed his own wrong and accused others, often his own accomplices, by an **appeal** of felony. In an age without any professional public police force (see **constables**), approvers or informers were used and encouraged by the government and sometimes paid a sum of money during their imprisonment. However to escape the gallows an approver's allegations had to be proved true by conviction of the accused before a jury, or by judicial combat (see **lists**). If he was successful the approver was spared his life in return for imprisonment or abjuring the realm (see **sanctuary**). Some approvers were **pardoned** by the King. But if he failed he was executed.

(B) In many Shakespearian contexts 'to approve' means to give or have proof ('approved' often bears the intensified sense of well-proven). To 'approve' may also mean to put to the test of experience (OED II), or else to to commend something (to state a good opinion of or hold a high estimation of it). But in several places the legal meaning in which an 'approver' is one who informs upon and accuses others (OED approver 1), and therefore expresses (what might be seen as moral) disapproval of them, may also have bearing.

OTH contains a great many instances of 'approve' or its derivatives applied in one or other of its non-legal senses. But when Othello angrily encounters Cassio and others in a drunken fight, he asks for an informer to reveal the original culprit, and offers a degree of immunity to him:

> Give me to know
> How this foul rout began, who set it on,
> And he that is approved in this offence,
> Though he had twinned with me, both at a birth,
> Shall lose me. What, in a town of war
> Yet wild, the people's hearts brimful of fear,
> To manage private and domestic quarrel
> In night, and on the court and guard of safety!
> 'Tis monstrous.
>
> (OTH 2.3.202–10)

He then, fatally, asks 'Iago, who began 't?', and Cassio is the one informed upon, or 'approved'. Although Iago has other motives than to save his own neck, his testimony is, as in the case of an 'approver', self-serving, and is, as in some such cases, malicious.

In a possibly even more exact application, an approver accuses another and proceeds to trial by battle when Thomas Mobray enters the **lists** to do battle with Bolingbroke. Mowbray does this, as the herald says, 'Both to defend himself and to approve / Henry of Hereford, Lancaster, and Derby / To God his sovereign and to him disloyal' (R2 1.3.112–14). This trial by battle may therefore be seen as both Mobray's defence against an **'appeal'** of **treason** made against him by Bolingbroke (1.1.4), and as a trial of Bolingbroke on an appeal made by Mowbray as an approver (1.1.27). Neither combatant has confessed to treason, so the full legal sense of an 'approver' does not exactly apply to Mowbray. However Mowbray does make a partial confession of a serious fault:

> For Gloucester's death,
> I slew him not, but to my own disgrace
> Neglected my sworn duty in that case.
> For you, my noble lord of Lancaster,
> The honourable father to my foe,
> Once did I lay an ambush for your life,
> A trespass that doth vex my grieved soul;
> But ere I last received the Sacrament

> I did confess it, and exactly begged
> Your grace's pardon, and I hope I had it.
> (1.1.132–41)

Therefore the word 'approve' in the herald's speech may suggest a meaning beyond simply 'to prove'.

The false accusations of high **treason** brought against Gloucester in CYL 3.1.95–123 bring in sequence his bitter attack on his accusers (142–71), their call for the protection of those who will bring accusations of treason (173–6), Gloucester's **murder**, and Henry VI's call, too late, that the Protector's enemies: 'Proceed no straiter 'gainst our uncle Gloucester / Than from true evidence, of good esteem, / He be approved in practice culpable' (CYL 3.2.20–2). A possible link here of 'approve' with approvers' tendencies to give false evidence is emphasised by Queen Margaret's following hypocritical words: 'God forbid any malice should prevail / That faultless may condemn a noble man! / Pray God he may acquit him of suspicion!' (23–5).

Similar contexts where 'approve' may carry connotations of 'accuse' occur at HAM A.N.27–8 (in a 34-line passage in Q2 replacing Folio HAM 5.2.107, in which addition Hamlet mocks Osric's high-flown verbiage), LRF 3.5.11, CYM 2.4.23–6, and in a possible paradox amidst forensic metaphors at TNK 1.3.64–6.

Perhaps the most intriguing possible allusion to the paradoxical legal meaning wherein an 'approver' was in fact a disapprover (in Freud's term 'approve' was thus a 'primal word') is in the famous initial approval of Macbeth's pleasant castle:

KING DUNCAN   This castle hath a pleasant seat. The air Nimbly and
                    sweetly recommends itself
                    Unto our gentle senses.
BANQUO   This guest of summer,
                    The temple-haunting martlet, does approve
                    By his loved mansionry that the heavens' breath
                    Smells wooingly here.
                                (MAC 1.6.1–6)

The paradox of the procreative martlet approving Macbeth's citadel, soon after headquarters for the murder of children, may obliquely reference the paradoxical legal use of the term 'approve' for condemn.

(C) See under **appeal**, Baker, 1990b, pp 574 and 579, and Bellamy, 1973, pp 125–34. Baker, 1986b, pp 290–1 explains that, although not abolished, approving was replaced in the seventeenth century by a mainly similar practice of 'turning king's evidence'.

attorneys (A) The lawyers known as attorneys-at-law are discussed under **lawyers**. An 'attorney' and the verb 'to attorney' are also used by Shakespeare to mean acting as an agent on another's behalf. The law of agency held that relations of agency existed between master and servant, or principal and agent in various situations. The common law provided remedies against agents in default in actions of account (see under **audit/account**), although the principles for vicarious liability were not settled until the end of the seventeenth century.

(B) The term 'attorney' referring to an attorney-at-law appears in jocular and/or disparaging Shakespearian contexts. Scoffing Lavatch says 'As fit as ten groats is for the hand of an attorney' (AWW 2.2.20). Grieving Queen Elizabeth requests 'scope' for words of calamity, although these are only 'Windy attorneys to their client woes' (R3 4.4.127).

An 'attorney' as an agent is mentioned for instance in 1H6 5.5.121–2, where the Earl of Suffolk remarks aside 'And yet methinks I could be well content/ To be mine own attorney in this case'. By this he means he would rather be wooing the desirable Margaret for himself rather than, for politic reasons, on Henry's behalf. Yet at 5.7.55–6 Suffolk says of the King's match with Margaret 'Marriage is a matter of more worth / Than to be dealt in by attorneyship', arguing it should not be a mercenary matter.

In R3 4.4.344 King Richard for politic reasons alone wishes to woo a princess by proxy, and so exhorts her mother Queen Elizabeth to 'Be the attorney of my love to her' (on such marriages see **pre-contract**, and on this context see **usury/interest**). Several other Shakespearian uses of 'attorney' as noun or verb similarly indicate a substitute or substitution, as in: ERR 5.1.101; AYL 4.1.88; MM 5.1.382; WT 1.1.27.

'Attorneys general' as used by Shakespeare in R2 2.1.204 (and 'attorneys' in R2 2.3.233) has the sense of an attorney acting under a general authority from his principal to act in all legal matters, rather than a special power of attorney limited to a specific matter (on these passages see **sue his livery**). The King's Attorney General, one of the government law officers, first appeared in the fifteenth century, and in 1613 Francis Bacon was appointed to the office by James 1. It was as Attorney General that Bacon in 1616 drew up the decree that brought an end to the dispute between Coke and Ellesmere. The Attorney General is not so named by Shakespeare but is probably the one referred to as 'The King's attorney' in AIT 2.1.16.

(C) Unsettled early modern legal aspects of the forms of agency, as reflected in drama, are discussed in Braunmuller, 1990. On the legal-historical background see Holdsworth, 1903, vol 3, pp 382–7; vol 8, pp 222–9, 472; Baker, 1990b, pp 414–5, Braunmuller, 1990 and under **audit**.

The use of 'attorney' in R3, and how knowledge creates a criminal accessory there, are discussed in terms of 'theatricality' in Day, 1991. See under **murder** for a discussion of criminal agency.

The illegality of Richard II's Parliamentary Committee denying to **exiled** Mowbray and Bolingbroke powers of attorney is treated in Gohn, 1982, pp 947–8n.

audit/account (A) Under the Statute of Westminster II, c.11 (1285) an audit would be required when actions on a writ of 'account' were taken against 'servants, bailiffs, chamberlains and all manner of receivers'. Auditors could be appointed by the parties privately, if they agreed. When medieval auditors found arrears, they had drastic powers to commit the accountant to prison without further trial. By the fifteenth century it was settled law that after an action of account the accountant who owed a debt could not claim *nihil debet* and wage his law (Thorne, 1985a, p 263; on wager of law see **debt**). The action of account was first used against bailiffs, but came to be used between business partners and joint traders, and against guardians and other agents.

An imprisoned accountant could seek review in the Court of Exchequer, but the very fact that the auditor could imprison him without any other court's action was used by Coke in an odd argument for the proposition that only 'courts of record' could imprison or fine. Coke's claim was that auditors were judges of record. On this basis he may have suggested in a reversed argument that prerogative courts without records, such as Requests, Chancery, High Commission, and **star chamber** lacked the power to imprison or fine. He did not go so far as this in his political battle against the Royal prerogative, but did apply his theory to support the restoration of the former judicature of parliament, which had been in abeyance since the fourteenth century and was revived just after Shakespeare's time (see Thorne, 1985a on Coke and courts of record).

Various actions for **debt**, especially for obligations under seal (see **recognizance**, **statutes**, **bonds**), and actions **on the case** (such as eventually for *indebitatus asumpsit* – see Baker, 1990b, pp 413–19) had stronger powers of compulsion, and had partly displaced actions of account by Shakespeare's time. By the mid seventeenth century efficient procedures for taking accounts that had developed in the Chancellor's **equity** Court completed the displacement of the old action of account.

The Church courts also required **executors** to produce an account of goods or lands in an estate. However these courts had little power to enforce compliance. The Chancery Court increasingly challenged the Church courts' continuing testamentary **jurisdiction** over 'probate, the grant of administration, the supervision, distribution, and recovery of legacies' (see **inheritance** and Jones, W. J., 1967, p 402). The great advantage of Chancery, according to ibid., pp 403–4, was that it could demand a sworn account of the disposition of the property in an estate which could be challenged, which reduced the profitable 'sharp practice' of some executors of wills.

(B) In several Shakespearian contexts either 'audit' or 'account' refers to a reckoning of goods or wealth. Thus Timon's steward Flavius has brought him 'accounts' (TIM 2.2.129–32); that these go unheeded explains the legal situation in the play (but see **debt**). Later Flavius offers Timon 'If you suspect my husbandry or falsehood, / Call me before th' exactest auditors / And set me on the proof' (TIM 2.2.152–4), exactly as befits an agent similar to the medieval English bailiff.

In a metaphor naming a relation with a bailee, but concerning honour rather than money, Prince Hal replies to his father's remarks on Hotspur:

> Percy is but my factor, good my lord,
> To engross up glorious deeds on my behalf;

> And I will call him to so strict account
> That he shall render every glory up,
> Yea, even the slightest worship of his time,
> Or I will tear the reckoning from his heart.
> (1H4 3.2.147–52)

Speaking of [ac]count and audit, Lady Macbeth uses a similar metaphor in reverse, welcoming Duncan with the fulsome: 'Your servants ever / Have theirs, themselves, and what is theirs in count / To make their audit at your highness' pleasure, / Still to return your own' (MAC 1.6.25–8). Accounts for goods or money feature also in MV 4.1.414, ROM 1.5.117 and 5.1.44–8, R2 1.1.128- 31, TNK 5.4.58–60, and AIT 3.2.211–14, and inventories are mentioned in 2H4, COR, CYM, and AIT.

Accounts are also often mentioned figuratively in relation to a final justifying of one's life to heaven. In metaphors in HAM (discussed below), and in CYM, the word 'audit' actually appears in this connection. In CYM 5.5.121 Posthumus' reference to an 'audit' by the gods mixes primary implications of moral accountancy (paying his life for a life he has taken) with secondary ones of the gods taking a final account of his own life.

Clarkson and Warren, 1942, pp 267–8 claim that the mocking speech in which Olivia gives 'schedules' of aspects of her 'inventoried' beauty (TN 1.5.233–8) reflects testamentary language, and in particular the initial inventory required of **executors**. Her speech does arise in a context concerning mortality, in reply to the complaint: 'Lady, you are the cruell'st she alive / If you will lead these graces to the grave / And leave the world no copy' (1.5.230–2). Yet Speed's listing of his beloved's mixed virtues (TGV 3.1.294–358), which Clarkson and Warren mention as a parallel, does not arise in a similar context.

The connection of 'audit' with testamentary matters is most explicit in SON 4, concluding:

> Then how when nature calls thee to be gone:
> What acceptable audit canst thou leave?
> Thy unused beauty must be tombed with thee,
> Which used, lives th' executor to be.

Imagery of **inheritance** (together with that of **debt**) is dominant in this sonnet, which contains 'legacy', 'bequest', 'given thee to give' as well as 'tombed' and '**executor**'. The audit mentioned is clearly a summing up at death.

Hamlet muses that the 'audit' of old King Hamlet's lifetime and sins is known only to heaven (HAM 3.3.82). Here, as in the SON 4, the term 'audit' refers to a final summing up, suggesting the term's testamentary use.

In a sarcastic figurative usage deliberately conflating the fiscal with the testamentary types of 'audit', Henry VIII says to Cardinal Wolsey:

> You are full of heavenly stuff, and bear the inventory
> Of your best graces in your mind, the which
> You were now running o'er. You have scarce time
> To steal from spiritual leisure a brief span
> To keep your earthly audit.
>
> (AIT 3.2.138–42)

Here Henry ostensibly praises Wolsey's spirituality, but actually refers ominously to his great wealth. Wolsey's wealth in goods or 'stuff' is referred to twice again in the scene in terms of an actual 'inventory' (in 3.2.125, and 3.2.452).

(C) See Jones, W. J., 1967, pp 400–17, and Clarkson and Warren, 1942, pp 280–1. On difficulties met in attempts to appoint an official auditor to the Court of Chancery see Jones, W. J., 1967, pp 280–1.

On Coke's argument concerning auditors and courts of record see Thorne, 1985a. This discusses the action of account, as do: Belsheim, 1931 (at length); Plucknett, 1956, pp 28, 365, 389, 448–9; Milsom, 1981, pp 275–82; Baker, 1990b, pp 410–13.

On Elizabethan playwrights' references to an executor's inventory or 'audit' see Clarkson and Warren, 1942, pp 286–8.

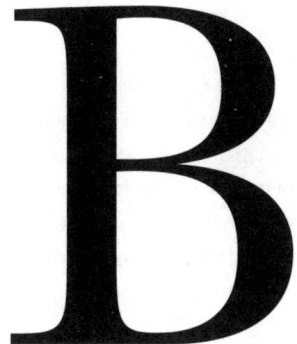

banishment See **outlawry/banishment/exile**.

bar The 'bar' of the court was the rail placed in front of the table at which the officers of the court sat, dividing the judges and court officers from the lawyers arguing the case before them. (Shakespeare does not mention, but no doubt knew of, the 'bar' dividing the benchers and readers from the students at the **Inns of Court**.)

An actual 'bar' is mentioned twice in a description of the trial for **treason** of Buckingham in AIT 2.1.1–40. This recounts how 'the great Duke' was initially found guilty 'and condemned upon 't', but then he:

> Came to the bar, where to his accusations
> He pleaded still not guilty, and alleged
> Many sharp reasons to defeat the law.
> The King's attorney, on the contrary,
> Urged on the examinations, proofs, confessions,
> Of divers witnesses, which the Duke desired
> To him brought *viva voce* to his face –
> At which appeared against him his surveyor,
> Sir Gilbert Perk his chancellor, and John Car,
> Confessor to him, with that devil-monk,
> Hopkins, that made this mischief.
>
> (AIT 2.1.13–23)

His ordeal continues:

> All these accused him strongly, which he fain
> Would have flung from him, but indeed he could not.
> And so his peers, upon this evidence,
> Have found him guilty of high treason. Much
> He spoke, and learnedly, for life, but all
> Was either pitied in him or forgotten.
>
> (AIT 2.1.25–30)

Lastly 'he was brought again to th' bar to hear / His knell rung out, his judgement', and

> he was stirred
> With such an agony he sweat extremely,
> And something spoke in choler, ill and hasty;
> But he fell to himself again, and sweetly
> In all the rest showed a most noble patience.
>
> (AIT 2.1.32–7)

Here 'the bar' is actually part of a court, and being brought to it is synonymous with being brought to the court.

Witnesses coming to 'the bar' signify the tribunal of his bad conscience in Richard III's last soliloquy, in which he realises the nature of his past deeds: 'Perjury, perjury, in the high'st degree! / Murder, stern murder, in the dir'st degree! / All several sins, all used in each degree, / Throng to the bar, crying all, "Guilty, guilty!"' (R3 5.5.150–3).

In the final act of H5, Burgundy brings the Kings of France and England together at a 'bar and royal interview' (5.2.27), indicating that a legal resolution of their contention is to be found.

Many instances of 'to bar' in Shakespeare indicate an impediment to, or the blocking of, a right, claim, or action. What is barred is frequently either royal succession or an **inheritance**.

bargain and sale (A) This became a common means of **conveyancing** of **land** after the enactment in 1536 of the Statute of Uses (27 Hen. VIII, c. 10; see **use**), before which it was a means to transfer an **equitable** right, but not the legal title to the property. Prior to 1536, when the legal owner and a purchaser agreed on a sale of land, and money or valuables were paid or pledged to be paid, but a legal conveyance of the land had not been completed, the title in law remained with the bargainor (the vendor). However in such circumstances the equitable Court of Chancery held that a **use** was raised in which the bargainee (the purchaser) was the *cesti que use*, and the legal title was then held by the bargainor for the bargainee. After the Statute of Uses most uses (with some exceptions discussed in **use**) were automatically 'executed' (converted into legal estates). So the equitable estate of a *cesti que use* created by a bargain and sale became a legal estate, and the conveyance was effected.

Because it was possible to raise a secret use by means of an oral bargain and sale, and secret conveyancing was seen as an evil making landholding insecure and depriving the King of feudal dues, slightly later in 1536 a further Statute of Enrolments (27 Hen. VIII, c. 16) was passed requiring that bargain and sale transactions, to be valid, must be made in writing, **indented**, sealed and registered within six months in a 'court of record' (on courts of record see under **audit**).

(B) There may be some anachronism in CYL, the events of which are set c. 1450, when York laments, 'So York must sit and fret and bite his tongue, / While his own lands are bargained for and sold' (CYL 1.1.230–1).

(C) See: Holdsworth, 1903, vol 4, pp 424–5, 467–8; Clarkson and Warren, 1942, pp 136–9; Simpson, 1986, p 188. On the Statute of Enrolments, see Kaye, 1988.

bastard/bastardy (A) A bastard was an illegitimate child. Under canon law the parents had sinned by conceiving a child outside a marriage and should be punished. Part of the punishment fell on the child, because the status of bastardy conferred certain civil disabilities. For example, under rules of canon law a bastard could not be ordained as a priest (unless a dispensation was granted – see Neill, 1993, p 277, which mentions the Bishop of Winchester in 1H6). At common law, by a legal fiction, an illegitimate child was *filius nullius*, the child of no one. In the twelfth century Glanvill wrote that this meant he or she had no rights of **inheritance**, so bastards could not inherit real property (**land**) from either parent, and themselves had no **heirs** except those born of their body; no collateral heirs could inherit from them. Apart from these disabilities the common law considered bastards had the same rights at law as any free person.

Treatment of the illegitimate child led to a conflict between Church and common law courts. Disputes about the validity of a marriage, and the punishment of marital and sexual offences were heard in the Church courts, but any disputed inheritance of real property was determined by the common law courts. So, in theory, questions of bastardy were referred to the Church courts for a bishop's certificate of legitimacy in much the same way as questions about the validity of a **marriage** (see **pre-contract**). If the bishop's decision on legitimacy resulted in disputed claims to the inheritance of real property, these claims had to be heard in the king's common law courts.

The problem was that the common law and canon law applied different rules to determine illegitimate status, which could have substantial effect on the outcome of arguments about the inheritance of real property. The main cause of dispute between Church and common law courts concerned the particular circumstance known as 'special bastardy'. Here a child was born and the parents married subsequently. Under canon law a subsequent marriage legitimised a child, but the common law did not accept this, holding such a child still illegitimate and therefore incapable in inheriting real property. To avoid the problem of having to accept the bishop's certificate, in the thirteenth century the common law courts asked the Church courts to certify that the child had been born after marriage, not whether or not the child was legitimate. The bishops objected to having their authority circumvented in this way and the often told story is that they suggested that 'the barons change the common law to accord with the canon law'. In the Provisions of Merton (1236) 'all the Earls and Barons replied with one voice that they did not wish to change the laws of England which were customary and had been approved' (see Adams, 1946, p 369 and Baker, 1990b, p 558). So from this time until the law was changed by the Legitimacy Act 1926 the common law courts did not accept that a certificate of legitimacy provided by a Church court was conclusive as to legitimacy, although they would accept as conclusive a bishop's certification of illegitimacy. The common law kept to itself the right to determine cases of 'special bastardy'.

The common law courts made further encroachments on the Church court's **jurisdiction** in the fifteenth century by declaring that it was not necessary to obtain a bishop's certificate in cases of disputed title to land unless the action was 'proprietary'. This meant that the claimant used a 'writ of right', which was an expensive, cumbersome process that could even lead to a trial by battle (see **lists**). But in cases of disputed title where the claim was 'possessary' and the parties were able to use possessary assizes and 'writs of entry', then the bishop's certificate was not needed. So if the dispute was formulated as 'born before marriage' and not bastardy, and the action commenced by possessary assize and not writ, it would be tried in the king's court by **jury**. The Church courts objected to what they claimed were tricks of wording.

There were other differences between the canon and common law findings of illegitimacy. Canon law bastardised children born from an adulterous relationship, but the common law had a strong presumption against a finding of illegitimacy for a child born to a married woman. In common law, for example, if a husband was in France at the time when conception might have taken place then the child was held to be legitimate (the husband could have sailed home at night – Helmholz, 1969, p 370). This evolved into the 'four seas' test which held that as long as the husband was not impotent and he was in the kingdom at any time at all during the pregnancy then the child was legitimate (see Keeton, 1930, pp 1–7). The rule was quaintly expressed in a case reported in a Year Book in 1406 as 'Whosover bulleth my cow, the calf is mine' (Keeton, 1930, p 7; Helmholz, 1969, p 370). The four seas test was used until 1732, and then abandoned 'on account of its absolute nonsense' (quoted ibid.).

Canon law held that in certain circumstances children born in marriages made in good faith were not bastardised if the marriage of their parents was later annulled (see **divorce**), for example following the subsequent discovery of a previously unknown **impediment** such as affinity. The English common law courts did not agree, and held that while divorce for the impediments of consanguinity and affinity did not make a child illegitimate, divorce on account of a prior **pre-contract** did. As a result, if a question of legitimacy and inheritance was before the king's court, and the cause of possible illegitimacy was pre-contract, then the king's courts would issue the writ asking the Church court to determine the legitimacy, knowing the result would be decided in the same way in both jurisdictions. But if the cause was consanguinity or affinity, then the king's court refused to refer to the Church court.

25

Some limited exception to the rigid position of the common law arose in the complex circumstances of a *bastard eigné*. Here the requirement was that an elder son was born before his parents marriage, then later a second son was born to the same parents but after their marriage. If the elder took possession of his inheritance and no objection was raised at the time, then after the elder's death his son was able to inherit. But, in general, marriage of the parents did not remove bastardy in common law until 1926.

There was great concern about the social problem of the support of illegitimate children who were abandoned or born to single mothers. In many cases fathers, if identified, could be ordered to support their illegitimate offspring (see Helmholz, 1977). Mothers also could be punished, for instance under an Act of 1609 specifying the incarceration for one year of women who had a bastard chargeable to the parish, but Osborne, 1960, pp 67–9, shows the inability of some **justices of the peace** to enforce this. On the roles of the Poor Laws, Church courts, and parishes generally see under **poverty**.

In some circumstances a finding of bastardy conferred an advantage and was actively pursued. Illegitimacy brought with it the advantage of free status to the child of a **villein**, on the basis that a bastard had no father (see Adams, 1946, pp 378–81). Some bishops were happy to oblige by conferring this privilege of bastardy in their Church courts even where it was not strictly merited (Baker, 1990b, pp 558)

(B) Illegitimacy is referred to in nearly every one of Shakespeare's plays. In particular, insults such as 'bastard', 'bastardy', 'whoreson', 'half blooded fellow', 'bastard blood . . . / Contaminated, base, / And misbegotten blood' (1H6 4.6.20–2), are flung with force in most of them.

Thus the word 'bastard' is mainly used in derogatory, bitter, or darkly comic contexts. Yet scurrilous Thersites revels in his 'bastard' birth, mind, valour, learning (TRO 5.8.8–10). 'Bastard', meaning sweet wine, is certainly not disparaged in 1H4 2.5.26 and 72.

The legal fiction of a bastard being *filius nullius* reflects in the bantering between Speed and Launce in which the former alleges 'she hath many nameless virtues', and the latter says 'That's as much as to say "bastard virtues"' (TGV 3.1.310–11), and also in Charmian's bantering 'belike my children shall have no names' (ANT 1.2.31).

Bastardy is thematically important in some Shakespeare plays because it apparently motivates unscrupulous or envious malignity (JN 2.1.562–99, ADO 1.3.10–34, LRF 1.2.1–22), and/or because it has bearing on questions of inheritance of real property (**land**). Brennan, 1990, also suggests that Biblical resonances make blasphemous (as well as subversive) the bastard son Edmund's attempt to usurp legitimate Edgar (on scriptural condemnations of bastardy also see Neill, 1993, pp 276–8).

One Shakespearian reference to bastardy that might seem merely tasteless bawdry may actually have arcane, but important, overtones. Sokol, 1998 relates Launcelot Gobbo's strange excuse for 'the getting up of the Negro's belly' in MV 3.5.36–40 to an obscure and repulsive English law against miscegenation, and to a theme of prejudice central in the play.

The reply made in 1H6 5.6 by the Shepherd, her father, to Joan's proud claim to bastardy, connects with issues of some legal subtlety. Although Joan had claimed shepherd ancestry in 1H6 1.3.51, at her trial she denies her father with: 'Decrepit miser, base ignoble wretch, / I am descended of a gentler blood. / Thou art no father nor no friend of mine' (1H6 5.6.7–9). The Shepherd replies just as an English ecclesiastical court would require: ' . . . 'tis not so. / I did beget her, all the parish knows. / Her mother liveth yet, can testify' (5.6.10–12). His reply however is not in accord with English common law, which would not allow parents to testify on legitimacy, but rather looked no further to determine legitimacy than to the married status of the mother and to the father's presence within the kingdom during any part of the time of pregnancy.

Parallel issues arise in the legitimacy trial of Philip Faulconbridge in JN 1.1. King John in his council, serving as the court, finally arranges a compromise between the two brothers Philip and Robert Faulconbridge who are contesting their late father's attempt to **disinherit** the elder son Philip using a deathbed **will**. The younger son Robert alleges:

> large lengths of seas and shores
> Between my father and my mother lay,
> As I have heard my father speak himself,
> When this same lusty gentleman was got.
> Upon his deathbed he by will bequeathed
> His lands to me, and took it on his death
> That this my mother's son was none of his;

> And if he were, he came into the world
> Full fourteen weeks before the course of time.
>
> (JN 1.1.105–13)

But, according to common law, no note can be taken of the 'four seas' rule, since the father had not been abroad during all of his wife's pregnancy. So King John replies correctly by reciting the common law rule that married women cannot bear bastards:

> Sirrah, your brother is legitimate.
> Your father's wife did after wedlock bear him,
> And if she did play false, the fault was hers,
> Which fault lies on the hazards of all husbands
> That marry wives. Tell me, how if my brother,
> Who, as you say, took pains to get this son,
> Had of your father claimed this son for his?
> In sooth, good friend, your father might have kept
> This calf, bred from his cow, from all the world;
> In sooth he might. Then if he were my brother's,
> My brother might not claim him, nor your father,
> Being none of his, refuse him. This concludes:
> My mother's son did get your father's heir;
> Your father's heir must have your father's land.
>
> (JN 1.1.116–29)

As Philip Faulconbridge physically resembles Richard Coeur-de-lion, he is offered and is content to accept an arrangement to 'bequeath' the disputed land to Robert, accept a knighthood, and be renamed 'Sir Richard and Plantagenet' (1.1.160–2). This royal connection makes him glad to be landless and known as a bastard (164–6).

Gladness to be allied to a man of quality by bastardy is also heard when a Trojan warrior known as 'bastard Margareton' boasts himself 'A bastard son of Priam's' (TRO 5.5.7 and 5.8.7). Conversely, Costard says of the witty page Moth 'O, an the heavens were so pleased that thou wert but my bastard, what a joyful father wouldst thou make me!' (LLL 5.1.71–3).

It is quite otherwise when Gloucester admits, speaking of embarrassment about his bastard son Edmund, 'I have so often blushed to acknowledge him that now I am brazed to 't' (LRF 1.1.8–10). The

28

bastard Edmund's very odd ideas of what proves love, discussed under **subcontracted**, may be connected with this reluctant acknowledgement. In any case, the exchange at the play's start between Gloucester who is embarrassed to confess to Edmund's illegitimate paternity yet boastful of the 'good sport at his making' (LRF 1.1.22), and the noble Kent who tries to be gracious about Edmund, does reflect a turnabout of social attitudes circa 1606. Not long before then, according to social historians, many high born fathers did not blush to acknowledge their bastards openly, and with pride. Stone, 1979a, p 663, claims, perhaps with exaggeration, that in early sixteenth century England 'in practice, if not in theory . . . the nobility was a polygamous society'. Gillis, 1985, pp 12–13, states that 'The aristocracy also continued to give pride of place to kin and lineage . . . in sixteenth-century Lancashire, many lived in open adultery. They were shamed neither by their concubines nor by their bastards'. A change from these attitudes is sometimes attributed to Puritanism, and/or to the Elizabethan Poor Laws. However, according to Flandrin, 1979, pp 180–4, both Catholic and Protestant Europe in the same period generally saw the final decline of widespread medieval toleration for the institution of concubinage. This adds, p 182, that by the early seventeenth century those living in open concubinage 'had virtually disappeared from sight: only kings and the most powerful lords still reared their bastards in public'.

Writing on the cusp of such changes, Shakespeare shows Gloucester at first ashamed of Edmund, keeping him from the court until a brief visit, and then intending 'away he shall again' (LRF 1.1.32). The thrusting Edmund, publicly called by his father a 'whoreson' (1.1.23), compensates for his status so effectively that he even overcomes the legal disability to be an heir, persuading Gloucester to seek means to make him 'capable' to inherit 'land' (2.1.82–4). The anachronism in a play set in ancient Britain of indicating a legal means to disinherit the legitimate heir of lands (a means not available before the Statute of Wills 1540 – see **wills**) is consistent with reflections in the play of up-to-date social attitudes of Shakespeare's time condemning bastardy.

There are hints in WT that Perdita's alleged bastardy might make her more than usually available as a prince's concubine. This is expressed crudely in the source, Greene's *Pandosto*, but only insinuated in WT. Baby Perdita's beauty causes even a country Shepherd to supposed her birth to have been due to an illicit court-intrigue: 'Though I am not bookish, yet I can read 'waiting-gentlewoman' in the scape'

(WT 3.3.70–1). Her bastardy is accepted by Antigonous (3.3.42–5), and note is taken of the likelihood she has had higher origins than her station by Polixenes (4.4.156–9) and Camillo (4.4.578–9). Such perceptions may mesh with Perdita's worries least Florizel 'wooed me the false way' (4.4.151), and make more poignant her shunning of hybrid flowers 'Which some call nature's bastards' (4.4.83). That her concerns have point is borne out by remarks in other Shakespeare plays suggesting that female bastards are actually raised to be employed in prostitution. Thus speaking of her 'conscience' the Bawd of PER speaks of 'bringing up of poor bastards – as I think I have brought up some eleven', and Boult replies 'Ay, to eleven, and brought them down again' (PER S.16.13–15), and Mistress Overdone of MM says ominously of Kate Keepdown's year old illegitimate child 'I have kept it myself' (MM 3.1.461).

(C) On bastardy laws and their influence in England see: Pollock and Maitland, 1898, vol 2, pp 382, 396–9; Farrer, 1917; Adams, 1946; Osborne, 1960; Helmholz, 1969; Helmholz, 1977; Baker, 1990b, pp 557–9.

On bastardy in English renaissance drama see Neill, 1993 and Findlay, 1994. On bastardy as portrayed by Shakespeare see Draper, 1938, and Williamson, 1986, pp 81–5, 91–9. On the bastardy trial of Faulconbridge in JN see: Keeton, 1930, pp 1–9; Phillips, O. H., 1967, p 186; Phillips, O. H., 1972, pp 85–6; Hamilton, D. B., 1992, pp 34–42. On the attempted **disinheriting** of the bastard in JN see Clarkson and Warren, 1942, pp 212–15. On how contemporary ideas about bastardy inform Edmund's boasts of bastards' superiority, and generally shape Edmund's role, see Elton, W. R., 1966, pp 131–5. On the alleged bastardy and vulnerability of Perdita in WT see Sokol, 1994a, pp 116–41.

On the rapidly changing rate of illegitimacy in Shakespeare's era see: Shorter, 1976, pp 332–3; Laslett, 1977, pp. 102–55; Levine, D. and Wrightson, 1980; Laslett, 1983, pp 153–74. A steep drop in illegitimacy in the decades just following Shakespeare's career was often connected by earlier social historians with 'the brief reign of the Puritans' (Laslett, 1977, p 106). It is associated with 'Puritan reformers . . . and Poor Law administrators' also in Neill, 1993, p 273. However more recently social historians have contested the notion that the influence of Puritanism produced a sexual revolution in mid seventeenth-century England. To explain reduced bastardy Wrightson, 1980 posits an alternative to 'models centred upon the influence of political or ideological change'. Fear of increased legal sanctions in the 1620s against couples who had ante-nuptial sexual relations is cited for a reason in Houlbrooke, 1984, p 81. Ingram, 1985, concludes, p 159, that in the English seventeenth century 'harsher attitudes to illicit sexuality . . . could occur in the absence of any strong Puritan drive'. Laslett, 1983, p 162, also holds that Puritanism alone may not have directly caused the drop in illegitimacy rate at around 1650. For a list of sources of similar revised historical views, and of literary interpretations founded on earlier beliefs in the significance of Puritanism for a changed attitude to women, see Cook, 1991, p 13, notes.

Widmayer, 1995 makes a case that bastard bearing was sometimes very severely punished in Shakespeare's age, and applies this to MM.

battery (A) In its legal uses 'battery' referred to an unlawful physical attack on a person. It was a **trespass**, rather than a **felony**. Neither intent nor negligence was alleged, only the deed. The only possible responses were 'guilty or 'not guilty'; special pleas of mishap, 'negligence in the sense of inadvertence', or any other special circumstances were not formally admissible (see Baker, 1990b, p 456).

In formal pleadings all defendants were alleged to 'assault, beat and wound . . . with force and arms namely with swords and staves' so that the plaintiff's 'life was despaired of'. The **jury** could hear the particulars of the defence, but the pleadings would not normally mention them. Only a few formal defences were possible: these included self-defence; that lawful force was used by a **constable** or other officer in his duty; that the action was part of a medical treatment.

(B) Although it may be directed against a person, 'batt'ry' is more a military than a personal assault in erotic metaphors in LC 23, LC 277, and VEN 426. The term is used similarly in RDY 3.1.37, JN 2.1.447, PER S.21.34–8, and with a degree of irony in COR 5.4.21, ANT 2.7.106, CYM 1.4.21. (Military uses of the term are literal in 1H6 1.6.43 and H5 3.3.90.)

Several contexts in other plays mention or allude to an action of battery. A cynical use of the justification of self-defence arises in ROM 1.1.37 , where intending to fight on seeing the Montague servants, one of the quarrelsome Capulet servants suggests that he and his fellows provoke the Montague men to the first action: 'Let us take the law of our side. Let them begin.' (noted by Campbell, J., 1859, p 97).

Hamlet imagines a skull dug up to be that of a formerly litigious lawyer, and asks 'Why does he suffer this rude knave now to knock him about the sconce with a dirty shovel, and will not tell him of his action of battery?' (HAM 5.1.97–100). The circumstances make the fixed wording of the writ of battery, that 'his life was despaired of', even more fictional than usual.

Although this resembles one of his famous malapropisms, **constable** Elbow is not wholly daft when he threatens 'mine action of battery' when the cause is actually for an action of slander (MM 2.1.172–5); the reason is discussed under **slander**.

Sir Andrew Aguecheek makes a threat against Sebastian: 'I'll have an action of battery against him if there be any law in Illyria. Though I struck him first, yet it's no matter for that' (TN 4.1.33–5). Heard, 1883, pp 30–1, notes that here with characteristic foolishness Aguecheek 'supposes *son assault demense* [self-defence] is not a good plea to an action of trespass for an assault and battery'.

(C) See Baker, 1990b, pp 456–9; ibid., p 629, prints a specimen writ. On *son assault demense* see Milsom, 1981, pp 47 and 296. See Campbell, J., 1859, p 97, and Heard, 1883, pp 30–1.

beggary See **poverty/beggary**, and also **vagrant/vagrom man**.

bequeath See **will/testament**.

bills (A) In Shakespearian legal or quasi-legal contexts 'bills' are one or more of: 1) documents used to promise payment in commerce, or used as promissory instruments for arranging **debt**; 2) lists of accusations brought to a court; 3) any written documents used in law or commerce (OED n3 1.a); 4) heavy sharp-edged weapons; 5) a means to proposing **statutes** for legislation.

The plaintiff's 'bill' beginning a Chancery suit was 'an intelligible statement of claim and nothing more' (Yale, 1965, p 50). The flexibility and simplicity of this procedure compared with the use of formally worded writs (for an example, see **battery**) in the common law courts, coupled with the fact that Chancery's equity **jurisdiction** allowed the 'discovery' of any relevant documents to a case, made Chancery attractive to litigants. However Shakespeare made very sparing specific reference, if any at all, to the Chancellor's equity jurisdiction (see under **equity**).

The common law courts too used a bill procedure in certain circumstances. These included when suits were initiated against the court's own officers, or against prisoners in the custody of the court. When it was still itinerant, following the King's travels around the kingdom, the medieval Court of King's Bench allowed proceedings to be begun by bill against local defendants. Such bills were not enrolled (entered onto a court record after payment of a fee), and therefore were less costly to use, and they were quicker and cheaper to get, than writs which had to be obtained from the royal secretariat (Chancery) in London. The non-enrolled process by bill also encouraged a negotiated settlement of disputes before the case came to trial by **jury**, for such a settlement would minimize costs to the plaintiff and cause no immediate nor lasting embarrassment to the defendant. (These and other technical advantages of the King's Bench bill procedure are detailed in Blatcher, 1978, pp 109–13.)

After the Court of King's Bench settled in Westminster, only those defendants present in the county of Middlesex, or held in custody in the King's Bench prison, could be sued by its popular bill. Some plaintiffs resorted to having defendants arrested on false claims to achieve this end. Such ruses became unnecessary after 1542 because the King's Bench allowed plaintiffs to issue bills claiming (fictitious) trespass, known as a 'bill of Middlesex' to arrest a defendant. Once this was accomplished the plaintiff could begin the genuine action against the defendant. By a further legal fiction, the writ of *latitat* (he lurks and roams), the King's Bench could order the arrest of a defendant by a local sheriff in any part of England (Baker, 1990b, p 51). The result was that the court of King's Bench took a great deal of litigation away from Common Pleas, which continued to require writs.

(B) Shakespeare's use of 'bills' as instruments of debt sometimes suggests that these are 'bill of exchange'. But they may be also legal

bonds, for sealed bonds with conditional defeasance written in English, as opposed to the more usual but not legally required Latin, were 'sometimes distinguished by being called bills' (Simpson, 1966, pp 393–4).

Shakespeare's 'bills' may also be mere reckonings (as of tavern charges in CYM 5.5.253). Uses of 'bills' referring to more substantial debts undertaken or due for payment are mentioned in SHR 4.2.90, and (ambiguously with sense (2)) in WIV 1.1.9. The presentation of bills or bonds due for payment dominates the action of TIM 2.2 (starting from the Folio stage direction tln 656), and TIM 3.4.

Simpson, 1966, pp 393–4 makes it clear (citing *Core's Case* (1536) Dyer 20a at 22b) that fixed forms of wording were not required for validity of a **bond**, but that it was wise to follow the traditional formula which began '*Noverint universi per praesentes* . . . '. Wording parodic of the English translation of such a 'bill' appears in a jocular context in AYL 1.2.114–15, where Rosalind describes Le Beau's 'three proper young men': 'With bills on their necks: 'Be it known unto all men by these presents'. Here there may be a submerged pun on 'bills' as weapons, for the young men are prospective (albeit wrestling) combatants.

The same wording arises among puns using the language of legal instruments of **debt** which inform Pandarus' commentary on Troilus' impassioned 'You have bereft me of all words, lady' (TRO 3.2.53), leading to a mutual kiss with Cressida. Always obscene Panadrus says:

> Words pay no debts; give her deeds. But she'll bereave you o' th' deeds too, if she call your activity in question. What, billing again? Here's "in witness whereof the parties interchangeably".
>
> (TRO 3.2.54–7)

'Billing' of course connotes a 'bill' as an agreed financial instrument, while simultaneously denoting mutual interchange of a different sort. Pandarus suggests in his next phrases, 'Come in, come in. I'll go get a fire', that the lovers do further 'deeds' in privacy.

The violent tearing up of a 'bill' in the sense (2) of a list of accusations is specified by the Folio stage direction to 1H6 3.1 (tln 1203–4), although Shakespeare avoids mention of the important growth of bill procedure in specific courts.

Bills of **outlawry** are mentioned in JC 4.2.225; see under **witch** on bills accusing witchcraft.

Sense (4) of 'bill' sometimes arises in Shakespearian references to crude or improvised weaponry generally, as in CYL 4.7.142, R2 3.2.114, and punningly in TIM 3.4.88. A 'bill' as weapon may also indicate a specific type of edged weapon 'used by **constables'** of the watch till late in the 18th cent.' (OED n1 2.b). Thus the watch in ROM 1.1.70 attempt to restore order with 'Clubs, bills and partisans!'. In ADO 3.3.39–40 **constable** Dogberry bids the peerless men of his watch to slumber, warning 'Only have a care that your bills be not stolen.'

In ADO 3.3.171, this same watch's bills are punningly confounded with 'bills' of debt in sense (2), made dangerous by the scheme of 'taking up' commodities. A parallel pun appears in CYL 4.7.141–2 (on these puns, see under **commodity**).

Painted halberds, as used by the watch, are referred to as 'brown bills' in CYL 4.9.12 and LRF 4.5.91 / LRQ S.20.90–1, in contexts of roguery and madness respectively.

There is a punning reference to a bill in senses (2), (3), and (4) simultaneously in SHR 4.3.143–50. Here 'bill' associates with commercial documents, legal accusations, and a a type of weapon, and all this is conjoined with a typical indecent pun about tailors:

GRUMIO   Error i' th' bill, sir, error i' th' bill. I commanded the sleeves should be cut out and sewed up again, and that I'll prove upon thee though thy little finger be armed in a thimble.

TAILOR   This is true that I say. An I had thee in place where, thou shouldst know it.

GRUMIO   I am for thee straight. Take thou the bill, give me thy meteyard, and spare not me.

(SHR 4.3.143–50)

The passage also presents a parodic challenge to trial by battle, an anachronism of recurrent interest to Shakespeare, described under **lists**. The weapons proposed are, in some sense, the batons allowed to the lower degree of combatants in such trials (as in CYL 2.3), but the cause of the challenge does not match any legally allowed (such as a 'Writ of Right', 'appeal of treason', etc. – see under **appeal**). Some light may be thrown on the odd folklore of combative tailors by the unexpected statistics of the professions of violently criminal sanctuary-men, noted under **sanctuary**.

Reference to bills in sense (5) arises in H5 and WIV, in serious and facetious contexts respectively. In H5 1.1.1–99 a 'self bill' proposed under Richard II and reintroduced under Henry V arouses church-men's fear of a law to confiscate **lands** left to the Church. Some legal and historical aspects of this fear are discussed under **statute**. In WIV 2.1.26–7 Mistress Page is so outraged with Falstaff's attempted seduc-tion she avers: 'Why, I'll exhibit a bill in the Parliament for the putting down of men'. A nexus of Windsor's provincial or domestic affairs and the central legal institutions of London is a running jest of this play.

(C) On the rise of bill procedures to bring common law actions see Knafla, 1977, p 117 and Blatcher, 1978, pp 110–53.

On bills as instruments of debt see under **bond** and **debt**.

On the fears of the clergy at the start of H5 see Clarkson and Warren, 1942, pp 10–12, and on the long history of laws prohibiting 'mortmain', the leaving of lands to corporations such as the Church, see ibid., pp 242–3, and under **perpetuities**.

On the Elizabethan development of the system of bringing 'bills' to propose legislation in Parliament, and for details of the ensuing devel-opment of parliamentary procedural strategies, see Neale, 1976, pp 369–88, and under **statute**.

bond (A) The 'bond', 'double bond', or more completely 'penal bond with conditional defeasance', was a deed, or sealed instrument of obli-gation often used for arranging **debt** popular because it ensured timely repayment. It was very widely used in Shakespeare's period whenever substantial funds were borrowed, as it offered lenders both strong security and great ease of enforcement.

Such a document, unlike so-called covenants of debt, allowed enforcement of penal obligations. These penalties would arise unless the bond's condition (timely repayment) was fulfilled. The mere physical possession of an uncancelled bond allowed certainty of per-formance of its obligation (the penalty), for as long as the bond was acknowledged by the defendant as his own deed he had no recourse in law but to fulfil the obligation it imposed.

Common law courts would not look into any question except whether the condition written on the back of the bond ('endorsed') was fulfilled. Sometimes the bond referred to a separate **indenture** which listed several conditions to be fulfilled. If the condition was met, the obligation in the deed was cancelled. If it was not, and the bond was intact, the obligation (penalty) could not be avoided in law.

Thus payment of a monetary debt could be ensured because unless the debt was paid on time, with the consequence that the actual bond was cancelled, destroyed, or delivered over to the debtor, then a penalty would be enforced. A typical penalty for a money bond was forfeiture of property worth twice as much as the amount of the debt.

The legal onus was on the debtor to defend against the penalty, not on the creditor to enforce the condition (Simpson, 1966, p 397). Nor, where the express terms of an instrument in the form of a bond were available, were the common law courts normally willing to look into the 'real causes of the transaction' in question (ibid., p 400). This accounts for the popularity of the 'peculiarly topsy turvey' (ibid., p 411) institution of penal bonds, for lenders would not have to face any chancy and expensive litigation in order to be repaid.

In fact even if a borrower repaid the creditor, but had the misfortune or folly not to recover his bond after repayment, or if it was snatched back by the creditor, the penalty in the bond could be enforced in common law. (Baker, 1990b, p 369, explains that even if the uncancelled bond was snatched, only a writ of **trespass** could be used in hope of recovering damages.) Only a cancelled bond was unenforcable. Thus the Court of King's Bench concluded that the amount owed on a bond had to be paid twice because 'although the truth be that the plaintiff is paid his money, still it is better to suffer a mischief to one man than an inconvenience to many, which would subvert a law' (*Waberley v Cockrel* (1542) 1 Dyer 51a).

This very problem of the law requiring a double payment if a paid-up bond remains uncancelled was discussed in the first philosophical dialogue of St. German's *Doctor and Student* (c. 1523):

> it is not the lawe of Englande that yf a man that is bounde in an oblygacyon pay the money without acquytance . . . that therefore the law determyneth that he ought of right to paye the money eftsones for that lawe were both agaynst reason and conscyence but troughth it is that there is a generall maxyme in the lawe of England that in an accyon of dette sued upon an oblygacion the defendant shall not plead that he oweth not the money or that he has paid it. . . . And because it should be a hurte to many yf an oblygacyon should be so lightly avoyded by a bare word. Therefore the lawe specyally

preventyth yt hurte . . . And yet intendyth not nor commaundyth not that the money of right ought to be payde agayne but settyth a generall rule which is good and necessary to all the people & that euery man maye well kepe without it be through his owne carelessness or defaute and yf suche defaute happen in any persone whereby he is without remedye at the common lawe: yet he maye be holpen in equity.

(St German, 1975, pp 77–9)

The last phrase reflects how from the fifteenth century the Court of Chancery was increasingly willing to offer equitable relief from conditions of bonds where the common law courts were not. So the happy situation, for lenders, of penal bonds being unquestionable was eroded, and in the time of Elizabeth 'petitions for relief [from bonds in Chancery] became very common' (Simpson, 1966, p 416).

As Baker, 1979, p 271, explains, Chancery gradually offered more relief and eventually 'the use of bonds to obtain an extortionate advantage over a contracting party was seriously curtailed'. This adds that by the sixteenth century 'it was established that it was inequitable for the obligee to recover a sum which exceeded his actual loss arising from the breach of condition, and obligors could obtain relief in Chancery against penalties which they had incurred at law'. Nevertheless conditional bonds still gave 'procedural advantages', and they remained very popular instruments of debt until long after Shakespeare's time (Baker, 1990b, p 370).

(B) In SON 87, 117, 134, and 142 a 'bond' appears among metaphors of debt and monetary repayment, colouring the concerns of love.

In Shakespeare's plays the legal meaning of a 'bond' as an obligation sometimes links with the concept of emotional 'bonds'. In many Shakespearian contexts human 'bonds' are powerfully affectional, as in the description of the cousins in AYL 1.2.265- 6 'whose loves / Are dearer than the natural bond of sisters'. But sometimes they show elements of extreme rigidity, and/or give opportunities for extracting extortionate advantages or penalties, and in that way resemble aspects of monetary bonds that were being eliminated legally by Shakespeare's time.

In Macbeth's terrific imprecation, 'Come, seeling night, / Scarf up the tender eye of pitiful day,/ And with thy bloody and invisible hand / Cancel and tear to pieces that great bond / Which keeps me pale'

(MAC 3.2.47–51), the primary significance is of the severing of the human obligation to behave humanely toward fellow men. But both 'sealing' and the image of a hand tearing up may also allude to the creation and cancellation (by physical destruction) of a monetary bond. Later, when Macbeth resolves to kill Macduff despite the witches' reassurances, he says: 'But yet I'll make assurance double sure, / And take a bond of fate thou shalt not live' (MAC 4.1.99–100); here there is an allusion to the extra assurance of a conditional or 'double' bond.

Cordelia's fateful response: 'I love your majesty / According to my bond, no more nor less' (LRF 1.1.92–3) unflinchingly delineates her obligations. She states truly that her obligation is sure, although Lear takes her to mean primarily that it is limited. In addition to this, *King Lear* contains three other mentions of bonds (LRF 1.2.106; 2.1.46–7; 2.2.351), and one of 'fond bondage' (1.2.50), all in contexts concerning relations between children and parents. At least two of these are surrounded by confusions of love and pelf (1.1.36–119; 1.2.48–9). A proper appreciation of human bonds, what is owed, what is needed, and how much it is proper to demand, is crucially deficient in Lear's kingdom and family.

Actual monetary bonds are often mentioned by Shakespeare. ERR names these five times in connection with the play's farcical treatment of **debt** (4.1.13; 4.2.49 and 50; 4.3.31; figuratively in 4.4.126). Bonds of humanity are mentioned in TIM 1.1.148 and men's words as bonds in TIM 1.2.64; unpaid monetary bonds are seen, and twice mentioned in connection with the play's tragic treatment of bankruptcy (TIM 2.1.33 and 2.2.37). John of Gaunt may be metaphorical in speaking of England being 'bound in shame / With inky blots and rotten parchment bonds' (R2 2.1.63–4 – on the context see **lease**), but the Duchess of York is literal when she hopefully suggests that the seditious 'writing' hidden by her son may be 'nothing but some bond that he is entered into / For gay apparel 'gainst the triumph day' (R2 5.2.65–6).

More lightheartedly, Falstaff outrageously suggests that he has lost to pickpockets 'three or four bonds of forty pound apiece, and a seal-ring of my grandfather's' (1H4 3.3.101–3). This of course is a lie, but indicates that the physical possession of a bond was all important. We learn later that a wise tradesman refuses to accept Falstaff's bond (2H4 1.2.32).

The most famous Shakespearian money bond is of course Shylock's, which has for its terrifying forfeit a pound of human flesh. It is interesting that the stipulation of the exact nature of this penalty varies between MV 1.3.147–50 and 4.1.229–30 (see Sokol, 1995a). The variation in a way matches the shifting legal nature of the bond itself, which Shylock at first calls 'single' (1.3.144), but which is clearly a double bond since it carries a penalty with conditional defeasance.

Simpson, 1966, p 420, explains that penalties *in terrerem* were allowed to individuals as well as the state in Shakespeare's age, and adds, p 421, 'Shylock's bond . . . neatly illustrates the fact that the best pledge of all is the body of the contractor, which in early law he could have used as security'.

In fact Shylock's attempted revenge mirrors the barbaric customs of some early English local or borough courts involving 'punishments [which] included mutilation and allowed participation by the victim' (Selden Society, 1987, p 93). But even in such local courts 'bonds with penalties were not always enforced' (ibid., p 94, referring to London and Lincoln courts objecting to penalties in double bonds – see also Bateson, 1906, p 208).

So even local courts did not always enforce bonds. A crucial question about MV is whether the law represented in the play considers non-enforcement or equitable relief for Antonio, and if it does not, why.

Tucker, 1976, pp 99–100 even suggests the adequacy of Elizabethan common law to apply equitable relief in its judgment on a bond like Shylock's, without needing recourse to Chancery. However, it appears that the common law followed Chancery in this practice only from about 1670 (Simpson, 1966, p 418).

Instead of offering equitable relief, Portia supports Shylock when he argues that the law regulating his bond cannot be overturned, and indeed insists that Shylock may have his unreasonable penalty if he wishes. The play offers no answer to the paradoxical demand that individual mitigation be overlooked, lest, in Portia's words, in the precedent of the alteration of a "decree established . . . many an error by the same example/ Will rush into the state' (MV 4.1.216–19 – see **precedent**). For further considerations, see under **equity**.

A curious image in CYM 3.2.35–9 involving a wax seal, bonds, lovers, and prison, is discussed under **on the case**.

(C) On conditional or 'double' bonds see Baker, 1990b, pp 368–71, and in greater detail Simpson, 1966.

On the relief available in equity from conditional bonds see: Jones, W. J., 1967, pp 441–5; Henderson, 1974; Baker, 1979, p 271. On an actual case probably known to Shakespeare, see Berry, H., 1993.

On the question of the 'merry bond' and alleged equity in the trial of MV generally see references listed under **equity**. Several peculiarities of Shylock's bond are discussed in Sokol, 1992 and Sokol, 1995a.

branded (A) Branding was a punishment inflicted on criminals convicted of a **felony** who were able to escape a sentence of death by hanging by pleading 'benefit of clergy' in mitigation of the sentence. If their plea was accepted by the judge, then the convicted criminal was branded on the thumb (with a T for thief, or an M for murderer), and freed. Thus the Act 4 Hen. VII, c.13 required 'Every suche persone so convicted for murdre, to be marked with a M. upon the brawne of the lefte thumbe', for benefit could be used only once, and this identification helped ensure that. (Ben Jonson was so branded after he killed a fellow actor in a fight).

Benefit of clergy was one of several ways in which the harshness of the punishments imposed by the early criminal law was mitigated. Others methods of avoiding sentence of death were to seek a **pardon**, or to take **sanctuary**, or by the refusal of sympathetic **juries** to indict or convict.

The practice of allowing benefit of clergy in mitigation of sentence developed out of the separation of religious and secular jurisdictions after the Norman Conquest. The Church claimed that clerics accused of crimes should be tried in ecclesiastical courts. This was resisted by secular authority, which considered a convicted cleric should receive the same punishment in common law courts as any other convicted felon. In the twelfth century Thomas Becket, Archbishop of Canterbury, argued that this was unjust because a cleric would be punished twice for the same offence, once in the King's Court and then again in the ecclesiastical courts. Henry II argued that on the contrary the injustice was the disparity of treatment between lay and clerical prisoners. A series of scandalous cases in which Royal justice was notoriously circumvented by the use of benefit of clergy exacerbated the worsening dispute between King and Archbishop. Henry's argument with Becket culminated in Becket's murder in Canterbury Cathedral on 29 December 1170, and made Becket into a saint. After this the King capitulated;

41

a claim of benefit of clergy gave complete immunity from secular **jurisdiction** to criminous clerks.

The punishment awarded by ecclesiastical courts to clerics who were convicted felons was penance, sometimes excommunication, together with disparagement, or public humiliation, whereas in the common law courts the mandatory sentence for **felonies** was death by hanging. By the fifteenth century clerical status was very loosely defined by common law courts, and in this way was extended to many who were only marginally connected to the Church, if at all. A prisoner presented visible evidence to the court of clerical status, such as clerical garb or tonsure, but eventually the reading test alone was used. Although the choice of reading was supposed to be random, as long as an accused felon could read Psalm 51, verse 1, clerical status was assured. This was known as the 'neck verse' and could be learnt by heart, so clerical status became a legal fiction used to mitigate the death penalty. There are reports of judges encouraging prisoners to read (lending eyeglasses), and of gaolers arranging tuition for the illiterate before trial. Even a married man could claim benefit of clergy, for clerics below the rank of subdeacon could marry as long as they were not bigamous. Bigamy in this context was taken to include marrying again after a first wife's death, or marrying a widow; by I Edw. VI, c.12 (1547) bigamy was no longer a bar. By the same Act, peers of the realm did not have to read and were excused branding. After 1576 (18 Eliz. c.7) those receiving benefit of clergy were not handed over to ecclesiastical authorities at all, but could be discharged at once or could be imprisoned for one year.

Despite the relative generosity in findings of clerical status, it seems many prisoners did not plead benefit of clergy until after they were found guilty and sentenced. At first sight this pattern of behaviour seems puzzling, but it probably offered the best chance of avoiding sentence. If clerical status was pleaded before a trial then a jury would not be cautious about returning a 'guilty' verdict. Then if a plea of clerical status was rejected all was lost. For this reason many prisoners preferred first to seek a 'not guilty' verdict.

Some attempt was made by common law courts to restrain what was known as 'clergy'. Not all crimes were clergyable; for example **treason** was not, and in 1512 **murder** and certain kinds of **robbery**, and in 1576 **rape**, were also declared non-clergyable. But most **theft** was clergyable and theft made up by far the largest number of cases of felony. The process of statutory withdrawal of clergy from offences continued, and helped serve the purpose of shaping the criminal law, until the legal fiction of clergy was abolished in 1827.

It is calculated that by the end of the sixteenth century up to half of those convicted for offences punishable with death were successfully able to claim clergy. Many were branded more than once, which indicates that the rule that benefit of clergy could only be claimed once was not strictly applied. The reading test was abandoned in 1706, and the statutes 21 Jac. I c.6 (1624) partially and 3 Will. & Mar. c.9 (1691) fully extended the right to claim clergy to women, abandoning any pretence that the felon was in clerical orders. Branding, which did not serve for identification, was replaced by whipping in the early eighteenth century.

Before the abolition of abjuring by Henry VIII, branding on the thumb with the letter 'A' was also used to mark those who, having taken sanctuary, chose to abjure the realm rather than stand trial (see under **sanctuary** for details of abjuring).

(B) Jack Cade boasts to his confederates 'I fear neither sword nor fire' but one of them replies 'methinks he should stand in fear of fire, being burned i' th' hand for stealing of sheep' (CYL 4.2.60–5). This, and that Cade had been 'whipped three market days together' (4.2.59) for some lesser crimes, makes him an opponent of the legal process. He is also particularly opposed to those who 'can write and read' (and especially if they dared teach literacy to others, 4.2.86–90). Therefore, in his absurd indictment of Lord Say, Cade includes the charges of abetting the teaching of reading and printing of books, and that:

> Thou hast appointed justices of peace to call poor men before them about matters they were not able to answer. Moreover, thou hast put them in prison, and, because they could not read, thou hast hanged them when indeed only for that cause they have been most worthy to live.

> (4.7.38–43)

Cade's charges that Say has been erecting grammar schools and building (anachronistic) paper mills, lead up to this complaint about favouring the literate – yet it appears that Cade himself had memorised his 'neck verse'.

The branding of disreputable offenders is alluded to many other times by Shakespeare, as when Richard III is berated by Queen Elizabeth:

> Hid'st thou that forehead with a golden crown,
> Where should be branded – if that right were right –
> The slaughter of the prince that owed that crown,
> And the dire death of my poor sons and brothers?
> Tell me, thou villain-slave, where are my children?
>
> (R3 4.4.140–4)

In Shakespeare's use, 'brand', except when it signifies a 'firebrand', almost always carries figurative connotations of a shaming mark (as in OED 4b). So SON 111 has 'my name receives a brand'; HAM 4.5.117 has 'brands the harlot'; LRQ S.2.10 has 'Why brand they us with "base, base bastardy"'; ANT 4.15.76–7 has 'branded / His baseness'; WT 2.1.73–4 has 'These petty brands / That calumny doth use'; AIT 3.1.127 has 'branded with suspicion'. A particular punishment, or perhaps the mark of an abjurer, is imaged when Palamon berates Arcite: 'Be as that cursed man that hates his country, / A branded villain' (TNK 2.2.203–4).

(C) See: Holdsworth, 1903, vol 3, pp 293–302; Plucknett, 1956, pp 439–47; Gabel, 1969, pp 25–9, 71–91, 116–27; Baker, 1990b, pp 586–9; Bellamy, 1973, pp 151–5; Baker, 1978, pp 326–34; Baker, 1986b, pp 292–3. Wilson, R., 1990, pp 25–8, treats benefit of clergy in relation to Shakespearian comedy in a Foucauldian context.

burglary (A) The legal definition of the crime of burglary was complex and not settled during the sixteenth century. It was disputed that house breaking was a **felony** at all unless it was accompanied by murder. Details of the definition (for instance that from 1450 it was a night-time offence, with widely varying definitions of 'night', or that until 1547 uninhabited houses could not be burgled, or that it included from 1587 putting hooks through windows, and from 1616 shooting through a hole in a wall) are not significant to Shakespeare's use, but the fact of the difficulty of definition may be.

(B) Shakespeare may have spoofed the uncertain definition of 'burglary' in his one employment of the word. 'Burglary' is heard in the pat and idiotic assurances of the **constables'** of ADO:

SECOND WATCHMAN	Marry, that he had received a thousand ducats of Don John for accusing the Lady Hero wrongfully.
DOGBERRY	Flat burglary, as ever was committed.
VERGES	Yea, by mass, that it is.

(ADO 4.2.45–9)

See **slander** on false sexual accusations.

(C) Complexities in the nature of burglary are discussed in Bellamy, 1973, p 44; Baker, 1978, pp 325–6; and Herrup, 1987, pp 170–2. Difficulties of its definition are outlined in Baker, 1990b, pp 604–5, and sixteenth century lawyers' discussion of the definition is noted in Baker, 1986i, p 315. On itinerant burglar gangs see Beier, 1985, p 131–4.

chattels (A) In English law property can be of two kinds, personal (or movable) property, and 'real property' which is **land**. The term 'chattels', derived from law-French, refers to movable or personal property, including money. Because English land law was so closely tied to feudalism, it developed separately from the law relating to movables. In particular, the doctrines of tenures (see **land**) had no application to chattels.

The laws of real property and personal property had different rules for **conveyance**, **inheritance** and **wills**, and 'real property' and personal property were protected by different court actions in Shakespeare's time. A real action protected the possession of real property by giving the right to recover the land itself. Chattels were protected by actions which more usually allowed for the award of damages alone (see **conversion**), and the property itself was not recovered.

A **lease** of land, known as a 'term of years absolute', was not recognized as land because originally it did not fall within the feudal framework of lords and landholding. A lease was not subject to the doctrines of tenures and estates but instead regarded as a commercial venture, usually entered into as security for a loan. To distinguish it from real property a lease was called a 'chattel real'.

(B) Petruchio deliberately mocks or confuses legal concepts when he abducts or 'rescues' Kate after the wedding but before the wedding feast:

Nay, look not big, nor stamp, nor stare, nor fret.
I will be master of what is mine own.
She is my goods, my chattels. She is my house,
My household-stuff, my field, my barn,
My horse, my ox, my ass, my anything,
And here she stands, touch her whoever dare.
I'll bring mine action on the proudest he
That stops my way in Padua. Grumio,
Draw forth thy weapon, we are beset with thieves.
Rescue thy mistress if thou be a man.
Fear not, sweet wench. They shall not touch thee, Kate.
(SHR 3.3.100–10)

This miscellany of real property and chattels, house, household stuff, fields, oxen, etc., received different treatment in English law. Petruchio's muddling of all together seems done deliberately in order preposterously to underline complete 'ownership' of his wife as property. But Petruchio's words 'I'll bring my action . . . ' may also draw attention to his deliberately farcical and eccentric behaviour, for by including 'chattels' and landed property in his list he makes a nonsense of his threat to bring a legal action, leaving only a threat of physical 'action'.

Pistol's characteristic verbal extravagance inspires his redundant charge to his wife: 'Look to my chattels and my movables' (H5 2.3.45). More grimly, a writ is sued against Wolsey 'To forfeit all your goods, lands, tenements, / Chattels, and whatsoever, and to be / Out of the King's protection' on account of his **praemunire** (AIT 3.2.343–5).

(C) On the law relating to chattels and chattels real, see Baker, 1978, pp 209–20; Simpson, 1986, pp 74–6; Baker, 1990b, pp 337- 42, 427–53.

Chief Justice (A) The Chief Justice was the senior judge of the Court of King's Bench, and as such one of the three most important **Justices** in early modern England. The others were the Lord Chancellor who sat in the Court of Chancery, and the Master of the Rolls.

In medieval and early modern England the judiciary, though small in number, were responsible for much of the development of the English common law (see **precedent**). By Shakespeare's time most judges were not clerics, but had previously practised as **serjeants** in the King's Courts (on serjeants-at-law see under **lawyers** and **justices**). All were the King's servants, and appointed and paid by him. They were therefore removable by him.

(B) The sole Chief Justice in Shakespeare is an important minor figure of 2H4. Perhaps significantly, in the Folio stage directions (tln 2880, 3248–9), as in the text, the Chief Justice of 2H4 is addressed as 'Lord Chief Justice' only in the play's later scenes (after 5.2) when he is, or is about to become, triumphant. His explicit role as the direct adversary of Falstaff's anarchic disregard for the rule of law reinforces his implicit role as the symbolic opposite to Falstaff's crew's, and the play's rural **Justices of the Peace's**, good-order-defying hankering for power through favouritism.

The Chief Justice's symbolization in 2H4 of the 'bold, just, and impartial spirit' of true lawfulness (5.2.115) replaces Hotspur's symbolization in 1H4 of chivalric honour, in so far as both are opposed to Falstaff's dishonourable lawlessness. But while Falstaff symbolically 'kills' honour when he dishonourably stabs Hotspur's corpse in 1H4, he cannot sustain his pretended deafness to the Chief Justice when the latter prevails at the end of 2H4. So, although Hotspur represents the more glamorous adversary, the Lord Chief Justice represents the more admirable and durable opposing principle to Falstaff's riot and excess.

The famous, perhaps historical, action of the certainly boldly independent-minded Chief Justice Sir William Gascoigne, who was reputed to have imprisoned Henry V when he was Prince of Wales, is recalled in the first words spoken of his Shakespearian counterpart: 'Sir, here comes the nobleman that committed the / Prince for striking him about Bardolph' (2H4 1.2.54–5). Questions of its authenticity aside, this often recounted legend illustrates an issue of profound significance for Shakespeare's age. Is the law empowered to command royalty?

Certainly Shakespeare treats the delicate issue of prerogative with circumspection. His Lord Chief Justice states only that he bears the king's authority to rebuke and imprison the royal **heir apparent**, and this intermediate position between judicial autonomy and delegated prerogative is wholly approved. Thus, in testing the Chief Justice, Prince Harry asks with apparent indignation:

> . . . How might a prince of my great hopes forget
> So great indignities you laid upon me?
> What – rate, rebuke, and roughly send to prison
> Th' immediate heir of England? Was this easy?
> May this be washed in Lethe and forgotten?

Although expecting a heavy reprimand, the Lord Chief Justice replies:

> I then did use the person of your father.
> The image of his power lay then in me;
> And in th' administration of his law,
> Whiles I was busy for the commonwealth,
> Your highness pleased to forget my place,
> The majesty and power of law and justice,
> The image of the King whom I presented,
> And struck me in my very seat of judgement;
> Whereon, as an offender to your father,
> I gave bold way to my authority
> And did commit you. If the deed were ill,
> Be you contented, wearing now the garland,
> To have a son set your decrees at naught –
> To pluck down justice from your awe-full bench,
> To trip the course of law, and blunt the sword
> That guards the peace and safety of your person,
> Nay, more, to spurn at your most royal image,
> And mock your workings in a second body?

The law is thus aligned with the king's second body, which is the immortal monarchy. The prince then upsets all expectations with 'You are right Justice, and you weigh this well' (2H4 5.2.67–101).

Here the story might be seen to end, with Shakespeare 'on the fence' concerning the balance of regal and judicial powers. Yet, as pointed out in Merchant, 1964, p 117, in the successor play H5, Prince Hal metamorphoses into both a theoretical-minded and practical-minded monarch who deeply concerns himself about principle and legality.

A similar jurisprudential problem to the one informing the parable in 2H4 of royalty resisting the embodiment of royal justice is poignantly

49

expressed in Lady Constance's claim that 'There's law and warrant . . . for [her] curse':

> When law can do no right,
> Let it be lawful that law bar no wrong.
> Law cannot give my child his kingdom here,
> For he that holds his kingdom holds the law.
> Therefore, since law itself is perfect wrong,
> How can the law forbid my tongue to curse?
> (JN 3.1.110–16)

As Ian Ward, who surveys the debate over Shakespeare and theories of law and monarchy, says: 'Constitutionally, it seems, Shakespeare is still to be claimed' (Ward, I., 1996, p 286).

(C) On the historical, and on Shakespeare's fictional, Chief Justice Gascoigne see: Keeton, 1930, pp 155–62; Merchant, 1964, p 117; Phillips, O. H., 1967, p 198.

Taft, 1995 holds that the actions of the Lord Chief Justice in 2H4 suggest he stands not for profound justice, but 'just for law and order'. But for most critics the role of the Lord Chief Justice raises issues having constitutional importance. Hamilton, D. B., 1983 offers a valuable discussion of Shakespeare's contexts and the question of the king being subject to law (mainly in relation to R2), identifying in many Elizabethan commentators a doctrine descending from the thirteenth century Henry of Bracton holding that kings are made by and are bound by the law. Hamilton claims recent historical work supports this position, which diverges from widespread Shakespearian editorial 'glosses that derive their authority from nineteenth-century scholarship'. Gohn, 1982, commenting also on R2, offers an opposite position, claiming Shakespeare altered the historical fact in favour of absolutism. The debate far is from closed, as seen in: Barton, A., 1994, pp 136–60; Ward, I., 1995, pp 59–89; Ward, I., 1996, 1997; Hutson, 1996, pp 265–8.

civil doctor (A) Lawyers who practised Roman civil law (mainly in the ecclesiastical courts) were known as civilians, or civil doctors. They were graduates of Oxford or Cambridge and sometimes had studied at other continental European Universities. Civilians were members of Doctor's Commons, founded in the late fifteenth century.

In 1534, after the controversy over the royal **divorce**, Henry VIII prohibited the teaching of canon law in England, and so it was after this date that civilian lawyers took over the work of the English Church courts. Civilian lawyers also practised in the Court of Admiralty, the Court of Requests, the Council of the North and the Council of the Marches of Wales, and could act as experts in international law. However in Shakespeare's age civilians were altogether less important and less numerous than common lawyers, probably numbering some two hundred to about two thousand common lawyers. In terms of professional and academic standing the civil doctor ranked alongside a serjeant-at-law (see under **lawyers** and **justices**), although civilians were much less likely than these to come from the gentry or nobility and much more likely to be commoners. Civilians were also more frequently employed in government office than common lawyers (Levack, 1973, pp 3, 9–16).

Doctors of civil law conducted the Church courts' 'instance' jurisdiction over marriage, probate, defamation, perjury and tithes. They also conducted *ex officio* cases in the Church courts, which included the trial of spiritual crimes, and offences against public and private morality. This jurisdiction covered a very wide variety of matters, for instance heresy, fornication and adultery.

Civil doctors were also prominent among the officials of the Court of Chancery. Whether Chancery masters' civilian training had a very significant influence over the Chancellors' **equity** jurisdiction is a matter of debate; for the contemporary theorist Edward Hake, who was influenced by the Elizabethan civilian lawyer Sir Julius Caesar, however, it was a matter of firm belief (see the third of Hake's three unpublished dialogues in Hake, 1953).

Although Edward Coke's views on the distinctiveness of the English common law were in part propagandistic, it is no doubt true that English common law did persist and strengthen at a time during which other European countries (including Scotland) saw a 'reception' of civil or Roman law. Maitland's famous lecture, 'English Law and the Renaissance' (Maitland, 1901) attributes the continuation of English legal traditions while many continental traditions were being subordinated to Roman-based codification to the unique existence in England of establishments teaching the indigenous law, the **Inns of Court**. Varied views, including intensifications, corrections and other insights have been offered on this thesis, including those in several essays bearing Maitland's lecture's title: Kelley, 1974; Thorne, 1985d, Baker, 1986d, and Sharpe, K. and Brooks, 1976. Interestingly, Sharpe, K. and Brooks, 1976, especially pp 135–8, points out that many Inns of Court men had previously studied civilian law at Oxford or Cambridge, and so even common lawyers had civilian training.

One of the most important civilian lawyers of Shakespeare's time was Dr John Cowell (1554–1611), Regius Professor at Cambridge from 1594, master of Trinity Hall from 1598 until his death, and Vice Chancellor of Cambridge University in 1603 and 1604. At its foundation in 1350 Trinity Hall was intended for the training of canon and civil lawyers. As mentioned, the teaching of canon law was suppressed in 1534. The fortunes of the civil law were further advanced in 1540 when Henry VIII founded a chair in the subject. Trinity Hall had close links with the practising lawyers of Doctor's Commons. Cowell was also a protege of Richard Bancroft, and in 1604 helped prepare a list of canons repugnant to Puritanism. Then the energetically intellectual Dr Cowell in 1605 attempted to put English common law into a civilian framework, but by 1607 aspects of his enterprise led to political uproar. He had a particular enemy in Edward Coke, who derisively called him 'Dr Cow-heel'. The political differences between Coke, who championed the independence of common lawyers and parliamentarians, and Dr Cowell, who defended a nearly absolute royal prerogative, reached crisis over Cowell's heavily slanted 'definitions' of 'King', 'Parliament', 'Prerogative of the King' and 'Subsidy' in a law dictionary, Cowell, 1607. Eventually King James responded to the resulting outrage, ordering that this Dictionary be suppressed by proclamation (Larkin and Hughes, 1973, vol 1, pp 243–5). Cowell died soon after.

(B) Shakespeare implicitly recognises that the canon law was at issue in Henry VIII's divorce of Queen Katherine, and that it was suppressed soon after his divorce. Canonists or civil doctors are mentioned explicitly in the Folio stage direction to AIT 2.4: 'Trumpets, Sennet, and Cornets. Enter two Vergers, with short siluer wands; next them two Scribes in the habite of Doctors . . . ' (tln 1332–4). They are further mentioned when Henry complains of a spiritual and religious malaise due to his marriage:

I meant to rectify my conscience, which
I then did feel full sick, and yet not well,
By all the reverend fathers of the land
And doctors learned.

(AIT 2.4.200–3)

As mentioned above, the divorce-led English Reformation did not
bring a Roman Law 'reception' to England (although some argue it
nearly might have), but did leave canon law in bad repute and its
teaching suppressed at Oxford and Cambridge. Perhaps for allied
reasons, misanthropic, misogynistic and law-hating Timon rants to
Alcibides:

I not desire to know. Follow thy drum.
With man's blood paint the ground gules, gules.
Religious canons, civil laws, are cruel;
Then what should war be? This fell whore of thine
Hath in her more destruction than thy sword,
For all her cherubin look.

(TIM 4.3.58–63)

Civil law was in current use in Shakespeare's England in the courts
of Request and Admiralty; these two prerogative jurisdictions were
intended respectively to protect poor against rich, and to adjudicate
international merchant disputes. Perhaps for such reasons, or perhaps
because of its continental setting, the lawyers in MV are repeatedly
called 'doctors', meaning civil lawyers. Ironically, the Paduan Doctor
Bellario's substitute, Portia cross-dressed as Doctor Balthasar of Rome,
is described mistakenly by ring-duped Bassanio: 'No woman had it, but
a civil doctor' (MV 5.1.210).

More doubtfully, other doctors of civil law may be referenced by
Shakespeare. A problem of definition may arise. As explained in
Levack, 1981, pp 108–15, the membership of the civilian profession
was undefined, for Doctors Commons was an 'informal association'
and no other body controlled admission to the profession (p. 113).
Ibid., p 112, adds that sometimes clerics practised canon law as 'inci-
dental to their main profession'. But Levack, 1973, p 20, focusing on
the period 1603–41, describes some professional regulation by Doctor's Commons, and, pp 63–6, details actions taken by James I and

Charles I against appointments of untrained clerics to civilian judicial posts.

In light of these ambiguities, Shakespeare may refer to another civil doctor. His historical source in Hall (and More's) *Union*, states explicitly that the 'Doctor Shaw', named only in the Folio version of R3 (tln 2191, following R3 3.5.100), was Rafe Shaa, a doctor of divinity 'of more learning than virtue, of more fame than learning'. However, because Shaw's testimony was used to allege (falsely) that both Edward and his children were illegitimate, the issues that Doctor Shaw addresses are of canon law (see **bastardy**).

Claudio's strange comparison, 'But then is an ape a doctor to such a man' (ADO 5.1.197–8), may refer to a doctor of physic, or possibly a learned civil doctor.

The 'churlish priest' of HAM 5.1.235 who limits Ophelia's 'Maimed' funeral rites (5.1.214ff – see **self-slaughter**) is identified the speech head of the second quarto text of HAM as 'Doct.' Draper, 1936, p 233, suggests that this indicates a 'Doctor of Civil Law', and probably one 'of the Church of England'.

(C) For discussion of Jacobean conflicts over civil law see Merchant, 1964, pp 109–17 and Ives, 1964, p 74, and Sharpe, K. and Brooks, 1976. Ives, p 78, sees a greater gulf between civilians and common lawyers than do many later studies, but not greater than does Kelley, 1974, which carries to an extreme Maitland's views of the difference between English and continental law. Kelley's position is replied to by Sharpe, K. and Brooks, 1976, and sympathetic views are taken of Coke and others also in Gray, C., 1980; Berman, 1994.

See Levack, 1973 on the English civilian lawyers under the early Stuarts, and Levack, 1981 on their profession from 1500–1750. On the history of Doctor's Commons see Squibb, 1977.

On the civilians and Chancery see Jones, W. J., 1967, especially pp 111, 266, 301, 381. This detailed study generally finds that the civilian lawyers associated with Chancery did not greatly influence the Chancellor's equitable jurisdiction. However, Yale, 1965, pp 49–50, attributes to the use of civilian procedural devices much of the popularity of that jurisdiction.

On the English Canons of 1603–4, see under **impediment**, and on the relations of common law and Church courts see under **jurisdictions** and **praemunire**.

On the avoidance of a 'reception' of Roman civil law in England see: Maitland, 1901; Kelley, 1974; Sharpe, K. and Brooks, 1976; Thorne, 1985d; Baker, 1986d.

On the Dr Cowell scandal see Simon, 1968a for detail, and for its background see McIlwain, 1918, pp 308–10 and Sokol and Sokol, 1999b. Levack, 1973 treats this affair pp 101–6, and the wider context of civilians and Royal powers pp 81–117; Kelley, 1974, especially pp 29–40, characterises the conflict between Coke and systematizers and civilians such as Cowell as a symptom of English insularity resisting continental subtlety and historicism; this article, pp 42–5, especially praises the 'legal humanism' of the English civilian Thomas Smith.

Bate, 1995, p 28, suggests that Roman civil law, exemplified for instance in Saturnius 'chilling' insistence in TIT 4.4.54 that Martius and Quintius 'died by law', is opposed in the play with the English common law associated with Titus' appeal to **precedent**. Bate suggests that civil law was in 1594 'associated with arbitrary government'. This would be in accord with later political campaigns, following the accession of James.

Kerr, 1992, in a discussion connecting legal uses of evidence with classical rhetoric (in this resembling Altman, 1978 and Hutson, 1994), like Bate alleges a 'darker side' of civil law informs arbitrary judgment in TIT.

However the employment of a 'civil doctor' in MV does not convey a notion of a 'darker side' of civil law to most legally interested critics of the play (except possibly Campbell, S., 1992). On how one alleged connection of law in MV with Roman law is unlikely, see Barrett, 1983.

In a discussion of marriage in HAM, Jardine, 1991, pp 137–8, suggests that the English canons of 1603, the church laws applied by civil doctors, were left in a 'kind of deliberate limbo'. See under **impediment** on these canons.

Lindley, 1996, especially pp 337–49 makes careful use of historical distinctions between common law and ecclesiastical **jurisdictions** and principles in a re-evaluation of the pardon of Barnadine in MM.

Marcus, 1988, especially pp 152 and 166n, connects the Roman setting of CYM with the Jacobean question of union with Scotland, and comments on how Roman civil law was used by advocates both pro and anti-union.

clemency See **pardon/clemency**.

co-heirs (A) A co-heir shares equally in an **inheritance**. In early modern England the customary rule of inheritance known as **primogeniture** allowed the eldest son to take all his deceased father's property, thus excluding the interests of sisters or any younger brothers. But if a man died leaving no sons to inherit then different customary rules were applied which allowed daughters to inherit in preference to any collateral male. An only daughter took the whole inheritance, but otherwise sisters shared in the inheritance equally, which was known as co-parceny. This rule came into use following the *statutum decretum* of Henry I. However inheritance of the Crown was excluded from the co-parceny rule, and an eldest sister took to the exclusion of others (Baker, 1990b, p 306).

In certain parts of Britain, mainly Wales and Kent, another customary rule known as gavelkind, allowed equal sharing by male co-heirs of land (see **inheritance**). Land from dissolved monasteries in Kent was 'disgavelled' by 31 Hen. VIII, c.3 (as well as all land in Wales by 34 & 35 Hen. VIII, c.26) indicating desires of the new landowners to prevent partition (Baker, 1978, p 209; see also Bonfield, 1983, p 22). All these customary rules of inheritance could be excluded by a **will** after the 1540 Statute of Wills.

(B) In WT 2.1.146–52 Antiginous horribly threatens, if he learns that Hermione is truly unfaithful:

> I have three daughters: the eldest is eleven;
> The second and the third nine and some five;
> If this prove true, they'll pay for 't. By mine honour,
> I'll geld 'em all. Fourteen they shall not see,
> To bring false generations. They are co-heirs,
> And I had rather glib myself than they
> Should not produce fair issue.

(C) See Baker, 1990b, pp 306–7 on the complexities of coparceny. The concept is also discussed in Clarkson and Warren, 1942, pp 218–19, where a reference in AYL 1.2.16–19 to a sole daughter's presumptive inheritance which she wishes to share with a female friend is unconvincingly related to co-parceny. Kentish gavelkind is mentioned in relation to *King Lear* in Wilson, R., 1993, p 221, although Lear has only daughters and co-parceny applied in all counties.

commodity The term 'commodity' had a peculiarly complex range of meanings, and widely diverse implications of these meanings are often fused in Shakespeare's uses.

'Commodity' may refer to trade-relations generally, and 'commodities' to the goods of legitimate trade. Also 'a commodity' of something may be a shipment, parcel or job-lot of specified trade goods. Such meanings normally convey valuations only of the useful or practical, but cynical or ominous overtones are heard when Falstaff identifies his initial group of recruits as a job-lot or 'commodity of warm slaves as had as lief hear the devil as a drum' (1H4 4.2.18–19).

In other contexts 'commodity' can mean convenience, personal advantage, expediency, acquisitiveness, opportunity, or self-interest. For example Falstaff, ill with intemperance, says he will sham a war wound to gain a pension and 'turn diseases to commodity' (2H4 1.2.246–51). Thoroughgoing cynicism informs an encomium of 'commodity' by the amoral **bastard** Faulconbridge, in which greed, ambition, and dishonesty are seen as universal traits, and essential for success:

> That smooth-faced gentleman, tickling commodity;
> Commodity, the bias of the world . . .
> This sway of motion, this commodity,
> Makes it take head from all indifferency,
> From all direction, purpose, course, intent;
> And this same bias, this commodity,
> This bawd, this broker, this all-changing word . . .
> And why rail I on this commodity?
> But for because he hath not wooed me yet -
> Not that I have the power to clutch my hand
> When his fair angels would salute my palm,
> But for my hand, as unattempted yet,
> Like a poor beggar raileth on the rich . . .
> Since kings break faith upon commodity,
> Gain, be my lord, for I will worship thee.
> (JN 2.1.574–99)

In Faulconbridge's sense, 'commodity' is a term for selfishly seeking personal gain.

Seeking gain is associated with commerce or moneylending when cynical Parolles names a woman's virginity as a 'commodity' to be used as 'principle' allowing a rapid large 'increase' (AWW 1.1.145–51). Indeed 'commodity' could denote trade itself, as in Antonio acceptance that Shylock must be granted his bond to defend 'the commodity that strangers have / With us in Venice' (MV 3.3.27–8).

Moneylending, commerce and cynicism combine in a particular trick used to elude the Elizabethan **usury** laws, known as 'taking up a commodity'. In this despised practice moneylenders evaded the legal restriction of interest on loans to 10% (see **debt**) by means of a fictitious sale to the borrower of a 'commodity' of overpriced goods. The borrower would purchase the goods on credit from the moneylender and then obtain cash by immediately reselling them for a much lower price, usually to the moneylender himself. When the debt became due the difference between the amount of credit nominally advanced and the money actually taken by the borrower in the 'sale' of the goods amounted to effective interest paid far beyond the legal maximum. Often the goods in question had very little intrinsic value, and so were referred to as 'a commodity of brown paper, or the like' (OED, commodity 7.b).

Thus the 'drawing of young gentlemen into security for commodities of tobacco and phillizellas and such unnecessary stuffs' was one of the new abuses dealt with by the enterprising court of **Star Chamber** (Baker, 1985, p 45). The ruinous luring of the improvident into this travesty of genuine trade is described by writers such as Robert Greene.

Shakespeare did not dramatise the actual process of this abuse, but did often allude to it. So Pompey describes a 'young Master Rash' imprisoned for debt: 'he's in for a commodity of brown paper and old ginger, nine score and seventeen pounds, of which he made five marks ready money' (MM 4.3.4–7). In ERR 4.3.4–6 the bewildered Antipholus of Syracuse wonders that 'Some [strangers] tender money to me . . . / Some offer me commodities to buy', with a likely humorous shading toward 'taking up commodities', as the play is centrally concerned with unpaid debt.

In ADO, a similar oblique allusion dovetails into a complex pun involving also **constables'** bills and bills of exchange. After two comic mentions in the scene of constables' 'bills', their weapons of office (see **bills**), the arrested Borachio and Conrad jest about 'taking up commodities': 'We are like to prove a goodly commodity, being taken up of these men's bills' (ADO 3.3.170–2).

A somewhat similar pun on 'commodities' and 'bills' appears when a fellow rebel asks Jack Cade 'My lord, when shall we go to Cheapside and take up commodities upon our bills? (CYL 4.7.141–2). 'Bills' here refers to the rebels' edged weapons, or workmen's tools and mattocks, used to take 'commodities' (goods) by illicit force. But the phrasing also travesties Elizabethan commercial language concerning credit, in which **bills** are documents, and commodities trade goods.

constable (A) The Lord High Constable and Earl Marshal presided over the court which by the later middle ages had jurisdiction over military matters arising outside England. This included the discipline of the army, appeals of **treason** or **felony** committed outside the **jurisdiction**, and in times of war rules of martial law, including questions of prisoners of war and prizes, or payment of ransom. (Similarly, the Court of the Lord High Admiral of England dealt with matters arising out of the jurisdiction on the high seas.) The Court of the Lord High Constable and Marshal went into decline in 1521 after Henry VIII beheaded the Duke of Buckingham, the last holder of the office of Lord High Constable (on his trial as represented in AIT see under **bar** and **treason**). In order to avoid bringing an **appeal** against Sir Francis Drake, Elizabeth refused to agree to a new appointment. Under James I the Earl Marshal's court revived to deal with coats of arms and other honours; this was among the concilliar courts which developed out of the King's council, and which followed civil law procedure and not common law (see **civil doctor**).

In contrast to the Lord High Constable, the high constable and the petty constable were the representatives of local authority in Tudor England. The origins of the office are obscure, but opinion in sixteenth century considered that the constable's authority replaced that exercised by community elders pre-conquest (Lambard, 1583). In medieval England the country was divided into shires, then subdivided into hundreds and tithings, or groups of ten men, who stood as pledges or securities for each other for maintaining the king's peace. The representatives of hundreds and tithings were known by the old names of tithingman, borsholder or **headborough**, which may reflect names given to ancient local rulers. The 'constable' was a later name said to mean 'hold of the king' (ibid., p 5 – although OED suggests 'count or officer of the stable'). He was the unpaid representative of the hundreds, one of whose most important duties was to be answerable for his community's wrongdoing, or breaches of the king's peace, at the hundred court or before the **sheriff**'s 'tourn', a biannual visitation.

The local community, through the constable, could be amerced, or fined, for wrongdoing. The distinction between high constable and petty constable reflects the difference between larger and smaller communities. Probably the high constable once had a military role to perform for the king.

When royal justice expanded in the fourteenth century the constable found himself in a dual role. He was answerable to the King as the representative of royal justice and also to the **sheriff** and other members of the hundred as their appointee. From the Statute of Westminster 1380 onwards several **statutes** added to the constable's responsibilities, for policekeeping, supervising weights and measures, enforcing statutes, regulating wages and **apprenticeships**, and supervising the collection of taxes. By the seventeenth century the constable was expected to assist the sheriff, for example by executing warrants, and was a recognised agent of royal authority. Constables were issued with lengthy 'articles', lists of matters on which they should make reports, either to the sheriff's court, to the **Justice of the Peace**, or by the seventeenth century to the royal **justices** at the assize courts. In this way their activities were closely supervised, and they were held personally responsible to account for any default of duty.

A sixteenth century description of constable's duties includes the remark that when the constable arrests an offender he must be conveyed to gaol. The constable must be careful to guard the offender well because if he escapes through the constable's contrivance or negligence then the constable himself will be fined by the justices. Also 'if the arrest were for felonie, then by a willing escape, the officer himself becomes a felon also' (Lambard, 1583, pp 22–3).

It has been argued that after the early seventeenth century the importance of the constable declined, while that of other parish officials, for example churchwardens and overseers to the poor, increased (Holdsworth, 1903, vol 4, pp 121–5). However more recent studies of local records indicate that the police and administrative functions of constables increased in late Tudor and early Stuart England (Kent, 1986). Constables retained a central role in policekeeping, organizing watch and ward, **hue and cry**, arresting and guarding prisoners, and executing warrants. The constable also acted as the sheriff's agent in collecting fines and imprisoning offenders in the stocks.

Other miscellaneous civil functions of constables included organising and supervising the work of the community on 'common days' to maintain highways, licensing alehouses, registering recusants and, most importantly, responsibility for administering the vagrancy acts. These acts required the constable to see that **vagrants** were whipped and sent onwards to the parish of their birth, or imprisoned in Houses of Correction, and to issue them with the certificate which they needed to travel from parish to parish.

Local custom appears to have dictated who would serve a term of office as a constable. He would be chosen from a number of property holders, and the duty to serve often rotating among them supposedly for a term of one year. The duty was often attached to ownership of a certain house or land, in much the same way as the duty to serve as a member of a **jury** attached to ownership of particular hereditaments. As a result it was not necessarily the most substantial local property owner who would be chosen. If the property holder was ineligible, being for example a woman or a priest, they would be expected to provide a substitute who could serve.

Once selected the constable was confirmed in office at the court **leet** of the hundred or manor, and would take his oath of office there. By the sixteenth and early seventeenth century, as the parish increased in importance as an administrative unit, the appointment might be made by the parish vestry. Alternatively in Shakespeare's time the justice of the peace sometimes appointed the constable to office (by 1662 this exercise of authority was confirmed by an Act of Parliament).

Once appointed the constable would be expected to perform his office unpaid, although he could claim an 'allowance' to cover the expense he would otherwise have to meet from his own resources. There can be little doubt that the office was onerous and some were reluctant to accept it. In 1608 the Privy Council discussed a proposal to allow men to avoid service by payment of a sum of money. Recent research into local records shows that some refused to hold office or complained about the length or frequency of office, and also indicates extensive use of substitutes by those reluctant to serve themselves. However the incidence of such objections was not extensive, and most accepted the office without complaint (Kent, 1986, p 74). But, by the 1630s, the increased number of very unpopular of taxes to be collected by constables (for example ship money), did lead to more complaint.

Shakespeare and some contemporaries (e.g. Francis Bacon in his

'Office of the Constable', Bacon, 1872, vol 7, p 751) portray the Elizabethan constable as uneducated, possibly illiterate and generally of low social status. It appears however that the difference in the wealth, education and social standing of the constable varied in different parts of the country. The constable's social status and education reflected the prosperity of his particular community, for in general it was the more wealthy men of the area who were eligible for office. In the countryside they were often yeomen (Kent, 1986, p 82).

It has been argued by social historians that especially before the 1620s or 30s petty constables were typically reluctant to enforce rigorously laws that could excite conflict within their communities, or which might incite reprisals against them in their villages or towns. Instances of resulting dereliction of duty include negligent policing of alehouses, apprenticeship, and sometimes even bawdry or **theft** (Wrightson, 1983, esp. p 24 and passim). Investigations show many cases of poor men taking constables' offices for pay, or under duress, and also of negligent, drunken or disorderly constables. Yet these were not typical; many constables were able, substantial citizens. There was a wide local variation in petty constables' educational attainments: in 1642 their bare literacy varied from 93% in Dorset, through 50% in Warwickshire, down to 0% in Westmorelandshire (ibid., pp 26–9, p 28).

(B) In AIT 2.1.103, the disgraced Duke of Buckingham, now mere Edward Bohun, laments on his way to execution that he was once Lord High Constable of England. As mentioned above, he was the last of that office.

In H5 the haughty Lord High Constable of France is the first called to the field by King Charles (3.5.40), and is the first listed among the French Lords killed at Agincourt (4.8.92).

The rest of Shakespeare's constables are of a lowly sort, although the ambiguity of their title may be exploited in the quibbling clown Lavatch's claim to have an answer to all questions, metaphorically, 'From beyond your duke to beneath your constable' (AWW 2.2.29).

In the Shakespearian instances, law enforcement by constables is often derided or defied. In WIV 4.5.112 Falstaff complains that a 'knave constable' had set him in the stocks (see **wise woman**); in ROM 1.4.40 Mercutio urges Romeo to nocturnal escapades with 'Tut, dun's the mouse, the constable's own word'; in TMP 3.2.25–6 the reeling drunk Trinculo declares 'I am in case to jostle a constable'.

Although he appears in several scenes of LLL and often speaks, mere absurdity dominates the presentation of constable Antony Dull. Self-identified as the Duke's 'farborough' (LLL 1.1.182 – an alternate spelling of **thirdborough**), Dull is consistently malaprop and maladroit. In his final reply in the play (prior to offering to do a country dance or bang a tabor) he establishes that his mentality is true to his name:

HOLOFERNES: goodman Dull! Thou hast spoken no word all this while.

DULL: Nor understood none neither, sir.

(LLL 5.1.142–4)

More historical interest arises from the comic characterisations of the petty constables in ADO and MM, who despite their witless methods do help enforce justice.

Constable Elbow's malapropisms and muddling so confuse the courtroom in MM 2.1 that, without the astuteness of Justice Escalus, the accused Pompey would have escaped altogether. Elbow's madcap accusations somehow concern a brothel, a dish of stewed prunes, and some insult to his own pregnant wife. Escalus is partly bemused and indulges in undignified witticism himself, but he detects the dangers posed by Pompey to the fatuous Froth, whom he warns (MM 2.1.196–9). Escalus rightly detects Pompey to be 'partly a bawd howsoever you colour it in being a tapster' (2.1.208–12), but (although the legal shambles initiated by Elbow includes Pompey's full but unrepentant confession), Pompey is released with a warning. Escalus next examines the ineffectual Elbow himself, who admits to having been constable of his ward for 'seven year and a half', repeatedly taking the place of those responsible to fulfil the office in exchange for 'some piece of money'. This abuse is a matter that Escalus will pursue, and he commands Elbow: 'Look you bring me in the names of some six or seven, the most sufficient of your parish' (2.1.260–1).

The constables Dogberry and Verges of ADO are hardly less bumbling than Elbow in their methods, and Dogberry in his pretentiously inaccurate parroting of official phraseology is certainly not less malaprop than Dull or Elbow. Yet Dogberry and Verges, together with the inimitable watch of Messina, dominate four and a fraction scenes of the play, and speak about 7% of its text. They also take the main part in the unravelling of the plot's complications. Moreover, despite their

63

ineptness, Dogberry and Verges do clarify their 'better's' tendency to misapprehension, and so contribute to the play's thematic concerns.

At their first appearance Verges urges Dogberry to 'charge' or instruct the watch (ADO 3.3.7). Dogberry duly bids them: continue illiterate; permit any man, particularly a vagrant, who will not 'stand' or submit upon command, to go freely; sleep on duty; not meddle with drunkards, thieves, or even crying babies (3.3.1–84). These derelictions of duty are all justified by exquisite comic logic, skitting various jurisprudential questions. Thus 3.3.55–9 raises the issue of public order v excessive judicial **mercy**:

DOGBERRY   The most peaceable way for you if you do take a thief is to let him show himself what he is, and steal out of your company.
VERGES   You have been always called a merciful man, partner.

Similarly 3.3.71–9 links with the question of how far the king's justice may go in dealing with royalty (see under **Chief Justice**):

DOGBERRY   You, constable, are to present the Prince's own person. If you meet the Prince in the night you may stay him.
VERGES   Nay, by 'r Lady, that I think a cannot.
DOGBERRY   Five shillings to one on 't with any man that knows the statutes he may stay him. Marry, not without the Prince be willing, for indeed the watch ought to offend no man, and it is an offence to stay a man against his will.

Moreover, as seen in editorial glosses tracing back to Steevens, Dogberry's and Verges' conclusions (3.3.62–70) that the watch should make a limited attempt to wake negligent nurses to attend their crying charges may be a 'burlesque upon the Statutes of the Streets' of 1595 (White, E. J., 1987, p 68). Whether the passage alludes to these laws or not, it does raise, with wonderfully apropos imagery, the issue of the boundary between a nanny state's and an individual's responsibilities.

Immediately following their session of training in laxness, the Messina watch miraculously apprehend Conrad and Borachio, and succeed in making them stand (on the two culprits' replies on being taken see **commodity**). But in 3.5 Dogberry and Verges manage only to bemuse Leonato with their garbled account of this arrest. He, (unlike old

Escalus in MM) misses a serious abuse on account of its clownish narration, and so sends the watch off to perform their own (self-styled) 'excommunication' of the suspects. In 4.1, a rational Sexton makes sense of the plot (such an officer is pertinent here, as the sexual **slander** in question would be a matter for the **jurisdiction** of a Church court). Nevertheless in 5.1.201–22 Dogberry puts the matter so badly that the prince Don Pedro remarks, again bemusedly, 'This learned constable is too cunning to be understood'. Next, happily, Borachio confesses. The constables and watch in ADO thereby finally assist true justice, despite ineptitude.

Although Shakespeare's bumbling constables sometimes manage proper vigilance where their 'betters' fail, he made them seem worse in capability than contemporary records seem to bear out. Why he did this remains unexplained.

(C) On the Lord High Constable and Earl Marshal of England and of France see Meron, 1993, p 12, and Baker, 1990b, pp 141–3.

Lambard, 1583 sets out the duties of constables and is a valuable resource. Generally see Holdsworth, 1903, vol 4, pp 122–5. The recent historical studies in Wrightson, 1983 and Kent, 1986 argue that Elizabethan petty or village constables did not wholly deserve the ridicule and criticism they received in their own period and since.

The portrayal of the inefficiency of petty constables, no doubt exaggerated satirically by Shakespeare, is mistaken for an historical record in Keeton, 1930, pp 47–54. While giving a detailed lawyer's account of the activity of the constables of ADO, White, E. J., 1987, pp 69–74 is more circumspect in alleging Shakespeare's own 'deep seated dislike for constables'. Draper, 1943, pp 572–5, gives a historically informed reading of the same scenes, bringing out the hilarity of their travesties of legal procedures and terminology. On the historical authenticity of Dogberry giving a 'charge' to the watch see ibid., p 569, and Phillips, O. H., 1967, pp 196–7.

The sorts of criminality that a local constable would have had to deal with in 1602 is indicated both statistically and anecdotally in Knafla, 1983. The statistics given in this essay confirm a contemporary view of an increase in crime, and the ripe anecdotes make Dogberry's advice to his watch to avoid as far as possible all contact with reprobates seem quite good sense.

The bulk of commentary on Shakespeare's constables focuses on

Dogberry's strangely successful performance of his duties. Drawing on accusations heard in the era, Frasure, 1934, and Draper, 1943, alleged realism in Shakespeare's and his contemporary dramatists' depictions of useless and possibly corrupt constables. However Spinrad, 1992, citing more recent historical studies, suggests that Dogberry and even Elbow are 'true heroes', not enforcing oppression or enacting oppressive surveillance, yet able to defend their communities from harm 'when government is ineffectual' (p. 178).

contract Nearly every one of the numerous mentions of a 'contract' or of 'contracting' in Shakespeare's plays refers to a spousal contract (as seen in 1H6, R3, ROM, 1H4, WIV, AYL, HAM, TN, AWW, MM, LRQ, LRF, CYM, WT, TMP). The few exceptions to such uses include mentions of peace treaties as 'contracts' in 1H6 and CYL, and Gonzalo's phrase 'contract, succession, / Bourn, bound of land, tilth, vineyard, none' (TMP 2.1.157–8), which is a portion of his utopian fantasy taken nearly exactly from Florio's translation of Montaigne's 'Of the Cannibals'.

Generally, modern contract law was in a nascent state in Shakespeare' time: on its early manifestations see under **debt**, **on the case**, and **account**. On the legalities surrounding marriage contracts see under especially **pre-contract**, and also **impediments** and **divorce**.

convert/conversion (A) In law, 'conversion' is wrongfully to appropriate another's **chattels** for personal use.

The action of detinue was the original remedy to protect the security of personal property, but like the action of debt this action often brought considerable disadvantages to the plaintiff (these included the possibilities of wager of law, or of incomplete compensation; see **debt**). From the fifteenth century conversion increasingly became subject to actions **on the case** (see Simpson, 1987c). To avoid actions of detinue, a legal fiction was contrived called 'trover and conversion', which alleged that misappropriated goods had been lost by the plaintiff and then found by the defendant and retained. The application of this fiction, like the fiction that an *assumpsit* could be applied to all **debts** (see under **on the case**), was at first resisted by the Court of Common

Pleas, but during Shakespeare's lifetime it was established as an accept-able basis for actions on the case (Baker, 1990b, p 450).

Thus during Shakespeare's period the old writ of detinue was replaced by a range of actions on the case. These included those for conversion where there was withholding and misconduct, for *assumpsit* where there was an undertaking and nonfeasance, and for damages where goods were altered, destroyed or lost.

(B) To 'convert' something is mainly used by Shakespeare to indicate an altering of its use or nature. However, Timon's stream of curses, including:

> Obedience fail in children! Slaves and fools,
> Pluck the grave wrinkled senate from the bench
> And minister in their steads! To general filths
> Convert o' th' instant, green virginity!
>
> (TIM 4.1.4–7)

may gain in force from a legal overtone in which the 'conversion' of virginity was by wrongful seizure, e. g. **rape**.

The term 'converted' also may carry sinister overtones in wealthy Portia's declaration to her successful suitor, the impoverished Bassanio, that:

> Myself and what is mine to you and yours
> Is now converted. But now I was the lord
> Of this fair mansion, master of my servants,
> Queen o'er myself; and even now, but now,
> This house, these servants, and this same myself
> Are yours, my lord's. I give them with this ring,
>
> (MV 3.2.166–71)

'Converted' is strangely placed here, especially in a play where misap-propriated rings, theft of money, and illicit means to marriage are prominent. Of course Jessica's marriage was accompanied by the actual conversion of Shylock's goods. It has been suggested sometimes that Portia traduces her father's **will**, therefore taking his goods illicitly, by passing hints to Bassanio during the casket test just before these lines.

Possible dark resonances in MV of 'convert' are especially arresting

67

because to convert could also mean to change religious faith. Jessica becomes a Christian in order to marry Lorenzo (MV 2.3.21). Otherwise, in English law, Lorenzo would be subject to dire punishments (see Sokol, 1998). Jessica later explicitly mentions 'converting Jews to Christians' amid oddly cynical banter about religious conversion (MV 3.5.17–34 – see ibid. on the legal overtones of this scene). Finally a conversion 'presently' to Christianity is forced upon Shylock (4.1.384) at the culmination of the play's trial scene. But in 5.1.292 Shylock is still referred to as 'the rich Jew'.

(C) For accounts of conversion and detinue see Milsom, 1981, pp 366–79, Simpson, 1987c, and Baker, 1990b, pp 413–14, 447–52.

Oldrieve, 1993, pp 95–7 links forced conversion with the legal and political plight of those finding themselves outside of the (often changing) established religions of early modern England.

conveyance (A) Conveyance is the term for the legal transfer of ownership of property from one person to another, in particular the transfer of **land**. By Shakespeare's time it was possible to effect such a transfer in a number of ways, although none were without difficulties.

In Shakespeare's age land law and conveyancing continued to be governed by a feudal framework of rules, although the medieval feudal structure to land-holding had become inappropriate as trade, commerce and population expanded. Historians have long argued over whether or not it was possible to **inherit** or to alienate (transfer to another) land at the time of the Norman Conquest, largely because such dealing with land did not fit well with the doctrine of tenures (on this doctrine see **land**). According to the orthodox theory, William I introduced the 'feudal system' to England. The feudal relationship between lord and tenant can be seen as personal and contractual. The tenant offered homage and fealty to the lord. In return the lord warranted (guaranteed) the tenant's title, providing compensation if it was defective. The kind of tenure granted by the lord determined the kind of services required by him, for example knight service, and in turn the different tenures determined which feudal incidents were payable by the tenant to the lord. For an example see the payment made when a tenant who had been a **ward** of the King was **suing his livery**.

The problem was to retain the relationship even if the tenant alien-ated the land. Until the Assize of Northampton in 1176 it had been necessary for the tenant's heir to pay a fine on admittance to the land, and in theory the lord could refuse a new heir or a new tenant.

The medieval form of conveyance was **enfeoffment** (investment) with livery of seisin. Seisin meant possession and demanded a degree of physical delivery of the land itself. Enfeoffment meant the grant of the land, and the requirement for livery of seisin was originally met by attendance on the land and a symbolic handing over of a clod of earth. The grant did not have to be by deed, but such a deed called a 'charter' was often executed as an additional record to the feoffee's public appearance on the land itself. In order to ensure the record was not lost or stolen, a copy could be entered onto court rolls, or executed in duplicate and then torn into two pieces. Each party would then keep part, called an **indenture**.

After the Statute of Uses 1536 a method of conveying land was devised which avoided formal livery of seisin. The Statute was aimed at executing a use of land (see under **use**), but it also executed a contract for a **lease**. So if a lessor contracted with a lessee for a lease and then subsequently granted a **reversion** of the same land to the same lessee, the whole interest amounting to the freehold passed from grantor to grantee without the need for livery of seisin. This method of con-veyancing was in use at the start of the seventeenth century and may have been known to Shakespeare.

Another form of conveyancing recorded by a deed (actually men-tioned by Shakespeare) was effected by legal fictions known as **fine and recovery**. Both fine and recovery and conveyance by deed of lease and release continued in use from Shakespeare's time until the nineteenth century.

Obtaining secure title by **purchase** was a particular problem because earlier defects in title were difficult to remedy later (Thorne, 1985i, p 202). Remote titles, hidden either by ignorance, error, or intent to defraud, could be suddenly produced to defeat present possession. This problem was exacerbated in the sixteenth century because most of the land of England was held in **use**. It was concern about the lack of any secure way of recording title to land that led landowners and their lawyers to adopt some of the expedients discussed above. Both vendor and purchaser were anxious to prove good title because a defective title no matter how long ago in the past could affect present possession.

The situation was open to fraud, and falsification of deeds was not uncommon. So in order to deter **thieves** and fraudsters, many deeds were stored in massive heavy chests.

A quite different popular understanding of the word 'conveyance' that was current in Shakespeare's time indicated theft with an overtone of contrivance or slight-of-hand (OED 4 and 11b).

(B) The complexities and uncertainties of land conveyancing seem to have impressed Hamlet when he mused on the skull of a lawyer:

> Will his vouchers vouch him no more of his purchases, and double ones too, than the length and breadth of a pair of indentures? The very conveyances of his lands will hardly lie in this box; and must th' inheritor himself have no more, ha?
>
> (HAM 5.1.105–9)

On this context, which includes mentions of fines and recoveries, see **fine and recovery**.

The meaning in which 'conveyance' indicates an underhandedly cunning or especially light-fingered removal inspires a number of Shakespearian uses in which it suggests furtive **theft** or worse:

> I am come to survey the Tower this day.
> Since Henry's death, I fear there is conveyance.
> (1H6 1.4.1–2)

> If this inducement move her not to love,
> Send her a letter of thy noble deeds.
> Tell her thou mad'st away her uncle Clarence,
> Her uncle Rivers – ay, and for her sake
> Mad'st quick conveyance with her good aunt Anne.
> (R3 4.4.265–9)

NIM   The good humour is to steal at a minute's rest.
PISTOL 'Convey' the wise it call. 'Steal'? Foh, a fico for the phrase!
> (WIV 1.3.25–6)

The last discussion, between professional thieves, suggests that if filching can be done in the time of a minim (that is, the smallest possible subdivision of musical time), it might be called 'convey' with a sense of conjuring away.

(C) See: Barton, J. L., 1976; Simpson, 1986, pp 119–37. On deceit in land purchasing, and the remedies, see Baker, 1990b, pp 383–4.

On Elizabethan dramatist's uses of the concept and term conveyance see Clarkson and Warren, 1942, pp 102–62. For a claim that several aspects of conveyancing are metaphorically applied by Shakespeare in WIV, and especially 'fraudulent conveyancing' see Ross, 1994.

copy (A) In **land** law 'copy' can refer to land held 'by copy of the court roll'. In medieval England this was known as villein tenure, and was therefore associated with **villein** or unfree status. The villein's title was entered onto the manorial court-roll, and his land was held according to the customs of the manor. Any disputes would be heard in the manorial court, not the central royal courts. By Shakespeare's time villeinage had died out and villein tenure was known as copyhold, no longer linked to any social status. As a consequence it became possible for copyholders to recover land (to gain or regain legal possession of it) in the King's courts in much the same way as freeholders, by the action of ejectment (see **lease**). Copyhold land could be inherited, and copyholders could create life estates or **entails** of copyhold land so that it descended to specified **heirs** (usually the eldest male). So by the seventeenth century copyholders had attained security of tenure, although the method of **conveying** land from one person to another still remained different from that of freeholders.

(B) Several contemporary playwrights alluded to copyhold tenure, some contracting this to 'copy'. Shakespeare only doubtfully did so, in the sinister marital exchange:

MACBETH	O, full of scorpions is my mind, dear wife!
	Thou know'st that Banquo and his Fleance lives.
LADY MACBETH	But in them nature's copy's not eterne.
MACBETH	There's comfort yet, they are assailable.

(MAC 3.2.37–40)

As noted by Paul S. Clarkson and Clyde T. Warren (Clarkson and

Warren, 1940), editors have frequently supposed that 'copy' here refers to the terminable nature of copyhold tenure. Clarkson and Warren deny this, for several reasons. One is an allegation of anachronism; they point out that the pre-conquest era of Macbeth (in Holinshed, 1040–1054) had no copyhold tenure, while in Shakespeare's time this tenure was no longer easily terminated by the will of Lords through their courts. But such an argument is not very strong, considering Shakespeare's insouciance with regard to greater anachronisms, such as the clocks striking three in *Julius Caesar*. More convincingly, they point out that no other Elizabethan dramatist refers to copyhold being easily terminable, and that copyhold was thought of as secure in Shakespeare's time.

There are other non-legal meanings of 'copy' more suited to the resonances of the passage. The uses of 'copy' in SON 11 and in WT 1.2.124 and 2.3.100 refer to how nature copies a parent in their child. If we consider the witches' show of the long string of Banquo's royal progeny (MAC 4.1.128ff), Lady Macbeth's hopeful use of the term 'copy' may be seen to mean progeny.

(C) An historical background is given in Clarkson and Warren, 1940, and somewhat expanded in a chapter of Clarkson and Warren, 1942, pp 37–48. Despite making reference to this, Muir, 1977, p 83n, suggests that 'the *legal* sense of *copy* may be an 'undertone of the passage'.

For discussions of the history of copyhold tenure see: Baker, 1990b, pp 347–50; Baker, 1985, p 52; Milsom, 1981, pp 163–5; Holdsworth, 1903, vol 3, pp 491- 510; Pollock and Maitland, 1898, pp, 369–70, 375; and especially Simpson, 1986, pp 144–72.

coram This word is used by the idiotic Slender in WIV 1.1.4–5 to refer to Justice Shallow, 'In the county of Gloucester, Justice of Peace and Coram'. Commentators have claimed that Slender's 'coram' refers either: (1) proudly to his uncle being a member of the 'quorum' of dignitaries required to act as a 'commission' of *oyer and terminer* (meaning hear and determine – see under **Justices of the Peace**); (2) or confusedly to the Latin 'coram' meaning 'before', which is used in legal phrases such as 'a writ of coram nobis' (bring before us), to be 'brought under coram' (to be called before a tribunal), etc.

Despite the syntax, the second meaning is not impossible, for Shallow has just threatened to have Falstaff called before the **Star Chamber**. On the other hand, Shallow himself appears to take up the first meaning from his nephew, by paralleling 'coram' with the actual office of **custalorum** (WIV 1.1.6). White, E. J., 1987, p 29, refers to only the second meaning, while Phillips, O. H., 1967, p 196, prefers the first.

It is probably most in keeping with Slender's simplicity to find him as inaccurate in the use of the term 'coram' as in his attribution to the self-styled 'Custalorum' Shallow of an office of 'Ratolorum too', which in fact is a malapropism for *custos rotalurum'*, the same office.

custalorum This is the contraction used in WIV 1.1.6 of the term *'custos rotalurum'*, a keeper of the shire records, required by 34–5 Hen. VIII, c. 27 53. A 'custalorum' could have been an important **Justice of the Peace** like Shallow, but OED 2 also cites Brougham's 1862 *British Constitution*, xvii:274, 'The Lord Lieutenant, or rather the Custos Rotulorum in each county'.

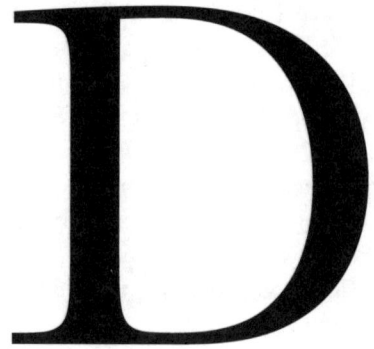

debt (A) The medieval writ of debt was one of the earliest forms of personal action that the royal courts considered, other than actions in **land** law. Of course any sort of obligation could be enforced by writs of covenant, but the royal courts would not enforce an obligation in a covenant unless it was incorporated into a deed under seal. Unwritten agreements therefore had to rely on actions in debt or detinue. Like the writ of detinue to which it was very closely allied, an action for debt was a claim to recover **chattels** withheld; the difference was that in an action for debt the property claimed was not an actual specific thing, but instead a certain sum of money or a measured quantity of generic 'fungibles' (such as ten bushels of barley). Actions of debt were sometimes collusive, intended to put an obligation on record in the court (in a way parallel with the collusive **fine** used in **conveyancing**). If the creditor brought the action in the king's court in an attempt to collect a contested debt, a defence was almost always available through 'compurgation' in a trial by 'wager of law'. This meant that the alleged debtor could swear that he did not owe the debt, and that this would be accepted as true if a specified number of 'compurgators' (usually eleven) would swear (not that they had any knowledge of the debt, but) that his oath was clean. Despite later complaints that this procedure was corruptible, there are indications that at least in the fifteenth century it was not as easy to be dishonest in such a way as it might seem (Simpson, 1987c, p 94).

An action of debt could be taken only if there was a *quid pro quo*, which is to say if there was an obligation arising from some visible transfer of goods, services, or utility (for example, valuables, labour received, or rent due). The basis of the debt could not be mere words, such as a promise to give a sum of money or to perform a deed in the future. However a debt could be validly founded on words alone if there was an evident *quid pro quo* as well as a verbal agreement. Of course written documents, if they existed, could be used to prove a debt, and these would have a much higher evidential value than any verbal allegations (similarly, sealed deeds could not be overturned by unsealed documents – see **bonds**).

There were several shortcomings to the action of debt. At least in the fifteenth century it was held that because the dead could not wage their law, verbally founded debts died with the debtors. Complexities of determining *quid pro quo* could leave creditors in multi-party transactions with no recourse for debt collection. Insurance claims could be seen as gambling wins and therefore became uncollectable. Also, the legal procedures in an action of debt became very complex, and legal and court fees were high. And, at least in some instances, trial by wager of law became an empty ceremony, as compurgators could be hired from among the minor court staff or on the streets who would swear for a fee.

Frustrated lenders could and did turn for relief to merchant tribunals, local courts, Church courts, and sometimes for larger sums to the court of Chancery. They also increasingly used sealed and/or registered documents, such as **bonds**, **indentures** and **statutes** staple or merchant, when arranging credit. However commercial life often required an uncomplicated and rapid means of trading on credit, or means for making purchases or investments without excessive delay and formality (as in today's stock exchanges and auction rooms). Verbal agreements, and even gestural agreements are to this day used in commerce (where 'my word is my bond'). In either a small rural community, or a compact urban merchant community, where creditworthiness could be assessed by reputation (as in MV), compurgation may have been a reasonable means of regulating debt (it was abolished only in 1833, although its use was much declined in early modern England).

By Shakespeare's time an alternative to the writ of debt existed, and was much used. Actions for trespass **on the case** for debt enabled the development of means of debt collection through the king's courts that overcame many of the disadvantages of actions on writ of debt. Finally it was established following *Slade's Case* (1597–1602) that nearly all debts could be recovered by an action on the case called *assumpsit* (see under **on the case**).

(B) The London world which Shakespeare addressed was very familiar with credit and creditors. Shakespeare, unlike many of his later critics, seems generally to have had a sympathetic view of the benefit in repayment of loans to the continuing economic well-being of his community.

The word 'debt' or a derivative appears in most of Shakespeare's plays and extended poems. The concept of an obligation, usually with its figurative force deriving from financial dealings, appears in all.

Early modern England saw a vigorous traffic in credit. Borrowed money was required by many, including those with mercantile interests (like the character Antonio in MV), landowners or their heirs seeking ready cash, and a new breed seeking large sums to enable the magnificent self-presentation then befitting lofty ambitions (men such as Sir Francis Bacon, characters such as Bassanio in MV). Perhaps in answer to such needs, the law's handling of obligations to repay borrowings underwent significant change in the years just before and during Shakespeare's lifetime.

The modes of borrowing and lending referred to in Shakespeare's plays include the despised practice of **usury**, the use of conditional or double **bonds**, the illicit ruse of selling fictitious **commodities**, and the important new forms of enforcement of indebtedness using actions on the case.

In TGV 2.7.75–6 Julia says, mistakenly, of Proteus, 'His words are bonds, his oaths are oracles, / His love sincere, his thoughts immaculate'. In the quibbling context of TN3.1.20, Feste says 'words are very rascals since bonds disgraced them'. Both contexts, although concerned with love, use images of **bonds** as instruments of financial obligation. Feste's mention of words having become 'very rascals' may even hint that an increasing use of sealed bonds has showed up the rascals whose hired words had 'disgraced' compurgation.

Actual debt collection is mentioned in SHR 4.4.24, and is the motivation in 2H4 2.1 of the legal altercation and street- brawl discussed under **sergeant** and **pre-contract**. Debt collection also features centrally in ERR, TIM and MV; and 2H4 and ERR allude to actions for debt on the case.

76

(C) See: Plucknett, 1956, pp 362–5, 631–4, 665–70; Milsom, 1981, pp 250–75; Baker, 1990b, pp 87–8, 365–73, 395–6, 441–5. On the Church courts' important varied involvements with the law of debt see Helmholz, 1987c, *passim*, and on **executors** and debt see Helmholz, 1987f. Tudor social and economic changes resulting in new uses of old forms for debt are considered in Thorne, 1985i, pp 206–9. On the developing law of contract see Simpson, 1975 and Baker, 1986h. Also see under **bond**, **statute** and **on the case**.

On Shakespeare's treatment of the law of debt generally, see Keeton, 1930, pp 79–89, which chapter, pp 81–4, raises some particularly interesting questions about TIM. Draper, 1934 addresses debt in TIM in terms of the Elizabethan background, but does not detect the same anomalies.

Many critics of MV suggest that Belmont in the play is an idyllic place of all-giving in love, and oppose it to mercantile Venice with its laws demanding repayment of loans. For discussion of such views, and different perspectives, see Sokol, 1998.

In Jordan, C., 1994, CYM is seen as a play built around a notion of contracts, and particularly of words given in good faith binding the conscience. This essay, pp 36–8, makes reference to *Slade's Case*. Spinosa, 1993 and Spinosa, 1994 connect MV with an argument that *Slade's Case* established changes in the law of obligation marking a major transformation of English society.

Considering TMP and TIM, Wilson, L., 1994, suggests that social implications of *Slade's Case* illuminate a notion of 'performance' both in law and in the theatre. Gulley, 1996, considering MM, also connects legal activity to theatrical 'performance'.

disinherit Although the word 'disinherit' is explicitly used in only two of his plays, the notion of disinheritance is found frequently in Shakespeare's work.

In RDY 1.1.171–6 the weak King Henry VI agrees to disinherit his own heir in favour of Richard Duke of York and his heirs. The exact conditions on which Henry gives away the succession of his crown (1.1.195–201) are discussed under **entail**. The word 'disinherit' is not used in this agreement, but it does specify that to ensure a peaceful reign Henry will deny his son's rights to the throne. Thereafter Henry sadly, and Queen Margaret and Prince Edward angrily, repeatedly use the term 'disinherit' (RDY 1.1.194, 1.1.226, 1.1.227, 1.1.251, 2.2.24). Prince Edward's disinheritance seemingly matches early medieval traditions of royal succession by election discussed under **inheritance** and **election**. It is confirmed by an 'act of Parliament' mentioned in RDY 1.1.250, which is revoked by a 'new act' mentioned in RDY 2.2.91.

In R3, set on by Richard of Gloucester, a bogus 'wizard' predicts that 'that by 'G' / [King Edward IV's] issue disinherited should be' (R3 1.1.56–7). This prophesy, contrived to be the downfall of George Clarence, ironically proves true thanks to Gloucester's own plots and murders.

King Lear does not actually disinherit Cordelia by denying her a share of his kingdom for a **dowry**, but he does effectively deprive her of inheritance by making an *inter vivos* gift of all he has to her two sisters. Nevertheless, as noted under **co-heirs**, in the absence of a male heir the succession of the Crown was excluded from the rule of co-parceny, and the eldest daughter took all. In WT the disinherited royal princess Perdita is not only denied a dowry and succession, but is threatened with infanticide (see under **bastardy** and **murder**).

Aside from royalty, several **heirs** presumptive are disinherited in Shakespeare plays; most are recalcitrant daughters. Thus the old Athenian father angry that Timon of Athens's mere servant is courting his only child, threatens to disinherit her. He speaks of choosing an alternate 'heir': 'If in her marriage my consent be missing, / I call the gods to witness, I will choose / Mine heir from forth the beggars of the world / And dispossess her all' (TIM 1.1.140–3 – discussed under **endowed**).

Old Capulet would also impose his marriage choice on Juliet, or else he will disinherit her: 'An you be mine, I'll give you to my friend. / An you be not, hang, beg, starve, die in the streets, / For, by my soul, I'll ne'er acknowledge thee, / Nor what is mine shall never do thee good' (ROM 3.5.191–4). For similar reasons, old Egeus in MND 1.1.44 threatens to kill his daughter and sole heir, an extreme form of disinheritance. The Duke of Milan in TGV 3.1.68–79 pretends to threaten his female heir presumptive similarly, saying he will take a new wife, and thereby may get a son (this is discussed under **dowry**).

Unless the father chose to make an *inter vivos* gift of all he possessed (and even then in many cases as alienation of land was not always possible), in England before the 1540 statute of **wills** disinheritance of a male heir was not easily achieved. Gloucester does attempt to disinherit Edgar (LRF 2.1.82–4), but a father's deathbed will disinheriting a male heir is declared invalid by King John (JN 1.1.129 – discussed under **bastard**.)

Disinheritance unless she obey the rule of the casket test is also seemingly threatened by the peculiar conditions of Portia's father's will, which are probably invalid (or would be in English law, see under **will**).

Gohn, 1982, p 948, describes the questionably legal manoeuvres in R2 by which King Richard effectively disinherits Bolingbroke, and also points out the suppression in R2 of the fact that, in usurping Richard, Bolingbroke overrode the claim of the infant Earl of March to succeed to the throne (but this is expounded at length in 1H6 2.5).

divorce (A) In Shakespeare's time the word 'divorce' had two meanings, neither of which corresponds to the modern law of divorce. Briefly, in the first meaning, the marriage was annulled when the Church courts found a 'dirimentary **impediment**' making the marriage void *ab initio*. In such a divorce *a vinculo matrimoni* the parties were free to marry again. In the second kind of divorce granted by the Church courts, known as divorce *a mensa et thoro*, husband and wife were freed from the duty to cohabit, but not free to remarry.

There is some lack of agreement among historians about the early legal and social history of divorce in England. The early church had allowed divorce for certain matrimonial offences including adultery, and in Anglo Saxon England divorce and remarriage had been available. In the early middle ages the church had not been able to make clear distinctions between marriage and concubinage, because no universally agreed formula for contracting a valid marriage existed in Europe. According to views in Flandrin, 1979, pp 180–4; Stone, 1979a, pp 662–3; Gillis, 1985, pp 12–13; Cook, 1991, pp 186–9, concubinage was widespread in Europe up to the sixteenth century (when attempts at vigorous regulation began, which were not very successful until the early seventeenth century). Other historians consider that divorce was readily available in medieval England, for many arranged their own affairs and divorced and remarried at will (see Brooke, 1981, pp 18–26 on the easy matrimonial practices of earlier medieval clergy and nobility, and on more popular practices see Smith, R. M., 1986, pp 52–69 and Sheehan, 1996, pp 38–76). The conclusion reached is that marriage during the middle ages was unstable and insecure. But this view is not universally accepted. The same scarcity of records of divorce litigation in medieval Church courts that leads some historians to believe informal divorce was common, leads others to conclude that divorce was rare (Helmholz, 1974, pp 75–6).

The lack of certainty about what was needed for a valid marriage led Pope Alexander III in the late twelfth century to attempt, unsuccessfully, to introduce the requirement for some form of church ceremony to enter into a legal marriage. Instead the Roman Church accepted the doctrine of consent, which held that a valid marriage was contracted solely by the consent of both parties and that the Church had no role to play in legal formalities. At about the same time, theologians held that marriage was a sacrament, and once contracted before God created an indissoluble bond between husband and wife. These two theories of marriage – that it was a sacrament and that it was created solely by consent of the parties – lasted until the Council of Trent for much of the Church of Rome, and until the Marriage Act 1753 for the Church in England (see under **pre-contract** and **marriage**).

By Shakespeare's time the post-Reformation English Church held matrimony was not a sacrament, but a holy estate, but still could not be ended by the will of either party, but only by the death of one of the parties. Despite this position, the Church courts did grant a divorce *a vinculo* in limited circumstances; if an impediment could be proved the marriage was annulled and had never existed. Serious consequences could follow: the wife was barred from **dower**, and any children born during the marriage might be bastardized (for details, see under **bastard**).

A renowned comment by Maitland suggested that the very complexities of the impediments of affinity and of consanguinity meant that it was nearly always possible to find some relationship that would prevent, or importantly, dissolve, a marriage. Consequently divorce was often possible when 'spouses who had quarrelled began to investigate their pedigrees and were unlucky if they could discover no impedimentum dirimens' (Pollock and Maitland, 1898, vol 2, p 393). Recently this 'hoary tradition in English historiography' has been doubted (Sheehan, 1996, p 84; see also Ingram, 1987, p 146). Sheehan, p 85, claims that to date the subject has not been studied fully, but agrees that the Church's stress on marriage by consent alone, requiring no formalities, did create a dilemma in late medieval and early modern England. It was all too easy for couples to be ignorant of, or choose to forget, an impediment.

Helmholz has conjectured that the reason why very few cases of divorces based on impediments are found in Church court records is that popular opinion believed marriages contracted within the prohibited degrees would not prosper (Helmholz, 1974, p 79–80). Another possible reason for few cases was the strict rules as to proof, and especially the difficulty of proving distant relationships in an age without many written records. Parties were dependent on the memories of witnesses for long-past marriages or connections. The nobility and gentry were more likely to claim the impediments of affinity and consanguinity than other people, and certainly Henry VIII made great use of arguments of impediments of affinity to achieve his aim of divorcing several of his wives. Henry's divorce history is discussed below.

In the case of a divorce *a mensa et thoro*, a declaration by the Church court allowed the parties to a marriage to live apart but not to remarry. This was available in several circumstances: adultery; sodomy; 'spiritual fornication' (by which was meant apostasy or **heresy**); and cruelty or fear of future injury (Helmholz, 1974, p 100; Baker, 1990b, p 562). As today, a reconciliation following the adultery or cruelty which appeared to condone the wrong done acted as a bar to the future grant of such an order. It is uncertain whether or not the grant of a divorce *a mensa et thoro* absolved a husband from the duty to maintain his wife as well as the duty to cohabit; fathers always had a duty to maintain their children though (whether or not legitimate, see Helmholz, 1977).

The lack of many recorded cases for divorce *a mensa et thoro* was possibly because many people made their own private arrangements or turned to unofficial arbitration for their marital disputes. But the Church did not recognise private agreements to separate, and upheld the duty to cohabit. When cases of divorce *a mensa et thoro* did reach Church courts the judge often acted as a mediator, or a 'rather heavy-handed marriage counsellor' (Helmholz, 1974, p 101; also see Poos, 1995).

It seems the normal rules about the need for evidence which applied in annulment were not insisted on for divorce *a mensa et thoro*, leaving the court free to counsel the parties to reach an accommodation with each other. In an age where physical abuse of wives was legal and acceptable (within limits), and where most women had no independent means of livelihood, and where the duty to cohabit was stressed by parents, parish, and church, the Church court's intervention (sometimes initiated *ex officio*) must have offered a degree of protection from domestic violence.

Men were often ordered to offer sureties for future good behaviour in return for resumed cohabitation, and where an order for divorce was made the court sometimes added a requirement for alimony. But if the parties were unable to compromise then the case was decided on legal merits and it was necessary to prove actual force or injury before an order was granted, using the 'constant man' test (on this see **impediments**).

Henry VIII's marital problems provide an illustration of the difficulties and limitations of the canon law of divorce in early modern England. In 1509 he married Katherine of Aragon, the widow of his deceased elder brother Arthur. The marriage was *prima facie* within the prohibited degrees and therefore void (the law was not changed until 1921), but Pope Julius II granted a dispensation from the impediment of affinity which allowed the marriage to go ahead. That dispensation appears to have been incorrect because if, as was claimed, Arthur's marriage was unconsummated, no impediment of affinity arose between Katherine and Henry. But the impediment of 'public honesty' did, which prohibited marriage between people related through a pre-contract, even a contract dissolved by mutual agreement or by death. However no questions were raised until years later when Henry determined to divorce Katherine and marry Anne Boleyn, and became immersed in arguments of canon law. In 1528 Pope Clement VII sent his legate, Cardinal Campeggio, to England and Henry's case was argued before a specially convened legatine court in 1529.

It seems that Henry intended to argue that the Pope's dispensation was invalid because the marriage between Katherine and Arthur had indeed been consummated. At this point Katherine complicated matters greatly by producing a copy of a second papal bull, in the form of a brief, which appeared to grant the dispensation necessary for her marriage with Henry to take place whether or not her marriage to Arthur had been consummated. Cardinal Wolsey probably correctly concluded both bulls had been very badly drafted, but this did not advance the King's cause. The King argued instead that he had been twelve years of age and therefore too young to consent when the marriage with Katherine had been arranged and later had protested against the marriage. Moreover the arrangement for the marriage was supposed to ensure peace between England and Spain, but by the time it actually took place this was not in issue and therefore not a valid reason to grant a papal dispensation.

Finally, Henry married Anne Boleyn privately, and the newly appointed Archbishop of Canterbury, Thomas Cranmer, announced the marriage to Katherine void for reasons of affinity. A proposal for the reform of marriage laws was drawn up by Cranmer, who considered that a divorce *a mensa et thoro* offended against the duty to cohabit insisted on by the Church. He drafted a new marriage code which allowed divorce followed by remarriage for marital misconduct, adultery, cruelty, desertion and 'bitter enmity'; these proposals came to nothing, although for a while there was some uncertainty about the effect of a divorce *a mensa et thoro*.

In 1548 the Marquis of Northampton divorced his wife *a mensa et thoro* and then remarried, his second marriage being confirmed by a 1552 Act of Parliament (repealed in 1553). The validity of such a remarriage following divorce *a mensa et thoro* was overruled by **Star Chamber** in *Rye v Fuljambe* ((1602) Moore K. B. 683). Divorce by private Act of Parliament for a wife's adultery (not for the adultery of a husband) did not become a possibility until 1670 when Lord Roos divorced by this means and remarried (see Stone, 1990, pp 301–13).

(B) The word 'divorce' is sometimes used by Shakespeare simply to mean a separation of things formerly united, but most often this occurs in a marital context.

The mere separation of the members of a family caused by a sea accident is called 'this unjust divorce of us' in ERR 1.1.104. In the same play marital divorce for reasons of adultery, recalling earlier practice, is alluded to when Adriana berates her seeming husband:

> How dearly would it touch thee to the quick
> Shouldst thou but hear I were licentious,
> And that this body, consecrate to thee,
> By ruffian lust should be contaminate?
> Wouldst thou not spit at me, and spurn at me,
> And hurl the name of husband in my face,
> And tear the stained skin off my harlot brow,
> And from my false hand cut the wedding ring,
> And break it with a deep-divorcing vow?
>   (ERR 2.2.133–41)

She adds, following the doctrine of 'one flesh' to its illogical limit (see

marriage), that his adultery would make her adulterous, and therefore he must abstain:

> I am possessed with an adulterate blot;
> My blood is mingled with the crime of lust.
> For if we two be one, and thou play false,
> I do digest the poison of thy flesh,
> Being strumpeted by thy contagion.
> Keep then fair league and truce with thy true bed,
> I live unstained, thou undishonoured.
>
> (ERR 2.2.143–9)

Her cleverness and intense jealousy avail her little though, for unbeknown to her she addresses her brother-in-law.

A pointed use of a notion of divorce for adultery appears in King Lear's extreme reaction to a possible failure by Regan to welcome him. If she were to fail, his figure of speech states, she must be illegitimate: 'If thou shouldst not be glad / I would divorce me from thy mother's shrine, / Sepulchring an adultress.' (LRF 2.2.302–4 / LRQ S.7.292–4).

The trial of Hermione in WT, beginning with an 'indictment' alleging adultery and conspiracy (WT 3.2.11–20), is for high **treason**. There seems to have been no move to dissolve the marriage and legally bastardize the children, but one child is left exposed to die, and the other dies of grief. In an historical parallel, in order to bastardize Princess Elizabeth, Cranmer on Henry VIII's behalf claimed the marriage with Anne Boleyn had been void. Although the reasons were never made public, the impediment of affinity occasioned by Henry's prior affair with Anne's sister could have been argued, or else a pre-contract for another marriage previously entered into by Anne. Yet later, as there were no children, Henry executed but did not divorce the adulterous Katherine Howard, although evidence of a prior pre-contract entered into by Katherine could have been used by Henry to prove his marriage with her was invalid.

Later in WT an actual 'divorce' is named. The disguised King Polixenes unmasks and interrupts a public celebration of the handfasting of his son and Perdita with the line 'Mark your divorce, young sir' (WT 4.4.417). However, whether the pair are married at that point depends on the meaning of their having joined hands when the Shepherd said 'Take hands, a bargain; / And, friends unknown, you shall bear witness to 't' (4.4.381–2). Surely they are just about to say the words necessary for a *de praesenti* spousal, and their gesture may already be seen as having been sufficient to show the consent required to make a valid marriage (see **pre-contract**). As Polixenes himself has just acknowledged, a father's consent was not required for marriage (see **impediments**), although his advice might well be sought: 'Reason my son / Should choose himself a wife, but as good reason / The father, all whose joy is nothing else / But fair posterity, should hold some counsel / In such a business' (4.4.406–10). If the young couple were married, an outraged father (even a royal one) could not 'divorce' them at will. The king's words, like his following threats to Perdita, are tyrannous.

Fury also inspires Bolingbroke's accusations against King Richard's misleaders, and perhaps minions, Bushy and Green. While extra-legally condemning them to death, 'to wash your blood / From off my hands' (R2 3.1.5–6), Bolingbroke claims 'here in the view of men' that:

> You have misled a prince, a royal king,
> A happy gentleman in blood and lineaments,
> By you unhappied and disfigured clean.
> You have, in manner, with your sinful hours
> Made a divorce betwixt his queen and him,
> Broke the possession of a royal bed,
> And stained the beauty of a fair queen's cheeks
> With tears drawn from her eyes by your foul wrongs.
> (R2 3.1.8–15)

Ironically, as a consequence of his usurpation, Bolingbroke himself draws tears from Richard's Queen, when she is forced to separate from her husband. In a scene filled with their sorrows, Richard says: 'Doubly divorced! Bad men, you violate / A twofold marriage: 'twixt my crown and me, / And then betwixt me and my married wife' (5.1.71–3). Here Richard objects to an extra-legal divorce from bed and board.

A similar divorce without Church sanction is proclaimed by Gloucester from his ambitious duchess Eleanor in CYL 2.1.209–11: 'I banish her my bed and company, / And give her as a prey to law and shame / That hath dishonoured Gloucester's honest name'. This does not protect him from the consequences of her offence of **heresy** in using **witchcraft** (see under **treason**).

85

The strong minded Queen Margaret also privately proclaims her separation *a mensa et thoro* from the weak King Henry VI:

> But thou preferr'st thy life before thine honour.
> And seeing thou dost, I here divorce myself
> Both from thy table, Henry, and thy bed,
> Until that act of Parliament be repealed
> Whereby my son is disinherited.
>
> (RDY 1.1.247–51)

Divorce is also mentioned in relation to the marital difficulties of Helena, Desdemona and Imogen. Helena and Bertram are married by a 'contract' sealed by public handfasting and subsequent 'ceremony' mentioned in AWW 2.3.177–81, though under very odd circumstances (see **ward**, **pre-contract**, and Mukherji, 1996). When Helena at last reveals that she has both the ring and a child of Bertram, fulfilling the seemingly impossible conditions he has set for his acknowledgement of their marriage, he says to the King in his amazement 'If she, my liege, can make me know this clearly / I'll love her dearly, ever ever dearly' (AWW 5.3.317–18). Helena's reply is 'If it appear not plain and prove untrue, / Deadly divorce step between me and you' (5.3.319–20). Here the pat couplets express two conditionals 'if – then' that may be unravelled. A divorce could well seem deadly to Helena who has risked her reputation in the 'bed trick'. Despite Helena's risk and Bertram's induction into a settled marriage through humiliation, it is suggested that all will 'end well' by Lafeu's response to these lines: 'Mine eyes smell onions, I shall weep anon' (5.3.322).

Asking 'Are you fast married?', Iago warns the newly married Othello that Brabantio's political authority is great: 'the magnifico is much beloved, / And hath in his effect a voice potential / As double as the Duke's' (OTH 1.2.11–14) Iago adds, 'He will divorce you, / Or put upon you what restraint or grievance / The law, with all his might to enforce it on, / Will give him cable' (OTH 1.2.14–17). Again (paralleling WT, and implications in MND, ROM, and CYM) the myth is that a powerful father may force the divorce of an unwanted son-in-law. Historically, although well-connected families did sometimes sorely oppress their children's unwanted spouses, they could not force divorces legally (a brutal English medieval case in which such a forced divorce was prevented by the Pope is recounted in Brooke, 1981, pp 31–2).

In the same play, Desdemona in her desperation asks Iago for help and advice, averring that she 'ever did, / And ever will – though he do shake me off / To beggarly divorcement – love him dearly' (4.2.159–62). It is notable here that she has perfectly grasped what is unjustly suspected of her: 'I cannot say "whore". / It does abhor me now I speak the word. / To do the act that might the addition earn, / Not the world's mass of vanity could make me' (4.2.165–8). Friendless and isolated from all she had known, like the traditional 'patient Griselda' she still sees beggarly divorce as her worst possible fate.

Imogen's marriage to Posthumus may be on an ambiguous standing or based only on a pre-contract (see Barton, A., 1994, pp 3–30). Yet Imogen, Posthumus himself, and others repeatedly call him her 'husband' (CYM 1.1.8, 1.1.86, 1.1.97, 1.6.3, 2.1.60, 3.4.14, 3.4.55, 3.4.131). Posthumus also accepts, and even in anger uses for her, the term 'wife' (CYM 1.1.114–18, 2.5.7). Moreover Imogen herself calls Cloten 'A foolish suitor to a wedded lady' (CYM 1.6.2). Yet her father, King Cymbeline, wishes to separate her from his erstwhile **ward** Posthumus, calling him merely 'her minion' (2.3.39). In pursuit of Imogen for himself, Cloten decries her adherence to a marriage 'contract' with Posthumus on the basis of an assumed aristocratic superiority to plebeian forms:

> The contract you pretend with that base wretch,
> One bred of alms and fostered with cold dishes,
> With scraps o' th' court, it is no contract, none.
> And though it be allowed in meaner parties –
> Yet who than he more mean? – to knit their souls,
> On whom there is no more dependency
> But brats and beggary, in self-figured knot,
> Yet you are curbed from that enlargement by
> The consequence o' th' crown, and must not foil
> The precious note of it with a base slave,
> A hilding for a livery, a squire's cloth,
> A pantler – not so eminent.
>
> (CYM 2.3.110–21)

His arrogance, and readiness to proclaim ad hoc a divorce allowing remarriage, possibly reflects the aristocratic mores described above as waning in Shakespeare's time. It certainly occasions Imogen's fury.

Is Imogen's marriage invalidated by 'The consequence o' th' crown'? Royal birth was not an impediment allowing a divorce *a vinculo matri-moni*. Iachimo, discussing Posthumus's 'banishment', remarks on the fame of his 'lamentable divorce' (CYM 1.4.18–19), but that would seem to be only his enforced marital separation due to his **banishment**. But a 'horrid' and actual 'divorce', allowing the marriage of Imogen with the despicable Cloten, is named by a courtier in 2.1.60–1. To avoid this Imogen flees the court and 'Cloten, whose love suit hath been to me / As fearful as a siege' (3.4.134–5). She will not hear of a divorce on the casual basis in which Roman gentry and early European royalty are said to have indulged (see Brooke, 1981, pp 22–6). Although Imogen is presented in a Roman Empire setting, she has the outlook of Shakespeare's age.

Finally AIT partly enacts the events of the divorce of Queen Katherine and Henry VIII. An interesting legal point is Katherine's refusal to accept Cardinal Wolsey as her judge because of his lack of impartiality (AIT 2.4.73–82), which *recusatio* was indeed an allowed objection in the Church courts (see Helmholz, 1987d). Commentators have generally noted that in AIT's treatment of the divorce Shakespeare follows sources closely, is diplomatic to all parties, and makes no reference to the non-consummation of Arthur's marriage.

(C) On divorce *a vincula* and *a mensa et thoro* see Pollock and Maitland, 1898, vol 2, pp 392–6; Helmholz, 1974, pp 74–107; Houlbrooke, 1979, pp 67–75; Ingram, 1987, pp 143–50; Baker, 1990b, p 565; Carlson, E. J., 1994, pp 75–8, 83–5, 91–5; Sheehan, 1996, pp 68–76. On the history of divorce and separation see: Brooke, 1981; Smith, R. M., 1986; Ingram, 1987; Phillips, R., 1988; Stone, 1990; Poos, 1995; Laurence, 1994, p 47–54; Sheehan, 1996. On canon law and Henry VIII's divorce see Thurston, 1904, and Scarisbrick, 1974, pp 218–316, 367–75, 452-56, 479–84, 554–9.

On the divorce trial of Queen Katherine as depicted in AIT see: Keeton, 1930, pp 206–16; Phillips, O. H., 1967, p 186; and Phillips, O. H., 1972, pp 86–7. On the canon law (as opposed to civil law, pp 34–5) background of the *recusatio* in Katherine's challenge to Wolsey, see Helmholz, 1987d.

double voucher For an explanation of this complex device used in

conveyancing, and for discussion of the context of its twice naming in HAM 5.1.102 and 5.1.105–6, see **fine and recovery** and **voucher**.

dowager/widow (A) In early modern England the widow's position in law was reputed to be an enviable one. This contrasted with her position during marriage when she was subject to *coverture* arising from the doctrine that husband and wife were one person in law (see **marriage**). As a result of *coverture* the married woman suffered proprietary disabilities at law, but if she became a widow her legal personality revived and she was once more able to hold property and enter into contracts in her own name, and to earn money and keep it.

Widows of the aristocratic and gentry classes, and often widows of merchants, benefited from the financial arrangements made with their husbands before their marriage. As dowagers they could receive **dower**, a one third life interest in all their deceased husband's lands. In Shakespeare's time, after the Statute of Uses, it was more likely that the arrangement made would have been for **jointure**. They would therefore have been in receipt of an agreed annuity raised by way of a rent charge on the deceased husband's lands. Either way, for the duration of her life the widow was able to do as she thought fit with property secured to her by dower or jointure, although she could not alienate it. Widows of men less wealthy, or not in possession of land, might benefit from a **bond**, secured by a double penalty, arranged by her husband with a third party before his death. All widows might also continue to benefit from 'pin money', which was money which had been set apart for their own private expenses during the marriage. Again this was arranged before marriage by husband and wife, or more usually between the husband and the wife's family.

A widow was able to recover to her own use and possession all the real property that she had brought with her into the marriage, and also any property she had been given or inherited later. Although during her marriage all of a wife's property was held by her husband in his name, and he was entitled to all the profits from it, if her husband had alienated her real property (**land**) the widow was able to recover it from the third party. But any personal property a wife brought into the marriage became her husband's absolutely. Therefore, on widowhood if nothing of her personal property remained the widow had no rights and could not pursue any one now in possession of what had once been hers. She had claims only to any specific legacy of personal property made to her in her husband's **will**, and to her 'paraphernalia', by which was meant personal clothing and jewellery. However the latter was subject to claims against the husband's estate from creditors.

A man was able to make specific gifts to his wife in his will, and so a widow could benefit from property left to her and dispose of it as she wanted. A widow was also able to make her own will, a right from which as a wife she had in most cases been excluded because of *coverture* unless by agreement with her husband (some borough customs also allowed wives to make wills). It has been suggested that women (at least those who were eligible to do so) were more likely to make a will than their husbands (Erickson, 1993, p 206). Some married women not eligible also made wills, which were readily administered by the Church courts because of the importance placed by Church teaching on gifts of alms, particularly last gifts of alms (such wills were accepted unless an objection was made by the widower; see Sheehan, 1996, p 36). If the argument that women were more likely than men to make wills is correct, the reason might be because intestate husbands left widows who were automatically entitled to dower and to administer their husband's estate, whereas a widow's intestate estate had no such obvious administrator nor beneficiary (unless there were young children to provide for).

Widows frequently acted as executrix or administrator of their husband's estates, particularly among merchant classes and in boroughs (see Brodsky, 1986, p 145, and under **executor**).

Often-heard remarks that a widows' positions were enviable needs more careful examination, for many rapidly remarried and so resumed *coverture*. Marriage during Shakespeare's period was notoriously fragile because of early deaths through disease, particularly in towns, and many women chose to remarry. Studies made of widows in metropolitan English towns reveal that in London wealthy widows or the very poor seldom remarried, but widows from craft and trade backgrounds frequently did so, within an interval of often less then one year (Brodsky, 1986, 128–34). Younger widows were more likely to remarry single men, though overall a pattern emerges of widows marrying men younger than themselves.

A widow's decision to not remarry but to manage her deceased husband's trade on her own account appears to have been most possible to achieve for the wives of London craftsmen and tradesmen. But such a choice was hampered by the 'forces of patriarchalism and fraternalism institutionalised in the household and . . . in about eighty London companies which held a jurisdiction over virtually all trades and a myriad of craft specialities' (Brodsky, 1986, p 141). Possibly for this reason married women and widows appear infrequently in registers of **apprentices** or of freedom of companies.

Many husband's wills reveal constraints put in the way of widow's remarriage, by stipulating this would result in a forfeiture of property, bringing into question the apparent freedom and power of widows in early modern England. Widows have been presented in literature and in recent social historical studies as overly powerful rich old ladies who prevented heirs from enjoying their inheritance for decades, sometimes outliving them (see for example the pattern found by Archer, 1984 in late medieval landed families). But others point out that this perspective assumes the superior claim of **primogeniture**, and overlooks the claims of wives, younger sons and daughters (Erickson, 1993, p 221) which were in practice often acknowledged by husbands.

To lay excessive stress on patrilineal descent also overlooks the fact that many powerful dowagers had been heiresses in their own right before marriage, and on widowhood once more held property that had been theirs (Spring, 1993, p 41).

On the many special legal conditions applied in widowhood, and on some allied social circumstances, see also under **appeal**, **branded**, **dower**, **dowry**, **inheritance**, **jointure**, **poverty**, **marriage**, **sanctuary**, **treason**, **wills** and **waste**.

(B) It seems that the appellation 'dowager' was first applied to Henry VIII's sister, Mary Tudor, Dowager of France (OED). So it was a new title when applied by Henry to his wife Katherine of Aragon, as represented in AIT.

The questioning in AIT by Henry VIII of 'this our marriage with the dowager, / Sometimes our brother's wife' (AIT 2.4.177–8) presages Henry's first **divorce**. Cramner's machinations are reported by Suffolk:

> Shortly, I believe,
> His second marriage shall be published, and
> Her coronation. Katherine no more
> Shall be called 'Queen', but 'Princess Dowager',
> And 'widow to Prince Arthur'.

> (AIT 3.2.67–71)

The result is that the second marriage of widowed Katherine, and her royal status, is annulled and invalidated.

Usually Shakespeare's plays reflect disapproval of remarriages of widows (but not of Marianna's second chances encouraged in MM 5.1.421–2 – discussed under **dower**). But disapproval is not expressed of remarriages of the 'widowers' named as such in AWW 5.3.71 and ANT 2.2.126.

Widows make particularly bad wives in TIT, SHR and CYM. Tamora instigates much of the rank evil in TIT (see under **rape**). In SHR, once disappointed Hortensio resolves to marry a widow, mistakenly hoping for 'Kindness in women' if 'not their beauteous looks' (SHR 4.2.41). What he gets is a practised shrew; when Tranio says 'he'll have a lusty widow now, / That shall be wooed and wedded in a day' Bianca comments ominously 'God give him joy' (4.2.50–2). The mother of Cloten who becomes queen to King Cymbeline does not even merit a name, and only evil comes of this 'widow / That late he married' (CYM 1.1.5–6).

In H5 2.1 we learn that Nell Quickly, the self-styled 'poor widow of Eastcheap' of 2H4 2.1.71, has remarried absurdly, despite a prior troth-plight (see under **impediment**). The social circumstances suggest a probably irregular or illicit marriage.

The rapid remarriage of widowed Queen Gertrude is subject to serious impediments, including 'affinity' and possibly 'crime' (see under **impediment**). Her 'incest' clearly inspires Hamlet's disgust, but he is also opposed generally to remarriage of widows. Thus when he hears the player Queen's conventionally virtuous: 'Both here and hence pursue me lasting strife / If, once a widow, ever I be wife', he comments 'If she should break it now!' (HAM 3.2.211–13)

Lust is often implied to motivate the remarriage of widows, in contexts of disapproval. In the course of the chaotic investigation of the accusations of **Constable** Elbow, the magistrate Escalus replies with an eloquent interrogative to Pompey's information on Mistress Overdone:

ESCALUS   What trade are you of, sir?
POMPEY   A tapster, a poor widow's tapster.
ESCALUS   Your mistress's name?
POMPEY   Mistress Overdone.
ESCALUS   Hath she had any more than one husband?

POMPEY   Nine, sir – Overdone by the last.
ESCALUS   Nine? –

(MM 2.1.190–6)

Likewise another Pompey, in ANT 2.1.35–8, uses the word 'widow' to figure forth lust: 'let us rear / The higher our opinion, that our stirring / Can from the lap of Egypt's widow pluck / The ne'er lust-wearied Antony.' The lustful sisters widowed Regan and the would-be widowed Goneril plot evil remarriage in *King Lear* (see **subcontracted**). Timon of Athens says in his disgust with humanity's relation to 'gold': 'This is it / That makes the wappered widow wed again. / She whom the spittle house and ulcerous sores / Would cast the gorge at, this embalms and spices / To th' April day again.' (TIM 4.3.38–42).

Despite evidence of such disapproving attitudes in plays by Shakespeare and many contemporaries (especially Chapman's *The Widow's Tears*), for economic reasons, 'widows were at a high premium in the London marriage market' of Shakespeare's time (Elliott, 1981, pp 83–4 and passim). Thus Brodsky, 1986 contrasts disapproving male dramatists' attitudes with the fact that rapid re-marriage was frequent among the widows of late Elizabethan London.

Another social issue concerning widowhood that overlapped with legal matters was the possible resentment on the part of a younger generation of some widows' control of extensive property. A dowager aunt is regarded benignly in Lysader's: 'I have a widow aunt, a dowager / Of great revenue, and she hath no child, / And she respects me as her only son' (MND 1.1.157–9). But at the start of the same play, Theseus images youthful frustration in a comment on the slowness of the passage of four days between his **pre-contract** and the solemnisation of his marriage thus: '. . . but O, methinks how slow / This old moon wanes! She lingers my desires / Like to a stepdame or a dowager / Long withering out a young man's revenue' (1.1.3–6).

(C) See: Elliott, 1981; Archer, 1984; Brodsky, 1986; Brundage, 1992; Erickson, 1993, pp 205–22; Spring, 1993, pp 39–65; Sheehan, 1996, pp 194–8.

dower (A) Shakespeare uses the term 'dower' in three ways. One use, in which the term is interchangeable with 'dowry', indicates the marriage portion, the gift made by the woman's family to the man upon marriage. This derived from the feudal *maritagium* and is discussed under **dowry**. Another use of 'dower' is in contexts where 'jointure' would be the technically correct term; the confusion of terms is significant particularly in MV, and is discussed under **jointure**.

A third use of 'dower' by Shakespeare, discussed here, is the one usual in English law. It indicates the gift of property made by the husband to the wife on marriage, which would become available to her on widowhood. This endowment in time became a right and did not depend on the husband's gift. Thus a **widow's** or **dowager's** legal right to dower, amounting to a life interest in one third of her deceased husband's estate, was set out in ecclesiastical and common law. However, by Shakespeare's time these rights were often partly circumvented.

To examine this in more detail, during the middle ages canonists in Europe generally developed the law relating to dowry, but in England the concern of common lawyers was with dower as a widow's right, and so this use of the term became the most common. Both church and common law developed rules regulating widow's rights, which by the twelfth century became legally binding.

In England it was said that the widow had the special protection of 'God and the king'. But although early Canon law took special care of the position of the widow, protection of her interests did not evolve as part of the church's law on marriage. Instead she was regarded as a *miserabilis persona*, a poor person specially deserving of charity and protection. It was on this basis that her property rights were protected, and her right to choose not to remarry upheld (Sheehan, 1996, p 18, and on the origins of this see Brundage, 1992). The church in England placed importance on the endowment of the bride at the church door with property that would be hers as a widow. This ceremony became part of the sacramental liturgy of church marriage, although it was never required for validity.

While questions of the validity of **marriage** and of **divorce** were the preserve of the ecclesiastical courts, questions of real property were not. It seems that the church did not question the common law's right to determine disputes about **land** between husband and wife, and that therefore questions of dower were seen as the concern of the common law from the early middle ages. The Coronation Charter of Henry I in 1100 promised that widows of his barons would be assured of their dower, and confirmed their right not to be forced to remarry. This latter promise was not honoured, and notoriously high fines were extracted from widows in return for remaining unmarried or to secure dower. As a result of the barons' dissatisfaction, Magna Carta and its variously amended reissues of 1215, 1217 and 1225 confirmed a widow's right to dower and to choose not to remarry, but with ambiguities and confusions that produced a period of 'transition' (see Loengard, 1993). Eventually it was settled that dower was to be assigned from all the lands a husband held at the date of his death, and all property held at the time of marriage and subsequently acquired (Plucknett, 1956, p 566).

There is disagreement among historians about whether some formal ceremony was needed before a widow could claim dower. Following Bracton, some historians hold that the common law demanded that a right to dower was dependent on the prior endowment of the bride by her husband at the church door (Pollock and Maitland, 1898, vol 2, p 375; Plucknett, 1956, p 566; Loengard, 1985; Biancalana, 1988, pp 257 and 288–92; Carlson, E. J., 1994, p 29; Outhwaite, 1995, p 5). Others suggest that dower was a widow's right at common law whether or not this ceremony had taken place (Archer, 1984, p 17; Sheehan, 1996, p 21). Smith, R. M., 1986, pp 62–3), holds that really the problem was largely the practical one of obtaining sufficient independent evidence from witnesses that the marriage had taken place, other than just the widow's word, to allow the court to award dower in disputed cases.

In a celebrated case of 1225 (translated from Bracton in Ward, J., 1995, p 44) dower was denied to a long term concubine who was married privately to James de Carduville at the close of his life. The basis of the court's decision refusing dower was that by entering into a death bed agreement the husband had 'acted for the salvation of his soul and in peril of death'; words which throw doubt on the sincerity of his consent to his spousals, without which there can be no valid marriage. But this decision does not suggest that common law would not recognise an unsolemnised marriage, or that endowment at the church door was essential for the award of dower. Smith, R. M., 1986, pp 63–4, points out that all the cases cited in Pollock and Maitland, 1898, vol 2, p 374, of 'disputed dower in "death-bed" marriages' involved problems about lack of evidence rather than any principle of law. The problem of the widow's claim to dower is therefore closely tied to the question of establishing a valid marriage in early modern England (see **pre-contract**).

By the end of the thirteenth century the common law accepted that dower was to be calculated as a freehold life estate in one third of the deceased husband's real property. If it was greater, the heir was allowed to reduce the widow's share to this amount by the Writ of Admeasurement. But in some local circumstances custom would allow the widow more, so in gavelkind (see **co-heirs**) the widow was allowed a life interest in half the husband's property.

If real property was alienated by a husband after the marriage, or by the heir after the death, then the widow could use the common law Writs of Dower, and of Entry and Right of Dower against the heir in the heir's court to recover it (Plucknett, 1956, p 567). Yet dower was not part of the feudal order because it was not a form of tenure; the widow did not hold her land from her husband's lord, and did not owe services for it (see **land**). Dower was rather 'an internal arrangement within the inheritance' (Milsom, 1976, p 168; Baker, 1990b, p 308). The widow held from her deceased husband's heir, and he owed the services for it. So to enter her dower the widow would sue out a writ to obtain it from the heir (Bonfield, 1983, p 6). Similarly, if the property was in the hands of a third party, then she would have to join the heir to sue (Milsom, 1976, p 167). The widow's rights could set up grave tensions within the inheritance, and conflicted with a lord's right to **wardship**. Also, because dower was a life interest, it extended beyond any remarriage (see **dowager/widow**).

Lands held in **use** were not subject to dower, so from the fourteenth century and until 1536 uses were very frequently employed to bar dower. The Statute of Uses 1536 executed most uses (see **use**), so that those lands would have been subject again to dower. However a special clause of the Statute (27 Hen. VIII, c. 10 4) was inserted to allow jointures to bar dower (see **jointure**). Spring, 1993, pp 47–9, argues that the Statute was a 'husband's charter' depriving most widows of dower, and that it could have been written in other ways so as to avoid the problems of a sudden great transfer of lands to widows. Following from this argument, the preamble of the Statute which claimed it executed uses in order to eliminate fraud on widows is an inversion of the truth. But Bonfield, 1983, p 6, points out that there were some advantages to a widow to receive a **jointure** instead of dower.

Dower rights in land could also be barred by agreement with the wife in a collusive court action which was then recorded as a fine (see under

fine and recovery and **marriage**). Such agreements to bar dower in order to alienate land unburdened were frequent.

In a curious analogy to dower, after the wife's death, as long as a child of the marriage had been born alive, and even if it did not outlive its mother, an English widower became a tenant by 'curtesy', and was entitled to a life interest in all her real property. Tenancy by curtesy continued even after remarriage by the husband.

(B) Depriving widows of their customary rights is listed by Salisbury among exemplary 'sins' that are not excused by oath-taking:

> It is great sin to swear unto a sin,
> But greater sin to keep a sinful oath.
> Who can be bound by any solemn vow
> To do a murd'rous deed, to rob a man,
> To force a spotless virgin's chastity,
> To reave the orphan of his patrimony,
> To wring the widow from her customed right,
> And have no other reason for this wrong
> But that he was bound by a solemn oath?
> (CYL 5.1.180–8)

The 'customed right' could be dower of one third of the husband's property, or half as in some borough customs, or even all, as was customary with **villein** tenure (Plucknett, 1956, p 567).

In RDY, a widow's hope for what she calls 'dower' is threatened by the lustful King Edward IV, who is called 'the bluntest wooer in Christendom' (3.2.83). Lady Elizabeth Grey approaches Edward for help to recover her dead husband's lands, and he sets a condition:

KING EDWARD   To tell thee plain, I aim to lie with thee.
LADY GREY   To tell you plain, I had rather lie in prison.
KING EDWARD   Why, then, thou shalt not have thy husband's lands.
LADY GREY   Why, then, mine honesty shall be my dower;
            For by that loss I will not purchase them.
KING EDWARD   Therein thou wrong'st thy children mightily.
LADY GREY   Herein your highness wrongs both them and me.
            But, mighty lord, this merry inclination
            Accords not with the sadness of my suit.

	Please you dismiss me either with ay or no.
KING EDWARD	Ay, if thou wilt say 'ay' to my request;
	No, if thou dost say 'no' to my demand.
LADY GREY	Then, no, my lord – my suit is at an end.

(RDY 3.2.69–81)

Thus this widow resists becoming a royal 'concubine' (3.2.98 – see discussion under **divorce** and **bastard** of such informal customs). In consequence Edward marries her, despite a possible **pre-contract** with Princess Bona; Richard III later makes political use of this irregularity in R3 3.7.174–81 (see under **impediment**).

Petruchio's arrangements with Baptista for Katerina's dower show him both acquisitive and unusually generous. In an age when dower rights were typically barred by jointures, as described above, Shakespeare has Petruchio seemingly say that he will not do this with any of his property provided that Baptista provides an agreed large sum for Kate's **dowry**: 'for that dowry I'll assure her of / Her widowhood, be it that she survive me, / In all my lands and leases whatsoever' (SHR 2.1.123–5). It seems that Petruchio offers no fixed amount of jointure, but an interest in all of his property (which he says in 2.1.118 has been increasing), as in dower. This arrangement is to be enshrined in legal documents: 'Let specialties be therefore drawn between us, / That covenants may be kept on either hand' (2.1.126–7 – see under **jointure** on the context).

Before Shakespeare's time a **felon's** goods were confiscated and dower was lost to his widow (Plucknett, 1956, p 567). Yet Clarkson and Warren, 1942, pp 204–6, is sceptical of any technicality in relation to dower in MM. This argues that by 1551 dower was allowed to the widows of some felons, and so Marianna's treatment following Angelo's punishment (MM 5.1.419–22) should not be connected with issues of dower. It does however seem likely to us that both confiscation and the death penalty would apply to Angelo for **treason**, which did bar dower. In a further complication, by the rules of pre-contract Angelo is Marianna's husband, but they were not married in the face of the church. Arguably, this too might have been seen to prevent dower. Both to protect Marianna from the scandal of an illicit but not illegal marriage (see **pre-contract**), and to assure her attractiveness for re-marriage (see **dowager/widow** and **dowry**), the Duke orders her to be publicly married to Angelo just before his execution:

Consenting to the safeguard of your honour,
I thought your marriage fit; else imputation,
For that he knew you, might reproach your life,
And choke your good to come. For his possessions,
Although by confiscation they are ours,
We do enstate and widow you with all,
To buy you a better husband.

(MM 5.1.416–22)

The rare usage of 'to widow' (OED), meaning to assure a widow's financial security, is treated further under **jointure**.

Some of the uses of the term 'dower' by King Lear are peculiar. When he announces that he has 'a constant will to publish / Our daughters' several dowers' (LRF 1.1.43–4) he refers to two married and one unmarried daughter. 'Dower', as often in Shakespeare, means **dowry** with reference to Cordelia (this is clear in 1.1.108: 'Thy truth then be thy dower', and in 1.1.191, 1.1.256, and 2.2.385). With respect to the other two daughters the 'dower' Lear names at first seemingly denotes an intended *inter vivos* gift of lands. But Lear's language has another legal resonance when he gives to Regan an 'ample third of our fair kingdom' and offers Cordelia a chance for 'third more opulent than your sisters' (1.1.80 and 86). A third was the common law proportion of estates reserved to widows as dower. Lear's odd gift giving hints toward an act of leaving his estate on death to three wives, as in a bizarre version of dower, not giving it in life to three daughters. The ambiguities of Lear's family relations, and of his giving and not quite giving away his royal state while, he says, 'we / Unburdened crawl toward death' (1.1.40–1), are crucial in the play.

(C) See: Glanvill, 1993, pp 58–9; Pollock and Maitland, 1898, vol 2, p 375; Plucknett, 1956, pp 566–9; Bonfield, 1983, pp 1–10; Archer, 1984, p 17; Loengard, 1985; Smith, R. M., 1986, pp 62–5; Biancalana, 1988; Baker, 1990b, pp 308–10; Brundage, 1992; Spring, 1993, pp 42–9; Laurence, 1994, p 229; Sheehan, 1996, pp 21–4. On medieval widows' legal battles for dower see Walker, 1993 and Loengard, 1993. There is a detailed discussion of forms of dower in Coke, 1628, sections 36–55 (book 1, leaves 30–41).

Ranald, 1979 calls the 'widowhood' in SHR 2.1.123–5 a 'jointure', but seems to conflate the term with 'dower' in a note pp 69–70. Boose,

1982, p 344, note 13, follows Ranald. Boose, 1988, p 245, again suggests a **jointure** is implicit in Petruchio's marriage settlement in SHR, and this leads to Kate's ritual prostration and offering of her hand for stepping on in 5.2. (We see the implication of dower, not jointure, in the term 'widowhood' of SHR.)

On Marianna's dower in MM see Clarkson and Warren, 1942, pp 202–6, and our discussions above and under **jointure**.

dowry (A) Shakespeare used the term 'dowry' to refer to the property given on marriage to the husband by a wife's friends or family (although in Shakespeare's use **dower** sometimes has this meaning too).

The Roman practice of making a gift on marriage, the '*dos*', was accepted by the Christian Church and was once common throughout Europe. During the middle ages the English common law understanding of '*dos*', **dower** and **dowry** came to differ from the rest of Europe. In England the term dower was reserved for the gift made on marriage by the husband to the wife (to take effect only on widowhood). The term dowry, the bride-gift made by the woman's family to the man was at first called a marriage-gift, or *maritagium* (see Glanvill, 1993, p 69), and later a marriage **portion**. Both dowry and dower mean endowment of a woman on marriage, but in one case by her father and in the other by her husband. Dowry, dower and **jointure** were terms used mainly by the landed aristocracy, while others used marriage settlement, agreement, covenant or portion to describe their arrangements.

The *maritagium* was a gift of property made to husband and wife and their **heirs**. If this was land it was not a gift in **fee-simple** but instead the donor remained seised of the **land** for three generations to ensure the new family was successfully established. If the new line failed (for example if no children were born, or the wife died) then the property reverted to the donor's family, preventing **inheritance** by the husband's collateral relatives. This arrangement was established by the twelfth century, and was protected by the Statute *De Donis Conditionalibus* 1285. The *maritagium* influenced the subsequent development of doctrine of estates in **land** through the **entail**, which was used to benefit younger sons and other family members and not exclusively daughters on marriage.

By Shakespeare's time the dowry or bride-gift provided by the wife's family was commonly known legally as a **portion**, while the husband's endowment of his wife was most often described as **jointure**. An examination made of Chancery records of marriage settlement litigation among the aristocracy during the seventeenth century finds a reciprocity between portion and jointure. The amount of portion brought into a marriage was reflected in the amount of jointure agreed to provide for a widow. In aristocratic families the pre-marriage agreement was likely to limit the wife's jointure to her widowhood alone; if she remarried the husband's family were anxious to ensure her jointure ended. In contrast, in the pre-marriage negotiations the wife's family would attempt to negotiate a jointure for life. The amount of the woman's portion on marriage was therefore a very important factor in these complex negotiations. There is evidence that throughout the early modern period the cost of portions rose steeply (Stone, 1979a, p 645). The ratio between portion and jointure is said to have risen from 5 : 1 to 10 : 1 during the seventeenth century (Erickson, 1993, p 119, but see Reynolds, 1996, p 331). By the eighteenth century, draft agreements set out in precedent books, used by lawyers and interested parties, presupposed a ratio of 10:1 between portion and jointure, and they provide examples of both jointures for life or limited to widowhood (Erickson, 1993, p 120).

While the rise to the 10:1 ratio applied in families of the aristocracy, chancery records indicate that gentry families and merchant families did not see such a dramatic rise in the cost of portions. Erickson, 1993, p 121, considers that this could be explained by the different use made of portions. Families of peers were more likely to use a cash portion to purchase land to provide income from rents or to purchase an annuity for the widow. Land prices were sharply rising at the time. Gentry, merchant, and yeoman families were not so likely to purchase land. Instead evidence from the probate of wills of married yeomen indicates their marriage agreements provided the widow with a cash sum, or **bonds** secured by a double penalty, which matched in value the portion that she brought into the marriage (ibid., p 129–30). Even the wills of those below the level of yeomen reveal they had marriage agreements which left small sums for a widow.

The conclusion to be drawn from evidence of legal records and from literature is that negotiations over marriage portions were of great importance in early modern England for all social classes. For the

101

landed aristocracy a large dowry brought an increase in wealth and social standing to the man, and it was used to provide for the woman's support in widowhood. For gentry and merchant families whose marriage portions did not increase at the same rate as the aristocracy's, dowry still remained a significant part of marriage negotiations. Women from families of yeomen status and even daughters of poorer craftsmen attempted to bring some property into their marriage. Their marriage agreements were often made orally, but when found reported in wills or litigation show that the understanding between husband and wife was that the portion would be returned to the wife on widowhood in the form of some kind of provision for her.

(B) The 'dowry' is also sometimes called 'portion' and sometimes (in one of its meanings, as described under **dower**) 'dower' by Shakespeare. For him the 'dowry' is always given by the brides or their families to their husbands.

The 'dowry' (or in the sense of bride portion 'dower') is referred to in many Shakespeare plays, and surprisingly often features as a portion by some accident not paid (TGV 3.1.78–9; MM 1.2.137–9 and 3.1.219–32; LRF 1.1.128–9), and/or as riches that exists mainly or only in the form of the prospective bride's virtues (TGV 3.1.78; LRF 1.1.108–20; WT 4.4.384–5; TMP 3.1.53–4).

Marianna's and Juliet's missing or delayed dowries are crucial in MM (see under **pre-contract**), and so may be Isabella's, by implication. McFeely, 1995, p 214, substantiates a suggestion made in Kliman, 1982, pp 138–9, which is that Isabella would need no dowry to become a Poor Clare. If the Clares were not absolutely 'the only possible refuge for dowerless Isabella', as Kliman suggests, McFeely shows they were unlike 'most orders [that] required dowries'. McFeely, p 211, points out that dowries for daughters were sometimes explicitly provided in the Middle Ages by the wealthy 'for their marriage or entering a religious house'.

In TGV an expected dowry is threatened with non-payment when Silvia's father, the Duke of Milan, pretends to withdraw his support from her in order to fool Valentine into revealing his plans for elopement with her. Despite the fantastic nature of this ruse, the Duke's description of how he has decided to re- marry and not be dependent on his daughter may illuminate a social practice in which care in old age is expected in return for material support:

Proud, disobedient, stubborn, lacking duty,
Neither regarding that she is my child
Nor fearing me as if I were her father.
And may I say to thee, this pride of hers
Upon advice hath drawn my love from her,
And where I thought the remnant of mine age
Should have been cherished by her child-like duty,
I now am full resolved to take a wife,
And turn her out to who will take her in.
Then let her beauty be her wedding dower,
For me and my possessions she esteems not.

                                        (TGV 3.1.69–79)

This pretended mood, if not its covert purpose, seems realistic. A parallel sort of motive is implied in the connection between King Lear's withdrawal of Cordelia's marriage portion (the odd nature of which is discussed under **dower**) and his relinquishing of his original plans for old age, 'to set my rest / On her kind nursery' (LRF 1.1.123–4).

'Dowerless' (meaning doweryless, LRF 1.1.256 and 2.2.385) Cordelia is willingly married by the King of France, who is therefore disparaged by Lear for being 'hot-blooded' (2.2.385). The anti-erotic implication of this is borne out in Lear's subsequent misogyny, echoing one notion of 'manliness' of the age.

In Shakespeare's age marriage portions were frequently crucial for marriages to proceed. Particularly in political life dowries were sometimes very great. This is seen, for instance, when much of France is demanded for Katherine's marriage portion in H5. The young Henry V uses considerable diplomacy and wit in this negotiation. He avoids the disastrous excessive publicity of Cordelia's wooing (see under **election**), and having dismissed the court audience woos Katherine with:

No, it is not possible you should love the enemy of France, Kate. But in loving me, you should love the friend of France, for I love France so well that I will not part with a village of it, I will have it all mine; and Kate, when France is mine, and I am yours, then yours is France, and you are mine.'

                                        (H5 5.2.171–6).

This is one of many ways in which Hal as Prince and private man brings those two aspects of himself together to advantage.

Likewise, having ascertained their consent to marriage, King John says concerning the marriage of his niece Blanche to Louis the Dauphin of France,

> Then do I give Volquessen, Touraine, Maine,
> Poitou, and Anjou, these five provinces,
> With her to thee, and this addition more:
> Full thirty thousand marks of English coin.
> Philip of France, if thou be pleased withal,
> Command thy son and daughter to join hands.
> (JN 2.1.528–33)

The purpose of this match is to obtain a dowry and a powerful ally.

Similarly King Henry VI at first accedes to a marriage with lady Bona, knowing this will bring 'a large and sumptuous dowry' (1H6 5.1.20) and probable peace with France. When soon after he is influenced by Suffolk to marry Margaret with no dowry at all, and less political advantage, the English nobles complain, and Suffolk chides:

> A dower, my lords? Disgrace not so your King
> That he should be so abject, base, and poor
> To choose for wealth and not for perfect love.
> Henry is able to enrich his queen,
> And not to seek a queen to make him rich.
> So worthless peasants bargain for their wives,
> As market men for oxen, sheep, or horse.
> Marriage is a matter of more worth
> Than to be dealt in by attorneyship.
> Not whom *we* will but whom his grace affects
> Must be companion of his nuptial bed.
> And therefore, lords, since he affects her most,
> That most of all these reasons bindeth us:
> In our opinions she should be preferred.
> For what is wedlock forced but a hell,
> An age of discord and continual strife,

Whereas the contrary bringeth bliss,
And is a pattern of celestial peace.
(1H6 5.7.48–65)

Soon after, Henry's adventure in the individualistic 'heroics of marriage' (of a sort that Rose, 1988, pp 186–235 argues came to dominate
Jacobean tragicomedy) begins to have disastrous consequences.

   In Romance or comedy, in accord with literary conventions, marriage with dowerless maids is sometimes less momentous. Marina,
Miranda, and Perdita are first presented as having small or no dowries
beside their virtues (WT 4.4.385; TMP 3.1.54), but prove to be fit
matches for princes (see under **poverty/beggary**).

   A strangely contrary remark of Bassanio in MV seemingly opposes
the convention that comeliness brings its own dowry, objecting to out-
ward show in terms of a stolen dowry:

So are those crisped, snaky, golden locks
Which makes such wanton gambols with the wind
Upon supposed fairness, often known
To be the dowry of a second head,
The skull that bred them in the sepulchre.
(MV 3.2.92–6)

Although the King in AWW says of Helena 'Virtue and she / Is her own
dower', he adds there will also be a supply for her marriage of 'honour
and wealth from me' (2.3.144–5). This economic and social realism in
the offer of a dowry may not go far enough for Count Bertram.

   See under **ward** on the question of disparagement. Also, the forced
marriage of Bertram, even with a good dowry, is an offence against an
ideal of free choice of a marriage partner enunciated by Suffolk of 1H6
(cited above). Such an ideal is enacted by numerous Shakespearian
lovers who marry in the absence of parental consent and of dowry
arrangements. A tension between the operation of a distinctly economic 'marriage market' in Shakespeare's milieu (such as described in
Elliott, 1981), and the model many social historians describe of a relatively free choice of marriage partners for many of Shakespeare's middling class contemporaries (see (C) below), may underlie peculiar ironies
of AWW. For one, the unhallowed 'bed trick' is offered by Helena as a
holy means to provide virtuous but poor Diana's dowry: 'Doubt not but

heaven / Hath brought me up to be your daughter's dower' (AWW 4.4.18–19). And the King repeats the nearly disastrous intervention he had first made for Helena's sake by offering a dowry for Diana: 'If thou be'st yet a fresh uncropped flower, / Choose thou thy husband and I'll pay thy dower' (5.3.328–9).

(C) See under **jointure**, **dower** and **dowager/widow**.

On the *maritagium* see Plucknett, 1956, pp 546–57; Baker, 1990b, pp 310–11; and also Ward, J., 1995, pp 16–17. See Erickson, 1993, pp 79–97, 114–22, 129–39, on the form taken by marriage portions as evidenced in Chancery litigation and in probate of wills of married men.

Historians writing about a tendency to relatively autonomous choices of marriage partners in Shakespeare's middling class milieu include: Macfarlane, 1986, pp 119–147, especially p 124; Houlbrooke, 1984, pp 72–3; Cook, 1991, pp 69–103, especially, p 87; with examples found in Macfarlane, 1970a, pp 95–8; and with some reservations expressed in Laslett, 1983, pp 102–4.

On dowries for nuns, and Isabella in MM, see Kliman, 1982 and McFeely, 1995.

election (A) In political uses 'election' means the choosing of a leader, as opposed to following a pattern of succession fixed by customary rules of law such as **primogeniture**. Some early medieval traditions of English kingship also allowed for election, as noted under **inheritance**.

After much debate on whether or not it is lawful for a king 'to make his heire whomsoever he shall thinke good, or leave his kingdome to whome hee will' (on which point canon law and the Bible seem to contradict), Henry Swinburne's important legal treatise on **wills** concludes realistically that such a question is likely 'in the end to be decided and ruled by the dead stroke of uncivill and martial cannons, rather than by any rule of civill or canon lawe' (Swinburne, 1590, leaves 66–7).

In other legal uses 'election' is a choice between two rights where there is an implied condition that the enjoyment of one must exclude the other. This is connected with the 'old, basic and wide' doctrine of election in **equity**: 'a person may not accept a benefit and reject an associated burden . . . a person may not choose between parts of a single transaction' (Martin, J. E., 1997, p 839).

(B) Shakespeare's often uses 'to elect' or 'election' to refer to either a personal choice, or the choosing of leaders. 'Election' refers to the choosing of kings or high officials of Shakespeare's Rome, Scotland, medieval England, and Denmark.

Some of Shakespeare's sources treat succession to the English throne

107

by election as unjust **disinheritance** of a rightful heir, as do Henry VI, Queen Margaret, and Prince Edward of RDY (1.1.194, 1.1.226, 1.1.227, 1.1.251, 2.2.24). In other political contexts, Emperors, Kings or Regents are said to be 'elected' in TIT 1.1.235, 1H6 4.1.4, CYL 1.3.165, HAM 5.2.66 and 5.2.306, MM 1.1.18, and PER S.8.32, and the king's election in Scotland is also an important aspect of MAC. The Roman people's power to take a (largely ceremonial) part in the choosing of a consul is named 'election' repeatedly in COR.

In RDY 1.1.171–6 we see the future line of English kings chosen by election rather than by descent, on account of the weakness of Henry VI (see under **disinherit**). Rules of royal descent are also ignored in R2, when Bolingbroke's effective *coup d'etat* makes Richard elect him king, and this cuts out the claim of the infant Earl of March (which claim is elided in the play – see Gohn, 1982 – but is expounded in 1H6 2.5).

Danish succession by election is indicated by Hamlet's remarks that Claudio has 'Popped in between th' election and my hopes' (HAM 5.2.66) and 'But I do prophesy th' election lights / On Fortinbras. He has my dying voice.' (5.2.306–7)

'Election' of another legal sort may be named when Burgundy is asked to make a choice between Cordelia without any **dowry** or not at all in LRF 1.1.201–4 / LRQ S.1.192–5. Burgundy replies to Lear's question whether he will 'take' or 'leave' her as wife with: 'Pardon me, royal sir./ Election makes not up in such conditions' (1.1.205 / S.1.196). Keeton, 1967, p 46, argues that Burgundy's reply depends on the equitable doctrine of 'election'. If this is so, then seemingly Burgundy means that the legal doctrine of election does not properly apply forcing him to have either no hope of marrying Cordelia, or no hope of receiving a marriage portion. The reason would be because originally there had been no such condition made implicitly or explicitly on his courtship.

If it is one, Burgundy's use of 'election' constitutes a very strained legal allusion. Yet its gnomic expression might match his shuffling embarrassment at saying that he will only take Cordelia with a good dowry. In terms of ideals discussed under **dowry**, Burgundy is certainly shown up when his rival France accepts that Cordelia 'is herself a dowry' (LRF 1.1.241).

(C) Gohn, 1982, especially pp 948, 950, 952, 956–9, considers the portrayal in R2 of the election by Richard of Bolingbroke as his successor, interpreting it as if an invalid devise of land made under duress, and pointing out that physical pressures on Richard were much greater in historical fact than in the play.

Jardine, 1991, pp 132–5, discusses HAM in terms of an unlawful **marriage** resulting in complications over a blood '*line*' in which there is a '*usurpation*' of Hamlet's regal rights (p. 133). Election is not discussed.

In Keeton, 1967, p 46, the equity expert George W. Keeton asserts that in LRF 1.1.204–5 'election is used in its legal sense', as noted above.

endowed Shakespeare's generally uses 'to endow with' to mean to make a gift of, and 'endowed with' to mean having a certain quality. But in ADO and TIM when an unmarried woman is said to be 'endowed', this means she has a certain **dowry** for her marriage.

With typical hyperbole, Benedict says of Beatrice: 'I would not marry her though she were endowed with all that Adam had left him before he transgressed' (ADO 2.1.234–6). The suggestion is that if her remote ancestor Adam were able to give her Eden for her dowry, it would not tempt him to marry her.

Timon of Athens makes a generous gift to his servant Lucilius to enable him to marry, following negotiations with the bride's father. These include:

TIMON	How shall she be endowed
	If she be mated with an equal husband?
OLD ATHENIAN	Three talents on the present; in future, all.
TIMON	This gentleman of mine hath served me long.
	To build his fortune I will strain a little,
	For 'tis a bond in men. Give him thy daughter.
	What you bestow in him I'll counterpoise,
	And make him weigh with her.

(TIM 1.1.143–50)

As seen under **dowry** and **jointure**, advance financial arrangements made by family or friends of early modern marriage partners could be very costly. Five talents represents a considerable debt in TIM 1.1.97, so to counterbalance a dowry of three talents will require a 'strain' or sacrifice.

enfeoffment (A) A feoffment is a grant of **land** made by a feoffor (grantor) to a feoffee (grantee). This grant is of land held in **fee-simple**, the most absolute form ownership known to English law. To enfeoff means to invest some one with the grant of the land.

(B) In 1H4 3.2.68–9 Henry IV warns Prince Hal that 'the skipping King' Richard II lost his majesty because he 'Grew a companion to the common streets,/ Enfeoffed himself to popularity'. This metaphoric use indicates a complete giving of himself.

(C) Shakespeare's use of the term 'enfeoffed' is discussed in Clarkson and Warren, 1942, pp 111–12. See under **land**, and **use**.

entail (A) An entailed estate, or fee tail, was an estate in **land** created by a donor which restricted the donee's ability to alienate (transfer to someone else) the land. Land granted to A using the words 'to A and the heirs of his body' would devolve on A's heirs after his death and A could not alienate during his lifetime.

When the grant of land was made it was necessary to include the words 'of his body'. If these exact 'words of procreation' were omitted, or replaced for example by 'to A and his heirs', a **fee-simple** estate would be created instead of an entailed estate and A could alienate immediately.

An entailed estate could be limited by the donor to descend to only male **heirs**, called a fee tail male, or only female heirs, or to the heirs resulting from a specified marriage. In this way a donor tried to ensure that land remained within the immediate family, by arranging that A takes take a life estate, and on his death A's heirs as specified by the donor would take life estates and so on. During the term of A's life estate, A's heirs had an interest in **remainder**. If A's heirs failed, then on A's death the property reverted to the donor, or the donor's estate. Therefore the donor or his estate was said to have an interest in **reversion**. Of course such an arrangement could be deliberate, to ensure the return of the property to the donor's family after A's death.

Creating an entailed estate was possible because of the statute *De Donis Conditionalibus* 1285, but that statute said nothing about how long such an estate was to last. So in theory it could last indefinitely, for in every generation the heir could prevent alienation. This has been

110

famously described as the creation of a 'juridical monster' (Milsom, 1981, p 177) and was regarded as unwise, a struggle between the interests of the 'living and the dead' (ibid. p 178; see also under **perpetuities**). The late sixteenth and early seventeenth century saw much debate and uncertainty about when the entail could be 'barred' (broken, cut), and therefore converted to a **fee-simple** and alienated. Several cases held devices for perpetual entails to be void, including: *Cholmeley v Humble* (1595) B. and M. 160–1; *Germyn v Arscott* (1595) B. and M. 159; *Cobett v Cobett* (1600) B. and M. 158–62; *Mildmay v Mildmay* (1602) B. and M. 163–4; *Hethersal v Mildmay* (1605) B. and M. 164–6.

In Shakespeare's time entails could be barred by devices known as **fines and recoveries** (see that heading for details), but Baker, 1978, pp 204–8 suggests reasons why entails continued to be used despite the ease of destroying them: the tenant in tail was restrained during his minority; they discouraged disloyal division of a patrimony; attempts were made to find legal devices to prevent barring. By the late sixteenth century it was settled that common recovery would bar remaindermen and reversioners (*Capel's Case* (1581) 1 Co. Rep. 61). *Partington v Rogers* (1613) 10 Co. Rep. 35 held to be invalid any limitation of an entail that restrained the use of recoveries, thus preventing perpetual entails.

Finally the entail should be distinguished from the 'strict settlement' (familiar from nineteenth century literature) which did succeed in allowing estates to follow one another in succession without the possibility of being barred, but did not take its final form until after 1640.

Both Sir Edward Coke and his enemy Sir Francis Bacon disapproved of entails, partly because of their complexity and partly because they made **conveyancing** uncertain, protected landowners from creditors, and could prevent the property of **felons** or **traitors** going to the crown; however St German and others in the sixteenth and seventeenth centuries argued for their retention or reform (see Bonfield, 1983, pp 16–21).

(B) In AWW 4.3.280–3 Paroles calumniates Dumaine, claiming that for a trivial sum 'he will sell the fee-simple of his salvation, the inheritance of it, and cut th' entail from all remainders, and a perpetual succession for it perpetually'. On the first metaphor here see **fee-simple**. The phrase 'cut the' entail' used here shows that 'Shakespeare indicates that he knew that entails could be barred' (Clarkson and

111

Warren, 1942, p 132). The passage shows also Shakespeare's awareness of the legal problem presented by **perpetuities**.

In RDY 1.1.195–9 (in the quarto text only) the verb 'to entail' is used by Henry VI when he sadly offers the succession due to his own son to Richard Duke of York and his heirs:

> I here entail
> The crown to thee and to thine heirs for ever,
> Conditionally, that here thou take thine oath
> To cease this civil war, and whilst I live
> To honour me as thy king and sovereign . . .

According to Clarkson and Warren, 1942, pp 58–60, here and again at RDY 1.1.236 where Queen Margaret repeats the same language, Shakespeare misuses the term 'entail' because 'the crown' is not land, and because the word 'heirs' rather than the required words 'heirs of his body' is used. Although technically correct, this analysis overlooks the liveliness of a figurative use of the familiar legal concepts in the passage.

(C) For a detailed explanation of entails see Simpson, 1986. For a brief summary see Simpson, 1987b, pp 145–9. For general discussion see: Baker, 1978., pp 51–2; Baker, 1990b, pp 311–12, 318–21; Clarkson and Warren, 1942, pp 54–63. Bonfield, 1983 describes in detail the development during Shakespeare's period of the strict settlement from judicial constructions concerning entails with contingent remainders, to which was added the protection of the remainders by trustees. For an account of entails, settlements and inheritance as these affected heiresses see Spring, 1993, pp 27–35.

equity (A) Shakespeare makes few references to this term but because there a tradition of critical discussion of 'equity in Shakespeare', a brief discussion the Elizabethan law of equity becomes relevant.

In current day legal usage, 'equity' is not synonymous with justice in a broad sense. The classical definition is found rather in Maitland, 1936, p 1: equity means the system of legal rules, procedures and principles which before the Judicature Act of 1873 were applied by the court of Chancery, and until the English Civil War also by lesser equity courts (including the central Court of Requests, and regional equity courts).

A wider sense of the word 'equity' long in use indicates justice and fairness in general, and some historians have attempted to equate ideas of justice and fairness with medieval Chancery judgments. Such attempts have met difficulties. Milsom, 1981, p 82, warned that 'few beginnings are as elusive as that of the Chancellor's equitable jurisdiction'. Records were not kept of Chancery proceedings until the sixteenth century; this lack of evidence has tempted many to conjecture. Two such conjectures are refuted in Post, 1983, pp 78–9, which finds that medieval Chancery's equitable jurisdiction was neither based in civilian law (see **civil doctor**), nor particularly distinctive 'in the legal character of its judgments'.

The Chancellor's court derived from the royal secretariat, the descendant of the Anglo Saxon *scriptorium*. Indeed to Elizabethan times and beyond the Chancellor still presided over the issue of royal writs and grants. By the fourteenth century petitions were addressed directly to the Chancellor, who eventually was said to give judgements in equity. Yet records indicate that it was not until after 1460 that Chancery's equitable jurisdiction became significant in terms of numbers of cases (Guy, 1983).

Medieval legal thinking appears not to have considered that common law and equity were separate bodies of rules (Post, 1983, pp 83–4). But by the sixteenth century a distinct theoretical basis was propounded for equity. The generally accepted view was that 'any general rule must work injustice in particular cases, and therefore that the application of positive law should be subject to some dispensing power in the interest of higher justice' (ibid., p 88 – see: St German, 1975, p 96; West, W., 1601, p 174; Cowell, 1607, N2v-N3r; Lambard, 1635, pp 46–7). An appeal to higher justice for such correction was of great antiquity (*Nich. Eth.* 1137a–1138a); according to S. F. C. Milsom, the unique English innovation was the institution of a system of equity and a system of common law as separate bodies of rules (Milsom, 1981, pp 88–91).

Yet the English equity courts of Shakespeare's time developed only in certain distinct areas of concern. In or near Shakespeare's time there was some expansion of scope for grants of equitable relief in financial disputes (see under **mortgage** on the developing 'equity of redemption', and see under **bond**), but the early modern equity courts operated mainly in matters involving real property (**land**) and the **uses** under which this was often held.

In practice, and as reflected much in contemporary discussion, the Elizabethan courts of equity did not freely apply 'conscience' to correct defects of positive law. The authoritative modern introduction to the famous dialogues in *Doctor and Student* (c. 1523; Barton, J. L., and Plucknett, 1975, pp xi–lxvii) makes abundantly clear that attempts to equate a court of 'conscience' with contemporary English equity lead Christopher St German not only to crucial ambiguities, but indeed to 'outright self-contradiction'. West, W., 1601, p 176, mentions that only 'the common people terme the Chauncery the Court of Conscience', and offers alternatively, p 174: 'Equitie as some other say, is a reasonable measure, containing in it selfe a fit proportion of rigor . . . a ruled kind of Justice'. West and others point out that, instead of applying only conscience, equity had developed its own structures and principles.

Neither did English equity in Shakespeare's time offer free '**pardon** for crimes. Only in exercising one of its administrative functions as a royal secretariat did the multifaceted Chancellor's department have to do with issuing pardons (see Bellamy, 1979, pp 218–19, 223–4). Several contemporaries of Shakespeare saw clemency as a function 'onely proper to the Prince' (West, W., 1601, p 175; see also William Lambard quoted in Dunkel, 1962, p 276). Nor, despite some claims by sixteenth century theorists, did equity's jurisdiction consider abstract 'mercy'. So St German holds that 'Equytye . . . is temperyd with the sweetness of mercye', but immediately offers as examples legal questions having nothing to do with clemency (St German, 1975, pp 95–9; similar confusion appears in West, W., 1601, p 174).

There is an instructive contradiction in William Lambard's 1591–1598 treatise, *Archeion*. Lambard first holds that the common law part of the Chancellors' 'double *Jurisdiction*' is 'limitted in power', but that the other part, concerning '*Equitie*', is by contrast 'meere absolute, and infinite' (Lambard, 1635, p 48). Yet later on Lambard wonders 'whether it be meet, that the *Chancellor* should appoint unto himselfe, and publish to others any certaine *Rules* & *Limits* of *Equity*, or no' (p 74). Then he offers suggestions for the regulation of the equitable jurisdiction (pp 74–7; on these proposed reforms see McIlwain and Ward, 1957 pp 158–9). This inconsistency in Lambard's treatise, which first proposes an infinite scope for and then propose the definite limitation of the equity jurisdiction, points toward Lord Chancellor Nottingham's clear delineations of limits in the later seventeenth century (in Yale, 1965).

Another common historical presumption that needs clarification is the notion that there was an unbroken consistency in the disagreements between common law courts and other competing courts such as Chancery from the times of Henry VIII to those of James I. In fact in the late Elizabethan period these conflicts were abating, and greater harmony was being sought. This late sixteenth century phase is dated from about 1591 by S. E. Thorne in his preface to Hake, 1953, pp xi-xii; its existence is strongly argued throughout Jones, W. J., 1967 and further set in context in Yale, 1965, pp 10–11. Several of Shakespeare's contemporaries remark on it in: Lambard, 1635, pp 71–2; West, W., 1601, p 176; Hake, 1953. However, during the later part of Shakespeare's career, renewed and intensely political struggles between equity and common law took place. Rivalry between competing jurisdictions was exacerbated by the personal rivalry between Sir Edward Coke, Chief Justice of Common Pleas, and the Lord Chancellor, Lord Ellesmere. This led to the famous crisis of 1616 when the exasperated King James dismissed Coke from office (see under **praemunire**, and: Thomas, G. W., 1976, p 508; Baker, 1969, p 369; Dawson, 1941, p 128; Yale, 1965, p 12).

(B) Shakespeare several times refers to the general concept of 'equity' or rightful lawfulness, as in: RDY 1.1.124, 'by right and equity'; 1H4 2.3.8, 'there's no equity stirring'; CYL 3.1.146 'equity exiled'; JN 2.1.241 'downtrodden equity'. But judgments in the actual English prerogative **jurisdiction** of equity in Shakespeare's age were not based on rightfulness and conscience acting without rules or precedent, despite misapprehensions of some critics and editors.

As discussed at length in Sokol and Sokol, 1999b, an explicit reference to the equity jurisdiction appears in the 1605–6 Quarto version only of *King Lear*:

> Thou robed man of justice, take thy place;
> And thou, his yokefellow of equity,
> Bench by his side.
>
> (LRQ S.13.32–4)

Following this command Lear convenes a court in which sit a Bedlam beggar, whom he has just addressed as a 'most learned justicer', a coarse servant, and his Fool. The hallucinating Lear arraigns a rough piece of furniture, a 'join-stool', as if it were Goneril, and an equally imaginary Regan. Satiric intent is evident, for this, like other 'mad' speeches by Lear, challenges the worldly authority of justice (see Merchant, 1964, pp 121–3). Ironically, this mad trial scene may present a view of how justice could be executed. Cases that concerned important legal or political matters were sometimes heard before all the justices of England sitting together (see under **precedent** and **plantation**).

MM and MV are playtexts in which a supposed 'equity versus law' theme has been much discussed, although neither contains any allusion to Chancery or other equity courts, nor any explicit representation of equity principles or procedures. The relation of equity with MV is made complex, however, because of the absence in that play of any reflection of the equitable relief from an unfair conditional ('double') bond that was available and well known to be so in Shakespeare's time (see under **bond**). Despite very numerous readings that find concepts of equity crucially relevant to the play, what is most notable legally is that no equitable relief from Shylock's bond is mentioned during the trial scene or elsewhere (this is noted in: Pollock, 1914, p 175; Windolph, 1956, p 55; Denning, 1986, p 30; Sokol, 1992; Holmer, 1995, pp 212–13, 327–9; White, R. S., 1996, p 164). No single reason for this omission has been agreed.

(C) On equity in Shakespeare's time see: West, W., 1601; Cowell, 1607; Ashe, 1609; Lambard, 1635; Keeton, 1930; Dawson, 1941; Hake, 1953; Windolph, 1956; Ives, 1964; Merchant, 1964; Jones, W. J., 1967; Baker, 1969, 1978; St German, 1975; Gray, C., 1976, 1980; Knafla, 1977.

On the late Elizabethan abating of jurisdictional conflicts see references cited above, and also Tucker, 1976 and Hill, 1988, pp 40–53.

For references on 'equity of statute' see under **statute**.

Discussions of Shakespeare in relation with concepts of 'equity' in philosophical, rhetorical and jurisprudential traditions that were more or less divorced from the practice of lawcourts in the plays are found in: Altman, 1978; Wilson, L., 1991; Hutson, 1994, 1996.

It may not be particularly significant that Shakespeare himself had personal experience of equity litigation, because such an experience was widely familiar to property owners in his era, but for records of how Shakespeare's family lost a Chancery action to recover lands lost in a forfeit mortgage see Chambers, 1930, vol 2, pp 35–41. This case is expanded upon as influential on plays in: Phelps, 1901 (the documents translated pp 157–70); Dickinson, 1962, p 292; Knight, 1974, pp 98–104.

On a supposed treatment of equity in MM see: Dickinson, 1962; Dunkel, 1962; Levin, 1996. For allied views concerning 1H4 see Phelps, 1901 – which contains many of the historical points later alleged relevant to MM or MV.

Various claims for the relevance of equity to the trial in MV include: Keeton, 1930, p 18; MacKay, 1964; Andrews, 1965; Saunders, 1984; Wilson, R., 1990; Cohen, S. A., 1994. Such claims were not common in the hundred years of diverse international lawyer's wranglings about MV wittily summarized in Phillips, O. H., 1972, pp 91–118. The reason is that, as Keeton, 1930, p 19 states, 'Equity is not mercy'. Portia actually asks for human mercy, not equitable remedies, and then not obtaining it ripostes with positive law, indeed statute. Notice of the distinction of English equity from the trial in MV is taken in: Pollock, 1914, p 175; Windolph, 1956, p 55; Tucker, 1976, pp 99–100; Denning, 1986, p 30; Sokol, 1992; Holmer, 1995, pp 212–13, 327–9; White, R. S., 1996, p 164. See also Posner, 1988, p 94 and Weisberg, 1992, pp 207–10.

A number of critics finding 'equity' in MV have associated or equated that with a merciful 'New Law' overcoming a merciless Old Testament concept of strict legal construction. Sokol, 1998 argues that Shakespeare in MV showed a far greater grasp of the Bible than such commentary supposes; other discussions opposing the error of supposing MV indicts a merciless 'Old Law' include Slights, 1980, p 359; Weisberg, 1992, pp 93–104; Halio, 1993, pp 60 and 62; Hamilton, M. A., 1993, pp 128n, 133; Holmer, 1995, pp 232–3; Yaffe, 1997.

On 'equity' in *King Lear* see Keeton, 1967, pp 33–5, which warns, p 33, 'too much should not be read into' the solitary reference to Chancery in the play (not noting its absence from LRF), and Sokol and Sokol, 1999b.

espousal See **spousal**.

executors (A) The medieval church held it to be sinful to die intestate, or without a **will**, and also thought that 'failure to appoint an executor in a will amounted to virtual intestacy' (Jones, W. J., 1967, p 401). By Shakespeare's time executors were no longer the general heirs, but instead independent friends or lawyers who nevertheless could still be residuary legatees. The executors' duties were to ensure that the testator's property was distributed according to his wishes which were set out in his last will and **testament**. To this end the executors brought the will to the judge in the Church court and produced two witnesses to swear that it was genuine.

During this period rules developed for the regulation of the conduct of executors. They were made accountable to the court for their actions, and by a statute of 1529 had to make a detailed itemised inventory of the deceased man's property and produce it in court before administration of the estate was handed over to them. Failure to make an inventory was serious, and could result in an order making the executor personally responsible to meet payment of the legacies. To compel performance the courts made executors enter into formal bonds and give sureties. Executors were also expected to produce an account after completion of the administration (see **audit**), but evidence from some courts shows they did not appear to do so very frequently (see Jones, W. J., 1967, pp 403–4, and Houlbrooke, 1979, p 114).

Many complaints are recorded in Elizabethan Chancery Court cases about dishonest executors and the Church courts' failure to deal with them, and about delay, abuse and the burden of fees (see Jones, W. J., 1967, pp 403–4, and **audit**). These complaints can lead to the conclusion that the Church courts were inefficient in administering probate of wills, and that there was great concern about dishonest executors. There were difficulties in ensuring that residuary legatees who acted as executors make full account for their actions. But recent examination of some Church court records has led to doubts about drawing too hasty a conclusion on the Church courts' ineffectiveness (see Helmholz, 1990, pp 79–80 and **wills**). There is more to be learned by investigation of Church court records.

Also, in a study of late Elizabethan London, Brodsky, 1986, p 145, finds that '80 per cent of married testators appointed their wives as sole executors of their wills', and argues, pp 144–6, that many men formed with their wives their 'deepest affective bonds' (see **dowager/widow**).

118

So trust in their executors may have been common among men in Shakespeare's London milieu.

(B) The appointing of executors for wills is referred to in the poetic lamentations of Richard II: 'Let's choose executors and talk of wills – / And yet not so, for what can we bequeath / Save our deposed bodies to the ground?' (R2 3.2.144–6). This usage is consistent with Richard's wish to emphasise, with pathos, his imminent non-royal status (see **will** on this passage).

An 'executor' with testamentary functions appears also figuratively (in accord with the dominant imagery) in SON 4, which is discussed under **audit**.

In addition to indicating anyone who executes a task, as in TMP 3.1.13, 'executor' had a specific denotation of 'executioner' (OED 2). It is thus used in H5 1.2.203.

(C) See Jones, W. J., 1967, pp 400–17, and especially pp 410–16 on the 'theoretical principle that the office of executor was a trust'. See also: Houlbrooke, 1979; Helmholz, 1987f; Helmholz, 1990.

Clarkson and Warren, 1942, pp 258–81 details the functions of executors, and describes their reflections in Elizabethan drama.

exile See outlawry/banishment/exile.

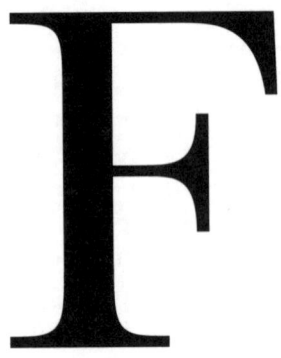

fee farm 'Fee farm' was a free tenure (see **land**) in which land is held in **fee-simple** (which means it is heritable and is held for as long as there is an heir for the time being) for a perpetual fixed rent and no other service. By the late sixteenth century, as other forms of tenure disappeared, this was probably a form of 'socage' tenure.

Shakespeare's one clear use of this term conveys obscene and perhaps derogatory implications against Cressida. Pandarus urges Trolius 'Rub on, and kiss the mistress', and then remarks 'How now, a kiss in fee farm!' (TRO 3.2.48–9). This typically sniggering image of Pandarus may suggest a kiss of perpetual duration, yet one that is paid for annually.

It is possible that a tenure in fee farm is also implied in the derogatory description of a piece of land in a passage of Q2 *Hamlet* described under **fee-simple**: 'a little patch of ground / That hath in it no profit but the name. / To pay five ducats, five, I would not farm it . . . ' (HAM A.J. 9–11, added at the end of 4.4). A derogatory implication attaches also to John of Gaunt's description of how England: 'Is now leased out – I die pronouncing it – / Like to a tenement or pelting farm' (R2 2.1.59–60); on this and other land law images surrounding it see Gohn, 1982, pp 956–8.

fee-simple (A) A fee simple represents the closest English **land** law comes to absolute ownership of land. It is necessary to qualify absolute

120

ownership in this way because of the operation of the doctrine of **tenures**, which states that all land is held of the Crown. So traditionally English land law, when faced with competing claims to land, has been most concerned to decide who has the better right to possession of the land, rather than establishing absolute rights.

The word 'fee' denotes that the fee simple is an estate in land that is capable of inheritance by the owner's heirs (see **land** for an explanation of the workings of the doctrines of tenures and estates). However a fee simple estate could be alienated in Shakespeare's time without any need to obtain the permission of an **heir** presumptive or apparent. In this context an 'heir' can be someone who inherits by descent from an ancestor, or by **will** or by intestacy, or by **purchase**.

The word 'simple' denotes that this is not an estate that has been 'cut down', so that the fee simple will not terminate on the happening of a given event. For example a life estate terminates on the death of the tenant. A fee simple could therefore last indefinitely, as long as there were heirs capable of inheriting.

If the heirs failed, then the fee simple 'escheated' to the person with superior title, for instance the tenant **in capite**. Eventually, with the abolition of most forms of tenure in the seventeenth century, most superior titles are today vested in the Crown.

(B) 'Fee-simple' is most often employed by Shakespeare figuratively, and often facetiously. It is used metaphorically or metonymically to represent something actually or hopefully possessed absolutely.

Yet, to be 'sold in fee' literally indicates an alienable estate in land held in fee simple in a Q2 addition to HAM. The worthlessness piece of land bloodily battled for by Fortinbras is there described by a Captain as 'a little patch of ground / That hath in it no profit but the name. / To pay five ducats, five, I would not farm it, / Nor will it yield to Norway or the Pole / A ranker rate, should it be sold in fee' (A.J. 9–13, at the end of HAM 4.4). It is ambiguous whether Hamlet is envious when he shows himself contemptuous of Fortinbras' mindless zeal for his rights and honour. The particular sort of fee mentioned here may be **fee farm**.

Jack Cade's reference to Alexander Iden's 'fee-simple' is metonymic for his land held in fee simple, on which the hunted rebel Cade, degraded to near-animal existence, is a 'stray' (CYL 4.9.25).

ROM 3.1.30–3 displays the tendency of Shakespearian youths to jest with technical legal terms, perhaps in imitation of **Inns of Court** men in the audience. This jesting merges into Mercutio's ominous defiance of a warning about being killed:

BENVOLIO   An I were so apt to quarrel as thou art, any man should buy the fee-simple of my life for an hour and a quarter.
MERCUTIO   The fee simple? O, simple!

In AWW 4.3.280–3 Paroles calumniates Dumaine using several land law metaphors, claiming that for a trivial sum 'he will sell the fee-simple of his salvation, the inheritance of it, and cut th' entail from all remainders, and a perpetual succession for it perpetually.' On this passage see **entail** (which explains **remainder**) and **perpetuity**.

The humorous notion of a (near-absolute) fee-simple made over to the devil arises again in WIV 4.2.195–8, where Mistress Page says of the defeated Falstaff: 'The spirit of wantonness is sure scared out of him. If the devil have him not in fee-simple, with fine and recovery, he will never, I think, in the way of waste attempt us again'. See under **fine and recovery** for explanation of how this fictional action made possession even surer, and under **waste** on the bawdy significance here of another land-law term.

In the quarto version only of TRO, scabrous Thersites' imprecations include 'the rivelled fee-simple of the tetter' (AA 6, an elaboration of 5.1.17–21). This images the surface of a human body (like a piece of land) in the total possession of a 'tetter', a skin disease like that of Hamlet's poisoned father.

A more difficult metaphor in which 'fee-simple' may be entangled appears in MAC 4.3.197. Macduff asks if the ill news he has been warned about is public or intensely private: 'The general cause, or is it a fee-grief / Due to some single breast?'. As in the usage of 'fee simple' to indicate a person's life in ROM above, this usage foreshadows disaster.

(C) On the history of the fee simple, and particularly how it became alienable, see Barton, J. L., 1976, which wisely concludes 'it is dangerous to attempt to deduce the practical functioning of [past] institutions from what is assumed to be the inherent logic of their structure'. Also see: Simpson, 1986, pp 56, 85, 89–90; Baker, 1990b, p 301.

For a discussion of Shakespeare's uses of 'fee-simple' see Clarkson and Warren, 1942, pp 4 and 50–4.

felon/felony (A) In the middle ages, a felony was a crime of such seriousness that it breached the feudal relationship between lord and tenant and merited the confiscation by the lord of the tenant's lands. But by the thirteenth century the rights of feudal lords to seize the lands of felons, following the king's right to hold the land for a year and a day with **waste**, had ceased. All felonies were capital offences, and were 'pleas of the crown'. This originally meant that they were matters in which the king had an interest, in contrast to 'common pleas' which were matters between subjects in which the king had no interest. 'Pleas of the crown' became a synonym for criminal law.

In Shakespeare's time a felony was a serious crime which was punished with death usually by hanging, and forfeiture of property to the king. To merit this, it had long been thought necessary that the offender had an intention to do wrong, and was mentally fit to understand what they did. However there were and are significant philosophical and judicial difficulties in defining or applying such a requirement for a felonious *mens rea* (see Sayre, 1932 and Baker, 1990b, pp 596–9).

The list of capital felonies included treason, petty treason, murder, burglary, larceny and arson. Rape was usually a felony, but most other sexual crimes were tried by the Church courts which punished with penance or excommunication. Incest was not a secular crime until the twentieth century, but 'bestiality became a capital offence in 1543 and, with one brief interval [1553–62], remained so until 1861' (Thomas, K., 1983, pp 38–9). Sodomy, first became a felony in 1533–4 (25 Hen. VIII, c.6), and numerous subsequent early modern **statutes** modified, continued, or extended this (on these statutes see Smith, B. R., 1991, pp 41–53, which also discusses the rarity of convictions).

For further legal historical details on the felonies named by Shakespeare see under **treason**, **murder/homicide**, **burglary**, **robbery** and **rape**.

Lesser crimes, which were punished with fines, imprisonment or corporal punishment, were called **trespasses** or misdemeanours (Baker, 1990b, pp 572–3). Misdemeanours included assault and **battery**, making threats, and administrative offences such as using non-standard weights and measures. The development of the law of misdemeanour was an achievement particularly of the court of **Star Chamber**.

Prosecution of felonies was either by **appeal** of felony, which was private prosecution by the victim or family, or by indictment which was the sworn accusation of the **jury** of presentment (grand jury). Because of the interpretation put on Magna Carta 1215 it was said that no man could be put on trial for an offence punishable by imprisonment or death without indictment first by a grand jury of his peers. However, as Baker, 1986b, p 263 points out, this traditional view ignores prosecution by appeal of felony.

Both felonies and misdemeanours could be tried by jury before either the **Justice of the Peace** at the quarter sessions, or by the royal **justices** when they came to the county on assize. But by the Marian statutes 1554–5 (1 & 2 P. & M. c.13, and 2 & 3 P. & M. c.10) justices of the peace were required first to examine those accused of felony and any witnesses, and then to pass on certified information to the royal justices to be heard at assize. During Elizabeth's reign the process of removing serious crimes from the Justice of the Peace at quarter sessions was continued, and additional offences (for instance forgery) were added to the list of crimes reserved to assize judges. Also, as Justices of the Peace became overloaded with administrative tasks such as regulating weights and measures (see **Justice of the Peace**), they increasingly chose to refer serious or difficult cases to the royal justice on assize.

(B) Jack Cade's plans for social reformation include a determination to 'make it felony to drink small beer' (CYL 4.2.69). Gonzalo's plans for his utopian kingdom would, together with outlawing work, eliminate, 'Treason, felony, / Sword, pike, knife, gun, or need of any engine' (TMP 2.1.166–7). In double paradox, an anarchist would retain, and a sentimental libertarian eliminate, felony.

Alcibiades posits, to defend a military friend's spontaneously violent crime, the paradox of a 'felon / Loaden with irons wiser than the judge, / If wisdom be in suffering' (TIM 3.6.49–51). Here, as often, 'felon' is a term of disparagement. For instance, 'felon' is the provocative epithet that causes an at-first-unwilling Romeo to fight following Paris's 'I do defy thy conjuration, / And apprehend thee for a felon here' (ROM 5.3.68–9).

The Protector Humphrey Duke of Gloucester is accused of having devised 'Strange tortures for offenders, never heard of, / That England was defamed by tyranny' (CYL 3.1.122–3). He replies:

> Why, 'tis well known that whiles I was Protector
> Pity was all the fault that was in me,
> For I should melt at an offender's tears,

And lowly words were ransom for their fault.
Unless it were a bloody murderer,
Or foul felonious thief that fleeced poor passengers,
I never gave them condign punishment.
Murder, indeed – that bloody sin – I tortured
Above the felon or what trespass else.

(124–32)

This **mercy** toward all but thieves and murderers encompasses both felony and **trespass**. See under **jury** on torture.

(C) See: Plucknett, 1956, pp 424–30; Milsom, 1981, pp 403–6; Baker, 1990b, pp 594–9; Bellamy, 1973, p 33–6. On modes of trial see Cockburn, 1972, p 90.

Boehrer, 1994 argues a connection of the felony of bestial buggery with MND, and offers statistics of actual occurrences, pp 147–50. An analogy between bestiality and religious miscegenation made in Coke's *Institutes* is argued to be important to MV in Sokol, 1998.

Discussions treating Shakespeare's plays and poems in relation to homosexual desire range from Stewart, 1949 which finds repressed homosexual desire behind the jealousy in WT, through a wide-ranging investigation in Smith, B. R., 1991. Thompson, 1994, pp 4–7, surveys similar recent work.

On *mens rea* in felony see especially Sayre, 1932 and Baker, 1990b pp 596–9. For a philosophical account of guilty minds in MM see Grene, 1992. For an historically informed and sensitive account of Macbeth forming a guilty intention see Wiggins, 1990. For a discussion alleging that a concept of 'modular intentions' informs HAM see Wilson, L., 1993; on the author of HAM presenting us with a lawmaker-like intention see Wilson, L., 1991.

fine and recovery (A) Fines and recoveries were two different legal fictions used in the **conveyancing** (the legal transfer of title) of land. Both depended on fictitious legal actions in which the court, the vendor, and the **purchaser** of **land** colluded to achieve their common purposes. These were to facilitate the transfer of title to the land, and then to have the desired title entered on the court's records, which gave an undisputed record of the title.

The **fine** was an agreement which settled a fictitious 'disputed' action for title to land. The terms of the agreement between the parties were entered onto a parchment which was then torn into three (an **indenture**). Each party took one part and the third part, the end of the parchment known as the 'foot of the fine', remained in the court as a record of the compromised legal action. The statutes 4 Hen. VII c.24 and 32 Hen. VIII c.28 confirmed that a fine would bar heirs of **entailed** land, allowing the **disinheritance** of what (probably) Sir Francis Bacon called 'disobedient, negligent, and wasteful' sons (Bonfield, 1983, p 16).

A common **recovery** was a more complex legal fiction which developed from the warranty of title which a tenant in tail (see **entail**) could give a third party on alienation of the land, provided the subsequent heirs in tail were left with lands of equal value descending from the same donor. By the sixteenth century this had become a collusive legal action, depending on the actions of a **voucher** for warranty of title. The procedure was that a stranger brought a claim for the land against the tenant who then named a third party to vouch for his title. The third party, or vouchee would then default and the stranger could claim the **fee-simple**. In theory the **heirs** in tail could claim against the vouchee, but from the late fifteenth century the whole process had been turned into an accepted device for barring the heirs. Finally in *Capell's Case* (1581) common recoveries were held to bar not only heirs but **remaindermen** and **reversioners** as well (again see **entail**). The vouchee was a landless court official, later called the 'common vouchee', who would receive payment for his part in the legal fiction.

The common recovery described above would not bar all possible claimants to the land. It was considered correct that all claiming under the same title as the tenant were barred, but not those who could claim under another title. Simpson, 1986, pp 135–7, gives the example of A, a tenant in tail, who wrongfully grants the land to B who regrants it immediately to A. The whole purpose of this exercise would be to resettle on terms more beneficial to A. If A then subsequently effected a common recovery, A's heirs would not be barred because their claim to the land rested on the older, original entail and not the later arrangement with B. It was in order to ensure that all possible claimants were barred that the **double voucher** made its appearance. This worked as follows: the tenant in tail would grant the land to C, and the real purchaser would then bring the collusive action against C who vouched the tenant in tail who in turn vouched the common vouchee, the man of straw. This was held to bar the heirs of any title whatsoever that the tenant in tail had possessed, although the use of treble vouchers is also recorded.

(B) The actually separate terms 'fine' and 'recovery' are coupled together or used in close proximity in several jocular Shakespearian contexts. Perhaps they were equivalently great dilemmas for learning, and their coupling suggests an **Inns of Court** student jest.

A joke about the devil taking Falstaff's soul 'in fee-simple, with fine and recovery' (WIV 4.2.195–8) is contexualized in the entry for **fee-simple**.

In both ERR and HAM, the contexts of 'fine and recovery' are quibbles over time and death. Although the jests are flimsy, there is a resonance in these two legal terms with time and death, or at least attempts to overcome death and eclipse time; both fines and recoveries were means to defeat **perpetuities** (again see **entail**).

In the first context, Dromio of Syracuse cites 'a rule as plain as the plain bald pate of Father Time himself':

DROMIO OF SYRACUSE There's no time for a man to recover his hair that grows bald by nature.

ANTIPHOLUS OF SYRACUSE May he not do it by fine and recovery?

DROMIO OF SYRACUSE Yes, to pay a fine for a periwig, and recover the lost hair of another man.

(ERR 2.2.69–77)

When Hamlet speculates that a skull thrown up by the gravedigger had been a lawyer's, he produces a stream of legal quibbles, including (HAM 5.1.103–4): 'Is this the fine of his fines and the recovery of his recoveries, to have his fine pate full of fine dirt?'. The context of this is filled with legal terms:

HAMLET Why might not that be the skull of a lawyer? Where be his quiddits now, his quillets, his cases, his tenures, and his tricks? Why does he suffer this rude knave now to knock him about the sconce with a dirty shovel, and will not tell him of his action of battery? H'm! This fellow might be in 's time a great buyer of land, with his statutes, his recognizances, his fines, his double vouchers, his recoveries. Is this the fine of his fines and the recovery of his recoveries, to have his fine pate full of fine dirt? Will his vouchers vouch him no more of his purchases, and double ones too, than the length and breadth of a pair of indentures? The very conveyances of his lands will hardly lie in this box; and must th' inheritor himself have no more, ha?

HORATIO   Not a jot more, my lord.

HAMLET   Is not parchment made of sheepskins?

HORATIO   Ay, my lord, and of calf-skins too.

HAMLET   They are sheep and calves that seek out assurance in that.

(HAM 5.1.95–114)

The overall thrust of the passage is to indicate the futility, the sheep and calf like folly, of seeking assurance in holding property, however firmly legally, in the face of death. Judging by the volume of his conveyances, this lawyer is imagined to have acquired huge amounts of property. (See separate entries for **quillet**, **tenures**, **battery**, **statute**, **convey-ance**, **purchase**, **recognizance**, **voucher**, **double voucher**.) Also the prolific production on sheepskin or calfskin parchments of legal documents, written by lawyers and law clerks for fees, is probably satir-ized. The excess of one Chancery scrivener was soon after punished by Lord Chancellor Ellesmere by forcing him to parade wearing the excessive pages he had written arrayed around his head.

(C) On fines and recoveries see Baker, 1978, pp 204–8 and Simpson, 1986, pp 122–37. On the social and economic contexts that made the 'bare faced fraud' (p. 202) of the common recovery acceptable to the Tudor law courts, see Thorne, 1985i. Interestingly, Edward Coke's con-temporary treatise on fines, Coke, 1764, pp 211–78, emphasizes the antiquity and therefore integrity of English common law. On Coke and 'fictions' see Gray, C., 1980 and Thorne, 1985g.

On Shakespeare's uses of fine and recovery see Clarkson and Warren, 1942, pp 127–33. Ibid., p 128, presents a close analysis of the puns in the four instances of 'fine' in Hamlet's graveyard speech. A similar analysis is found in Phillips, O. H., 1972, p 121.

headborough See **thirdborough** and **constable**.

HEIR (A) At common law an 'heir' describes a person who inherits property by descent rather than by will (see **inheritance** and **will**). The legal doctrine *nemo est heres viventis* meant that the living could have no heirs, only the dead, because only at death can the heir be conclusively determined. But the term 'heir' in general use included the wider meaning of the **heir-apparent** of the living, and sometimes Shakespeare uses this meaning.

(B) The term '**heir**' appears in all but five of Shakespeare's plays. In fact the five exceptional plays also contain allusions to heirs. MND 5.2.35 and 5.2.40 mentions first-born 'issue'; TN 1.5.108, an 'eldest son'; TRO 4.1.66, breeding 'inheritors'; MAC 3.1.62–5, 'a fruitless crown/ . . . No son of mine suceeding'; and MM concerns a notably heirless Duke who appoints a young surrogate successor, but then marries.

Sometimes Shakespeare's 'heirs' are children of living fathers, as in 1H4 4.3.74 or MV 4.1.93, and sometimes inheritors from deceased ones as in SHR 2.1.117 or JN 1.1.56.

Celia's legally imprecise reference to Rosalind becoming an 'heir' to her usurping uncle has attracted adverse critical commentary, as detailed in Clarkson and Warren, 1942, p 219. Celia's generosity may seem hyperbolic in:

129

> You know my father hath no child but I, nor none is like to have. And truly, when he dies thou shalt be his heir; for what he hath taken away from thy father perforce, I will render thee again in affection.

(AYL 1.2.16–19)

Yet Clarkson and Warren are probably over-ingenious in suggesting that the sister-like affection between the cousins could result in co-parceny (see **co-heirs**). Celia probably means only that she will return voluntarily Rosalind's stolen patrimony, the inheritance that Rosalind as the **heir apparent** of the usurped Duke lost because it had been 'taken away' by Celia's father.

In civilian law (see **civil doctor**), as opposed to common law, an 'heir' could also denote an **inheritor** under a will. A usage based on this sort of possibility is seen in TIM 1.1.140–3 (on the context see under **disinherit**). However (despite her own guise as a civil doctor) Portia, an inheritor very much subject to 'the will of a dead father' (MV 1.2.23–4), is not called an 'heir', but 'a lady richly left' (1.1.161).

Carroll, 1992, p 214, suggests that just as in R3, also in *King Lear*, the 'principle of lineal succession is denounced, desired, and finally achieved', and points out, p 219, that the title page of LRQ identifies Edgar as 'sonne and heire to the Earle of Gloster'. In view of Gloucester's attempts to make the illegitimate Edmund legally 'capable' of inheriting his land (LRQ S.6.85), Carroll remarks that 'in this case "sonne and heire" is no redundancy'.

(C) See Clarkson and Warren, 1942, pp 200–19, Jardine, 1991 on HAM, and Carroll, 1992.

heir-apparent This is the term for someone who will be **heir** so long as they outlive the ancestor (in law an ancestor can be an antique collateral relative) from whom they will inherit.

Shakespeare explicitly writes 'heir-apparent' in: CYL 1.1.150; 1H4 1.2.57, 2.2.43, 2.5.272, and 2.5.369; PER S.10.37. In all of these cases the reference is to the inheritance of a throne.

Heir-apparent is abbreviated to 'apparent to the crown' in RDY 2.2.64, although there Prince Edward's right of succession is in question (see RDY 2.2.91–4). Being the royal 'heir apparent' is the central issue jested and punned about in 1H4 1.2.56–7, 2.2.43, 2.5.272 and 2.5.369. The term is used paradoxically in 'Our heir-apparent is a king! / Who dreamt, who thought of such a thing?' (PER S.10.37–8), when Pericles who might inherit the throne of Pentapolis is discovered to be the King of Tyre. Even more oblique is Leontes' comment to Hermione concerning Polixenes 'Next to thyself and my young rover, he's / Apparent to my heart' (WT 1.2.177–8); however as Mamillius, the 'young rover' of the passage, is actually heir-apparent, a link to the legal concept is evident.

Finally the child King Henry VI's uncle and Protector, the Duke of Gloucester, is identified as 'the next of blood/ And heir apparent to the English crown' (CYL 1.1.149–50). It has been objected (for instance, in Clarkson and Warren, 1942, pp 198–200) that he is 'heir presumptive', not 'heir apparent', for he is currently the nearest relation but would be supplanted in the succession if Henry later had a child. The technical term 'heir presumptive' is not used by Shakespeare.

heresy (A) Heresy was the offence of departing from the authorised doctrines of the Church, and was defined by canon law. In England it was tried in the middle ages by the ecclesiastical courts, but then the guilty person was turned over to the common law courts for punishment, which was to die by being burned alive at the stake.

During the religious struggles of the early and mid sixteenth century many Catholics and Protestants were tortured and burned as heretics. **Witchcraft** also was punished as heresy.

But by Shakespeare's time the statute 1 Edw. VI, c.12 had repealed all previous English legislation on heresy. So Pollock and Maitland, 1898, vol 2, p 552, argues that since under Elizabeth I and James I 'there were no statutes that punished heresy with death', any burning of heretics in their age had to draw illogically on common law tradition. Ibid. comments: 'assuredly it was hard to find any logical theory which would send heretics to death and yet not admit that papal decretals were not still valid law in England'. Before the reformation not all papal decretals were binding, but those on heresy were.

In fact the burning of a heretic was rare in Shakespeare's England, although it was still possible until 1677. In 1612 Coke (unsuccessfully) argued that a writ to do so was illegal (see Holdsworth, 1903, vol 1, p 618). Langbein, 1977, p 184, claims that the last heretics to be burnt alive in England were the Unitarians Bartholemew Legatt and Edward Wightman, in 1612.

(B) Some of Shakespeare's allusions to being burned alive for heresy may possibly recall the famous martyrdoms of the earlier sixteenth century. Threatened for truth-telling by King Leontes who says 'I'll ha' thee burnt', steadfast Paulina replies 'I care not. / It is an heretic that makes the fire, / Not she which burns in 't.' (WT 2.3.114–16). She thereby alleges the tyrannous king is a heretic to truth, and not herself.

The senselessness of burning heretics is suggested by King Lear's Fool's satirical 'prophesy' of a future time of paradoxical impossibilities,

> When priests are more in word than matter;
> When brewers mar their malt with water;
> When nobles are their tailors' tutors,
> No heretics burned, but wenches' suitors,
> . . .
> When every case in law is right;
> No squire in debt nor no poor knight;
> When slanders do not live in tongues,
> Nor cutpurses come not to throngs;
> When usurers tell their gold i' th' field,
> And bawds and whores do churches build
>   (LRF 3.2.81–92)

The Fool's figure of wenches' suitors being heretics aligns with a notion of a lover committing heresy several times repeated by Shakespeare (MND 2.2.147, ROM 1.2.93, ADO 1.1.219–20, TN 1.5.218, CYM 3.4.81–2). In these usages heresy is a metaphor for a lover's defection from a mistress, or for a sceptic's rejection of love itself.

Some of Shakespeare's figures of lovers' heresy refer to imagined or actual written papers: 'I have read it. It is heresy.' (TN 1.5.218); 'The scriptures of the loyal Leonatus, / All turned to heresy?' (CYM 3.4.82). These writings contain the 'heresy' of a lover's inconstancy or insincerity.

In other cases there is pointedly no doctrinal meaning to a lover's 'heresy'; his defection reflects only the willfulness of passion. Such usages may suggest in reverse an arbitrary absurdity in bloody doctrinal disputes. So, having fallen out of love with Hermia, Lysander falls into loathing of her, and explains:

> For as a surfeit of the sweetest things
> The deepest loathing to the stomach brings,
> Or as the heresies that men do leave
> Are hated most of those they did deceive,
> So thou, my surfeit and my heresy,
> Of all be hated, but the most of me
>   (MND 2.2.143–8)

The cruelty of hating a woman just because she was formerly loved is paralleled with a passionate hatred of a faith formerly endorsed, now called 'heresy'. This image may convey a sardonic view of the murderous sectarian conflicts of the sixteenth century.

Although faithfulness is claimed, immaturity is in evidence when, after Benvolio predicts that Romeo will meet a greater beauty than Rosaline, Romeo replies:

> When the devout religion of mine eye
> Maintains such falsehood, then turn tears to fires;
> And these who, often drowned, could never die,
> Transparent heretics, be burnt for liars.
> One fairer than my love! – the all-seeing sun
> Ne'er saw her match since first the world begun.
>   (ROM 1.2.90–5)

Oxymoron and copious paradox are the leading figures here, and convey no emotional depth. The metaphoric reference to burning heretics in this poetic wrangling shows a kind of conceited cleverness, but also cavalier disinterest in the cruel treatment of heretics.

In MV 2.9.81–2 Nerissa says to Portia: 'The ancient saying is no heresy: / Hanging and wiving goes by destiny'. This quip wryly accepts that marriage choice is fated, but a usage of 'heresy' in a context concerning marriage may also resonate with the play's subplot in which a Christian marries a Jew. If Jessica had not **converted**, under English common law her marriage would have been a crime, with the punishment of burning alive (Coke, 1797, 3rd Institute, p 89; the resonances in MV are investigated in Sokol, 1998). If Lorenzo had converted, his heretical apostasy would also have merited burning alive. Although after 1215 the Church no longer directly inflicted such punishments, in an unusual and famous case of 1222 (remarked on by Bracton, Holinshed and others), Archbishop Stephen Langton handed over a Deacon, who had converted to Judaism after marriage, to the **sheriff** of Oxford. The latter promptly burnt him alive without further trial, contrary to Magna Carta (see **jury**). This case is discussed in Pollock and Maitland, 1898, vol 2, p 584 and in Maitland, 1911a at length.

In JN 3.1.62–273 the sort of political differences that made the persecution of heretics so bloody in Europe are reflected in Shakespeare's presentation of a dispute involving the same Stephen Langton. Cardinal Pandolph, a papal legate, demands that King John explain why he has prevented Langton from taking up the Archbishopric of Canterbury. John rejects Pope Innocent's authority to question him (see under **interrogatories**), adding:

> that no Italian priest
> Shall tithe or toll in our dominions;
> But as we, under God, are supreme head,
> So, under him, that great supremacy
> Where we do reign we will alone uphold
> Without th' assistance of a mortal hand.
> So tell the Pope, all reverence set apart
> To him and his usurped authority.
> (JN 3.1.79–86)

This act of defiance, linked by John with false 'juggling **witchcraft**' in the sale of the Pope's 'corrupted **pardon**' (90–7) brings two prompt consequences. One is the excommunication of John, to which Pandolf appends: 'blessed shall he be that doth revolt / From his allegiance to an heretic; / And meritorious shall that hand be called, / Canonized and worshipped as a saint, / That takes away by any secret course / Thy hateful life' (100-5). The other consequence of the accusation of heresy is destruction of the new founded peace between England and France, and resumption of war.

The investigation of religious non-conformity or heresy in Shakespeare's time (especially in the prerogative Court of High Commission) often involved interrogation under oath, for in no other way could suspects' private beliefs be tested. Political conformity was imposed in similar ways, involving imposed oath-taking.

Swearing on oath, even if forced, was believed effective because of fears of damnation. But Cummings, 1997 argues that the early modern English public became cynical when forced to swear allegiance to fluctuating creeds. This article begins with accounts of contradictory reports in **Star Chamber**, under oath, about the martyrdom of sixteenth century English heretics. It then refers to the much-hated ex-officio oaths which required suspects to reveal their inner thoughts, and also to the obscene, or more often blasphemous, expletives that were newly legally repressed in Shakespeare's age. The essay then turns to OTH, finding a number of trial-like passages in the play (especially in the quarto) parodying legal procedures, and also both types of swearing. Then, p 225, Cummings paraphrases Iago's remarks in OTH 3.3.138–46 that even slaves may have private thoughts (these remarks are treated under **leets** and **slave**) with the proverb 'thought is free', but adds ironically 'except (that is) in a heresy trial'.

Refections of contemporary objections to swearing oaths may be seen in many other Shakespearian contexts, such as 'It is great sin to swear unto a sin, / But greater sin to keep a sinful oath' (CYL 5.1.180–1, discussed under **dower**), or 'I'll take thy word for faith, not ask thine oath; / Who shuns not to break one will sure crack both' (PER S.2.125–6).

Allied points concerning law, truth-telling and damnation in Shakespeare are investigated in Frazier, 1985. This notes first that an important legal decision, reported in 1792, linked the exemption of deathbed declarations from the rules against hearsay evidence with Shakespeare's Lord Melun's dying assertions:

> What in the world should make me now deceive,
> Since I must lose the use of all deceit?
> Why should I then be false, since it is true
> That I must die here, and live hence by truth?
> (JN 5.4.26–9)

Many lawyers and judges have quoted this passage, but Frazier shows that Shakespeare's treatments of dying declarations in a wide range of plays produce a much more varied and complex understanding than in this single example. Edmund's unexpected truth-telling in a futile attempt to save Cordelia and Lear (LRF 5.3.218–22) is said by Frazier

135

to be Shakespeare's most 'interesting' dying speech, but the most 'pro-vocative' is Desdemona's in OTH 5.2.132–9. In this Desdemona attempts to exculpate Othello, but he in turn says 'She's like a liar gone to burning hell / 'Twas I that killed her'. Would Desdemona be con-demned by a spiritual court for such a charitable lie? Emilia thinks not, responding: 'O, the more angel she, and you the blacker devil!'. Dying words here are not equivalent to reliable sworn testimony, although they do keep a faith.

Bloody conflicts and personal disaster follow cross-accusations of 'heresy' in AIT. Although acknowledging that she is 'virtuous / And well deserving', Cardinal Wolsey objects to Anne Boylen on account of her birth ('A knight's daughter / To be her mistress' mistress?') and because she is a 'spleeny Lutheran' (AIT 3.2.95–100). He is also con-cerned about the rise of Anne's supporter Cranmer, whom he calls 'An heretic, an arch-one' (3.2.103). But Anne and Cranmer rise, while Wol-sey falls under charges of **praemunire** (3.2.341) and corruption. Then the **divorce**-led English Reformation progresses, but its promoter Cranmer is in his turn accused of being 'A most arch heretic, a pesti-lence / That does infect the land' (5.1.45–6). This is formalised in the Lord Chancellor's accusation that Cranmer and his chaplains have widely taught 'new opinions, / Diverse and dangerous, which are her-esies' (5.2.51–2). The enemies call for a 'reformation' (5.2.54) against the progress of the Reformation, but Henry supports Cranmer. Despite taking a very cautious or balanced stand on the issues, the play does seem to imply that ambition, jealousy, and power-play, as much as belief and doctrine, inspired Henrician conflicts over heresy. A most interesting part of the diplomatic balancing of assessments in the play is Wolsey's double epitaph at 4.2.1–75.

(C) See on heresy: Pollock and Maitland, 1898, vol 2, p 552; Holds-worth, 1903, vol 1, p 618; Baker, 1986b, pp 279–80; and on Elizabeth's moderating hand post 1580, Neale, 1934, pp 249–53.

Hamilton, D. B., 1992, pp 34–58, discusses the hated *ex officio* oaths required by the ecclesiastical Court of High Commission in relation to JN, making an analogy between **bastards** and religious dissenters. On trials on oath for heresy, related to OTH, see Cummings, 1997. Frazier, 1985 very interestingly considers deathbed statements in Shakespeare where fears of damnation may (or may not) elicit truth in JN, R2, MV, 1H4, HAM, MAC, OTH, LRF and CYM.

On 'an heretic . . . makes the fire' in WT 2.3.114–16 see Khanna, 1988.

homicide Homicide as an act is discussed under **murder/ homicide.**

In Shakespeare's use 'a homicide' denotes a murderer in 1H6 1.3.4 and 5.6.62, and in R3 1.2.125, 5.2.18, and 5.5.200. 'Homicidal' is also the word Mistress Quickly twice has in mind, or does she, when Falstaff resists her attempt to arrest him for **debt** (see also arrest **on the case**). In reply to Falstaff's stand against the **sergeant** she has appointed, 'Away, varlets! Draw Bardolph! Cut me off the villain's head! Throw the quean in the channel!', Quickly sputters:

> Throw me in the channel? I'll throw thee in the channel! Wilt thou, wilt thou, thou bastardly rogue? Murder, murder! Ah, thou honeysuckle villain, wilt thou kill God's officers, and the King's? Ah, thou honeyseed rogue! Thou art a honeyseed, a man-queller, and a woman-queller.
>
> (2H4 2.1.45–55)

Perhaps 'man-queller' and 'woman-queller' allude to **manslaughter**?

hue and cry (A) Raising the 'hue and cry' was one of the means of enforcing law and public order used in medieval England. All adult able-bodied men within a county or shire were grouped together into tithings (ten families) and hundreds, and all such men were supposed to be within the system known as frankpledge. Twice a year the **sheriff** visited hundred courts on his tourn to 'view the frankpledge', and members of tithings and hundreds were under a duty to present wrongdoers for punishment. Failure to present wrongdoers resulted in a fine imposed on all within the group. Most wrongdoers were caught in the act or just afterwards, but if the offender was not apprehended it was the duty of anyone within the tithing to raise the 'hue and cry' to search for and pursue him.

The duty to make the arrest and keep the suspect in custody until he was brought before the sheriff belonged to the **constable**, but ordinary citizens could make an arrest if there was good reason to do so, for example if the hue and cry had been raised. If a man was fleeing to **sanctuary**, then no one was supposed to hinder him unless the hue and cry had been raised. Although by Shakespeare's time the system of frankpledge had fallen into disuse, raising the hue and cry was still employed to catch wrongdoers.

(B) The first of Shakespeare's two instances of 'hue and cry' follows the Gads Hill **robbery**. A Sheriff says to Prince Hal 'First, pardon me, my lord. A hue and cry / Hath followed certain men unto this house' (1H4 2.5.513–14). Asked 'What men?', the Sheriff's reply is 'One of them is well known, my gracious lord, / A gross, fat man' (2.5.515–17). Hal then shields the unworthy Falstaff with a lie – this context is further discussed under **sheriff**.

Another Shakespearian instance of a failure of 'hue and cry' is even more farcical. In an odd bye-plot of WIV, the Host of the Garter Inn at Windsor has his horses stolen in a confidence trick involving a supposed German duke. When the Host discovers that he has been duped he cries out to Bardolph 'Hue and cry, villain, go!' and 'Fly, run, hue and cry, villain. I am undone', and implores Falstaff 'Assist me, knight. I am undone' (WIV 4.5.84–6). Certainly Bardolph seems an accomplice in the horse taking, and Falstaff may be also (see Ross, 1994, p 158), so the Host calling for Falstaff's and Bardolph's aid in raising the 'hue and cry' is destined to scant success. The obscure horse-stealing subplot, probably involving a vengeance on the Host for a practical joke he had played on Evans and Caius, may have had topical political significance, and is argued in Ross, 1994 to be related to the abuse of fraudulent **conveyancing**.

(C) On hue and cry see Pollock and Maitland, 1898, vol 2, pp 578–80; Plucknett, 1956, p 430; Baker, 1990b, pp 8, 29, 574; Hudson, 1996, pp 61–9.

I

impediments (A) A valid **contract** of **marriage** could not be entered into if an impediment to the marriage existed. Canon law held that many varied circumstances would constitute such an impediment, including lack of capacity on the part of either party to contract marriage, or prohibitions on marriages between parties related in some way. Evidence of an impediment would act to prevent a marriage taking place, and could also be produced in a suit for **divorce** *a vinculo matrimoni*.

A lack of capacity for a marriage arose when either party was unable to give valid consent, as in cases of insanity. In a contract *per verba de praesenti* (see **pre-contract**), infants were unable to consent until they reached the age of puberty, taken to be twelve years for women and fourteen for men. The age of consent for a pre-contract *per verba de futuro* was only seven years, but when the child reached puberty the marriage could be avoided as long as consummation had not taken place. Despite the theoretical possibility of infant marriages, in practice the age of marriage for most people in early modern England was relatively late, on average the late twenties, although the nobility and gentry sometimes arranged early marriages for their children for dynastic reasons.

A lack of capacity to consent to marriage could also be proved if duress was used to coerce the parties. The agreement of parents or guardians was not required for marriage, while pressure amounting to duress from parents or anyone else amounted to an impediment. Claims of such impediments of 'force and fear' involving violence, threats, or inducements have been found in both **divorce** cases and in **pre-contract** litigation records (see Helmholz, 1974, p 90). Witnesses were required to give evidence of the severity of the force used. The test applied by canon law was the 'constant man or woman test': was the force or fear used sufficient to sway a 'constant' person? If so, this pressure amounted to an impediment. The courts appear to have required evidence that a high degree of force was used, inducing actual injury, or fear of this.

It has been suggested that such cases have not been found in great numbers because later consent to the marriage, implied by subsequent apparently willingly entered sexual relations or cohabitation, was held to 'purge the effect of force and fear' and ratify the marriage (see ibid., p 91, and Swinburne, 1686, p 223). Reluctance to give evidence, late marriages, English social customs in which many young people were in service away from their families, and early death of parents must also go some way to explaining lack of many claims of duress. On the relative autonomy of children in English marriage choices see: Macfarlane, 1986, pp 119–47, especially p 124; Houlbrooke, 1984, pp 72–3; Cook, 1991, p 87, Macfarlane, 1970a, pp 95–8. Laslett, 1983, pp 102–4 presents a pattern in which parents 'at least of yeoman stock' take a larger initial role; Stone, 1979b, p 183, emphasizes the 'authoritarian control by parents over the marriage of their children' which 'lasted longest in the richest and most aristocratic circles'. However Outhwaite, 1995, p 58, argues that it distorts the truth to insist that parental consent to marriage was not needed, claiming that parents could stop a church marriage at the banns stage if their children were under twenty one.

After lack of capacity, the most important impediments were due to affinity and consanguinity. Complex lists of the four prohibited degrees of relationship existed to act as guides to help avoid such impediments.

Affinity was a pre-existing relationship between the parties created by a former marriage or carnal relationship outside marriage. Affinity extended to the first, second and third cousins of a spouse or a person with whom one has had sexual intercourse. Affinity was also created by 'spiritual' connections with god-parents and their relations.

Consanguinity was a blood relationship between the parties within the prohibited four degrees. This meant approximately that all people descended from a common great-great-grandfather were barred from marriage with each other. The law of consanguinity remained complex, although the Marriage Act 1540 set out simplified prohibited degrees of relationship based on Leviticus. Then in 1563 Archbishop Parker's *Admonition to All Such as Intend to Marry*, a book containing a table of prohibited relationships, was ordered to be displayed in every parish church in order to clarify the requirements.

Any pre-existing marriage contract with a third party entered into by one of the parties to the marriage acted as an impediment, and could be argued in a multi-party suit for **divorce**. But again not many such cases have been discovered among court records, and difficulties of proof must have been a deterrent.

The impediment of 'crime' prevented a married man who had committed adultery with a woman from marrying that woman after the death of his wife. The woman was said to be 'polluted by the adultery' and the impediment to their marriage was permanent, although it is suggested that this prohibition on marriage was disregarded in practice (Helmholz, 1974, pp 94–5) and difficulties in proof (it was necessary to show that the second marriage had been contracted during the life of the first wife) meant that it was not often used successfully as a reason for divorce.

Swinburne, 1686, pp 223–4 also mentions as impediments lack of valid consent occasioned by furore and drunkenness. Sexual frigidity (impotence) too could prevent a valid marriage being contracted, the problem being again one of proof. Other impediments were error of person, error of condition, religious vows, or unknowing marriage to someone of servile status (Helmholz, 1974, p 100).

The 'dirimentary impediments' acceptable as grounds for annulling a marriage (see **divorce**) were lack of capacity, affinity, consanguinity, duress, impotence, mistake of person, the existence of a pre-contract, a religious vow of celibacy, or difference of cult. Canon law distinguished between different causes of impotence, ranging from physical deformity to natural frigidity. Helmholz's investigations in Canterbury and York find all cases to have been brought by wives against husbands, and details the astonishing hands-on methods ordered by the courts to establish the wives' claims. Helmholz concludes that these methods appear to have been practical local innovations, not recommended by the Church of Rome or any canonists (Helmholz, 1974, pp 87–90).

The new Canons of the Church of England of 1603–4 included Canon 99, which made void any marriage within prohibited degrees, re-enacting the table of 1563 (Bullard, 1934, pp 106–7). The next, Canon 100 (ibid.), prohibited marriage and **contracts** of marriage for those under twenty one, without parental consent. It did not declare such marriages void. Parliament did not enact the 1603–4 Canons, and indeed passed a bill declaring that no recent (within ten years) or future church Canon could result in loss of life liberty or goods unless it was confirmed by a **statute** (ibid., p xvii). So, despite contrary assumptions of some Shakespeare critics (for instance Hamilton, D. B., 1992, pp 121–3), the 1603–4 canons 99–108 concerning marriage and divorce had at best equivocal force unless they reiterated older Church laws.

(B) The famous context of 'impediments' in sonnet 116, as is usually the case in Shakespeare's poems, uses law terms highly figuratively: 'Let me not to the marriage of true minds / Admit impediments. Love is not love / Which alters when it alteration finds, / Or bends with the remover to remove.'

The term is used much more literally when an 'impediment' due to a feigned act of illegal adultery between the spousal and marriage ceremony is 'discovered' in ADO. When villainous Borachio says of Claudio's intended marriage 'I can cross it', Don John says prophetically of the means: 'Any bar, any cross, any impediment will be medicinable to me' (ADO 2.2.3–7). Don John then alleges Hero's adultery when he is asked by Claudio 'If there be any impediment, I pray you discover it' (3.2.83–4). When at the start of the marriage ceremony Hero and Claudio are asked (as was traditional according to Cook, 1991, p 162): 'If either of you know any inward impediment why you should not be conjoined, I charge you on your souls to utter it', Claudio tries Hero's conscience with a bitter 'Know you any, Hero?' (4.1.12- 15). After some more sarcasm, Claudio tell Hero's father 'Give not this rotten orange to your friend. / She's but the sign and semblance of her honour. / Behold how like a maid she blushes here! / O, what authority and show of truth / Can cunning sin cover itself withal!' (4.1.32–6).

Claudio's refusal to marry Hero on the grounds of impediment is valid, since following a **pre-contract** *per verba de futuro* if one party commits adultery with a third person then the other party is free to dissolve the contract (Swinburne, 1686, p 237). On the other hand, if sexual relations had taken place between the two parties to a contract *per verba de futuro*, this would make their relationship into a valid if irregular marriage. In accord with this law, Claudio adds in response to the suggestion that it was he that has had sexual relations with Hero, that if true this would 'extenuate the forehand sin' (4.1.50).

142

In the course of dynastic negotiations over a marriage of Antony with Octavia, possible impediments to a marriage are obliquely referenced when Cleopatra's name is mentioned by Caesar. Antony's reply is 'I am not married, Caesar' (ANT 2.2.126–9), and when concluding the agreement he says 'May I never / To this good purpose, that so fairly shows, / Dream of impediment!' (2.2.151–3). In the absence of a valid pre-contract to marry Cleopatra (and none was possible while Fulvia lived, due to the impediment of 'crime') this was true for Shakespeare's age; the relations of Antony and Cleopatra, one of the very few cohabiting couples in Shakespeare, were not an impediment to Antony's marriage with another.

An inquiry into Malcolm's suitability for kingship elicits from him the following confession:

> there's no bottom, none,
> In my voluptuousness. Your wives, your daughters,
> Your matrons, and your maids could not fill up
> The cistern of my lust, and my desire
> All continent impediments would o'erbear
> That did oppose my will. Better Macbeth
> Than such an one to reign.
>
> (MAC 4.3.61–7)

This is a testing lie; the impediments here to his assuming rule may be in some analogy with the integrity required in spousals. Using perhaps a similar metaphor, Iago proposes to Roderigo that his passion for Desdemona will be furthered 'by the displanting of Cassio'. He suggests that thereby 'So shall you have a shorter journey to your desires by the means I shall then have to prefer them, and the impediment most profitably removed, without the which there were no expectation of our prosperity' (OTH 2.1.275–9). Here again an 'impediment' to lust features in a context involving adultery.

The impediment of affinity should have prevented the marriage of Claudius and his sister-in-law Gertrude. In accord with Leviticus 18.16 and 20.21, Hamlet properly calls his mother's second marriage to his uncle 'incestuous' (HAM 1.2.157). Hamlet's father's ghost calls Claudius moreover 'that incestuous, that adulterate beast' (1.5.42), indicating that he had seduced Gertrude during her first marriage, probably adding the impediment of 'crime'. The ghost however urges

Hamlet to intervene only against Claudius's current 'damned incest' (1.5.83).

According to Brooke, 1981, p 26, from the twelfth century onward church authorities became less concerned about obscure forms of incest than about the stability of marriages, and so began to limit **divorce** based upon claimed impediments of remote affinity or consanguinity. However a deceased brother's wife was so well within the prohibited degrees of affinity that marriage with her remained sinful until recently. So Hamlet hopes to revenge himself when his uncle 'is drunk asleep, or in his rage, / Or in th' incestuous pleasure of his bed' (3.3.89–90), and finally kills him calling him 'thou incestuous, murd'rous, damned Dane' (5.2.276). The impediment of affinity could not be more clearly emphasised.

Impediments due to the existence of a prior marriage **pre-contract** are wilfully ignored or defied by several Shakespeare characters, most importantly two kings. When Henry VI asks the Lord Protector Gloucester, to 'give consent / That Marg'ret may be England's royal queen' (1H6 5.7.23–4), the reply is dusty:

> So should I give consent to flatter sin.
> You know, my lord, your highness is betrothed
> Unto another lady of esteem.
> How shall we then dispense with that contract
> And not deface your honour with reproach?
>
> (5.7.25–9)

However Suffolk, the marriage's promoter, counsels Henry to ignore his pre-contract with the daughter of the Earl of Armagnac, on the cynical grounds 'A poor earl's daughter is unequal odds, / And therefore may be broke without offence' (5.7.34–5). Henry, in his weakness, accepts the advice.

In R3 3.7.4–5 Richard colludes with Buckingham to allege that one or more similar impediments of pre-contract have invalidated the marriage of Edward IV, and therefore bastardized Edward V (a pre-contract with Princess Bona is alleged, and also one with Lady Elizabeth Lucy). In an ensuing charade of Richard's reluctance to reign, Buckingham pretends to have to persuaded Richard to take the throne:

You say that Edward is your brother's son;
So say we, too – but not by Edward's wife.
For first was he contract to Lady Lucy –
Your mother lives a witness to his vow –
And afterward, by substitute, betrothed
To Bona, sister to the King of France.
These both put off, a poor petitioner,
A care-crazed mother to a many sons,
A beauty-waning and distressed widow
Even in the afternoon of her best days,
Made prize and purchase of his wanton eye,
Seduced the pitch and height of his degree
To base declension and loathed bigamy.
By her in his unlawful bed he got
This Edward, whom our manners call the Prince.
                              (R3 3.7.167–81)

Therefore, Buckingham urges, Richard must take the throne, 'If not to bless us and the land withal, / Yet to draw forth your noble ancestry / From the corruption of abusing times, / Unto a lineal, true-derived course' (R3 3.7.187–90). The story of the pre-contract with Lady Lucy, from More's *History of King Richard III*, has no other Shakespearian expression. But as described by Shakespeare, the sequence in Edward IV's marriage negotiations with Princess Bona comprises an embassy of Warwick to France to woo her, arranged in RDY 2.6.89–90, then the 'bluntest' wooing of Lady Elizabeth Grey in RDY 3.2.69–81 (discussed under **dower**), then the acceptance of Edward's proposal by Lady Bona immediately followed by the arrival of news of his new marriage to Lady Grey in RDY 3.3.139–66. This sequence is complicated by delays due to messengers, an incalculable time scale, and conflicts between personal and dynastic reasons to marry, making the truth of Richard's (albeit cynical) allegations of bigamy and bastardy due to pre-contract uncertain.

We learn in H5 2.1.18, with no such ambiguity, that Pistol had married Nell Quickly despite the impediment of Nim's prior 'troth-plight to her'. The resulting multi-party dispute is settled in a private way, not in court, as such matters must often have been by those of less than lofty station. The resulting gaps in official records may be deceptive.

The impediment of Isabella's impending religious vows is overlooked when the Duke twice proposes marriage to her in MM 5.1. It is true that she is 'yet unsworn' (1.4.9), and still only a 'novice' (1.4.19) sister of Saint Clare. However in a medieval case outlined in Brooke, 1981, pp 32–3, the mere intent of the bride, Christina of Markyate, to follow a religious life was enough to give rise to an annulment. Brooke reports that in this case the husband was willing to support her demand for a **divorce** after he had became convinced that she was 'radically opposed to consummating the marriage'. Some readings of MM 5.1 suggest that congruent attitude may be implied in the silence of Isabella.

Helena and Bertram are married by a 'contract' sealed by public handfasting and subsequent 'ceremony' (AWW 2.3.177–81), and so Bertram's two subsequent offers to marry others may be seen as bigamous. However his attempted seduction of Diana with promises to marry her after Helena's death (revealed in 4.2.72, 5.3.266–7) constitutes an invalid conditional pre-contract *per verba de futuro*, due to the impediment of 'crime' (see Helmholz, 1974, pp 94–8). On the other hand his willingness to a match with Maudlin (seen in 5.3.77) is not disallowed by impediment, for it follows only an invalid (and insincere) conditional contract with Diana, and it postdates his belief that Helena is dead (as seen in AWW 4.3.54–67, 4.3.91).

A wild set of propositions about marriages prohibited due to impediments of affinity, and even of bigamy, form the basis of bitter sarcasms in LRF 5.3.68–82. These are discussed under **subcontracted**.

The impediments alleged to invalidate the marriage of Henry VIII with Katherine of Aragon, as presented in AIT, are treated under **divorce**.

(C) For an overview on marriage impediments see Baker, 1990b, pp 560–2 and Swinburne, 1686. For discussion of these in connection with **divorce** see Helmholz, 1974, pp 76–100, and Ingram, 1987, p 145.

Nelson, 1984 mentions but does not pursue the legal aspect of 'impediments' in SON 116; this is more concerned with **pardon** in a 'matrimonial cause', as in ADO. In a theoretical and personal discussion involving women's agency and 'the relationship between cultural history and textual studies' Jardine, 1991 addresses questions of consanguinity and unlawful marriage in HAM. Ranald, 1979 discusses various supposed irregularities in or impediments to marital **pre-contracts** or marriages in SHR, ADO, MM, and AWW.

in capite (A) A tenant *in capite* or tenant in chief held **land** directly from the king. This had certain consequences in the context of feudal relations. By the time that actual services had been commuted to money payments (about 1200) all **tenures** carried with them recognised consequences, the most important of which were financial. The monies payable by the tenant to the lord were known as feudal incidents; the most onerous payments of all were due to the king from his tenants in chief. So much so that when a tenant in chief died the king's official called the escheator took over all the lands and conducted an inquiry into what payments were due to the king before the **heir** could take possession.

In particular, the king was entitled to *primer seisin* of a tenant in chief's land, which meant he could take one year's profit from the land. The king could also claim the valuable feudal incident of **wardship**, and additionally had prerogative rights of wardship over all the tenant in chief's lands, whether or not they were held from the crown. The rights that the king had over a tenant in chief were particularly lucrative, and this explains the king's interest in maintaining the system as a source of crown revenue.

(B) Reserving to himself the mythical right of the first night (which was never legal in England), Jack Cade uses the language of English **land** law: 'There shall not a maid be married but she shall pay to me her maidenhead, ere they have it. Married men shall hold of me *in capite*. And we charge and command that their wives be as free as heart can wish or tongue can tell.' (CYL 4.7.118–22). He apparently intends to make the services of all wives (improperly seen as property) feudal incidents due from his tenants in chief, their husbands. '*Caput*', meaning 'head', no doubt makes 'in capite' into one of the numerous puns of Shakespeare's age on cuckold's horns, as well as a pun on maidenhead.

Cade's proclamations and speeches are crowded with legal allusions. According to Campbell, J., 1859, pp 76–7, in claiming his rights over all wives, Cade nearly precisely recites an exact legal formula: 'as free as tongue can speak or heart can think', the construction of which was determined by the Court of King's Bench and recorded in the Year Book, Hil. Term, 10 Hen VII, fol. 13, pl. 6.

(C) See under **land**.

incest Incest was 'not a secular crime at all until the twentieth century' (Thomas, K., 1983, p 39) in England. It was a frequent topic of drama from ancient times. Shakespeare is among a number of early modern dramatists who explored this topic.

Richard II's wish to marry Elizabeth within prohibited degrees of consanguinity in R2, and Claudius' marriage within prohibited degrees of affinity in HAM, are partially or wholly politically motivated. AIT indicates that Henry VIII's concern over incest was concurrent with his hope for a male heir, as well as with his desire for Anne Boylen.

Possible overtones of parent-child incest in *King Lear*, speculated upon under **dower**, are more obscure, as are the more famous possible complexes of Hamlet. PER, CYM, WT and possibly TMP repeatedly adumbrate incest. They do this sometimes forthrightly, but often indirectly; for instance had Hermione been guilty as charged in WT, Florizel and Perdita would have been half brother and sister. Such matters have been more often treated by critics in terms of social or individual psychology than of law.

The unsteady outlines of canon law prohibitions against incestuous marrying are discussed under **impediments**, and in relation to the Henrician marriages under **divorce**. McCabe, 1993, pp 30–55 reviews the tangled and shifting definitions of incest in supposed 'natural law', the law of classical civilisations, and in ecclesiastical law. This reviews treatments of incest in early modern drama, including Shakespeare, as does Taylor, 1982.

indenture (A) An indenture was a deed recording an agreement between parties entered onto paper or parchment which was then torn or cut into two or more pieces, with one part going to each party. Only the original parts would match: the purpose was security. In Shakespeare's time the indented or serrated form was essential, and this shape made an indenture without the need for any words to state the fact.

Indentures were used to **convey** title to land, but also for other purposes. In particular the sealing of such deeds was used in agreements binding **apprentices** to their masters. 'Indentures' could therefore be a synonym for an apprenticeship.

(B) While being promised aid, young Arthur is kissed 'As seal to this indenture of my love' in JN 2.1.20. A metaphoric connection between kissing and sealing appears again in the song in MM 4.1.5–6: 'But my kisses bring again, bring again,/ Seals of love, though sealed in vain, sealed in vain.' The same metaphor appears in VEN 511–16, SON 142, and TRO 3.2.193. In TRO 3.2.56–7 a mutual kiss observed by Pandarus, 'What, billing again?', is described in the exact terms of a clause in an indenture: 'Here's "in witness whereof the parties interchangeably"' (on the context of this see under **fee farm**).

Indentures are alluded to or mentioned three times in 1H4, in varied contexts. First King Henry refuses Hotspur's demand that he ransom Mortimer, saying: 'Shall our coffers, then, / Be emptied to redeem a traitor home? / Shall we buy treason, and indent with fears / When they have lost and forfeited themselves?' (1H4 1.3.84–7). 'Indent with' here is figurative, drawing its force from 'make an agreement by indenture'.

Next Prince Hal unkindly teases Francis the apprentice tavern drawer, remarking on the remaining length of his indentures:

Five year! By 'r Lady, a long lease for the clinking of pewter. But Francis, darest thou be so valiant as to play the coward with thy indenture, and show it a fair pair of heels, and run from it?

(1H4 2.5.44–7)

The normal term of apprenticeship was seven years (although there were exceptions of longer terms as noted in Sokol, 1994b), so Francis faced a tedious time to serve.

Next, in 1H4 3.1.67–83, we see the rebel forces agreeing 'interchangeably' to divide the realm they mean to conquer into three portions by sealing 'our indentures tripartite'. The form of their indentures is correct, which contrasts with the illegality of their actions. The parallel mentions of 'indentures' in 1H4 in scenes alternating between the serious settings of high political conflict, and the comically demotic setting of a Eastcheap tavern, provides a microcosm of the structure of the play.

The skull meditated upon by Hamlet is imagined to be a **lawyer**'s, a deceased **conveyancer**'s, who now possesses little land, only his grave. Hamlet wonders that 'his vouchers vouch him no more of his purchases, and double ones too, than the length and breadth of a pair of indentures?' (HAM 5.1.105–7). The jesting here depends on how an assurance of **purchases** of land by using **vouchers** (actually conveyancing fictions), or the greater assurance given by **double vouchers**, finally yields a piece of ground not much larger than the

149

physical size of a pair of indentures (see under **fine and recovery** on the context).

One of the two mentions of 'indenture' in PER is made by the assassin Thaliart. Antiochus has ordered him to kill Pericles merely 'Because we bid it' (S.1.200), and after describing his fear of doing otherwise, Thaliart remarks wryly that 'if a king bid a man be a villain, he's bound by the indenture of his oath to be one' (S.3.8–9). The mention of a legallly binding 'indenture' and indeed an 'oath' here helps raise in a darkly comic mode (for Pericles escapes, but at great cost) questions of royal prerogative and moral covenants. (On Thaliart's mission see under **murder**; on swearing oaths and duress see under **heresy**; on the separation of lawfulness from royal will see under **chief justice**.)

The other use of 'indenture' in PER is made by Marina, who means by this an **apprenticeship**. She counsels the bawd Boult:

BOULT   What would you have me do? Go to the wars, would you, where a man may serve seven years for the loss of a leg, and have not money enough in the end to buy him a wooden one?

MARINA   Do anything but this thou dost. Empty
Old receptacles or common sew'rs of filth,
Serve by indenture to the public hangman –
Any of these are yet better than this.

(PER S.19.195–202)

Thus, associating the gallows and brothel, she advises Boult to follow a path similar to the one Pompey has followed in MM.

(C) The instance from 1H4 3.1.67–83 is discussed in Clarkson and Warren, 1942, pp 120–3. One of the instances from TRO is discussed in Campbell, J., 1859, p 78.

inheritance (A) In England during the middle ages customary rules of descent divided a man's personal property (**chattels**) on his death into three parts. One third belonged to his widow, one third, known as the *legitim*, belonged to his children, and one third was available to the testator to leave as he wished. Charitable or pious gifts were often made from this remaining third. If a man had only a wife, or only children, then one half his property was available to the wife or the children, and one half was available for him to leave as he wished. If a man had neither wife nor children then all his personal property was his to dispose of as he wished.

Married women could not own property in their own name, so these rules did not apply to them. In theory they could not make **wills** at all without the consent of their husbands, but the Church courts encouraged them to do so for the good of their souls and did not hesitate to administer such wills. Single women were able to devise their personal property as they wished. If they died intestate then the same rules applied to them as to intestate men.

The administration of the estates of those who died intestate was in the hands of administrators appointed by the Church court; they were usually the next of kin. These administrators could sue or be sued in the same way as **executors**, but scandal sometimes followed an ecclesiastical court's failure to control their activities.

The inheritance of the real property (**land**) was subject to various customary laws. There were 'strong traditions' at the time of the Norman Conquest that land should be divided equally between sons (Baker, 1990b, p 303). It was also traditional that an ancestor should nominate his own heir, which benefited Kings William I, William II, Stephen and John, who were crowned despite the existence of closer relatives. (ibid. – see **election**). There were other regional customs or traditions such as gavelkind, the equal division of land between sons, which was common in Wales, Kent and in East Anglia (see under **co-heirs**), and the custom known as borough English, or ultimogeniture, applicable in many rural manors, in which the youngest son inherited all the land.

However in most of England by the twelfth century the common law protected **primogeniture** in descent of land. The reason usually advanced for this was the military needs of the Normans post-Conquest. The rules for inheritance rested on patriarchal principles, and land descended in the male line. For women the rules of inheritance depended on whether they had any brothers alive capable of inheriting. If so, daughters' rights to inherit were deferred to brothers' rights. Only if there were no sons did daughters inherit, in which case they took equally as coparcenors (see **co-heirs**).

The detailed rules applied for the descent of real property, known as

151

the *parentelic scheme*, meant that all people within the *parentela* of a person could inherit. Lineal descendants of the deceased were traced first, then lineal descendants of the deceased's father. Lineal descendants were preferred to collateral descendants, and of collateral descendants brothers and sisters took before uncles and aunts. If the land in question had descended from the father's side of the family it could only descend on the father's side and any relatives of the mother were excluded. If there were no relatives capable of inheriting on the father's side then the land escheated and returned to the lord. The same rules in parallel applied if land descended from the mother's side of the family, but in this case it was possible for the inheritance to ascend through the male line. In general however inheritance could not ascend, only descend, so parents could not inherit from their children. Despite patriarchal primogeniture, in the absence of sons collateral male relatives were not preferred to daughters, so that a daughter took property in preference to an uncle.

Dower and 'curtesy' were also customary rules that limited free testation of land. See **wills** on further issues surrounding free testation.

Briefly, in the situation established by Shakespeare's time different kinds of property were treated by law in different ways, and were subject to different rules for descent by will or by intestacy. It had always been possible to make a will for personal property but land had only been devisable by will, which overrode rules of customary descent, since the Statute of Wills 1540 (however see **uses**).

The Church courts administered both wills of personality (chattels) and estates of the intestate. Administrators appointed by these courts by Shakespeare's time often scandalously divided the remaining estate between themselves after paying **debts**. It was not until the Statute of Distributions 1670 that a statutory scheme for distribution was laid down which administrators had to follow.

Common law courts administered wills of real property (**land**). Complications arose because many wills were mixed, containing gifts of both land and personality. During Shakespeare's period the Church courts maintained their right to administer the personality part of such wills. Also sometimes a will did not dispose of all a man's estate, and again the Church courts would administer both the property bequeathed and the part treated under laws of intestacy.

(B) Inheritance is a factor permeating all of Shakespeare's imaginary worlds. Like **heir**, the words 'inheritance' or 'inherit' appear in most of Shakespeare's plays.

'Inheritance' is sometimes used by Shakespeare to indicate qualities received by what we now call genetic means (2H4 4.2.114, AWW 1.1.38 and 1.2.22). To 'inherit' sometimes means to receive, inhere (within), or possess (ROM 1.2.28, LRQ S.20.121 / LRF 4.5.123, COR 2.1.196 and 3.2.68). But mainly 'inherit' has to do with the legal descent of property.

The returned **exile** Bolingbroke justifies himself to his uncle York in terms of 'inheritance':

> What would you have me do? I am a subject,
> And I challenge law; attorneys are denied me;
> And therefore personally I lay my claim
> To my inheritance of free descent.
>
> (R2 2.3.132–5)

His inability to use more legal means raises an issue between the pre-rogative of kings and the King's law, discussed for instance in Hamilton, D. B., 1983.

One strange figurative use of 'inherited' is made by the Athenian Senator who pleads with the conquering Alcibiades to spare those citizens innocent of his exile:

> All have not offended.
> For those that were, it is not square to take,
> On those that are, revenges. Crimes like lands
> Are not inherited
>
> (TIM 5.5.35–8)

The notion of descent of guilt to the guiltless is here distinguished from the legalities of inheritance. In ages earlier than Shakespeare's lands may or may not have been devisable by will, but they had long been inheritable; these lines must mean 'crimes are not inherited like lands'.

An allied old 'idea that "corruption of the blood" should follow conviction of a serious crime' (Baker, 1990b, p 572) was partly miti-gated in Shakespeare's age, by which time not all **felonies** resulted in the felon's children's **disinheritance**. In fact some felonies did still result in this until 1870 (on some that didn't in Shakespeare's age, see the English witchcraft statutes of 1542 and 1604 discussed under **witch**). Attainture for **treason** makes questionable what Rosalind proposes, that: 'Treason is not inherited, my lord' (AYL 1.3.60).

The Archbishop of Canterbury tells Henry V that his claims to France are just, 'For in the Book of Numbers is it writ, / "When the son dies, let the inheritance / Descend unto the daughter"' (H5 1.2.98–100). He repudiates the counter-claim that the 'law Salic' supposedly local to France (1.2.11) bars such inheritance. The basis of the Archbishop's long argument (1.2.33–95) is not that local customary law cannot override the canons of inheritance, but that these laws are not properly applied to France.

(C) See: Clarkson and Warren, 1942, pp 197–210; Simpson, 1986, pp 56–63; Baker, 1990b, pp 304–7; and on the *legitim* Helmholz, 1987h.

Inns of Court (A) In early modern England lawyers received their education in the common law at one of the legal Inns, the most important of which were the Inner Temple, the Middle Temple, Gray's Inn and Lincoln's Inn, known as the Inns of Court. The English common law was not taught at Oxford or Cambridge until the eighteenth century. After Henry VIII's suppression of the teaching of canon law there, civil law alone was taught at the Universities. Civilians, or **civil doctors** were educated in the Universities to prepare them to practice in the ecclesiastical and some other prerogative courts such as Requests and Admiralty.

The early history of the Inns of Court is obscure. Records of the Inns began in the fifteenth century with the Black Books of Lincoln's Inn in 1422. Middle Temple's records began in 1501, Inner Temple's slightly later in 1505, and Gray's Inn's in 1569. But these records are mostly concerned with financial transactions, and so do not readily provide information on early organisational structure, or indeed purpose. The Inns were first described as teaching institutions by Sir John Fortescue, Chief Justice of the King's Bench, in his treatise on English law, *De Laudibus Legum Angliae*, published c. 1470. This led later historians to believe that the Inns were first founded as institutions in which students gathered around teachers of the law who gave legal instruction by lectures. However more recent historical investigations indicate that the origin of the Inns in the fourteenth century was rather as houses rented during the legal term by practising lawyers (Thorne, 1985c, p 138; Prest, 1972, p 4).

In the fourteenth century the Inner Temple and Middle Temple took over the tenancy of the buildings once owned by the Knights Templar, while Gray's Inn was originally the London residence of the Lords Grey of Wilton which was tenanted by law students at around the same time. The early details of Lincoln's Inn are disputed, but probably it was once the town house of Henry de Lacy, Earl of Lincoln.

The change from lodging house to college in the universities in England, Paris, Bologna, and throughout Europe, has been described as a 'momentous development' (Prest, 1972, p 4), and as a 'revolution in educational thought' (Thorne, 1985c, p 144). The early development of London's legal Inns can be seen as part of this movement. By the mid sixteenth century the Inns of Court were so successful as teaching institutions that they were generally known as the Third University of England.

Early records of student admissions to the Inns are incomplete, but do indicate that the sixteenth century saw a dramatic rise in the number of students. By 1600, 250 students were admitted, double the number of 50 years earlier. During the four legal **terms** the students, or 'inner barristers', were expected to be in residence. Legal education was given by means of lectures, moots and attendance at court. It was also necessary for the student to 'keep commons', in other words to eat a required number of meals with fellow students. Lectures, known as readings, were given to the students by Readers of the Inns in the summer and Lent vacations; these concentrated on making detailed sequential examination of chapters of statutes and the common law derived from the statute.

A student who joined an Inn as an inner barrister sat within the **bar** of his Inn during legal exercises for probably about seven years. When he had achieved sufficient proficiency in the legal exercises he would be 'called to the bar'. It is uncertain what this meant exactly (see Baker, 1990b, p 184), but the call to the bar was certainly an internal degree of the Inn marking the transition from being an 'inner barrister' to an 'outer or utter barrister', one of those who stood outside the bar as pleaders. Orders of 1559 and 1574 were the first known to establish the connection between a call to the bar and the right of audience in the courts; utter barristers were allowed a right of audience five years after call (Simpson, 1970, p 252–3).

An utter barrister of at least ten years could be required to give readings to students, and so became a Reader at his Inn. As a Reader he now became a bencher of the Inn and would take part in its government. He would also take his place as a judge in student moots. Moots were student disputations on common law which were regarded as very important training exercises in debate and analysis. Students would also gain their legal education by attending court, sitting in special places set aside for them in Westminster Hall and **Star Chamber**. In Westminster Hall the students sat in wooden cribs, sometimes referred to as 'pecunes', listening to the legal argument and taking notes which were later entered into commonplace books. Surviving legal literature indicates that manuals, statutes and year-books of cases circulated widely among students both before and after the introduction of printing.

By the mid fifteenth century attendance at an Inn was considered a satisfactory argument to support a claim to be 'learned in the law', in other words to have attained sufficient professional status to defend against a charge of 'maintenance', or interfering in litigation for profit.

There were also at one time nine or ten Inns of Chancery, lesser Inns which also functioned as societies of lawyers, and in Tudor times these drew teachers from the Inns of Court, and acted as preparatory institutions for them. Despite their name, they were not connected with the Court of Chancery in any way, although they may once have trained Chancery clerks. By Shakespeare's time the four Inns of Court had achieved such success that the Inns of Chancery had lost much of their status as teaching institutions. Their decay in the seventeenth century meant they attracted fewer numbers of students, and some ceased to exist altogether while others operated once again as rooming houses.

Not all members of the Inns of Court intended to practice as pleaders; some were **attorneys**. But the four Inns of Court attempted to regulate legal education by requiring all members to study for the bar, which led to a declaration in 1614 excluding attorneys. These then congregated in the Inns of Chancery, together with solicitors and law clerks (see **lawyers**).

The four successful Inns of Court embarked on ambitious rebuilding plans between 1550–1640. Brick and stone buildings five or six stories high built around courtyards rapidly replaced the medieval timber houses. Prohibitions on building issued by Elizabeth's government in 1574 indicate concern at the spread of London but were ignored in practice. Middle Temple Hall, twice mentioned by Shakespeare, was begun in 1562 and finished about 1574, and was greatly admired, being 'the only structure of comparable expense and size erected during this period' (Prest, 1972, pp 18–19).

Some students who sought admission to the Inns did not intend to practice law. During the late sixteenth century and early seventeenth century time spent at the Inns was considered part of a gentleman's education, in much the same way as the Grand Tour accompanied by a tutor and entourage would be later. It was considered useful, possibly essential, for a gentleman to have some knowledge of the English common law; knowledge of **land** law was especially necessary in order to administer or direct the administration of estates and arrange family settlements. A gentleman was also expected to acquire sufficient legal knowledge to understand the functions and concerns of the **Justice of the Peace** and **sheriff**, and play a part in the administration of justice and government in the provinces.

In an age when rank and status was of much importance, a student of the Inns of Court was automatically conferred with the title of gentleman. Fortescue had emphasised the gentlemanly status of students, and that tuition was available in non-legal gentlemanly pursuits such as dancing and 'all games proper for nobles, as those brought up in the King's household are accustomed to practice' (Fortescue, 1949, p 119). Studies of the social background and status of students at the Inns reveals about 40% of the entrants were sons of the nobility, and 80% were from the landed gentry and nobility combined, much higher figures than at the Universities (Prest, 1972, pp 30–1; Prest, 1967, p 20). A stay at the Inns of Court was very costly; to the costs of residence, house fees and commons, had to be added the expense associated with maintaining a position in fashionable London society (expensive clothing, eating, gaming and perhaps theatre-going). At the Inns of Court, unlike the Universities, no scholarships were available for the poor but able student. Few Inns of Court students were from non-gentry or non-peerage families, but despite several attempts by the Inns at different times to exclude all except those of good parentage, the sons of prosperous merchants and yeoman continued to attend. A successful legal practice was thereafter the foundation of many fortunes.

Wilfred Prest argues that the influx to the Inns of the sons of the aristocracy and gentry in the later sixteenth century meant a gap developed between the 'career' and amateur law students. The gentlemen

157

formed a group apart and took care to maintain the distinction. Prest also suggests that sneers at lawyers' avarice and lack of 'polite' or classical learning had a social connotation which was understood and echoed by the poets and playwrights, who at the same time also satirized the pretensions of the Inns of Court gallant (Prest, 1972, pp 40–1).

Maitland has famously argued that the common law survived in England at a time when the reception of Roman Law vanquished other national customary legal systems in Europe because of the unique and vigorous teaching in the English common law undertaken at the Inns of Court (Maitland, 1901; see **civil doctor**). But some more recent scholarship considers that Maitland overestimated the impact of Roman Law in renaissance Europe, as well as underestimating its influence within England (see Sharpe, K. and Brooks, C. 1976, Baker, 1986d, Thorne, 1985d).

(B) Shakespeare refers to Inns of Court or Chancery in three places. These must be contexualized with the facts that some of his plays were produced in the Inns, and that fashionable young students of the Inns (such as John Donne) certainly numbered in the audiences of the public playhouses (see: Ives, 1964, pp 64, 78–9; Keeton, 1967, pp 10–13, 27; Phillips, O. H., 1967, pp 79–82; Cook, 1981).

Earnest Prince Harry in his preparations for war says to the ever-facetious Falstaff:

> Jack, meet me tomorrow in the Temple Hall
> At two o'clock in the afternoon.
> There shalt thou know thy charge, and there receive
> Money and order for their furniture.
> The land is burning, Percy stands on high,
> And either we or they must lower lie.
>
> (1H4 3.3.201–6)

This 'Temple Hall' was a site let out by 1388 to the Inns of Court societies of the Inner Temple and Middle Temple (Baker, 1990b, p 183). Its naming by Prince Harry as the place for a rendezvous to prepare Falstaff for a role in the war arises in a tense and serious context, for the Prince speaks tersely while sending out important dispatches. Yet this meeting and the war itself will not transform the always irresponsible Falstaff; likewise the Prince's connection with

Falstaff marked by the meeting at the Temple does not portend well for the serious enterprise of suppressing civil dissension.

Indeed civil dissention is ignited near the Temple Hall in scene 2.4 of Shakespeare's earlier-written and earlier-performed play 1H6. This scene portrays a dispute between young nobles, argumentative students, in the rose garden outside the Temple, met there because, as Suffolk says, 'Within the Temple hall we were too loud. / The garden here is more convenient' (1H6 2.4.3–4).

The rose garden scene of 1H6 (containing many legal references given fuller consideration under **quillets**) is fictional, but reflects a pungent Elizabethan reality. The York–Lancaster contention over the throne is imagined to flare up in a clash between hotheaded young men studying at an Inn of Court. These men would have been similar to the sort of actual 'students' of the Inns who were in fact not much involved with studies, but rather more with fighting and high living.

Suffolk, clearly only a nominal student, communicates in one phrase bravado and brutal threat: 'Faith, I have been a truant in the law, / And never yet could frame my will to it, / And therefore frame the law unto my will' (1H6 2.4.7–9). Warwick adds:

> Between two hawks, which flies the higher pitch,
> Between two dogs, which hath the deeper mouth,
> Between two blades, which bears the better temper,
> Between two horses, which doth bear him best,
> Between two girls, which hath the merriest eye,
> I have perhaps some shallow spirit of judgement;
> But in these nice sharp quillets of the law,
> Good faith, I am no wiser than a daw.
>
> (1H6 2.4.11–18)

Such a student disparagement of 'nice' legality looses all charm or humour when we see it leading to bloody war and national disaster.

In a lighter vein, stimulated by meeting his former companion John Falstaff, Justice Shallow's past days and especially nights at Clement's Inn are fondly remembered in his Gloucestershire dotage. As if time stood still, Shallow asks, for instance, after Jane Nightwork, who had been a 'bona-roba' during her wild youth more than 55 years previously (2H4 3.2.195–207).

Just before indulging in such distant recall, Shallow tells Silence

159

about his son studying at Oxford, who 'must then to the Inns o' Court shortly' (2H4 3.2.12). This progression from University to an Inn was a common pattern for the training of lawyers; in it Shallow junior betters his father as Clement's Inn was one of the Inns of Chancery, a lesser institution than an Inns of Court. Shallow continues:

SHALLOW   . . . I was once of Clement's Inn, where I think they will talk of mad Shallow yet.

SILENCE   You were called 'lusty Shallow' then, cousin.

SHALLOW   By the mass, I was called anything; and I would have done anything indeed, too, and roundly, too. There was I, and little John Doit of Staffordshire, and black George Barnes, and Francis Pickbone, and Will Squeal, a Cotswold man; you had not four such swinge-bucklers in all the Inns o' Court again. And I may say to you, we knew where the bona-robas were, and had the best of them all at commandment. Then was Jack Falstaff, now Sir John, a boy, and page to Thomas Mowbray, Duke of Norfolk.

(2H4 3.2.12–25)

This boastful name-dropping is followed by a splendidly confused mixture of meditations on long-dead companions and their long- past high-jinx with canny comments on the current price of livestock. Indications of cyclical or seemingly timeless rural rhythms thus mix with reflections on mortality, recalling the play's overall concern with 'the passing of an old order' (Eure, 1975, p 401) in England's political and legal life.

Despite his judicial dignity, **Justice of the Peace** Shallow's memories of when he 'lay at Clement's Inn' include cheerful recollections of wenching and brawling. Thus he recalls Falstaff as a forward boy:

The same Sir John, the very same. I see him break Scoggin's head at the court gate when a was a crack, not thus high. And the very same day did I fight with one Samson Stockfish, a fruiterer, behind Gray's Inn. Jesu, Jesu, the mad days that I have spent! And to see how many of my old acquaintance are dead.

(2H4 3.2.28–33)

This prepares for a continuation of the scene in which Falstaff as a recruiting officer desperately abuses his authority, stimulating Justice Shallow to remember the glories of his student days' military drill:

> I remember at Mile-End Green, when I lay at Clement's Inn – I was then Sir Dagonet in Arthur's show – there was a little quiver fellow, and a would manage you his piece thus, and a would about and about, and come you in and come you in. 'Ra-ta-ta!' would a say; 'Bounce!' would a say; and away again would a go; and again would a come. I shall ne'er see such a fellow.
>
> (2H4 3.2.276–83)

Finally Shallow's vanity and credulous foolishness attract Falstaff's larcenous designs, which he reveals in a soliloquy:

> I do see the bottom of Justice Shallow. Lord, Lord, how subject we old men are to this vice of lying! This same starved justice hath done nothing but prate to me of the wildness of his youth and the feats he hath done about Turnbull Street; and every third word a lie, duer paid to the hearer than the Turk's tribute. I do remember him at Clement's Inn, like a man made after supper of a cheese paring. When a was naked, he was for all the world like a forked radish, with a head fantastically carved upon it with a knife. A was so forlorn that his dimensions, to any thick sight, were invisible. A was the very genius of famine.
>
> (2H4 3.2.297–309)

In the quarto text only, not the folio, Falstaff adds immediately following this a revelation that Shallow's pastimes were not at all innocent:

> yet lecherous as a monkey; and the whores called him 'mandrake'. A came ever in the rearward of the fashion, and sung those tunes to the overscutched hussies that he heard the carmen whistle, and sware they were his fancies or his good-nights.
>
> (A.C. 1–5)

The implication that London's law students had been fashion-affecting whoremasters and brawlers since medieval times would no doubt have tickled many in Shakespeare's audiences, some them the students themselves.

(C) See: Fortescue, 1949, pp 117–21; Bedwell, 1909; Holdsworth,

1903, vol 2, pp 493–512; Prest, 1967; Simpson, 1970; Prest, 1972; Baker, 1978, pp 125–37; Baker, 1986e; Baker, 1990b, pp 178–85; Thorne, 1985c. On the Inns and the English non-reception of Roman Law see Maitland, 1901, and Baker, 1986d. The contribution of legal discussion in the the Inns to the refinement and development of criminal law is discussed in Baker, 1986j, pp 313–15.

interest See **usury/interest**.

interrogatories To examine upon interrogatories meant to question formally a witness or a person accused.

This term is used twice in succession in MV, the second instance echoing Lorenzo's initial proposal: 'Let us go in, / And 'Let us go in, / And charge us there upon inter'gatories, / And we will answer all things faithfully' (MV 5.1.297–9). Campbell, J., 1859, p 52, claims that the exact phrases 'charge upon interrogatories' and also 'will answer all things faithfully' belong to the legal procedures following a complaint for contempt.

A 'Name to interrogatories' denotes a legal right to question, which King John denies is within the scope of the authority of Pope Innocent: 'What earthy name to interrogatories / Can task the free breath of a sacred king?' (JN 3.1.73–4).

Contrastingly, cowardly Parolles, believing himself a captive of enemies and prepared to betray and slander his friends, willingly says 'I beseech you let me answer to the particular of the inter'gatories. Demand them singly.' (AWW 4.3.187–8).

King Cymbeline, responding to the joyful mood accompanying the (not yet quite complete) disentangling of the play's intricate plots, comments: 'But nor the time nor place / Will serve our long inter'gatories' (CYM 5.6.392–3). This avoidance of close interrogation accords with a shift in Cymbeline's diction from a formal and legalistic rigidity, as seen in 3.1.46–61, to his verbally supple and sinewy acceptance with gratitude of peace in 5.6.477–86.

Parker, 1985 connects the questioning of a criminal suspect point by point with 'delation', a word this essay finds related to the complex Shakespearian word 'dilation'. It detects this process echoed or mocked in LLL, ERR, and OTH. A similar process may be reflected in the first 'recognition' scene PER S.21, with its repeated forensic-like questions and answers.

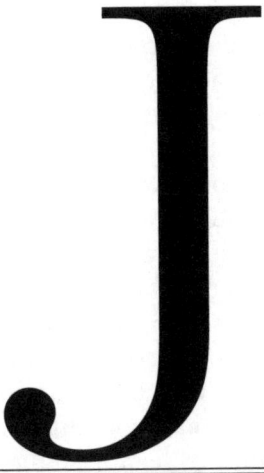

jointure (A) A jointure was the term used for an estate in land held jointly by any two or more people. By Shakespeare's time this had come to mean property to benefit the wife alone, used to provide for a wife after her husband's death (see **dowager/widow**). At first a joint estate in land (either freehold or **leasehold**), for husband and wife, it came to be a life estate limited to the wife which had to come into being immediately on the husband's death, with no intermediaries such as executors or trustees. By the sixteenth century it could take the form of an annuity based on a rent-charge on the property granted to the widow.

A widow's right to **dower** attached to **lands**, freehold or **entailed**, that her husband either held at the time of marriage or acquired later. However the importance of the right to dower was less than might be imagined because it did not attach to land held in **use**, and by 1535 the majority of land in England was actually held in use (Clarkson and Warren, 1942, p 135). After 1536 the Statute of Uses executed most uses, and the beneficiary was treated in law as the legal owner of the land, so dower might have once more been able to attach to all of her husband's lands. But section eight of the Statute specifically prevented such a result from occurring if the widow was already in possession of a jointure. So the effect of the Statute of Uses was to encourage land-owners to make pre-nuptial agreements offering jointures in consideration for the exclusion of dower.

The jointure to be available to a widow was typically negotiated between the bride's family and the groom before the marriage. If a jointure was agreed after the marriage had taken place, then the woman could elect whether to accept it or instead take up her right to dower (Bonfield, 1983, p 5, supposes this might be to protect wives from compulsion to accept less valuable jointures after marriage). The prospective husband's agreement to provide a jointure was very often contingent upon the payment by the bride's father of a marriage portion, or **dowry**, and typically the cost of the jointure was actually met by the property transferred with her at marriage. Eileen Spring comments that a falling ratio between value of the bride portion and value of the widow's jointure in the seventeenth century indicates a decline in the bargaining power of women; by the end of the century the amount of portion was twice as high in relation to jointure as it had been in 1550 (see Spring, 1993, p 50). By the eighteenth century the ratio was settled at a customary 10%.

The negotiations over dowry and jointure could be complex if the parties involved were land-owning aristocracy, gentry, or wealthy merchants. They were less so for brides of yeomen and others, where less property meant the estate could not be subdivided and yet realistically provide for widows and heirs. Erickson, 1993, p 130, finds that in such families it was not uncommon for husbands to use the bride's portion to purchase a **bond**, protected by a double penalty, which reverted to the wife after the husband's death.

(B) The quid pro quo aspect in arranging of jointures is seen clearly in the ill-fated negotiations for the marriage of Edward IV and the sister of the French queen. Thus King Louis says:

> Then, Warwick, thus – our sister shall be Edward's.
> And now, forthwith, shall articles be drawn
> Touching the jointure that your king must make,
> Which with her dowry shall be counterpoised.
> Draw near, Queen Margaret, and be a witness
> That Bona shall be wife to the English king.
> (RDY 3.3.134–9)

In the event neither jointure nor marriage materialise, for Edward contracts another marriage before the conditions of this one are agreed (see **impediments** and **pre-contract**).

In her pique because Orlando has been late for their rendezvous, Rosalind/Ganymede jests about a strange sort of jointure:

ROSALIND   Nay, an you be so tardy, come no more in my sight. I had as lief be wooed of a snail.
ORLANDO   Of a snail?
ROSALIND   Ay, of a snail; for though he comes slowly, he carries his house on his head – a better jointure, I think, than you make a woman. Besides, he brings his destiny with him.
ORLANDO   What's that?
ROSALIND   Why, horns, which such as you are fain to be beholden to your wives for. But he comes armed in his fortune, and prevents the slander of his wife.

(AYL 4.1.48–58)

This imagery is apt, for Orlando is without property and indeed homeless, and a 'jointure-house' was one specifically settled on a woman for her jointure.

More seriously, a jointure is offered to Anne Page on behalf of the idiotic Slender:

SHALLOW   He will maintain you like a gentlewoman.
SLENDER   Ay, by God, that I will, come cut and long-tail, under the degree of a squire.
SHALLOW   He will make you a hundred and fifty pounds jointure.
ANNE   Good Master Shallow, let him woo for himself.

(WIV 3.4.44–9)

Reynolds, 1996, pp 314–15, notes that the amount of this jointure seems 'generous', as it amounts to half of Slender's present annual income (which was just mentioned in 3.4.32). But ibid. still holds that Shallow's offer on Slender's behalf is nearly 'demonic', for both emotional and practical reasons. Practically, on marriage Anne will bring seven hundred pounds in ready money from a grandfather (1.1.46–59), as well as a **dowry** from her father (1.1.55). Eventually, Slender's estate derived from Shallow would be likely to produce **dower** far in excess of the offered jointure. So, as ibid., p 323, notes, and Spring, 1993, confirms, 'in Shakespeare's day, the jointure was employed chiefly as a means ... of restricting [the widow's] entitlement to dower in

165

the cause of preserving the landed estate' (see also Stone, 1979a, pp 642–5).

Finance plays a leading role in the marriage negotiations in SHR. It appears in 2.1.114–25 that in exchange for a large **dowry** Petruchio will not bar Katerina's **dower** in any of his 'lands and leases whatsoever'.

An analysis of their wooing shows that this unlimited offer is not repeated by any of Bianca's wooers. Although Baptista says that who-ever 'That can assure my daughter greatest dower / Shall have my Bianca's love' (2.1.339–40), he uses the term 'dower' imprecisely. For (as discussed under **dower**) in Shakespeare's age the amount of a widow's dower was set by common law (as a one third life interest in the hus-band's total estate including that acquired after marriage), and so was not negotiable in advance of marriage, or indeed knowable at that time. Therefore the fixed amounts offered by Bianca's suitors would have been properly-called 'jointures'.

First old Gremio boasts of his wealthy household, implying untruly that his wife would share in its possession (see **marriage**), and then he vaguely suggests she will inherit from him (2.1.342–58) Then the nego-tiation and terminology becomes more precise when Lucentio's proxy Tranio offers a specific (pre-arranged, limited) 'jointure' for Bianca:

> I'll leave her houses three or four as good,
> Within rich Pisa walls, as any one
> Old Signor Gremio has in Padua,
> Besides two thousand ducats by the year
> Of fruitful land, all which shall be her jointure
> (SHR 2.1.362–6)

Gremio then makes a counter-offer, adding 'an argosy' and Tranio tops this with three argosies plus 'twice as much whate'er thou off'rest next' (368–76). This contending to give a bigger jointure makes for a ridicu-lous auction, with the absurdity increased because Tranio the servant has no real basis on which to make his offers.

As Tranio is young, and he cites 'his' (that is Lucentio's) father's wealth as his to dispense, Baptista objects that the 'dower' he offers is unsafe, and says: 'let your father make her the assurance, / She is your own. Else, you must pardon me, / If you should die before him, where's her dower?' (2.1.383–5). This call for an assurance from the bridegroom's father matches the advice in a discussion of 'Dowment by the assent of the father' in Coke, 1628, section 40 (book 1, leaves 35–6): 'That it behooveth the wife to have a Deed of the father, to proove his assent and content to the endowment'. In further accord with the image of an absurd auction, Hortensio's offer is kept in reserve if Lucentio's father is not produced. All this represents, or maybe parodies, negotiations over jointure.

The materialistic world of Italy also informs Capulet's and Montague's reconciliation, where the end of their feud is linked verbally first to a tragic 'jointure', then to a golden object:

CAPULET   O brother Montague, give me thy hand.
This is my daughter's jointure, for no more
Can I demand.
MONTAGUE   But I can give thee more,
For I will raise her statue in pure gold,
That whiles Verona by that name is known
There shall no figure at such rate be set
As that of true and faithful Juliet.

(ROM 5.3.295–301)

(C) See: Clarkson and Warren, 1942, pp 81–4; Bonfield, 1983, pp 1–10; Baker, 1990b, p 309; Spring, 1993, pp 47–52; Erickson, 1993, pp 25–6, 92–3, 102–5, 129–30, 138. Bonfield, 1983, pp 47–54 describes the gradual development of jointures into the strict settlement of the later seventeenth century.

Boose, 1982, p 329, remarks on the tragic 'jointure' in ROM.

Boose, 1988, p 245 suggests a jointure is implicit in SHR, which leads to Kate's ritual prostration and offering of her hand for stepping on in 5.2; on this see under **dower**.

Reynolds, 1996 treats jointure in WIV.

jurisdiction (A) There was a wide variety of courts in early modern England, and it is worthy of note that Shakespeare does not mention them, nor does he mention the often-disputed boundaries of their jurisdictions. He makes very few references to any particular court of law of his age, alluding only to the quarter sessions of the **Justices of the Peace**, the low-level local **leets**, **Star Chamber**, and the civilian jurisdictions that would employ **civil doctors**.

Nevertheless the activities in the royal courts of law would have been familiar to many of Shakespeare's contemporaries in London, and to those who came to London to conduct their legal business during the legal **terms**. Surveys of how the courts would have appeared to members of Shakespeare's audiences are found in Ives, 1964, and Baker, 1985. The royal judges regularly toured the country on assize, and their visits, which were major public occasions, brought royal justice to the county towns (see **justice/justicer**). Shakespeare and his audiences were without doubt aware of the differences between the local, ecclesiastical, common law, and prerogative courts of their time. To list a few, there were the courts of Queen's (or King's) Bench, Common Pleas, Chancery, Exchequer, Star Chamber, High Commission, Wards, Staples, Admiralty, Requests, the Universities, the City of London's Orphans, and many other varied local manorial, market, merchant, borough or special ecclesiastical jurisdictions. Generally the common law courts by Shakespeare's time were encroaching on all other jurisdictions, and they would eventually take over all local and prerogative jurisdictions except Chancery.

The Church courts were also well known to Shakespeare's litigious age, as their jurisdiction covered many secular aspects of everyday life, for example validity or annulment of **marriage**, probate of **wills**, sexual offences, and defamation (see **slander**). These Church courts included the two Archbishop's prerogative courts in the north and south of England, the consistory courts of the bishops, the archdeacon's courts, and the deanery and 'peculiar' jurisdictions which operated at parish level. The Archbishop of Canterbury's Court of Arches located in London acted as an **appeal** court, but the Archbishop's court at York did not appear to do so. In these courts civilian lawyers (see **civil doctor**) followed civilian procedures and practised ecclesiastical law, which was an amalgamation of the canon law of the western church, papal codes, and Roman law. Part of the history of their relations with the King's courts until Shakespeare's time is outlined in **praemunire**.

Although long established practices directed certain kinds of legal action to particular courts, in the sixteenth century procedural innovations on the part of some courts (especially Queen's or King's Bench; see **bills**), and new social and economic needs (see for instance under **debt**), resulted in competition and conflict between jurisdictions. The common law courts (especially King's Bench) were rapidly expanding their business, taking over, for example, the work of traditional merchant law tribunals (see Plucknett, 1956, p 663; but also see Baker, 1986f).

The common law courts were not arranged in a hierarchical scheme allowing a modern type of **appeal** procedure. Rather, conflicts resulted in the issue of injunctions, writs or prohibitions by means of which one court attempted to restrain the encroaching activities of another. While recent studies have shown that co-operation was an important feature of the relations between the various Elizabethan courts and their personnel (discussed in Sokol and Sokol, 1999b), competition for business between these courts led to notorious conflict. Some jurisdictional disputes which took place provided the battleground for intensely politicized struggles (for example, conflicts between puritans and the Court of High Commission, which replaced the Papal Court after the English reformation). Many of the royal prerogative courts, such as Admiralty, Requests, **Wards** and **Star Chamber** came under attack from anti-royalist lawyers or from parliament, and eventually of these only Chancery was left in place at the Restoration.

(B) Shakespeare almost never even alluded to the jurisdictional relations, peaceful or otherwise, between the different law courts of his time. He stayed clear of references to such dangerous matters, although he did once allude to the late Elizabethan ideal of jurisdictional co-operation (in LRQ). But after the notorious and very public clash between the King and the Lord Chief Justice Coke, Shakespeare (or his colleagues) later took care to eliminate this allusion in a revision in LRF (see Sokol and Sokol, 1999b, and see under **equity** and **praemunire** for details of the conflict between James, Elllesmere and Coke).

It is uncertain whether Shakespeare kept clear of certain legal absurdities, however ripe for satire, because it was taken for granted that law 'worked that way', or because he was leery of straying onto dangerous grounds for humour. It is equally difficult to be sure if he was even generally influenced, when thinking about concepts of justice, by anomalies arising from contemporary tensions between competitive English jurisdictions, such as the civilian Admiralty and common law King's Bench (see under **jury** on such a possibility in MV).

Although in general Shakespeare avoided the issue of conflict of jurisdictions, there is an exception of sorts in some of the accusations that Henry VIII made against Cardinal Wolsey. These include: 'First,

169

that without the King's assent or knowledge / You wrought to be a legate, by which power / You maimed the jurisdiction of all bishops' (AIT 3.2.311–13). The charges against Wolsey conclude:

> Because all those things you have done of late,
> By your power legantine within this kingdom,
> Fall into th' compass of a praemunire –
> That therefore such a writ be sued against you,
> To forfeit all your goods, lands, tenements,
> Chattels, and whatsoever, and to be
> Out of the King's protection. This is my charge.
>
> (339–45)

These matters concern a foreign jurisdiction, rather than conflicts of English ones.

Shakespeare's only other use of the word 'jurisdiction' is placed in the mouth of Jack Cade, who frequently traduces legal terminology. Cade begins by punning on the name of a hapless noble, Lord Say, abducted by his followers: 'Ah, thou say, thou serge – nay, thou buckram lord! Now art thou within point-blank of our jurisdiction regal' (CYL 4.7.23–5). He continues, punning obscenely and apeing a tribunal of justice, making varied accusations including:

> What canst thou answer to my majesty for giving up of Normandy unto Mounsieur Basimecu, the Dauphin of France? Be it known unto thee by these presence, even the presence of Lord Mortimer, that I am the besom that must sweep the court clean of such filth as thou art. Thou hast most traitorously corrupted the youth of the realm in erecting a grammar school; and, whereas before, our fore-fathers had no other books but the score and the tally, thou hast caused printing to be used and, contrary to the King his crown and dignity, thou hast built a paper-mill. It will be proved to thy face that thou hast men about thee that usually talk of a noun and a verb and such abominable words as no Christian ear can endure to hear.
>
> (CYL 4.7.25–38)

Many commentaries, including Campbell, J., 1859, pp 73 and 76–7, have noted that Cade here adopts two standard legal formulae. These are: for the opening of a **bond** 'Be it known unto thee by these presence' (also punned upon jocularly by Rosalind in AYL 1.2.114–15); and for the condemnation of seditious publications offending the 'King his crown and dignity' by using words 'as no Christian ear can endure to hear' (see **libel** and **treason** on offences made by use of words). One might add that Cade's charges echo the Athenian accusations of corrupting the youth made against Socrates. Of course the implication is not that Cade is learned. His anarchic regime portrays, in parody, traits opposite to those appropriate to any 'regal' or even lesser 'jurisdiction'.

(Cade's neat characterization of his 'jurisdiction' as an devastating weapon in 'point blank' range parodies centuries in advance some currently fashionable views on early modern discipline and punishment, which are sharply brought into doubt in Herrup, 1985.)

(C) Attempts by parliament to take over part of the Church courts' jurisdiction are discussed under **statute**. Views of this jurisdiction and its complex interactions with the common law jurisdiction, reflecting newer research, are found in Helmholz, 1969, 1974, 1977, 1979, 1987c, 1990; Houlbrooke, 1979; Ingram, 1981, 1987; Donaghue, 1983.

The jurisdictions of the Church or 'bawdy' courts are discussed in relation to MM in Lindley, 1996. Hamilton, D. B., 1992, pp 34–58 discusses the hated *ex officio* jurisdiction of the ecclesiastical Court of High Commission in relation to JN. See under **praemunire** on jurisdictional issues concerning these courts.

Sokol and Sokol, 1999b maintains that contemporary jurisdictional conflicts between the courts became too charged politically for safe theatrical treatment. This discusses widely held views claiming on the contrary that the jurisdictional issues leading to the crisis of 1616 are reflected in one or another of Shakespeare's plays. Such views regarding 1H4 are found in Phelps, 1901, which is a prototype for many later arguments. MM is similarly treated in Dickinson, 1962; Dunkel, 1962; Levin, 1996, but the most widespread applications of similar notions are made to MV, as in: MacKay, 1964; Andrews, 1965; Saunders, 1984; Wilson, R., 1990; Cohen, S. A., 1994.

jury (A) The jury has an ancient history in English law, and its origins are not clear. The origins of the presentment (grand) jury, rather than the trial jury, may lie in the duty owed by the community (the people in

tithings) to present wrongdoers to the **sheriff**. However there are contrary indications that in medieval England responsibility for prosecution lay with public officials rather than the community. Alternately, the
Carolingian inquisitions, which were royal administrative devices for
making fiscal investigations, have been claimed as the ancestors of the
grand jury, and this tradition may well have influenced the compilation
of the 1080 Norman Doomsday survey of England.

Despite obscure origins it is certain that in the twelfth century the
reforms of Henry II introduced the system of prosecution by jury that
formed the basis of later developments. The Assizes of Clarendon 1166
and of Northampton 1176 required local officials to produce **juries**
made up of twelve members of the local community to present certain
crimes including **murder**, **robbery**, forgery of coins, arson, and
theft. These presentments were made to the **justices** in Eyre, or later
on assize (circuit) and the accused was brought to trial. In cases of theft,
local courts retained some jurisdiction, and the ecclesiastical courts
heard some criminal matters too, but in general all **felonies** were
categorised as 'pleas of the crown', including **homicide**, and tried
before the royal justices.

Once a prosecution was started in this way, the supernatural modes
of proof were employed, including trial by battle (see under **lists**),
compurgation (see under **debt**), and the ancient ordeals of fire and
water. The history of the modes of proof sheds light on legal thinking,
judicial organization, the psychology of ordinary people and their attitudes towards the supernatural (see Van Caenegem, 1973, p 62). A
presentment jury decided which suspect underwent which ordeal, after
looking at extrinsic evidence. But after priestly involvement in ordeals
was forbidden by the Fourth Lateran Council in 1215, another form of
proof was needed in criminal trials, and within a few years suspects
were being offered the alternative of a jury verdict. (Compurgation was
not affected and was in use in Shakespeare's time. This survival gave
rise to a great increase of actions for **trespass**, which did require jury
trial; see under **on the case**).

At first a verdict by jury was offered only to appeals by **approvers**
(see under **appeal**). Then the offer was extended to all criminal suspects, who had to choose between prison or jury trial. An unfortunate,
cruel, result of this development was that the suspect who refused trial
by jury was liable for punishment *prisone forte et dure* (see **pressing**). The
word prison was (mis)interpreted as *peine* and the suspect who refused

jury trial was taken to prison and subjected to either a very strict regime or was loaded with heavy weights until he was pressed to death.

By Shakespeare's time the change from irrational to more rational methods of proof had already taken place, although trial by battle remained a theoretical possibility (see **lists**). The jury of presentment sometimes numbered up to twenty nine, but more usually consisted of twelve freemen. All of these were local men of substance, with land worth at least 40 shillings a year (the duty was often attached to owner-ship of particular hereditaments; see **constables**), and had usually held local office. Grand jurors were chosen by two men appointed for the purpose by the bailiffs of the hundred, and they attended court both at quarter sessions conducted by the **Justices of the Peace**, and when the royal **justices** came into the area on assize. The justice of the peace received and investigated complaints, then the grand jurors heard the crown's evidence of the wrongdoing. If they considered the accusation was genuine, they endorsed the **bill** or petition *billa vera* which became the presentment or indictment, and if not they endorsed it *ignoramus*.

It was considered unconstitutional (on the basis of Magna Carta, 1215) for any man to be tried for **felony** unless he had been first indicted by a grand jury, or else **appealed** by a private complainant. Neither the King nor his government could accuse a man and bring him to trial for his life without indictment by his peers. The grand jury began its slow decline in England after pre-trial examination of the accused by the Justices of the Peace was put in place under Mary (1554–5 1 & 2 P. & M. c.13, and 2 & 3 P. & M. c.10).

Both felonies and misdemeanours (less serious offences not punish-able by death; see **trespass**) could be prosecuted by indictment, but prosecution of misdemeanours could also be begun by an 'information' put forward by either a private person as an informer, or by a law officer (see **Star Chamber**). Informers were often paid and great public dis-like attached to informations laid by the crown's law officers in King's Bench and Star Chamber later in the seventeenth century. In 1692, because it was politically unacceptable, statute forbade trial on informa-tion alone.

The petty jury (trial jury) was also composed of twelve local freemen of substance and good standing. They were summoned by the **sheriff** to attend court and acted as a public inquest into the wrongdoing, presided over by the judge. While the trial jury appeared in England after 1215, elsewhere in Europe an inquisitorial procedure developed,

173

where the judge directed production of evidence, directed the interrogation of witnesses, and gave judgment. In England the existence of the trial jury meant that pre-trial confessions were not essential to the legal process; therefore torture was used rarely, and was seen as contrary to English law (see Langbein, 1974, pp 206–7, Baker, 1986b, p 21, and especially Langbein, 1977). As a result the jury has been long revered as a bastion of English liberties. Yet in fact not all non-capital criminal cases took place before a jury, for from the fifteenth century onwards statute introduced procedure for minor misdemeanours to be tried summarily. From the sixteenth century **Star Chamber** tried serious cases of misdemeanour, such as for misprison of treason, without jury.

Whether or not juries were independent judges of fact in early modern England is a question that has received various answers. Although Baker, 1986i, pp 305 and 310–12, stresses the independence of the jury during the early modern period, he acknowledges that until *Bushell's Case*, 1670, jurors could be fined if the judge considered the verdict was contrary to his instructions. Nevertheless in theory the jurors and not the judge decided the case because the judge could not alter a jury verdict. The right of the accused to challenge jurors, and the collective responsibility of jurors for their verdicts, are matters also said to have ensured some degree of independence from control by the prosecution.

On the other hand, Langbein, 1978, pp 284–300, argues that juries were controlled by judges and their autonomy severely restricted in various ways long after the end of the judges' ancient powers to impose instant fines for disobedience. Disobedient or otherwise defaulting jurors could even be bound over to appear in **Star Chamber** to be punished for misconduct. Grand juries could be controlled by judges or sheriffs by 'packing', and often met with coercion or threats by judges to ensure a bill of presentment was found or Parliamentary statute upheld.

Because of this arguable lack of autonomy, the apparent willingness of early modern period juries to reach verdicts contrary to law, or to mitigate sentence, has been much commented upon (Lawson, 1988, p 117). Many juries found a lesser offence where a more serious one had been charged, for instance by finding stolen goods to be less valuable than claimed so that the defendant would escape death (see under **robbery/theft**, **pardon** and **murder**). For hard to determine reasons, the frequency of such 'partial verdicts' increased steadily from about 1590, according to Cockburn, 1988, pp 171–4. Such behaviour on the part of juries has been hailed as evidence of the continued existence of a communal understanding of guilt or innocence, which persisted despite the powerful presence of royal justices (see, for instance, Herrup, 1985; however Cockburn, 1988, p 173, suggests judges may have influenced juries to indict on lesser charges). There is also evidence that grand juries could refuse to give effect to government statutory policy, for example by refusing to find recusancy bills presented at an assize (Cockburn, 1972, p 114). Whatever the case, the social composition of the jury, all of whom met a residence and property qualification and who were likely to be craftsmen, substantial citizens, yeomen or even possibly gentry, in theory made for a less deferential body of men than might be imagined.

However royal justices often complained about the quality of men appearing as jurors, while sheriffs had difficulty empanelling sufficient jurors who were unpaid for undertaking their public role. Justices complained that inefficient minor local officials either warned every freeholder to appear at the assize, which resulted in none coming, or warned none at all. The unfortunate result could be that some long-suffering jurors were required to sit on numerous panels, or that to remedy the deficit bailiffs empanelled men attending the assize on the day, a custom which did not ensure impartial disinterested juries. Undoubtedly to be a juror must have been an arduous physical experience, especially because the practice was for one jury to hear several cases, one after the other, and then be sequestered to reach agreement on all of them. In order to remove them from the possibility of influence and to encourage agreement, juries were sequestered without food, water, or heat until they had reached an agreed verdict. Baker, 1990b, p 89, reports records of Tudor jurors being fined for eating sweets.

Because criminal defendants were never allowed special pleading and could plead only the general issue (guilty or not guilty), it has been argued that no real development took place in criminal law until modern times (see Milsom, 1981, p 403). In contrast others have identified important developments in early modern criminal law in which the institution of the jury has been instrumental. Baker, 1986i, p 305, writes that once proof by jury took the place of the ordeals it became possible to consider the evidence in particular cases. The process of demystification of a verdict could begin. This inevitably produced a tension between judge and jury and from this tension developed the law of evidence and the substantive criminal law.

175

Green, T., 1976, p 491, argues that in Tudor England procedural changes in criminal trials and statutory changes to benefit of clergy (see under **branded**) had a 'profound effect' on the development of the substantive law. Procedurally, in a criminal trial any plea of benefit of clergy was now made after conviction and not before, so the evidence was considered by the jury. Statutory changes meant benefit of clergy was denied to an increasing number of felonies (see under **murder**). The Marian Bail statutes of 1554–5 put the responsibility for prosecution into the hands of the Justices of the Peace, who now heard preliminary evidence. This meant that the jury now weighed the evidence presented to it by witnesses, rather than consulting their own knowledge of the defendant. The result of all these changes was that detailed evidence was now heard in open court, allowing a jury and the justice to define substantive law (such as in distinctions achieved in early modern England between excusable homicide, or manslaughter, and culpable homicide, or murder).

Although Elizabethan juries considered the facts in these ways, defendants and their witnesses were not allowed to give sworn evidence at the trial, but prosecution witnesses could.

(B) The highway **robbery** at Gads Hill involved loud threats of violence as in Falstaff's flamboyant 'What, ye knaves! Young men must live. You are grand-jurors, are ye? We'll jure ye, faith' (1H4 2.2.88–9). As 'jure' puns on 'injure', and evidence suggests that grand jurors were at least from late Elizabethan times increasingly drawn from relatively substantial citizenry (the evidence is reviewed in Green, T. A., 1988, pp 377–8), this attack combines Falstaff's typical disregard for respectability and law with his quaint disavowals of his own advanced age (see **Chief Justice**).

Juries alone could decide capital offences in England, reflected in an image used by Timon of Athens in his rant: 'jurors on thy life' (TIM 4.3.343). This English legal detail arises, quite typically, despite a non-English setting.

The same aspect of the English legal system is reflected in MV, despite specifically indicated differences of legal setting from English common law. Even in Shakespeare's England juries were not used by certain civilian, prerogative and summary **jurisdictions** (including Chancery, Requests, High Commission, Admiralty, **Star Chamber** and 'pie poudre' law-merchant tribunals – on which see Sokol, 1992). It is very interesting that the court in the trial of Shylock v Antonio (mainly discussed under **equity**) applies summary justice, and also takes the advice of a **civil doctor**; this may imply a civilian jurisdiction. Yet at the end of that trial a bystander alludes to common law trial by jury. Twelve jurors, as required in England for a capital trial, are 'wittily' referenced by foul-mouthed Gratiano, who says to the defeated Shylock, forced to **convert** to Christianity: 'In christ'ning shalt thou have two godfathers. / Had I been judge thou shouldst have had ten more, / To bring thee to the gallows, not the font' (MV 4.1.395–7).

The trials seen in the Vienna of MM are also without juries. Yet a reference is made in MM, as in MV, to an English-style jury trial for a capital offence. This allusion to a 'sworn twelve' arises when, in reply to Escalus' question regarding Claudio's offence, 'Whether you had not sometime in your life / Erred in this point which now you censure him, / And pulled the law upon you', Angelo argues that judges and jurors need not be saints:

> 'Tis one thing to be tempted, Escalus,
> Another thing to fall. I not deny
> The jury passing on the prisoner's life
> May in the sworn twelve have a thief or two
> Guiltier than him they try. What knows the law
> That thieves do pass on thieves? . . .
> You may not so extenuate his offence
> For I have had such faults; but rather tell me,
> When I that censure him do so offend,
> Let mine own judgement pattern out my death,
> And nothing come in partial. Sir, he must die.
> (MM 2.1.14–31)

Consistent with this position, eventually Angelo condemns himself, and requests only that 'No longer session hold upon my shame, / But let my trial be mine own confession. / Immediate sentence then, and sequent death, / Is all the grace I beg' (5.1.368–71).

Two less surprising Shakespearian references to juries are set, not in mythical foreign places, but in Henry VIII's England. The first is in an allegation that justice rather than tyranny is seen in the politically engineered fall of Buckingham, because he was tried by jury. An outraged kinsman by marriage, the Earl of Surrey complains to Cardinal Wolsey:

> Thy ambition,
> Thou scarlet sin, robbed this bewailing land
> Of noble Buckingham, my father-in-law.
> The heads of all thy brother cardinals
> With thee and all thy best parts bound together
> Weighed not a hair of his. Plague of your policy,
> You sent me deputy for Ireland,
> Far from his succour, from the King, from all
> That might have mercy on the fault thou gav'st him;
> Whilst your great goodness, out of holy pity,
> Absolved him with an axe.
>
> (AIT 3.2.255–65)

Wolsey's reply is a denial, offering, 'How innocent I was / From any private malice in his end, / His noble jury and foul cause can witness' (3.2 268–70).

In another instance later in AIT Archbishop Cranmer complains of his political enemy, sarcastically mentioning 'mercy': 'Ah, my good lord of Winchester, I thank you. / You are always my good friend. If your will pass, / I shall both find your lordship judge and juror, / You are so merciful' (5.2.92–5). Thus, although elsewhere representing opinions that juries are subject to imperfection, Shakespeare here indicates the advantage to justice and mercy of separate juries and judges.

(C) Generally see Bellamy, 1973, pp 121–4, 140–51; Green, T., 1976; Baker, 1978, pp 103–16; Green, T. A., 1985; Baker, 1986b pp 266–70; Baker, 1986i, pp 305, 310–13; Baker, 1990b, pp 85–90. On the history of juries see: Langbein, 1974, pp 140–55; Van Caenegem, 1973, pp 62–84; Groot, 1988b. On jury trial and judicial torture see Langbein, 1977, pp 9, 77–80.

The disputed question of the degree of autonomy of early modern juries is considered in: Cockburn, 1972, pp 111–24; Green, T., 1976; Langbein, 1978, pp 284–300; Herrup, 1985; Green, T. A., 1985, pp 105–52; Cockburn, 1988; Lawson, 1988; Green, T. A., 1988. Connections between certain cases of jury mitigation of accidental killings with the *deodand* are suggested in Wilson, L., 1994, pp 72–3 (see **murder/ homicide**). Judicial means to direct or even override jury decisions on damages in actions **on the case** for **slander** are explained in Helmholz, 1987e. Bullying by Edward Coke of a presentment jury which refused to bring charges of **praemunire** is vividly recorded in a document printed in Thorne, 1985f.

Hayne, 1993, pp 27–9, suggests that jury mitigation was common and places the conclusion of MM in this context.

justices/justicers (A) Early royal justices were men without specific legal training who acquired their legal expertise in the course of their service to the king. However by the thirteenth century the records identify judges who spent many years in office and might be called professional. Probably many had previously trained and practised as **serjeants**-at-law, (see under **lawyers**). But some of those recruited by the king to act as legal advisers or as judges in his courts are known to have been canon lawyers, or civilians (see **civil doctor**) who trained in Roman law at Bologna and other Universities (Brand, 1992, pp 154–7). By the fourteenth century training as a serjeant-at-law had become the only route to judicial office in the Courts of Common Pleas and King's Bench and the commissions of assize which brought royal justice to the counties. Judges in other courts, for example the barons of the Exchequer, and masters in Chancery, were often but not always serjeants. By the sixteenth century the serjeants had lost their primacy and barristers began to be appointed to judicial office, the first recorded being John Ernle who was appointed **Chief Justice** of Common Pleas in 1519. By Shakespeare's time many justices, including Sir Edward Coke, had not previously been serjeants. All twelve common law judges were made members of the two serjeants' **Inns of Court**, and so had chambers in close proximity to the serjeants.

All judges were appointed by the king and could be removed from office by the king at his pleasure, and were the king's servants. Once appointed all judges received salaries and their court robes from the crown. All supplemented their salaries by charging fees in return for acting as arbitrators, or by accepting gifts in return for giving advice. Baker, 1990b, pp 190–1, notes that it is difficult to assess the independence of the judiciary, for while medieval judges sometimes received direct instructions from the Crown, they also often made decisions against the Crown's interest. Ibid. also argues that factors including the professional training of judges and the influence of the constitutional writings of Fortescue (Chief Justice of King's Bench 1442–61) helped produce a general principle of the independence of the judiciary. The

179

story of the young Prince Henry and Chief Justice Gascoigne, who insisted that a Prince was not above the law, was popular during the sixteenth century (see **Chief Justice**).

In the early seventeenth century James I clashed with his judges on several occasions, famously in 1608 summoning all the judges to demand compliance with his request that suits involving a Crown interest should be stayed if he wished. Several judges were dismissed from office by James and then Charles I, including in 1616 Sir Edward Coke, then Chief Justice (see **equity** for the story of conflict between jurisdictions and Coke's dismissal).

In early modern England royal justice was frequently delivered when the king's judges visited the provinces on assize. The visit of the justices spared the litigant an expensive sojourn in London for himself and his witnesses. It also meant that prisoners accused of criminal offences could be tried locally by the assize judges on commissions of gaol delivery. The country was divided into six circuits, and by 1485 bi-annual visitations were the rule although the more remote northern counties were visited only once a year. So twice a year, during the Lent vacation (in February and March) and the Trinity vacation (in July and August – see **terms**), two of the king's justices, or sometimes a justice and a serjeant-at-law, (sometimes, though rarely, two serjeants-at-law) received their commissions and rode out from Westminster on each circuit to hear pleas and deliver gaols in each county town or other centre. At each assize town the red-robed justices would be met by **sheriffs** and local officials, and lodged for the duration of their stay at local expense, sometimes in some splendour but often very poorly. Sheriffs were allowed to charge the Exchequer for the feasts given the justices when they arrived and sumptuous banquets were common under Elizabeth until suspicion of corruption led the Exchequer to take control of expenditure in 1574.

The visiting justices' lodgings and courtrooms were often poorly maintained. Judges in early modern England clearly needed good health and stamina; illness and death on account of the rigours of the circuit were common. In 1577 the 'Black Assizes' resulted in the deaths of both assize judges, the clerk of the assize, the lord lieutenant, sheriff, coroner and about 400 other people who were officials, spectators and prisoners. Gaol fever frequently killed both prisoners and judges, and judges' personal safety from assault while travelling could not be ensured. In return for their work on circuit the judges were paid an annual salary which in 1611 was £20 per annum, but this figure was supplemented by generous daily allowances from the crown and present-giving by local sheriffs and gentry. By the early seventeenth century the present-giving was reduced to small formalized token gifts of money.

The opening session of the assize was preceded by attendance at church, at which lengthy sermons were preached to the assembled justices, assize officials and litigants by specially chosen clergy. In the early seventeenth century these sermons were used to put forward royal policy. After church all attended court, where the justices' commissions were read out, local officials handed in their records (for example the examinations and informations from the justice of the peace), and a grand or presentment **jury** of respectable men was called and sworn. Next the justices addressed the assembled dignitaries and citizens, imparting their instructions on government policy, which acted as a vehicle for propaganda on religious and other issues of royal concern. In this way Tudor and early Stuart governments used the justices on assize to dispense their administrative and political as well as judicial authority.

(B) The Justices or Justicers prominent in MM (Angelo, Escalus and an unnamed justice), as well as those mentioned in LRQ and COR, have no specified rank in the judiciary of their play's diverse or imaginary times and places. They are however attached to central courts and are therefore above the rank of the local **Justices of the Peace** seen or mentioned in many plays.

In the majority of the trial scenes represented by Shakespeare the presiding judge is the actual or effective head of state, as in JN, R2, MV, OTH and WT. Impartial justice is notably absent in at least the latter two of these trials, where King Leontes judges his own case and where the Duke of Venice favours Othello for military reasons.

In MM there is a central image of the head of state Duke Vincentio delegating his judicial authority to lower ranking officers acting as his deputies, yet retaining supervisory and manipulative powers. The play begins with Vincentio giving a 'commission' (1.1.13) to dispense justice to Escalus, and a more potent 'commission' to determine justice and to act as the duke's full deputy to Angelo (1.1.44–7). Vincentio then withdraws, but actually remains in disguise to oversee, and eventually correct, the work of his justices. The image of such a controlling role for a head of state might have been highly gratifying to King James, whose public statements were often in favour of independent English common law, but whose personal views were probably different. On a memorable occasion in 1608, through the agency of Archbishop Bancroft, James informed the assembled judges of England that, as they were actually the delegates of the Crown, James could decide a crucial jurisdictional dispute himself (see Usher, 1903; Bowen, 1957, pp 261–4). However, whether Vincentio's covert surveillance over and eventual manipulation of the judiciary is presented in a way that entirely favours the Duke of Vienna's behaviour is open to question.

The Archbishop of Canterbury presents an image in H5 1.2.202–4 of an orderly beehive requiring a 'sad-eyed justice with his surly hum / Delivering o'er to executors pale / The lazy yawning drone'. The sentences of English justicers could be capital, but they were not empowered to dispense **pardon**; this distinction is overridden in MM 1.1.44 because Angelo as judge is also acting head of state, and thus has the power to decide between 'Mortality and mercy in Vienna'.

(C) See: Plucknett, 1956, pp.231–44; Baker, 1990b, pp 189–91; Brand, 1992, pp 27–9. King James's collision with the judiciary is outlined in Merchant, 1964 pp 115–17 and is discussed in Sokol and Sokol, 1999b. The justices on assize are discussed in Cockburn, 1972.

MM has had much discussion as a locus for the exposition of the relations between a head of state and his judiciary. Actual Jacobean contexts of this issue have been traced recently in relation to the play in, for instance, Knight, 1988, Hotine, 1990, Bernthal, 1992, Kernan, 1995, Powers, 1996. Discussions doubting that Vincentio emerges unscathed from Shakespeare's representation include Bawcutt, 1984, Hammond, 1986, and Sokol, 1991.

Green, J. M., 1995 considers *King Lear* in terms of the Jacobean secular criminal law and of Christian Last Judgement, but does not discuss at length the justices or 'justicers' (LRQ S.13.17 and S.13.51) who enacted the former.

Justices of the Peace (A) The Justice of the Peace has been described as one of the 'most influential class of *men* in England' (our italics) in the England of Elizabeth I (Trevelyan quoted in Gleason,

1969, p 1), important for a dual role as local government administrator and local justice.

The authority of a justice of the peace rested on his appointment by the king to a body of men known as a commission of the peace. Originally, in the twelfth century, this commission was made up of knights of the shire acting as a militia to preserve the peace in the countryside, organising a local military defence and guarding against insurrection or unrest. In later medieval England the role of the Justices of the Peace was expanded to include the administration of local government and dispensing local justice, acquiring much of the authority lost by the **sheriff**.

The system for itinerant royal government, the Eyre, had fallen into disuse in the first half of the fourteenth century, proving both inadequate to meet the local demand for royal justice and at the same time unpopular because of the heavy fines that the visiting royal judges could impose on the country. The alternative decided upon was to use members of the existing commissions of the peace to undertake police and judicial functions, achieved initially by the periodic issue of special commissions of '*oyez and terminer*' and 'gaol delivery'. So the unpaid Justice of the Peace, drawn from the country gentry, instead of the sheriff or the Eyre, took on the major role of inquiring into and punishing wrongdoing in the countryside on behalf of the king.

The appointment in Tudor and Stuart England of Justices of the Peace was by means of a document called a commission of the peace, drawn up for each county by the king's council. The commission lasted until the issue of the next commission, so that in theory power remained with the king who could revoke the authority. In practice few commissions were revoked. The commission was in several parts: the first part appointed the Justice of the Peace and gave him authority to make inquiries, issue warrants, take 'informations', and hear examinations of witnesses; another clause appointed the Justice of the Peace or a certain number of them, to a quorum (see **coram**), to act as a commission of *oyer and terminer* (hear and determine); a final clause appointed a record keeper, the custos rotolorum (see **custalorum**). The commission would require the Justices of the Peace to hold quarter sessions during each of the four legal **terms**. Originally the Justice of the Peace would inquire into and try all felonies, trespasses and other offences. But by the second half of the sixteenth century the serious capital criminal offences, **felonies**, were referred to the assizes, the twice yearly meetings of the royal **justices** who would visit the countryside as assize commissioners on circuit to dispense royal justice.

A series of statutes from the mid fourteenth century onwards extended the authority derived from commissions and custom of Justices of the Peace. By the reign of Elizabeth I their duties had grown to be extensive and very various. In fact it is difficult to be precise about what these duties were (see Lambard, 1582). As well as judicial work at the quarter sessions, the Justices of the Peace were charged by general and special commissions and by statute with the performance of many civil administrative functions (in some places carried out at intermediate petty sessions). These ranged from overseeing alehouse licenses and weights and measures to wage regulation under the statutes of labourers and administration of the Poor Law (see **poverty**).

In contrast to France, England did not develop a paid class of local bureaucrats but instead used the unpaid services of the local knights of the shires on an *ad hoc* basis. In medieval England a high proportion of those named in the quorum were lawyers, trained at the **Inns of Court**, but after the mid sixteenth century lay Justices of the Peace predominated. Despite the lack of payment, danger or hostility from neighbours, and the heavy burden of work, there appears to have been little reluctance to take up office, so it is suggested that the honour and prestige, and the influence and power in the countryside that came with the office must have been great enough to compensate (Gleason, 1969, p 115). In Tudor and Stuart England most country gentry would expect to be included in a local commission as a mark of their rank (Neale, 1976, p 21, suggests widespread clamouring for the honour). While playwrights made them a subject of satire, and **Star Chamber** heard of corruption, many have remarked on the creation of effective local government in the person of the Justice of the Peace (see Holdsworth, 1903; Stone, 1979a, citing Coke and Maitland, 1911b; but see Kent, 1973, pp 51–3, Williamson, 1986, p 93; Lander, 1989).

(B) A verbal sketch of a Justice of the Peace – imaging a responsible, comfortable, substantial, grave, late-middle-aged gentleman – typifies Jacques' fifth age of man: 'the justice, / In fair round belly with good capon lined, / With eyes severe and beard of formal cut, / Full of wise saws and modern instances' (AYL 2.7.153–6). Another elderly Justice of the Peace furnishes Rosalind with a simile when she facetiously laments lovers' often-broken promises to be punctual, 'Time is the old justice that examines all/ such offenders' (AYL 4.1.189–90). A view of the ineptitude of seven Justices of the Peace flavours Touchstone's humorous praise of a judicious 'if', forming part of his disquisition on giving of the lie:

I knew when seven justices could not take up a quarrel, but when the parties were met themselves, one of them thought but of an 'if', as 'If you said so, then I said so', and they shook hands and swore brothers. Your 'if' is the only peacemaker'

(AYL 5.4.96–100).

A facetious reference to several grave Justices of the Peace similarly flavours the larcenous pedlar Autolycus' outrageous claims for a trumpery ballad that he would sell as truthful: 'Five justices' hands at it, and witnesses more than my pack will hold' (WT 4.4.281–2).

However Shakespeare's levity about Justices of the Peace in some contexts does not preclude seriousness about their function in others. Thus an anarchic murder by Jack Cade's rebels follows absurd charges condemning Lord Say for appointing Justices of the Peace: 'Thou hast most traitorously corrupted the youth of the realm in erecting a grammar school. . . . Thou hast appointed justices of peace to call poor men before them about matters they were not able to answer' (CYL 4.7.30–40). For further discussion of Cade's mock-legal indictment of Lord Say see especially **jurisdiction** and also **branded** and **treason**.

The questioning of an earthly justice's right to punish immorality is central to MM, finding voice especially in Isabella's pleading in 2.2.59–145 followed by Angelo's 'Thieves for their robbery have authority, / When judges steal themselves' (2.2.181–2). An even more drastic doubting of judicial impartiality informs Lear's terrific rant:

. . . A man may see how this world goes with no eyes; look with thine ears. See how yon justice rails upon yon simple thief. Hark in thine ear: change places, and handy-dandy, which is the justice, which is the thief? Thou hast seen a farmer's dog bark at a beggar? . . . An the creature run from the cur, there thou mightst behold the great image of authority. A dog's obeyed in office.
Thou rascal beadle, hold thy bloody hand.
Why dost thou lash that whore? Strip thy own back.
Thou hotly lusts to use her in that kind

185

For which thou whip'st her. The usurer hangs the cozener.
Through tattered clothes great vices do appear;
Robes and furred gowns hide all. Plate sin with gold,
And the strong lance of justice hurtless breaks;
Arm it in rags, a pygmy's straw does pierce it.
None does offend, none, I say none.

(LRF 4.5.146–64)

In a somewhat similar vein King Claudio, finding himself unable to pray, berates earthly justice while lamenting his untenable position before heavenly justice:

In the corrupted currents of this world
Offence's gilded hand may shove by justice,
And oft 'tis seen the wicked prize itself
Buys out the law. But 'tis not so above.

(HAM 3.3.57–60)

The seriousness of a Justice of the Peace being corruptible is mitigated by a tone of near-idyll in the rural scenes of 2H4. The elderly Gloucestershire Justices of the Peace Shallow and Silence reminisce over pleasures and profits past in so timeless a manner that Shallow is transported back 55 years, to his imaginary vigorous youth spent at Clements Inn (see **Inns of Court**), when he kept company with the page Jack Falstaff. This and a comic stream of similar nostalgia allays serious audience concerns over the Justices of the Peace countenancing Falstaff's dishonest recruiting in 3.2, the rank exercise of judicial favouritism in 5.1, and superannuated carousing climaxing in collapse or in plans to suborn the realm in 5.3. No harm is meant to be sharply felt in these farcical proceedings.

Yet there is satire of an abuse when, implying an assumption of its normality, Shallow's servingman Davy is offended that Shallow has not shown favouritism in judging a lawsuit. Speaking of an unworthy litigant, Davy says:

I grant your worship that he is a knave, sir; but yet God forbid, sir, but a knave should have some countenance at his friend's request. An honest man, sir, is able to speak for himself, when a knave is not. I have served your worship truly, sir, this eight years. An I cannot once or twice in a quarter bear out a knave against an honest man, I have little credit with your worship. The knave is mine honest friend, sir; therefore I beseech you let him be countenanced.

(2H4 5.1.36–44)

To this request to bend justice in order to gratify his serving man once or twice at each quarter session, Shallow replies, 'Go to; I say he shall have no wrong.' In 5.1.55–77 Falstaff comments on this travesty, in which Gloucestershire justice is so far from impartial, making facetious allusions to London's legal life (see under **terms**).

A later appearance of Justice Shallow in WIV casts him as the promoter of his nephew's, the idiotic Master Slender's, doomed marriage suit. The play begins with Shallow exclaiming against Falstaff for poaching his deer: 'Sir Hugh, persuade me not. I will make a Star Chamber matter of it. If he were twenty Sir John Falstaffs, he shall not abuse Robert Shallow, Esquire.' This threat of **Star Chamber** proceedings is backed up by Shallow's claim to the dignity of being a Justice and a **custalorum**. Old Shallow's legal bluster leads on to boastful threats showing him an unfit officer of the *peace*: 'Ha! O' my life, if I were young again, the sword should end it' (1.1.36–7). He again absurdly boasts a pugnacious disposition:

Bodykins, Master Page, though I now be old and of the peace, if I see a sword out my finger itches to make one. Though we are justices and doctors and churchmen, Master Page, we have some salt of our youth in us. We are the sons of women, Master Page.

(2.3.41–5)

In the combative, competitive, and greedy world of WIV, the venial Justice Shallow is portrayed less indulgently and more satirically than in 2H4.

(C) Merchant, 1964, pp 112–13, lists contemporary books offering guidance to Justices of the Peace. The most valuable of these is Lambard, 1582. In this manual William Lambard, bencher of Lincoln's Inn, Justice of the Peace in Kent and later a master in Chancery, complained of the heavy burden of the office. Wrightson, 1983, pp 24–6, maintains that Justices of the Peace often delegated downward toward petty **constables** the more onerous or unpopular tasks of law enforcement.

187

Kent, 1973, pp 51–3 demonstrates that opposition in Elizabethan and early Stuart parliaments to proposed legislation intended to regulate personal conduct often took the form of an expressed distrust or dislike of giving summary jurisdiction, discretion over punishment, or other powers to Justices of the Peace. These concerns were 'sometimes attributed to the inferior origins of many who held the office and to their desire to use it for personal profit' (p 52). An allied fear was that incontinent gentry might be reprimanded by their social inferiors, be they Justices of the Peace or lesser officers such as petty **constables** (pp 53–5).

Discussions of Justices of the Peace include: Maitland, 1911b (which predicts a decline of the 500 year old institution); Osborne, 1960; Bellamy, 1973, passim; Kent, 1973, pp 51–5; Elton, G. R., 1974, pp 59–60; Neale, 1976, pp 19–21; Baker, 1986b, pp 275–8; Wrightson, 1983; Williamson, 1986, pp 91–9; Baker, 1990b, pp 29–31. For historical accounts of Justices of the Peace in detail see Gleason, 1969; Lander, 1989. Langbein, 1974, pp 5–125, offers the view that especially after 1555 Justices of the Peace took the role of prosecutors of crime, and Langbein, 1977, p 186, responds to objections to this theory.

On Shakespeare's Justice Shallow see Draper, 1937, Phillips, O. H., 1967, pp 199–200, and Keeton, 1930, pp 39–47, which argues Shallow's role is a caricature of his office but not (as sometimes proposed) of Sir Thomas Lucy. On the legally sanctioned but morally unjust intentions of Shallow in WIV see Reynolds, 1996.

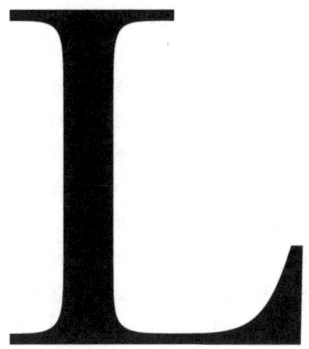

L

land (A) Land as property is known as 'real property', in contrast to **chattels**, which are 'personalty'. English law treats as land not only the land itself but anything attached to it, under it, or indeed over it. In addition, many incorporeal rights over land, such as a right of way, or easement, can be treated as real property.

English land law in Shakespeare's time had shed some of its feudal past but the structure still rested on the doctrines of **tenures** and estates, as it still does. The doctrine of tenures was introduced at the Conquest 1066. What is known as the 'feudal system' has been much debated by historians. The term itself was a product of the eighteenth century while 'feudalism' appeared in the nineteenth century. However lawyers accept the legal structure set out by Littleton's *Tenures*. The first of many printed versions of Littleton appeared in 1481, and in 1628 Edward Coke published a glossary, *Coke on Littleton* (Coke, 1628), as the first part of his *Institutes* (Coke, 1797). Briefly, according to Littleton's scheme, all land was held by the King who then parcelled it out to tenants in chief (***in capite***) in return for services. The services described by Littleton ranged from military tenures such as knight service (the duty to supply the King with a specified number of equipped fighting men for a certain number of days in the year), to agricultural service known as socage tenure, to spiritual tenure such as frankelmoin. The King's tenants in chief in turn made grants of land to their tenants by subinfeudation in return for a variety of services and so on. At the end of the feudal chain or ladder the **villeins** held land in unfree agricultural tenure, working the lord's land on a number of days a week in return for their holding.

This feudal structure to landholding lasted into the early modern period (indeed some ghostly features still exist), and it was often argued that the reason was because of the King's need to ensure a military force was available. But recent opinion considers the King's need for revenue as more important than raising an army. After all, money would pay for knights and an army. By the twelfth century some services, particularly knight service, had been commuted to money payments made by the tenant to the immediate lord. By the sixteenth century these payments or rents had lost most of their economic value through inflation.

But nevertheless, the doctrine of tenures remained important for two reasons. First, the 'feudal incidents' of tenure had retained their economic value to lords. Feudal incidents were payments made by the tenant to the lord on the happening of certain events; these payments became a property right for the lord. For example a lord would exact a customary payment from a tenant when an **heir** was admitted to the land. Very much more valuable were the feudal incidents of **wardship** and **marriage**. If a tenant died leaving an underage heir then the lord took the profits of the land until the ward came of age. In addition the lord could arrange the marriage of the heir and demand a payment if the heir did not consent. As the King was the ultimate lord, he had most to gain from these incidents, which brought a very significant part of royal revenue. The King also had most to lose if the feudal incidents were evaded by tenants. This was especially so after the Statute *Quia Emptores* in 1290 had enacted that any alienation of land was to be by substitution of one tenant for another instead of by subinfeudation, the creation of lesser estates. The consequence was that by Shakespeare's time many intermediate lords had disappeared from the feudal ladder, and, increasingly, most land was held of the King.

In the early thirteenth century, the duty of inquiring into the crown's rights to feudal incidents was taken away from the **sheriff** or itinerant **justices**, and given to specially appointed royal officials known as escheators; this reflected the importance to royal revenue. Complaints about the Crown's enforcement of feudal incidents formed the subject matter of many charters and petitions, including the Coronation Charter of Henry I, Magna Carta 1215, the Statute of Marlborough 1267, and the Statute of Uses 1536.

190

The most important method of evading feudal incidents was effected by the **use**, when the tenant, here called feoffor, conveyed the land to feoffees, or trustees, to hold for the benefit of the *cestui que use*, who could be his heir or even himself. As the feoffees now held the legal estate there was no question of feudal incidents arising, for example on the death of the tenant. It was in order to stem this loss of revenue that Henry VIII enacted the Statute of Uses in 1536, which ensured the legal estate remained with the beneficiary and not the feoffees. The estate therefore once more became liable for feudal incidents.

The second reason for the importance attached to the doctrine of tenures was because of the notion of lordship and vassalage, and the reciprocal rights and duties which resulted from this relationship. For example the right to hold a law court could be a concomitant of a particular lordship, and a tenant could have a duty to attend and act as a **juror**. In this way many administrative and governmental functions attached to possession of land and the doctrine of tenures. Most feudal tenures (except socage tenure) were swept away by the Tenures Abolition Act 1660, which confirmed legislation passed during the Commonwealth. But in Shakespeare's time the doctrine of tenures still played its role and the feudal incidents attached to it raised much revenue for the Crown.

The doctrine of estates, the second basic building block of English land law, dealt with the nature of a tenant's interest in land. Whereas the doctrine of tenures asked how the tenant held land, whether by military tenure or agricultural or whatever, the doctrine of estates dealt with how long the estate would last. 'An estate in the land is a time in the land, or land for a time' (*Walsingham's Case* (1593) 2 Plowd. 555.). For example a life estate or a **fee-simple** is the largest estate known, and lasts until the last tenant for the time being dies without heirs. By Shakespeare's time the tenant's rights to alienate the land by **conveyance**, or disposing of it by **will**, or charging it by way of **mortgage**, were settled.

(B) The term 'land' appears in nearly every play of Shakespeare, for it signalled a dominant theme of both law and society. The assumptions of the English system of land law permeate innumerable aspects of the actions of the plays, where, for instance, **primogeniture**, **suing livery** or **wardship** are in question.

The legal definition in which 'land' includes anything built on it gives the point to Ford's simile, in which he says a poor return in a sexual pursuit (of Mistress Ford) is 'Like a fair house built on another man's ground, so that I have lost my edifice by mistaking the place where I erected it' (WIV 2.2.209–11 – this is commented on in Heard, 1883, pp 14–15). A bawdy pun mixed with the legal language of possession in this comparison matches his sexually jealous obsession.

Oddly, allegations of sexual misdeeds and legal strife over an edifice built on another man's ground were also entangled in crucial events in the history of the Shakespearian theatre. These culminated in the nocturnal removal from formerly leased ground of the timbers of The Theatre, which were reassembled to make the first Globe playhouse. Three years later the furious former landlord deposed that, a lease permitting it notwithstanding, this was 'contrary to the laws', and was 'outrageous, violent and riotous' (Schoenbaum, 1986, p 208). Ibid., pp 207–9, gives a brief account of these events, and Berry, H., 1993 details the complex erotic and financial conflicts, and the lawsuits, leading up to them.

Just a few places in Shakespeare's plays where legal significance specifically attaches to the word 'land' include:

PETRUCCIO   Then tell me, if I get your daughter's love,
             What dowry shall I have with her to wife?
BAPTISTA   After my death the one half of my lands,
             And in possession twenty thousand crowns.
PETRUCCIO   And for that dowry I'll assure her of
             Her widowhood, be it that she survive me,
             In all my lands and leases whatsoever.
             Let specialties be therefore drawn between us,
             That covenants may be kept on either hand.
                                          (SHR 2.1.119–127)

             Well, push him out of doors,
             And let my officers of such a nature
             Make an extent upon his house and lands.
             Do this expediently, and turn him going.
                                          (AYL 3.1.15–18)

             Got 'tween a sleep and wake? Well then,
             Legitimate Edgar, I must have your land.

> Our father's love is to the bastard Edmond
> As to th' legitimate. Fine word, 'legitimate'.
> . . .
> Let me, if not by birth, have lands by wit.
> All with me's meet that I can fashion fit.
> . . .
> May have due note of him – and of my land,
> Loyal and natural boy, I'll work the means
> To make thee capable.
> (LRF 1.2.15–18; 172–3; 2.1.82–4)

> TIMON   Let all my land be sold.
> FLAVIUS   'Tis all engaged, some forfeited and gone,
> And what remains will hardly stop the mouth
> Of present dues. The future comes apace.
> (TIM 2.2.142–5)

These show how fully meshed land law was with almost every legal issue, including **marriage**, **bastardy**, **debt** and criminality.

(C) For an historical introduction to land law see: Bean, 1968; Milsom, 1981, pp 99–118, 116–239; Simpson, 1986, pp 1–24; Baker, 1990b, pp 255–294. For discussion of the history of feudalism see Watkin, 1979 and White, S. D., 1975. For a discussion on the heritability of fees see Thorne, 1959, and Barton, J. L., 1976. On the greatly increased and very profitable market in land in some regions of England during Shakespeare's period, resulting in a massive transfer of land 'from crown and peerage to a gentry closely allied with, in fact indistinguishable from, the merchant class' (p 202) see Thorne, 1985i. On the legal questions about lands taken in colonial ventures, see **plantation**.

Clarkson and Warren, 1942 closely considers Shakespeare's use of land law. Other discussions include: Keeton, 1967; Phillips, O. H., 1967; Hamilton, D. B., 1983; Ross, 1994; Spinosa, 1995.

Gohn, 1982, especially pp 948, 950, 952, 956–9, finds questions in R2 of royal succession and of descent of land in close analogy with one another, often linked in imagery or by metaphor.

lawyers (A) In early modern England the term 'lawyer' embraced more than one kind of legal practitioner, each performing different functions. Shakespeare mentions two types of practitioners by name, the **attorney**, and the civilian lawyer or **civil doctor**, as well as using the appellation lawyer[s].

The main division among lawyers was between those who practised the common law and those who practised the civil law derived from Justinian's *Corpus Juris Civilis*. Attorneys, solicitors, utter-barristers and serjeants-at-law were common lawyers, while civil doctors were the inheritors of the classical law tradition; on these see under **civil doctor**.

Wilfred Prest claims that the history of advocacy in early modern England is also the history of the rise of the professions such as medicine, law, the church (Prest, 1986, p 1). Certainly the legal profession went through a fundamental transformation between the mid sixteenth and the mid seventeenth century, taking on its modern forms.

Shakespeare does not make any reference to **serjeants**-at-law, but in medieval and early modern England these lawyers were important figures in the legal and public world. Until the seventeenth century they were the senior advocates and before 1519 all judges were appointed from their ranks. J. H. Baker remarks that the emergence of the Common Law was more or less coincident with the appearance of the professional judge, and professional practitioners, the serjeants-at-law, followed soon afterwards (Baker, 1990b, p 177).

Serjeants-at-law attended the Court of Common Pleas with the plaintiff, where they recited the plaintiff's 'count', or claim. Educated at the **Inns of Court**, where they entered as apprentices, serjeants were created by the Crown. In medieval England when serjeants were admitted to their Order, the Order of the Coif, grand ceremonies with great feasts took place which lasted for several days; the King himself often attended and the serjeants took an oath and distributed gold rings. But by Shakespeare's time the serjeants had begun to lose their pre-eminent position. Written pleadings had replaced oral pleadings, so serjeants main function of reciting the count was gone. Also, changes in the way in which royal justice was heard in the regions meant more cases were initially heard out of London at assize by *nisi prius*. This was the procedure by which a defendant would be ordered to attend the King's central court by a given date 'unless before then' the King's judges came to the county on assize. The twice yearly assize would hear the case and take the jury's verdict back to Westminster for deliberation and judgment by the assembled judges. Serjeants did not have a monopoly at assize. Moreover, serjeants did not have sole right of audience before all central courts, only the Court of Common Pleas. In the sixteenth and seventeenth centuries the serjeants faced competition from other lawyers, as the Court of King's Bench began to expand its business taking on some of the work that previously was the sole preserve of Common Pleas (see **bills** and Blatcher, 1978). Even so throughout the middle ages and into early modern England Common Pleas still conducted the largest share of all legal business (see Thorne, 1985d, p 412, on its proud, and profitable, conservatism) and remained the busiest court. Then when Elizabeth granted Francis Bacon the office of 'Queen's counsel extraordinary' in 1594 she created a new rank which took precedence over that of the serjeant. James I appointed a King's counsel and his successors followed with many more, so eventually it became less rewarding for lawyers to take the serjeants' Order of the Coif. James followed Elizabeth's practice of selling the coif and judgeships, but in his reign this became 'an open scandal', and in 1603 the rumour that a serjeant had paid £800 for his coif led contemporaries to comment that 'argent makes serjeant' (Baker, 1984, p 110). But despite scandal, increased numbers, and competition from king's counsel, in Shakespeare's time many eminent lawyers were still serjeants-at-law, and two thirds of all judges were serjeants.

Not all the apprentices in the Inns of Court became serjeants; many practised in the other Westminster Courts or outside London as 'utter-barristers' or 'outer-barristers', so called because they were sufficiently trained in the law to argue a case outside the **bar** of their Inn. In 1546 a Proclamation restricted rights of audience in courts (other than Common Pleas) to utter-barristers or other lawyers who had been members of an Inn of Court for a minimum of eight years. The apprentice was, more or less, the ancestor of the modern barrister. Some apprentices also seem to have acted as **attorneys**, at least some of the time.

The profession of attorney was ancient, and had developed at the same time as that of serjeants-at-law, although the attorneys-at-law of early modern England are a diverse and difficult to define group of lawyers. By the start of the seventeenth century attorneys were attached to particular courts, and some had a monopoly (for example to **Star Chamber**, see Brooks, 1986, p 25). They could receive training in the law at one of the **Inns of Court**, although moves to exclude them from the Inns began in 1556. It was more likely that they attended one of the lesser Inns of Chancery. It has been argued that it was even more likely that they trained by acting as clerk in an attorney's office (Brooks, 1986, p 152). Before attorneys could practise they were examined by the judges, and their names were then entered onto a roll. They were subject to discipline by the judges, and had to swear to be of good behaviour. Punishment for misbehaviour was the removal of their name from the roll, and it is said that they were literally ejected from the court, physically 'cast over the bar' (Baker, 1986e, p 84).

The attorneys' function was to take steps necessary for the progress of a case through its various procedural stages. They acted as agents for litigants, frequently attending to legal business in the Westminster Courts when the plaintiff or defendant was not there in person. In the mid-sixteenth century, once oral pleadings gave way to written pleadings, the task of preparing and exchanging these fell to attorneys. Attorneys could be general practitioners too, giving advice on legal questions. They were the largest group of lawyers in early modern England (300 were attached to Common Pleas in 1580). Their numbers caused considerable concern in late sixteenth and early seventeenth century England (Brooks, 1986, p 20).

Shakespeare's was a litigious age. It is difficult to point to any one reason for this, but the expansion of trade, commerce, population, and wealth had increased the demand for law. It also appears that during the sixteenth century the nobility became less inclined to settle their differences by resorting to violence and increasingly turned instead to the law, for the number of **Star Chamber** actions for riot and affray fell. For whatever reasons, overall there was an unprecedented increase in the volume of litigation between the mid sixteenth century and mid-seventeenth century, after which the levels fell. Particularly between 1580 and 1606 the business in the Courts of King's Bench and Common Pleas nearly doubled (Brooks, 1986, pp 75, 107). It was no longer possible for the judges of Common Pleas to control the work of all lawyers, and the numbers of lawyers who worked in other courts, including those outside London, increased dramatically.

According to Baker, 1986c, p 85, contemporaries attributed the rise in litigation to the activities of attorneys, although this does seems a complaint familiar to any age. In fact attorneys were in competition with other lawyers, and during the late sixteenth century were restricted to working in the court they were attached to. Nevertheless concern was real, reflecting fears that an ordered cohesive society was breaking down and that increased numbers of lawyers, particularly attorneys, were encouraging law suits for their own gain instead of working to reconcile adversaries (Brooks, 1986, pp 132–6). Lord Keeper Egerton in a speech to parliament in 1601 called attorneys 'Petty Fogers and Vipers of the Common Wealth' and called for a limit on numbers in order to reduce litigation (Brooks, 1986, p 139).

Like attorneys, court officials and clerks also advised the public, advised litigants, and conducted litigation, functions which overlapped with those performed by attorneys-at-law. By the early seventeenth century, court clerks were in fact by far the largest group of lawyers acting in the court of King's Bench. Although justice was royal justice, and the courts were royal courts, the structure of the bureaucracy differed from court to court. There were different numbers of officials in each of the courts, with different names and performing different functions. Most courts had their own rules of procedure which had developed over the years. In Common Pleas officials were mostly appointed by the Lord Chief Justice, and in Chancery some were appointed by the Lord Chancellor and some by the Master of the Rolls. In the prerogative courts of **wards** and **Star Chamber** they were appointed by **letters patent**. Office holding was regarded as a form of property, and as only nominal salaries were paid, all court office holders depended on fees charged to litigants for their income (Brooks, 1986, pp 12–15). Numerous underclerks were employed by the office holders, many of whom have left no record. Both office holders and their underclerks wrote and issued the originating and judicial writs which authorised courts to act, or ordered a defendant to appear.

Lawyers other than attorneys-at-law or court officials undertook a range of work, including practice as manorial stewards, court-keepers, scriveners, attorneys in borough courts, town clerks and under-sheriffs (Prest, 1972, p 4). Legal documents were also drawn up by notaries. Many who called themselves lawyers had never been members of an Inn of Court and therefore had had no traditional legal training. As 'solicitors' they practised in a number of ways, often before 1546 acting for a litigant in court (hence soliciting), but their early history is obscure. In 1590 *Broughton v Prince* established the necessity of a call to the Bar as the minimum qualification for the right of audience before a superior common law court, which restricted advocacy in court to the serjeant-at-law or the apprentice-at-law such as the utter-barrister (Baker, 1986c, p 129). Solicitors also performed clerical work, acting as a steward or auditor or paymaster of a large household.

There was much concern among judges in the common law courts about the increase in numbers of solicitors because of the lack of regulation or supervision of their training or practice. In the late sixteenth and early seventeenth century the judiciary waged war against the solicitors, using the laws against maintenance to prevent solicitors taking on work they considered only competently undertaken by attorneys and barristers (see Baker, 1986j). Maintenance was the criminal and tortious offence of interfering or meddling in litigation without good cause, and it could be severely punished with fines and loss of fees. Lord Keeper Egerton was determined to rid the law of solicitors, famously calling them in court 'caterpillars of the common weal' (*Att.-Gen. v Kinge* (1596), noted by Baker, 1986c, p 141). He was not the only judge to employ such invective against the upstart solicitors. Parliament too brought in **bills** in 1580 and 1601 to suppress frivolous suits and pettifogging solicitors, but these did not become law. A further, successful, attempt to regulate the activities of solicitors was made in 1606 when an Act was passed which regulated their fees, and in so doing had the effect of achieving some recognition for the profession.

(B) Shakespeare's references to attorneys-at-law, discussed under **attorney**, imply mockery or even reproach. Perhaps similarly, when planning to impersonate a male lawyer, Portia tells Nerissa: 'I have within my mind / A thousand raw tricks of these bragging Jacks / Which I will practise' (MV 3.4.76–8). This mockery of men, focused on swaggering, may be also anti-lawyer, focused on 'tricks'.

In theory all separate judicial authority grew out of the King's Council, and therefore Lord Keeper Egerton's phrase, noted above, about upstart solicitors being 'caterpillars of the common weal' may have been echoed in Bolingbroke's phrase: ' . . . Bushy, Bagot, and their complices, / The caterpillars of the commonwealth, / Which I have sworn to weed and pluck away' (R2 2.3.164–6. But see 1H6 3.1.73–4 'Civil dissension is a viperous worm / That gnaws the bowels of the commonwealth', and the CYL 4.4.35–6, in which 'scholars, lawyers, courtiers, gentlemen' are called 'false caterpillars' (commented on below).

If not similarly damning, at least impolite is Lear's wise Fool's simile for 'nothing' paid for with 'nothing', implying that lawyers will talk only for fees: 'like the breath of an unfee'd lawyer' (LRF 1.4.128). Neither is Hamlet polite about the skull he supposes to be that of a land-grabbing lawyer (HAM 5.1.95–109; the passage and the land acquisitiveness of the rising 'professional' class of lawyers is discussed at length under **fine and recovery**). Timon curses, 'Crack the lawyer's voice, / That he may never more false title plead / Nor sound his quillets shrilly' (TIM 4.3.153–5); the difficulties and complexities of obtaining safe title to **land** are discussed under **conveyancing**. **Quillets** describes legal quibbles used to trick, so Timon expresses condemnation of lawyers who would employ such devices.

In an effort to disrupt her spousal to Posthumus (on which see under **divorce** and **marriage**), villainous Cloten plans to corrupt Imogen's attendant by making her his agent: 'I will make / One of her women lawyer to me' (CYM 2.3.71–2). The metaphor implies a relationship of bought loyalty, and perhaps reflects fears in connection with the great expansion in litigation and numbers of lawyers (particularly attorneys and solicitors) in Shakespeare's age.

In the fanciful Queen Mab speech, 'lawyers' are described as being as susceptible as are parsons to dreams of venal temptation,

> Sometime she gallops o'er a lawyer's lip,
> And then dreams he of smelling out a suit;
> And sometime comes she with a tithe-pig's tail
> Tickling a parson's nose as a lies asleep;
> Then dreams he of another benefice.
> (ROM 1.4.77–81)

Hamlet lists among typical frustrations that could provoke a strong temptation to a 'quietus make/ With a bare bodkin' ('quietus' as part of a legal phrase is discussed in Merchant, 1964; Bland, 1988): 'The pangs of disprized love, the law's delay,/ The insolence of office, and the spurns/ That patient merit of th' unworthy takes' (HAM 3.1.74–6). Litigation could indeed run ruinously for many years (see for instance Berry, H., 1993), and lawyers could be blamed.

Perhaps not despair to the point of wishing 'the Everlasting had not fixed / His canon 'gainst self-slaughter!' (HAM 1.2.131–2), but at least some dark humour seems implicit in Rosalind's remark that time 'stays', or stands still, 'With lawyers in the vacation; for they sleep between term and term, and then they perceive not how time moves' (AYL 3.2.322–4). It would seem this refers to the tardiness of lawsuits due to the paralysis of legal business outside of the brief legal **terms**. A similar implication is conveyed in Falstaff's means of expressing, by reckoning the slowness of legal actions, a goodly long time: 'the wearing out of six fashions – which is four terms, or two actions' (2H4 5.1.72–3).

In his disquisition on varieties of melancholy Jacques says that the 'lawyer's [melancholy] is politic', meaning contrived for effect (AYL 4.1.13). In TIM 2.2.107–11 the fool lists the lawyer along with the lord, the 'philosopher', and 'all shapes that man goes up and down in from fourscore to thirteen' as lustful 'whoremasters'. The general calumny may be heightened here by particular imputations about law students discussed under **Inns of Court**.

All these references reflect popular or populist wryness about lawyers. Yet in SHR 1.2.278–9 lawyers are seen, at least in their professional relations, more genially. This contains a proposal that the adversaries in a love-cause: 'do as adversaries do in law – / Strive mightily, but eat and drink as friends.' A rare wholly honourable appearance of a 'lawyer' in Shakespeare is in 1H6 2.4.56–8, where an unnamed Lawyer joins Richard Plantagenet's faction because Somerset's 'argument' is 'wrong in law' (however the New Arden editor thinks this legalistic, and not based on justice).

Departing from populist aspersions, or indeed any reflection of the campaign in the courts against particularly the 'lower' branch of the legal professions between the 1590s and 1606, the depiction of law and lawyers shifts to another level when in CYL Shakespeare contemplates an anarchic destruction of legal order. There is no doubt that the play condemns Jack Cade's brutal popular rebellion (see **sergeant**). Cade's followers aim to 'kill all the lawyers' (CYL 4.2.78) and call 'All scholars, lawyers, courtiers, gentlemen/ . . . false caterpillars and intend their death' (CYL 4.4.35–6 – perhaps parodying the title of Stephen Gosson's 1579 pamphlet, *The Schoole of Abuse, Conteining a plesaunt inuectiue against Poets, Pipers, Plaiers, Iesters, and such like Caterpillers of a Commonwelth*). The murderous intent here reflects not a popular dislike for lawyers, but rather a recognition of their essential role in good social order, as is emphasised in Boyarsky, 1991.

It is suggested in Barton, S. D. P., 1929, p 83, and Campbell, J., 1859, p 93, that the 'solicitor' referred to in OTH 3.3.27 (indeed in a context nearly equivalent to LLL 2.1.29) is a lawyer. This seems to us stretched. Less improbable is the suggestion in Barton, S. D. P., 1929, p 85, and Campbell, J., 1859, p 36, that the 'good counsellors' mentioned in MM 1.2.98–9, named as parallel with bawds in lacking 'no clients', are implicitly lawyers.

(C) On the history of the legal professions, in particular attorneys, barristers and solicitors see: Holdsworth, 1903, vol 2, pp 484–93; Baker, 1986e; Ives, 1964, pp 73–86. Also see Brand, 1987, especially for an analysis of increase in the volume of litigation and of numbers of lawyers. On the history of the bar and barristers see: Prest, 1972; Prest, 1986; Baker, 1986a. On solicitors and attorneys see especially Brooks, 1986 and Baker, 1986j. On civilian lawyers see under **civil doctor**.

lease (A) In Shakespeare's time a lease was an interest in **land** that was held for a term of years. The lease in many ways appears similar to a life estate (see **entail**) but it was treated differently in law. A life estate was subject to the 'doctrines of tenures and estates' (see **land**), and therefore could exist within feudal relationships. But despite the fact that a long lease could last for much longer than a life estate, there were doubts about whether the doctrine of tenures and estates applied to it, and leases fell outside the framework of feudal relations. No lessee ever did homage for a lease; there was no relation of lord and vassal between lessor and lessee.

The lease was not regarded as a freehold estate, but a **chattel**. As a result the lessee did not have available to him the remedies for recovery including remedies for disseisin (loss of possession) and the real actions, which were available to the holder of either a **fee-simple** or a life estate. Eventually, by the close of the medieval period, the lessee developed his own remedy, the action of ejectment. This was originally a form of writ of **trespass**, *eiectio firmae*, which allowed an ejected lessee to recover damages. By the early fifteenth century specific recovery of the land for the term of the lease was granted. The advantages to the lessee were considerable: a simpler procedure and title tried by **jury**. These advantages were apparent to freeholders and from about 1570 an action in ejectment using fictitious leases was commonly used by freeholders seeking possession. The device worked as follows: the real plaintiff, out of possession but believing he had good title to the disputed land, granted a lease to a friend, John, the nominal plaintiff.

John then began an action claiming to have been ejected by the actual possessor of the land. If John won he released his interest to the real plaintiff. By the early seventeenth century ejectment was the most usual way to try disputed title, and the legal fiction became formalized. The nominal plaintiff, called Shamtitle or John Doe, claimed to have been ejected from the land by Richard Roe. This nominal defendant then took no action, which forced the occupier, who was the real defendant, either to defend his title or to have judgment entered against him by default. The action of ejectment and the fictitious characters Doe and Roe were to continue until the mid nineteenth century property law reforms.

Because (before 1926) the lease was seen not as an estate in land but as a means of raising money by landowners, it came to be classified as a 'chattel real', a term which recognized its dual nature. A lease would not pass to an heir on the death of a tenant, but to his **executors** to be dealt with as personalty, and a lease could not be **entailed**. In Shakespeare's time two cases relaxed these rules to an extent. Entails of leaseholds were held not possible, but testators could leave a life interest in a lease in a **will**, and leave an interest in **remainder** (*Manning's Case* (1609) 8 Co. Rep. 94b, and *Lampet's Case* (1612) 10 Co. Rep. 46b.).

In Shakespeare's time then, from the freeholder's point of view, a lease was seen as a means of raising money in much the same way as did a **mortgage**. With the decline of feudalism the 'husbandry lease' became the common form of landowning for those who farmed the land, but were not possessed of sufficient capital to **purchase** the free estate.

The duration of the term of the lease was not settled by law, but it could not be indeterminate. Very long leases were considered with suspicion as possible devices for fraud; the length of a lease was impugned in 1612 (*Cotton's Case* (1612) Godbolt 192). Despite this, in Shakespeare's time there was still as yet no limit to the length of a lease, so a 1000-year lease was possible.

(B) The technical, metaphorical and colloquial uses of this legal term tend to merge as they often do in Shakespeare, especially as it is used in metaphors in SON 13, 18, 107, 124, and 146. (Compare with **waste**, and Clarkson and Warren, 1942, pp 102–6 on dramatists' uses of **purchase**.)

202

An image of the long or tedious duration of a lease is perhaps implicit in Prince Hal's suggestion that the **prentice** Francis has a 'long lease' to run in his **indentures**, and mischievously suggests breaking the agreement (1H4 2.5.40–54).

Conversely, the impermanence of a lease is foremost in uses such as in Macbeth's exultation:

> Rebellious dead, rise never till the wood
> Of Birnam rise, and on 's high place Macbeth
> Shall live the lease of nature, pay his breath
> To time and mortal custom.
>
> (MAC 4.1.113–6)

Where a more exact significance in land law is adumbrated, a frequent implication is often that the leasing of lands is something untoward, to be pitied or disparaged. For the hungry and hunted Jack Cade deciding to break from cover, the precarious and terminable nature of his life is metaphorically a 'lease': 'But now am I so hungry that if I might have a lease of my life for a thousand years, I could stay no longer' (CYL 4.9.4–6). He says this just after he speaks of Alexander Iden's **fee-simple**, the mode of possession of the traditional landed classes. It is not surprising that Iden, the fee simple-owning yeoman, vanquishes Cade, the upstart rebel whose life is likened to a dubious lease.

In TGV 5.2.25–9, the 'possessions' of the foolish suitor Thurio are said to be pitied by Silvia because 'they are out by lease'. Though Thurio speaks of his lands, which he hopes may help win her, Steevens conjectured that when Proteus says [she] 'pities them' he means she pities his poor possession of wits.

Even more disparagingly, King Richard II's supposed 'leasing' of the lands of England is twice condemned by the dying John of Gaunt. He says this first in his famous oration on 'This other Eden, demi-paradise':

> This land of such dear souls, this dear dear land,
> Dear for her reputation through the world,
> Is now leased out – I die pronouncing it –
> Like to a tenement or pelting farm.
> England, bound in with the triumphant sea,
> Whose rocky shore beats back the envious siege

> Of wat'ry Neptune, is now bound in with shame,
> With inky blots and rotten parchment bonds.
>
> (R2 2.1.57–64)

He repeats this disparagement of leasing one's land to his nephew Richard's face, when he tells him that *he* is moribund, for 'Thy deathbed is no lesser than thy land' (R2 2.1.95), and:

> Why, cousin, wert thou regent of the world
> It were a shame to let this land by lease.
> But, for thy world, enjoying but this land,
> Is it not more than shame to shame it so?
> Landlord of England art thou now, not king.
> Thy state of law is bondslave to the law,
> And –
>
> KING RICHARD   And thou, a lunatic lean-witted fool,
> Presuming on an ague's privilege.
>
> (R2 2.1.109–17)

Aspects of this second passage are discussed in Hamilton, D. B., 1983, and under **waste**.

Yet, despite such attitudes depreciating mere commercial uses or holding of land, the monetary worth of leases of land are distinctly referred to as valuables during the negotiations for a **dowry** in SHR 2.1.123–5 (see under **dower**). Thus Petruchio agrees: 'And for that dowry I'll assure her of / Her widowhood, be it that she survive me, / In all my lands and leases whatsoever'. It seems that SHR exhibits a radical viewpoint less concerned about the feudal implications of land-holding than the monetary worth of property.

(C) For a history of early leases and later developments see Simpson, 1986, pp 247–55. This discusses the rise of husbandry leases as related to the beginnings of the evils of landlords' absenteeism. On playwrights' reflections of leasehold see Clarkson and Warren, 1942, pp 67–9.

leet Courts leet were the local courts of the hundreds (also see **sher-iff**) that met annually or semi-annually to examine minor criminal and civil disputes and to oversee the tithing system. By Shakespeare's time the system of leets was fragmented and these courts often privately held by lords of the manor (see Baker, 1990b, pp 29, 32, 33; Milsom, 1981 pp 15–16). Coke printed an idealized description of the operation of 'Leets ou Courts des Views de Frankpledge' in the preface of 9 Co. Rep. (Coke, 1826, vol 5, pp vii-viii). Among the points made are that

> every hundredor shall assemble once a year, and not only freeholders, but all of the hundred, as well strangers as denizens, from twelve years upwards [excepting] all religious people and Clerks, Earls, Barons, and Knights, married women, persons dumb and deaf, diseased, bastards and lepers, and those that are dezeiners elsewhere.

They were to enquire of 'offences personal . . . and to the Commonality', but 'not by bondmen or women, but by the oaths of twelve freeman at the least, for a bondman cannot indict a freeman'. In another context Coke argued that leets were 'courts of record' with powers to extract fines (see Thorne, 1985a, pp, 265–6; on the context of Coke on courts of record see under **audit/account**).

Christopher Sly begins the Induction of SHR mad-drunk and threatening to answer the Hostess's challenge 'by law'. Later he is told by one of his supposed servants that in the past fifteen years he had spoken none,

> but very idle words,
> For though you lay here in this goodly chamber
> Yet would you say ye were beaten out of door,
> And rail upon the hostess of the house,
> And say you would present her at the leet
> Because she brought stone jugs and no sealed quarts.
> (SHR Ind.2.82–7)

Leets would have been a place to complain of unsealed measures (as noted in Campbell, J., 1859, p 53), and they were courts appropriate to Sly's social standing (just as **Star Chamber**, threatened by Shallow at the start of WIV, was appropriate to his). The words that are said to be 'idle' (insignificant) of course actually hearken to Sly's lowly origins.

Having tempted Othello to ask for 'thy worst of thoughts', Iago cunningly says of his own 'vile and false' thinking that he would not utter it:

As where's that palace whereinto foul things
Sometimes intrude not? Who has that breast so pure
But some uncleanly apprehensions
Keep leets and law-days, and in sessions sit
With meditations lawful?

(OTH 3.3.142–6)

Here sitting in sessions at leets probably refers to the comprehensive composition of leet day meetings at which all sorts (with the exceptions mentioned above) attended. For further discussion of this context, see under **slave**.

legacy See **will**.

letters patents These are documents, usually issued by a king, recording agreements or grants of rights, offices or titles. Letters patents concerning rights to inherit property are withdrawn ('called in') by King Richard in R2 (on this and its illegality see **sue his livery**).

Likewise Henry VIII withdraws from Cardinal Wolsey the great seal of England, although Wolsey claims:

the King,
Mine and your master, with his own hand gave me,
Bade me enjoy it, with the place and honours,
During my life; and, to confirm his goodness,
Tied it by letters patents.

(AIT 3.2.247–51)

Letters patents, sealed with the great seal itself, express the royal will, which in some cases may be as easily revoked by will: the winner in AIT is Sir Thomas More (3.2.394–5).

Srigley, 1994 identifies as a direct reference to letters patents the obscure phrase concerning the players that Polonius reads aloud in HAM 2.2.402–3 (especially as in the second quarto): 'For the law of writ and the liberty, these are the only men'. Srigley first describes the letters patents issued to the King's Men on May 19, 1603 which granted 'unprecedented' privileges, dignity and status to the company. These

206

named one Lawrence Fletcher as well as Shakespeare, and in content recalled a similar licence granted to Fletcher in Scotland in 1599. Srigley proposes that the Scottish licence in turn echoes verbally Polonious' words. Following on from this, his article suggests that Shakespeare's company played HAM, and possibly even added local topical allusions to it, at Cambridge and Oxford in 1603.

See Bolton, 1988 on Ricardian law reports and Bolingbroke's letters patents. On connections that might have been drawn by Elizabethan audiences between letters patents and monopolies see Hexter, 1980.

libel/slander (A) The law relating to defamation was in a state of lively development in Shakespeare's time. The two terms 'libel' and 'slander' were not distinguished as they are now; either could arise from written or spoken words (Plucknett, 1956 p 490; Baker, 1990b, p 506). Indeed libels, according to Coke's report of the important case *De Libellis Famosis* (1605) 5 Co. Rep. 125a, could be *sine scriptus* and even be by pictures, signs (emblems) or lyrics sung (cited in Milsom, 1981, p 389). Moreover, varied actions in different tribunals could treat defamation as a tort (wrong) meriting recompense for damages, or a trespass (crime) meriting penance or punishment.

Local or Church courts heard most actions for defamation before 1500. Technically, in Church law, the *defamatus* was a person with a reputation that is so bad that it is an accusation of wrongdoing and he is tried; if acquitted those who have maliciously spread the false rumours and calumny 'among good and grave persons' are guilty of a crime and face excommunication (Plucknett, 1956, p 484). This clear-cut medieval definition and procedure ran up against problems. For instance, it could not deal with envious or greedy imputations against professional competence. Also, following *Circumspecte Agnis* (1285) the Church courts were protected from prohibitions from common law (see under **jurisdictions**) when punishing defamation as a sin, but were not protected if they allotted damages to victims. Milsom, 1981, p 381, describes how this limitation may have been unofficially circumvented.

The lack of opportunity for damages and for actions in defence of professional competence first brought cases for defamation to the king's courts in the period just before Shakespeare's time. Earlier, one special sort of defamation was dealt with by royal justice under a series of statutes beginning in 1275, defining an offence know as *Scandalum*

Magnatum. This 'slander of magnates' was the political and criminal offence of abusing the higher clergy or nobility, threatening the social order. The re-enactments of 1554 and 1559 made explicit that they were to counter 'sedition'. The offence could in theory be dealt with by **Justices of the Peace**, but in practice was often tried without reference to the statutes by the king's council in **Star Chamber** which inflicted punishments of mutilation. The common law courts tried civil damages arising from *Scandalum Magnatum*, and here 'defendants could not justify by claiming that the words were true' (Plucknett, 1956, p 486).

The common law gradually became more involved with defamation following a principle that Church courts could not try defamatory allegations of matters that were not themselves determined by the Church. The king's courts therefore, as early as the fifteenth century, heard complains of false imputations of **villeinage**. By Shakespeare's time four categories of use of defamatory words were admitted for trial in royal courts as actions **on the case**: accusations of **felonies** or lesser offences; accusations of professional incompetence; accusations of 'spiritual' matters such as **heresy** or adultery which resulted in temporal losses (where there was therefore a claim for 'special damages'); and imputations of the two specified diseases syphilis or leprosy (see Baker, 1990b, pp 497–500). There was a flood of such actions, which the common law courts attempted to restrain. Their most colourful means to do this was to apply the principle *in mitiori sensu* whereby defamatory words were construed in the mildest possible sense. So in in a 1599 the words 'pocky whore' were interpreted as possibly meaning small pox, so not actionable (ibid., pp 501–3 provides this and more absurd examples).

Slanders alleging that common law crimes had been committed possessed some interesting qualities. Plucknett, 1956, p 493, explains that the crimes alleged in this type of slander were usually of a sort where insulting words were also likely to be used, so that 'it was almost common form when counting on an assault and battery to add allegations of insult too'. A further peculiarity of actions for slander in which a common law crime was imputed was that these 'retained as a relic of their early association with trespass the rule that damages were at large, and this in spite of the fact that actions **on the case** were normally actions for special damages' (ibid.).

(B) The word 'slander' and its derivatives appear in most of Shakespeare's plays and in all of his groups of poems. There are fewer

208

instances of the word 'libel' in Shakespeare's plays, but as the two concepts are not wholly distinct for his age, both terms for defamation will be treated here.

The word 'slander' has its root in common with 'scandal'. Therefore, in some of Shakespeare's uses the reputation of an agent suffers from a 'slander' caused by his own actions, and not initiated by an envious or malevolent other. Thus Antipholus of Ephesus is warned not to break down the door of his own house in broad daylight:

> If by strong hand you offer to break in
> Now in the stirring passage of the day,
> A vulgar comment will be made of it,
> And that supposed by the common rout
> Against your yet ungalled estimation,
> That may with foul intrusion enter in
> And dwell upon your grave when you are dead.
> For slander lives upon succession,
> For ever housed where once it gets possession.
> (ERR 3.1.99–107)

This warning uses **land** law imagery to indicate that scandal may gain a kind of **fee-simple** freehold **tenure** on reputation very hard to dispossess.

Because 'slander could mean 'scandal', it could refer to a merited, as well as an unmerited, disgrace (OED slander n. 3 & 4 and v. 1 & 2). The early modern courts held that even a truthful condemnation (or allegation of bad reputation) made by a private party could be slander, on the principle that 'a grievance should be addressed by law, and not by the party himself using force, or circulating extra-judicial accusations' (Plucknett, 1956, p 490 thinks this a view post 1605; Baker, 1990b, p 506, holds that it was 'exploded' post Henry VIII; Helmholz, 1990, pp 64–5 doubts that even Church courts accepted truth as a defence against defamation). Correspondingly, 'slanders' which are truthful, or believed to be, are named in: ERR 4.4.68; R3 3.3.12; R2 1.1.61 and 1.1.113; AYL 4.1.58; HAM 1.3.133 and 2.2.199; ADO 2.3.44 and 3.1.84; MM 1.3.43 and 2.4.111; CYM 1.1.72, 2.5.26 and 3.5.76.

Nevertheless in Roman law, common law, English **statute**, and most usually for Shakespeare himself, a slander is an malicious lie or calumny.

Thus Juliet proposes 'That is no slander, sir, which is a truth' (ROM 4.1.33). This particular meaning of 'slander', requiring a falsehood, often appears even in plays where the same word has another meaning.

Slander is confused with another personal affront that is legally actionable when Constable Elbow mistakes Pompey's word 'respected' for '[carnally] suspected' and he blurts out:

> If ever I was respected with her [his wife], or she with me, let not your worship think me the poor Duke's officer. Prove this, thou wicked Hannibal, or I'll have mine action of battery on thee.

To this double malapropism bemused Justice Escalus adds 'If he took you a box o' th' ear you might have your action of slander too' (MM 2.1.170–5). Yet Elbow is not entirely daft; the very frequent actual conjunction of actions for slander with disorderly 'trespasses to the person', as noted above, might have amused lawyers, or those familiar with typical courtroom occurrences, in the audience.

Again in an angry context the vain Cloten sputters threats after being named by Imogen as less worthy than Posthumus or even 'His meanest garment'. She replies 'Ay, I said so, sir. / If you will make 't an action, call witness to 't.' (CYM 2.3.129–48).

Although the word 'libel' derives from 'little book', **Star Chamber** explicitly concluded that libels 'could lie as much in speech as in writing' (Milsom, 1981, p 390, which adds that the court was nonetheless preoccupied with writing). In fact, only one of Shakespeare's three 'libels' is apparently verbal.

Titus Andronicus, feigning madness, publishes (by most ingenious means) written complaints against the justice of the state and its rulers. Saturninus protests:

> And now he writes to heaven for his redress.
> See, here's 'to Jove' and this 'to Mercury',
> This 'to Apollo', this 'to the god of war' –
> Sweet scrolls to fly about the streets of Rome!
> What's this but libelling against the Senate
> And blazoning our unjustice everywhere?
> A goodly humour, is it not, my lords? –
> As who would say, in Rome no justice were.
>
> (TIT 4.4.13–20)

Similar seditious acts in Shakespeare's time were sometimes punished in Star Chamber by severing of hands (but Titus has himself already severed his hand).

Richard of Gloucester boasts in soliloquy that he has covertly arranged a smear campaign against his brother George:

> And therefore since I cannot prove a lover
> To entertain these fair well-spoken days,
> I am determined to prove a villain
> And hate the idle pleasures of these days.
> Plots have I laid, inductions dangerous,
> By drunken prophecies, libels and dreams
> To set my brother Clarence and the King
> In deadly hate the one against the other.
> And if King Edward be as true and just
> As I am subtle false and treacherous,
> This day should Clarence closely be mewed up
> About a prophecy which says that 'G'
> Of Edward's heirs the murderer shall be.
>
> (R3 1.1.28–40)

The malice boasted here is matched by covert cunning. In like cases investigated by Star Chamber, the anonymity of the source of a libel became of particular interest, exacerbating the offence (Milsom, 1981, p 390).

The 'libels' mentioned by Palamon in his prayer are wittily obscene writings, such as were widely circulated in Shakespeare's England. Claiming purity, Palamon says to Venus:

> I have never been foul-mouthed against thy law;
> Ne'er revealed secret, for I knew none; would not,
> Had I kenned all that were. I never practised
> Upon man's wife, nor would the libels read
> Of liberal wits. I never at great feasts
> Sought to betray a beauty, but have blushed
> At simp'ring sirs that did. I have been harsh
> To large confessors, and have hotly asked them
> If they had mothers – I had one, a woman,
> And women 'twere they wronged.
>
> (TNK 5.2.30–9)

211

Here defamation appears in the form of misogyny.

(C) On the relations of Church courts and royal courts concerning defamation see Helmholz, 1990, pp 51 and 56–69, and Helmholz, 1987b, pp 9–12. On **Star Chamber** on sedition and libel (which it never clearly differentiated) see Barnes, 1977. On common law damages for slander see under **on the case**, and see Helmholz, 1987e. On a rise in early modern Church court cases for sexual slander see Sharpe, J. A., 1980 and Ingram, 1987 pp 292–319. Gowing, 1996 interprets the detailed content of such slander.

Slander in MM (some of which is seditious) is treated in Kaplan, 1990.

Widmayer, 1995, especially pp 192–4, finds an aim to protect reputation and in particular avoid sexual slander in MM in accord with particular social and legal trends of Shakespeare's age.

Sexual slander against a woman in ADO is treated in Cerasano, 1992, and in WT in Kaplan and Eggert, 1994.

lists (A) The lists were places appointed for trial by battle. Trial by battle, also called 'judicial combat' or 'wager of battle', was one of the early methods of proof by ordeal used to decide the outcome of trials in early medieval England. Other early customary methods of proof included ordeal by iron or by water, and 'wager of law', which was proof by the oath of compurgators (see **jury** and **debt**). These latter ancient methods of proof are thought to predate the introduction of Christianity, but the Normans brought trial by battle with them from Normandy in 1066. At first its use was reserved only to Normans, but it eventually spread to the English.

These early methods of proof did not take account of factual evidence. In criminal cases guilt or innocence was decided by reference to the supernatural: God judged rightness or wrongness and his decision was revealed in the outcome of the ordeal. Some have thought this too simplistic an explanation because studies of thirteenth century French custom indicate that the defendant could argue an 'exception' to the accusation (that the actions did not constitute the wrongdoing charged), even in trials using customary methods of proof (Brand, 1992, p 4). In 1215, at the Fourth Lateran Council, Pope Innocent III prohibited priestly involvement in ordeals because of objections to tempting God.

212

As a result all ordeals were abandoned as a method of proof except for trial by battle, which did not have priestly involvement as an essential ingredient. Trial by battle remained possible until 1819, when it was finally abolished by statute (59 Geo. 3, c.46). However by the seventeenth century battle was very rare.

Trial by battle was allowed by law in three different circumstances. Firstly, it was used to try disputes over ownership of land commenced by service of a Writ of Right. Secondly, it was used in **appeals** (private prosecutions) which by Shakespeare's time could only be criminal. Lastly, chivalric battles, a formalised exercise similar to jousting, took place in the Constable and Marshal's Court.

Most litigants in cases of civil appeal did not themselves fight, but employed champions who were professional fighters, to do battle on their behalf. But if the case was a criminal appeal then a hired champion was not allowed and the parties had to fight in person or by some other appropriate person, such as a relative. However, some cases show the appellee offering to fight either 'by his own body' or by his freeman, or even his servants, which seems arguably very similar to providing a hired champion.

Battle following issue of a Writ of Right was not allowed at all between **co-heirs**, or those related by the whole blood. If one party did not want to risk battle he had to leave court immediately before battle was offered. Otherwise he had to be able to produce his champion rapidly, because once battle had been pledged in court then arrangements about date and venue would be made.

There were detailed rules for the steps to be taken at each stage in the preliminaries to the battle. The presiding judge appointed knights to act as masters of ceremony, or 'keepers of the field'. These knights arranged for the oaths to be taken by the combatants, and supervised the proper conduct of the battle. The combatants or their champions in civil battles took oaths against employing sorcery to help them, and sometimes seemed to swear not to eat or drink. They were shaved and anointed and received absolution.

Any kind of interference with the battle was severely punished (for this and other details of arrangements see *Lowe v Paramour* (1571) Dyer 301A). For interference with battles in the Constable and Marshal's Court, punishment was loss of life or limb, or forfeiture. One man who had assisted his brother in a battle abjured the realm (see

213

sanctuary) for 12 years until he was **pardoned**, because of his fear of the penalties he would otherwise face (Russell, 1980a, p 115).

Cases also provide details of the arena used for the fight. The ground should be a level area of 20 square yards covered with gravel, sand and rushes. There should be a raised dais for the judges, with a **bar** for the **serjeants**-at-law (on these see under **lawyers** and **justices**). There were detailed rules about the positions to be taken by the combatants on the field of battle. If the offence was one punishable by death then the fight was to the death. The fight could be on horseback or on foot, and the fight could be with swords or by batons, which were presumably stout wooden staves. In London most battles were fought at Tothill Fields, now partly covered by Vincent Square SW1, while many chivalric battles took place at Smithfield.

A trial by battle following a criminal appeal of **felony** was brought by the victim, or nearest family if the victim was dead. Appealable crimes included **treason**, **homicide**, **robbery**, assault and **battery**, **rape**, and larceny. Once the appeal was brought, the defendant could ask for trial by battle and the appellor could be imprisoned if he refused the defendant's request. In general, as women were prevented from fighting they were not allowed to bring appeals of felony except for murder and rape (see **appeal**), but otherwise the rules for criminal trial by battle did allow fights between near relatives. The rules did not allow battle between people of different social rank, as between a lord and his tenant, or a master and his servant, unless the case was one of **treason**. Battle was also prohibited between Christians and Jews, or if any party was infirm, under 14 or over 60 years old, or female. In Wales for some extraordinary reason twins were said to count as one person, so an appellor could in theory face two opponents in battle.

Battles were sometimes terminated by agreement reached by the parties at the field itself, even during the fight. Such an agreement was regarded as binding on both parties, and a payment was made to the crown. If no settlement was reached, the fight could be halted at any stage if a combatant cried 'craven', meaning he craved his life, but this was considered a disgraceful thing to do.

By Shakespeare's time, although judicial combat was not obsolete, no battle for a civil case had probably taken place since the fourteenth century. The last battle in a criminal case that was actually fought was *Whitehorn v Fisher* in 1456. Therefore the case of *Lowe v Paramour* in 1571, (a case of disputed title to land where the tenant called for trial by battle), caused contemporary astonishment and much antiquarian interest. The dispute was settled with personal help from Queen Elizabeth before the date set for the battle, but nevertheless a token fight took place on the appointed day with great ceremony. The champions were preceded onto the field by a band of fifes and drums and the event took place before the Lord **Chief Justice** and other judges. After the exchange of a few token blows, stage-managed to satisfy the great public interest, the crowd 'dispersed shouting "Long live the Queen"' (Russell, 1980a, p 127).

(B) Challenges followed by actual trials by battle feature in: CYL 1.3.27–39, 1.3.180–226 and 2.3.59–109; much of R2 1.1 and 1.3; LRF 5.3.83–145 (LRQ S.24.80–150). Unfulfilled challenges to such battles, all following charges of having treasonous ancestry or being a 'traitor', are found in 1H6 2.4.96–8, PER S.9.51–3 and TMP 1.2.467–76 (see **treason** and **appeal**). A parodic challenge to battle in SHR 4.3.143–50 is discussed under **bills**. The terms 'lists' or 'royal lists' with reference to the place assigned for an actual trial by battle appear in CYL 2.3.47–55, R2 1.2.44–52 and 1.3.26–45, and appear in more figurative contexts concerning a chivalric battle in 1H6 5.7.31–3 and an erotic enterprise in PER S.1 104–6. Challenges to a chivalric trial by battle over factional allegiances arise in 1H6 3.8.28-45, and are suppressed by the king in 4.1.78–194. A factional dispute and 'attainder' over the killing of Woodstock erupts at the moment of Bolingbroke's triumph (R2 4.1.7–97), but the resulting challenges of multiple 'appellants' to do battle are ordered by him to 'rest under gage / Till we assign you to your days of trial' (4.1.95–7). In the event several of those accused enter into a rebellion and are defeated, preventing the trial.

The limitations on the use of a champion in an **appeal** of **treason** described above might seem to validate Goneril's claim, made when Edmund is defeated by the disguised Edgar in a trial by battle: 'By th' law of arms thou wast not bound to answer / An unknown opposite. Thou art not vanquished, / But cozened and beguiled.' (LRF 5.3.143–5, and nearly LRQ S.24.148–50). However, the disguised 'champion' (LRF 5.1.33, LRQ S.22.45) produced to prove Edgar's appeal is Edgar himself, who has moreover given Albany a paper proving Edmund's guilt. So when the masked champion is revealed he is seen to be both worthy and an injured party: as Edgar says of himself, 'no less in blood than thou art, Edmund. / If more, the more thou'st wronged me' (LRF

5.3.158–9; similarly LRQ S.24.163–4). Interestingly, in these words Edgar allows Edmund a degree of equality, and also rights to chivalry, although according to contemporary treatises cited in Elton, W. R., 1966, pp 132–3, Edmund as a **bastard** should have been barred from trial by combat. (But otherwise, as noted above, there was no bar to judicial combat between near relatives.)

CYL contains a trial by battle on an **appeal** of treason between an **apprentice** Peter Thumpe and his master, the armourer Thomas Horner. This is made complex by the implicit petty treason (see under **treason**) in the public disclosure of the private if treasonous words of a master by his apprentice (on the socio-political implications of betrayal by a household member see Bernthal, 1991). Yet, as noted above, in an exception to the general rule, unequals could fight in an appeal of treason.

In the event the feeble and fearful-seeming Thumpe (CYL 2.3.56–7) is able to defeat the stronger-seeming Horner; it is left ambiguous whether divine intervention, or Horner's excessive quaffing, is the main cause of the outcome. The weapons allowed in the 'lists and all things fit' (2.3.54) are a version of batons, not weapons of chivalry. (The folio stage direction, tln 1118–19, says Horner's are: 'his Staffe, with a Sand-bagge fastened to it'.) The combatants, although unequal, are both men positioned to 'scour . . . armour' (CYL 1.3.195), not to use it.

Differences of the treatments in CYL and in its sources of an historical trial by battle between an armourer and his apprentice, and CYL's representation of political machinations lying behind a court faction's interest in the battle, are among matters well-discussed in Bernthal, 1991.

Bornstein, 1976 argues that humanistic objections to trial by combat confronted a cult of chivalry in Shakespeare's time, and that Shakespeare implied his sympathy with the former. It is true that some satire on fashionable swordplay features in comedies such as AYL and TN, and a more serious critique of a cult of honour is implicit in 1H4 and COR. But the ceremonious chivalry seen at Simonides' court (PER S.6-S.7) is not disparaged, and the values of Hotspur and even Coriolanus are given mixed treatment. Although, as noted under **appeal**, there were objections to private prosecutions that could lead to trials by battle, adverse views did not extend to ceremonial tilting, which continued at court. Chivalric exercises were particularly evident at the celebration in 1613 of the tenth anniversary of James I's accession (on

Shakespeare's personal involvement with these see Chambers, 1930, vol 2, p 153, and the comment in Sokol, 1994a, p 20).

It is often noted that the trial by battle that fails to be fought between Bolingbroke and Mowbray is crucial for R2. A few details may be highlighted. In Shakespeare's play the Marshal protects the lists in accordance with the laws (R2 1.3.42–5), farewell speeches are made, and all attention is focused on the combatants. At this point Richard suddenly stops the fight (1.3.118), drawing all the attention to himself. According to Gohn, 1982, p 947, in doing this he acted within his rights. Yet as Mowbray was his agent (see under **murder**) in the death of Woodstock, perhaps he feared exposure in the trial; also, Richard seemingly loves the limelight, which he effectively gains by stopping the fight before it begins.

As noted above, Queen Elizabeth did not deny her public a spectacle of a fight in the lists of 1571. Unlike Richard in 1398, she allowed the public the pleasure of a stirring event. Yet, childless like him, she did once compare herself with Richard II. She is recorded by the lawyer William Lambard (on whom see Dunkel, 1965, **constable**, **equity**, **Justice of the Peace**, and **pardon**) to have said: 'I am Richard II, know you not that? . . . this tragedy was played 40 times in open street and houses' (see Schoenbaum, 1986, pp 217–19). Elizabeth's remark has often been taken to refer to Shakespeare's play R2, and the bribing of Shakespeare's company to perform R2 on the day of the Essex rebellion.

(C) See Plucknett, 1956, pp 113–20, 417–18; Milsom, 1981, p 4–5, 130–1, 285–6; Baker, 1978, p 116; Baker, 1990b, pp 85-8; Russell, 1980a; Russell, 1980b; Russell, 1985.

Gohn, 1982, pp 946n and 961–4, maintains that Shakespeare was accurate historically in R2 when portraying the Court of the Constable and the Marshal, in which **homicides** and **treasons** allegedly committed abroad (as alleged against Mowbray) were tried by combat. However, as Plucknett, 1956, p 205, and Bellamy, 1970, p 145, make clear, the restriction of the Court of the Constable and the Marshal to try treasons committed abroad was enacted just after the time of Richard, by 1 Hen. IV, c. 19.

On the various trials by combat in Shakespeare see Keeton, 1930, pp 170–82, and Edelman, 1992, pp 146–58. On the trial between Thumpe and Horner see Bernthal, 1991 and Levine, N., 1994. On trials by combat in R2 see: Bornstein, 1976; Ranald, 1987, pp 201–2 (which cites Bracton); Bolton, 1988 (which disputes Bornstein).

Keeton, 1967, pp, 31–2, finds in SON 46 a reference to trial by battle in real (**land**) actions, an assessment which is doubted in Simon, 1968b, pp 34–5.

manslaughter The legal distinctions between murder and manslaughter, which were different in Shakespeare's time than in ours, and were changing then, are described under **murder/homicide**. One of the factors that could make killing more excusable was if it happened in 'chance medley', which was a killing which took place in the heat of a quarrel. This could result in the defendant taking **sanctuary** followed by abjuration (self-**banishment**), or in a grant of pardon, or a claim for benefit of clergy (see **branded**).

The distinction of 'chance medley' is implicit in the limited punishment allotted Romeo for killing Tybalt. Despite having promised death to street brawlers (ROM 1.1.93–4), the Prince only **outlaws** and '**exiles**' Romeo, although saying 'Mercy but murders, pardoning those that kill' (ROM 3.1.185–96). This mitigation of the death sentence is later revealed to Romeo:

ROMEO	What less than doomsday is the Prince's doom?
FRIAR LAURENCE	A gentler judgement vanished from his lips:
	Not body's death, but body's banishment.

(3.3.9–11).

Romeo did not seek this; but mitigation of homicide by self-defence is deliberately sought by hot blooded Capulet servants who frown or bite their thumb at passing Montague men in order to provoke them to violence, saying 'Let us take the law of our side. Let them begin' (ROM 1.1.37).

Alcibiades argues that acting in 'hot blood' should excuse a killing, particularly by a soldier. But what Elizabethans called chance medley is not acceptable to an Athenian senator, who replies to Alcibiades' plea for mercy for his friend with:

> Your words have took such pains as if they laboured
> To bring manslaughter into form, and set quarrelling
> Upon the head of valour – which indeed
> Is valour misbegot, and came into the world
> When sects and factions were newly born.
> He's truly valiant that can wisely suffer
> The worst that man can breathe, and make his wrongs his outsides
> To wear them like his raiment carelessly,
> And ne'er prefer his injuries to his heart
> To bring it into danger.
>
> (TIM 3.6.26–35)

The mention of 'The worst that man can breathe' seems premonitory of an English legal position dated to 1666, that words alone are not sufficient provocation to reduce murder to manslaughter (cited in Holdsworth, 1903, vol 8, p 303).

marriage (A) Questions of marriage and its consequences appear in every Shakespeare play. This section will look mainly at the economic and socio-legal consequences of marriage. Other aspects of the law of marriage, formation and dissolution, are treated elsewhere. These are indicated here briefly. Provided there were no **impediments**, then making a marriage valid in law in early modern England required only the consent of the two parties to the marriage. Making a valid marriage is discussed under **pre-contract** (see also **spousal**). Marriages were ended by death (see **ward** and **heir**), or could be terminated very exceptionally by **divorce** or annulment. Property settlements were often arranged in advance of marriage after negotiations between the parties, their families and friends. Consideration of the woman's **portion** on marriage or marriage settlements for the couple (see **dowry** and **jointure**), were matters of social custom as well as private legal arrangements between the parties and their families, but a **widow's** right to **dower** was regulated by law.

When a man and woman entered into a valid contract of marriage, certain legal consequences followed. The most significant was the effect of the doctrine of the unity of the person, which held that husband and wife were one person in law. In practice that person was the husband. Legal, religious, and popular ideas accepted the concept of patriarchal authority which regulated the relations between individual family members and between the family and the outside world.

In law, an unmarried woman was known as a '*feme sole*'. She could **purchase**, hold and alienate property, and enter into contracts in her own name. But once married she became a '*feme covert*', which had consequences on property rights, in contractual relations, and in criminal law. A wife could not make contracts in her own name, although she could enter into contracts as the agent of her husband. She could not sue or be sued in her own name. Yet the principle of 'one person' was not wholly consistent: she was not liable for her husband's **debts**, neither was she liable for his crimes. Moreover, in criminal law a woman's capacity to commit any crime and therefore her criminal liability was not affected by marriage. A husband was not liable for his wife's crimes, although courts were willing to presume the wife had been coerced by the husband if her crimes were committed at his command. It is thought that this was a response to the court's inability to allow a woman to plead benefit of clergy (see **branded**).

The wife was subject to the husband's guardianship and authority, for he was her *baron* or lord. Therefore if she killed her husband she was guilty of the serious **felony** of petty **treason**. For this the punishment was burning to death, whereas if a man killed his wife then the less cruel punishment for **murder** applied, which was to be hanged.

There was no concept of community of ownership of property between husband and wife in England in Shakespeare's time, although such a system of community did exist in some other parts of Western Europe, and may have existed to a certain extent in England in the earlier Middle Ages. On marriage a woman had no legal interest in any matrimonial property. Therefore the legal status of a married woman differed considerably from that of an unmarried woman. The married woman was not dead in law, like a member of a religious order, and she did not suffer from a general lack of legal capacity, but she lacked the capacity to own property in her own name. Any personal property she owned vested absolutely in her husband, and he could deal with it as he wished. This included money, furniture, jewellery and clothing. This notion was taken to its logical limits, so that for example a husband could not in law make a gift of any personal property to his wife during the marriage; this would be giving to himself. If a wife was convicted of a **felony** then no note was taken of **chattels** she might own for the purposes of forfeiture, because she was presumed to own none (see Holdsworth, 1903, vol 3, p 527). As a wife could not own personal property, she did not have the right to make a **will**. This last theoretical disability on married women met with resistance from the Church courts who had **jurisdiction** over the administration of the estates of personal property, and over intestate estates. Roman law had allowed married women testamentary freedom and canon lawyers were anxious to defend a wife's rights because of the theory of merit and grace in almsgiving. A 'final gift of alms' in a will was particularly encouraged by the church, and in practice it seems that married women did leave personal property in wills which the Church courts administered, and that husbands did not object (see Sheehan, 1996, pp 26 and 28). However Helmholz, 1993 concludes, p 175, that married women's testaments become rare after 1450.

This regime for a woman's personal property was subject to exceptions in certain parts of the country, where borough custom in some towns allowed a woman to hold property, and to leave property by will. So the customs of London allowed women to hold property and trade in their own names. But in general even a woman's earnings were her husband's property, although by the end of the seventeenth century the **equity** Court of Chancery allowed a wife to save 'pin money' (money for personal spending), for her own use.

Any real property (land) belonging to the woman also vested in her husband during marriage. But unlike personal property, a wife's real property did not vest in her husband absolutely. During the marriage he had 'seisin' (see **land**) and was entitled to all profits from the property, but he was not free to alienate the wife's land without her consent. If he did so, the widow or her heir may have been able to recover it after the husband's death.

Because her real property vested in her husband, a woman could not alienate her own land during marriage without her husband's consent. If they did agree to sell land, a husband and wife together would levy a **fine** in the Court of Common Pleas, which was a settlement of fictitious suit at law, the agreement being recorded in court as a 'final concord'. In such cases the judge was supposed to question the wife alone to ensure her agreement to alienate was genuine and not forced by the husband. This process was also effective to bar **dower**, for she would be asked if in her free will she resigned her rights to dower in the land sold (Plucknett, 1956, pp 567 and 568). The adequacy of safeguards in such a practice seems open to question.

By Shakespeare's time the equity jurisdiction in the Court of Chancery allowed property to be held in trust for a woman's own separate use, and such property was not subject to the doctrine of *coverture*. By the end of the middle ages **uses** in favour of married women were upheld by Chancery, and some years after the Statute of Uses Chancery upheld similar devices called 'trusts' protecting wives' separate property. However such an arrangement was vulnerable to the danger that a wife might be prevailed upon to agree to alienate her trust property to her husband, or for his benefit. Therefore a clause known as a 'restraint on anticipation' was often inserted in deeds settling property on married women which prevented them from alienating. This worked by postponing a wife's absolute interest in the property until such time as she was **widowed**. If she attempted to alienate before then the estate was forfeited, which would act as a deterrent. But although such clauses were common after 1800 it is not known how much they were in use before then.

An unsettled question is whether marriages by *verba de praesenti* only, or indeed those marriages without full church ceremony (see **precontract**), avoided the disabilities and cancelled any benefit to women from *coverture*. Swinburne, 1686, claimed (p. 108) that such a marriage brought with it none of the legal consequences of coverture respecting property:

> Albeit they that do Contract Spousals *de praesenti*, be very Husband and Wife, in respect of the Knot or Bond of Matrimony . . . ; yet do not these Spousals produce all the same effects here in *England*, which Matrimony solemnized in the face of the Church doth, whether we respect the Legitimization of their Children, or the Property which the Husband hath in the Wife's Goods, or the Dower which she is to have in his Lands.

Elsewhere Swinburne draws a parallel between the difference in treatment accorded by ecclesiastical and common law courts to **bastards** and on a *de praesenti* only marriage. He claims that at common law 'no more is [a wife by spousal contract alone] to have any Dower of the same Lands . . . because as yet, she is not his lawful Wife, at least to that effect' (Ibid., pp 233–4.

Whether Swinburne is correct on English law is open to doubt. He certainly made a strong case by claiming that although it was formerly held otherwise, in the present a man can make 'a Feoffment' to such a wife which is in common law 'good, as being made, not unto his Wife, but unto a single Woman, and another Person in Law'. Even more strangely, because ecclesiastical law governed married women's **chattels**, he continued (pp. 234–5): 'Concerning Goods, the like may be said of them as hath already be spoken of Lands', stating this was a difference between 'Civil and Canon Laws' and 'the law of this Realm'. He also alleged that a women in such a marriage may make her own will (which a *feme covert* could not), but if her husband died intestate she 'cannot obtain the *Administration* of his Goods'.

Such absolute statements are sometimes incorrectly summarized by the simple claim that the common law did not recognize a spousal *de praesenti* as a marriage. Pollock and Maitland, 1898, vol 2, pp 383–5, makes it clear that this was not the case, but points out the problem that 'a marriage might easily exist and yet be unprovable'. To determine even if an unsolemnized marriage, although valid, was 'no marriage for purely possessory purposes' (as proposed in ibid., p 384), requires evidence which is extremely difficult to obtain. Marriages involving families or individuals with substantial property were inevitably preceded by lengthy negotiations often involving detailed complex conditions (see Smith, R. M., 1986, pp 66–7). Agreements reached were secured by the use of trusts, **bonds**, **jointures**, etc. Because such matters were settled in advance of marriage, in writing ('Let specialties be therefore drawn between us, / That covenants may be kept on either hand' (SHR 2.1.126–7)), there was not much subsequent litigation.

Moreover, even if common law courts did show a 'theoretical preference' for solemnized marriages, it is not certain that local manorial courts did the same (ibid., p, 65). There are some early dower and inheritance cases involving land in which a **pre-contracted** marriage prevailed over a marriage in the face of the church (ibid., pp 59–60). The inheritance rights of children of unsolemnized marriages were upheld by Bracton and Glanville, and in early case law (p. 62). There is disagreement among historians concerning a wife's rights of dower following an unsolemnized marriage; see under **dower**.

(B) According to the teachings of the church, man and wife were one flesh, and this was taken to give dominance to the man. Popular homilies and conduct books stressed the husband's role as governor in the house, likening it to the status of a king. His wife, children and household servants had a corresponding duty to submit to this authority (see Ingram, 1987, p 143).

The doctrine of 'one person' in a marriage, that person being the husband, is parodied in Pompey's quibbling reply to the Provost's 'Can you cut off a man's head': 'If the man be a bachelor, sir, I can; but if he be a married man, he's his wife's head, and I can never cut off a woman's head' (MM 4.2.1–5). It is more passionately expressed in ERR 2.2.122–32, where Adriana complains:

> How comes it now, my husband, O how comes it
> That thou art then estranged from thyself? –
> Thy 'self' I call it, being strange to me
> That, undividable, incorporate,
> Am better than thy dear self's better part.
> Ah, do not tear away thyself from me;
> For know, my love, as easy mayst thou fall
> A drop of water in the breaking gulf,
> And take unmingled thence that drop again
> Without addition or diminishing,
> As take from me thyself, and not me too.

The doctrine of *coverture* is rehearsed at the **contracting** of Portia with Bassanio, when she avers:

> But the full sum of me
> Is sum of something which, to term in gross,
> Is an unlessoned girl, unschooled, unpractised,
> Happy in this, she is not yet so old
> But she may learn; happier than this,
> She is not bred so dull but she can learn;
> Happiest of all is that her gentle spirit
> Commits itself to yours to be directed
> As from her lord, her governor, her king.
> Myself and what is mine to you and yours
> Is now converted. But now I was the lord

> Of this fair mansion, master of my servants,
> Queen o'er myself; and even now, but now,
> This house, these servants, and this same myself
> Are yours, my lord's. I give them with this ring.
>
> (MV 3.2.157–71)

However, she immediately makes a condition that the ring be protected absolutely or else it will 'be my vantage to exclaim on you'. As she will scheme to overturn Bassanio's pledge to keep the ring, it is uncertain just how 'unschooled' she will prove.

Claiming in effect that persons incorporated as 'one' must not be of two minds, Portia of JC insists on knowing her husband Brutus's business:

> You have some sick offence within your mind,
> Which by the right and virtue of my place
> I ought to know of. And upon my knees,
> I charm you by my once-commended beauty,
> By all your vows of love, and that great vow
> Which did incorporate and make us one,
> That you unfold to me, your self, your half,
> Why you are heavy, and what men tonight
> Have had resort to you – for here have been
> Some six or seven, who did hide their faces
> Even from darkness.
>
> (JC 2.1.267–77)

The burden of this plea is implicitly denied in Macbeth's 'Be innocent of the knowledge, dearest chuck' (MAC 3.2.46).

The transfers of property preceding marriages are realistically shown to be matters of complex negotiation for instance in SHR, AWW and H5. Not so in MV where the transfer is absolutely to the husband without limit or conditions, as noted above. The only preliminary to the mutual spousal contract called in MV 3.2.193 'the bargain of [their] faith' is the gift of a ring, and perhaps the scroll's suggested 'loving kiss' (3.2.138). (On how such expressions of intent may suffice to make a marriage see under **pre-contract**). Then Portia tells Bassanio that he is lord of all that she possesses. It is not sure if this immediate all-giving is a poetic feature of fabulous and romantic Belmont. It could be a recognition that spousals alone (without further ceremony or sexual consummation) conferred on husbands 'one person' property rights, despite Swinburne's demurs noted above.

The marriage of Posthumus and Imogen is accepted as complete by themselves and others, as detailed under **divorce**; for example in CYM 2.5.7 even in anger Posthumus calls her a 'wife'. Yet CYM 2.5.9–13 indicates that this marriage has not been consummated; for a possible explanation see Barton, A., 1994, pp 3–30.

(C) On the legal consequences of marriage see: Swinburne, 1686 and notes on this in Derrett, 1973 and Baker, 1993; Pollock and Maitland, 1898, vol 2, pp 364–436; Holdsworth, 1903, vol 3, pp 520–33; Baker, 1990b, pp 545–57; Carlson, E. J., 1994. See also Ingram, 1985, pp 141–5; Smith, R. M., 1986; Laurence, 1994, pp 228–30, 234–5; Outhwaite, 1995; Helmholz, 1993; Sheehan, 1996, pp 20, 25, 26–8, 186–93.

English social historians generally challenge earlier theories in Stone, 1979b of sixteenth century patriarchal tyranny ruling over unaffectionate households. See: Macfarlane, 1979; Laslett, 1983, pp 119–20; Ingram, 1987, pp 143–4; Wrightson, 1982, pp, 106–18; and Cook, 1991, pp 12–13. Stone, 1993, p 15, remarking on sixteenth-century Englishwomen's training to 'postures' of 'total submission' shows little retreat.

Outhwaite, 1981 contains a useful survey of work on marriage and society, identifying many areas of incomplete knowledge, and poses a series of provocative questions relating to claims made in Stone, 1979b.

mercy See **pardon/clemency**.

mortgage (A) At common law a mortgage was a pledge of land as security for borrowing. The **debt** was secured by the transfer of real property, either fee simple or lease, (see **conveyancing**) from the borrower to the lender. If the borrower repaid the debt on the agreed date, the redemption day, then by means of a covenant in the agreement he had a right to re-enter the land. Later, during the sixteenth century covenants were made agreeing re-conveyance to the borrower. This arrangement allowed creditors to claim against debtors' lands, normally prohibited at common law (see under **usury/interest**). Also by the sixteenth century the recognition that the mortgage was a security for a debt and not an estate in the land meant that the borrower was allowed to remain in possession of the land unless he defaulted in payment.

In Shakespeare's time the Court of Chancery began to intervene on the borrower's behalf and prevented the borrower from loss of his property in certain circumstances, for example if the date of redemption was missed and payment was made late. However the development of 'the equity of redemption', the borrower's right to redeem, took place after Shakespeare's time at the end of the seventeenth century.

(B) A 'mortgage' is mentioned by Shakespeare only in SON 134, where it is referenced figuratively in a context dominated by the language of **debt**. The sonnet includes also mentions of **bonds**, **usury**, and **statutes** merchant or staple.

(C) See Simpson, 1986, pp 242–7. See also: Holdsworth, 1903, vol. 3, pp 128–31, Plucknett, 1956, pp 603–8; Baker, 1990b, pp 353–6. On claimed 'equity of redemption' and MV see Andrews, 1965 p. 65.

murder/homicide (A) The term 'homicide' covered all kinds of felonious or non felonious killing (see **felony**; Shakespeare also used 'a homicide' to refer to the killer as well as the offence – see under **homicide**). The modern law of homicide, which clearly distinguishes between serious and less serious forms of killing, developed from procedural changes introduced into criminal trials in the sixteenth century.

In Anglo-Saxon and early Norman England capital punishment was reserved for those who killed 'by stealth'. After the Conquest, William I imposed a heavy murder fine or *murdrum* on the community for any Norman (but not Englishman) found unaccountably dead in the neighbourhood. The fine could be avoided by 'presentment of Englishry', which was proof that the victim was English. The amercement of a community for a murder gradually went out of use, and it was abolished in 1340.

The notion of murder as stealthy killing incorporated deliberate killing by ambush or by poisoning. Such evil killings, or murders, were considered incapable of remedy: they were 'bootless' crimes and the killers were hanged. But other forms of killing (accidental killings or killings in sudden quarrels) were punished by a system of compensation payments made to families of the victim by the killer or his family.

Primitive vengeance for killing, in the style of the blood feud (as in TIT and HAM), was reflected in both the prosecution of murder by **appeal** of felony and in the deodand; both had an ancient history but were still in use in Shakespeare's England. The deodand was an animal or inanimate **chattel** that had inadvertently caused death, which was seized and confiscated by the Crown. The appeal of felony, the right of the next of kin to pursue the killer by means of a private prosecution, remained an important alternative to indictment by **juries** of presentment (grand juries) throughout the middle ages and in early modern England. Many such appeals were begun but then never came to trial, probably because they were compromised by the parties after payment of compensation.

In the twelfth century Henry II's reforms replaced local justice with trial by royal **justices** for homicide. The Assizes of Clarendon 1166 and of Northampton 1176 required local officials to produce juries made up from members of the local community to present certain crimes, which included murder. After the Assize of Clarendon the earlier distinction between types of killings that were emmendable (by payment to next of kin) and killings that were bootless, was obliterated. All killings were **felonies**, and so all killers were liable for punishment by hanging. However justifiable homicide (killing a thief caught in the act, or official killing) or excusable homicide (accidental killing, or killing in self-defence) were not treated as capital offences. Instead all cases of homicide were investigated by a jury convened by the Coroner, a local royal official, who presided over an inquest into causes of death. Then after presentment at the assizes the accused was tried before the **justices** on their next visit to the area, and after 1215 by a trial jury made up of local men. A convicted killer was sentenced to death and hanged quickly, but royal **pardon** spared the life of an excusable or justifiable homicide. In the later thirteenth century cases of homicide involving misadventure or self-defence, being *prima facie* eligible for pardon, were immediately reported to the crown by the justices (Statute of Gloucester (1278) 6 Edward I, c.9). However the grant of a royal pardon did not prevent forfeiture to the crown of the excusable felon's goods, which appears to be a penalty imposed in return for the grant of a pardon. Nor did it prevent the victim's family from later bringing an appeal of felony against the pardoned felon. The convicted felon who

229

was hanged also suffered penalties which affected his family's right to inherit: his **lands** and his **chattels** were forfeit to the crown.

Thus, although the substantive law did not distinguish between an accidental killing and an intentional one, in practice only intentional killing was a capital offence. As well as the use of pardons, mitigation of capital offences was undertaken by juries who, by means of their control of the evidence presented at a trial, acquitted many defendants (more than half according to investigations of records undertaken by Green, T., 1976, p 432; also see Lawson, 1988, p 119., and Cockburn, 1988, p 173). Often facts were fitted to a formula of excusable self-defence. That is to say, the homicide was presented as an act of 'last resort' in which the fleeing defendant was said to be constrained by an assailant against a hedge, or wall or ditch and killed in one single act of self-defence (see Green, T., 1976, p 429). Alternatively the jury found that the defendant killed by accident, and so was eligible for pardon in the thirteenth century, and by the fourteenth century was systematically acquitted.

Of course royal pardons could be granted for any homicide at all. The King's liberal use of pardons for intentional killers gave rise to many complaints during the fourteenth century, and led to the enactment in 1390 of a statute which declared that in future no royal pardon was to be allowed for certain crimes, including '*Murdre, Mort d'ome occis par agait, assaut, ou malice prepense*' (13 Rich. II, Stat. 2, c.1).

Many historians have regarded this Act as the first statutory description of the requirement for 'malice aforethought' in murder. Kaye, 1967, p 369, disagrees (outlining an historiography, pp 366–8), arguing rather that by 1390 the word 'murder' had already acquired a wider meaning than killing by stealth, and by then referred to any culpable homicide at all. If Kaye's reading of the word 'murder' in the statute is correct, then the grant of a royal pardon to any kind of culpable homicide was restricted, and no distinction in law was made between murder and manslaughter until much later developments in the sixteenth century (when distinctions were drawn between deliberate killing and 'chance medley' described below).

However an alternative discussion of the 1390 statute in Green, T., 1976, p 465, supports earlier readings. This suggests that the use of the term 'malice aforethought' modified homicide, so that while royal pardons were still available for simple homicide, such grants were restricted in cases of murder as stealthy killing. So the 1390 statute which aimed to restrict royal powers of pardon to certain forms of homicide was in line with earlier popular understanding of the difference between excusable and capital homicide. Whatever the intention of the drafters of the 1390 statute, the effect of any distinction made in the law of homicide was short-lived, because no change had been made in the rules of criminal liability; all felonious homicides were still *prima facie* capital offences and Reports show that the king soon after began pardoning all sorts of homicides.

Next, during the fifteenth and sixteenth centuries, use of benefit of clergy to mitigate capital punishment increased greatly (on benefit of clergy see **branded**). If a defendant claimed benefit of clergy, the jury's reluctance to convict for 'simple' homicide (not murder) was overcome, because the jurors knew conviction would not necessarily result in a death sentence (see ibid., p 475). Then, in a series of statutes passed between 1496 and 1547 (12 Hen. VII, c.7 (1496), 4 Hen. VIII, c.2 (1512), 23 Hen. VIII, c.1, ch. 3–4 (1531), 1 Ed. VI, c.12 ch. 10 (1547) certain homicides, called 'murders with malice prepense', were excluded from benefit of clergy. Also by Tudor times the wording of indictments made clear the distinction between murder and other homicides, for lesser homicide was by then known as **manslaughter**. In 1578, the earliest reported verdict of manslaughter, *Salisbury's Case*, clearly explained the need for malice aforethought in conviction for murder.

So by Shakespeare's time some malicious intent to kill, a particular *mens rea* known as malice prepense, was required before a man was hanged for murder. But by then the notion of intent or 'malice prepense' was being extended to include malice 'either expressed' by the murderer himself, or 'implied by law' (Coke, 1797, 3rd Institute, p 47), which is to say presumed to apply under specified circumstances. Coke in his Third Institute (published 1628) considered malice to be implied in several situations: where a violent killing took place in the absence of provocation; where there was killing by poison; in the killing of an officer of the law; in a killing when carrying out an unlawful act; in the cruel killing of a prisoner 'by the dures of the gaoler' or in an unauthorized execution (ibid., pp 51–2). Watkin, 1984, p 290, suggests that in Shakespeare's period malice was implied by law from external circumstances where there was genuine malice prepense not 'obvious to the eye of the beholder'. But alternately Sayre, 1932, p 997, convincingly comments that implied malice allowed courts to refuse clergy

231

to a defendant where, because of the nature of the killing, public opinion demanded more severe penalties regardless of the motivation of the killer.

The meaning of implied malice was also extended to include homicide by wanton negligence, and even some unintentional killing. A witting accomplice to murder – for instance anyone who has employed, assisted, failed to stop, sheltered, or misdirected the pursuers of a murderer – was considered to be a murderer himself. A master could be found guilty of a murder carried out by his servant. The master's or principal's instructions need not be carried out precisely for him to be found to be an accomplice and guilty of an agent's crime; so if M says 'use a knife' and the agent uses a gun, M is still guilty. Moreover, neither threats of death nor even a royal warrant would exculpate an agent who carried out a murder, who shared guilt with his principal.

Because of extended use of 'implied' malice aforethought, the term murder was transformed in the seventeenth century to encompass all those acts considered to be the worst kind of felonious killing (Sayre, 1932, pp 997–8 and 1016–26). However the term 'murder' probably also recalled its earlier meanings in some of its many Shakespearian uses, that is a killing by stealth, or a secret killing where the unknown perpetrator was an underhanded criminal who evaded identification and escaped before the **hue and cry** could be raised.

In summary, the most important change in the law of homicide in early modern England was the increased use made of benefit of clergy, claimed after a trial had taken place, to distinguish between excusable and culpable homicide. By Shakespeare's time homicide might be either murder with malice aforethought, or manslaughter, which included accidental killing and also homicide in 'chance medley', which was a killing which took place in the heat of a quarrel. Manslaughter was still punishable by hanging and forfeiture of property, but the sentence could be avoided by **sanctuary**, or **pardon**, or benefit of clergy. Even if execution was avoided, **branding** in the case of benefit of clergy, and abjuration of the realm with branding in the case of sanctuary, and forfeiture of goods in all cases would still result.

The exclusion of chance medley, killing in a sudden quarrel, from culpable homicide can only be understood in the social context of the time when quick fights and sudden brawls which resulted in death were common. Such a fatal fight was not considered to have taken place with malice prepense. In 1600 the distinction between chance medley and murder was revised (*Watts v Brains*, Cro. Eliz. 778), and the test for murder became instead the issue of provocation. In 1604 this change was underlined by removing cases of death by stabbing from benefit of clergy (1 Jac. I, c.8). This statute was said to have been enacted because of the many violent fights between Englishmen and Scotsmen at King James's court. If a man stabbed another who had neither drawn a weapon, nor attacked first, and the stabbed person died within six months, then the attacker was guilty of murder (Holdsworth, 1903, vol 4, p 501).

Another felonious homicide that was punished by confiscation was suicide, or *felo de se* (see **self-slaughter**). Yet certain forms of killing were excluded from punishment in secular courts. Infanticide was 'considered something less than homicide in medieval England' and punished with penance by the Church courts (Helmholz, 1987g, p 164; see also 163 and 167); following an Act of 1624 there was an increased tendency to convict and execute for murder women killing newborn illegitimate children (Laslett, 1983, pp 174–5). An unsuccessful attempt to kill was not murder (until the nineteenth century). There had been no specific doctrine of attempt in medieval English law. Instead certain offences, in particular **treason**, were defined to include an unsuccessful attempt. So attempts to murder husbands by wives, or masters by servants, were punished as petty treason (Kiralfy, 1992, p 95). For a certain period of time in the early fourteenth century, criminal attempt was punished according to the medieval maxim that the will should be taken for the deed, but this was short-lived and attempted crime was only punished as a **felony** when it could be encompassed into treason or petty treason.

Certain categories of people escaped liability for murder, including the mentally incompetent and those under seven years of age. The test to establish criminal responsibility for both children and those of unsound mind was whether the offender knew what they did was wrong. This is a remnant of the old canon law notion that an offence requires a 'guilty mind'.

(B) The word 'murder' is extremely common, and is in widely varied use in Shakespeare's plays. In figurative uses it can represent any sort of

233

killing, as in killing a fly (TIT 3.2.54), in hunting quarry (LLL 4.1.8), or even by a dangerous windstorm at sea: 'Yet Aeolus would not be a murderer' (CYL 3.2.92).

At another extreme from the metaphorical, murdering is the actual occupation of a number of minor Shakespearian figures seen assassinating with or without compunction (or refusing to do so) on promises of reward. To add to gruesome realism, a description of suffocation worthy of forensic science describes murderers' handiwork in CYL 3.2.160–78. An interesting case of attempted murder by use of an agent arises in PER. Thaliart is handed 'poison' and given 'gold' by Antiochus, and he agrees to kill Pericles (S.1.193–201). But when leaving to pursue the fleeing Pericles, Thaliart assures Antiochus 'If I can get him in my pistol's length / I'll make him sure enough' (S.1.210–11). As indicated above, this change of the specified murder weapon by his agent makes Antiochus no less a murderer.

In ROM 'murder' is used often, both figuratively and literally, to denote all sorts of metaphorical or actual killing. In Romeo's lament over his **banishment** he speaks of the law's **mercy** as murder: 'Thou cutt'st my head off with a golden axe, / And smil'st upon the stroke that murders me' (ROM 3.3.22–3), and in his comment upon paying for illegal poison he calls greed 'murder': 'There is thy gold – worse poison to men's souls, / Doing more murder in this loathsome world, / Than these poor compounds that thou mayst not sell' (5.1.80–2; on the passage see **poverty**).

But such a broad notion of 'murder' is not the one implicit when Cordelia claims upon being effectively **disinherited**: 'It is no vicious blot, murder, or foulness' (LRQ S.1.219 / LRF 1.1.227) Cordelia's 'vicious blot' implies malice aforethought. But murder as chance medley is implied when despicable Oswald cries out 'Help, ho, murder, help!' (LRQ S.7.29–40 / LRF 2.2.30–41) rather than meet Kent's challenge to fight. (Under the 1604 statute of stabbing Kent would have been guilty of murder if he killed Oswald, since Oswald refuses to draw a weapon; it is interesting that the 1606 play casts the light of sympathy on Kent rather than Oswald.) Indeed, many in Shakespeare's plays cry 'murder' when fearful of their safety (for instance in MND 3.2.26, SHR 5.1.51). Also many killings in hot blood are called 'murder', as they are repeatedly in ROM.

Yet premeditation and stealth are important elements in many Shakespearian contexts of 'murder'. The means to a series of political killings planned in soliloquy by Richard of Gloucester in a 'cold pre-meditation for my purpose' (RDY 3.2.133) will include the use of evil stealth:

> Why, I can smile, and murder whiles I smile,
> And cry 'Content!' to that which grieves my heart,
> And wet my cheeks with artificial tears,
> And frame my face to all occasions.
>
> (3.2.182–5)

Iago hypocritically denies 'iniquity', claiming 'Though in the trade of war I have slain men, / Yet do I hold it very stuff o' th' conscience / To do no contrived murder. I lack iniquity' (OTH 1.2.1–3). He proceeds to wound from behind, stab in the dark, and conspire to ruin utterly Othello and Desdamona.

'Premeditated and contrived murder' (H5 4.1.161) is listed by Henry V together with other undetected guilty crimes that may be punished by God through war, if they escape human law. Having just fraudulently deplored the 'murder' of Polonius, which was an unpremeditated accident, Claudius enlists the willing Laertes into a conspiratorial plot to kill Hamlet 'Under the which he shall not choose but fall; / And for his death no wind of blame shall breathe; / But even his mother shall uncharge the practice / And call it accident' (HAM 4.7.64–7). Not even revenge, but only policy, drives the king's dark plans to do an undoubted premeditated murder, by poison, through use of an agent.

'Caitiff' is a term suggesting either pity or contempt in numerous Shakespearian uses; perhaps it carries both shades of meaning at once in a subtle context in which King Lear speaks of the 'great gods' exposing 'close pent-up guilts'. Among those with hidden sins, Lear bids a 'caitiff, to pieces shake, / That under covert and convenient seeming / Has practised on man's life' (LRF 3.2.55–7 (LRQ S.9.55–7)). Premeditation to kill here, as in the case of Richard of Gloucester or King Claudio, is secretive and deceitful, but seems fully conscious.

Premeditation has a more complex course in MAC, starting when Macbeth first considers 'My thought, whose murder yet is but fantastical' (MAC 1.3.138); this progression in which self-deceit plays a role is well treated in Wiggins, 1990.

Murder is claimed, but stealth or premeditation are not evident, in some of Richard II's imagined

> sad stories of the death of kings –
> How some have been deposed, some slain in war,
> Some haunted by the ghosts they have deposed,
> Some poisoned by their wives, some sleeping killed,
> All murdered.
>
> (R2 3.2.152–6)

Hector being slain in battle is also called a 'murder' in TRO 5.11.4–6, on account of the dishonouring of his corpse.

Criminal liability for murder on account of killing through negligence is implied in Lepidus' image of a grossly incompetent surgeon: 'we do commit / Murder in healing wounds' (ANT 2.2.21–2).

Although not a **felony**, an attempted, but not successful, murder was a serious **trespass**, punished in Shakespeare's England by **Star Chamber**. It is avenged by the populace of Tarsus against Cleon and Dionyza; on this Gower comments nearly ultimately in the play: 'The gods for murder seemed so content / To punish that, although not done, but meant' (PER S.22.122–3).

Another deed on the fringe of murder was infanticide, as noted above. The killing of actual children in MAC and R3 is murder, but the slaughter of newborn infants imaged in MAC 1.7.54–9 and 4.1.30–1 and the exposure of infant Perdita might not have been seen in the same light. Antigonous seems punished for exposing Perdita, although he leaves money and a scroll with her, saying 'Blossom, speed thee well!' (WT 3.3.45); Queen Hermione has called the ill-treatment of baby Perdita a 'murder': 'My third comfort, / Starred most unluckily, is from my breast, / The innocent milk in it most innocent mouth, / Haled out to murder' (WT 3.2.97–100). In 1610 this sinful act may have been especially shocking (in common with Lady Macbeth's resolve to 'dashed the brains out' (MAC 1.7.58)). For, although statistics are undoubtedly hard to confirm, and some infant mortality may have been non-accidental, according to Laslett, 1983, p 174, the rate of infanticide in 1610 in London was at the vanishingly small level of about 3 per 100,000.

(C) See: 'Britton,' 1865, vol 1, p 38; Bracton, 1968, vol 2, p 379; Stephen, 1883, pp 23–78; Holdsworth, 1903, vol 3, pp 310–16; Plucknett, 1956, pp 442–6; Kaye, 1967; Bellamy, 1973, pp 53–8; Kaye, 1977, pp 4–8; Baker, 1978, pp 303–16; Baker, 1986i; Baker, 1990b, pp 596–9,

600–3. On the nature and transformations of notions of malice prepense in relation to the idea of *mens rea*, see Holdsworth, 1903, vol 8, pp 434–7, Sayre, 1932, and especially Green, T., 1976. On infanticide see Laslett, 1983, pp 174–5 and Helmholz, 1987g.

Emphasizing the aspect of **jury** involvement, Green, T. A., 1985 considers killings in self-defence (pp. 38–46), stealth as an aspect of murder (pp 53–9), the border between manslaughter and excusable homicide (pp 125–6), and similar topics.

Accounts of investigations of murder by **Justices of the Peace** in Shakespeare's time are detailed in Langbein, 1974, pp 45–54. On deodands see Sutton, 1997 and Braunmuller, 1990, p 191.

The first part of Braunmuller, 1990, pp 179–91, contains a survey of the law as it stood in Shakespeare's time in relation to agency and accomplices in murder, while the second part discusses agency in Elizabethan drama. Day, 1991 describes, in a discussion of the play's 'theatricality', how being presented with knowledge of murder creates an accessory to it in R3.

Draper, 1933, p 90, points out that the murder of a master by a servant was severely punished as petty **treason**, but claims that contrarily a servant 'might kill in defence of his master and be absolved from murder', relating this to 'the bravery of the Capulet and Montague underlings'. Their attempts to fight and perhaps kill without legal liability are noted under **battery** and **manslaughter**.

See Campbell, R., 1985 on the punishment of women for killing a husband or master, which was by burning for 'petty **treason**'. See Kiralfy, 1992 on the treatment of criminal attempt as petty treason.

Watkin, 1984 offers an analysis of the law of homicide at about the time of the writing of HAM, and matches this to the many killings in the play. The treatment in MM of the convicted murderer Barnadine is astutely analysed in Lindley, 1996.

on the case (actions/arrest) (A) Legal actions in the royal courts for **trespasses**, seeking punishment and amends for transgressions, originally had to be initiated by writs obtained from Chancery alleging a wrong done 'with force and arms against the king's peace'. This form of words was settled in the thirteenth century, with the required phrasing taken from the **appeal** of **felony**. Such writs were formulaic quite regardless of the actual facts in question which may bear little resemblance to the wording of the writ (see for instance the fictional form of words cited under **battery**, which would encompass many possible harms). Details of circumstances could not be included in such writs except in a subsidiary position following '*cum*' (with), used to claim aggravation or give further explanation.

Because local courts could not usually deal with suits for more than 40 shillings, many fictional allegations of '*vi et armis*' were made to bring the matter before the royal courts. By 1360 this phrase and also '*contra pacem*' could be omitted from writs. The courts also allowed litigants to bring suits for a non-forcible wrong alleged to be vaguely 'in like case' to a corresponding suit for a forcible wrong (but the wording in records was quite variable – see Kiralfy, 1951, pp 50–4). From the 1340s or earlier there was a gradual rise of such suits, in which the writs were quite verbose in specifying particular circumstances, and often a '*cum*' clause became the crucial part. By the early fifteenth century actions for non-forcible trespasses begun by writs created especially for them became known as 'actions on the case', or actions

238

for 'trespass on the case'. (Within 100 years of Shakespeare's lifetime these actions and a resulting law of 'torts' became the corner-stone of all civil law.)

By the 1380s it was settled following a series of cases that a trespass on the case, like any trespass *vi et armis*, must be tried by a **jury**, rather than by an ordeal of compurgation or 'wager of law' (see Baker, 1990b, p 75; on wager of law see under **debt**). Actions on the case, brought in the Courts of King's Bench or Common Pleas, began to be used more and more widely, sometimes to address wrongs in areas not otherwise remedied, and sometimes because they brought advantages in areas overlapping other **jurisdictions** or forms of action. For instance, actions on the case were bought for account (see **audit/account**), **debt** or detinue, **conversion**, covenant, deceit, negligence, nuisance, and even defamation (see **libel/slander**). However a general principle, holding that actions on the case should be barred when legal remedies using older writs were available, limited the development of 'case' until the early seventeenth century, when this principle was increasingly overlooked.

One particular type of action on the case of great importance was the action of *assumpsit*. By the fifteenth century many such actions came to the royal courts, alleging that the defendant 'took upon himself' (*assumpsit super se*) to do a service which was done badly or dishonestly, causing loss to the plaintiff. From about 1560 a doctrine subsequently crucial in contract law arose that to bring an action of *assumpsit* required an element of mutuality, or so-called 'consideration'. By Shakespeare's time actions of *assumpsit* applied to a wide range of matters, including 'misfeasance' (such as arising from negligence in performing professional services), certain forms of 'nonfeasance' (no performance), deceit (as in giving false warranties), and even breach of promise of marriage (see **pre-contract**). From the start of the sixteenth century, writs of *assumpsit*, often alleging deceit, were used to sue for unpaid **debts** in the Court of King's Bench. From about 1540, the court of Common Pleas, which had the monopoly for actions on writs of debt, objected strenuously and litigants found themselves in trouble. By the 1590s the Court of Exchequer Chamber, which then included no King's Bench judges, began to overturn on error all King's Bench judgments for debt that were based on *assumpsit*. Finally, the much discussed and rather mysterious *Slade's Case* (B & M, pp 420–41) was tried between 1597 and 1602 before all the judges of England, with the result (however reached) that

239

nearly all debts thereafter could be recovered in King's Bench by an action of *assumpsit*.

All unpaid debts, including those entered into verbally (and, from 1610, even implicitly), became nominal trespasses. However a perhaps fictional allegation of deceit in their non-paying debtors was not a material advantage to creditors. The actual advantages of *assumpsit* to creditors were other, and many. These included that an action of *assumpsit* was possible in many circumstances where an action of debt was not (for example, against **executors** who could not wage law, or in cases involving commercial **bills** of exchange), that actual losses beyond the amount of the original debt could be recovered, that the cost of bringing an action in King's Bench was less than in Common Pleas, that **bills** unlike writs were not recorded before action and thus they encouraged out-of-court settlements, and that the barristers who argued in King's Bench had much lower fees than the **serjeants** of Common Pleas (see **lawyers**). Another possible advantage, which recent authorities think may have been overly stressed by earlier historians, was that wager of law was not allowed in actions of *assumpsit*.

Although actions on the case became very popular during or just after Shakespeare's time for collection of all manner of debts, their rise may not have signalled quite the revolution of society, or even of commercial life, sometimes claimed. Thorne, 1985i, pp 206–9, points out that the new economic needs of Tudor England were generally well served by adaptation of older forms for ensuring **debt**, including **recognizances**, **statutes** and **bonds**, and suggests that historians have given false prominence to *Slade's Case* and other cases involving *assumpsit*. Likewise, Baker, 1986f, pp 349–52, explains how long prior to *Slade's Case* merchants were able to recover debts on commercial bills through royal courts including Chancery. Moreover, Simpson, 1966, p 421, points out that based on statistics (for instance for 1572) published in Kiralfy, 1951 'we must guard against the notion that *assumpsit* triumphed as rapidly as is sometimes assumed'. The history of the development of the modern law of contract has great intellectual interest, but within it the initiation of far-reaching innovations may have had less impact on their immediate times than is sometimes thought.

An allied issue is a sometimes alleged change in societal outlook in Shakespeare's age, away from dealings in good faith, that has been associated with the rise of *assumpsit*. But Helmholz, 1987a actually finds canon law's *causa fidei laesionis seu perjurri*, and not equity's remedies, to be the likely actual source of the common law's development of *assumpsit*. This essay, pp 277–81, notes many similarities between *assumpsit* and *fidei laesio*, but also notes as the greatest difference that the former could offer consequential damages, while the latter could offer only an order to perform an original promise plus public penance. Such a difference provided a strong practical reason for the growth of *assumpsit*. For instance Simpson, 1986, p 337, points out circumstances in which action on the case would produce damages while prosecutions for breach of faith in spiritual courts would not produce any material recompense at all for the injured party (as for example in cases of professional libel or slander).

For concerned contemporaries, innovations in uses of 'case' and also in greater availability of **bill** procedure appeared to be mainly **jurisdictional** issues. Thus Knafla, 1977, pp 120–1, notes Lord Chancellor Ellesmere's dismay at the degree of discretion newly allowed to common law judges on account of plaintiffs' enlarged freedom to set down particular circumstances both in actions of *assumpsit*, and in actions on bills to which access had been greatly extended by King's Bench. Ellesmere's kind of concern, that the common law courts were preempting the Chancellor's jurisdiction, has been taken more literally than need be by some modern critics. These do not include D. E. C. Yale, whose seminal introduction to Hake, 1953 makes it clear that Edward Hake's calling actions on the case 'equity of the Common lawe' represents only a viewpoint (pp xx-xxiii). Indeed, although some contemporary lawyers feared that relative freedom from formality in actions on the case might threaten the courts of **equity**, of all the prerogative courts only the equity jurisdiction of Chancery survived the joint triumph of parliament and common lawyers in 1645.

As noted under **bills**, initiating common law actions while sidestepping the strict forms dictated by formal writs was long available if the defendants were in the county where King's Bench happened to be sitting, or were either officers of or in the custody of any royal court; these possibilities existed long before the sixteenth century. On the interesting relations between King's Bench bills and actions on the case see: Kiralfy, 1951, pp 45–8; Plucknett, 1956, pp 640–1 and 644–5; Blatcher, 1978, pp 160–2; Milsom, 1981, p 64. Kiralfy suggests that the informality of bill procedure neither inspired nor eased the creation of case.

Arrest for debt (as often seen in Shakespeare) was by 'mesne process' using the writ of *capitas ad respondendum*. This process was extended in 1285 to actions of account (see **audit/account**), in 1351 to writs of debt, and in 1504 to actions on case (19 Hen. VII, c.9; see Plucknett, 1956, p 389 and Baker, 1990b, p 76). It was not very efficient, due to poor incentives offered to arresting officers (see **sheriff**), and Baker, 1990b, p 76). Defendants who did not appear could be **outlawed**, which was also not efficient (ibid., p 77). Imprisonment of debtors was possible by writs of *capitas ad satisfaciendum* (ibid., p 79), a dire proceeding but less so than the remnants of Anglo-Saxon **slavery** for unpaid debt (see Plucknett, 1956, pp 389–90).

(B) The slave Dromio of Syracuse, much given to punning, indicates that his master has been arrested 'on the case' for debt, and seeks help from his mistress:

ADRIANA	Why, man, what is the matter?
DROMIO	I do not know the matter, he is 'rested on the case.
ADRIANA	What, is he arrested? Tell me at whose suit.
DROMIO	I know not at whose suit he is arrested well,
	But is in a suit of buff which 'rested him, that can I tell.
	Will you send him, mistress, redemption – the money in his desk?
ADRIANA	Go fetch it, sister. This I wonder at,
	That he unknown to me should be in debt.
	Tell me, was he arrested on a bond?
DROMIO	Not on a bond but on a stronger thing:
	A chain, a chain – do you not hear it ring?
	(ERR 4.2.41–51)

It is interesting that Dromio refers to an arrest on an action on the case, but Adriana either mishears this, or is confused, and asks about an arrest on a bond. Actions for debt on conditional bonds, such as afflicted Antonio of MV, were of an older sort but were still very much noted and used in Shakespeare's time (see especially Simpson, 1966).

In the same gallows-humour punning context we hear a great deal more about arresting officers and their buff coloured suits or jackets (ERR 4.2.35–55). Slightly later one of these officers complains of the

242

liabilities he faces when arresting debtors: 'He is my prisoner. If I let him go, / The debt he owes will be required of me' (4.4.118–19). The same threat is faced by the 'naughty jailer' whom Shylock thinks 'so fond / To come abroad with [Antonio] at his request' (MV 3.3.9–10).

Mistress Quickly in 2H4 2.1.30–1, in appointing officers to arrest Falstaff for debt, says her 'exion is entered, and my case so openly known to the world'. This is no doubt sexually equivocal (as is its entire context), but the meaning of 'exion . . . my case' is as nearly related to 'action on the case' as is her later 'thou hempseed' (2.1.60) is to 'thou **homicide**'.

CYM contains two unexpected images of imprisonment for debt. In one Imogen breaks open a sealed letter from Posthumus, exclaiming merrily:

> Good wax, thy leave. Blest be
> You bees that make these locks of counsel! Lovers
> And men in dangerous bonds pray not alike;
> Though forfeiters you cast in prison, yet
> You clasp young Cupid's tables.
>
> (CYM 3.2.35–9)

She has far less cause than she thinks for joy, for Posthumus intends to have her killed; her images perhaps correspondingly are unthinkingly dark. Locks and bonds themselves are restraints, and the 'bonds' she refers to are sealed instruments of debt which if defaced will become forfeit (see **bonds**); moreover she images the forfeiters as imprisoned debtors.

Just after this, in a second instance, imprisonment for debt is again imaged when Guiderius complains to his guardian of his and his brother Arviragus' rural **exile** and small experience of the world. He admits 'Haply this life is best, / If quiet life be best', but says 'unto us it is / A cell of ignorance, travelling abed, / A prison for a debtor, that not dares / To stride a limit' (CYM 3.3.29–30 and 3.3.32–5). Here imprisonment for debt is an image of limitation, and stands in ironic opposition to the warning given to Guiderius and Arviragus: 'Did you but know the city's usuries, / And felt them knowingly . . . ' (CYM 3.3.45–6).

(C) On the theory and the rise of action on the case see: Plucknett, 1956, pp 372–3; Milsom, 1981, pp 285–313; Simpson, 1987c; Helmholz, 1987a; Baker, 1990b, pp 71–5. Kiralfy, 1951 is a classic study of actual actions on the case up to 1700, excluding those for debt. This contains a good discussion on the origins and theory of case, pp 1–48.

On damages given by **juries** in actions on the case for **slander** see Helmholz, 1987e.

On *assumpsit* see: Kiralfy, 1951, pp 137–50; Simpson, 1966, p 421; Plucknett, 1956, pp 637–50 and 668–9; Simpson, 1975, and especially pp 199–315, 406–505, 574–98; Knafla, 1977, pp 117–18; Milsom, 1981, pp 316–60; Ibbetson, 1982; Baker, 1990b, pp 374–96, 416–24, 547. On 'consideration' see Ibbetson, 1982 and Baker, 1986h. On the historical and jurisprudential complexities, and the later misunderstandings, of *Slade's Case* see especially Baker, 1986g.

Despite the reservations of legal historians noted above, some have associated the sixteenth century expansion of *assumpsit* with a secularisation of society. For instance Helmholz, 1987a, p 288, suggests that the rise of *assumpsit* evidenced a 'secularisation in men's attitudes which occurred during the late fifteenth and sixteenth centuries', and Helmholz, 1987f, pp 320–1 discusses on adjacent pages the rise of *assumpsit* and a decline in popular belief that it was proper for the church to deal with testamentary debt. Yet, Jones, N. G., 1997 questions whether an action of *assumpsit* could be understood as based on an implied **use** in favour of a beneficiary; if so, then it would be concerned with acting in good faith.

An increase in uses of 'case', and especially of *assumpsit*, has been associated with social transformation by several Shakespeare critics. In a discussion bearing on MV, Hutson, 1994 connects the reduced formality of pleadings in actions on the case with the supposed freedom of 'equitable practice' in 'Chancery' (p. 146), and propounds the view that, in a massive social change c. 1500–50, 'equity at common law' displaced conscience from spiritual *fidei laesio* (pp. 139–48; however see Helmholz, 1987a, as noted above, on the source of *assumpsit* in *causa fidei laesionis seu perjurri*). A 'misogny of equity' is then traced (pp. 149–51).

Arguments alleging a new social outlook implicit in the rise of *assumpsit* and the outcome of *Slade's Case* are applied to the worlds of MV in Spinosa, 1993 and Spinosa, 1994 and to notions of 'performance' with suggested applications to TIM and TMP in Wilson, L., 1994.

Jordan, C., 1994 connects several themes in CYM to obligation in debt, and particularly notes *Slade's Case*, pp 36–8. Although this essay seems to confuse the meaning of a 'writ', it suggests an explanation in themes of the play for the legal imagery noted above.

On imprisonment for debt also see under **audit**. A use of mesne process in arrests for debt in ERR, MV and 2H4 is noted in Campbell, J., 1859, pp 39, 49 and 70. Ibid., p 50, notes Shylock's veiled threat against the Jailer of an action for 'escape'.

outlawry/banishment/exile (A) During the middle ages a sentence of outlawry could be imposed by a court on a convicted criminal, or more usually as a result of the non-appearance and subsequent indictment of someone on a criminal **appeal**. Usually perpetrators of crimes were either caught red-handed, or not at all, and due to the lack of a police force only a small percentage of crimes committed were ever brought to trial. In many cases the accused fled too far to be pursued, or took **sanctuary**. As no trial could take place without the presence of the defendant and judgment in default was not available, the absent defendant was finally proclaimed an outlaw.

First, every attempt had to be made to secure the defendant's attendance by issue of a series of *mesne* writs, and if this failed then a sentence of outlawry was pronounced. Although proclamation of outlawry was a royal right, the **sheriff** took the preliminary steps by calling on the defendant to appear at five successive county courts. Finally outlawry was proclaimed, which had serious consequences because the defendant was now outside the protection of the law.

If captured, a fugitive outlaw would be hanged, and an outlaw resisting arrest faced summary execution. If an outlaw escaped arrest and remained at large he would lose all his property. His personal property (**chattels**) was forfeit to the King, while his **land** went first to the King for a year and a day and for **waste**, and then escheated to his lord, just as in **felony**.

The same process and punishment of outlawry used against non-appearing criminal defendants also attached from the middle ages to actions of **trespass** and **account**, and by the statute 25 Edw. III, stat. 5, c.17 to **debt**, detinue, and replevin. Outlawry was also attached to actions **on the case** in 1504 by 19 Hen. VII, c.9. But in contrast to criminal outlawry, although there was forfeiture of goods (until the 1870 Forfeiture Act 33 & 34 Vict., c. 23), here outlawry was not equivalent to a sentence of death.

In medieval England criminal bands were familiar in many parts of the country, forming a threat to public order and royal authority. The system of outlawry was held responsible for the creation of these bands because after pronouncement of sentence of outlawry fugitives banded together in forests or remote areas for mutual support and protection. These bands could be large (in the late fourteenth century William Beckwith's outlaw band is said to have numbered 500 men), but smaller groups of 20 or so were more common. Sometimes the leaders of the bands were members of the gentry, and leaders of gentle birth were much esteemed. Often it was clear that outlaw bands were supported by local magnates, and they were reputed to be actively employed by them to settle feuds. Religious houses also employed outlaws to settle arguments with neighbours, and monks were reported to be active members of bands holding people to ransom (see Bellamy, 1973, p 73).

Those people who provided outlaws with passive help such as food or shelter, could be punished as 'receivers', while those who commissioned outlaws to carry out crimes were known as 'maintainers'. These latter were often men of high social status who took a large percentage of the outlaws' profits. Outlaw bands **robbed**, poached, extorted, kidnapped, and **murdered** (see Bellamy, 1973, pp 78–80). Large scale poaching was profitable; one outlaw who led a band specializing in park-breaking and raiding was known as 'Frere Tuk'.

Outlaws appear to have been regarded with both fear and admiration by contemporaries. When brought to justice many were acquitted. Medieval kings dealt with outlaws by using a mixture of threats and bribes, both offering money for the capture of outlaws and accepting money from them for the purchase of **pardons**. They would also grant pardons to former outlaws as reward for military services, and induce outlaws to reform by offering appointments to office or promising gifts of land.

By Shakespeare's time the lawlessness of medieval outlaw bands was a memory. Also, by the end of the fifteenth century legal outlawry was not the personal calamity it had been, leading to an 'inclination to flee blindly, or take to the woods and become a professional robber' (Bellamy, 1973, p 105). Outlaws would simply lie low with friends or move to another district to await a pardon. In the Elizabethan world outlawry was still used as a punishment, but pardons were readily purchased and a sentence of outlawry seemed not to prevent holding even royal office. Elizabeth is said to have complained about the number of outlaws sitting as members of parliament (Baker, 1990b, p 77n).

Outlawry as the possible origin of abjuration or banishment is discussed in Holdsworth, 1903, vol 3, pp 303–4. A connection between the two is seen frequently in Shakespeare's plays. Although mainly a memory in England, banishment was a punishment in the Roman Empire and medieval Europe. Deportation to an island was a statutory Roman punishment for sexual and state offences. Ovid was famously banished, possibly for a sexual intrigue with Augustus' daughter, and Shakespeare's audiences were also familiar with Dante's famous exile from Florence following a political reversal.

Although mentioned in Magna Carta, exile was not, by name, a judicial penalty in Elizabethan England. However, it was effectively imposed upon unrepentant religious non-conformists by the Act (1592–3) 35 Eliz. c.1. This demanded that if potentially 'seditious Sectaries' did not attend the English Church and take Communion there for a month, or if they participated in any illegal 'Exercise of Religion', and after a further three months in prison they did not conform, then they are compelled to 'abjure this realm of England . . . forever'. Failing that, or on a return without permission, they became **felons** without 'benefit of clergy' (see under **branded**).

Thus, although abjuration of the realm by **sanctuary** men had been prohibited by 22 Hen. VIII, c.14 (also 28 Hen. VIII c.1, 32 Hen. VIII, c.3), forced abjuration could be imposed on Elizabethan Roman Catholics, which amounted to repatriation or exile. Shakespeare may have been very sensitive to such matters, as members of his own family may have been only reluctantly or outwardly conforming communicants.

(B) Shakespeare's plays look mainly to the fierce reputations of mythical, medieval or classical outlaws, or to severe political banishments; they do not seem to reflect the diluted outlawry of his age.

Outlawed men, some singly and some in gangs or military bands, feature repeatedly in Shakespeare's plays in all genres. Most of Shakespeare's works contain allusions to 'banishment', 'exile', or a legal sentence to leave a court, city or country on pain of death. Such banishment confers the status of outlaw in the sense of 'outside the protection of the law'.

Various associations of banishment and outlawry arise in Shakespeare's works. In the text and stage directions of AYL, where the old Duke's men are repeatedly called 'banished' or in 'exile', according to the Folio stage direction to 2.6, they are first seen (presumably dressed) 'like Out-lawes' (tln 972). A similar association may be suggested in a close collocation of the two terms 'banished' and 'outlawed' in Gloucester's speech at LRF 3.4.154 and 3.4.157.

The notion that an exile who returns without leave becomes an outlaw is made clear in the case of Bolingbroke. Gohn, 1982, p 947, claims that 'Shakespeare's audience clearly was aware of the novelty of the penalty' when Bolingbroke is 'banished' from England for six years 'upon pain of life' (R2 1.3.133–237). When 'the banished Bolingbroke repeals himself' prematurely (R2 2.2.49), he is a man outside the law. Almost like a medieval 'receiver', York gives Bolingbroke shelter (R2 2.3.158–60). He receives military support from the Percys and others. In a later play these events are described contemptuously by Hotspur:

> And when he was not six-and-twenty strong,
> Sick in the world's regard, wretched and low,
> A poor unminded outlaw sneaking home,
> My father gave him welcome to the shore
> (1H4 4.3.58–61)

Thus outlawry, like **poverty**, is treated with disdain.

A contemptuous view of outlawry with hints about medieval 'maintenance' (see above) is heard during the mutual denunciations of Gloucester and the Bishop of Winchester, including the choice invective:

GLOUCESTER   . . . Thou bastard of my grandfather.
WINCHESTER   Ay, lordly sir; for what are you, I pray,
             But one imperious in another's throne?
GLOUCESTER   Am I not Protector, saucy priest?
WINCHESTER   And am not I a prelate of the Church?
GLOUCESTER   Yes – as an outlaw in a castle keeps
             And useth it to patronage his theft.
             (1H6 3.1.43–9)

The Church is compared with a lord profiting from outlawry, or even perhaps aligned with the Religious houses employing medieval outlaws described above.

Again in accord with medieval fact and legend, an organised band of outlaws are met in TGV 4.1. These men are serious criminals, some of

248

high station, who have been banished from various Italian cities (TGV 4.1.42–52). Like the fabled English outlaw bands, they inhabit wild places and prey on passing travellers. One of them even alludes to Robin Hood and Friar Tuck (TGV 4.1.35). The outlaws' sympathy for Valentine is aroused upon confirming that he has been banished from Milan for the 'small fault' of **manslaughter** (TGV 4.1.30, 4.1.57). When Valentine is discovered to be well spoken, possessed of 'the tongues' of 'A linguist', and 'beautified / With goodly shape', the band decides to elect him their 'king', 'general', 'commander', or 'captain' (TGV 4.1.32–65; the miscellany of ranks may indicate a lawless band). Although these outlaws already observe limits in their depredations (TGV 4.1.71), Valentine's honourableness seems contagious, for the member of his band who captures Silvia remarks: 'Come, I must bring you to our captain's cave. / Fear not. He bears an honourable mind, / And will not use a woman lawlessly' (TGV 5.3.11–13). Naturally the 'reformed, civil, full of good, / And fit for great employment' men of the band are at last pardoned and rewarded (TGV 5.4.150–7).

Despite looking 'like Out-lawes' (as mentioned above), the usurped and banished Duke Senior and his lordly followers of AYL practice even more fabulously gentlemanly behaviour in the forest of Arden. Their depredations extend only to deer, not the 'passengers' of TGV 4.1.1. Yet they live according to the bone-crushing wrestler Charles 'like the old Robin Hood of England'. Charles adds romantically of the Duke 'They say many young gentlemen flock to him every day, and fleet the time carelessly, as they did in the golden world' (AYL 1.1.111–13). Such harmless outlawry is confined to the comedies, and not all of them; PER for instance features rapacious, if chaste, pirates.

Outside the comedies, banishment is generally viewed far more seriously by Shakespeare. When the tribune Sicinius arouses the people against Coriolanus the range of proposed punishments is: 'be it either / For death, for fine, or banishment' (COR 3.3.14–15), and the outcome is banishment (COR 3.3.103–47). Coriolanus himself brackets punishment by 'Vagabond exile' with 'the steep Tarpeian death', 'flaying', and being 'pent to linger / But with a grain a day' (COR 3.3.92–4), but he still stubbornly refuses to bend to the people. Unlike Socrates, who believed his identity so Athenian that he chose death over exile, Coriolanus leaves Rome and takes with him an individualistic ability to fight and enact revenge. The warrior Alcibiades, banished in TIM 3.6.96–101, does just the same in Athens; these two outlawed 'heroes', one puritanical and the

249

other over-ripe, do not need their cities to be themselves. In a curious sense the warlike Queen Margaret of R3 also seems to discount banishment when she returns to plague Richard with curses. In the the Folio text of R3 only, Richard asks her 'Wert thou not banished on pain of death?', and she replies 'I was, but I do find more pain in banishment / Than death can yield me here by my abode' (A.B. 1–3, following R3 1.3.166; tln 636–8). Her maledictions are terrific and defiance heroic.

Heroes defy it, but to more ordinary women and men in Shakespeare, banishment is very damaging. In CYL 2.3.9–16 the Duchess of Gloucester is banished, and in 2.4 she is led through the London streets barefoot while wearing a white sheet and carrying a candle to shame her, en route for exile (see under **sheriff** and **witch** on the context). In the civil confusions following Julius Caesar's assassination, reports vary, but Messala holds that 'That by proscription and bills of outlawry / Octavius, Antony, and Lepidus / Have put to death an hundred senators' (JC 4.2.225–7).

The romantic image of banishment to the Forest of Arden of AYL becomes harsher and more strenuous in the Welsh mountains of CYM. Banished Belarius expresses a preference for the bracing wilds over the confining court, adding to a Roman martial ideal the Christian commonplace that humbleness induces piety (CYM 3.3.1–107; see **poverty**). But when he hears Cloten seeking 'those runagates' he assumes that by these Cloten means himself and his purported sons, and therefore fears an 'ambush' because 'We are held as outlaws' (4.2.64–9). The naturally noble Guiderius is then subject to the insulting epithets of the braggart Cloten, including 'villain mountaineers' 'slave' (see under **slave**), 'robber', 'law-breaker', 'villain', 'varlet', 'injurious thief' (4.2.73–88), and 'traitor' (4.2.121). Guiderius replies by cutting off Cloten's royal head. To Belarius' horrified response to this act, 'What hast thou done? . . . We are all undone' (4.2.118 and 124) Guiderius replies with a recitation of the jurisprudential basis of outlawry:

> Why, worthy father, 'what have we to lose
> But that he swore to take, our lives? The law
> Protects not us: then why should we be tender
> To let an arrogant piece of flesh threat us,
> Play judge and executioner all himself,
> For we do fear the law?
>
> (4.2.125–30)

Nevertheless, on a return to civilisation the killing of Cloten in a fair fight ('chance medley'; see under **murder**) is almost a calamity, until Prince Guiderius, as one of the 'outlaws' (4.2.139), is discovered to be Cloten's superior.

(C) See: Holdsworth, 1903, vol 3, pp 303–6; Plucknett, 1956, pp 385, 430–1; Bellamy, 1973, pp 69–88 and 105–6; Baker, 1990b, p 77; Hudson, 1996, p 69. On the earlier Elizabethan **treason** acts, especially 27 Eliz., c.2, applied to Jesuits and foreign-trained Seminarians, see Bellamy, 1979, pp 69–76.

For a discussion of banishment and R2 see Gohn, 1982, p 947. Breen, 1994 notes errors regarding the proclamation of Edgar's banishment in LRQ S.21.

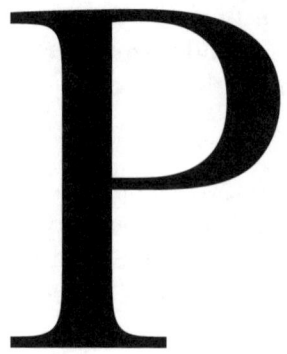

pardon/clemency (A) Pardons absolved a convicted criminal from punishment. They were, for instance, typically given to those who killed accidentally (see under **murder/homicide**).

No special pleading was possible in criminal law; a defendant must plead the general issue, guilty or not guilty. There was therefore a need to mitigate the harsh and inflexible criminal law in England in which all **felonies** were punished by death. Various means of mitigating or avoiding punishment were available in medieval and early modern England, including pleading benefit of clergy (discussed under **branding**), or using sanctuary with or without abjuration (discussed under **sanctuary**). There was also a possibility that **juries** of presentment (grand juries) would refuse to bring indictments where their sympathies were aroused. A sympathetic trial jury could also diminish the seriousness of crimes, for example by deliberately undervaluing proceeds of **theft** so that the accused would not be executed for felony (see Cockburn, 1972, p 127). There is evidence also of the selective dismissal by the Court of King's Bench of certain indictments referred there on writs of *certiorari*. It seems that, at least sometimes, minor technical 'flaws' were discovered which invalidated indictments in cases where off-the-record details suggested an extra-legal reason for mitigation (see Baker, 1986i, pp 305–10, especially 308–9).

The very frequent incidence of mitigation of punishment for crime in Shakespeare's England has been said to be the result of a view of human nature in the age. Sinful behaviour was not then regarded as an exception against a background of normal human purity and correctness. Rather, the virtue of all men and women was constantly challenged, and so all owed sympathy to those who transgressed. In the light of this, Herrup, 1985 analysed the supposed 'inefficiency' of criminal law in Shakespeare's England (particularly in East Sussex), and found 'considerable leniency' operated in practice (p. 106). The relative infrequency with which indictments were brought against the accused, or convictions upheld, or (if convictions were obtained) capital punishment was imposed, is argued to have been built into the system of trial by **jury**, which required a unanimous verdict. Following a close consideration of contemporary values and rhetoric, and of statistics, Herrup's essay proposes that rehabilitation as much as punishment may have been the aim of criminal justice in the age.

Juries were so likely to find means to minimise or forgive crimes, either at presentment or at trial, that some contemporaries of Shakespeare felt a need to insist that clemency was a function 'onely proper to the Prince' (West, W., 1601, p 175; juries' refusals to indict was also repeatedly deplored by William Lambard – see Read, 1962 passim, and Dunkel, 1962, p 276). Their objection was against usurpation of the royal prerogative power to grant a pardon.

Despite some claims to the contrary, the **equity** jurisdiction of the Court of Chancery could not offer 'pardon' for crimes. The king or more rarely parliament issued pardons, and Chancery's involvement was entirely administrative, exercising its function as a general secretariat to the crown. Bellamy, 1979, pp 218–19, explains that 'special' pardons for particular cases were granted by the crown, while 'general' pardons extending for some fixed period were also occasionally offered by royal proclamation or by parliamentary acts. Following the announcement of general pardons, applicants had to register their names and obtain sealed documents from Chancery for a small fee (or sometimes freely). Some applied for such documents as a protection from being charged in the future, but general pardons registered in advance of charges were not automatically accepted by courts.

(B) More than half of Shakespeare's works contain references to granting mercy or pardoning offences. Only a selected survey of instances is possible.

Numerous interpretations of pardon in Shakespeare (and also in Shakespeare's England) apparently follow from Michel Foucault's

Discipline and Punish, as for instance Kernan, 1995, pp 58–9. These apply Foucault's thesis to Jacobean England, claiming that the public pardoning of criminals served the state's aims of subjugation. In an interesting instance, Spencer, 1996 suggests that pardons asserted prerogative power, but finds that prerogative power was limited during the 'criminal' wars of H5; Henry taking lands by force is able to pardon Williams for **slander**, but not Bardolph for **theft**. Although some Foucauldian commentaries on pardon in Shakespeare do not acknowledge their source, such an application to a broad range of plays in Wilson, R., 1990 clearly does acknowledge it.

A particularly subtle application to AIT of somewhat atypical Foucauldian ideas is found in Schreiber-McGee, 1988, which describes, pp 197–8, how the repeated image of a 'single voice' in the play relates to a pardon.

Berger, 1981 amusingly argues that an imposition of 'mercifixation' characterises Portia in MV, who in her excessive generosity practices a kind of 'negative usury'. This irreverent comment on the speaker of the play's 'quality of mercy' homily (MV 4.1.181–99) is among the few that does not approach repeated mentions of 'mercy' in the play (especially in the trial scene) with awe. For fuller discussion of the traditions of Shakespeare criticism on the trial by (or of) law in MV see under **equity**.

MM contains Isabella's powerful and famous arguments urging 'mercy' and 'pardon' (MM 2.2.50–159), recalling in some ways the non-Foucauldian concepts of clemency brought out historically in Herrup, 1985 (discussed above). Indeed MM ends with a string of pardons, clustered around the Duke's extremely interesting line 'I find an apt remission in myself' (5.1.497). Despite that, this play explores at length the problematics of excessive judicial leniency. Having just set free the self-confessed unrepentant bawd Pompey, **Justice** Escalus states a central concern of the play succinctly: 'Mercy is not itself that oft looks so. / Pardon is still the nurse of second woe' (MM 2.1.272–3).

In another instance in the same play, judicial upholding of Lucio's false denial of the paternity of his child (MM 4.3.163–7) is not a credible outcome of the laxness in prosecution of sexual offenders in Vienna. This child would have been granted support from him both under canon law, and the Elizabethan Poor Law of 1576 (see Helmholz, 1977, **poverty** and **bastardy**).

Only by wholly ignoring the obvious theological implications in

Prospero's epilogue, pleading 'As you from crimes would pardoned be, / Let your indulgence set me free' (TMP 5.Ep.19–20), can an exclusively secular political/legal interpretation be placed, as it often is, on the extremely frequent mentions of pardoning offences in TMP.

A connection of a theatre audience with a merciful (perhaps heavenly) judge viewing human frailty also arises, in metaphor, in Shakespeare's sole passage containing the abstract noun 'clemency' ('clement' appears in CYM and STM). This is spoken at Elsinore, by the visiting players' Prologue:

> For us and for our tragedy
> Here stooping to your clemency,
> We beg your hearing patiently.
> (HAM 3.2.142–4)

Hamlet's immediate scoffing comment on this 'posy of a ring' (3.2.145), followed by his disruptive commentary during the ensuing performance, may seem to us merciless. But, as portrayed by Shakespeare, many in the noble audiences of meta-theatrical spectacle are sharply judgemental, and express this in an unbridled way during enactments (LLL 5.2 and MND 5.1). Shakespeare's choral presenters of spectacle also express a need to pray for the 'patience' of their audiences (H5 Pr.33 and WT 4.1.15). A concept of pardoning permeates Shakespeare's meta-theatrical gestures, suggesting that actors need indulgence in a way parallel with all men, who must hope for better applause from heaven than they deserve. The 'deceiver' who is 'pardoned' in TMP 5.Ep.7 is both an ambiguous and universal figure, a part of Prospero and every one of the audience addressed as 'you'.

(C) On pardons see: Pollock and Maitland, 1898, vol 2, pp 474–84; Bellamy, 1979, pp 218–25; Baker, 1990b, pp 584–5, 589–91. On the purchase of royal pardons in the middle ages see Bellamy, 1973, pp 85–6 and 190–8.

On mitigation or clemency offered by Elizabethan juries see especially Herrup, 1985, and under **jury**.

Nelson, 1984 finds SON 116 concerned with the pardon of an errant lover, as in ADO, and posits that the position expressed resembles that of a tolerant Church court judge (see under **civil doctor**) acting in a matrimonial cause concerning an **impediment**.

Jordan, W. C., 1982 is among the essays that properly distinguishes pardon and mercy as treated in MV from the activity of the English Chancery **jurisdiction**; see under **equity** for others. Berger, 1981 amusingly sees granting mercy as Portia's means to wresting power in MV.

Lindley, 1996 analyses punishment and pardon in MM, especially of Barnadine, with admirable lucidity; this finds that both details of the text and **jurisdictional** issues of Shakespeare's time raise doubts that the pardon in the play is used simply as a bid for power. Bernthal, 1992, p 253, suggests the pardons of Angelo, Lucio, Barnadine and Claudio in MM 'give a theatrical echo of the surprise pardons of Markham, Cobham and Grey, and Raleigh's stay of execution'. This points out calculation, theatricality, and two apparent resurrections in King James's 1604 proceedings. Wilson, R., 1990 exemplifies fully Foucauldian readings of MM; Lindley, 1996 points out among other problems with these is the secrecy of the 'execution' of Barnadine.

In a study of the jurisprudential aspects of Shakespearian comedy, especially, MV, MM, and TMP, Denvir, 1987, p 836, suggests it is best to view Portia, Isabella, and Prospero as judges faced with the problems of offering mercy.

McCune, 1994, especially pp 186–90, outlines how a 'public outcry' against the threat to public order, danger, and abuse in excessive pardoning of offenders found voice in pre-Shakespearian Tudor drama. The historical background elucidated has relevance to the problemisation of clemency in MM.

patent See **letters patents** for possible overtones of several uses denoting permission or licence, as for example when the Countess of Rousillon says that by the absent Count Bertram's 'authority [Lavache] remains here, which he thinks is a patent for his sauciness, and indeed he has no pace, but runs where he will' (AWW 4.5.65–7).

perpetuity (A) The term 'perpetuity' means a settlement of **land** which restricts inheritance, alienation and other dealings with the estate by the heirs into the future.

The modern doctrine of perpetuities, which strikes down any attempt to settle land for longer than the time span of a life or lives in being plus twenty one years, was developed with many vacillations and much perplexity through cases between the end of the fifteenth century and early eighteenth century.

In Shakespeare's time landowners and their **conveyancing** lawyers made efforts to create perpetual settlements in a number of ways, all of which failed (until the later seventeenth century). First attempts were made to create unbarrable **entails** by inserting clauses in deeds which made any attempt by life tenants to bar the entail and alienate a reason to allow the donor or his estate to re-enter (take over; see **fines and recoveries**). A series of cases from the late sixteenth century, including *Mildmay's Case* (1606) 6 Co. Rep. 40a and *Mary Portington's Case* (1613) 10 Co. Rep. 35 held such clauses to be void. Then lawyers experimented with creating 'perpetual freeholds' by a providing for a series of life estates, but this too was struck down in *Lovelace v Lovelace* (1585) (discussed in Simpson, 1986, p 315), and again in *Mary Portington's Case*.

An alternative form of perpetual settlement attempted was the entailed use. Briefly, in a use the legal estate was held by feoffees (trustees) for the benefit of the *cestui que use* (beneficiary). The Statute of Uses in 1536 enacted that the legal estate passed to the *cestui que use* (for more detail, see under **use**). But the law was unsettled about how far the Statute had any effect on an entailed use. However *Chudleigh's Case* (1595) 1 Co. Rep. 113b held that the Statute of Uses applied to such settlements too, so attempts to create perpetuities based on these failed.

Landowners were always concerned to secure dynastic succession through settlements of land (often through marriage arrangements involving **dowries** and **jointures**). They were probably also always concerned to retain freedom to alienate land if the need arose. In Shakespeare's time, such contrary needs, and the requirements of a changing society, made particularly contentious the unsettled part of **land** law dealing with perpetuities.

(B) In AWW 4.3.280–3 the relation of **entails** with perpetuities is wittily inverted, as the Devil will get perpetual possession perpetually in a surer manner than any human entail could arrange: 'he will sell the fee-simple of his salvation, the inheritance of it, and cut th' entail from all remainders, and a perpetual succession for it perpetually.'

King Lear on the contrary does attempt to set up a perpetual entail, although he fails to use precisely the right form of words ('heirs of your body' — see **entail**) to do so:

257

Of all these bounds even from this line to this,
With shadowy forests and with champaigns riched,
With plenteous rivers and wide-skirted meads,
We make thee lady. To thine and Albany's issues
Be this perpetual.

(LRF 1.1.63–7)

(C) On the evolution of the rule 'against' perpetuities through the seventeenth century and the political leanings of the lawyers involved see Haskins, 1977. On perpetuities in early modern England see especially Bonfield, 1983, pp 13–15, 22–4, 36–46. See also Simpson, 1986, pp 208–19 and Simpson, 1987b. References to perpetuities in Shakespeare are noted in Barton, S. D. P., 1929, pp 75–6 and Phillips, O. H., 1967, p 202, but oddly not in Clarkson and Warren, 1942.

plantation (A) 'Plantation' was the word in Shakespeare's time for establishing a colony (OED 4a). We can distinguish two issues that gave rise to the legal discussion of plantation in the period. One is the legal justification for the acquisition of **lands** which may have belonged to someone else, and the other the legal problems which emerge from setting up the constitution and administration of the plantation.

In the early years of the seventeenth century there was an intense controversy over the justification and legitimacy of the new English plantation in North America. Shakespeare was probably aware of the controversy over this issue, because long included among the putative sources of *The Tempest* are a number of New World texts, including tracts and a letter describing the miraculous salvation of a tempest-beset vessel of the 1609 supply expedition to the Jamestown colony in 'Virginia' (see Bullough, 1975, vol 8, p 240; Muir, 1972, p 200).

The question of legitimacy of settlement in non-Christian lands had been argued at first by Dominican jurists concerned with the treatment and the status of New World peoples in Spanish colonized lands. Notorious aspects of this debate fed into a long pamphlet war between Protestant and Catholic antagonists (see citations below). The English position was that the donation of the New World to Spain and Portugal by Pope Alexander was of dubious legality. How could he give away what was not his to give, for the legal maxim held *nemo dat quod non habet*? Moreover if the purpose of Spain's territorial claims was to convert the inhabitants to Christianity, then this purpose had manifestly failed. Instead the Spanish had enslaved the native inhabitants (see **slave**).

The English claimed to be able to do much better. Many pamphlets and sermons concerned the legitimacy, or otherwise, of taking land from native Americans. The doctrine of *terra nullius* allowed the occupation of empty land, but were lands occupied seasonally by ambulatory groups empty? Some pamphlets advanced James' lawful claim by right of succession from his immediate predecessor, claiming that Elizabethan voyages of discovery to the New World were made with the intention of planting English colonies in 'places not already possessed and inhabited by subjects of other Christian Princes' (Johnson, 1609, B1r). Potential Native American claims were discounted because the Virginia Company had no intention of supplanting the 'Indians' or invading their rights and possessions. Instead the Virginia Company intend 'mutual interchange and commerce' and the conversion of native inhabitants 'not by raging cruelties' as the Spanish had done, but by 'faire and loving means' (C2v).

Another argument raised was that the Native Americans had no particular property in any part or parcel of Virginia, but only a general residence or occupation right. Therefore they could not complain that a wrong was done to them even if the whole land was taken from them, although there was no such intention to take from them by force their rightful inheritance. Also the Native Americans were willing to sell as much land to the English as they wanted, so unless it was by **inheritance** or **election** there could be no more lawful entry onto the land than that taking place (Gray, R., 1864, pp 23–7). The legal contradictions raised in these arguments are profound. If the 'Indians' have no proprietary rights to the land how are they able give good title if they sell it to the English?

The nearly disastrous conflicts in 1609–10 at Jamestown between the English settlers and the united forces of Algonkian native inhabitants was a likely inspiration for Francis Bacon's 1625 essay 'Of Plantations':

> I like a plantation in a pure soil; that is, where people are not displanted to the end to plant in others. For else it is rather an extirpation than a plantation.
>
> (Bacon, 1994, p 88)

But Bacon had expressed contrary views in an earlier composition; in

1608 he presented an essay to King James on the plantation of Ireland, in which he urged James to undertake this project because 'unions and plantations are the very nativities or birthdays of kingdoms' ('Certain Considerations Touching the Plantation in Ireland Presented to His Majesty, 1606' in Bacon, 1872, vol 11, p 116). Bacon addressed both the legal justification for plantation and constitutional arrangements, presenting the King with plans for the good administration and government of such a plantation which closely resembled the constitution of the Jamestown Settlement set out in 1606 in the first Virginia Company Charter (Bemiss, 1957).

Some of the legal and constitutional bases on which England was to 'plant' colonies abroad were settled in an important legal decision of 1609. This decision found an alternative to a political 'union' of England and Scotland; it may provide the key to the difference between Bacon's 1625 views on plantation in uninhabited places and his earlier views on colonizing Ireland, which as we have seen bracketed 'unions and plantations'.

The accession of King James VI of Scotland to the English throne as James I, in 1603, left the question of the status of inhabitants of both England and Scotland unsettled. James wanted the union of England and Scotland under one Crown. He was opposed by the House of Commons, who argued that his succession had no effect on the separate legal systems of England and Scotland, and therefore a union of the two countries could only be achieved by an Act of Parliament. James opened the Parliamentary Session of 1606/7 with a strong plea for an Act of Union. The House of Commons and House of Lords debated the question over several months. Bacon introduced the debate in the House of Commons, while in the House of Lords ten leading judges were asked for their advice which was in favour of automatic naturalisation of the *postnati*, as those born in Scotland after James' succession were known (see Cobbett, 1806, vol 1, pp 1071–96). Despite this persuasive authority, the House of Commons refused to pass either an Act of Union or a declaratory Act for the automatic naturalisation of *postnati*.

Within a few months Robert Calvin's case was brought before all the judges of England. Although Francis Bacon insisted that *Calvin's Case* was 'no feigned or framed case' (Bacon, 1872, vol 7, p 641), there is little doubt that it was brought in both King's Bench and Chancery in order to bind every possible tribunal. Discussion by all the judges was the highest judicial authority and would create a **precedent** and so settle the question of the *postnati*, which the opinions given to Parliament could not. Francis Bacon, the Solicitor General, was counsel for the plaintiff and represented the crown's interest. The case was argued before Lord Ellesmere, the Lord Chancellor, Sir Thomas Fleming, Chief Justice of the King's Bench, Sir Edward Coke, Chief Justice of Common Pleas and the other leading judges (for published responses see: (1609) 7 Co. Rep. 1; Ellesmere's judgment reprinted in Knafla, 1977, pp 205–353; Bacon's arguments reprinted in Bacon, 1872, vol 7, pp 641–79). Briefly, the facts were that in 1608 Robert Calvin, an infant, claimed through guardians that he had been disseised, that is deprived, of land in London. The defendants argued that Robert ought not to be heard because he was an alien, born in 1606 in Edinburgh, and aliens could not hold freehold land in England.

The Court found in favour of Robert Calvin, and held that *postnati* could hold land in England. Francis Bacon argued that the 'allegiance of subjects to hereditary monarchs, which is corroborated and confirmed by the law, but is the work of the law of nature . . . as the common law is more worthy than the statute law; so the law of nature is more worthy than them both' (ibid., p 647). So for Bacon naturalization of alien Scots and their right to hold land in England was based not on the allegiance of the subject to a particular system of laws, or on any 'consent' given by the subject or by the representatives of the populace in Parliament, but on the personal bond of allegiance that existed between subject and monarch. Although Coke was later to fight to subject the King's prerogative powers to parliamentary control (see Berman, 1994 and under **praemunire** and **equity**), he agreed in his report on the case that allegiance and obedience is owed by every subject to his Sovereign; homage can be owed to a lord as an incident of tenure, but this can be respited, whereas allegiance cannot. So Coke emphasized that allegiance was the more permanent and lasting bond between King and subject. Even if a subject is outside the realm he owes allegiance which 'cannot be local or confined within the bounds thereof' ((1609) 7 Co. Rep. 9a). Therefore 'that leigance is a quality of the mind, and not confined within any space' (ibid.). For Ellesmere, all prerogatives derived from the natural body of the sovereign (Knafla, 1977, p 68; see also Kantorowicz, 1957, pp 14–16, and Coke 7 Co. Rep. 9b) but could be broken down into two parts: absolute prerogative revealed in the King's private will and prerogative revealed by the King's laws. Subjects owe a personal allegiance to the King who can

261

command all his subjects 'that bee under his obedience wheresoever they bee in the world' (Knafla, 1977, p 235). So for Coke, Bacon and Ellesmere allegiance would be owed by a subject when abroad because the King's power extended beyond the bounds of the Kingdom (see Dummett and Nicol, 1990, p 61).

These three and the other judges in *Calvin's Case* in 1608 probably had in mind not only the problem of the *postnati* of Scotland but also the status of the recent plantations of English people in Virginia. Settlers in Virginia were required to take oaths of allegiance to the English king, and the settlement was provided with laws by means of the King's prerogative. Therefore while it is true that the Virginian settlement was not at issue in the case, the legal basis of such arrangements were examined in it. *Calvin's Case* provided a forum for discussion of 'every aspect of allegiance and subjecthood' (Dummett and Nicol, 1990, p 59), and particularly of how the status of subject is attained. In his judgment, Coke addressed the question of the right of a King to legislate for other lands in some detail, considering Ireland, France, Jersey, Guernsey and the Isle of Mann as well as Scotland. People are divided into 'aliens' and 'subjects' ((1609) 7 Co. Rep. 17a). Subject status can be acquired by birth or gift. Aliens can be 'friend' or 'enemy', but infidels cannot be anything other than perpetual enemies, because between Christian and infidel there is perpetual hostility (ibid.). Coke went on to draw a distinction between conquest of a kingdom of a Christian King and that of an infidel: in the former the existing laws would continue in force until altered by the Conqueror, but in the latter the laws would immediately be abrogated, for such laws would be against Christianity, and against the laws of God and nature. Until new laws were enacted, the King through his appointed judges must judge the infidels by natural equity (see Virginia Council, 1906a, p 14). In any event the King's mandatory writs are not tied to any place but run outside the Kingdom if addressed to subjects (1609) 7 Co. Rep. 20a). Birth of a person outside the King's dominions but to parents who owe allegiance and obedience will make them a subject of the king. So it is the fact of the allegiance owed that makes the difference between an alien, friendly or otherwise, and a subject.

Bacon, who was a council member and shareholder in the Virginia Company and so shared the widespread fears during 1609–10 of the loss of English investment, prestige, and lives at Jamestown, referred more directly to plantations when he wrote of 'original submissions' to authority which are more natural and more ancient than the law. The first of these concerned 'paternity' or 'patriarchy'; when a family grew too numerous to contain itself within one habitation, and some branches were forced to plant themselves elsewhere, then this second branch naturally yielded 'an obeisance to the eldest line of the family from which they were derived' (Bacon, 1872, vol 7, p 645). If 'diverse families of English men and women plant themselves at Middleborough, or at Roan, or at Lisbon' and live and marry among themselves, then their descendants will be naturalized, and so 'you may have whole tribes and lineages of English in foreign countries' (p 652). It has been said that the doctrine of personal allegiance to the King was the link which would eventually bind the whole empire.

(B) Beginning 'Had I plantation of this isle, my lord' the rather confused old Lord Gonzalo outlines his plan for establishing an ideal colonial commonwealth on what he thinks to be a fertile but uninhabited island (TMP 2.1.149–74). The paradoxes of his speech are rich. For one, Shakespeare has Gonzalo plagiarize his supposedly utopian ideas, and also much of his very language, from John Florio's translation of Montaigne's essay 'On the Cannibals' where it discusses the strangeness of the actual polity of some indigenous peoples of Brazil. And the notion of applying the doctrine of *terra nullius* is further undermined when the 'isle' of the play turns out to have fantastic inhabitants who are at first hospitable and then hostile to the European intruders.

The background to these paradoxes was an actuality. Accounts of the 1609 foundering on an uninhabited Bermudan island and 1610 salvation of the crew and passengers of the ship *Sea Adventure* en route to America inspired the plot of *The Tempest* of 1611. What the *Sea Adventure* survivors found in 1610 at the dangerously threatened Jamestown settlement is also reflected in *The Tempest*. Jamestown was on the point of destruction thanks to disorder and rebellion of its European settlers, and to the effective trade embargo of the once-hospitable Algonkian inhabitants of the region. Despite the existence of carefully drafted laws, the weak governing of the colony was largely to blame for this. Correspondingly, the play displays a range of European plots and rebellions, and also shows both Ariel's exotic spirits and island-born Caliban turning from feeding to attacking the sojourners.

Caliban is aggrieved with Prospero because: 'This island's mine, by Sycorax my mother, / Which thou tak'st from me' (1.2.333–4). His

263

complaints reflect the issue of many discussions of colonial land seizures in English pamphlets and sermons, and in Bacon's essay. Caliban, although said to be lustful, ugly and deformed (and ill-smelling), also has a poetic capacity to appreciate beauty, and at the play's end says he will seek 'grace'. His (and Ariel's) mixed characteristics express the contradictory contemporary European views of America's native inhabitants.

The Tempest departs from the actual story of American settlement by the English when it finally shows Prospero and his fellow Italians abandoning the 'isle' and making a rapid journey home. (However, the Virginia settlement nearly met this fate in 1610.) Prior to this it reflects a range of attitudes in the sojourners on the play's island. Some see plantation as an opportunity for re-making society from a new start (2.1.149–74), others assume that a distance from Italy obliterates former ties of allegiance and fealty (2.1.244–73), and some run riot in anarchic rebellion.

(C) Despite a characteristic claim that an unresponsive silence as seen in TMP typifies 'the characteristic trope by which European colonial regimes articulated their authority over land to which they could have no conceivable legal claim' (Barker and Hulme, 1985, p 200), there were many articulate contemporary discussions of the legal and/or moral justification (or otherwise) of English plantation. The pamphlet controversy included: Ainsworth, 1608; Higgons, 1609a, b; Hoby, 1609; Johnson, 1609; 'True and Sincere Declaration,' 1610; Floyd, 1612; 'True Declaration,' 1844; Gray, R., 1864. Other documents containing contemporary sermons, arguments, or laws concerning plantation include: Keymis, 1596; Crashawe, 1610a, b; Strachey, 1844, 1953; 'Reasons Against Publishing,' 1906–35; Virginia Council, 1906a, b; and Bacon, 1872, vol 7, pp 661–2.

For a review of and response to part of the huge discussion of plantation and TMP, see Sokol and Sokol, 1996.

Questions of legitimacy in national expansion by war, as related to H5, are also addressed in Spencer, 1996.

portion This was the common term in legal documents for a dowry or gift on marriage made to the husband (see Sheehan, 1996, p 16). Shakespeare often uses this term, but uses 'dowry' even more frequently. An equivalence is implied in 'the portion and sinew of her fortune, her marriage dowry' (MM 3.1.222–3). The term 'portion' appears in this sense also in 1H6, SHR, LRQ, LRF, WT, TNK. See **dowry**.

poverty/beggary (A) During the sixteenth century a transformation took place in the perception of poverty, and for the first time the English parliament began to legislate for universal secular provision for the relief of the 'deserving' poor. This process culminated in the Elizabethan Poor Law of 1601.

The causes of poverty in England were various. The population had increased, probably doubling from 2.5 million in the early sixteenth century to about 5 million in the late seventeenth century. At the same time the incidence of outbreaks of the plague declined, and mortality fell. By the early seventeenth century a series of bad harvests at the end of the sixteenth century, and the cost and stress of the war with Spain, had led to inflation of the price of basic foods, increase in rents, and decline in real wages. The accelerating breakdown of feudal relations, and enclosures of common land all encouraged migration from countryside to towns. This in turn brought a great increase in urban population, leading to overcrowding and disease. Between the 1520s and 1600 London in particular grew from about 50,000 people to 200,000, and most of this increase was the result of migration.

In addition to these demographic and economic changes, the Henrician Reformation brought disruption in the traditional means for the relief of poverty. Between 1530 and 1540 some 800 monasteries, religious foundations and chantries were closed. The destruction of these institutions had grave consequences for the poor because, through almshouses, doles, education, and hospitals, they had been the main providers of relief for the old, the sick, and orphans.

The church had funded such institutions through tithes, a proportion of which was applied to poor relief, and by encouraging gifts of alms to pious causes in **wills**, and directing a proportion of an intestate's goods to pious causes (see **inheritance**). Wills of personalty and intestacy were administered by the Church courts, which developed many of the principles and rules applicable to the modern law of charity. Charitable gifts were privileged, for instance by the doctrine of *cy pres* by which gifts were applied to alternate charitable causes if they would otherwise fail.

265

After the Reformation, bequests to charitable causes fell. Protestant, puritan and Catholic humanist ideas promoted notions of godly reform. In France and Germany humanist inspired ideas of social reform led to schemes for the intervention by the state to provide institutions to care for the poor. In London humanist influence, allied to private philanthrophy and civic pride, was responsible for the founding (or reorganization) of several London hospitals between 1544–57, each providing for particular needs: St. Bartholomew's and St. Thomas' to care for the sick, Christ's to care for foundlings, Bridewell for idle rogues and Bedlam for the insane (Slack, 1988, p 120; Slack, 1990, p 16). Important legal developments took place. In an attempt to encourage the secular giving of alms, Chancery upheld charitable **uses**, allowing special privileges for charitable gifts. In 1601 the Charitable Uses Act provided for commissioners to oversee charitable foundations. This Act distinguished between a gift for a superstitious (meaning a false religious purpose), and a gift to relieve poverty. The former had been forbidden by Henrician statutes suppressing chantries, but the post- Reformation state now wanted to encourage secular support for charitable causes.

These measures provided an insufficient answer to the problems of poverty, and more radical measures were sought to replace the church's work. Distinctions were increasingly made between those who were seen as the deserving poor, who should receive help, and the undeserving, who should be punished. The deserving poor were the widows and orphans, the sick and the old, while the undeserving poor were the idle beggars, or the wandering **vagrants**. In Shakespeare's time large groups of wandering vagrants caused alarm and fear in towns and villages, while local indigents burdened the parish. The Tudor Poor Law statutes addressed these problems by combining help for the deserving poor, with punishment for 'incorrigible rogues', those deemed undeserving.

Under Henry VIII, first Thomas Wolsey, followed by Thomas Cromwell, began to formulate a policy for the relief of poverty. A statute passed in 1531 identified the problems of poverty and vagabondage and introduced the idea of legalized begging. Parish officials were instructed to make collections of alms to be distributed to the parish poor, and search out the transient poor and ensure they were returned to their parish of birth or where they had lived for the previous three years. Returning transients were to be provided with food and lodging at 10-mile intervals on their homeward route. All beggars were to be registered, and those considered deserving were to be issued with certificates of eligibility which authorized them to beg in a particular location. But the able-bodied poor were to be whipped and returned to their own parish. The punishment for re-offending was a further whipping, and the upper part of the offender's ear was cut off. A third offence was a **felony** and could result in hanging. A later short-lived Act of 1536 attempted to make begging and private almsgiving unlawful, and to instead introduce compulsory parish almsgiving into the 'common box' on Sundays and holy days to provide for the maintenance of the deserving poor, while vagabonds were to be put to work and pauper children to be provided with apprenticeships. This act marked the transition from hundred and court **leet** to the parish in the local organization of relief for the poor (Slack, 1990, p 17–18).

Another statute, short-lived because it proved unworkable, was passed in 1547. This demanded weekly collections of alms and prohibited all begging, both of which met with resistance in all levels of society. Vagrants who offended were to be enslaved for two years (see **slavery**). Further abortive or short-lived statutes in 1552, 1555 and 1562 all attempted to introduce compulsory almsgiving.

A statute of 1572 set out further, more effective, plans for the central regulation of problems of poverty, using the same mixture of punishment and help. **Justices of the Peace** were given responsibility to survey the poor, and powers to assess all within each parish for compulsory taxation to support local poor relief. Each parish was responsible for its own poor, and vagrants were to be forcibly returned to the parish of their birth. The office of Overseer of the Poor was set up with a duty to seek out rogues and vagabonds and put them to work. The harsh punishments to be meted out to vagabonds caused initial opposition to the bill in parliament; vagrants were to be whipped and bored through the ear for a first offence, followed by hanging for a second offence (these provisions were replaced in 1593 by a return to whipping). A later Act of 1576 supplemented the 1572 Act by requiring the Justices to provide work for the idle poor, and Houses of Correction for those who refused to work. This Act also empowered Justices of the Peace to order fathers to support their illegitimate offspring, relieving parishes of this expense and enforcing a long-standing provision of canon law (see Helmholz, 1977).

An Act of 1598 (later consolidated in the 1601 Poor Relief Act with the earlier acts) largely established the Elizabethan Poor Law. The churchwarden and two substantial householders in every parish were appointed by the Justice of the Peace to act as Overseers to the Poor, with duties primarily to provide outdoor relief. This included finding **apprenticeships** and employment for needy children, setting up schemes of work in Workhouses as outdoor relief for the unemployed, and building cottages on waste land to house poor families. The whole scheme was to be financed from local rates set by the Justice of the Peace, which was an idea unique to England at the time. In addition, the undeserving poor were controlled and punished. Native 'sturdy rogues' and 'vagabonds' were set to work in Houses of Correction, while vagrants, who were the responsibility of the **constable**, were punished by whipping and returned to their parishes of birth. The death penalty for a third offence was reintroduced in 1604. Dangerous and incorrigible rogues were brought before the Justices at the quarter sessions and could be **banished**.

In the late sixteenth and early seventeenth century the Privy Council produced instructions for Justices of the Peace in the form of a series of Books of Orders which were circulated throughout the country inform-ing them on what steps they should take to provide for the poor in a particular crises, such as harvest failure, or outbreak of plague, and generally on administering local provision for the poor. Although the Act of Settlement was not enacted until 1662, a principle had already been established in the earlier vagrancy statutes that each parish was responsible for its own poor. This principle has been much criticised for creating needless bureaucracy and expense, interfering with mobility of labour, and causing much suffering because each parish to acted to ensure it was not taking on the responsibility and meeting the cost of providing for the poor from other parishes. It has also been regarded as providing a 'useful cushion' for the poor, and importantly providing the poor with an acknowledged right to support at public expense in times of need (see Slack, 1990, pp 37–8 for a summary of these views).

(B) Nearly every play or group of poems by Shakespeare contains mul-tiple instances of the word 'beggary' or a derivative. The works lacking such words, 1H6, STM, VEN, WIV and TNK, are not real exceptions, as each of these contains one or more references to 'poverty' or to the 'poor'.

Images of poverty abound in Shakespeare's writing. Poverty is presented with valuations varying from that of a holy state, through to the pathetic, the comic, the despicable, and the frightening.

The self-pitying rhetoric of Richard II uses images of mendicant pilgrims or religious orders to figure the loss of his kingship:

> A God's name, let it go.
> I'll give my jewels for a set of beads,
> My gorgeous palace for a hermitage,
> My gay apparel for an almsman's gown,
> My figured goblets for a dish of wood,
> My sceptre for a palmer's walking staff,
> My subjects for a pair of carved saints.
> (R2 3.3.145–51)

This personal mawkishness is a poor reflection of the old traditions of holy indigence. These traditions involved a supposedly universal symbiotic relationship of rich and poor, in which charity relieves need while poverty reminds the rich to value the holiness of Christ's poverty. The latter function leads to Lear's new resolution to 'take physic, pomp . . . ' (LRQ S.11.30 / LRF 3.4.33 – see below).

In what seems a mixed reaction to an increasingly uncharitable age, Shakespeare's plays are ambiguously situated in relation to Reformation objections to mendicant religiosity. There is a sardonic glance at the allied issue of the purchase of salvation by giving alms, when King John scorns the monetary 'purchase' of a Papal 'pardon', calling it a 'juggling witchcraft' (JN 3.1.95). In Shakespeare's England, both sale of indulgences and mendicant orders were prohibited. Yet in several of his continental, medieval, or fabulous settings, Shakespeare does portray religious figures in mendicant orders, that is friars. These dramatic contexts reflect both their good intentions, and their reputation for worldliness. So, although with good if worldly aims, Shakespeare's friars or apparent friars become involved in dubious covert practices such as enacting seeming necromancy, arranging clandestine **spousals**, or the bid-trick.

Shakespeare displays mixed reactions to traditions of philosophical austerity perhaps affiliated to pious asceticism, Young Shakespearian would-be ascetic philosophers are mocked by their easy capitulations to erotic temptation in LLL and SHR (but not the older Jacques of AYL). But Shakespearian lovers who express traditional self-abnegation

269

('naughting') in terms of poverty are perhaps more sincere, as in 'I do forgive thy robb'ry, gentle thief, / Although thou steal thee all my poverty' (SON 40), or in Biron's repentant 'I am a fool, and full of poverty' (LLL 5.2.380).

Shakespeare's characters express varied Renaissance notions relating to poverty, other than the ascetic ideal. Renaissance scepticism about worldly rank is heard often, as in Lear's 'mad' social insights, or in Hamlet's sardonic:

> we fat ourselves for maggots. Your fat king and your lean beggar is but variable service – two dishes, but to one table
>
> (HAM 4.3.23–5)

But alternately, Coriolanus thinks of the killing of the Roman poor as a loss of 'musty superfluity' (COR 1.1.226) or 'musty chaff' (5.1.26), and the less shocking Calpurnia believes: 'When beggars die there are no comets seen; / The heavens themselves blaze forth the death of princes' (JC 2.2.30–1). Yet others of Shakespeare's works (some discussed below) take sympathetic note of economically struggling figures, and give prominence not only to princes.

Quite often the implied valuation of a pauper in a Shakespeare play is ambiguous or mixed. In particular, Christopher Sly is called 'Begger' in the Folio stage directions and speech prefixes of SHR, and by the Lord in the Induction. Sly identifies himself as 'by birth a pedlar, by education a cardmaker, by transmutation a bearherd, and now by present profession a tinker' (SHR Ind.2.17–19). The wide variety of his occupations speaks either to habitual failure, or to keen initiative in the face of hardship. It is also ambiguous whether the jest in Sly's temporary transformation from poverty to riches rests in portraying Sly's social ineptitude, or in portraying Sly's enterprising spirit.

A perhaps beguiling wiliness appears in the antics of Autolycus of WT. Sokol, 1994a, pp 167–82, argues that his dubious ploys are audience-testing, rather than instructive (as seemingly thought by Simon Forman). Autolycus portrays downward social mobility as opposed to Sly's (or the Clown's in WT) upward mobility. Like Sly, Autolycus has also by his own account practiced a wide variety of callings. Once 'a servant of the Prince ... whipped out of court', Autolycus then became 'an ape-bearer, then a process-server – a bailiff – then he compassed a motion of the Prodigal Son, and married a tinker's wife . . . and having flown over many knavish professions, he settled only in rogue' (WT 4.3.86–98). The itinerant and showmanlike (using bears or puppets) activities of Sly and Autolycus are considered under **vagrant**. Here it is emphasized that, in a mode similar to 'coney-catching' narrators, Shakespeare reflects a fascination with ingenious if dishonest poverty. The Elizabethan taste for portrayals of cunning roguery may even suggest folkloric dissidence from orthodoxies about 'degree' and station.

Her father's poverty is used in an insult in the Yorkist Edward Plantagenet's defiant description of the marriage of Henry VI to Queen Margaret: 'he took a beggar to his bed' (RDY 2.2.154). Heterogamy, as figured in the hoary tale of a king who loves a beggar maid, has varied expositors in Shakespeare's comedies. These range from the absurd Don Armado in LLL 1.2.104–11, 4.1.64–79 (on the context see under **precedent**), through the viciously obscene Lucio of MM 3.1.389–9 ('not the Duke? Yes, your beggar of fifty; and his use was to put a ducat in her clack-dish'), to the high born Oliver of AYL, Lysimachus of PER, Florizel of WT, and Ferdinand of TMP who love and would marry apparently lowly lasses. Of course Viola, Marina, Perdita, and Miranda are not what they seem; within the conventions of Romance or romantic comedy their apparent poverty is a benign accident temporally befalling the well born. But the noble **outlaws** following Duke Senior in AYL experience their temporary privations alongside permanent residents of Arden born to permanent economic limitation. At the play's end the folk of the forest are left in their relative want, while asceticism in the forest provides some of the court with an opportunity for permanent penance and religiosity.

Shakespeare exposes flaws in characters who vigorously assert so strong a feeling for the differences of 'degree' that they despise the poor. To his discredit, Coriolanus is often scabrous against the Roman poor, and rails against the image of giving anything to 'beggars':

> For the mutable rank-scented meinie,
> Let them regard me, as I do not flatter,
> And therein behold themselves. I say again,
> In soothing them we nourish 'gainst our Senate
> The cockle of rebellion, insolence, sedition,
> Which we ourselves have ploughed for, sowed, and scattered
> By mingling them with us, the honoured number

271

> Who lack not virtue, no, nor power, but that
> Which they have given to beggars.
>
> (COR 3.1.70–8)

In CYM the odious Cloten appears even worse when he proposes that, unlike impoverished Posthumus, he is too grand to be bothered with legal and ethical decencies concerning marriage **contracts** fit only for 'meaner parties . . . to knit their souls, / On whom there is no more dependency / But brats and beggary, in self-figured knot' (CYM 2.3.113–16 – see under **pre-contract**).

Indeed, not even despising the poor, but only mentioning a wide distinction of status or 'degree', borrows a moral taint from Leontes' tyrannical insistence on Hermione's adultery: 'Lest barbarism, making me the precedent, / Should a like language use to all degrees, / And mannerly distinguishment leave out / Betwixt the prince and beggar' (WT 2.1.86–9 – on the context see under **precedent**).

A regime in which the Poor Laws distinguished worthy from unworthy beggars, yet the community retained an older belief that need itself justifies help, is reflected in several Shakespearian sequences in which the formerly prosperous receive much-needed charitable help from the penniless. This is seen in AYL 2.7.88–134, and on his own report even haughty Coriolanus accepted a succour from a 'poor man' (COR 1.10.81–2). The most extended instance is in PER, when the naked shipwrecked Prince Pericles seeks help from poor fishermen. Pericles first says to them 'He asks of you, that never used to beg' and receives a wry reply: 'No, friend, cannot you beg? Here's them in our country of Greece gets more with begging than we can do with working' (PER S.5.103–6). Such rumours of well-off beggars or sham invalids, and their wiles, found their way into coney-catching texts (and are reflected in H5 3.6.68–82, 5.1.84–5). Pericles, however, does receive charitable help, for he shows himself clearly destitute:

PERICLES   What I have been, I have forgot to know,
          But what I am, want teaches me to think on:
          A man thronged up with cold; my veins are chill,
          And have no more of life than may suffice
          To give my tongue that heat to crave your help,
          Which if you shall refuse, when I am dead,
          For that I am a man, pray see me buried.

MASTER	Die, quotha? Now, gods forbid 't an I have a gown here! Come, put it on, keep thee warm. Now, afore me, a handsome fellow! Come, thou shalt go home, and we'll have flesh for holidays, fish for fasting-days, and moreo'er puddings and flapjacks, and thou shalt be welcome.
PERICLES	I thank you, sir.
SECOND FISHERMAN	Hark you, my friend, you said you could not beg?
PERICLES	I did but crave.
SECOND FISHERMAN	But crave? Then I'll turn craver too, an so I shall scape whipping.
PERICLES	Why, are all your beggars whipped, then?
SECOND FISHERMAN	O, not all, my friend, not all; for if all your beggars were whipped I would wish no better office than to be beadle.

(PER S.5.112–34)

This recalls the punishment of all but licensed beggars under the English statutes (see above, and **constable**). Prince Pericles approves the 'honest mirth' of these poor labourers, and soon after overcomes his pride concerning the need to beg from them, saying he indeed means to 'beg of you, kind friends' (S.5.179). In such a scene, even where one fisherman is humorously called 'Patchbreech', there is no contempt of poverty.

Neither is Katherine of Aragon at all contemptuous of poverty when she says of her loyal followers 'they are the poorest, / But poverty could never draw 'em from me' (AIT 4.2.149–50).

Yet, in a different dramatic register, Falstaff treats derisively the ragged recruits he has gathered for the army:

PRINCE HARRY	I did never see such pitiful rascals.
FALSTAFF	Tut, tut, good enough to toss, food for powder, food for powder. They'll fill a pit as well as better. Tush, man, mortal men, mortal men.
WESTMORLAND	Ay, but Sir John, methinks they are exceeding poor and bare, too beggarly.
FALSTAFF	Faith, for their poverty, I know not where they had that, and for their bareness, I am sure they never learned that of me.

273

PRINCE HARRY   No, I'll be sworn, unless you call three fingers in the
                ribs bare. But sirrah, make haste. Percy is already in
                the field.

                (1H4 4.2.64–75)

Here Falstaff's squalid view of these 'food for powder' is overlooked by
Hal, for whom the running joke of Falstaff's obesity apparently lightens
inhumanity.

Indeed, a contemptuous attitude toward poverty is implicit in
numerous Shakespearian interchanges in which allegations of starvation for food season abusive speech. The contexts for these are often
military flyting (1H6 1.7.16 and 3.5.1–8; CYL 1.1.132; H5 4.2.16–29),
or Falstaffian humour (1H4 2.5.248–51; 2H4 3.2.299, 3.2.307–9 and
5.4.18–30). It is probably also intended to be discrediting to Jack Cade
that he admits 'famine' has been his vanquisher (CYL 4.9.60 and
4.9.75). Some kind of humorous aspersion is intended in the naming of
'Master Starve-lackey' (MM 4.3.13), of 'Robin Starveling' (MND
1.2.54, etc.), and of 'Doctor Pinch' (ERR 4.4.48, etc.). The poverty of
the would-be exorcist Pinch is delineated with particular contempt by
the chief victim of his quackery, who describes him as 'a hungry lean-
faced villain, / A mere anatomy, a mountebank, / A needy, hollow-
eyed, sharp-looking wretch, / A living dead man . . . pernicious slave'
(ERR 5.1.238–42 – see under **wise man** and **slave**).

When it comes to effrontery, buffoonery, and poverty entangled,
Falstaff takes all prizes, and draws all in, even the **Chief Justice**:

LORD CHIEF JUSTICE   To punish you by the heels would amend the
                      attention of your ears, and I care not if I do
                      become your physician.

FALSTAFF   I am as poor as Job, my lord, but not so
                      patient. Your lordship may minister the potion
                      of imprisonment to me in respect of poverty;
                      but how I should be your patient to follow your
                      prescriptions, the wise may make some dram
                      of a scruple, or indeed a scruple itself.

                                . . .

LORD CHIEF JUSTICE   Well, the truth is, Sir John, you live in great
                      infamy.

FALSTAFF   He that buckles himself in my belt cannot live
                      in less.

LORD CHIEF JUSTICE	Your means are very slender, and your waste is great.
FALSTAFF	I would it were otherwise; I would my means were greater and my waist slenderer.

(2H4 1.2.125–44)

Here the usually clear-headed Chief Justice falls into the trap of making jests on Falstaff's girth, yet manages first to mention the stocks as a punishment for idle poverty. Interestingly, in WIV 4.5.110–13, Falstaff admits he is indeed stocked (as a **wise woman**!) by a **constable**.

The deeply impoverished, as opposed to idle labourers or rogues undergoing shallow dearth, are not shown humorously by Shakespeare. The famine in Tarsus of PER S.4 presents a horrible image of degraded suffering, until outside relief is offered. This offer of mass relief accords with the practice in England, which was increasingly effective until periodic mass starvation was eradicated by the end of the seventeenth century.

The consequence of hard poverty on an individual is portrayed in the sale for money of the conscience of the apothecary approached in ROM for illegal poison. The interchange is chilling:

ROMEO	. . . Famine is in thy cheeks,
	Need and oppression starveth in thy eyes,
	Contempt and beggary hangs upon thy back.
	The world is not thy friend, nor the world's law.
	The world affords no law to make thee rich.
	Then be not poor, but break it, and take this.
APOTHECARY	My poverty but not my will consents.
ROMEO	I pay thy poverty and not thy will.

(ROM 5.1.66–76)

Rather more sympathy is shown toward the 'houseless poverty' of the Fool in *King Lear*, which when noticed by him causes Lear to reflect:

> Poor naked wretches, wheresoe'er you are,
> That bide the pelting of this pitiless storm,
> How shall your houseless heads and unfed sides,
> Your looped and windowed raggedness, defend you
> From seasons such as these? O, I have ta'en

275

Too little care of this. Take physic, pomp,
Expose thyself to feel what wretches feel,
That thou mayst shake the superflux to them
And show the heavens more just.

(LRF 3.4.28–36)

Such a call for sympathy and greater sharing to 'show the heavens more just' was reflected also in society's attempts through law at distributive justice.

Such an historical context may help us read constable Dogberry, who is one of the 'poor Duke's officers' (3.5.19), 'but a poor man' (3.5.25–6). It is not necessary that Dogberry's former receipt of charity from a hospital or the like is (as some editors think) a discredit to him when he cries out with habitual gratitude 'God save the foundation' (ADO 5.1.309). Although alms could appear in a humorous metaphor like Costard's 'alms-basket of words' for miscellaneous lexical discards (LLL 5.1.39), if Dogberry had been a foundling he would not differ from Perdita, the 'bairn' of whom the Shepherd says 'I'll take it up for pity' (WT 3.3.74).

The concept of 'charity' is named in the majority of Shakespeare's plays, is implicit in nearly all, and is never disparaged.

(C) The most important English poor law **statutes** are summarized in Slack, 1990, which also has a good bibliography.

On English charities see Jones, G., 1969 pp 3–56 and Chesterman, 1979, pp 10–35. For an outline of the historical background see: Wrightson, 1982, pp 139–142, 144, 180–2; Slack, 1988; Slack, 1990, pp 9–34. On the problem of 'masterless men' see Beier, 1985, and under **vagrant**. On orders issued by the King's Council to Justices of the Peace following the disastrous harvest of 1608 see Osborne, 1960, p 77.

On support orders for **bastards** see Helmholz, 1977. On Jacobean punishments of mothers whose bastards were chargeable to the parish see Osborne, 1960, pp 67–9.

Studies by social historians such as Laslett, 1983 have thrown much light on early modern poverty in England.

Berry, R., 1988 considers social 'class' and Shakespeare's plays; Patterson, 1989 throws considerable doubt on notions that Shakespeare reflected only an elitist position. For a useful bibliography of work arguing whether there is or is not social–political 'subversion' in *King Lear* see Patterson, 1984, p 59.

McDonald, 1995, pp 121–5, outlines the economic troubles leading to dearth and displacement in the 1590s, and gives a careful account of the debates and five **statutes** concerning poverty or its causes of the 1597/8 Parliament. This then finds reflections of the same issues in several plays of 1599, including AYL and H5. It reads AYL as imaging an ordered agrarian world offering hospitality and self-reliance, and imaging contrary displacement and hunger, and it locates in H5 the problems of fake veterans, vagabonds and rogues (see under **vagrant**).

In a discussion of Elizabethan taverns and moral irregularities in relation to MM, punishments of single mothers are considered as severe oppression in Widmayer, 1995.

Ives, 1985, pp 26–8, outlines the harsh economic circumstances of Shakespeare's age, and finds Shakespeare not very responsive or sympathetic to its victims; in a reply disagreeing with this, Carroll, 1991 discusses the implications of the language used by Shakespeare concerning poverty, especially in CYL, *King Lear* and WT.

Cohen, D., 1993 considers the 'obsessive concern' portrayed in TIM with contrasts of poverty and wealth an indication of a transition from **villeinage** to capitalism, notes a distortion of values in the play, and finds the tragedy 'revolutionary'. Wilson, R., 1993, pp 83–117, argues that COR concerns the (unhappy) rise of a 'market economy' in which the Elizabethan Poor Law played an important part.

praemunire (A) This offence was to prosecute in a foreign court a suit which was triable in an English **jurisdiction**, and in particular to turn from an English court to the Papal courts. Praemunire was first created by the Statutes of Provisors of 1351 and 1353; the offence was named by a key word in the writ issued to summon the person accused to appear in the King's courts. The Statute of Winchester of 1393 specified that confiscation of property followed a *praemunire* action. Penalties were reduced in Elizabethan times, and it was sometimes brought into use for other purposes, such as against **debtors** who tried jurisdictional ploys to avoid payment (Knafla, 1977, p 168). However Shakespeare never alludes to these uses.

The boundaries of jurisdiction between the ecclesiastical and royal courts were supposed to have been settled by the early fourteenth century, by *Circumspecte Agatis* 1285 and *Articuli Cleri* 1315 (see Baker, 1990b, p 149, and Dawson, 1941, p 128). But the royal courts still issued writs of *praemunire*, first to prevent suits being taken to Rome, then to prevent papal legates asserting their authority in England. Later the royal courts also issued writs of prohibition to intervene in litigation in ecclesiastical courts within England, for example asserting the common law's exclusive right to hear cases of real property (**land**).

In 1529 Cardinal Wolsey, Lord Chancellor from 1515, was indicted for *praemunire*. Before his fall Wolsey had been much disliked by common lawyers for his apparent disregard for the common law and his interference with its courts (Baker, 1990b, p 123; Baker, 1978, p 77). By 1613 (when AIT portrayed these events) a momentous sequel was in process. In the series of jurisdictional challenges mounted by common lawyers leading up to the crisis of 1616, the **Chief Justice** Sir Edward Coke first turned his attention to the ecclesiastical courts and newer prerogative courts, and then finally against the Court of Chancery. He challenged the jurisdictions of the ecclesiastical courts for example in *Fullers Case* ((1607) 12 Coke Rep. 41), in which Dawson, 1941, p 129, says 'occasion was seized to claim the broadest power in common law courts to define the limits of the ecclesiastical jurisdiction'. Coke also attacked the minor **equity** Court of Requests, for example in *Penson v Cartwright*, Cro. Jac. 345 (1614), and questioned among other things the use of *ex officio* oaths by the Court of High Commission which compelled people to incriminate themselves (see *Prohibitions del Roy* (1608), 12 Coke Rep. 63). He also attacked the provincial equity courts of the North and the Welsh Marches with writs of *habeas corpus* and prohibition (the advisory opinion in 12 Coke Rep. 50; see Dawson, 1941, pp 129–30). Eventually Coke directly addressed the long-standing dispute about the right of Chancery to reopen judgments at common law, relying on the statute 4 Hen. IV, c.23 (1403) that judgments in the king's courts were to be left in peace unless reversed by attaint or writ of error, and on the *praemunire* statutes. In *Heath v Ridley* (1614) 2 Bulstrode 194, Cro. Jac. 335, Coke at King's Bench refused to obey a Chancery injunction, and in *Wright's Case* (1614) Moore KB 836, 1 Rolle Rep. 71 he considered prohibitions against Chancery. Coke's actions in the *Earl of Oxford's Case* (1615) 1 Rep. Ch. 1 incurred the particular enmity of Francis Bacon and Lord Chancellor Ellesmere. Under Coke, King's Bench issued writs of prohibition and *habeas corpus* against the Court of Chancery, and finally in 1616 considered using *praemunire* in *Glanville's Case* (Cro. Jac. 344 (1614); see Baker, 1969, pp 379–83).

(B) There is a clear reference in AIT to the *praemunire* of Cardinal Wolsey, to whom Suffolk says:

> Lord Cardinal, the King's further pleasure is –
> Because all those things you have done of late,
> By your power legantine within this kingdom,
> Fall into th' compass of a praemunire –
> That therefore such a writ be sued against you,
> To forfeit all your goods, lands, tenements,
> Chattels, and whatsoever, and to be
> Out of the King's protection. This is my charge.
>
> (AIT 3.2.338–45)

If Shakespeare indeed wrote these lines, he was reflecting the historical record. So Keeton, 1967, p 31, points out that this passage 'uses the very words of the Statute of *praemunire* [16 Rich. II, c. 5], but, of course, Shakespeare would find these words in any account of the fall of Wolsey'. AIT then accurately indicates the confiscation and **outlawry** that arose.

Shakespeare avoided any allusion to dubiously correct extended uses of writs of *praemunire* in English jurisdictional disputes, as well as all jocular or figurative uses of '*praemunire*' such as those noted in OED 3.

(C) On the development of *praemunire* following the English reformation see Baker, 1990b, pp 150–1. On uses of *praemunire* to limit the jurisdiction over **debt** of the Church courts, see Helmholz, 1987f.

On the *praemunire* charges against Wolsey see Scarisbrick, 1974, pp 301–10. On the mainly accurate reflection in AIT of these charges see Keeton, 1967, p 31, and Phillips, O. H., 1972, p 138.

On the events leading to Coke's use of *praemunire* and his dismissal in 1616 see Usher, 1903; Dawson, 1941, p 137, Baker, 1969; Thomas, G. W., 1976; Knafla, 1977, p 170, Gray, C., 1976, and Thorne, 1985f.

On the *ex officio* business of the Church courts see under **civil doctor** and **pre-contract**. On *ex officio* oaths and an alleged connection with the question of the property of the **bastard** in JN see Hamilton, D. B.,

1992, pp 34–58, which mentions, p 50, two **statutes** proposed in 1593 to make officials who administered such oaths guilty of *praemunire*.

precedent (A) English law is often described as a common law system of law. When common law is used in this sense a distinction is made between the English legal systems and others, such as the civilian legal systems (see **civil doctor**). Used in another sense common law is said to be one part of English law, along with statute law. In this context common law means case law, or judicial law, as opposed to legislation (on this see **statute**, **bills**), and is to be found in the decisions of judges. This law can be found in the *ratio decidendi* of a case, that is the judge's finding of law in any legal decision which will act as a precedent and bind decisions in inferior courts.

The doctrine of precedent existed to a certain extent in early modern England and was closely linked to the declaratory theory of common law. According to this theory the common law had always existed, so that judges did not make the law but merely pronounced it. So it was only necessary to know what the law was in any given situation, which could be discovered by looking at prior decisions. Although the declaratory theory now rests on the doctrine of binding precedent, or *stare decisis*, the latter is of relatively recent origin. A doctrine of binding precedent requires judges not to depart from rules of law found in previous decisions, and so such a doctrine must in turn depend on the existence of a comprehensive system of law reporting. The Council of Law Reporting was eventually set up in 1865 to produce the *Law Reports* (although before that date individual named reports had appeared).

The modern doctrine of binding precedent also requires the existence of a hierarchy of courts, so that each court stands in a definite relationship to other courts, and an inferior court is bound to follow the decisions of the superior court. Again this hierarchy is of relatively recent origin, developing from the system of courts set up in the nineteenth century (Judicature Acts 1873 and 1875). It was only in 1898 that the House of Lords held it was bound by its own previous decisions (although in 1966 it held it could depart from previous decisions).

In medieval and early modern England there was no hierarchy of courts in general, and courts did not consider themselves bound by decisions in other courts. Also when precedents were applied they could arise from much earlier rather than from more recent cases. Moreover, in medieval and early modern England, when judges did defer to precedents these were less likely to be found in individual decisions and understood more as the 'common learning', or a collective understanding, of the common law. This common learning could sometimes be found in legal treatises, sometimes arose from discussions that took place in the courts at Westminster Hall, and sometimes from discussions between judges and lawyers at **Serjeants'** Inn or the **Inns of Court**. Some very important 'leading' cases were submitted to the common opinion of all the judges and **serjeants** (on serjeants-at-law see under **lawyers** and **justices**), who met in Exchequer Chamber at Westminster. Such opinions were often considered the highest judicial authority in the country (see Baker, 1990b, p 226).

The medieval oral system of pleadings used in the royal courts had allowed for tentative legal argument between lawyers and judges which continued until the issue was considered sufficiently settled, and only at this point were the pleadings said to be fixed. However in the sixteenth century a change took place because of the introduction of written pleadings. This meant that pleadings were settled before the case was heard, and this ended the practice of informal legal discussion in court. As a result the locus of collective learning was shifted from preliminary discussions to the case itself, and gradually these matters appeared in case reports. By the late sixteenth century there are instances when precedents were cited in court, and evidence that the modern distinction between *ratio decidendi* (which was binding) and *obiter dicta* (merely general remarks that are not binding) was recognised.

Another change that took place in the sixteenth century was the effect brought about by the introduction of printing, allowing for wide dissemination of treatises, reports and, for instance, Coke's monumental *Institutes*. Legal publishers like Richard Tottel (also of the important poetic *Miscellany*) propelled a change in the common law from a predominantly oral culture to a written one.

Before the introduction of printing in about 1470, the plea rolls recorded only the decisions reached. Fuller legal reporting was found in the Year Books, which were collections of legal arguments probably intended for students which date from the late thirteenth century. The authors of the Year Books are anonymous, and judges and lawyers are for the most part not identified in them. Within a short period of time after printing was introduced the manuscript Year Books were collected and printed, and the first named reports of cases (Port, Spellman, Dyer and Plowden) appeared in the mid and late sixteenth century. Eleven volumes of Coke's famous *Reports* were edited between 1600–16 (two further reports were printed in 1658 and 1659).

Printing also made possible other developments which laid emphasis on the importance of individual judicial decisions. These included the publication of Abridgements of past reports, and the publication of comprehensive legal treatises, the first and most important being Sir Thomas Littleton's *Tenures* which was in print by 1481, and by 1550 more often reprinted than the English Bible. The treatises formed a canon of 'authoritative' texts, and together with named law reports began the process of forming the modern doctrine of judicial precedent.

The principles of historical jurisprudence made explicit in the seventeenth century (see Berman, 1994), in which common law's authority derives from forms and principles supposedly unchanged since 'time out of mind', paradoxically provided the flexibility for early modern common lawyers to adjust the law to meet the needs of the society of their time.

The above mentioned declaratory theory, in which the common law has always existed and judges merely pronounce it, was clearly articulated in Shakespeare's era, notably by Sir Edward Coke. By means of selective and sometimes distorted uses of precedents, Coke in particular forged hugely influential opinions suited to new societal circumstances and moral outlooks. Thorne, 1985g gives three varied examples of his methods of employing counterfeit medievalism, or forging 'spurious Latin maxims', or bluntly inventing 'precedents'. Thorne's lecture, generally in praise of Coke, even puts forward a 'theorem' (p. 227) to the effect that in Coke's legal arguments 'the longer the list of authorities reconciled, the greater the divergence from the cases cited'. The three examples given are of the *Case of the Monopolies, Darcy v Allein* (11 Co. Rep. 84v, 1602), of the *Case of the Tailors of Ipswich* (11 Co. Rep, 53), and of the interpretation in Coke, 1628 of a technicality of medieval **land** law. In the first two examples Coke argued against royal and guild monopolies respectively as being in restraint of free exercise of handicraft trades. Thorne holds that in the first case Coke's many cited authorities 'are hardly convincing precedents' (p. 230), and particular that his reliance on Magna Carta's guarantees of freedom and liberty involves a wild distortion of the source. In fact, as we note under **letters patent** in relation to HAM 2.2.402–3 (as discussed in Srigley,

1994), Shakespeare's use of 'liberty' may well refer to monopoly-like special privileges, and not to liberties as understood in Coke's promotion of commercial liberalism. In the second case discussed by Thorne, in which the existing precedents and indeed **statutes** simply went against Coke, Thorne, p 232, says that the precedents 'were quietly ignored – a frequent occurrence in Coke's writings and one that makes them so misleading as a guide to the law of the middle ages'. Instead, in what Thorne calls 'an outrageously unhistorical statement', Coke asserted that his position against guilds 'is and always has been the common law'. While Thorne applauds Coke's exuberantly re-creative legal readings to serve social change in these two cases, in his third example (pp. 234–7) he deplores Coke's unhistorical misunderstanding of certain medieval land law principles, which created 'illusory' questions and initiated 200 years of legal problems.

Thus the use made of the doctrine of 'precedent' in Shakespeare's age enabled the common law to change and adapt while retaining a air of stability. New principles were formed and whole new areas of law developed (for example, the law of tort, or of contract), allowing the common law to match and triumph over rival prerogative **jurisdictions**, such as those of **equity** or **Star Chamber**, in innovative versatility.

(B) The word 'precedent' is most frequently used by Shakespeare without obvious legal connotations, referring to that which came before (sometimes such usages are adjectival, as in HAM, ANT and TIM). However in many places 'precedent' either has or shares in the meaning given in OED 2b (although the earliest example given is dated 1689): 'A previous judicial decision, method of proceeding, or draft of a document, which serves as an authoritative rule or pattern in similar or analogous cases'.

An obscure but interesting instance possibly arises when Don Armado and Moth discuss the old ballad of the King and the Beggar maid, which Armado wants to employ as a 'precedent'. The context may mirror or mock legal manoeuvres. Asked about the ballad, Moth says dismissively: 'The world was very guilty of such a ballad some three ages since, but I think now 'tis not to be found; or if it were, it would neither serve for the writing nor the tune'. Armado replies, oblivious to both Moth's critique and his own ridiculousness: 'I will have that subject newly writ o'er, that I may example my digression by some mighty precedent. Boy, I do love that country girl that I took in the park with the rational hind Costard. She deserves well' (LLL 1.2.106–13). In 'that subject newly writ o'er', to create a 'mighty precedent', one may be reminded of the re-writing of 'three ages' old precedents by early modern lawyers not for the sake of antiquarian concern, but to rationalize justification for actual innovations. That is to say, the common lawyers sometimes acted Armado-like, concocting high and ancient precedents to supply a gloss of antique nobility to current-day needs and desires.

In other instances 'precedents' in Shakespeare are simply the originals from which the manuscripts of legal documents are copied. Thus Lewis the Dauphin in JN 5.2.1–7 orders a copy of a document to be made and kept 'for our remembrance', and further orders Lord Melun:

> Return the precedent to these lords again,
> That having our fair order written down,
> Both they and we, perusing o'er these notes,
> May know wherefore we took the sacrament
> And keep our faiths firm and inviolable.

This may relate to Holinshed's implication that Lewis subscribed to Magna Carta.

In R3 3.6.1–14 a scrivener complains in soliloquy of his labours, and of the unjust uses of legal formality by Richard:

> Here is the indictment of the good Lord Hastings,
> Which in a set hand fairly is engrossed,
> That it may be today read o'er in Paul's –
> And mark how well the sequel hangs together:
> Eleven hours I have spent to write it over,
> For yesternight by Catesby was it sent me;
> The precedent was full as long a-doing;
> And yet, within these five hours, Hastings lived,
> Untainted, unexamined, free, at liberty.
> Here's a good world the while! Who is so gross
> That cannot see this palpable device?
> Yet who so bold but says he sees it not?
> Bad is the world, and all will come to naught,
> When such ill dealing must be seen in thought.

Forms of justice in a tyrant's world are cruel mockeries (on this see Bellamy, 1970, p 215, Carroll, 1992, and generally under **treason**).

In some more metaphoric uses Shakespeare uses 'precedent' to denote a prior example conveying a moral, if not strictly a legal, model. Prominent among these in its complexity is the gruesome use of a precedent from history in exoneration of violent slaughter in TIT 5.3.35–51:

[TITUS]	My lord the Emperor, resolve me this:
	Was it well done of rash Virginius
	To slay his daughter with his own right hand
	Because she was enforced, stained, and deflowered?
SATURNINUS	It was, Andronicus.
TITUS	Your reason, mighty lord?
SATURNINUS	Because the girl should not survive her shame,
	And by her presence still renew his sorrows.
TITUS	A reason mighty, strong, effectual;
	A pattern, precedent, and lively warrant
	For me, most wretched, to perform the like.
	Die, die, Lavinia, and thy shame with thee,
	And with thy shame thy father's sorrow die. [He kills her]
SATURNINUS	What hast thou done, unnatural and unkind?
TITUS	Killed her for whom my tears have made me blind.
	I am as woeful as Virginius was,
	And have a thousand times more cause than he
	To do this outrage, and it now is done.

The extreme bitterness and sarcasm in the circumstances of his address to Saturnius, whom he certainly does not honour as his 'mighty lord', complicates how we must take Titus's alleging a 'pattern, precedent, and lively warrant'. Titus calls his own despairing murder an 'outrage'; does he here posit, or spitefully mock, the idea of justification by 'precedent' and 'warrant'?

A precedent is a moral example again in RDY 2.2.26–33, where Henry VI is urged by Lord Clifford to be fierce in defence of his own offspring, as even normally mild birds or animals will be: 'For shame, my liege, make them your precedent!'. In R2 2.1.116–24 Richard II

says he spares John of Gaunt from death for 'unreverent' speech (see
treason) only because of their family relationship. Old Gaunt retorts
with bold sarcasm that Richard may as well kill him, as he had killed
'My brother Gloucester, plain well-meaning soul', an act which 'May be
a precedent and witness good / That thou respect'st not spilling
Edward's blood' (2.1.125–32; on other aspects of lese-majesty in R2 see
Gohn, 1982). With hidden doubleness, Leartes replies to Hamlet's
apology:

> I am satisfied in nature,
> Whose motive in this case should stir me most
> To my revenge. But in my terms of honour
> I stand aloof, and will no reconcilement
> Till by some elder masters of known honour
> I have a voice and precedent of peace
> To keep my name ungored; but till that time
> I do receive your offered love like love,
> And will not wrong it.
>
> (HAM 5.2.190–8)

This is a hypocritical gesture toward seeking a judgement based on
authorities and precedents in chivalry or 'honour', for Laertes has
already plotted with Claudius stealthily to murder Hamlet (see HAM
4.7.64–7, discussed under **murder**).

Edgar seeking a disguise in LRQ S.7.179–80 / LRF 2.2.176–7 may
slightly echo a legal use when he says that in reality 'The country gives
me proof and precedent / Of Bedlam beggars'. In CYM 3.1.72–5 the
'Pannonians and Dalmatians' warring for 'liberties' are called 'a precedent / Which not to read would show the Britons cold'. Leontes
suggests that he only forebears from calling Hermione a whore 'Lest
barbarism, making me the precedent, / Should a like language use to
all degrees, / And mannerly distinguishment leave out / Betwixt the
prince and beggar' (WT 2.1.86–9). Despite his fear of giving such a
precedent, his socio-linguistic chastity breaks down very quickly when
Leontes calls her 'A bed-swerver, even as bad as those / That vulgars
give bold'st titles' (WT 2.1.95–6). And Sebastian accepts Antonio's
model and tutelage in murder and usurpation of an elder brother: 'Thy
case, dear friend, / Shall be my precedent. As thou got'st Milan, / I'll
come by Naples' (TMP 2.1.295–7).

Most of these contexts of 'precedent' are at best only figuratively connected with legal precedents. In a context in which there is a specific and direct connection with law, Portia disguised as the young Roman **civil doctor** Balthazar offers 'his' opinion that in order to avoid presenting the world with an unfortunate example, Venetian commercial law must not be abrogated:

> It must not be. There is no power in Venice
> Can alter a decree established.
> 'Twill be recorded for a precedent,
> And many an error by the same example
> Will rush into the state. It cannot be.
> (MV 4.1.215–19)

Antonio, the merchant victim of this judgment, has previously explained the urgency of maintaining its principle for the sake of 'profit' or '**commodity**', saying there cannot be a precedent for overturning contracts between citizens and aliens in an international trading city:

> The Duke cannot deny the course of law,
> For the commodity that strangers have
> With us in Venice, if it be denied,
> Will much impeach the justice of the state,
> Since that the trade and profit of the city
> Consisteth of all nations.
> (MV 3.3.26–31)

Although his meaning is obscured by his typical clenched and gnomic syntax, Shylock reiterates the same point at the trial, warning that he must have the forfeit, or else 'If you deny it, let the danger light / Upon your charter and your city's freedom' (MV 4.1.37–8). The danger Shylock alludes to is ruin following loss of the confidence of alien traders; the resident alien Shylock says '*your* charter . . . *your* city'.

Portia's position echoes a report of a 1542 English case concluding that the amount owed on a **bond** had to be paid twice because 'although the truth be that the plaintiff is paid his money, still it is better to suffer a mischief to one man than an inconvenience to many, which would subvert a law' (*Waberley v Cockrel*, 1 Dyer 51a). The same idea that an 'error by the same example' might result from such a precedent was also discussed c. 1523 in the first dialogue of St German's *Doctor and Student*. St German's example concerns the problem that law requiring a double payment when a paid-up bond remains uncancelled, because

> there is a generall maxyme in the lawe of England that in an accyon of dette sued upon an oblygacion the defendant shall not plead that he oweth not the money . . . And because it should be a hurte to many yf an oblygacyon should be so lightly avoyded by a bare word.

This concludes that the careless debtor 'is without remedye at the common lawe: yet he maye be holpen in equity' (St. German, 1975, pp 77–9).

As discussed under **equity**, **bond** and **debt**, Portia does not propose such help or relief in equity. This may be because the precedent mentioned by Antonio and suggested by Shylock concerns matters more practical than philosophical; these adversaries both agree that in trading disputes a great international mercantile city cannot afford any doubts of its reputation for rendering even-handed justice. These views are possibly echoed even in the prefatory sonnet Edmund Spenser wrote for Lewkenor's *The Commonwealth and Government of Venice*, which values higher than even Venice's beauty and grandeur the city's 'policy of right' (Spenser, 1966, p 482).

Keeton, 1930, pp 27–9 argues that AIT blurred the historical sequence (confusing 1521 with 1525) in order to address issues of 'contemporary politics'. It does this in representing Henry VIII rebuking Cardinal Wolsey for heavy taxation without 'a precedent / Of this commission' (AIT 1.2.92–3), and then showing the king freely **pardoning** 'each man that has denied / The force of this commission' (1.2.101–2). Given a date about 1612 for AIT, it is certainly impressive that here Henry lectures Wolsey: 'We must not rend our subjects from our laws / And stick them in our will' (1.2.94–5), for this was when debates between royal prerogative and legal independence had become intense and dangerous (see Sokol and Sokol, 1999b).

(C) For a theory of the common law based on notions of historical precedent, relating it to a kind of customary law, see Simpson, 1987a. On a Tudor change toward the principle in which case law as opposed to 'common learning' founds the accepted precedents, see Baker,

288

1990b, pp 225–8. Plucknett, 1956, pp 342–50, gives a history of precedent emphasising a long and slow development. On the dangers and advantages of a flexible system of using precedents see Baker, 1990b, pp 225–30 and Thorne, 1985g. Kelley, 1974, especially pp 29–40, goes much further than Thorne in condemning Coke for historical 'innocence', 'intellectual insularity' and a common law 'guild-mentality' (Kelley brackets with Coke English legal antiquaries like William Lambard). Berman, 1994, is much more sanguine about Coke's and others' development of 'historical jurisprudence'. On the great importance of legal treatises to common law, and on the later decline of this, see Simpson, 1987d. On diverse factors affecting the survival of common law see Simpson, 1987e.

pre-contract (A) The complex issue in question is the formation of a legally valid **marriage**. Technically, Shakespeare's term 'pre-contract' is a misnomer for a **contract** of marriage. The terminological error is, however, instructive. The 'pre-' in the term implies that after such a contract further steps were needed to form a valid marriage. This was not in general true. But, as will be explained below, such a notion was certainly significant socially and at law.

Briefly, the rules of marriage formation established in the twelfth century by Pope Alexander III were still in force in Shakespeare's England. These held that even a private and verbal agreement to marry either immediately or in the future (*per verba de praesenti* or *per verba de futuro*) would immediately create a valid marriage, prohibiting marriage with any other person, and *de praesenti* contracts needed no further steps to confer full married status.

Therefore marriage in later medieval and early modern England was the concern of the church. Although the English common law dealt with disputes concerning real property (**land**) arising from marriage, from the mid-twelfth century until the mid-nineteenth century litigation about formation of marriage took place in the Church courts.

The jurisdiction of the Church courts was divided into non-contentious matters (mostly administrative such as probate of wills, or grant of marriage licences), and contentious matters. The latter could be brought as 'instance' cases, or else as *ex officio* cases. Instance cases were the most common contentious cases, and many of these were brought by one of the parties to an alleged marriage, asking for its enforcement.

Alternatively in multi-party instance cases the court typically considered competing claims presented by several parties claiming that the marriage they had entered into was valid. An example of the latter would be where a man had 'married' several women, all of whom claimed the validity of their contract.

Marriage was also often at issue in *ex officio* Church court cases. These were disciplinary prosecutions for moral and religious offences usually brought before the court by the Bishop himself, and sometimes on the report of suspicious circumstances made to him by a court official, parish officer, or occasionally a third party. The Bishop would then summon the accused to the court and order inquiries to be made in the parish.

Although the Church courts' records were in Latin, their proceedings were conducted in English, and so investigations could be conducted into aspects of everyday life. The large number of prosecutions for marital and sexual offences explains why the Church courts were colloquially known as 'bawdy courts'. The post-reformation Church courts continued to play an important role in the public regulation of private morality. They were often portrayed at best as ineffective, failing to pursue offenders, at worst as 'corrupt, inefficient and unpopular' – however such opinions are now regarded as suspect because they were based on evidence of contemporary puritans seeking more strenuous enforcement of public moral discipline, or of common law critics of the church's **jurisdiction** (Ingram, 1987, p 364).

An examination of records of several of the bishops' consistory courts shows that the overwhelming majority of matrimonial cases considered by them did not concern **divorce** or annulment, but instead the interpretation and enforcement of contracts of marriage (Helmholz, 1974, p 25; Ingram, 1987, p 189; Ingram, 1981, p 36). The reason for the large numbers of cases in the middle ages and early Tudor England concerning marriage contracts can be found in the lack of any agreed formula of words for entering into a valid contract, and in the difficulties surrounding the interpretation of words used in the contested cases (Helmholz, 1974, p 72).

These difficulties began in twelfth-century Europe, when canonists had disagreed on the requirements for the formation of a valid marriage (see Brundage, 1987, pp 229–55). One view, supported by Gratian and the Bolognese school, argued that all that was necessary to make a valid contract of marriage was the consent of both parties to the marriage. Subsequent consummation would then make the marriage indissoluble. But if such a contracted marriage was unconsummated, a second consummated contract would be valid and take precedence over the unconsummated first contract.

An alternative view was put forward by Peter Lombard and the Parisian school of canonists, who considered that if the formulation of Gratian was accepted difficult theological questions were raised about the nature of the marriage between the Virgin Mary and St Joseph. The alternative argument was that a contact of marriage could be made in two ways: by *verba de praesenti* or *verba de futuro*. The former, words of present consent, immediately created a valid marriage. Nothing more was needed. So an unconsummated contract using words of present consent would take priority over any subsequent marriage, whether or not consummated. However a contract formed by words of future consent was not indissoluble unless followed by consummation, and if unconsummated would not take priority over a subsequent consummated contract.

In the late twelfth century Pope Alexander III in a number of decretals accepted the views of Peter Lombard and the Parisian school, in which merely *verba de praesenti* formed a valid marriage. In England, the Council of Westminster 1175 made clear the need for mutual consent of the parties to form a marriage. The consent of parents, or other family, or lords, was not necessary for validity. Nor was endowment at the church door necessary (see under **dower**). Importantly, neither lack of public ceremony nor lack of priestly blessing would invalidate such a marriage.

The parties' consent, the sole fact to be established, could be given by words, or by signs such as the giving and receiving of a ring and handfasting (see Houlbrooke, 1985, p 344 and Swinburne, 1686, pp 10, 86, 203–12), or by the agency of a third party (Swinburne, 1686, pp 10, 154–92).

A contract *per verba de futuro* could be conditional, with for example a condition relating to payment of a marriage **portion**. In this case the contract did not become a valid marriage until the performance of the condition, unless the marriage was consummated.

In adopting Pope Alexander's consensual formulation of marriage the Western church also accepted an individualistic view of marriage, in which (in theory) the importance of control by family, feudal lord, kings or church solemnization was subordinated to individual consent (see Sheehan, 1996, p 40). However there is no doubt that the church strongly discouraged marriages that were made with lack of formality. In 1215 the Fourth Lateran Council demanded priestly involvement and public announcement of the marriage. In England this was interpreted as a requirement that parties to a marriage arrange for the publication of banns on three Sundays, and a public ceremony before a priest. This could be in the church at a mass, or at the door of the church, with an exchange of rings and **endowment** of the woman.

Any marriage that failed to meet the church's demands for solemnization was termed 'clandestine'; this term therefore covered a large variety of ways in which unsolemized consent could be given (Sheehan, 1996, p 47). In Shakespeare's time clandestine marriages frequently took place privately before willing priests, or in certain so called 'lawless churchs' outside the jurisdiction of bishops, known as 'peculiars', some of which were in prisons (see Outhwaite, 1995, pp 19–49).

In 1563 the Church of Rome at the Council of Trent addressed the difficulties of clandestine marriage, and introduced reforms that required marriage to take place before a priest. From 1564 these were applied, although not everywhere immediately, in Catholic Europe (see Brundage, 1987, pp 561–5). But the post-reformation Church of England did not follow Rome, and continued to apply the older canon law. Henry VIII had introduced a short-lived reform in 1540, stipulating marriages solemnized in church were valid despite any pre-contracts of marriage, but Henry's purpose was to validate his marriage to Catherine Howard rather than effect real reform. The statute was repealed eight years later.

So, even though the teaching of the Church of Rome was that marriage was a holy sacrament (after the Reformation the Church of England disagreed, holding it to be 'an honourable estate'; see Carlson, E. J., 1994, p 45), failure to go through church solemnization of marriage was not fatal to its validity. Clandestine marriages, although valid, were treated as a sin and punished in the Church courts; erring parties could be ordered to comply and to do penance, and any priests involved could be punished.

By the early seventeenth century, in England, even witnesses to clandestine marriages were severely punished, which made them reluctant to testify if questions about the marriage came to the Church courts. In the first decade of the seventeenth century the Bishop of London was so extreme that he actually forbade admission of any such evidence on the principle that the witness was *ipso facto* excommunicate (Helmholz, 1990, pp 71–3; Donaghue, 1983, pp 153–5 says that earlier there was similar practice in northern France, but not in England). Therefore 'clandestine' or private marriages posed serious problems of proof in contested cases.

As noted above a marriage *per verba de futuro* could be dissolved by mutual agreement if not consummated, but one *per verba de praesenti* could not. The distinction of tenses of a verb led to many difficulties of proof, not only because of lack of witnesses or their faulty memories. Making such a distinction legally crucial was 'was no masterpiece of human wisdom' according to Maitland because, 'of all people in the world, lovers are the least likely to distinguish precisely between the present and future tenses' (Pollock and Maitland, 1898, vol 2, pp 368–9).

Some recent investigations of records of consistory courts cast doubt on a former belief that clandestine marriages continued to be very common in late sixteenth and early seventeenth century England. For example, records of Wiltshire courts show that between 1570–1640 the amount of contentious marriage litigation fell sharply, and this was matched by a similar fall in disciplinary prosecutions for marriage contracts and for failing to have banns read (Ingram, 1987, pp 192–3). Such evidence has been used to suggest that during these years a change in popular understanding had occurred; the church's teaching and admonitions on the need for calling banns and going through a church ceremony had been generally successful, and led to a fall in numbers of clandestine marriages. As a result, it is claimed, ecclesiastical lawyers regarded unsolemnized marriage contracts as more or less unenforcable (ibid., pp 206–9). But these findings do not agree with evidence presented from Church courts in other parts of the country (Houlbrooke, 1985, p 351), and as a result the change in attitude of ecclesiastical courts and lawyers has been doubted.

While evidence for a decline in spousal litigation throughout the country remains inconclusive, it seems that popular opinion considered the church's blessing a necessary part of the formation of a valid marriage. Despite this, and despite the many problems which resulted from clandestine marriages, they continued in use and were not prohibited by law in England until Lord Hardwicke's Marriage Act of 1753. Yet it could be argued that the church's exact requirements on solemnization were not universally accepted. Old traditions of marriage in Europe and England which required some form of ceremony or ritual (such as giving away the bride) and consummation, although having no legal basis, long continued to be important. It has been suggested that the continuing numbers of clandestine marriages evidences the continuity of such traditions (Helmholz, 1974, p 31).

Many disputes over contracts to marry by *verba de praesenti* suggest a continuing popular belief that such words created an **spousal** only, and not a marriage (ibid., p 32). Michael Sheehan cites as evidence of deep-rooted uncertainty about solemnization reports from fourteenth century Ely of clandestine contracts employing a variety of extra-canonical acts, words, and rituals. Here

> unsophisticated men and women . . . tried to establish a relationship within the categories and procedures demanded by a custom which in part was the debris of a culture which no longer existed and in part was a ritual statement of a . . . different view of marriage.
>
> (Sheehan, 1996, p 57)

Not only the common people seemed unclear about the need for solemnization. Even the Queen's **attorney** general, Sir Edward Coke, went through a clandestine marriage in 1598 when he privately (and, as it later turned out, disastrously) married his second wife, Lady Elizabeth Hatton, the second daughter of Lord Burghley, without either a church blessing or a public ceremony. Coke and Lady Hatton were cited to appear before the Church court, and at probably some financial cost Coke obtained a dispensation on the basis that he was ignorant of canon law (! – noted in Outhwaite, 1995, p 23). Thomas Russell, the overseer of Shakespeare's own **will**, also undertook a clandestine marriage under complex circumstances detailed in Hotson, 1937, pp 125–40, 209–11. This situation was first mentioned as relevant to MM in Empson, 1952, p 286, and since has often been simplified in references to Shakespeare and pre-contract.

(B) 'Pre-contract' is a term for a spousal contract appearing only once in Shakespeare's plays (yet in a crucial place, discussed below), while marriage 'contracts' are named and/or appear in nearly all of the plays. Indeed a marriage contract is nearly the only referent of the term 'contract' when used by Shakespeare (see **contract**). Nevertheless, the social-historical significance of a notion of an arrangement in some sense prior to a further act, as implied in the term 'pre-contract', is crucial for understanding Shakespeare's treatment of the formation of marriage.

As detailed above, if there were no **impediments**, any contract showing a genuine consent to marry created a marriage. Therefore it was typical and correct for already contracted parties awaiting (or even in the absence of) solemnization to be referred to as a 'husband' or 'wife' (as are Kate in SHR 2.1.317 and Antonio in MM 4.1.70).

Yet there was simultaneously a widespread notion that unsolemnized 'betrothal' was different from a solemnized and consummated marriage, and so the language of Shakespeare's plays contains over a dozen references to the betrothed or betrothing, usually referring to eager lovers, and most probably indicating those having undertaken *de futuro* spousals and not yet having solemnized or consummated their union. So Falstaff as a recruiting officer plans to extort money from unwilling 'contracted bachelors, such as had been asked twice on the banns' (1H4 4.2.17–18).

A gloss on the status of Falstaff's victims as 'contracted bachelors' raises interesting distinctions. The thrice reading of banns to avoid **impediments**, followed by a public marriage ceremony in the 'face of the church' were strongly urged by English secular and religious authorities. Yet, as we have seen, 'contracted' legally meant married. 'Bachelors' was mainly used by Shakespeare to specify unmarried men (as in 'Are you a married man or a bachelor?' JC 3.3.8), but with some ambiguity. In MND 2.2.65, Hermia calls Lysander a 'virtuous bachelor' in a context in which their marital status following betrothal is at issue. Hermia denies Lysander's wish to sleep by her side, despite his claim that their 'Two bosoms [are] interchained with an oath; / So, then, two bosoms and a single troth' (MND 2.2.55–6). So, as far as Hermia was concerned, but not Lysander, betrothal is not marriage, which was the position of the church, if not of church law.

In MM quite contrary opinions are heard, in which betrothal makes a woman 'fast my wife' and and a man 'your husband on a precontract' (discussed below). Contradictions between and even within Shakespearian contexts (as in MM, discussed below), express powerful ambiguities: in the absence of the Tridentine regulations, but with the spirit of these rules officially emphasised to avoid 'sinfulness', early modern England was in a kind of marital limbo.

That limbo allowed for some dishonest practices. The process of marriage solemnization traditionally included a public lesson by a

clergyman to the prospective bride and groom, explaining the seriousness of the institution of marriage, and so Jacques exhorts Touchstone,
about to be married 'under a bush': 'Get you to church, and have a
good priest that can tell you what marriage is' (AYL 3.3.76–8). Yet
dishonest Touchstone prefers not, as detailed below. That *de futuro*
promises of marriage were were not always honestly intended was a
commonplace of comedy. So Lucio is said to have 'promised' Kate
Keepdown 'marriage' (MM 3.1.458–60), and Falstaff has egregiously
broken faith in a long relationship with a **widow** (during 'twenty-nine
years come peascod-time', she says in 2H4 2.4.387).

Proffering an insincere promise of marriage to seduce or for other
purposes was an offence. If accepted, such an offer constituted a valid
marriage contract, which if unfulfilled could result in fines and an order
to do penance in the Church courts. This situation is travestied when
the **Chief Justice** comes upon a street brawl between Falstaff and
officers attempting to arrest him for his **debt** to Mistress Quickly (on
the context see under **sergeant**). She, showing great attention to detail
(but not naming the two witnesses required in Church courts), before
the Chief Justice accuses Falstaff that he owes her:

> Marry, if thou wert an honest man, thyself, and the money too. Thou
> didst swear to me upon a parcel-gilt goblet, sitting in my Dolphin
> chamber, at the round table, by a sea-coal fire, upon Wednesday in
> Wheeson week, when the Prince broke thy head for liking his father
> to a singing-man of Windsor – thou didst swear to me then, as I was
> washing thy wound, to marry me, and make me my lady thy wife.
> Canst thou deny it? Did not goodwife Keech the butcher's wife come
> in then, and call me 'Gossip Quickly' – coming in to borrow a mess
> of vinegar, telling us she had a good dish of prawns, whereby thou
> didst desire to eat some, whereby I told thee they were ill for a green
> wound? And didst thou not, when she was gone downstairs, desire
> me to be no more so familiarity with such poor people, saying that
> ere long they should call me 'madam'? And didst thou not kiss me,
> and bid me fetch thee thirty shillings? I put thee now to thy book-
> oath; deny it if thou canst.

> (2H4 2.1.87–105)

Naturally, not minding false oaths (see under **heresy**), Sir John does
deny it, supplying a marvellous overplus of detail also:

296

My lord, this is a poor mad soul, and she says up and down the town that her eldest son is like you. She hath been in good case, and the truth is, poverty hath distracted her. But for these foolish officers, I beseech you I may have redress against them.

(2H4 2.1.106–10)

The Chief Justice is not impressed, and comes to the point succinctly:

You have, as it appears to me, practised upon the easy-yielding spirit of this woman, and made her serve your uses both in purse and in person . . . Pay her the debt you owe her, and unpay the villainy you have done with her. The one you may do with sterling money, and the other with current repentance.

(116–23)

The Chief Justice is unable at this early stage of the play tio do more than rebuke Falstaff, while later he takes charge of him; this progression symbolises the consolidation of the power of the king's law in the age leading to Shakespeare's time. The Chief Justice's rebukes without further action may also approximate to the 'rather heavy-handed' mediating role often played by judges when faced with domestic altercations in the bawdy courts of Shakespeare's own age (see **divorce**), or reflect possibly the weakness complained of by puritans of the existing legal means to control 'moral' offences (see Kent, 1973).

Where Shakespeare dramatised marriages involving important property or political negotiations, the contingent nature of a conditional contract makes the concept of a marriage 'pre-contract' unproblematic. Both Princess Margaret in 1H6 and Princess Katherine in H5 agree to marriage with kings of England conditionally on their fathers' approval, surely meaning political approval. The former responds with justified caution to Suffolk's proxy wooing (1H6 5.5.83), the latter directly to Henry V, but in 'broken English': 'Dat is as it shall please de *roi mon pere*' (H5 5.2.243–5).

An unconditional marriage contract by *verba de praesenti* required only an indication of present consent, and no particular words. Nor any words at all: legitimate marriage could be legally contracted 'by *Signs* only' (Swinburne, 1686, pp 86, 203–12). This is seen in WT as discussed below, and in ADO following Claudio's marriage-contracting words: 'Lady, as you are mine, I am yours. I give away myself for you,

297

and dote upon the exchange'. Hero speaks no audible lines in reply (only whispers in Claudio's ear), but may make her wishes known to the witnesses present by taking Beatrice's merry advice to: 'Speak, cousin. Or, if you cannot, stop his mouth with a kiss, and let not him speak, neither' (ADO 2.1.288–92).

Although such a mode of present consent was sufficient to make a valid marriage, and neither solemnization nor consummation were essential, a fuller process of establishing a marriage was usually portrayed by Shakespeare. While Fenton and Anne Page have been privately 'long since contracted' (WIV 5.5.215), they still secretly arrange for a vicar at church 'in the lawful name of marrying, / To give our hearts united ceremony' (4.6.49–50). This is to make their marriage 'so sure that nothing can dissolve us' (5.5.216).

The traditional sequence of espousal, marriage ceremony, and then consummation is seen in all of its stages, at least implicitly, both in MND and ROM. The interval between betrothal and consummation in MND extends from before the action to the last lines before the epilogue (5.1.356–63), while in ROM it extends from the 'contract' spoken of in 2.1.159 (which seems to be the *de futuro* betrothal in 2.1.184–98), to a clandestine religious ceremony just after the end of 2.5, to consummation between 3.2 and 3.5. Theseus and Juliet respectively express impatient desires, but not at all sourly (in MND throughout, beginning with 1.1.1–6; in ROM 3.2.1–31), upholding the traditional pattern.

In a humorous vein Rosalind says that time 'trots hard with a young maid between the contract of her marriage and the day it is solemnized. If the interim be but a se'nnight, time's pace is so hard that it seems the length of seven year.' (AYL 3.2.306–9). Here again the contract and the consummation of the marriage are separated by an anxious interval, and one acknowledging female desire.

In TMP Prospero makes a 'gift' of (willing) Miranda to Ferdinand, calling this transaction a 'contract' (4.1.8, 4.1.19). In fact they have already (they think) privately spoken *verba de praesenti*, Miranda saying 'I am your wife, if you will marry me' (3.1.83), and Ferdinand replying to her question 'My husband then?' with 'Ay, with a heart as willing / As bondage e'er of freedom. Here's my hand.' To this Miranda offers her reply in the form of a traditional handfasting: 'And mine, with my heart in 't' (3.1.88–91). Despite these spousals, however, Prospero insists that consummation must be deferred until 'All sanctimonious ceremonies may / With full and holy rite be ministered' (4.1.16–17). Ferdinand not only accepts this, but shows positive zeal for temporary frustration, saying:

> As I hope
> For quiet days, fair issue, and long life
> With such love as 'tis now, the murkiest den,
> The most opportune place, the strong'st suggestion
> Our worser genius can, shall never melt
> Mine honour into lust to take away
> The edge of that day's celebration;
> When I shall think or Phoebus' steeds are foundered
> Or night kept chained below.
>
> (TMP 4.1.24–31)

The last phrase recalls Theseus' description of his wedding day's ending: 'this long age of three hours' (MND 5.1.33), but unlike Theseus, Ferdinand expresses relish at how that feeling will give 'the edge' to 'celebration'.

Very different is Leontes' first recollection of his prolonged wooing, in which 'Three crabbed months had soured themselves to death', although this seems to have been the interval before the handfasting, for he describes it as 'Ere I could make thee open thy white hand / And clap thyself my love. Then didst thou utter, / "I am yours for ever"' (WT 1.2.104–7). More than a decade later a second handfasting between Leontes and Hermione takes place wordlessly (5.3.107–9 – see above on marriages contracted 'by *Signs* only'). Thus the outcome of the play's mysterious 'statue scene' creates, in a sense, a second valid marriage between married persons, which however natural in terms of the play's theme was of course irregular legally.

However, what may seem most irregular to us is not Shakespeare's portrayals of marriage between already married lovers, but rather of marriages contracted between strangers. Politically arranged spousal contracts between virtual strangers (often undertaken for imperial or dynastic reasons – see **spousal**), wooing and betrothal through intermediaries (see **attorney**), and marriages by proxy (see Swinburne, 1686, pp 157–90) were not uncommon in history, and feature as marriages enacted or attempted in 1H6, CYL, H5, ANT and R2.

In ADO, more preposterously than in Shakespeare's historical plays, a wooing by proxy is arranged (1.1.299–311) and enacted by means of disguise at a masked ball. Thus the shy Count Claudio arranges to contract for marriage with Hero by means of the social graces of Don Pedro (2.1.78–89). Then for Claudio, in accord with Shakespearian precedent and social tradition, in the interval between the contract and the marriage ceremony 'Time goes on crutches till love have all his rites' (2.1.334–5). During this interval, in a kind of Saturnine parody of the former arrangement of a proxy wooing, in 2.2 Don John and his cronies arrange a kind of proxy adultery, making Hero seem unchaste with a man other than Claudio. So the intended marriage is broken off on account of this 'impediment' (4.1.12–68 – see **impediment**). It is notable that although morally reprehensible (see Leonato's tone in 4.1.45–7), if Hero had had sexual relations with Claudio, there would not have been any impediment. For then the *de futuro* contract would have converted to a *de praesenti* contract equivalent to full marriage, and as Claudio says, her father will be able to 'say she did embrace me as a husband, / And so extenuate the forehand sin' (4.1.49–50)

Despite their accord with laws governing spousal contracts, the marital affairs in ADO may seem extravagantly complex. Yet they are not far removed from details of a bizarre case of a spousal resulting from confusion of the identity of the woman married, given by Swinburne as an exemplar for an extended legal discussion (Swinburne, 1686, pp 168–77).

In a wry response to such entangled matters, AYL presents for our (perhaps dark) amusement two cunning allusions to the social confusions and personal problems that in actuality sometimes reached Church courts when there was difficulty in determining if a marriage contract was valid. First Touchstone proposes to marry the 'foul' Audrey to relieve a sexual itch, saying 'Come, sweet Audrey. / We must be married, or we must live in bawdry' (AYL 3.3.86–7). He further explains, 'so man hath his desires; . . . so wedlock would be nibbling' (AYL 3.3.73–4). The vicar Sir Oliver Martext is willing to marry them under a tree (on Martext's sort of illicit 'calling' (3.3.98) see Outhwaite, 1995, pp 22–31). Martext then insists, wrongly, 'Truly [Audrey] must be given, or the marriage is not lawful' (3.3.63–4). Jacques volunteers to play this part, but warns that Martext will join them badly. Touchstone then admits: 'I am not in the mind but I were better to be married of him than of another, for he is not like to marry me well, and not being well married, it will be a good excuse for me hereafter to leave my wife' (3.3.81–4). Yet according to Helmholz, 1974, p 79, irregular marriages deliberately contrived quickly to collapse (as Jacques says in AYL 5.4.190, 'but for two months victualled'), were actually unusual, because 'not consistent with human nature'.

Touchstone's perhaps aberrant crudity parodies in advance the squabbling over valid terms for contracting a marriage 'in fun' of Orlando and Rosalind/Ganymede, a frolic which presents an extraordinary sort of 'limit case' for questions over spousals (as pointed out in Appendix B of Lathem, 1975). Rosalind in the disguise of the boy Ganymede, and supposedly play-acting herself, obtains and returns *de praesenti* vows with Orlando. It is notable that she particularly insists on the use of the present tense. Thus she makes him say 'I take thee, Rosalind, for wife', having rejected his ambiguously *de futuro* 'I will' with 'Ay, but when?' (AYL 4.1.124–9). She herself then replies definitively in the present tense 'I do take thee, Orlando, for my husband' (AYL 4.1.130–1). Marriage with a boy, of course, was not legal, but marriage by proxy was; could one be proxy for oneself? There is no sign in the play-acting here of the duress or mental reservation that could invalidate spousals, unless a spirit of teasing fun is reservation. Yet Swinburne, 1686, p 105 denies that matrimony is contracted when 'words of the present time are uttered in *Jeast* or *Sport*, for such wanton words are not at all obligatory in so serious a matter'. The issue, perhaps not yet fully known to herself, is if Rosalind is serious in her jesting.

The greatest perplexities for Shakespeare critics over marriage contracts (especially for those seeking idealized female heroines in the comedies) have arisen out of the dramatisation of the irregular and covert confirmation of marriages following valid spousals in wholly unrealistic 'bed tricks' – consummations in the seeming total absence of the element of 'pure and perfect' mutual consent essential to establish a marriage (Swinburne, 1686, pp 121, 131). Swinburne, pp 224–8 details the circumstances in which sexual intercourse following a *de futuro* contract was taken to imply the consent forming an immediate marriage – this is only when it is undertaken 'with that affection, which doth become Man and Wife'. The resulting anomaly in Shakespearian bed tricks in which not only the affection but also the identity of one party to intercourse is uncertain, has long been discussed, pre-eminently in relation to MM.

In this play Duke Vincentio, disguised as a friar, encourages Marianna covertly to substitute for Isabella and have sexual relations with Angelo, saying:

301

> Nor, gentle daughter, fear you not at all.
> He is your husband on a pre-contract.
> To bring you thus together 'tis no sin,
> Sith that the justice of your title to him
> Doth flourish the deceit. Come, let us go.
> Our corn's to reap, for yet our tilth's to sow.
> (MM 4.1.69–74)

The duke as friar therefore authorizes sexual relations, even obtained by stealth, where there is a 'pre-contract'. The problem long noted is that the same disguised duke formerly heavily condemned Juliet, pregnant following an apparent pre-contact with her lover. He asked her to 'repent . . . of the sin you carry', which strangely contrasts with his 'no sin' advice cited above.

The point of Vincentio's disapproval of Juliet is heavily driven home. Having elicited that she loves 'the man that wronged you', and therefore determined that whatever transgression there was was mutual, he encourages her to feel extra guilt, promulgating a double standard: 'Then was your sin of heavier kind than his'. He shows satisfaction at her shame, 'I do confess it and repent it, father. / . . . I do repent me as it is an evil, / And take the shame with joy', and then immediately multiplies her sorrow by telling her, falsely, that her lover will have to die (2.3.20–41).

What is the difference between what the duke encourages Marianna to do and condemns in Juliet? Juliet's lover Claudio has explained:

> Upon a true contract,
> I got possession of Julietta's bed.
> You know the lady; she is fast my wife,
> Save that we do the denunciation lack
> Of outward order. This we came not to
> Only for propagation of a dower
> Remaining in the coffer of her friends,
> From whom we thought it meet to hide our love
> Till time had made them for us. But it chances
> The stealth of our most mutual entertainment
> With character too gross is writ on Juliet.
> (1.2.133–43)

We have no reason to disbelieve him. The play also gives parallel motives for the omission of the public marriage ceremonies of Juliet and Marianna, when the duke says of the latter:

> She should this Angelo have married, was affianced to her oath, and the nuptial appointed; between which time of the contract and limit of the solemnity, her brother Frederick was wrecked at sea, having in that perished vessel the dowry of his sister. But mark how heavily this befell to the poor gentlewoman. There she lost a noble and renowned brother, in his love toward her ever most kind and natural; with him, the portion and sinew of her fortune, her marriage dowry; with both, her combinate husband, this well-seeming Angelo.
>
> (MM 3.1.215–25)

In the play's long resolving final scene, the fact that he spoke of marriage with Marianna is at first half-dismissed by Angelo, but finally he wholly admits he was 'contracted to' her (5.1.214–21; 5.1.372–3). The differences of the two cases are only that while awaiting the **dowry** (called by Claudio 'dower') Angelo and Marianna abstained from sexual relations, Claudio and Juliet did not. There is finally no more doubt that Angelo is Marianna's 'combinate husband' than that Juliet was 'upon a true contract' at least 'fast' Claudio's 'wife'.

One way out of the enigma of how the spousals of Juliet and and Marianna can seem so similar and be treated so differently is to allege that the 'true contract' Claudio mentions and Angelo's 'pre-contract' are not (as Harding, D. P., 1950 supposed) of the same sort. Earlier legal commentators offered a variety of opinions, but Schanzer, 1960, carefully argued that Claudio's is a spousal *per verba de praesenti*, while Angelo's is *per verba de futuro*; the bed-trick then converts the second type to the first. However Nagarajan, 1963 claims just the opposite distinction of the two cases, Roscelli, 1962, pp 216 and 217, flatly asserts both couples were espoused by *verba de praesenti*, and Alexander, 1967, p 433, finds the crucial distinction of the cases in the fact that the publicity in Marianna's contracting is absent in Juliet's. If the text of the play implies anything on such questions, it is not in its offering paradoxes like Marianna's 'I do confess I ne'er was married, / And I confess besides, I am no maid. / I have known my husband, yet my husband / Knows not that ever he knew me' (5.1.183–6) There might be some help in the duke's remark that Angelo's contract was for a set future time: 'the

303

nuptial appointed; between which time of the contract and limit of the solemnity, her brother Frederick was wrecked at sea, having in that perished vessel the dowry of his sister.' (3.1.216–19). This phraseology may suggest a *de futuro* contract, or possibly a conditional contract made in expectation of the dowry (on allowed and disallowed pre-contract conditions see Swinburne, 1686, pp 109–53).

In fact, there is not much room to suppose that the spousal contract Angelo entered five years earlier with Marianna was conditional. If it had been conditional upon a dowry, it would simply have been cancelled with its loss. But an unconditional, and unconsummated, *de futuro* contract could be cancelled only by mutual consent (clearly absent), or under specific circumstances. In particular, the 'Innocent Party' could be freed of such a contract if the other commits '*Fornication*, or if 'there is a Fame or common report that there is some lawful impediment' (Swinburne, 1686, pp 237, 238).

Such an impediment was alleged, but falsely, according to the duke's report: on loss of dowry Angelo had originally 'swallowed his vows whole, pretending in her discoveries of dishonour' (3.1.228–9). Angelo, while acting as 'judge / Of [his] own cause' (5.1.165–6), himself alleges that he had broken with Marianna 'in chief/ For that her reputation was disvalued / In levity' (5.1.218–20). If theirs had been only a conditional contract, Angelo would not have had reason to disparage Marianna's chastity or reputation in order to claim an **impediment** to marriage.

Some astute critics assess MM as deliberately offering disruptive or flawed arguments, and from this it would likely follow that providing easy answers to difficult questions was not part of Shakespeare's design for the play (see especially Hammond, 1986). Certainly, despite long critical debate, no agreed resolution of the marriage contracts problem has been reached.

Nevertheless, the language of MM concerning pre-contracts and marital rights does illuminate legal and moral issues raised by the play. The duke's condemnation of Juliet at first focuses on the 'sin' of her pregnancy; English Church courts condemned the sin of disobedience in her sort of transgression, but did not condemn it as fornication (Wenterdorf, 1979, p 135). Indeed, only the generally scurrilous Lucio, of all the figures in the play, characterizes Juliet's pregnancy as a natural blessing, when he says to Isabella:

Fewness and truth, 'tis thus:
Your brother and his lover have embraced.
As those that feed grow full, as blossoming time
That from the seedness the bare fallow brings
To teeming foison, even so her plenteous womb
Expresseth his full tilth and husbandry.

(1.4.38–43)

Lucio's imagery, notably, is the same as in the duke's 'Our corn's to reap, for yet our tilth's to sow' cited above in connection with the 'bed trick'. In a play with 'pregnant' used in three non-sexual contexts to indicate forensic or political astuteness, the transformation of the duke's language from equating a pregnancy with 'the shame you carry' to indicating the fertility of the impending bed-trick in 'our corn's to reap', surely represents an outlook changed to greater acceptance of sexuality. Even prudish Isabella mentions that the secret assignation with Angelo is set for the 'heavy middle' of the night (4.1.34), implying pregnancy. The play's use of contrasting types of images at different stages suggests that it sets out to expose two wholly different takes on sexual purity (and perhaps even structurally the dynamic whereby one may develop from the other – see Sokol, 1991), by exploring an area of legal ambiguity.

Taking a contrary view, some critics are dubious that English legal history may have bearing on a central concern in MM with laws regulating sexual behaviour. Scott, 1982 protests against views that English legal conditions are relevant to the play, offering instead that it exhibits the legal conditions of either post-Tridentine Catholic Europe, or else of some sort of 'self-enclosed' fairyland, denying, p 793, the 'kind of authenticity to which Henry Swinburn can attest' in a play which is not even a 'history' play. But, as we have seen, even in the distinctly self-enclosed Forest of Arden in AYL, also a non-history-play, references to actual problems of spousals proliferate like 'real toads in imaginary gardens'.

Indeed, questions of contracts of marriage arise relation to: TIT (see under **spousal**); LLL; MND; SHR; ROM; H5; WIV; AYL; ADO; TN; AWW; LRF and LRQ (see under **subcontracted**); WT; and TMP. The topic was clearly of great socio-legal interest, and must have been easily recognised by many in Shakespeare's audiences.

(C) For discussion of spousals see especially Swinburne, 1686, but note caveats in Reynolds, 1996, p 330, and under **marriage**. On Swinburne see Derrett, 1973 and Baker, 1993.

On Canon law and litigation over pre-contracts in the Church courts see: Helmholz, 1974, pp 26–73; Houlbrooke, 1979, pp 55–67; Ingram, 1981; Donaghue, 1983; Houlbrooke, 1985; Ingram, 1987, pp 125–218; Helmholz, 1990, pp 69–72; Outhwaite, 1995, pp 1–49; Carlson, E. J., 1994, *passim*; Sheehan, 1996, p 76. Finch, 1990 discusses the problem of clandestine marriage in the middle ages, and distinguishes it from the issue of parental control.

'Wrying but a Little' in Barton, A., 1994, pp 3–30, discusses almost all of the marriage pre-contracts in Shakespeare (and many in contemporary drama). Following this it investigates questions regarding the irregular status of the marriage of Posthumus and Imogen in CYM, uncovering a fascinating aspect of the sexual politics in the play too complex to be summarized.

Lowenthal, 1996 finds a transition implied in MND from the power of fathers to determine marriage choices to a consensual basis for marriage, but makes no reference to the legalities of marriage formation of Shakespeare's time. McGuire, 1989, closely considers Theseus' overriding of the older Athenian marriage laws (MND 4.1.178–80) in terms of Egeus' subsequent silence, differences of quarto and folio texts, and issues of theatrical performance.

Cook, 1991, pp 175–6, discusses the 'contract of eternal bond of love' (TN 5.1.154) between Olivia and 'Caesario', with a note indicating the variety of critics taking this as a 'spousal' *de futuro, de praesenti*, or neither, asserting that this 'spousal' before a priest must be distinguished from a wedding. Ibid. alleges, p 165, that consummation was legally necessary for 'dower and other rights'.

Mukherji, 1996 discusses spousal pre-contracts in relation to the unconsummated marriage of Bertram and Helena in ADO, correctly noting, p 183, that in Elizabethan law concerning the validity of a *de praesenti* marriage 'consummation was as irrelevant as solemnization', yet noting that in popular tradition both were viewed as essential. This discussion corrects Ranald, 1963, which even as updated in Ranald, 1987, pp 33–49, holds that Bertram could hope for a release from his marriage by remaining missing for a period of two or three years (this, according to Swinburne, was only true of *de futuro* spousals, probably on account of a presumption of death). Cook, 1991, pp 227–8, echoes Ranald on this.

The many essays which investigate the marriage contracts in MM include: Harding, D. P., 1950, which distinguishes prevailing Elizabethan views of morality from current legality; Schanzer, 1960, which applies the *de praesenti* and *de futuro* distinction; Wenterdorf, 1979 which offers an excellent survey of former critics and unusually clear legal-historical analysis; Ranald, 1979, pp 77–9, which seems to propose that Shakespeare should have applied post-Tridentine canon law; Cacicedo, 1995, pp 191–2 and 203, which approaches the subject with Foucault in mind and supposes 'common law practice' demanded church marriage; Carlson, C., 1996, which argues that marriage as represented in the play may be 'imprisoning'. Hamilton, D. B., 1992, pp 121–3, finds expositions of the technicalities of spousals less relevant to MM than the English Canons of 1604 (given in Bullard, 1934; on these see under **impediments**), and this unusual view is somehow linked with questions of extremism, absolutism and justice.

The Russell marriage has its best exposition in Hotson, 1937, as noted above, and is less over-simplified than usual in Scouten, 1975, p 70, although this does not note the legally binding aspect of spousals.

prentice (A) The conditions of labour and the training of **apprentices** was regulated by **statutes** including the 1563 Elizabethan Statute of Artificers. The normal duration of apprentice **indentures** was fixed at a standard of seven years, but there were variations, for example a lengthy 13 apprenticeship years for goldsmiths. The statutes applicable to labour required that 'in a large number of specified employments, the hiring must be for one year', but exceptions were allowed for shorter terms (Holdsworth, 1903, 4:331).

Defiance of a master by an apprentice was potentially an instance of petty **treason**. Yet, Cornish and Clark, 1989, maintain, pp 291–2: 'There is considerable evidence that, in line with human relationships generally, in-servants and wage-labourers treated their employers argumentatively, aggressively, truculently'.

(B) Apprentices were seen as having a lowly social rank in Shakespeare's portrayals and metaphors. On Bolingbroke's bitter 'long apprenticehood' named as a degradation in the quarto of R2 (R2 A.C.4 following 1.3.256), see **apprentice**.

To purport low social origin, Paroles adds to many false aspersions that Lord Dumaine 'was a botcher's prentice in Paris' (AWW 4.3.190). More seriously, Marina in PER S.19.199–202 tells the bawd Boult he would do better to:

> Do anything but this thou dost. Empty
> Old receptacles or common sew'rs of filth,
> Serve by indenture to the public hangman –
> Any of these are yet better than this.

Thus she suggests that he follow a path similar to the bawd Pompey's (although in MM 4.2.20–5 it is arranged that Pompey 'compound' with the executioner Abhorson to live with him and learn his trade for only one year).

Apprentices were part of the Elizabethan household, a part of the master's 'family' in the extended use of that notion common to the age (see Laslett, 1983). Yet insubordination and even collective insurrection of apprentices was a recurrent feature of early modern English life (see Bernthal, 1991, pp 51–2 and bibliography there). Accordingly, 'prentices' appear gathered in armed rebellion in STM, demanding the expulsion of resident aliens, as indeed unruly apprentices and others periodically did in Shakespeare's London (see under **sanctuary** and **statute**).

Implicitly, turbulent apprentices also would be among Jack Cade's followers. During an attack on lawyers, Cade himself says 'I did but seal once to a thing, and I was never mine own man since' (CYL 4.2.83–4), perhaps implying his own **indentures**.

In the same play the prentice Peter Thumpe accuses his master Jack Horner of high **treason**, and succeeds in maintaining his right in a trial by combat (discussed under **lists**). The backing of Thumpe by his fellow 'prentices', and of Horner by his citizen 'neighbours' is argued by Bernthal, 1991, pp 49–50, to portray 'a major rift in the Tudor ideal of organic family and political harmony'. Bernthal generally argues an ambivalent attitude toward the victorious apprentice in CYL. On the contrary, Levine, N., 1994, pp 205–11 suggests an element of respect in CYL generally (despite Cade's rebellion) for the will of the populace and for Thumpe.

An apprentice is not well respected, however, in 2H4. To pursue a jest, Prince Hal disguises himself as a 'prentice tavern drawer, first remarking facetiously: 'From a god to a bull – a heavy declension – it was Jove's case. From a prince to a prentice – a low transformation –

that shall be mine; for in everything the purpose must weigh with the folly.' (2H4 2.2.165–8). In his disguise Hal imitates the prentice drawer Francis, whom he had questioned in 1H4, revealing the harassed boy's desire to abscond:

PRINCE HARRY	How long hast thou to serve, Francis?
FRANCIS	Forsooth, five years, and as much as to –
POINS	Francis!
FRANCIS	Anon, anon, sir!
PRINCE HARRY	Five year! By 'r Lady, a long lease for the clinking of pewter. But Francis, darest thou be so valiant as to play the coward with thy indenture, and show it a fair pair of heels, and run from it?
FRANCIS	O Lord, sir, I'll be sworn upon all the books England, I could find in my heart –
POINS	Francis!
FRANCIS	Anon, sir!
PRINCE HARRY	How old art thou, Francis?
FRANCIS	Let me see, about Michaelmas next I shall be –
POINS	Francis!
FRANCIS	Anon, sir!

(1H4 2.5.40–55)

Hal's appropriation of the tavern drawer's language is linked with a theory of colonialist oppression (see **plantation**) in the famous essay 'Invisible Bullets', Greenblatt, 1988, replied to in Sokol, 1994c.

(C) For analysis of the applicable statutes see Holdsworth, 1903, vol 4, p 331. For discussion of the effects of the very longstanding 1563 Elizabethan Statute of Artificers see Cornish and Clark, 1989, pp 289–95. This discusses underage servants, p 287, noting that only **justices**, not masters, could imprison runaway servants, but that if death resulted from a master's beating, it would be considered to be death by misadventure unless 'so barbarous as to exceed all bounds'.

See Bernthal, 1991 and Levine, N., 1994 on issues surrounding apprentices generally and Peter Thumpe of CYL particularly.

See Sokol, 1994b on the possibility that in TMP Ariel serves Prospero under 13-year-long apprentice-like **indentures**, which are abated to a more propitious 12-year term.

press[ing] to death (A) In early modern England a prisoner indicted for a criminal offence, a **felony**, or misdemeanour (**trespass**), would be brought to trial. The clerk of the assize read out the indictment and then asked the prisoner how he would plead, either 'guilty' or 'not guilty'. If the prisoner pleaded 'not guilty', the next question was how they wished to be tried. Because ordeals of fire and water had ended in 1215 (following the decision of the Fourth Lateran Council; see under **jury**), there was really only one choice which was to reply 'by God and the country', meaning trial by a jury. The problem was that no prisoner could be forced to make such a choice, and the common law had not evolved any alternative to trial by jury apart from abjuring the realm (on this see **sanctuary**), or short imprisonment. The period of imprisonment was probably intended to be unpleasant enough to induce the prisoner to change his mind because a statute of 1275 held that prisoners who refused to elect jury trial were to be placed in a 'prison fort et dure'. Heavy irons and scanty food and water often killed prisoners who would not relent.

In the thirteenth century Britton wrote

> And if they will not put themselves upon their acquittal, let them be put to their penance, until they pay to do it; and let their penance be that they be barefooted, ungirt and bareheaded, in the worst place in the prison, upon the bare ground continually night and day, that they eat only bread made of barley or bran, and that they drink not the day they eat, nor eat the day they drink, nor drink anything but water, and that they be put in irons.
>
> ('Britton,' 1865, vol 1, pp 26–7)

This harsh regime appears to have been misinterpreted in practice from about 1300 (until the abolition in 1772) as '*peine fort et dure*', meaning the prisoner was pressed to death under heavy weights. Why any prisoner would prefer this terrible fate to a jury trial remains puzzling, but it may be that by dying unconvicted a prisoner could avoid forfeiture of his property, which would then descend to his **heirs**.

A refusal to choose jury trial did not always result in *peine fort et dure*. It was not available to those prisoners accused of high **treason**, petty larceny, or misdemeanour, or on appeals of felony (see **appeal**). Here, standing silent was treated as a conviction and the prisoner would be punished accordingly. So '*piene fort et dure*' was the punishment for those who refused jury trial in cases of felony or petty treason (Baker, 1986b, p 283 – on petty treason, see under **treason**).

(B) This cruel punishment is alluded to by Shakespeare in several surprising ways and places. Its motive and its effect are deftly, if obliquely, suggested when the eavesdropping Queen describes her suffering as she hears common gardeners speak of Richard's mismanagement of the state and of his subsequent fall. She says: 'O, I am pressed to death through want of speaking!' (R2 3.4.73). She suffers because she is prevented from speaking, while in the 'real' *peine fort et dure* suffering results from being unwilling to speak. Feeling suffocated under the intolerable weight of wishing to reply, she then breaks her cover to speak to them.

   In a still more subtle scene of hidden overhearing, Hero arranges to have her cousin Beatrice eavesdrop while she gossips about Benedick and his supposed love. Hero adds, for good measure, a description of Beatrice's unattractive 'carping':

> to be so odd and from all fashions
> As Beatrice is cannot be commendable.
> But who dare tell her so? If I should speak
> She would mock me into air, O, she would laugh me
> Out of myself, press me to death with wit.
> Therefore let Benedick, like covered fire,
> Consume away in sighs, waste inwardly.
> It were a better death than die with mocks,
> Which is as bad as die with tickling.
>
> (ADO 3.1.72–80)

The metaphorical pressing to death feared here is by means of Beatrice's skilled ridicule. This is imagined threatened on account of Hero or Benedick speaking, rather than not-speaking, in inversion of *peine fort et dure*. Perhaps a touch of retributive malice against her extra-articulate cousin inspires Hero's cleverness, displayed here.

   A metaphor using *peine fort et dure* to link willed silence with a furtive sexual act arises in an obscene context of TRO, typical of Uncle Pandarus:

> I will show you a chamber with a bed – which bed, because it shall not speak of your pretty encounters, press it to death. Away!

311

> And Cupid grant all tongue-tied maidens here
> Bed, chamber, pander to provide this gear.
>
> (TRO 3.2.203–7)

In MM, Lucio's similar typical obscenity colours his lament over his forced marriage to Kate Keepdown:

LUCIO   Marrying a punk, my lord, is pressing to death, whipping, and hanging.

DUKE   Slandering a prince deserves it.

> (MM 5.1.521–3).

Here the black-humour of the gallows and of the brothel are linked together, as they often are in this play.

(C) See: 'Britton,' 1865; Baker, 1986b, pp 283–4; Baker, 1990b, pp 580–1. Summerson, 1983 gives a detailed historical treatment of the evolution of *peine fort et dure*, and offers informed speculation, pp 123–5, on why it was (rarely) elected. This article, pp 121–3, also contains an interesting discussion of the parallel between 'standing mute' and thus refusing the common law and its protections, and **outlawry**. Langbein, 1977, pp 74–6, distinguishes *peine fort et dure* from judicial torture used to obtain specific information.

primogeniture (A) Primogeniture is the customary rule of **inheritance** in England by which the eldest male inherits from the parent, and younger sons and any daughters take nothing. Although historians have disagreed about when land became heritable after the Norman Conquest, it is generally accepted that primogeniture was introduced to England in 1066. The developments of the common law writ of right and of the assize of *mort d'ancestor* ensured inheritance to the eldest son as **heir**.

Although primogeniture always favoured the eldest male, the rule did not extend beyond the immediate family, so for example a daughter would inherit before a nephew. Landowners would seek to provide for daughters and younger sons through *inter vivos* gifts, marriage settlements (**dowry**, **jointure**) and **uses**. Also, because primogeniture was a customary rule, it could be expressly avoided once it was possible to leave land in a **will** by the Statute of Wills 1540.

312

For other customary rules of inheritance, in particular coparceny, gavelkind, and borough English, see under **co-heirs**. Bonfield, 1983, pp 15–16, underlines the social importance of primogeniture to the landowning elite, and, p 22, points out Henrician acts disgavelling Kent partially and all of Wales 'as evidence of increased acceptance of primogeniture' in this period.

(B) Primogeniture is named in Shakespeare only once, in Ulysses' famous speech listing aspects of endangered 'order': 'The primogenity and due of birth' (TRO 1.3.106). Yet the traditional concepts discussed above permeate nearly all discussion of inheritance in Shakespeare and in his age.

Thus a younger son Orlando complains to the heir Olivier that 'The courtesy of nations allows you my better, in that you are the first-born; but the same tradition takes not away my blood, were there twenty brothers betwixt us' (AYL 1.1.43–6). Likewise in JN, AYL and *King Lear* questions of inheritance by younger sons, **bastards** and daughters are crucial.

(C) See under **land**, **inheritance** and **wills**. Elton, W. R., 1966, p 132, considers how Edmund and Gloucester in *King Lear* undermine primogeniture.

purchase (A) This word had a specific legal meaning, and yet also other meanings. The legal meaning informs only some of Shakespeare's uses.

Legally 'purchase' meant the acquisition of property, especially **land**, by any means other than inheritance or descent from an ancestor. The distinction was not new, but its legal importance was made newly prominent in the important and highly technical *Shelley's Case* (1579–81, 1 Co. Rep. 88b-106b). This case, described as 'one of the deepest mysteries of the common law' (Simpson, 1986, p 96), was of such significance that on the Queen's express command it was removed from Queen's Bench to be tried by all the judges of England (see **precedent**). The outcome was the establishment of the 'Rule in *Shelley's Case*' (which applied until 1925), that where land was left to 'A and his heirs' these are words of limitation and not of purchase. Success as the heir's counsel in this case established the legal reputation of Edward Coke.

313

(B) The sense 'by other than descent' applies in several, but not all, of the Shakespearian contexts containing 'purchase'. Some of Shakespeare's uses link definitely, and some only link loosely, to this legal meaning of the term.

The term 'purchase' embraced acquisition for money, but also by other than monetary payment. This is clear in Prospero's relenting remark to Ferdinand: 'Then, as my gift and thine own acquisition / Worthily purchased, take my daughter' (TMP 4.1.13–14). In law, any gift, or anything gained by worth or service, was something purchased.

A more degraded meaning of 'purchase', involving a sense of the word suggesting seizing or plundering (OED 1), but also euphemistically leaning toward the legal sense, is applied to Nym, Bardolph and Pistol in H5 3.2.42–3: 'They will steal anything, and call it "purchase"'.

'Purchase' meaning to acquire by means of sexual allure appears twice in relation to the wooing and marriage of Lady Elizabeth Grey by King Edward IV. She says she will not 'purchase' her husband's seized lands at the cost of her sexual 'honesty' (RDY 3.2.72–3), and later Richard III has it alleged that this widowed lady 'Made prize and purchase of [Edward's] wanton eye, / Seduced the pitch and height of his degree / To base declension and loathed bigamy' (R3 3.7.177–9).

The legal distinction between obtaining by 'purchase' and obtaining by descent is implied when the dying King Henry IV tell his eldest son that his own 'purchased' crown will now descend through **primogeniture**:

> For all my reign hath been but as a scene
> Acting that argument. And now my death
> Changes the mood, for what in me was purchased
> Falls upon thee in a more fairer sort,
> So thou the garland wear'st successively.
>
> (2H4 4.3.326–30)

Succession was of course the opposite of purchase. So, although as Barton, S. D. P., 1929, p 71 notes, legally ' "usurpation" ' did not rank as a "purchase" ', the usage here of purchase is 'happy'. (Again 'purchase' as seizure by force may be implicitly linked with legal meanings.)

An allusion to the distinction of 'purchase' from 'inherit' may arise when Orlando says to Rosalind, disguised as a rustic, 'Your accent is something finer than you could purchase in so removed a dwelling'

314

(AYL 3.2.331–2). The context suggests that he guesses from her mode of speech that she is not by breeding a native of Arden; her cultured accent, since not purchased locally, must have been by obtained by inheritance or birth at a court or city.

Lepidus more straightforwardly uses the legal distinction of 'purchase' from 'hereditary' in a metaphor mitigating the misbehaviour of Antony, when he says 'His faults in him seem as the spots of heaven, / More fiery by night's blackness; hereditary / Rather than purchased; what he cannot change / Than what he chooses' (ANT 1.4.12–15).

A contrast of the legal senses of the words 'purchase' and 'inherit' may become entangled in Biron's wordplay at LLL 1.1.72–3: 'Why, all delights are vain, but that most vain / Which, with pain purchased, doth inherit pain'. A mention of a 'pardon, purchased by . . . sin' at MM 4.2.110 may complexly adumbrate the distinction of a purchased from an hereditary (original) sin.

In the law-term-saturated context of HAM 5.1.95–114 (discussed under **fine and recovery**), Hamlet imagines a dead lawyer's many 'purchases' of land, so numerous that his 'very **conveyances**' would overfill his coffin. As purchases were the acquisition of **land** by means other than descent from an ancestor, it seems that this imagined lawyer was skilled at obtaining for himself more land than he was born to. What may be reflected is that the nascent professional class of Shakespeare's age was acquiring huge amounts of land; for instance the lawyer Sir Edward Coke died possessed of 'ninety-nine manors, and twice that number had passed through his hands' (Thorne, 1985i, p 200).

(C) Campbell, J., 1859, pp 94–5, and many since have commented on the legal overtones of 'purchase' in 2H4 and ANT. Barton, S. D. P., 1929, pp 69–71, suggests that the technical legal meaning of 'purchase' was not only important in law, but also likely to be known to be important by Shakespeare's audiences. Keeton, 1967, pp 44–5, discusses *Shelley's Case*, and following Campbell, J., 1859, suggests Shakespeare may have had direct knowledge of Coke's advocacy (which seems to be doubted in an important review of Keeton, Simon, 1968b, p 37). Yet Clarkson and Warren, 1942, pp 102–6 suggest that the sense of 'by purchase' as 'not as an heir' was not exclusively available to those competent in legally technicalities, but was rather continuous with a range of meanings in general use in Shakespeare's time. *Shelley's Case*, and the possible allusion to 'purchase' in AYL, are discussed in Sokol and Sokol, 1999a.

quillets (A) This word means both 'a small piece of land' and also 'a verbal quibble'.

(B) In a very nice pun, Hamlet uses both of the dual senses of 'quillets' at once in: 'Why might not that be the skull of a lawyer? Where be his quiddits now, his quillets, his cases, his tenures, and his tricks?' (HAM 5.1.96–7 – in a context discussed under **fine and recovery**.) The alliterative word 'quiddits' here refers to scholastic 'quiddities', such as were involved in metaphysical arguments of excessive subtlety. Conveyancing was practiced by Hamlet's imagined lawyer, and arguments of almost metaphysical subtlety did arise in early modern legal cases and procedures involved with the **conveyancing** of **land**. So, most appropriately, 'quillets' here suggest simultaneously pieces of land (held by **tenures**), and the subtle legal fictions or 'tricks' used for protecting or devising these.

Similarly, the ranting against humanity of Timon of Athens includes an attack on conveyancing **lawyers**: 'Crack the lawyer's voice, / That he may never more false title plead / Nor sound his quillets shrilly' (TIM 4.3.154–5). Here, however, 'quillets' probably refers only to legalistic quibbling and/or verbal trickery.

'Quillets' refer to ploys sought when the men of Navarre hope for a way to circumvent their former oaths to accept a '**statute**' (LLL 1.1.17) prohibiting love, wishing for 'Some tricks, some quillets how to cheat the devil' (LLL 4.3.286). The legal reference of the context is made clearer still when Dumaine describes these tricks as 'Some salve for perjury' (4.3.287).

In a scene filled with legal images, 'quillets' are named during the quarrel in the Temple Garden that involves the picking of red and white roses (1H6 2.4 – see under **Inns of Court**). Although the young men involved are nominal law students, some are self-admittedly 'truant' and more dedicated to good living than to studies. Asked to 'judge' the case between the parties of Richard Plantagenet and Somerset, young Warwick avers:

> Between two hawks, which flies the higher pitch,
> Between two dogs, which hath the deeper mouth,
> Between two blades, which bears the better temper,
> Between two horses, which doth bear him best,
> Between two girls, which hath the merriest eye,
> I have perhaps some shallow spirit of judgement;
> But in these nice sharp quillets of the law,
> Good faith, I am no wiser than a daw.
>
> (1H6 2.4.11–18)

This boast of ignorance or indifference to justice is not matched in an unnamed 'lawyer' present, who says to Somerset 'Unless my study and my books be false, / The argument you held was wrong in law; / In sign whereof I pluck a white rose too.' Richard then asks 'Now Somerset, where is your argument?', and the reply is 'Here in my scabbard, meditating that / Shall dye your white rose in a bloody red' (1H6 2.4.56–61). Disparagement of 'nice' legal 'quillets' gives way to threatened violence.

These threats are fulfilled, and in the next play of the trilogy Suffolk's brutality increases. Unable to prove any of the admittedly 'trivial' (3.1.241) charges he has brought against Gloucester, Suffolk proposes to conspirators to kill him extra-legally, urging 'let him die':

> And do not stand on quillets how to slay him;
> Be it by gins, by snares, by subtlety,
> Sleeping or waking, 'tis no matter how,
> So he be dead; for that is good conceit
> Which mates him first that first intends deceit.
>
> (CYL 3.1.261–5)

Murderous tyranny gathers force, despising legality, dismissing considerations of justice and compunction as 'quillets'.

It appears however that 'quillets' in OTH 3.1.23 are verbal quibbles without legal overtones.

(C) Commenting on only one instance, White, E. J., 1987, p 109, supposes 'quillets of the law' is derived from *quidlibet*. It would thus indicate an incomprehensible 'thingamajig'.

rape (A) Rape was the sexual assault of a woman by a man, and in Tudor England was always treated as a common law offence, in contrast to sexual incontinence, fornication or adultery, which came under the **jurisdiction** of the Church courts. However some cases nominally treated as fornication or bastardy could really have been rape, for example cases in which Church courts heard allegations of sexual coercion that resulted in the birth of children (see Ingram, 1987, p 266).

In medieval England rape was considered a serious **felony**, but was sometimes leniently dealt with as a misdemeanour (see Brundage, 1993, pp VIII:73, **trespass**, and **felony**). Records suggest that the definition of the offence was ambiguous, for indictments for rape were often accompanied by charges of abduction and **theft** (on the development of a clear distinction of *raptus* involving abduction and forced intercourse from *rapina* involving theft see Brundage, 1993, pp VIII:63–6). Yet the medieval canonists held sexual rape to be an *enormis delicta*, and conviction led to *infamia* (ibid., pp VII:66–7 and 73–4).

Glanvill's late twelfth century treatise *On the Laws and Customs of England* considered rape the capital offence of violating a woman by force. A later marriage would not allow the offender to escape punishment because this would cause disparagement if men of servile status married women of good birth, or vice versa (Glanvill, 1993, p 175). Bracton's treatise *On the Laws and Customs of England*, written in c. 1220, held that if conviction was on indictment, the penalty for rape could be mitigated if the woman chose to marry the accused man. But Bracton stressed the serious moral failure of this offence which should be punished. As an example Bracton approvingly told the tale of the beautiful Jewish wife of a court jester in France, raped by her lord, who ran to the King for protection. The King insisted on punishing the nobleman despite his offer to marry his victim (Bracton, 1968, vol. 2, pp 414–19). But it seems that severe punishments only applied to rape of virgins, and for rapes of other women an unspecified lesser scale of punishments applied, probably given by the Church courts (see Post, 1978, 151–3).

The Statutes of Westminster I in 1275 and II in 1285 provided some definition of the offence and its punishments. By Westminster I the offence was either to take or ravish an under-age unmarried woman regardless of her consent, or to take or ravish an over-age or married woman without her consent. For Britton writing around the end of the thirteenth century the punishment was death whether or not the woman consented after the commission of the felony ('Britton,' 1865, p 55). The offender could be pursued either by **appeal** of felony (a private prosecution), or if no appeal was brought by indictment by a grand **jury** if indicted, the accused could be punished by a fine and two years imprisonment (the appalling conditions of prisons made such a sentence likely to result in death). But if the victim brought a successful appeal of felony, then the punishment was either death by hanging, or mutilation. This could be castration or blinding, but in practice sentences of punishment by mutilation do not seem to have been carried out because only one case has been discovered in the plea rolls (see Post, 1978, p 151) and it is not mentioned by later legal commentators. (Generally, by the fifteenth century physical punishments, apart from execution, were confined to whipping, the stocks and the pillory, and branding; mutilation as a punishment was reserved for offences committed in the court itself, such as threatening a jury or throwing a brick at the judge. Later **Star Chamber** did impose mutilation.)

The Statute of Westminster II made rape a capital felony whether brought by indictment or by appeal, and whatever the marital status or age of the woman. Neither was the virginity of a woman a deciding factor. The King maintained a right to claim the value of the property taken with an abducted wife, who lost all right to **dower** if she continued to live with her abductor. In 1382 another statute (6 Ric. II, c.6) extended the right to bring an appeal of rape to fathers, husbands or next of kin, and treated an eloping couple as dead for the purposes of

inheritance (see **disinherit**). Yet, despite the definitions and severe punishments set out in the Statutes of Westminster, until 1576 (18 Eliz., c.7) rape remained clergyable (see **branded**).

In general, women were allowed to bring an appeal of felony for only two reasons, rape, or the murder of their husband. An appeal of felony for rape could be compromised by a subsequent marriage. During the fourteenth and fifteenth centuries charges of abduction and rape were common, perhaps as Bellamy, 1973, p 58, conjectures, because women of the wealthier classes who wished to marry men other than those chosen by parents or guardians would arrange elopements to look like abductions. The abduction and subsequent marriage of a **ward** could result in financial loss to the crown, so after the elopement such a new husband would be compelled to purchase a **pardon**. The cost of pardons was listed according to the rank of the offender, as well as the nature of the offence itself, and pardon for rape cost the same as for **homicide**.

The facts that law allowed the compromise of appeals of rape by subsequent marriage, but also insisted on the imposition of fines and forfeiture whether or not the marriage took place, indicates that ravishment and abduction were seen as wrongs meriting compensation to the victim's family. The runaway daughter, or abducted adulterous wife brought disparagement and financial loss to their families. The idea of the wronged family is evident in other remedies available for a husband or father of a raped woman. Holdsworth, 1903, vol 8, p 427, explains that the common law, by analogy with a lord's right to wardship, treated the father's right with respect to children, wives or servants as proprietary. So while the daughter had the right to pursue her attacker for the physical injury done to her, the father had a right to pursue her attacker for the loss of her services to him as a result of her injuries. By the mid-seventeenth century the father's right was seen to lie in **trespass** (see actions **on the case**), and damages for his injured feelings could be included. A husband had a stronger claim because he was considered to have a proprietary interest in his wife's *consortium*, which was lost if his wife was raped or abducted.

In the seventeenth century Coke defined the felony of rape as 'unlawfull and carnall knowledge and abuse of any woman above the age of ten years against her will, or a woman child under ten years with her will, or against her will' (Coke, 1797, Third Institute, p 60). The offender should not receive benefit of clergy.

321

By Shakespeare's time, it appears that although rape was a felony, many cases were non-suited (not pursued), or compromised, or failed before the **justices**, because some technical exception to the charge was found. This was possibly because an agreement for financial compensation had been reached. Since the time of the Statutes of Westminster, the law of rape was also a 'law of elopement and abduction' which served the interests of families and 'inhibited the purposes of the woman herself' (Post, 1978, p 160; Stephen, 1883, vol 2, p 201, cites Bracton and includes abduction under his definition of rape). Rather than financial recompense to her family, the woman's own primary concern may have been to to bring her rapist to justice, or in cases of alleged abduction to marry according to her own wishes.

(B) Circumstances in which violent sexual rape is threatened are depicted by Shakespeare, for instance in TGV, PER, CYM, TMP. Rape actually occurs, crucially, in TIT and LUC.

Shakespeare also often portrays rape in the sense of an abduction of a woman enacted or planned, for instance in TGV, MND, MV, TRO, OTH and PER. This is often, but not always, followed by an irregular or 'clandestine' marriage (see under **pre-contract**).

Marriage by ritual abduction, as it is known in anthropology, takes a parodic form when Katerina is unwillingly abducted from her own wedding feast by Petruchio, who pretends to meet non-existent family resistance (SHR 3.3.105–11, commented on in Sokol, 1985). Here the family's wishes to be rid of Katerina override her desire to have her will. In a different kind of travesty, in the wild dramaturgy of PER Marina is carried off by pirates and sold into a brothel, but, crucially for the Romance, keeps her virginity.

The term 'rape' is used in a metaphor for violation and despoliation of a virginal victim in JN 2.1.97–8 ('done a rape / Upon the maiden virtue of the crown'). A section of Tarquin's soliloquy, LUC 197–210, emphasizes that rape of a (married) woman also degrades the perpetrator.

In accord with the same notion that being a rapist is highly discredible, in his calumny in AWW 4.3.255 Parolles alleges that Dumaine 'parallels Nessus' in his numerous 'rapes and ravishments'. Male sexual incontinence is never treated kindly by Shakespeare, especially in heads of state such as Edward IV (his attempted sexual coercion of Lady Grey in RDY 3.2.69–81 is discussed under **dower**). Other rulers or rulers-to-be are held culpable for unbridled lust, such Angelo of MM, and Malcolm in his (falsely) confessed 'voluptousness' (MAC 4.3.61–6).

Yet in a play built around the vicissitudes of sexual desire, Paris debates that his abduction of Helen of Troy should be defended in the name of Trojan honour (TRO 2.2.147–61). He argues: the 'soil of her fair rape' can be 'Wiped off in honourable keeping her' (2.2.147–8), as if valour could counterpoise adultery and abduction. However, his may belong to the sort of cases mentioned above where the abducted woman was not herself unwilling.

The most brutal and sadistic violent rape in Shakespeare is in TIT. Yet the first time the word 'rape' is heard in the play (TIT 1.1.401), it refers to an abduction of a willing woman, not to a violent assault. The calling of such an act a 'rape' is contested by the perpetrator Bassianus, who says ''Rape' call you it, my lord, to seize my own – / My true betrothed love, and now my wife?', and he invokes the protection of 'the laws of Rome' (1.1.402–4). What Bassianus has done is to carry off and marry Lavinia to whom he had been apparently **pre-contracted**, despite the dynastic plans of Titus and Saturninus. Thus he claims legality and that 'I [am] possessed of that is mine' (1.1.405).

It is important to view Bassianus' actions in contrast with the concurrent actions of Titus and his sons. Bassianus' abduction of Titus' daughter Lavinia appears in the same scene as the sacrificial hewing to pieces of the eldest son of Tamora by Titus and Lucius, and the slaying by Titus of his own youngest son Mutius, for siding with Bassianus. So Bassianus acts in the name of faithfulness and love, while the honourable men of Rome slaughter in the name of military and family discipline and pride.

Tamora, whose pleas for her son were disregarded by honour-besotted Titus, becomes Empress instead of Lavinia, and plans devious revenge (1.1.447–52). Then Aaron dissuades Tamora's two remaining sons Chiron and Demetrius from battling over Lavinia's love, and persuades them to join forces to rape her (2.1.60–136). This rape of course contrasts with her earlier consensual abduction. When the **murder** of Lavinia is urged on her sons by Tamora, she makes it clear that she has not only mischief but revenge in mind, and so is not displeased that they intend a rape (2.2.161–80).

The two brothers cruelly torture Lavinia, mutilating and raping her on top of her husband's bleeding corpse. This is done partly in revenge for Titus killing their eldest brother, and partly to spite Lavinia's marital

323

fidelity. These horrible deeds may be reminiscent of blood feud mutilations allowed by obsolete law (Selden Society, 1987, p 93). But the mental and physical oppression of Lavinia is nearly identical to that planned by brutal Cloten of CYM, who out of sheer spite intends to rape Imogen in a manner adding extra 'torment to her contempt' (CYM 3.5.137–45).

(C) See Glanvill, 1993, p 175; Bracton, 1968, vol 2, pp 414–9; 'Britton,' 1865, p 55; Coke, 1797, Third Institute, p 60; Plucknett, 1956, p 451; Holdsworth, 1903, vol 3, pp 316, vol 8, p 427–30; Bellamy, 1973, pp 58–9, 126, 195; Post, 1978; Baker, 1978, p 326; Kaye, 1977, pp 8–9; Ingram, 1987, p 266; Groot, 1988a; Walker, 1988; Baker, 1990b, 603; Hudson, 1996, pp 235–6. Brundage, 1993, pp VIII: 62–75 surveys the development by the end of the thirteenth century of the modern definitions and laws of rape from Roman and canon law origins.

For a survey of some recent discussions of rape in TIT see the introduction to Bate, 1995, especially pp 36–7. Rape in LUC is treated in terms of military siege and **treason** in Ranald, 1987, pp 153–72, and it is discussed in terms of social discontent and the law of treason in Nass, 1996.

recognizance (A) This was any obligation entered into before a court or a legal officer and enrolled there officially. These often registered **debts** (often before a clerk in the chancery of exchequer); examples are **statutes** merchant or staple. If a borrower who in this way had acknowledged indebtedness later defaulted, he would immediately be in a position of having been successfully sued on a writ of debt by the creditor.

(B) One clear Shakespearian instance is in HAM 5.1.101–3, where Hamlet speaks of a supposed dead lawyer's 'statutes, his recognizances, his fines, his double vouchers, his recoveries'. On this context see under **fine and recovery**.

Where 'recognisance' appears as the 'pledge of love' which is Othello's handkerchief (OTH 5.2.221), it mixes the legal implications of an acknowledged obligation with the non-legal meaning of a 'token, badge, emblem' given in OED 3.

(C) See Thorne, 1985i, p 206, and on the difference from **bonds** see Simpson, 1966, p 416.

remainder On the legal meaning, and the use of this term in the context of AWW 4.3.282, see under **entail**. See also **reversion**.

reversion (A) A reversion is a future estate in **land**, the possession of which is postponed until the determination of another interest. For the circumstances in which such an estate could arise and the legal definition of reversion see **entail**.

Because it was a **fee-simple** absolute a reversionary interest could be alienated by sale or gift or otherwise, and could be protected in the king's courts. A reversioner's or a **remainderman's** interest could be protected by the writs of 'formedon in the remainder' or 'formedon in the reverter'.

In popular terms a 'reversion' commonly denoted the right of succeeding to an estate by any means (OED I.1.b).

(B) 'Reversion' is used by Shakespeare in contexts, often metaphoric, concerned with anticipated or conditional possession.

King Richard II says bitterly that Bolingbroke behaves 'As were our England in reversion his, / And he our subjects' next degree in hope' (R2 1.4.34–5). Later Richard's Queen speaks metaphorically of her woes, caused by an unnameable anticipated event: 'something hath the nothing that I grieve – / 'Tis in reversion that I do possess –' (R2 2.2.37–8).

In 1H4 4.1.54 the 'sweet reversion' spoken of as cherished is the military force held in reserve on account of the supposed illness of the Earl of Northumberland.

Troilus offers to perform better in fact than others idly promise in anticipation, claiming that his deeds in love and not mere words will prove his desert: 'No perfection in reversion shall have a praise in present. We will not name desert before his birth' (TRO 3.2.89–91). Here 'reversion' in the language of land law combines with 'birth' in the language of sexuality (see Sokol & Sokol, 1999a).

(C) See Clarkson and Warren, 1942, pp 72–7 and under **entail**. Sokol and Sokol, 1999a contains an extended discussion of 'reversion' in TRO.

robbery/theft (A) Robbery was the offence of openly and forcibly taking property belonging to another. The taking could be accompanied by violence or threats of violence. Because it was a **felony** robbery was punished by mandatory sentence of death. By the early sixteenth century the mitigation of sentence known as benefit of clergy (see under **branded**) was not allowed for this crime.

Highway robbery was common in the late middle ages. Highwaymen were the most professional robbers of the time; many were described in indictments as 'notorious' meaning habitual criminals, a serious charge (Bellamy, 1973, p 42). Highwaymen operated singly or sometimes in bands, often preying on merchants travelling lonely stretches of road. One mid-thirteenth century robbery of merchants from France and Flanders at Alton was notorious for the scale of the merchants' losses, and because some of the highwaymen were identified as members of the King's household. Yet, despite the legends of Robin Hood, not many men of the gentry became professional highwaymen. **Outlawed** gentry sometimes did join the outlaw bands which frequented the forests and woods and also robbed.

Theft, or larceny, was an offence which need not involve violence. Instead the offence was primarily of dishonesty. The characteristic behaviour of a thief was furtive or stealthy taking of someone else's property, as suggested by the etymology of these words ('*fur*' meant thief, 'stealth' meant theft). A thief was someone who took secretly. Liability for theft in medieval and early modern England is said to have depended not on intent, but on what have been described as the two factors of 'possesorial immunity' and conduct conforming to agreed ideas of 'acting like a thief' (Fletcher, 1976, p 472–3). Nevertheless, some mental element in theft, *animus furandi*, had been seen as essential in the thirteenth century by Bracton, although not shortly afterwards by Britton, and case reports are unclear (Sayre, 1932, p 987). Also the teaching of the Church was always that punishment depended on moral guilt, which requires some conscious mental element, and this was translated in criminal law as an evil or blameworthy mind (see under **felony** on *mens rea*).

Possesorial immunity meant that criminal liability did not arise when property was intentionally transferred by an owner to a bailee, or other recipient, and subsequently misappropriated. Instead common law writs of detinue and trover could be used to pursue the dishonest bailee (see **conversion**). This immunity was then modified by statute in certain circumstances, so that for example servants who misappropriated property belonging to their masters were no longer protected from criminal prosecution after 1529. In 1473 the *Carrier's Case* formulated the rule of 'breaking bulk'. Here a bailee, a carrier, not only misappropriated the bailor's goods but broke open bales in order to do so, and he was no longer protected by his bailment but treated as a **felon** (see Fletcher, 1976, p 481–6). The case reports also that the carrier's demeanour showed he had another intent than carrying the goods, and therefore he was a felon (see Sayre, 1932, p 999).

Liability for theft attached to those whose conduct conformed to a popularly agreed notion of the manifest thief. Any intent to thieve was subordinated to evidence of suspicious conduct, although lack of intent could be raised as a defence by the suspect. A property owner who discovered a manifest thief with stolen goods had the right to summarily kill him in medieval England (see **taken with the manner**). By 1532 such killing of thieves and robbers caught breaking into houses was treated by statute as justifiable **homicide** (24 Hen. VIII, c.5).

However by Shakespeare's time a need for blameworthiness and a recognition of a *mens rea* were evident. Coke's *Institutes* requires a guilty intent for a guilty act (Sayre, 1932, p 988) although it was still not necessary to prove an *animus furandi* in robbery cases. By the later seventeenth century Hale would write that both will and intention were needed to make an offence capital (quoted ibid., p 993).

Grand larceny, the theft of property over the value of twelve pence, was a felony and was punished by hanging. Petty larceny, the theft of property valued at less than twelve pence, was treated as a misdemeanour (see **trespass**) and punished with whipping or the stocks. Jury mitigation of the death penalty was common in early modern England (see **pardon** and **jury**); so sympathetic juries would value stolen goods at less then twelve pence to spare the defendant's life (see Lawson, 1988, especially pp 151–2, and Cockburn, 1988, pp 171–2).

Larceny remained by far the most common offence prosecuted at either quarter sessions or assize, and it is calculated that approximately seventy percent of all criminal indictments were for larceny or related offences. In some area where population was dense and where poverty existed, the number could rise to ninety percent of crimes (Cockburn, 1972, p 97). This range of figures remained constant in early modern England where offences varied from cattle stealing in the countryside to pocket-picking, burglary and housebreaking in towns (ibid.).

After a robbery or theft was reported, local officials were supposed to raise the **hue and cry** and search for the miscreant. Once the suspect was found the **constables** and local parish officials put an 'information' (charge) before the justices at quarter sessions or assize. Alternatively a **Justice of the Peace** could examine a suspect, who was then indicted by the grand **jury** and tried before the royal justices at the next assize.

(B) The terms 'robber' and 'thief' are used literally or figuratively with great frequency by Shakespeare. The thief's timidity and/or stealth are sometimes emphasised (ERR 4.2.59, RDY 5.6.12, AYL 3.2.318–20, ADO 3.3.57, AWW 2.5.81 and 3.2.131), distinguishing him from a robber ('thief', oddly, is occasionally a term of endearment as well, in 1H4 3.1.231 and 2H4 5.3.58).

But a robber is also a 'thief' for many of Shakespeare's speakers, who make no distinction of the two offences. Speaking clearly of a highway robber, Gloucester in CYL 3.1.129 describes a 'foul felonious thief that fleeced poor passengers' while in CYL 4.9.33 Iden calls Cade 'a thief . . . come to rob my grounds'. Prince Hal says in mock innocence 'I rob? I a thief?' (1H4 1.2.136), then Falstaff says of Poins 'I am accursed to rob in that thief's company' (1H4 2.2.11). In MM 2.2.181 Angelo muses 'Thieves for their robbery have authority . . .'. Cloten in CYM 4.2.76–7 accuses Guiderius of being 'a robber . . . thief'. Moreover two poignant images in the sonnets are 'that sweet thief which sourly robs from me' (SON 35) and 'I do forgive thy robb'ry, gentle thief' (SON 40).

The two terms 'thieves' and 'rob' are used together particularly ripely in Timon's rant to a gang of thieves: 'Rascal thieves, / Here's gold . . . / Trust not the physician; / . . . he slays / More than you rob' (TIM 4.3.430–5). The terrific malediction continues to find all humanity and all nature a thief, and bids the thieves to 'Rob one another' (4.3.447).

To be a robber was disgraceful, and an allegation of this is used disapprovingly or in insults in: TIT 5.1.41; H5 3.6.102 and 4.1.165; MM 2.2.181; JC 4.2.75; LRF 3.7.39; ANT 4.15.23; COR 5.6.91; CYM 4.2.76; TMP 5.1.275, AIT 3.2.256.

Yet, in CYM 3.3.62, a victim of a metaphorical robbery understates

his bitterness – this is among many Shakespearian portrayals of for-
giveness of serious injury aside from those often noted in LRF 4.6.68
and TMP 5.1.20–32 (see **pardon**). In this passage Belarius recalls long
ago events that caused the loss of his reputation and position, and a
continuing twenty years of **outlawry**:

> Then was I as a tree
> Whose boughs did bend with fruit; but in one night
> A storm or robbery, call it what you will,
> Shook down my mellow hangings, nay, my leaves,
> And left me bare to weather.
>
> (CYM 3.3.60–4)

This allows as optional views of Belarius' misfortune that a natural
force of some sort, 'a storm', might have been accounted responsible,
or alternately 'robbery' might have been the cause of the loss of his
'fruit'. His image shows that he is no longer deeply concerned (in
contrast with Prospero) about the malice of those who destroyed his
favour and honour in long ago court intrigues (see on this passage under
treason).

The figure of the vagabond thief Autolycus is ambiguously presented, indeed as in Belarius' image, alternately as treacherous, or as a
force of nature. We meet him singing cheerfully of 'The white sheet
bleaching on the hedge', admitting roguery that he will 'in the stocks
avouch'. He then claims 'My traffic is sheets' (WT 4.3.5–23); sheets are
related to lawless sexuality (WT 1.2.329), but also **vagrants** like
Autolycus were often reputed to be laundry-stealers. He happily admits
he will be a 'snapper-up of unconsidered trifles' (sheets, and seduced or
cozened countryfolk), but that cowardice forestalls him from engaging
in highway robbery: 'my revenue is the silly cheat. / Gallows and knock
are too powerful on the highway. / Beating and hanging are terrors to
me' (4.3.25–9). Whether he is an artist in crime, or a criminal traducing
art, is considered in Sokol, 1994a, pp 167–82 (also see **poverty**).

Historically and in legend robbery was the livelihood of groups of
outlaws, which is reflected in TGV, but not AYL or CYM (see under
outlaws).

Robbery was also the livelihood of the pirates mentioned in CYL
4.1.108, R3 1.3.158, MV 1.3.22–3, HAM 4.6.15, TN 5.1.65–6, MM
1.2.7 and 4.3.68, ANT 1.4.48–54, and PER S.15.141–51. Pirates are

repeatedly called water thieves or robbers (CYL 4.1.109, MV 1.3.23, HAM 4.6.19, TN 5.1.70, and PER S.15.145). In practice, in some circumstances English pirates could be tried as traitors (see under **treason**), but privateers like Drake who preyed on foreign nations not officially at war with England were sometimes regarded with a blind eye with regard to crime. Their situation may resemble Antonio's of TN, who denies he was ever 'thief or pirate' although admitting himself 'on base and ground enough / Orsino's enemy' (TN 5.1.70–2).

The most extended representation of robbery in Shakespeare is the Gads Hill robbery by Falstaff's crew, who are in turn robbed of their booty by the Crown Prince and Poins. These capers are planned, take place, and have their aftermath, in 1H4 1.2, 2.1, 2.2, 2.3, 2.5, 3.3. The Gads Hill affair is not forgotten even after Hal has returned the money taken (1H4 3.3.179), and Falstaff has appeared to be a hero at Shrewsbury; it is mentioned by the Lord Chief Justice in 2H4 1.2.60–1, and alluded to by the dying King in 2H4 4.3.254.

The Gads Hill robbery's complex presentation embraces its valuation as both a brilliant jest, and also as a mark of Hal's potential degradation. The caper is proposed following a parody of puritan piety, mutually enacted by Hal and Falstaff:

PRINCE HARRY   I see a good amendment of life in thee, from praying to purse-taking.

FALSTAFF   Why, Hal, 'tis my vocation, Hal. 'Tis no sin for a man to labour in his vocation. Poins! Now shall we know if Gadshill have set a match. O, if men were to be saved by merit, what hole in hell were hot enough for him? This is the most omnipotent villain that ever cried 'Stand!' to a true man. (1H4 1.2.102–9)

Then Poins proposes a robbery, and Hal at first declines to join in,

PRINCE HARRY   Who, I rob? I a thief? Not I, by my faith.

FALSTAFF   There's neither honesty, manhood, nor good fellowship in thee, nor thou camest not of the blood royal, if thou darest not stand for ten shillings.

PRINCE HARRY   Well then, once in my days I'll be a madcap.

FALSTAFF   Why, that's well said.

PRINCE HARRY   Well, come what will, I'll tarry at home.

330

| SIR JOHN | By the Lord, I'll be a traitor then, when thou art king. |
| FALSTAFF | I care not. (1.2.136–46) |

But Hal is persuaded by Poins to join in his 'jest to execute that I cannot manage alone' (1.2.159–60). They will rob the robbers, the aim being to elicit from Falstaff 'incomprehensible lies'. The well-orchestrated twin robberies succeed with no one hurt (2.1.53–2.3.19) and Falstaff perfectly satisfies the expectation that he will first misstate his courage, and then excuse his cowardice (2.5.112–328). But this leads on to playacting involving 'lese-majesty' (see under **treason**), in which Hal plays himself and Falstaff plays the King chiding a dissolute Prince, and then they exchange roles (2.5.379–490). Hal is playacting all along, but before changing his role he hazards a potentially defiling brush with serious crime.

Constable Dogberry gives astute advice to his watch on avoiding being defiled in thief-catching:

DOGBERRY	If you meet a thief you may suspect him, by virtue of your office, to be no true man; and for such kind of men, the less you meddle or make with them why, the more is for your honesty.
A WATCHMAN	If we know him to be a thief, shall we not lay hands on him?
DOGBERRY	Truly, by your office you may, but I think they that touch pitch will be defiled. The most peaceable way for you if you do take a thief is to let him show himself what he is, and steal out of your company. (ADO 3.3.48–57)

In fact, the keepers of the king's peace often did fail to apprehend thieves. The malefactors who were caught were often taken 'red handed', or with the stolen goose under their arm. The law term for that was '**taken with the manner**', twice used by Shakespeare.

(C) On the particularly 'interesting history' of the definition of larceny see Plucknett, 1956, pp 446–52. This holds that the common law crime was uncertain, Coke's interpretations added confusion (see Coke, 1797, 3rd Institute, pp 106–10), and many uncoordinated statues were passed. See also: Bracton, 1968, vol 2, p 425; 'Britton,' 1865, vol 1, p 55–62;

Sayre, 1932, particularly pp 989, 993, 999–1,000; Fletcher, 1976; Baker, 1978, pp 316–23, 324–5; Baker, 1990b, pp 605–6; Bellamy, 1973, pp 42–53. On lone thieves and robber gangs see under **outlaws** and Beier, 1985, pp 137–8.

A connection of theft with economic hard times is demonstrated in Lawson, 1986; as noted under **vagrants**, after some delay, years of dearth caused increases in larceny.

sanctuary (A) Sanctuary was a legal privilege once accorded to all consecrated buildings or grounds. Taking shelter in a sanctuary was most often used by those accused of crimes, but it was no admission of guilt, and sanctuary was used as a refuge from enemies as well as a shelter from the law.

Once an accused person had gained entry into a privileged place they were safe from punishment by the royal or local justice. All churches could give sanctuary to a fugitive for forty days. Some great churches or monasteries claimed 'special' privileges, granted by the King or Pope or by 'prescription' (long usage), which gave them the right to give sanctuary to fugitives for an indefinite period of time, even permanently. The cathedrals of Durham, Beaulieu and Beverly, and the abbeys of Glastonbury and Westminster, had privileges which allowed them to offer fugitives indefinite sanctuary. In some places, for example Beverly, sanctuary extended a league beyond the buildings. Sometimes boundaries were marked by stone crosses and the church officers could fine anyone who pursued the fugitive into the privileged area. There were also secular sanctuaries, where a fugitive was safe from pursuit because it was said that neither the king's nor any lord's authority could be enforced within the boundaries. For example the county palatine of Lancaster, or the marcher lordships of Wales could offer fugitives immunity from pursuit for an indefinite period.

During the middle ages sanctuary was available for those accused of any offence, including **treason**. Many **debtors** also attempted to escape creditors by taking sanctuary, which led to **statutes** regulating creditors' rights (see Ross, 1994, p 161). For instance a statute of 1379 allowed **sheriff's** officers to seize the lands and goods of debtors who had made fraudulent **conveyances** of their property to avoid their creditors, and then fled to a sanctuary.

Once the fugitive arrived at the sanctuary she or he was supposed to surrender any weapons, make confession, pay a fee and swear to follow the rules set by the religious house. Some of the great religious houses entered the fugitive's name, occupation or status, supposed offence, and place of residence into a register; the registers from Beverly and Durham survive for the late fifteenth and early sixteenth centuries. In Durham during this period the largest number of those who sought sanctuary were accused of **homicide**. In Beverly most fugitives accused of violent crimes were tailors (!). In general, most fugitives were men, and most earned their living in some way from the land.

In some of the large religious houses fugitives undertook tasks such as bellringing and were well fed and housed. But fugitives in poor parish churches were dependent on the charity of the priest and church officers for food and shelter, and could be easily starved out after the expiry of forty days. In all cases the common law imposed a duty on the **constable** to inform the coroner about the fugitive's presence and organize a watch composed of men from the four nearest towns to prevent his or her escape.

Within the forty day period the fugitive had to choose between standing trial or abjuring the realm (swearing to leave the country for ever). Abjuration has been described as an 'English invention' (Baker, 1990a, p 9), and had serious consequences. The abjurer was treated as dead in civil law, so that his **widow** was allowed to remarry immediately. The abjurer's **land** and **chattels** were forfeit to the King, and even if a **pardon** was granted goods would not be returned.

If abjuration was chosen, then the fugitive confessed to the coroner, swore an oath witnessed by the coroner and local people at the church door, and was **branded** on the thumb with a letter 'A'. He then set off to walk to the nearest port, bareheaded and barefoot, escorted by men from the nearest towns. The medieval abjurer is described as wearing white sackcloth with a red cross on it, and carrying a cross. The route to be followed was prescribed by the coroner, and if the fugitive tried to escape, or deviated from the path, he could be executed summarily. Once the port was reached the fugitive had to embark on the first available ship, and if none was available then to remain in the port and each day wade out to sea to show intent until leaving England forever. Although a **pardon** from the king always remained possible, most abjurers were never heard of again.

In the earlier sixteenth century, Henry VIII became convinced that abjurers who were skilled and informed English soldiers were joining the French armies (Baker, 1990b, p 585), and so prohibited abjuration (22 Hen. VIII, c.14, 28 Hen. VIII c.1, 32 Hen. VIII, c.3). An act of 1592–3 (35 Eliz., c.1), discussed under **outlawry/banishment**, demanded abjuration of unrepentant religious non-conformists, partly reversing Henry's prohibition.

The very success of sanctuaries brought them into disrepute; in particular 'special' sanctuaries were seen as dens of thieves where the criminals could gather to plan and carry out further outrages. In a notorious instance the 'sanctuary men' of St Martin's-le-Grand raided the City of London in 1455–6 and participated in anti-alien riots (Bellamy, 1973, p 110). The notorious case of St John's Priory 1519 (*Pauncefoot v Savage* Keil. 188) caused public outrage because Savage, accused of a serious attack on a judge, took sanctuary.

After the reformation, Henry VIII took steps to restrict privileges of sanctuary. Sanctuary was abolished for those accused of treason by 26 Hen. VIII, c. 13 (on the steps leading to this see Bellamy, 1979, pp 91–3). Sanctuary men were forced to wear badges to identify themselves. Many sanctuaries were abolished altogether (by 32 Hen. VIII, c.12 1540 and by the abolition of monasteries), and the forty day rule was imposed on all those remaining. Although Henry substituted eight cities of refuge for the abolished religious houses, this was not successful (local inhabitants objected) and the scheme ended in the next reign. Sanctuary was abolished for those accused of serious **felonies**, for example **rape**, **homicide** and **robbery**.

The Henrican statutes were repealed in 1603, reinstating the privileges of sanctuary, but these were finally abolished in 1624 (21 Jac. I, c.28 s.7).

(B) Antipholus of Syracuse, assailed by his wife Adriana and by angry merchants, is urged by Dromio to 'take a house' (ERR 5.1.36). 'To take' a house may here echo a hunting term meaning 'to take cover in', and/ or echo a legal mode of evading creditors by 'keeping house' (see Lester, 1995, p 14 on a 1543 statute). It may possibly also echo language such as in the statute 4 Hen. VIII, c.2 (1512), 'If any murderer . . . hadde taken any Church or Churchyerd' (discussed under **murder**).

Antipholus runs into a nearby priory, also called an abbey, pursued by creditors, and also by Adriana intent on imposing Dr Pinch's therapy on him. The Abbess diagnoses Antipholus' distraction to be caused by Adriana's excessive jealousy and intends to cure him, declaring her house to be a place of sanctuary. So when Adriana bids her 'Good people' to 'enter' it and 'lay hold on him', a disagreement ensues:

ABBESS   No, not a creature enters in my house.

ADRIANA   Then let your servants bring my husband forth.

ABBESS   Neither. He took this place for sanctuary,
And it shall privilege him from your hands
Till I have brought him to his wits again,
Or lose my labour in essaying it.

ADRIANA   I will attend my husband, be his nurse,
Diet his sickness, for it is my office,
And will have no attorney but myself.
And therefore let me have him home with me.

ABBESS   Be patient, for I will not let him stir
Till I have used the approved means I have,
With wholesome syrups, drugs, and holy prayers
To make of him a formal man again.
It is a branch and parcel of mine oath,
A charitable duty of my order.
Therefore depart, and leave him here with me.

ADRIANA   I will not hence, and leave my husband here;
And ill it doth beseem your holiness
To separate the husband and the wife.

ABBESS   Be quiet and depart. Thou shalt not have him.

LUCIANA   Complain unto the Duke of this indignity.

                             (ERR 5.1.92–114)

Adriana indeed does intend to beg the Duke to 'take perforce my husband from the Abbess' (5.1.118), and does this (5.1.160–1). To investigate, the Duke summons the Abbess. But before any contest between Ducal authority and the right of sanctuary begins, the play's plot of lost identities and severed families unravels.

In RDY, Edward IV's queen, Elizabeth Grey, pregnant with the future Edward V, turns to sanctuary for safety and succour. She tells her brother Lord Rivers that she will flee Warwick's advance:

> I am informed that he comes towards London
> To set the crown once more on Henry's head.
> Guess thou the rest – King Edward's friends must down.
> But to prevent the tyrant's violence –
> For trust not him that hath once broken faith –
> I'll hence forthwith unto the sanctuary,
> To save at least the heir of Edward's right.
> There shall I rest secure from force and fraud.
> Come, therefore, let us fly while we may fly.
> If Warwick take us, we are sure to die.
>
> (RDY 4.5.26–35)

Then, in R3 2.4.65–72, after the death of her husband and following the imprisonment of her brother and others, Queen Elizabeth again decides to enter sanctuary. She takes with her the young Duke of York, her second son, and Edward the heir presumptive of the throne. This young Prince of Wales and then his brother are each in turn taken from her (later to be assassinated by Richard of Gloucester).

To argue the removal from sanctuary of the young Duke of York, brother to Prince Edward, Richard's agent Buckingham says of Queen Elizabeth:

BUCKINGHAM Fie, what an indirect and peevish course
Is this of hers! – Lord Cardinal, will your grace
Persuade the Queen to send the Duke of York
Unto his princely brother presently? –
If she deny, Lord Hastings, go with him,
And from her jealous arms pluck him perforce.

CARDINAL My lord of Buckingham, if my weak oratory
Can from his mother win the Duke of York,
Anon expect him. But if she be obdurate
To mild entreaties, God in heaven forbid
We should infringe the sacred privilege
Of blessed sanctuary. Not for all this land
Would I be guilty of so deep a sin.

BUCKINGHAM You are too senseless-obstinate, my lord,

> Too ceremonious and traditional.
> Weigh it not with the grossness of this age.
> You break not sanctuary in seizing him.
> The benefit thereof is always granted
> To those whose dealings have deserved the place,
> And those who have the wit to claim the place.
> This prince hath neither claimed it nor deserved it,
> And therefore, in my mind, he cannot have it.
> Then taking him from thence that 'longs not there,
> You break thereby no privilege nor charter.
> Oft have I heard of 'sanctuary men',
> But 'sanctuary children' ne'er till now.
>
> (R3 3.1.25–56)

Buckingham then joins Richard in alleging the **bastardy** of the two princes, Richard accepts the throne, and Elizabeth again takes sanctuary (4.1.93). Although Buckingham himself balks at the murder of the princes (4.2.21–6), his actions have allowed it. His glib dismissal of those who would preserve sanctuary as 'too ceremonious and traditional' is at best wretched folly, serving tyranny.

Laertes replies, when asked what he would 'undertake' to avenge Hamlet's killing of Polonius: 'To cut his throat i' th' church'. Claudius responds approvingly, 'No place indeed should murder sanctuarize. / Revenge should have no bounds' (4.7.99–101). There is a double villainy in Claudius' denying sanctuary and promoting private revenge, and worse villainy follows (see under **murder/homicide** on this context).

In a mood reminiscent of that in King Lear's speech beginning 'No, no, no, no. Come, let's away to prison' (LRF 5.3.8ff), the holiness of sanctuary is imaged in a paradoxical and extreme figure used by Arcite in TNK 2.2.71–95:

> Let's think this prison holy sanctuary,
> To keep us from corruption of worse men.
> We are young, and yet desire the ways of honour
> That liberty and common conversation,
> The poison of pure spirits, might, like women,
> Woo us to wander from. What worthy blessing
> Can be, but our imaginations
> May make it ours? And here being thus together,

We are an endless mine to one another:
We are one another's wife, ever begetting
New births of love; we are father, friends, acquaintance;
We are in one another, families –
I am your heir, and you are mine; this place
Is our inheritance: no hard oppressor
Dare take this from us. Here, with a little patience,
We shall live long and loving. No surfeits seek us –
The hand of war hurts none here, nor the seas
Swallow their youth. Were we at liberty
A wife might part us lawfully, or business;
Quarrels consume us; envy of ill men
Crave our acquaintance. I might sicken, cousin,
Where you should never know it, and so perish
Without your noble hand to close mine eyes,
Or prayers to the gods. A thousand chances,
Were we from hence, would sever us.

A pseudo-religion of male friendship allied with philosophical asceticism (as in LLL), here makes prison a sanctuary from the world (where sanctuary was usually protection from prison or worse). This paradox evolves into a double irony, when a 'quarrel' over a 'wife' later 'consumes' as well as 'severs' the two friends.

(C) On sanctuary see Bracton, 1968, pp 382–3; "Britton," 1865, vol 1, p 17; Holdsworth, 1903, vol 3, pp 303–7; Plucknett, 1956, p 431; Bellamy, 1973, pp 106–14; Baker, 1978, pp 334–6; Bellamy, 1979, pp 91–3; Baker, 1990b, pp 585–6; Baker, 1990a.

self-slaughter (A) Self-slaughter, or suicide, was a heinous crime, a form of homicide and therefore a **felony** in early modern England (see **murder/homicide**).

A suicide's death resulted in forfeiture of property to the crown, as in all convictions for felony, so a case of possible suicide was brought before the Coroner's Court for an inquest to be held. The Coroner, a royal official, and a petty **jury** heard the circumstances surrounding the death. If the jury decided that the deceased had killed himself, then a verdict of *felo de se* was returned, which resulted in severe penalties. In

339

addition to forfeiture of property, the church refused suicides a Christian burial. Instead the suicide was buried at night, often at a public road side or a cross road, and with a stake driven through the body, a terrible fate to contemplate. The only defence allowed to the crime of *felo de se* was that the suicide had been mentally deranged, *non compass mentis*, at the time of death, in which case the property penalties did not apply and the deceased was given Christian burial.

It was formerly thought that sympathetic early modern juries were quick to find suicides had been mentally ill at the time of their death (Holdsworth, 1903, vol 3, pp 315–16). But MacDonald, 1986 holds that juries construed the law very narrowly, indicating, p 310, that less than 2% of suicides were found *non compos mentis*. Sometimes juries even held that the deceased was *non compos mentis* and at the same time had meant to kill himself and was therefore guilty of self-slaughter. Suicides of 'gentle birth' were more likely to be found *non compos mentis* than ordinary people, but the overall proportions among these were still low.

Popular belief in the seriousness of the sin of suicide, and the crown's financial interest in a suicide's property, combined to produce very restrictive decisions. Only really raving lunatics were found insane, and evidence of lesser derangement was instead interpreted as agitation indicating the deceased had indeed contemplated felonious *felo de se*. It was more probable that an accidental death would be found to be a *felo de se* than that a suicide would be found to be accidental.

Even if a jury did return a verdict of insanity, there was no assurance that the deceased would receive a proper Christian burial. The church offered no clear guidelines on what form burial should take, and some priests only allowed the insane to be buried on the north side of the church, with the excommunicated and unbaptised, which caused much unhappiness and complaint.

In general, death by drowning was the second most common way to commit suicide in early modern England, and it was the most usual way for a woman to commit suicide. Drowning was the cause of the 1554 death in the important case of *Hales v Petit*, decided in 1560, which restated authoritatively that self-killing was **murder** (see Holdsworth, 1903, vol 8, p 304). As Shakespeare echoes this important case, its circumstances as reported by Plowden are of particular interest. The suicide, Sir James Hales, was a protestant and a **justice** in the Court of Common Pleas. He had been imprisoned in 1553 for upholding laws against Catholics even after Mary's accession to the throne. After his release he drowned himself in a shallow stream (like Ophelia) while of unsound mind. The question to be decided by the court was not Hales's suicide, which had already been judged a felony by the Coroner's Court, but whether a **lease** held jointly with his wife Margaret had been correctly forfeited to the crown. The crown had granted the lease to a third party, Petit, and in court Margaret Hales claimed against him that her joint interest in the lease had been protected by the right of survivorship which attaches to jointly held property (see **jointure**).

Therefore the issue before the court was whether the property passed to the wife at the moment of Sir James's death, before the forfeiture took place, or whether it was correctly forfeited because Sir James's act of suicide was completed before his death. Which had priority at the moment of death, the wife's interest or the crown's interest? Margaret Hale argued that her interest was first in time. Petit, the lessee, argued through his lawyer that Sir James's act of felony was committed during his lifetime, and that forfeiture related to that act of felony which consisted of three parts: the Imagination; the Resolution; and the Perfection. This latter was itself divided into two parts: the Beginning and the End. The Beginning is undertaking the act which results in the death, which is a sequel to the act itself. This contorted argument, parodied by Shakespeare, sought to place the felony first in time because the intention to commit a felony preceded the act of committing it.

Although *Hales v Petit* was a famous case worthy of Shakespeare's parody, logic chopping over suicide was not unknown elsewhere, for instance in an early sixteenth century discussion at Serjeant's Inn of the question as to whether 'repentance between the deed and the death was a defence' to suicide (noted in Baker, 1986i, p 315).

(B) There are many instances of actual suicide in Shakespeare's plays set both in classical and Christian periods.

Aside from these, Shakespeare reflected popular attitudes toward *felo de se* in some odd places. In his diatribe against female virginity Parolles suggests: 'He that hangs himself is a virgin: virginity murders itself, and should be buried in highways, out of all sanctified limit, as a desperate offendress against nature' (AWW 1.1.137–40).

Even mad people who commit suicide are imagined in hell by the Jailer's daughter in TNK 4.3.28–36:

341

Alas, 'tis a sore life they have i' th' other place – such burning, frying, boiling, hissing, howling, chattering, cursing – O they have shrewd measure – take heed! If one be mad or hang or drown themselves, thither they go, Jupiter bless us, and there shall we be put in a cauldron of lead and usurers' grease, amongst a whole million of cutpurses, and there boil like a gammon of bacon that will never be enough.

Such notions, even in TNK's ancient Greece, accord with the theology which vexes Christian Hamlet: 'Or that the Everlasting had not fixed / His canon 'gainst self-slaughter!' (HAM 1.2.131–2).

In Shakespeare's poems and plays suicide is sometimes a noble act, and sometimes a dreadful sin. It is argued to be cowardly in LUC 1821–7 and in JC 5.1.100–107, despite classical settings. Also, although in (just) pre-Christian times, Imogen begs to be killed because 'Against self-slaughter / There is a prohibition so divine / That cravens my weak hand' (CYM 3.4.76–8). But generally in classical Shakespearian settings suicide may be presented as noble, while in Christian settings it is usually sinful. Yet suicide is arguably ennobling in ROM and in OTH, despite Christian settings.

There are many contrasting attitudes shown to those who opt for death within Shakespeare plays. Because Lady Macbeth's death is suspected to be 'by self and violent hands' (MAC 5.11.36), she is damned further. Yet Macbeth may be partly ennobled by his resolution to fight to death: 'I cannot fly, / But bear-like I must fight the course' (5.7.1–2). Counselling Roderigo to satisfy his lust, Iago says, 'If thou wilt needs damn thyself, do it a more delicate way than drowning' (OTH 1.3.351–3); later Emilia cries 'I'll kill myself for grief' (5.2.199), and Othello does just this. In 'ill thoughts again', the salvaged Gloucester is instructed 'Men must endure / Their going hence even as their coming hither' (LRF 5.2.9–10). Yet the more terrific grief of Lear causes Kent to implore: 'Vex not his ghost. O, let him pass. He hates him / That would upon the rack of this tough world / Stretch him out longer' (5.3.289–91).

The most often noted Shakespearian treatments of suicide are in HAM. Horatio may express a Renaissance reception of classical and stoic ideals of noble suicide (echoed by Montaigne, Donne and Chapman) in his 'I am more an antique Roman than a Dane' (HAM 5.2.292). However Christian and popular abhorrence of self-slaughter feature when the play's topic is the burial of Ophelia. So when Hamlet first notes 'maimed rites', without knowing these are hers, he readily concludes 'This doth betoken / The corpse they follow did with desp'rate hand / Fordo it own life' (5.1.214–16). Grieving Laertes is furious with the priest on that account:

LAERTES   What ceremony else?

PRIEST   Her obsequies have been as far enlarged
As we have warrantise. Her death was doubtful,
And but that great command o'ersways the order
She should in ground unsanctified have lodged
Till the last trumpet. For charitable prayers,
Shards, flints, and pebbles should be thrown on her,
Yet here she is allowed her virgin rites,
Her maiden strewments, and the bringing home
Of bell and burial.

LAERTES   Must there no more be done?

PRIEST   No more be done.
We should profane the service of the dead
To sing sage requiem and such rest to her
As to peace-parted souls.

LAERTES   Lay her i' th' earth,
And from her fair and unpolluted flesh
May violets spring. I tell thee, churlish priest,
A minist'ring angel shall my sister be
When thou liest howling.

                          (5.1.219–37)

But, for the gravediggers Ophelia is allowed more ceremony than she deserves. Discussing how 'The coroner hath sat on her, and finds it Christian burial' they wonder if 'she drowned herself in her own defence?' (5.1.4–7). Their confusion about 'self-defence' (confounded with with *se offendio*, self offence) may parody how juries juggled in some homicide cases (see **murder**). What follows from the first gravedigger (5.1.10–22) very likely parodies the arguments in *Hales v Petit* (but see Rudden, 1984). This contains outrageous elaborations on the original legalisms:

FIRST CLOWN   Give me leave. Here lies the water – good. Here stands the man – good. If the man go to this water

343

and drown himself, it is, will he nill he, he goes. Mark
you that. But if the water come to him and drown
him, he drowns not himself; argal he that is not
guilty of his own death shortens not his own life.

SECOND CLOWN   But is this law?

FIRST CLOWN   Ay, marry, is 't: coroner's quest law.

(HAM 5.1.15–22)

Unconvinced, the second gravedigger attributes Ophelia receiving
Christian, if limited, rites to her privileged rank:

SECOND CLOWN   Will you ha' the truth on 't? If this had not been a
gentlewoman, she should have been buried out o'
Christian burial.

FIRST CLOWN   Why, there thou sayst, and the more pity that great
folk should have count'nance in this world to drown
or hang themselves more than their even Christian.

(5.1.23–9)

This is followed by an 'Adam delved' style egalitarian argument, com-
pleting the parody on several fronts.

(C) See the definition of suicide in Bracton, 1968, p 424; Hanford,
1912 reviews instances of suicide throughout Shakespeare's plays, concluding that Shakespeare evidences 'no moral theories' but follows 'laws
of art'.

On Horatio's attitude to suicide in Ham, see especially MacDonald,
1986, p 315.

In considering Ophelia's suicide, Holleran, 1989 argues that the
scenic pattern of the last portion of HAM resembles funeral rites, and
repeats the older view that coroner's juries usually sought to bring *non
compos mentis* verdicts. On the contrary, MacDonald, 1986 relies on new
surveys of coroners' juries and reveals a *non compos mentis* verdict
unusual. Ibid. argues finally that Shakespeare's treatment of suicide in
HAM demonstrates a 'prismatic imagination' which analyses and
makes visible a wide range of contradictory contemporary attitudes to
suicide, attitudes which are not resolved or fused into a single orthodoxy
by the play. This analysis accords with the notion of a complex treatment of suicide in the play propounded in Wymer, 1986, pp 29–36.

Wymer, 1986 also treats suicide in LUC (pp 96–110), ROM (pp 116–18), JC (pp 150–5), *King Lear* (pp 66–72), OTH (pp 90–5), ANT (pp 127–32), and other renaissance drama. This book finally argues, pp 157–8, that a 'less moralistic' popular view (indicated by sympathetic juries and in theatrical audiences finding sympathy with suicidal despair) confronted differing Christian and classical traditions to produce contemporary contradictory perceptions of suicide.

Rudden, 1984 defends the first gravedigger in HAM against editorial and critical charges of having made legal 'blunders', 'mistakes', or 'muddles'. Rudden replies specifically to the claim in Watkin, 1984, p 283, that the clowns 'make a mess of their legal analysis and woefully mistake their Latin tags', and very interestingly traces links between the language of the clowns' banter, the contemporary logician John Argall, *Hales v Petit*, and jurisprudential questions of causation and liability. Although it takes a rather light-heartedly adversarial stand on behalf of the first gravedigger's cogency, this essay opens a serious possibility that the clowns in HAM allude to issues carrying considerable moral and philosophical importance. (If so, the speech by a clown of HAM 5.1 with serious resonances parallels the well-known case of the clownish Porter in MAC 2.3 who jests about Jesuits' 'equivocation').

Not referencing *Hales v Petit*, Keeton, 1930, pp 54–6, attempts to find the legal ratio of the gravediggers' 'somewhat cryptic' analysis of the coroner's vedict on the death of Ophelia. Also without reference to that famous case, Draper, 1936 considers the operations of coroner's inquests, and concludes that the arrangement of Ophelia's funeral, involving a compromise between royal wishes and 'clerical prestige', in agreement with 'sheer contemporary realism'. Taking careful note of the parody of *Hales v Petit*, Windolph, 1956, pp 44–6, finds the gravedigger's analysis of Ophelia's suicide indicating 'Shakespeare was amusing himself at the expense of what he called "old father antic, the law"'. Jenkins, 1982 finds the Shakespearian clown's embellishments to *Hales v Petit* 'brilliant'. In an elaborate discussion Wilson, L., 1993, partly demurs, claiming, p 38, 'that Shakespeare's wit is anticipated by the law's own institutional wit'.

sergeant/serjeant (A) The title 'sergeant' or 'serjeant' applied to a wide variety of royal, feudal, municipal and legal appointments (on the high ranking serjeants-at-law see under **lawyers** and **justices**).

Shakespeare's uses are mainly limited to references to a minor official carrying a rod or mace and employed in arresting accused offenders, usually defaulting debtors, to bring them before a court.

(B) In addition to arresting officers, Shakespeare also does present military 'sergeants', who appear briefly in 1H6 2.1 and MAC 1.2. These are 'sergeants of a band', formerly a high military rank (OED 9). In the first instance the character is identified in the folio stage direction as a 'Sergeant of a band' (1H6 tln 675), and in the second as a 'bleeding Captaine' (MAC tln 16).

A metaphor of arrest by a sergeant has a grim aspect in Hamlet's 'this fell sergeant Death / Is strict in his arrest' (5.2.287–8). Often in Shakespeare, oblique references to arrest approached gallows humour; in his time arrest especially for **debt** was widely known and feared (see under **on the case**).

Accordingly, in a scene of ERR filled with Dromio of Syracuse's legal quibbles, an arresting officer is a subject for inventive euphemism. He is called, for instance, a 'back-friend, a shoulder-clapper' (ERR 4.2.37). Then Dromio proposes that time itself fears arrest:

> Time is a very bankrupt, and owes more than he's worth to season.
> Nay, he's a thief too. Have you not heard men say
> That time comes stealing on by night
> If a be in debt and theft, and a sergeant in the way,
> Hath he not reason to turn back an hour in a day?
>
> (ERR 4.2.57–61)

The next scene of ERR refers obliquely to the mode of **usury** involving the sale of fictional **commodities** (ERR 4.3.6), which leads on to a further string of Dromio's euphemisms for an arresting sergeant (ERR 4.3.13–40). Dromio finally unwraps his circumlocutions in a multiple pun, 'Ay, sir, the sergeant of the band: he that brings any man to answer it that breaks his bond' (ERR 4.3.30–1), entangling references to a military rank, an unpaid **bond**, and a supposedly unpaid-for chain (previously punned on as like a bond in 4.2.50–1).

In a similar facetious vein, an officer is employed by Mistress Quickly to arrest Falstaff for debt, and this action dominates the nearly 200 lines of 2H4 2.1. Quickly's officer Fang in this knockabout scene represents a sergeant, for his strong-armed assistant Snare is called his 'yeoman': as the **sheriff** of London, Sir Thomas More is appreciated for having 'made my brother Arthur Watchins Sergeant Safe's yeoman' (STM Add.2D.50–1).

Fang's attempt at making an arrest is enlivened with farcical brawling, legal charges laden with sexual innuendo, and Mistress Quickly's wild diction including her famous mistake of 'honeysuckle villain' for 'homicidal villain'. At the scene's end the ever resilient Falstaff procures a further loan from Quickly, rather than being arrested. Yet the scene's tone is darkened by the grim names Fang and Snare, and by the disrespect Falstaff shows to the **Chief Justice**.

In a passage appearing in the quarto CYL, and omitted from the Folio, dislike of the activities of arresting sergeants becomes actually deadly during civil disorder:

SERGEANT   Justice, justice, I pray you, sir, let me have justice of this fellow here.

CADE   Why, what has he done?

SERGEANT   Alas, sir, he has ravished my wife.

BUTCHER   Why, my lord, he would have 'rested me and I went and entered my action in his wife's proper house.

CADE   Dick, follow thy suit in her common place. You whoreson villain, you are a sergeant – you'll take any man by the throat for twelve pence, and 'rest a man when he's at dinner, and have him to prison ere the meat be out of his mouth. Go, Dick, take him hence: cut out his tongue for cogging, hough him for running, and, to conclude, brain him with his own mace.

CYL 4.7.126–40

In this instance sexual–legal innuendo is not at all funny, nor is the barbaric physical abuse described farcical.

Shakespeare may have often spoofed the unpopular roles of **lawyers**, petty **constables** and arresting **sergeants**, but the anarchy of Cade's rebellion also reflects their bothersome functions as necessary to social order.

(C) On arrest see under **debt**, **sheriff**, and especially **on the case**. For commentary on Dick the Butcher's hostile suggestion 'Let's kill all the lawyers' see Boyarsky, 1991.

sheriff (A) The sheriff, or 'shire reeve', already had an ancient ancestry by Shakespeare's time. Anglo Saxon England had divided the country into administrative and judicial areas called hundreds (see **leets**)
and shires, within which were the hundred and county courts. The
sheriff was the king's local official and chief representative in these
country areas.

After the Norman Conquest the sheriff's importance grew until he
had responsibility for revenue collection, gaols and courts. He was the
keeper of the King's peace and so had powers of arrest and committal.
Twice a year he visited each hundred in a sheriff's 'tourn' (Anglo French
'tour', meaning 'turn') to administer justice and review administration.
By the thirteenth century 'viscontiel writs' issued by the King's courts
(the Norman French term 'vice-comes' was used for 'sheriff') were
addressed to the sheriff for execution in the localities. The sheriff was
responsible for the appointment of the bailiffs of the hundreds, the
constables and other officials. He was personally accountable for
their actions, and so was required to be a landowner in order to have
sufficient means.

The judicial authority of the sheriff declined in the thirteenth century at the same time that the general Eyre was replaced by commissions given to **justices** of assize. The sheriff's decline has been seen as
the result of royal fears of the presence of mighty magnates in the
provinces. So later Kings, anxious to limit the power of the sheriffs,
demanded that they attend Exchequer Chamber in person to **account**
for revenue collected, and by 1340 reduced their tenure to one year.
The power to try 'pleas of the crown' (criminal cases) was removed
from the sheriff by 1215, in Magna Carta. The power of the sheriffs
was further curtailed by a **statute** of 1315 which prevented the sheriff's
office becoming hereditary, and made the office an unpaid judicial
appointment. But Bellamy, 1973, p 93, points out that the sheriff was
not a magnate but a local knight in temporary office; if his powers had
been increased he might have been able to counterbalance the power of
country magnates to the benefit of the royal justice (Elton, G. R., 1974,
pp 58–60, thinks otherwise). What is clear is that the sheriff's court
declined in popularity as royal justice introduced newer methods of
trial (the petty **jury**), and as a result the sheriff lost local standing and
prestige.

By the sixteenth century the sheriff's power had waned. He no longer
had control of the local military force (this had passed to the lord

lieutenants), and new forms of revenue raising meant the sheriff's tax collecting function was greatly diminished. The sheriff's judicial and administrative role declined as that of the **Justice of the Peace** became more important. When the right to hear pleas of the crown was taken from the sheriff it was given to the Justice. By Shakespeare's time the eclipse of many of the sheriff's functions by the Justice was well established and it had become the task of the Justice to enquire into and determine crimes at quarter sessions.

Nevertheless sheriffs did retain miscellaneous judicial and administrative functions, including the duty to receive and execute writs issued from the royal courts, enforce coinage and commercial regulations, keep the local gaol, and supervise executions of convicted **felons**. According to Baker, 1990b, p 76, the apprehension of prisoners was a duty that some sheriffs shirked, as they were not allowed expenses and were liable to pay damages for mistakes.

(B) Most of Shakespeare's sheriffs are seen as arresting officers acting faithfully, evidencing none of the reluctance to act that was a possible problem of the age.

Shakespeare's sheriffs are most often met in history plays arresting the King's adversaries and bringing (often nobly born) **traitors** to punishment. One exception appears in 2H4 4.3.97–9, where the sheriff of Yorkshire is said to wield military force: 'The Earl Northumberland and the Lord Bardolph / With a great power of English and of Scots, / Are by the sheriff of Yorkshire overthrown'. Also, Sir Thomas More features as one of the London sheriffs suppressing a riot in the fragment STM.

In CYL 2.4.17ff., following her exile for the crime of conjuration (see **witchcraft** and **outlawry/banishment**), the Duchess of Gloucester is accompanied through London by the sheriff or sheriffs of London (in fact two were annually elected). Her husband expresses to the Sheriff concern lest 'her penance exceed the King's commission', and receives the reply: 'An 't please your grace, here my commission stays' (CYL 2.4.75–7). The same Sheriff replies to the Duchess's own complaints with: 'It is my office, and, madam, pardon me' (2.4.103). Here, and generally, the sheriff in Shakespeare is polite, even humane, in fulfilling a grim duty, and there is no hint of any abuse of office.

The textual differences between folio and first quarto alter the figure who brings the defeated kingmaker Buckingham to execution in R3. The quarto makes him Sir Richard Ratcliffe, Richard of Gloucester's most constant ally, and this parallels Ratcliffe's role in bringing Rivers, Grey and Vaughan to their executions in 3.2. But in the folio an unnamed sheriff conducts Buckingham to death, perhaps because the lower rank and neutral office of a sheriff makes more acceptable the penitent Buckingham addressing him as 'fellow' (R3 5.1.10).

The two most typical topics of raillery heard on the stage of Shakespeare's age are cuckoldry and hanging. Accordingly, the sheriff's grim task of conducting the condemned to prison or execution is probably why their offices were attached to darkly humorous popular tags such as: 'Dancing on nothing at the Sheriff's ball' for hanging; 'Sheriff's Hotel' for prison; 'Sheriff's Picture Frame' for gallows (these phrases were recorded long after, but similar banter is heard on the stage of Shakespeare's era).

An inversion of gallows humour informs the scene in which insouciant Falstaff is so little concerned at being arrested for a capital crime that he hides from 'the sheriff with a most monstrous watch' (1H4 2.5.487–8), but is next discovered in his hiding place drunk and asleep. In this scene Prince Hal manages to shield his blasé friend because the sheriff shows great respect for royal rank.

When cowardly Parolles in a sense socially 'hangs himself' by calumniating unawares his disguised betters, he mentions a sheriff in his belittling testimony. Perhaps this naming carries a whiff of prison or gallows into his false claim that Lord Dumaine has gotten 'the sheriff's fool with child – a dumb innocent that could not say him nay' (AWW 4.3.191–3). This 'fool' would be a girl or woman of defective or weak intellect placed in a sheriff's care.

In TN 1.5.143, Viola/Cesareo obstinately waiting at Olivia's door likens herself to a 'sheriff's post', one of a pair of posts set up for displaying proclamations. Several jocular Elizabethan contexts cited in the OED for both 'sheriff' and 'post' indicate that Viola's image would probably have raised a smile, especially as it is repeated by the lugubrious Malvolio.

(C) See Holdsworth, 1903, vol 1, pp 65–82, vol 4, p 112; Plucknett, 1956, pp 92–3, 100–2, 169; Bellamy, 1973, pp 89–93; Harding, A., 1973, pp 13–31, 72–4, 115–16; Elton, G. R., 1974, pp 6, 58–60 (on reasons for the decline of sheriffs); Neale, 1976, p 73 (on sheriffs and parliamentary elections); Baker, 1990b, pp 16–19, 26–31; Hudson, 1996, pp 34–40.

slander See under **libel/slander**.

slave (A) On the status of slaves, see under **villein**.

Hunt, 1997, p 39, thinks it relevant that under English **vagrancy** acts enslavement was briefly possible as a punishment for sturdy beggary between 1547 and 1549, and again after 1572, but admits that there is virtually no evidence that these punishments were ever used. Slack, 1988, p 122, explains why the 1547 act was a 'spectacular failure' ('volunteer slaveowners did not materialize'). The reason for this 'failure' is further discussed in MacCulloch, 1988, pp 98–9.

According to Baker, 1990b, p 541, 'in England in 1700 there was no extensive use of slave labour, as in the colonies'. By then in England black liveried servants were status symbols, but they were not treated comparably with plantation slaves. Although some such servants may have been present in his time, Shakespeare takes no note of them. In Shakespeare's time the English New World **plantations** had not yet begun to use slaves, although they did soon after.

(B) Aside from in the treatment of witty twin slaves in the classically inspired ERR, and a few places indicating the lover's Petrarchan service to the mistress, the vast majority of Shakespeare's many uses of the term 'slave' appear in contexts of disparagement or verbal abuse.

An exception occurs in an account the warrior Othello gives to Desdemona of his wild adventures, including 'Of hair-breadth scapes i' th' imminent deadly breach, / Of being taken by the insolent foe / And sold to slavery, of my redemption thence' (OTH 1.3.135–7). Here, as Slights, 1997, p 383, points out, Othello's slavery is not seen as any disgrace to him. Yet later in the play the epithet 'slave' is repeatedly hurled with deadly hatred. This is no great paradox: that warrior Othello was captured and temporarily enslaved in foreign parts is seen as just exotic (yet Cheadle, 1994 thinks the questioning of Othello's marvellous adventures indicates a prejudice against him). The heroics of enslavement and escape are separate matters from the deployment of the word 'slave' as a rank and bitter epithet (in OTH 3.3.447, 4.2.136, 5.1.63, 5.2.250, 5.2.283, 5.2.298, 5.2.341).

Yet hypocritical Iago twice uses 'slave' differently. In OTH 3.3.160–6 Iago says he does not care for his money, but only his 'good name'; his 'purse', by which he means the actual coins in it, he disparages as having 'been slave to thousands' (OTH 3.3.163), by which he means in common use through circulation. In the context leading to this, Iago instances slaves in order to express that there is a baseline or minimum for human autonomy. He does not allege that slaves have any claims at all in a material sense (unlike Lear's 'basest beggars' in LRF 2.2.438). But Iago holds that they are still entitled to the privacy of their thoughts:

> Good my lord, pardon me.
> Though I am bound to every act of duty,
> I am not bound to that all slaves are free to.
> Utter my thoughts?
>
> (OTH 3.3.138–41)

Cummings, 1997 discusses the conception that 'thoughts are free' in the context of early modern English **heresy** and **treason** trials, as well as trials for adultery, noting that the much hated ex-officio oaths of the age would bind unwilling suspects to reveal their inner thoughts (despite Iago's claims for 'slaves').

Actual slavery was a foreign phenomenon for Shakespeare. He probably knew of the condemnation of the Spanish in a 1610 pamphlet often cited as a background source for TMP:

> to preach the Gospell to a nation conquered, and to set their soules at liberty, when we have brought their bodies to slavery; It may be a matter sacred in the Preachers, but I know not how justifiable in the rulers. Who for their meere ambition, doe set upon it, the glosse of religion. Let the divines of *Salamanca*, discusse that question, how the possessor of the west Indies, first destroied, and then instructed. ('True Declaration' 1844, p 6)

There is no indication that Shakespeare knew of English trade in slaves, which had its first beginnings in his time.

The morality of slave-owning is alluded to sarcastically when Shylock says he intends to use Antonio in no other way than the Venetians use:

> . . .   many a purchas'd slave,
> Which, like your asses, and your dogs and mules,

> You use in abject and in slavish parts,
> Because you bought them
>
> (MV 4.1.89–92).

Here Shylock reviles the Christians, by claiming to imitate their low moral stature. The bitterness in the passage may also reflect the legal status of Jews as the king's property in England between the Conquest and their expulsion in 1290 (see Holdsworth, 1903, vol 1, pp 45–6, and Pollock and Maitland, 1898, vol 1, pp 468–75). But such ownership was much more limited than that implied in Shylock's 'asses/slaves' equation; Pollock and Maitland, 1898, vol 1, p 471, explains: 'the Jew, though he is the king's serf, is a freeman in relation to all other persons' (also see Routledge, 1982). Shylock's remark on slavery raises questions perhaps central to the play over distinctions of human life, animal life, and material goods (see Sokol, 1998).

In the light of Shakespeare's repeated uses of 'slave' as a term of vilification, how can we understand the presentation of Caliban, identified in the First Folio's 'Names of the Actors' as a 'salvage and deformed slave'? He is seven times called Prospero's 'slave' in the text. Both Prospero's and Miranda's emphatic attitude toward their 'poisonous slave' Caliban, whose material services they 'cannot miss' (TMP 1.2.312–15), is abhorrence. Prospero hurls nauseous epithets at Caliban: 'A freckled whelp, hag-born'; 'Dull thing'; 'Thou earth'; 'Thou poisonous slave, got by the devil himself'; 'Thou most lying slave'; 'Filth as thou art'; 'Hag-seed'; 'malice'; and so forth until finally 'this thing of darkness I / Acknowledge mine.' (1.2.284; 1.2.286; 1.2.316; 1.2.321; 1.2.346; 1.2.348; 1.2.367; 1.2.369; 5.1.278–9).

Brown, 1985, p 68, finds 'mine' in the last remark to be Prospero's assertion of a property relation 'when apportioning the plebeians to the masters'. This does not accord with any of Shakespeare's other uses of 'acknowledge', which involve accepting a kinship, responsibility or guilt; what is acknowledged by Prospero may be the meaning of Caliban as a psychological projection, rather than proprietorial embarrassment (see Sokol, 1993).

Indeed Prospero becomes particularly testy when recalling that Ariel (apparently in pique) had called himself 'my slave / As thou report'st thyself', contrasting this ironically with how he had been Sycorax's mere 'servant' (1.2.271–2). When at last Prospero has 'bated' Ariel one full

353

year of his **indentures** (see under **prentice**), he expresses personal sorrow at their parting, but no proprietorial regret.

(C) On paradoxes of *habeus corpus* and imprisonment or slavery in Shakespeare's time see Baker, 1990b, pp 168–9, 537–44, which has a useful bibliography.

In discussions of the bearing of slavery on ERR and OTH, Hunt, 1997, and Slights, 1997 respectively find 'virtual de facto enslavement' (p 40) and 'commidification of people as property' (p 383) to be characteristic of oppressive early modern society.

On Ariel's servant status see Sokol, 1994b.

spousal/espousal Spousal was a term with several significances. It is a key part of the title of Henry Swinburne's important *Treatise of Spousals or Matrimonial Contracts* (Swinburne, 1686, written c. 1600). This, p 1, explains that the term spousal could be used to mean either a 'promise of future marriage', or 'Love gifts, and Tokens of the Parties betroathed', or the wedding ring itself as an 'assured Pledge of a perfect Promise'. Sometimes 'spousal' also indicated the feast or banquet celebrating a marriage, sometimes the '**portion**' or goods given in consideration of marriage. Swinburne claims, p 2, the distinction that common lawyers used the terms 'spousal' and 'matrimony' interchangeably, but until the actual celebration of marriage did not consider the couple one person (see **marriage**), but civilian lawyers and canonists considered spousals to be 'pure and perfect Matrimony'. This was because a spousal by words of consent in the present tense in canon law created a legally binding marriage (see **pre-contract**).

Shakespeare himself used the term 'spousal' as a synonym for a marriage or marriage ceremony only in contexts involving great dynastic significance. It seems to have been, for him, an exalted term bearing political import.

Thus the Roman Emperor Saturninus, in a stunning show of ingratitude to Titus Andronicus who had given him the throne, reneges on his promise to marry with Titus' daughter and chooses instead Tamora the captive Queen of the enemy Goths. He exits to the Pantheon saying: 'There shall we consummate our spousal rites' (TIT 1.1.334).

Less dishonourably, Henry V cements imperial gains in his political marriage with Katherine of France. Katherine's mother Queen Isabel comments:

> God, the best maker of all marriages,
> Combine your hearts in one, your realms in one.
> As man and wife, being two, are one in love,
> So be there 'twixt your kingdoms such a spousal
> That never may ill office or fell jealousy,
> Which troubles oft the bed of blessed marriage,
> Thrust in between the paction of these kingdoms
> To make divorce of their incorporate league
>
> (H5 5.2.354–61)

Isabel's metaphor of a secure 'spousal' of the kingdoms, with no fear of future **divorce**, conveys a vain hope, as revealed in the play's final chorus a few lines later.

Shakespeare used the term 'espouse' sometimes figuratively (LUC 20; H5 4.6.26), or in ludicrously rhetorical contexts (H5 2.1.75), but, like 'spousal', 'espousal' is generally used by his characters to indicate a politically important marriage.

It is interesting that in CYL 'espouse' is used twice to describe the proxy marriage of King Henry VI and Margaret, once implying an agreement made in the present tense (CYL 1.1.9) and once in the future tense (in the written 'articles of peace', 1.1.44). This difference raises a question of the status of a marriage, as discussed under **pre-contract**. A solution here may lie in Swinburne's rule governing marriage by a proxy or 'Proctor', that: 'A general Mandate to contract Marriage is not sufficient unless his [the actual husband's] Ratification do follow' (Swinburne, 1686, pp 171–2).

A contract for espousal is clearly expressed in the future tense in TIT when Saturninus says that he 'will . . . espouse' Lavinia 'in the sacred Pantheon' (1.1.240–2). The present tense appears implicitly when he subsequently says of Tamora: 'I lead espoused my bride along with me' (1.1.325). The brutality of these proceedings includes rank ingratitude to Timon (noted above), and also that Lavinia's required consent to break a *de futuro* contract with Saturnius (formed 1.1.271–3) is not sought. Nor is Lavinia's implied **pre-contract** with Bassianus (noted 1.1.51–2, 1.1.276) ever taken in account.

Even more brutal than the mythical Romans, Shakespeare's King

Richard III has his wife killed for dynastic reasons, and wooing by **attorney**, obtains Queen Elizabeth's 'consent' that 'He should espouse Elizabeth her daughter' (R3 4.5.18).

Yet 'espouse' does not always appear in Shakespeare's most callous political settings. Pericles at Diana's shrine describes himself as 'the King of Tyre, / Who, frighted from my country, did espouse / The fair Thaisa at Pentapolis' (S.22.22–4), precipitating the play's second recognition scene; 'espoused' is used here in a genuinely sacred context.

On the technicalities of espousal, see under **marriage** and **pre-contract**.

star chamber This court, which grew out of the King's Council, met from 1366 or earlier in a room at the Palace of Westminster with stars painted on the ceiling. By 1540 it had separated as a court of law from the King's Privy Council, with which it shared most members. The High Court of the Star Chamber, in which also sat the two **Chief Justices** and the Lord Chancellor, became increasingly important in Shakespeare's age and just after.

In Shakespeare's time the main concerns of Star Chamber were criminal rather than property matters. Previously it had dealt mainly with **land** law disputes, often introduced with fictional complaints of riot, unlawful assembly, or oppression (Baker, 1990b, p 136; Barnes, 1977, pp 319–20). After the 1560s Star Chamber ceased to deal with questions of title (ibid., p, 320), but fictional complaints of riot and the like easily could be, and often were, used by Elizabethan landowners to 'annoy one's neighbour' according to Neale, 1976, pp 21–2, or to gain tactical advantages in litigation in other **jurisdictions** (Barnes, 1977, p 320).

From Tudor times cases were increasingly brought to the Star Chamber by 'informations', which is to say charges were brought by private individuals (who might be 'common informers' working for rewards, or law officers). Such a mode of bringing a prosecution (which before 1690 also could be used to bring charges for misdemeanours to King's Bench) did not require the approval of a grand **jury**. Because Star Chamber cases were tried summarily, without indictment or trial jury, Star Chamber could not try **felonies**; constitutionally, trial for capital offences required a jury of one's peers. (This rule was not circumvented by Star Chamber, although the rule that **land** law is in the sole province of the common law was – see Guy, 1975, pp 123–4.)

Star Chamber procedure allowed the accused to give evidence in his own defence, unlike that of the common law courts. Although it could not condemn to death, the Star Chamber did order unusual corporal punishments (such as removal of ears – such cruel and unusual punishments were prohibited by the Bill of Rights of 1689). It has been long and widely alleged that its independence from the common law system was a license for Star Chamber to use torture in interrogation, but there is no evidence for this (Elton, G. R., 1974, p 416, claims that the privy council did sometimes authorise use of torture, but not for cases in the Star Chamber Court; see also Langbein, 1974, pp 206–7, and Langbein, 1977, pp 131, 206). Charles I made political use of Star Chamber to try unpopular cases (such as sedition or dissenting religious offences) which led to its abolition in 1641.

The main achievements of the Star Chamber jurisdiction were in the development of the law of serious misdemeanours, and of the law of inchoate offences such as conspiracy and (unsuccessful) criminal attempt. In addition to riot, Star Chamber dealt with cases of **libel**, forgery, fraud, conspiracy, perjury, corrupted jurors, extortion, vexatious litigation, maintenance, and corrupt parliamentary elections (Neale, 1976, p 73). Either before or after its 1641 abolition, most of Star Chamber's useful developments were taken over by King's Bench (under the Commonwealth called the Higher Bench).

(B) The country landowner Justice Shallow calls for a Star Chamber action against Falstaff and his cronies at the very start of WIV, claiming they have committed a 'riot' (WIV 1.1.1–31). Shallow, in reply to Falstaff's question 'Now, Master Shallow, you'll complain of me to the King?', answered 'Knight, you have beaten my men, killed my deer, and broke open my lodge' (1.1.102–5), which indicates Falstaff had committed a real offence, although it may draw some humour from an adumbration of common legal fictions used 'to annoy' country neighbours. The riot Shallow alleges in Falstaff's lawless intrusion onto his land reflects rather the violent park-breaking and deer-stealing attacks common at that time, some committed by gangs led by gentry (which were indeed treated as riot by Star Chamber, see Manning, 1993, pp 35–6, 38, 54–5, 59).

(C) On the High Court of Star Chamber generally see Plucknett, 1956, pp 195–7; Elton, G. R., 1974, pp 64–5, 82–3, 414–17, Barnes,

1977; Baker, 1990b, pp 137, 396; 156. On its development under Henry VIII see Guy, 1975. On its reflection in Shakespeare see Keeton, 1930, pp 24–6, 29–33. On Star Chamber's interest in certain fraudulent financial practices see under **commodities**. On Star Chamber and the law of maintenance as used against solicitors, see Baker, 1986j. On Star Chamber cases of poaching and 'tumultous' hunting heard as riot see Manning, 1993, pp 59–60.

statute (A) The term 'statute' had two main applications in Shakespeare's time. Most commonly it referred to a law, made either by an early King and his council, or by parliament, or by a municipality or other body.

The second use of 'statute' was as a short form of 'statute staple' or 'statute merchant'. These names for commercial instruments eliptically referred to the statutes that created them. The statute merchant, created by 13 Edw. I, 3, was a form of indebtedness acknowledged before special registries set up in a number of towns which conferred strong assurances to protect the creditor. The statute staple, set up by 27 Edw. I, ii, c.9 and 23 Hen. VIII, c.6, was a similar 'obligation of record entered into before mayors and **constables** of the towns of the Staple' (Jones, W. J., 1967, p 503). Land or goods could be the security for the **debt**. Where **land** was the security 'the lender became a tenant of the land until satisfied' and so he had great security (Baker, 1990b, p 354). Such 'statutes' were popular English forms for arranging a loan in the sixteenth century, and when disputed often resulted in Chancery actions (see **equity**). They were in declining use in the seventeenth century (Jones, W. J., 1967, p 5), due to increasing use of **bonds**.

(B) Parliamentary Acts or statutes were brought in from Tudor times onwards by the **bill** procedure, and earlier a 'bill' could be a petition to the king to pass a statute. So probably there is no anachronism in the language used in H5 in a discussion of the 1414 renewal of a 1404 proposal to bring in an Act to confiscate Church lands. This 'bill' or proposed statute is discussed with alarm by clerics:

CANTERBURY My lord, I'll tell you. That self bill is urged
Which in th' eleventh year of the last king's reign
Was like, and had indeed against us passed,

> But that the scrambling and unquiet time
> Did push it out of farther question.

ELY But how, my lord, shall we resist it now?

CANTERBURY It must be thought on. If it pass against us,
> We lose the better half of our possession,
> For all the temporal lands which men devout
> By testament have given to the Church
> Would they strip from us – being valued thus:
> As much as would maintain, to the King's honour,
> Full fifteen earls and fifteen hundred knights,
> Six thousand and two hundred good esquires;
> And, to relief of lazars and weak age,
> Of indigent faint souls past corporal toil,
> A hundred almshouses right well supplied;
> And to the coffers of the King beside
> A thousand pounds by th' year. Thus runs the bill.

ELY This would drink deep.

CANTERBURY 'Twould drink the cup and all.

(H5 1.1.1–21)

Such a statute, in line with the earlier Mortmain statutes (see under **will** and **perpetuity**), would shift wealth from the Church to the Crown; it seems that to prevent it the Church found reasons to support materially and ethically Henry V's claims to France (H5 1.1.80–2, 1.2.33–114, 1.2.130–5).

The 'statutes' or laws referred to by Shakespeare were often harsh. They are 'rigorous' against Syracusans in ERR 1.1.9, are said likely to prove 'biting' in CYL 4.7.15, are said to be 'strict' and have 'rigour' in MM 1.3.19 and 1.4.66 (but see below), are called 'piercing' in COR 1.1.81.

A bitter jest on Jack Cade's 'biting statutes' arises because he intends fearful tyranny: 'Away! Burn all the records of the realm. My mouth shall be the Parliament of England' (CYL 4.7.12–14). Yet even Shakespeare's tyrant Macbeth realizes that laws may prove civilizing: 'Blood hath been shed ere now, i' th' olden time, / Ere human statute purged the gentle weal' (MAC 3.4.74–5).

Dogberry thinks, or half-thinks, that 'the statutes' which make the watch representative of the 'Prince's own person' may allow the watch to arrest the Prince himself (ADO 3.3.71–9). Constitutional issues of a similar sort are expounded at length in 2H4 5.2.72–100. But the power of law may be overcome by force of arms. So Queen Margaret says of Henry VI that he 'Is prisoner to the foe, his state usurped, / His realm a slaughter-house, his subjects slain, / His statutes cancelled, and his treasure spent' (RDY 5.4.77–9). Likewise at his forced abdication Richard II lists his losses: 'My manors, rents, revenues I forgo. / My acts, decrees, and statutes I deny' (R2 4.1.202–3). Although records may preserve their memory, statutes are no stronger than the human will to maintain or enforce them.

The written 'statutes' sworn to by the court of Navarre in LLL 1.1.17 are specifically misogynistic and anti-erotic. Such anti-sexual provisions were not matched by statutes of Shakespeare's England, but there was considerable contemporary agitation in favour of passing new 'morality' controlling laws. This matter is most fully reflected in MM, in which the Duke of Vienna at first seems to applaud the city's existing 'strict statutes and most biting laws' controlling sexual conduct (MM 1.3.19). Actually in 1604, and often before, there had been been calls in parliament for strict laws regulating personal misconduct, intended to supplant **jurisdiction** over matters such as fornication, adultery or incest of the Church or 'bawdy' courts. But objections were made to intentions to extend such regulation, and several proposed bills were defeated (see especially Kent, 1973). It is claimed that community surveillance of sexual matters was extensive and deeply intrusive in Shakespeare's England (Quaife, 1979, especially pp 50–2, Laslett, 1983, p 180, but Ingram, 1987, pp 238–81 presents an image of greater tolerance). Yet laws punishing fornication were not passed until decades after Shakespeare's death.

Thus in MM Shakespeare managed to present some of the issues of a heated topical debate over the proposed statutes, but by using the tactics of drama did not take an easily discernible stance. Here, as frequently, he treads near-enough to partisan concerns to elicit sharp interest, yet kept far-enough from taking sides to avoid danger to himself or his theatre company.

Similarly, the Venetian statute discriminating against aliens expounded by Portia in MV 4.1.345–53 was posited by Shakespeare for a fictional locale, while in actuality calls for anti-alien laws were clamorous in his own time and place. The Venetian law is deplored in Kornstein, 1994, p 79–81 as a 'vile Alien Statute', because it gives *un*equal protection in law; but aliens had no guarantees of equal legal treatment in Shakespeare's age (see the discussion of alien status and *Calvin's Case* in the entry on **plantation**). In 1601 Elizabeth arranged to expel from England all 'Negars and blackamoors' (see Jones, E., 1965, pp 12–13). Yet in 1594 she seemed hesitant to punish the unfortunate Doctor Lopez (see Katz, 1994, pp 49–101. Indeed Jews were so *un*equally protected in her England as to have been officially outlawed since 1290. Although they were not enacted, other Elizabethan anti-Alien laws were repeatedly proposed, and economic surveys were undertaken to investigate their applicability.

Behind this agitation lay the presence of economically important alien sub-communities in England, especially in London. Although these were generally tolerated, their rights, for instance to trade and to employ English men and women, suffered periodic verbal attacks and occasional outbursts of unofficial anti-foreigner rioting. In STM London **apprentices** are seen rioting in just this way, and reflections of social questions concerning aliens arise in Launcelot Gobbo's ruminations on employment by Shylock (MV 2.2.1–29). Shakespeare explored live issues in MV in this way, and by inventing a fictional anti-alien statute along lines that were argued for in his time.

Less serious contemporary matters are reflected in the mention of 'statute caps' in LLL 5.2.281. These were woollen caps worn by the citizens on holidays in obedience with the statute 13 Eliz., 19 favouring the cappers' industry. Plebeian caps are several times alluded to by Shakespeare, mainly to indicate the sentiments of the populace, as in H5 4.7.98, and even in the imperial Rome of JC 1.2.245–6 and the republican Rome of COR 1.1.210–11.

Statutes staple or merchant are alluded to in SON 134, amid metaphors of debt, and in HAM 5.1.101–3 where Hamlet speaks of a supposed dead lawyer's 'statutes, his recognizances, his fines, his double vouchers, his recoveries' (on this context see under **fine and recovery**).

(C) On the transformation during Shakespeare's period of a former concept whereby 'in England, prior to the sixteenth century . . . all statutes did not bind all persons within its borders' see Thorne, 1985h, pp 172–5. This deals also with the so-called 'equity of statute', discussed below.

On the rise of the volume of parliamentary legislation in Shakespeare's era and concomitant improvements in the precision and recording of the wording of statutes see Baker, 1990b, pp 234–7. On the operation of statutes in relation to courts see ibid., pp 239–43. On the development during Elizabeth's time of much tighter procedures than formerly for the passage of statutes see Neale, 1976, pp 356–63.

On proposals for statutes regulating personal conduct in Shakespeare's time, and objections to these, see especially Kent, 1973, and also: Hammond, 1986, p 517; Williamson, 1986, pp 91–9; Ingram, 1987, pp 31–2; Hayne, 1993, pp 17–18. Widmayer, 1995 maintains that such statutes were in place and were often enforced in ways that were highly repressive, and applies this to MM.

On 'statute caps' see White, E. J., 1987, p 110.

On the alien statute in MV see Schotz, 1991; Kornstein, 1993; Kornstein, 1994, pp 79–81; Sokol, 1998.

On views in Shakespeare's age of judicial latitude in construction of statutes (sometimes called 'equity of statute') see especially the introduction to Hake, 1953, and the introduction in Thorne, 1942, pp 3–4, which notes demands on judges in Elizabeth's age to strike 'a progressively difficult balance between justice in individual cases and the dictates of an authoritative Parliament'. On the intellectual background see Maclean, 1992, and especially in relation to English law, pp 184–6. See also Hake, 1953 part III, Baker, 1990b, pp 239–43, and (on two crucial cases) Thorne, 1985e and Thorne, 1985b. A number of literary critical articles, such as Wilson, L., 1991, attempt to relate such concepts to Shakespearian drama.

An alternative to understanding the laws in MM in terms of man-made statute is offered in Bennett, 1993, which focuses on 'natural law'. Young, 1990 explores a similar theme in relation to *King Lear*; Keeton, 1967, p 67ff, and White, R. S., 1996 explore it more generally.

On statutes merchant and statutes staple see: Plucknett, 1956, pp 392–3; Jones, W. J., 1967, pp 5, 503; Baker, 1990b, p 354. Thorne, 1985i, pp 206–7, considers these instruments of debt in terms of a wider Tudor context.

subcontracted This term appears once, in a peculiar context of *King Lear* where it indicates a bizarre spousal contract (this context is given as a first instance in OED). Its use pertains to the discovery of the sensationally irregular situation in which Edmund had agreed to marry two sisters, both of them already married.

The use of 'contract' in the compound word 'subcontracted' refers, as usual in Shakespeare. to a marriage **contract**. Legally, as explained under **pre-contract**, unless there was an **impediment** such as that of affinity, an agreement to marry by *verba de praesenti* would create a valid marriage. Also, during the *coverture* which resulted from marriage all of a woman's property rights were transferred to her husband (see **marriage**).

In an interchange wildly burlesquing these concepts, the **widowed** Regan (who unknown to herself has already been poisoned out of jealousy by her married sister Goneril) says to Edmund:

> Take thou my soldiers, prisoners, patrimony.
> Dispose of them, of me. The walls is thine.
> Witness the world that I create thee here
> My lord and master.
>
> (LRF 5.3.68–71)

This declaration seems to be one half of a valid **spousal**, although her words in the present tense still need to be matched by Edmund's words or gestures of present consent.

Before this happens, the marriage is objected to by Albany in strange terms. He arrests Edmund 'on capital **treason**', and with him impeaches Regan for treason (the Folio has him join her 'in thy arrest' (tln 3028), but the Oxford LRF 5.3.76 and other editions adopt 'attaint' from 'in thy attaint' in LRQ S.24.81). Albany then proclaims to Regan:

> For your claim, fair sister,
> I bar it in the interest of my wife.
> 'Tis she is subcontracted to this lord,
> And I, her husband, contradict your banns.
> If you will marry, make your loves to me.
> My lady is bespoke.
>
> (LRF 5.3.77–82)

Albany's notion of a 'subcontract', a spousal contract for the betrothal to Edmund of the already married Goneril, is of course a deliberate absurdity. Yet, under that absurd premise, Albany properly contradicts the banns of Goneril's sister with Edmund on grounds of affinity (see **impediments**). To cap his mock-argument, Albany suggests that his

363

sister-in-law Regan approach him for marriage, which of course would be bigamous as well as incestuous (because of affinity). He then sarcastically offers a pseudo-logical justification for this suggestion, 'My lady is bespoke'.

His sarcasm, involving bitter mockery of the legal rules governing marriage formation, indicates that Albany knows of the affair between his wife and Edmund.

Edmund's dying comments on his dual amours use language redolent of sin and passion: 'I was contracted to them both; all three / Now marry in an instant' (LRF 5.3.203–4). He adds 'Yet Edmund was beloved. / The one the other poisoned for my sake, / And after slew herself' (LRF 5.3.215–17). Murder, suicide, bigamy, and incest are the unwanted son's proofs of love (see under **bastard**).

sue his livery (A) In medieval English **land** law, after the death of a tenant ***in capite*** who held land from the King, the infant heir became a **ward** of the King. When the heir reached majority (which was 21 one for males and 16 for females) before he could take up his inheritance he had to offer homage, swear an oath of fealty and make a payment to the King known as a relief.

The formal process by which the heir who would hold as a tenant in chief of the King applied to obtain possession of his lands was known as 'sue his livery'. For an heir who would hold of a lesser lord it was known as '*ouster le main*'.

The heir made payment of the equivalent of half a year's profit from the land. If the heir held some lands of the king as tenant in chief, and lands from other lords too, the king's right of prerogative wardship meant he would have rights over all the land. To avoid potential difficulties in a complicated situation, such heirs negotiated payment of 'special livery'.

There is an anachronism in some annotations to Shakespeare editions, which comment that in R2 and 1H4 suing livery relates to delivery of lands to an heir from the court of wards. Correcting these, Clarkson and Warren, 1942, p 30n, points out that this court only came into being in 1540 (by 32 Hen. VIII, c. 46), while the denial of the right to sue livery in Shakespeare's plays follows immediately the death of John of Gaunt in 1399. Suing livery was practised long before its administration was attached in 1541 (by 33 Hen. VIII, c. 22) to the court of wards.

(B) All three of Shakespeare's uses of 'sue his livery' (R2 2.1.202–11 and 2.3.128–35; 1H4 4.3.63–4) refer to Richard's revocation of the **letters patents** giving Bolingbroke the right to obtain his inheritance. The wording in R2, including mention of his 'attorneys general' (see **attorney**) follows Holinshed. Thus York warns Richard:

> for how art thou a king
> But by fair sequence and succession?
> Now afore God – God forbid I say true! –
> If you do wrongfully seize Hereford's rights,
> Call in the letters patents that he hath
> By his attorneys general to sue
> His livery, and deny his offered homage,
> You pluck a thousand dangers on your head
> (R2 2.1.199–206).

(C) On the Shakespeare passages involving suing livery see: Clarkson and Warren, 1942, pp 28–31; Bean, 1968, p 11; Bolton, 1988, pp 56–62.

Gohn, 1982, pp 947–8n claims that the acts of Richard II's Parliamentary Committee that denied to **exiled** Mowbray and Bolingbroke powers of **attorney** (to sue livery) were actually illegal. Bellamy, 1970, p 115, explains legal peculiarities in Richard II's use of treason laws against Bolingbroke, and in seizing the Lancastrian estates.

Hexter, 1980, pp 7–23, argues that, in order to appeal strongly to the sympathies of Elizabethan audiences, R2 emphasises (by selection from Holinshed) the justice of Bolingbroke's defence against Royal seizure of his property. Hexter claims that such audience interest did not arise because of concern about great estates in land held by a feudal military tenure, but rather that Shakespeare's audiences were composed of many possessed of trades or skills threatened by prerogative monopolies (the 1603 case of *Darcy v Allen* is cited as crucial), or possessed of small copyhold properties (see under **villein** and **copy**).

taken with the manner 'Taken in the mainour' or 'taken in the manner' means to be apprehended in the very act of doing something unlawful (OED mainour 2). It is related to 'taken with the mainour' which relates to **theft** only, mainour meaning the stolen goods found in a thief's possession (OED mainour 1).

The first form, concerning being caught in an illegal act of consorting with a woman in the Navarre of LLL (see under **statute**), although expressed by Costard as 'taken with the manner', is unmercifully punned upon alongside other legal quibbles in LLL 1.1.198–211. The second form is used literally in 1H4 2.5.317–19.

See: Cowell, 1607; Pollock & Maitland, 1898, vol 2, pp 579–80; Keeton, 1967, p 35; **robbery/theft**.

tenures (A) See **land** for discussion of the doctrines of tenures and estates.

(B) There is an indisputable reference to tenures in Hamlet's wondering 'Why might not that be the skull of a lawyer? Where be his quiddits now, his quillets, his cases, his tenures, and his tricks?' (HAM 5.1.95–7). See **fine and recovery** on this context.

Several other Shakespearian instances of 'tenure' in this sense are alleged in a note to Clarkson and Warren, 1942, p 16. (These are in Sonnet 61, H5 5.2.72, LUC 1310, JC 4.2.223.) None of these seem to be in **land** law or legal contexts, and we agree with the Oxford and others editors who read in the ambiguous spelling the non-legal word 'tenor' in all these places.

(C) See **land**.

terms (A) These were the four legal terms of the Westminster courts, during which the courts sat and legal business was transacted: Michaelmass (in October and November), Hilary (in January and February), Easter (in April and May) and Trinity (in May and June). In Elizabeth's time the number of days in these four terms amounted to only 99 in a year. Chancery however sat continuously.

During the law terms London filled with litigants, lawyers and interested parties. Law students from the **Inns of Court** were spectators in Westminster Hall where they acquired legal knowledge amidst the din of the concurrent sittings of King's Bench, Common Pleas and Chancery.

(B) Law terms are referred to humorously or wryly in AYL 3.2.323 and 2H4 5.1.72–3 (on these jokes see under **lawyers**). The familiarity of Shakespearian audiences with law terms, making quips on them amusing, was presumably due to the presence not only of defendants and litigants, but also of **Inns of Court** students and practising lawyers (called 'termers') in the audience (see Cook, 1981).

(C) See Baker, 1990b, pp 77–8 and 119.

testament In correct legal usage a 'testament' is distinguished from a will; a testament is a bequest of **chattels**, or personalty, while a will is a devise of **lands**, or real property. Aside from personal and real property, a third, hybrid, form of property was the **lease**, known as a chattel real. A chattel real was bequeathed by testament.

The legalities of both wills and testaments are discussed under **will**.

'Testament' is used correctly when it describes Bertram's ring: 'Of six preceding ancestors, that gem; / Conferred by testament to th' sequent issue / Hath it been owed and worn' (AWW 5.3.199–201).

Yet in other places lands are said to be left 'By testament', as for

367

instance in H5 1.1.9–10. Sometimes 'testament' is actually used in parallel with or as a synonym for 'will', as in 'The will, the testament!' (JC 3.2.155), and:

> But here's a parchment with the seal of Caesar.
> I found it in his closet. 'Tis his will.
> Let but the commons hear this testament.
> (JC 3.2.129–31)

The two terms are also paralleled in the Painter's cynical 'Performance is a kind of will or testament' (TIM 5.1.27–8), discussed under **will**.

theft/thief See robbery/theft.

thirdborough (A) This was a petty **constable** or his assistant. Citations of statutes in the OED suggests a confused nomenclature of the petty officers of the peace in English townships or manors. The distinctions perhaps implicit among the addressees of the 1512 Act 4 Hen. VIII, c.19 6 'Preceptes to the Constables Hedbouroghes Thirdbouroghes Subconstables Tythingmen Borsalders' are more blurred in the 1536 Act 28 Hen. VIII, c.10 6 addressed to 'Euery . . . Hedborowe, Thredborough, Borsolder, and euery other Lay Officer.' (Yet the Arden Edition editor of LLL indicates that Ben Jonson's *Tale of a Tub* distinguishes 'high constable, headborough, petty constable and thirdborough', the last being the lowest ranking and a tinker.)

(B) Any distinction of the offices of petty officers of the peace becomes farcical when drunken Sly replies to the Hostess's threats of the Headborough with 'Third or fourth or fifth borough, I'll answer him by I'll not budge an inch, boy. Let him come, and kindly' (SHR Ind.1.11–13).

Dogberry, who is repeatedly addressed as 'Master **constable**' (ADO 3.3.16, 4.2.8, 4.2.32, 4.2.61–2), and Verges who is identified in one scene's Folio stage direction and some speech prefixes as the **headborough** (ADO 3.5, tln 1595–1625) are not much distinguished in the Folio stage direction to 3.3, which introduces them as 'Dogberry and his compartner' (tln 1330).

Constable Dull, saying 'I myself reprehend his own person' (LLL

1.1.181), identifies himself as the Duke's (in the Folio spelling, tln 195) 'Tharborough', which OED identifies as a corruption of thirdborough. (See under **statute** on a parallel passage with similar jurisprudential implications in ADO.) The quarto spelling is 'farborough' (1.1.182)

(C) For the history and function of the office see **constable**.

traitor The legal implications of this term of opprobrium are discussed under **treason**, because 'traitors' in Shakespeare are almost always those guilty of treason (in accord with OED traitor 2).

Contexts in which this connection are made explicit abound: 'Condemned to die for treason, but no traitor' (1H6 2.4.97); 'treason's secret knife and traitor's rage' (CYL 3.1.174); 'I arrest thee, York, / Of capital treason 'gainst the King and crown. / Obey, audacious traitor' (CYL 5.1.106–8); 'hear / The traitor speak, and timorously confess / The manner and the purpose of his treason' (R3 3.5.54–6); 'Treason, foul treason! Villain, traitor' (R2 5.2.72); 'I do arrest thee, traitor, of high treason' (2H4 4.1.332); 'guard these traitors to the block of death, / Treason's true bed and yielder up of breath' (2H4 4.1.348–9); 'no instance why thou shouldst do treason, / Unless to dub thee with the name of traitor' (H5 2.2.116–17); 'Merely our own traitors. And as in the common course of all treasons . . . ' (AWW 4.3.22–3).

treason (A) Treason was considered the most serious criminal offence. Consequently, in early modern England the most terrible punishments were reserved for those found guilty as **traitors**.

Once a medieval **felony**, treason was made a statutory offence in 1352 (25 Edw. III, st.5, c.2). This act defined high treason as any of the following: plotting or imagining the death of the king, his wife or eldest son; violating his wife, or his eldest unmarried daughter, or the wife of his eldest son; making war against the king or helping his enemies to do so; forgery of the great seal or coinage of the realm; killing the treasurer, chancellor, or judges in court.

In all these cases a conviction resulted in a terrible death which was usually to be hanged, drawn and quartered. This meant that the convicted prisoner was hanged by the neck and cut down alive, his genitals cut off (to show his issue was **disinherited**), disembowelled, and his

369

heart cut out. These body parts were burnt at the place of execution. Then the head was cut off, and the dismembered corpse was sent to be boiled in a prison. All the traitor's lands and goods were forfeit to the king.

The 1352 Act 25 Ed. III, st.5, c.2 also defined 'petty treason' as the killing of a husband by his wife, a master by his servant, or of his superior by a monk. A conviction of petty treason resulted in escheat of lands and goods to the defendant's lord. A convicted man was punished by drawing on a hurdle and then hanging, while women guilty of petty treason were burnt to death. Although statutory and judicial changes were made in subsequent centuries the basic definition remained as set out in the fourteenth century statute. Petty treason was reduced to ordinary **murder** in 1828 (9 Geo. IV, c.31).

Appeals of treason (private prosecutions) were brought, often by accomplices as **approvers** (see Bellamy, 1970, pp 141–2). If the accusations were based on one man's word against another's with no other evidence, then the appeal could be tried by judicial combat which took place before the king (see **lists**). In the reign of Richard II several appeals of treason were brought in parliament. Such appeals in parliament were prohibited by 1 Hen. IV, c. 19, but appeals remained possible in the common law courts or, for misdeeds committed abroad, in the Court of the **Constable** and Marshal. Trials by battle on appeals of treason were common under Richard II and especially frequent during the realm of Henry VI (see ibid., pp 143–7). The possibility of bringing an appeal of felony for petty treason lasted until abolition in 1819.

Because treason was regarded as so heinous a crime, no accused was allowed to plead 'benefit of clergy' (see **branding**). The accused was not allowed the help of legal counsel until 1696 unless some special point of law applied, but from Tudor times the crown would be represented by prosecution counsel, such as the **attorney** general or solicitor general, a disparity that was criticized by contemporaries (Langbein, 1978, p 307). Defendants and their witnesses were not allowed to give sworn evidence (sworn defence witnesses were first allowed from 1696), although the prosecution could. Two prosecution witnesses were required, although in practice this was not always strictly applied. The judge took an active role, examining witnesses and the defendant, and instructed the **jury**.

The 1352 Act had provided that cases of doubtful treason, where the conduct complained of could be a felony or treason, should be discussed in parliament before the king, to establish the boundaries of the offence. Although a series of further treason statutes were enacted during the middle ages (on which see Bellamy, 1970), the most important legal developments in the definition of treason took place in Tudor England. Between 1485 and 1603, sixty-eight treason statutes were enacted, a remarkably large number (Bellamy, 1979, p 12). These were often a result of concerns about the succession following a royal marriage, remarriage, or **divorce**, or about religious supremacy. For example an Act of 1534 made treasonable any deeds or written or printed words impugning the regularity of Henry VIII's marriage to Anne Boleyn, the first time that words alone were made treasonable by statute. Soon afterwards the definition of treason was extended to words spoken maliciously against King Henry VIII, his Queen or royal heir. It was also treason maliciously to call the King either by written or spoken word, a heretic, a tyrant, a usurper, a schismatic or infidel. Most importantly, the courts extended the category of imagining the death of the king, made treasonous by statute in 1352, to include using words and writings against the king. Even if no direct intent was found in the words, an indirect intent could be implied and used to convict for treason. Examples of words used to form the basis of successful prosecutions include repeating gossip in the street or commenting in public on the king's person (see Bellamy, 1979, p 11). Subsequent acts of Edward, Mary and Elizabeth partly retracted these provisions, but also extended similar ones (see ibid., p 47, and Patterson, 1993).

The definition of treason was wide enough to encompass piracy (2 Hen. V, c.6 (1414)), on the basis that such activities interfered with the king's truce with other monarchs, and this statue was applied to make treasonous riots in London against foreigners in 1517 (Bellamy, 1979, pp 18–19). There is also a possibility that the 'treason of buggery' was punished under Henry VIII and earlier (Bellamy, 1979, pp 42–4), although sodomy became a felony by 25 Hen. VIII, c.6 (see under **felony**).

Parliament could also bring a **Bill** of Attainder to obtain a conviction for treason against those who fled from justice. This had been developed in the fifteenth century to use against rebel uprisings (on the complex history of this development, related to appeals of treason and also the 1352 statute, see Bellamy, 1970, pp 177–205). Attainder resulted in the forfeiture of all lands and goods to the king, and the loss of all civil rights or remedies (in a manner similar to the common law

371

outlawry, which had become diluted by Shakespeare's time). The attainted person's blood was said to be corrupt and therefore his family **disinherited**. In the sixteenth century, attainder was used in 1533, 1539–40, 1542 and 1549, and met with much criticism. When it was used against those who had not fled justice, as it was under Henry VIII and the Stuarts, its purposes were political; Plucknett, 1956, p 205, notes, 'Thomas Cromwell invented this abuse, and very properly was the first to suffer by it'.

The punishment accorded to those convicted of treason varied and was not always death. Men convicted of using seditious words could be whipped, put in the stocks, or mutilated. This mutilation was frequently cutting off ears or nailing a prisoner to a door in public by an ear, and more rarely loss of limb or other mutilation. Women convicted of using seditious words could suffer the punishment of the cucking stool. **Banishment** for treason was also ordered in 1585 when some Jesuits, seminary priests and a laymen were put on ship for Normandy. But for serious treason the punishment was death, a warrant being signed by the monarch. In London execution took place at Tyburn, although nobles were sometimes executed at the Tower. Some royal or noble traitors were spared the ordeal of being hanged, drawn and quartered, and beheaded instead, as were Mary Queen of Scots, Anne Boleyn and the Dukes of Norfolk and Essex.

For many convicted traitors punishment was made worse by the knowledge that their families would be punished too. The traitor's lands and goods were forfeit to the crown, and 'corruption of the blood' meant the disinheritance of their heirs, and loss of **dower** to their widows. A traitor's wife needed an act of parliament to retain lands which she had held in her own right or jointly with her husband. Sometimes the crown exempted the family from part of this penalty, or made grants or annuities to destitute widows and children; for instance lists of traitors' widows and families were found among Thomas Cromwell's papers, and it appears he personally supervised their relief.

The King redistributed a traitor's forfeited lands to those who petitioned him for it as a reward, or he sold it in return for **purchase** money. Before the 1534 Act a conviction for treason would result in the forfeiture of lands held in **fee-simple**, but (except briefly during the last part of the realm of Richard II, from 1397) it had been necessary to obtain parliamentary acts of attainder to forfeit **entailed** lands, or lands held in use (see **land** and **use**). Henry's Act of 1534 allowed for the forfeiture of all lands, whether entailed or in use or not (Bellamy, 1979, p 34).

Historians have been divided in assessing Tudor treason legislation. Some have considered it ferocious and illogical, making the offence whatever the crown or courts considered a heinous crime, while others held that it protected public order. For instance G. R. Elton considered the Tudor legislation extended treason to cover 'fundamental offences against King and realm' and to protect the Reformation (quoted in Bellamy, 1979, p 13, who disagrees).

(B) The word 'treason' appears one or more times in most of Shakespeare's plays and poems, as does the word 'traitor'. At least one of the two words appears in nearly all of Shakespeare's works. Shakespeare's uses of 'treason' and '**traitor**' are tightly linked, and the two terms will be discussed together here.

The prime biblical model of a traitor as betrayer is Judas Iscariot, who dissembled and hid his treachery. So, amid courtly banter, we hear, 'Judas Maccabeus clipped is plain Judas. . . . A kissing traitor' (LLL 5.2.593–4). In an aside, while giving a kiss to the crown prince, treason-intending Richard of Gloucester calls himself 'Judas' (RDY 5.7.33). Richard II claims that his three chief followers have become 'Three Judases, each one thrice-worse than Judas!', wrongly believing they have joined the treasonous Bolingbroke (R2 3.2.128). Richard later makes a similar accusation against former extollers who have indeed betrayed him (R2 4.1.161).

Traitors in Shakespeare's plays are repeatedly identified as being 'dangerous and unsuspected' (R3 3.5.22), acting in a Judas-like manner. Traitors are assumed to be liars, so Duke Frederick replies to Rosalind's denial of any wrongdoing: 'Thus do all traitors. / If their purgation did consist in words / They are as innocent as grace itself' (AYL 1.3.51–3).

However Frederick, a usurper himself, offers no evidence to justify **banishing** his innocent niece for treason. He offers for reasons only, 'Let it suffice thee that I trust thee not./ . . . . Thou art thy father's daughter. – there's enough.' (AYL 1.3.54 & 57). These proceedings expose two particular aspects of treason. One is that acting on mere suspicion of treason is unjust, and may well derive from jealous or malicious ill intentions. Bellamy, 1970, indicates that some English kings seemingly extended the unstable definition of the crime to whatever or whomever they especially disliked (or possibly because they wished to

373

retain forfeited property beyond the one year allowed them in cases of **felony**). A second contrary aspect, relating to the Judas kiss, is that evidence for establishing treason was often hard to gather because traitors are by nature deceitful as well as disloyal, so even just kings could appear somewhat arbitrary in dealing with traitors.

Underhandedness and dishonour also are inferred in treason accusations: 'he harbours treason. / The fox barks not when he would steal the lamb.' (CYL 3.1.54–5). So, such accusations arouse hot fury in Shakespeare's plays. Although Pericles owes little of a subject's allegiance to King Simonides, and Ferdinand owes none to Prospero, both are outraged at being called 'traitor' (PER S.9.47ff. and TMP 1.2.463ff.). Allegations of treason typically lead to outrageous violence or threats of violence, as in MAC 4.2.82–4, COR 3.1.176–81 and 3.3.71–85, CYM 4.2.121, and TMP 1.2.463–9. Indeed, because of the affront involved, an accusation of treason or the taint of treason often provokes challenges to a trial by battle in Shakespeare, as seen in 1H6 2.4.96–8, CYL 2.3.47–50, throughout R2 1.1 and 1.3, LRF 5.3.91–5, and PER S.9.51–9 (see under **lists**).

The notion that tyranny can label whatever it pleases as treasonous has already been noted in regard to Duke Frederick of AYL, who when asked by Rosalind 'whereon the likelihood [of her alleged treason] depends?' (AYL 1.3.56), blithely dismisses the need to give any plausible reason. Wholly absurd reasons are offered by Jack Cade, who tells his rabble: 'Fellow-kings, I tell you that that Lord Saye hath gelded the commonwealth, and made it an eunuch, and, more than that, he can speak French, and therefore he is a traitor!' (CYL 4.2.162–5). But the malignant nature of a false accusation of treason is best brought out in Richard III's sinister mode of alleging Lord Hastings's purported treason.

Richard acts, as he openly states, for publicity's sake, 'T' avoid the censures of the carping world' (R3 3.5.66), when he blatantly lies to the Lord Mayor of London concerning the just-slaughtered Hastings. He claims:

> So dear I loved the man that I must weep.
> I took him for the plainest harmless creature
> That breathed upon the earth, a Christian,
> Made him my book wherein my soul recorded
> The history of all her secret thoughts.

> So smooth he daubed his vice with show of virtue
> That, his apparent open guilt omitted –
> I mean, his conversation with Shore's wife –
> He lived from all attainture of suspect.
>
> (R3 3.5.23–31)

Buckingham then asserts without proof that Hastings had been the 'covert'st sheltered traitor that ever lived', plotting murder. The cowed Lord Mayor is then forced to proclaim Hastings's summary 'execution' just, despite absolutely no evidence offered against him, nor judicial proceedings used.

According to Bellamy, 1970, p 215, although the limits of treason were sometimes stretched by historical English kings or courts, this killing of Hastings corresponds with an audacious sort of proceeding which was actually practiced, although uniquely, by Richard III. This act, which Shakespeare's Richard mildly admits is 'against the form of law' (3.5.40), far surpasses in its viciousness the already unfair advantages of prosecutors over defendants in actual treason trials described above. In these, at least in theory, two prosecution witnesses were required to try treason (although not against Seminarians following 27 Eliz., c.2).

Henry VIII, who in reality destroyed many for alleged treason, is represented by Shakespeare as calling for a proper trial of Buckingham:

> He is attached.
> Call him to present trial. If he may
> Find mercy in the law, 'tis his; if none,
> Let him not seek 't of us. By day and night,
> He's traitor to th' height.
>
> (AIT 1.2.211–15)

Buckinham is betrayed by a servant, as was his own father (1.2.133–210; 2.1.122–4). His 'noble' trial before his peers is further discussed under **bar**.

Many treason trials in Shakespeare's plays are in a degree suspect, as in the trial of Hermione (conducted with a valid indictment (WT 3.2.12–20), but an unjust judge). In another instance, his long established honour had been stolen from Guiderius when 'in one night/ A storm or robbery, call it what you will' (CYM 3.3.61–2) result in his banishment. This happened after 'two villains . . . swore to Cymbeline / I was confederate with the Romans' (66–8 – on this context see under **robbery**); adherence to the two-witness rule did not prevent injustice.

Because treason accusations often led to highly publicised political trials, it was not uncommon for the king's prosecutors verbally to assault defendants (as in the notorious 1603 trial of Sir Walter Raleigh). We may note that Jack Cade's insulting repeated use of 'thou' in his parodic indictment of Lord Say for having 'most traitorously corrupted the youth' (CYL 4.7.22–44 – discussed under **jurisdiction**) predates a similar insulting use against Raleigh by Coke in the 1603 trial. Coke's 1603 use, however, is alleged in Keeton, 1967, pp 53–4 to have inspired Sir Toby Belch's advice on how to instigate a quarrel in TN 3.2.42–3.

Once treason by words alone had become a possibility, the accusations of informers in the household, or at the convivial table, with perhaps malicious motives, was an abhorred and feared danger (as seen in Ben Jonson's poem 'Inviting a Friend to Supper'). Just such a situation arises, with attendant complexities, when a master accused of having committed verbal treason pleads:

> My accuser is my prentice, and when I did correct him for his fault the other day, he did vow upon his knees he would be even with me. I have good witness of this, therefore, I beseech your majesty, do not cast away an honest man for a villain's accusation.
>
> (CYL 1.3.201–5)

This rather simple apprentice, Peter Thumpe violates an important rule of family discretion, even while he obeys the law meant for the king's protection that treason must be revealed. Bernthal, 1991 holds that Thumpe's act of betraying his master is excused, because it prevents him shielding a traitor to the king, but also argues convincingly that CYL presents political intrigues behind the publicity given Thumpe's accusation. These intrigues are not at all focused on royal or national safety.

The notion that treason infects the blood of descendants of traitors is presented by Shakespeare with some ambivalence. It is first denied in Rosalind's 'Treason is not inherited, my lord' (AYL 1.3.60), but she backs down from this in the following lines, 'Or if we did derive it from our friends, / What's that to me? My father was no traitor' (1.3.61–2). The idea of a bloodline tainted by treason losing its nobility is clear in a challenge to the ancestry of Richard Plantagenet:

SOMERSET	By him that made me, I'll maintain my words
	On any plot of ground in Christendom.
	Was not thy father, Richard Earl of Cambridge,
	For treason executed in our late king's days?
	And by his treason stand'st not thou attainted,
	Corrupted, and exempt from ancient gentry?
	His trespass yet lives guilty in thy blood,
	And till thou be restored thou art a yeoman.
RICHARD PLANTAGENET	My father was attached, not attainted;
	Condemned to die for treason, but no traitor –
	And that I'll prove on better men than Somerset
	(1H6 2.4.88–98).

'Attainted' blood is denied, yet Richard seeks and gains royal assent to re-ennoble his blood (1H6 2.4.116–20; 3.1.161–77). Husbands are said to be 'attainted' by treasonous wives, or men or women by treasonous lovers, in CYL 1.2.106 and LRF 5.3.76–7.

The word 'attainted' and its derivatives are used in over twenty Shakespearian plays or poems to express a fatally guilty condition, in many cases having to do with an accusation of treason. The word is attached to a concept of acquiring a 'tainted' or corrupted bloodline, an inherited penalty for serious sin (see under **inheritance**; we consider the specific rejection of this in 1542 and 1604 statutes discussed under **witch**). It is tempting to align at least some Shakespearian contexts of 'attainted' with the parliamentary Bills of Attainder described above. It seems however that Shakespeare mainly stays clear of the delicate issues surrounding parliament's disputed **jurisdiction** (on parliamentary judicature in Shakespeare's time see under **audit/account**).

'Attainture' is predicted in CYL 1.2.106 for Eleanor Cobham Duchess of Gloucester on account of her intrigues. In the play these result in her permanent banishment. Shakespeare's source in Hall's Chronicles identifies her trial and condemnation as under the authority of the Archbishop of Canterbury. However Bellamy, 1970, pp 126–7, 149, and especially 153–4, finds that it was the king's council that dealt with the question of her treason by conjuration, and that it was likely (since treason was never clergyable) that the several churchmen involved in her case investigated only such charges as **heresy** or **witchcraft**; these crimes led to the Duchess's abjuration. It therefore seems that Eleanor Cobham, although indicted as an accessory, was never actually tried for treason, although her accomplices were.

The analogy underlying the equivalence of petty treason with high treason is described explicitly in Katerina's now-notorious speech:

> Such duty as the subject owes the prince,
> Even such a woman oweth to her husband,
> And when she is froward, peevish, sullen, sour,
> And not obedient to his honest will,
> What is she but a foul contending rebel,
> And graceless traitor to her loving lord?
>
> (SHR 5.2.160–5)

Whether this speech shows Kate's capitulation to brain-washing, submission to violence, participation in a conspiracy, or even her triumph and vindication, has been much discussed.

(C) See Stephen, 1883, vol 2, pp 241–70; Pollock and Maitland, 1898, vol 2, pp 500–8; Plucknett, 1956, pp 204–5, 443–4; Bellamy, 1970; Bellamy, 1973, pp 31, 188–90; Langbein, 1974, pp 307–10; Bellamy, 1979; Baker, 1990b, pp 599–600. Smith, L. B., 1954 discusses the sometimes false confessions offered following Tudor treason convictions.

On the history of treason by words alone see Bellamy, 1970, pp 16, 107, 116–23, 145; Patterson, 1993. Van Patten, 1983 treats Henrician prosecutions of treason by words which were prophesies sometimes tinged with magic, a pattern that was initiated in the 1534 execution of the Nun of Kent.

On 'petty treason' see Bellamy, 1970, pp 225–31, and on the punishment of women by burning for petty treason see Campbell, R., 1985.

On the origins of acts of attainder see Bellamy, 1970, pp 123–6, 177–205.

Nass, 1996, relates the language and uses of English treason statutes to LUC; Ranald, 1987, pp 153–72, discusses LUC in terms of military siege and also treason

Treason and petty treason in CYL are analysed in Bernthal, 1991 and Levine, N., 1994.

Carroll, 1992 considers cynical or hypocritical violations of due process, form, and ceremony in R3. This essay often focuses on legal matters, including unjust accusations or illegal executions for treason (pp 204–5). The tyrannous treason prosecutions of the actual King Richard III are discussed (as anomalies) in Bellamy, 1970, p 215.

Several critics deal with issues of treason in R2. Hamilton, D. B., 1983 argues that in R2 Bolingbroke is forced to accuse Mowbray of treason when King Richard, shielded by a misused prerogative, is the guilty party. Gohn, 1982, especially p 946, explains that to make an accusation against the king would be lese-majesty, and that Shakespeare portrays Bolingbroke's behaviour as avoidance of treason. Ibid. adds that Shakespeare's alteration of the historical record in the latter part of R2 (so that Richard abdicates willingly and names his successor) was to avoid the image of a gross treason in usurpation. Bellamy, 1970, p 115, explains several peculiarities in Richard II's actual use of treason laws against Bolingbroke and Mowbray.

Bernthal, 1992 argues that the notorious 1603 treason trial of Sir Walter Raleigh (and the famous **pardons** of Markham, Cobham, and Grey) influenced the portrayal of accusations and pardons in MM. We give reasons above to doubt the claim in Keeton, 1967, pp 53–4, that Raleigh's trial inspired TN 3.2.42–3; that theory is questioned also in Phillips, O. H., 1967, p 199. Hotine, 1983 argues that before Raleigh's trial the spider represented a traitor (so Coke called Raleigh a 'Spider of Hell'), and that this helps explain the spider imagery in WT 2.1.41–7.

Chermely, 1987, suggests a possible influence on *King Lear* of the actual trial of Peter Berchet for treason, who was convicted and punished although he was mad.

Cunningham, 1994, suggests that the Henrician treason statutes concerning the succession, and particular details of the attainder for treason of Katherine Howard (attainted for sexual activities before her marriage to Henry VIII), inform the trial of female fidelity in CYM.

Dolan, 1992b, considers petty treason in TMP, and Dolan, 1992a,

1994, considers representations of domestic violence and wives' acts of petty treason.

trespass In the early middle ages the word 'trespass' was understood legally to mean a wrong. In the twelfth century Glanvill described pleas as civil (concerning **land** mostly) or criminal. For him criminal pleas encompassed all wrongs, although this did not mean that the wrongdoer was always physically punished as a criminal because it did not exclude the possibility of the payment of compensation to the victim by the wrongdoer. So in early law there was no distinction between a crime and a 'tort' (civil wrong), and crime was punished at the instance of the victim, not the state (see **appeal** of felony).

By the thirteenth century serious wrongs were categorized as **felonies**, while less serious wrongs were known as trespasses or misdemeanours. However somewhat confusingly the term 'trespass' continued to refer to all wrongs generally.

'Trespass' also became the term used to refer to civil wrongs or 'torts'. During the sixteenth and seventeenth centuries actions for the separate torts, pursued as actions **on the case** for trespass, assumed definite modern characteristics. (After approximately 1600 these actions on the case could include actions for unpaid **debts**.) But the emergence of the law of negligence was delayed until the twentieth century.

(B) Shakespeare usually employs 'trespass' to refer to a wrongful act generally, with no implicit technical legal meaning. (Similarly, he does not use the term 'misdemeanour' technically). However, in two places in *King Lear*, one only in LRQ and the other only in LRF, the term 'trespass' seems to refer to an offence particularly distinguished by its lesser importance, and meriting a punishment which is shaming and unpleasant rather than capital. Both contexts refer to the stocking for alleged brawling and insubordination of Lear's servant and messenger, the **banished** Earl of Kent in disguise. Regan and Cornwall thereby show disrespect to Lear. The quarto text makes this disrespect very clear in its use of the depreciating location 'common trespasses':

CORNWALL   Bring forth the stocks, ho! –
                  You stubborn, ancient knave, you reverend braggart,

	We'll teach you.
KENT	I am too old to learn.
	Call not your stocks for me. I serve the King,
	On whose employments I was sent to you.
	You should do small respect, show too bold malice
	Against the grace and person of my master,
	Stocking his messenger.
CORNWALL	Fetch forth the stocks! –
	As I have life and honour, there shall he sit till noon.
	. . .
GLOUCESTER	Let me beseech your grace not to do so.
	His fault is much, and the good King his master
	Will check him for 't. Your purposed low correction
	Is such as basest and contemned wretches
	For pilf'rings and most common trespasses
	Are punished with. The King must take it ill
	That he's so slightly valued in his messenger,
	Should have him thus restrained.

(LRQ S.7.120–41)

In LRF Gloucester's speech is cut short. But when Lear finds his servant in the stocks, the disguised Kent explains that he had quarrelled with the despicable Oswald, and 'Having more man than wit about me, drew'. Kent continues 'He raised the house with loud and coward cries. / Your son and daughter found this trespass worth / The shame which here it suffers' (LRF 2.2.218–21). Here less clearly, but still distinctly, a 'trespass' is a crime meriting a lesser punishment than a felony, but a punishment unfitting for a royal messenger.

(C) See **felony** and **on the case**.

use (A) The early 'use', ancestor to the modern trust, probably developed in response to particular needs. The example often used is of a medieval crusader or pilgrim leaving England who wanted someone to manage his lands on behalf of his children, so that if he died while abroad his infant children (unable to hold land themselves) would inherit. To achieve this he passed the seisin in the property to 'tutors' or 'curators', who held the land on behalf of the children. But in these early transactions the legal estate did not pass to the tutor.

By the thirteenth century the use was quite common. The landowner enfeoffed trusted friends or lawyers, who became 'feoffees to use' or trustees (see **enfeoffment**). The feoffees then held the land for the benefit of the person nominated by the landowner, who was the beneficiary of the use, or in law-French '*cestui que use*'. The beneficiary could be the landowner himself, or frequently a religious foundation such as the Franciscans whose order forbade owning land, or religious bodies anxious to avoid the Mortmain statutes (which forbade passing land to religious houses – see under **will** and also **bill**).

Before the Statute of Wills (1540) the use was often utilised to avoid the common law rules which prevented a landowner from devising (leaving) his land by will. To get around this problem the landowner transferred the land to friends during his lifetime with instructions that after his death they were to dispose of his property as he directed. The use also made any transfer of land, or **conveyance**, easier to accomplish because physical transfer of possession, or 'livery of seisin', was

382

not necessary to convey a use. Once land was in use, a *cestui que use* could enjoy most of the benefits of owning land without the burdens. The advantages were so great that 'by 1535 most of the land in England was held to uses' (Clarkson and Warren, 1942, p 135).

In the fourteenth century the Church courts appear to have had jurisdiction over the enforcement of uses, but it is not clear from records what remedies were available against a defaulting feoffee. The jurisdiction of the Church courts declined as that of the Lord Chancellor grew. By the mid fifteenth century the Lord Chancellor in the Court of Chancery was intervening on behalf of the *cestui que use* to enforce a use against defrauding feoffees, and on behalf of creditors who claimed to have been defrauded because land put in use was not readily available for payments of debts despite statutory attempts to make it so.

Tudor kings, interested in 'fiscal feudalism', became concerned about their loss of feudal revenue when landowners put their land in use. Once land was in use no one had seisin, and therefore no one was liable to pay 'feudal incidents' (see **land**) such as **wardship**. While all lords lost feudal incidents when land was put in use, the greatest loss was to the king. To address this problem statutes were passed in 1490 (4 Hen. VII, c. 17) and 1504 (19 Hen. VII, c. 15) subjecting the heir of an intestate *cestui que use* to feudal incidents.

But Henry VIII went further than this. First in 1535 he persuaded the judges to declare in *Lord Dacre of the South's Case* (B. and M. 105) that the common law had never allowed land to be devised by will. It was clear that wills of uses had been accepted as settled law before this case, but the King and his minister Thomas Cromwell, the Master of the Rolls, considered that a will of a use of land was the same as a will of land and therefore not valid. They argued that the use made conveyancing of land insecure because it allowed secret conveyances which could be used to defraud **purchasers** or creditors who did not know about the use.

Then in 1536 the Statute of Uses (27 Hen. VIII, c. 10) was enacted despite the objections of the Commons. This statute 'executed the use', that is vested the legal estate in the beneficiary, and so rendered him liable for payment of all feudal incidents. Not all uses were executed by the statute. Those which were not included uses of leasehold land (see **lease**), copyhold land (see **copy**), and active uses which were those which imposed some specific duty on a feoffee (for example in administering charitable purposes or collecting rents). Another important exception to the statute was the 'springing' or 'shifting' use. A simple example would be where a donor granted an estate to a feoffee for the use of A when he reached the age of twenty one. In this case until A reached the required age a use existed for the donor.

Generally the effect of Henry's Statute of Uses was to succeed in raising considerable revenue for the crown. But dissatisfaction with consequent restrictions on the ability to devise land led some landowning gentry to join in the 1536 rebellion known as the Pilgrimage of Grace. Following this, the Statute of Wills of 1540 (32 Hen. VIII, c. 1) allowed devises of land to all socage tenants, while tenants by knights service were required to retain one third for their **heirs** (see **land** for the doctrine of **tenures**). The Statute of Wills is generally regarded as Henry's concession to the Commons.

When Shakespeare wrote, the law of uses was still in a period of transition and unsettled after the Tudor legislation. Bonfield, 1983, p 36, cites widely varied judicial opinions of the usefulness and validity of uses post 1536. Legal draftsmen attempted ingenious ways around the Statue of Uses. So 'the late sixteenth and early seventeenth centuries may justly be called the age of the fantastic conveyance' (Simpson, 1986, p 198). For example, the Statute of Uses did not inhibit conveyancing by means of deed of lease and release, and a use could be imposed on the release (see **conveyancing**).

By the early seventeenth century the Statute of Uses was held not to execute a second use, or use upon a use. For example 'to A and his heirs to the use of B and his heirs to the use of and in trust for C and his heirs' would execute the use to B but not the use to C, which to distinguish it became known as a 'trust'. The reason usually given for this development was that the second use was initially considered void on account of the Statute of Uses and was therefore unaffected by it, but later the second use was enforced by the Lord Chancellor. The earliest known case was *Sir Moyle Finch's Case* in 1600 (4 Co. Inst. 85) which in fact concerned an active trust. By the later seventeenth century, during Lord Nottingham's term as Chancellor, trusts were enforced by Chancery and the modern law of trusts was developed.

(B) The 'use' in the sense of a legal trust is named only once by Shakespeare, but in a crucial place, when the phrase 'let me have . . . in use' is employed in MV. The phrase 'in use' occurs in: TRO 3.3.123; JC 3.1.268; ANT 1.3.44 but it does not carry legal significance in any of these places. (A quite different phrase 'gave him use for it' (ADO 2.1.260), which refers to a payment of interest, is discussed under **usury**.)

The passage of MV involving 'in use' arises in the much discussed trial scene between Shylock and Antonio, and it poses great difficulties of interpretation. Under the Venetian alien **statute** which condemns Shylock, one half of Shylock's goods are Antonio's and 'the other half / Comes to the privy coffer of the state/ And the offender's life lies in the mercy / Of the Duke only' (MV 4.1.350–3). The Duke offers to forego the death penalty and to reduce Shylock's forfeit to the state to a lesser fine if he shows 'humbleness'. However, Shylock shows no obvious contrition, and his adversary is asked by Portia, 'What mercy can you render him, Antonio?' (4.1.375). Antonio replies:

> So please my lord the Duke and all the court
> To quit the fine for one half of his goods,
> I am content, so he will let me have
> The other half in use, to render it
> Upon his death unto the gentleman
> That lately stole his daughter.
> Two things provided more: that for this favour
> He presently become a Christian;
> The other, that he do record a gift
> Here in the court of all he dies possessed
> Unto his son, Lorenzo, and his daughter.
> (MV 4.1.377–87)

These conditions are enforced by the Duke, with threats of death. Just what they mean has produced much critical disagreement.

It is certain, at least that 'in use' here does not refer to **usury**, although some critics have thought so. But the language of 'quit the fine for one half', and 'let me have/ The other half in use' has proved very difficult to interpret (in an odd way, parallel with the moral character of Antonio).

Among varied views taken are those holding that Shylock is 'stripped' of all his wealth, or that he retains half his wealth (minus the fine) and Antonio holds the other half in a use with Lorenzo as beneficiary, or that Shylock retains a life interest in all his goods.

In our view, if Antonio proposes to reserve to himself until Shylock's death an interest in all of Shylock's goods, including most of those that would have gone to the state, there is no meaning to the 'favour' he offers Shylock. He would then add little to the 'mercy' urged by Gratiano, which is to give Shylock a 'halter, gratis. Nothing else, for God's sake'. It would be moreover odd for Antonio to be allowed to appropriate for himself the half of Shylock's estate that has been generously returned to Shylock by the Duke. So, unless the point is to show Antonio exceptionally merciless and mercenary, the 'Shylock stripped' theory seems unlikely.

It seems rather that the only 'favour' that could be said to be offered to Shylock in the passage above is a life estate in half of his 'goods' (properly, uses applied only to real property – see **chattels**). Antonio will be the feoffee, and the *cestui que use* is Shylock. Lorenzo has an interest in **remainder**; after Shylock's death Antonio passes the property absolutely to Lorenzo. The language, however is somewhat ambiguous, and other more complex constructions have been offered. See part C below.

It is not clear either what form of recorded 'special deed of gift' (MV 5.1.292) could ensure that Shylock will leave all his *future* wealth to Jessica and Lorenzo. After 1540 wills of land could be made, but wills could be changed at any time until death. Also, before the 1837 Wills Act introduced the 'ambulatory will', a will spoke at the date it was executed, and not the date of death. So real property acquired post execution would not be included. Shylock's future wealth, 'all he dies possessed' of, could not be given in a will, nor of course in a present gift *inter vivos*.

(C) For a general survey of the development of the use see: Yale, 1957; Barton, J. L., 1965; Barton, J. L., 1966; Baker, 1977; Helmholz, 1979; Simpson, 1986; DeVine, 1989; Baker, 1990b, pp 283–95. For a brief explanation see Buck, 1994. See Clarkson and Warren, 1942, pp 133–43, on the use in relation to Elizabethan drama.

Spinosa, 1995 argues a relation between the legal history of uses and the vicissitudes of early modern personal identity, and connects both with the opening scene of *King Lear*.

Several treatments of the question of the 'use' in MV are summarised in Holmer, 1995, pp 216–17 and 330–1, which, p 330, reviews and opposes the acceptance by many critics of a 'Shylock stripped' reading. Holmer's own view is that Antonio is generous in that he takes his own half of Shylock's wealth given by law 'in use', and will render the augmented principal on Shylock's death to Lorenzo.

A far more complex reading is found in Andrews, 1965, pp 72–5, which contains flow charts showing two different trusts supposedly created at the trial, one being a use after a use and involving the possible *gap* that characterizes a 'springing use'. As is much of Andrews' book, this reading is ingenious or fantastic but not at all close to Shakespeare's text, and it contains elements of legal–historical anachronism.

Eure, 1975, p 409, finds no problem that Shylock's 'deed recorded in court is to insure his testamentary beneficence to his Christian daughter and son-in-law'. This otherwise agrees with Keeton, 1967, pp 146–7, that Shylock will have the use of all of his money until his death.

Posner, 1988, p 92, note 31, questions whether or not Shylock will be the beneficiary of the trust set up 'for Jessica' (*sic*) during his lifetime, but suggests 'it is as difficult as it is unimportant to determine which interpretation is correct'.

The problem of the deed of gift that Shylock is forced to record is treated with regard to the aspect of gifts, not wills, in Clarkson and Warren, 1942, pp 182–4. This does not mention the phrase 'in use' (which is odd seeing the lengthy treatment of uses in the book, as cited above). This concludes that Shakespeare was unconcerned with legal correctness.

The legal enigmas of the trial in MV have been the subject of an huge number of varied discussions. Many of these are referenced under the entries for **debt**, **equity** or **usury**. They include in addition: Hirshfield, 1914; Pollock, 1914; Keeton, 1930; Jardine, 1987; Schotz, 1991; Campbell, S., 1992; Weisberg, 1992; Rockwood, 1994.

usury/interest (A) Usury was the taking of interest on a loan of money. Aristotle had denounced it, arguing that money should not breed. The medieval church considered it a sin, and after the Third Lateran Council of 1179 usury was severely punished (Plucknett, 1956, p 302). Popularly, usury was often considered a serious offence, and usurers were demonized. This was done in English tracts of the early modern period such as those by Thomas Wilson (1572) and Miles Mosse (1595). Yet, as noted under **debt**, fiscal credit was crucial for the economic well-being of Shakespeare's society.

Taking money for the use of money was often viewed with distaste, but taking rent for the use of land was not considered sinful or illegal;

this was one of many ways in which **land** was differentiated from other valuables. Also, **mortgages** were legal in common law, although they could in effect be usurious. Although occasional disquiet was expressed in case law of the fourteenth century, lending on conditional **bonds** with penalties was also not treated by the English law as usury (see Baker, 1990b, p 370; Simpson, 1966, pp 412–15). However by Shakespeare's time the Chancellor's Court of **equity** was giving relief if these penalties were unreasonably high.

The Church courts in medieval England punished usury, but their exclusive control over the practice was taken over by early modern **statutory** provisions of the common law. A 1545 statute (37 Hen. VIII, c.9), although nominally punitive, effectively allowed the taking of interest, as long as it was set at less than 10%. That was because this statute made usury punishable as a **praemunire** only if interest was above 10%, and although it allowed the confiscation of lesser amounts of interest this provision was not in practice enforced, and became a 'dead letter' eventually eliminated in 1623 (Holdsworth, 1903, vol 8, pp 110–11).

Further statutes of 1571, 1597 and 1623 (13 Eliz., c.8, 39 Eliz., c.19, and 21 Jac. I, c.17) renewed or slightly modified the 1545 Act. These early modern statutes reinforced the common law's **jurisdiction** over usury, despite the fact that all of them contained clauses reserving the punishment of usury as a sin to the Church courts. In fact, actions in the Church courts on 'usury causes' became 'quite rare' (Helmholz, 1990, p 161, also Houlbrooke, 1979, p 40, although Helmholz, 1987i, p 338, cites some).

(B) In the Folio text only, Shakespeare's Richard III uses an image of taking a large gain in 'interest' on a 'loan' approvingly. This may be ominous, given the popular view of interest taking, and given Richard's grotesque character and intentions. Richard uses this figure when he solicits a mother of a family he has largely destroyed to help him to exploit her daughter in a dynastic marriage:

> The liquid drops of tears that you have shed
> Shall come again, transformed to orient pearl,
> Advantaging their loan with interest
> Of ten times double gain of happiness.
> (R3 A.K.34–7, following 4.4.273; tln 3106–9)

Yet there is no ill-intent evident when the negotiator Sir Walter Blunt attempts to reconcile Hotspur and his faction to Henry IV, offering:

> If that the King
> Have any way your good deserts forgot,
> Which he confesseth to be manifold,
> He bids you name your griefs, and with all speed
> You shall have your desires, with interest,
> And pardon absolute for yourself and these
> Herein misled by your suggestion.
>
> (1H4 4.3.47–53)

It does not seem that the extra 'interest' offered here to compensate for a delayed payment (of political gratitude) is implicitly sinful or wrong.

Witnessing the inflationary trend of their mutual courtesies, Speed puns upon 'interest' meaning Silvia's romantic interest (exceeding Valentine's), and 'interest' meaning numerical/monetary gain: 'He should give her interest, and she gives it him' (TGV 2.1.95–6).

Less benign and more literal references to monetary interest abound in TIM. First, in a figure of speech converging with actuality, the loyal steward Flavius comments that Timon's excessively generous 'promises fly so beyond his state / That what he speaks is all in debt, he owes / For every word. He is so kind that he now / Pays interest for 't'. Flavius continues, making his metaphor ominously literal and describing a possible **mortgage** or **statute** merchant, 'His land's put to their books' (TIM 1.2.197–200).

A negative view of moneylending for interest arises also when the **banished** soldier Alcibiades contrasts himself with 'the usuring senate' (TIM 3.6.108) of Athens: 'I have kept back their foes / While they have told their money and let out / Their coin upon large interest – I myself, / Rich only in large hurts' (3.6.104–7). It is significant that the sarcastic symmetry of this context stresses *large* interest, as if usury required more than moderate gain.

When funding his revenge, Timon instructs Alcibiades to 'Pity not honoured age for his white beard; / He is an usurer' (TIM 4.3.112–13). Slightly later Timon, again emphasising immoderate gains, questions loyal Flavius if his is 'A usuring kindness, and, as rich men deal gifts, / Expecting in return twenty for one?' (4.3.510–11).

The demonization of usury is half-mocked in the malapropism of the simple apprentice Peter Thumpe, when bringing an **appeal** of **treason** against his master:

QUEEN MARGARET   What sayst thou? Did the Duke of York
                 say he was rightful heir to the crown?
PETER   That my master was? No, forsooth, my master said
                 that he was and that the King was an usurer.
QUEEN MARGARET   An usurper thou wouldst say.
PETER   Ay, forsooth – an usurper.

(CYL 1.3.30–5)

It is certainly mocked in the responses of the gullible rustics of Bohemia to a new ballad telling of procreative wonders:

AUTOLYCUS   Here's one to a very doleful tune, how a usurer's wife was
            brought to bed of twenty money-bags at a burden, and
            how she longed to eat adders' heads and toads
            carbonadoed.
MOPSA   Is it true, think you?
AUTOLYCUS   Very true, and but a month old.
DORCAS   Bless me from marrying a usurer!

(WT 4.4.260–6)

Beatrice in ADO admits Benedick once 'lent' her his heart for 'a while', a loan for which she paid heavy interest or 'use'. She says that she 'gave him use for it, a double heart for his single one', presumably by giving her heart in return (ADO 2.1.260–1). Her metaphor for a failed romance involving monetary payment, linked to her further accusation that he won her heart by using 'false dice' (2.1.262), helps explain Beatrice's initial disdain for Benedick.

The taking of interest is associated with procreative sexuality in knavish Parolles's argument encouraging the loss of female virginity:

virginity is peevish, proud, idle, made of self-love – which is the most inhibited sin in the canon. Keep it not, you cannot choose but lose by 't. Out with't! Within t'one year it will make itself two, which is a goodly increase, and the principal itself not much the worse.

(AWW 1.1.142–7)

However his mention here of a 'sin in the canon' may also associate the passage with Parolles's promotion of Bertram's aim at an irresponsible sexual conquest (reported in AWW 3.5.16–28, 3.5.84–7).

Indeed bawdry (also under the canon law's jurisdiction) is often associated with usury in Shakespeare's works. The association is seen, for instance, in scurrilous Apemanus' address to 'Poor rogues' and usurers' men, bawds between gold and want' (TIM 2.2.58–9). He then addresses the servants of 'three usurers', who provide the occasion for his extended comparison of usury with whoremongery (2.2.89–105).

The same association of usury with prostitution arises in the bawd Pompey's florid lament on the legal closure of the brothels of Vienna: ''Twas never merry world since, of two usuries, the merriest was put down, and the worser allowed by order of law, a furred gown to keep him warm – and furred with fox on lambskins too, to signify that craft, being richer than innocency, stands for the facing' (MM 3.1.275–9). Is Pompey's complaint of the allowance of the less merry (monetary) usury 'by order of law' an oblique reference to the English usury statutes following that of 1545? The same contemporary allusion seems likely in COR, in a Citizen's complaint that the Roman senators: 'make edicts for usury to support usurers; repeal daily any wholesome act established against the rich; and provide more piercing statutes daily to chain up and restrain the poor' (COR 1.1.79–82).

Certainly Pompey's image of monetary usury dressed in furs, suggesting usurers as high status, well-dressed respectable-seeming men, chimes with Alcibiades's and Timon's complaints against the Athenian senators, and with Lear's rant against men of authority, including 'The usurer hangs the cozener. / Through tattered clothes great vices do appear; Robes and furred gowns hide all' (LRQ S.20.157–9; LRF 4.5.159–61).

Usury seems associated with covert wealth in Lear's Fool's prophesy of a time 'When usurers tell their gold i' th' field, / And bawds and whores do churches build' (LRF 3.2.91–2), but with fashionable ostentation in Benedick's mocking 'What fashion will you wear the garland of? About your neck, like an usurer's chain?' (ADO 2.1.178–9). As appropriate to a churchman, Friar Lawrence associates 'usury' with a sinful misuse of life (ROM 3.3.121–4), while the **outlawed** courtier Belarius associates it with metropolitan and courtly corruption ('Did you but know the city's usuries, / And felt them knowingly; the art o' th' court, / As hard to leave as keep' (CYM 3.3.45–7)). For the mad Jailer's

391

daughter of TNK 4.3.33–4, 'a cauldron of lead and usurers' grease' is handy in Hell to boil the damned. The outraged Duke of Gloucester adds usury to his verbatim list of drastic complaints against the Bishop of Winchester after the latter tears up a **bill** of written accusations (1H6 3.1.17); usury is for Gloucester a fitting adjunct to wickedness, lewdness, envious malice and **treason**.

There are clearly varied attitudes to monetary interest- taking shown in Shakespeare's plays. Among the plays there is also one major presentation of professional moneylending, in a context that leaves Shakespeare's critics divided. Shylock complains bitterly of Antonio's public denunciation of 'me, my bargains, and my well-won thrift – / Which he calls interest' (MV 1.3.48–9), and is offended that Antonio 'was wont to call me usurer: let him look to his bond' (3.1.43–4). As we have noted above, advancing money on conditional **bonds** was not subject to usury restrictions. But if the terms of a penalty were extreme, as in Shylock's bond, **equity** could intervene.

How contemporary audiences did take and have since taken the presentation of the moneylender Shylock has been much discussed. In particular, Shylock's Biblical defence of taking interest in 1.3.70–101 may have been understood in Shakespeare's time more complexly than now, as is argued in Sokol, 1998. Many commentators have offered approaches to the question; a range is noted below.

(C) See Holdsworth, 1903, vol 8, pp 100–13; Baker, 1990b, pp 353, 370. Helmholz, 1987i surveys the English Church courts' treatment of usury through to Shakespeare's time, and concludes that mitigation or moderation in their treatment of 'petty' usury may have anticipated the Tudor statutes' countenancing of moderate interest-taking.

See also 'On Usury' in Bacon, 1994, and the introduction and Thomas Wilson's treatise in Tawney, 1925. Draper, 1935 and Derrett, 1973, p 2, comment on Wilson's and other Elizabethans' writings on usury. Holmer, 1995, connects Miles Mosse's treatise with MV.

Mischo, 1995, considers laws regulating monetary interest and Tudor attitudes toward usury in relation to Shakespeare's 'Procreation Sonnets' (SON 1–17) and concludes that 'usury has been transformed into an expression of Christian charity', expressing 'an emerging economic order that was to link "usurious" profitability to moral rectitude'.

Mainly censorious contemporary views of usury are discussed in relation with MV in Draper, 1935; Pettet, 1945; Hinely, 1980, pp

392

224–5; Cohen, W., 1982; Hutson, 1994; Holmer, 1995. On a different tack, Portia's generosity is described as masterful 'negative usury' in Berger, 1981.

Elizabethan hatred of usury is argued to be the unifying central theme of TIM in Draper, 1934.

vagrant/vagrom man Vagrants were the wandering poor (see **poverty/beggary**). Unlike the poor labourer in his cottage, vagrants were often very visible. Figures derived from records of punishment kept by local constables and parish officials indicate that vagrant beggars in England in Shakespeare's time probably numbered thousands (Slack, 1988, p 93). Evidence derived from Bridewell records show that particularly in London there was an increase at the end of the sixteenth and early seventeenth century (ibid.). Bands of vagrants wandering about the countryside were feared for the social disruption, disease and criminality they were thought to bring with them, and were regarded as a danger to the commonwealth.

Some vagrants moved about the country in large well-organized bands, living on the edge of criminality. Others were individual transients, or sometimes destitute families. Many in search of work or escaping famine moved from countryside to town and from the north to the south of England. Such vagrants were mainly men, and mainly young, although women are identified in records too. Some vagrants were discharged soldiers, or runaway **apprentices**. Others were gypsies, and some were recorded as Irish moving in groups across England towards the south east. Wandering minstrels were specially identified as vagrants in the Act of 1572, to be punished unless they were employed by a member of the nobility, or had a special license granted by two **Justices of the Peace**.

Some vagrants were professional beggars and criminals, who chose a way of life, or so the literature of the period leads us to believe. A criminal underworld existed in cities, but otherwise criminal vagrants could be people caught up in opportunistic crime. The poor harvests at the end of the sixteenth century led to shortage of basic food, and outbreaks of famine and sickness. In such conditions many left home and began to wander in search of work. Attempts to correlate the outbreak of recorded crime in a particular area with the dates of bad harvests conclude crime did not rise as soon as conditions first deteriorated. However after a lapse of time (sometimes a year or two) people left famine areas, and much reported crime does appear to be connected to their subsequent migrations (Lawson, 1986, p 113). Petty crime, in particular petty **theft**, was typically undertaken by transients, for example the theft of clothes drying on hedges, or the theft of wood or foodstuffs. Groups of discharged soldiers moving about the country also appear connected to outbreaks of crime.

Vagrants were identified and punished by the Poor Law **statutes** with particular severity, reflecting the fear which they engendered. Government policy, set out in the Tudor Poor Laws consolidated in 1601, produced a system of punishment and control (see under **poverty**). The organized system depended on the parish, which supported its own poor through local taxes. Alms and the provision of outdoor relief in the form of work in workhouses for the destitute was combined with whipping and incarceration in Houses of Correction for rogues and the idle. Vagrants from other parishes were punished, provided with passes and returned to the parish of their birth, or last place of residence where they had not been whipped and ejected.

(B) The laws regulating vagrancy, and the social dangers of 'vagrom men', are made light of in Dogberry's charge to the watch, beginning:

> You are thought here to be the most senseless and fit man for the constable of the watch, therefore bear you the lantern. This is your charge: you shall comprehend all vagrom men. You are to bid any man stand, in the Prince's name.

Asked 'How if a will not stand?' Dogberry replies 'Why then take no note of him, but let him go, and presently call the rest of the watch together, and thank God you are rid of a knave.' This policy is explained by Verges' logic, 'If he will not stand when he is bidden he is

395

none of the Prince's subjects' (ADO 3.3.21–31). Such an attitude to policing is discussed under **constable**.

The disgrace in being a banished and **outlawed** 'wandering vagabond' is lamented in R2 2.3.119 and punishments including 'Vagabond exile' are defied in COR 3.3.93; here exile and wandering is a legal punishment. Foreign soldiers are impugned as vagrants by Richard III, who characterises Richmond's followers as 'A sort of vagabonds, rascals and runaways, / A scum of Bretons and base lackey peasants, / Whom their o'ercloyed country vomits forth / To desperate ventures and assured destruction' (R3 5.6.46–9). This is in accord with frequent allegations of the wretchedness of enemy troops in Shakespeare, discussed under **poverty**. Soldiers who became vagrants were often accused of inventing their honours, as is wordy Pistol by Gower in H5 3.6.68–82. Another such boastful soldier, Parolles, is accused of being 'a vagabond and no true traveller' in AWW 2.3.257–8.

A distinction of the 'vagabond' Parolles from a 'true traveller' accords with a Renaissance outlook in which wandering is not at all disgraceful if it is questing driven by 'Such wind as scatters young men through the world / To seek their fortunes farther than at home, / Where small experience grows' (SHR 1.2.49–51). Shakespeare's gentlemanly true traveller Petruchio, thus self-described, has 'thrust' himself into adventures 'to wive and thrive as best I may' (SHR 1.2.54–5) deliberately. Most other young travellers in Shakespeare's comedies go abroad perforce, or by accident, but all wive and thrive, or find husbands.

All these are distinguished from the untrustworthy vagrant, who will lie, steal, and wherever possible abuse hospitality. A prime Shakespearian example of vagrant is wandering Autolycus, (con) artist, travelling rogue, and casual seducer. He has a sharp eye for 'the doxy over the dale' and 'The white sheet bleaching on the hedge' (WT 4.3.2&5). He also blatantly abuses the charity of the Clown and the hospitality of the sheepshearers, cheating and stealing from them, but in a way repays this with his minstrelsy.

Like the sometime entertainer Christopher Sly (who had been among many other things a 'bearherd' according to SHR Ind.2.17–20 – the bear presumably presented for entertainment purposes), Autolycus has had a motley career including being the presenter of an 'ape', and of a 'motion' (puppet show) (WT 4.3.86–98). We first meet him as a ballad-selling, singing, thief. Some of the objections that might be made against him resemble those often heard against theatre folk on tour, which Shakespeare would have known well.

A more dangerous class of vagrants or vagrant gangs portrayed by Shakespeare are discussed under **outlaws**.

(C) See: Beier, 1974; Beier, 1985; Slack, 1988, pp 100–7; Lawson, 1986, and see under **poverty**. On evidence for large groups of vagrants see Beier, 1974 and Beier, 1985, pp 57–65. On wandering minstrels, ballad-sellers and entertainers see especially ibid., pp 96–9. Also see under **poverty/beggary**.

In addition to discussing a range of social legislation of 1597/8, McDonald, 1995 comments on the economic dearth that probably led to an increased vagrancy peaking around 1600 (pp. 122–3), and on contemporary efforts to reinforce provisions against vagabonds (p. 136). This essay finds H5 generally concerned with the problem of telling true war veterans from rogues, and it claims that the Folio text is mellower, especially toward Pistol, than the Quarto (pp. 137–8). The essay finally associates the problematic standing of the Elizabethan theatre itself with contemporary questions about vagrancy and masterless men.

The legal problem of distinguishing the idle vagrant 'rogue' from the deserving poor is also discussed in Mowat, 1994, which applies the concept of 'rogue' to Autolycus of WT.

villein (A) This term originally referred to legal status of a person who held **land** by villein **tenure**. Within the feudal scheme of land-holding the holder of land by villein tenure was the peasant who had the very lowest rank and formed the base of the feudal pyramid. He held land at the will of his lord in return for the performance of agricultural services. Socage tenure was also an agricultural tenure but this can be distinguished from villein tenure by the fact that a villein tenant's duties were not fixed; the villein had to carry out whatever agricultural tasks the lord assigned to him. In contrast a socage tenant's duties were fixed by the terms of his tenure. But although in theory the services of the villein were not fixed, in practice the customs of the manor made detailed definitions of such duties. Records of manor courts indicate many arguments between lord and villein about services due.

Villein status brought with it certain civil disadvantages, but while personally unfree, a villein was not a slave. **Slavery**, or serfdom, was

397

known in Anglo Saxon England, and seems not to have disappeared with the Conquest in 1066 because many peasants were identified as serfs in the Doomsday survey of 1086. The numbers of villeins was large, as many formerly free peasants were depressed in status and reclassified as unfree villeins after 1066.

Among the disadvantages of villein status was the fact that villein tenure was 'allodial', meaning the villein was tied to the land, and that rights to the villein's services could be bought and sold with the land. If he left the land he could be forcibly returned. All the villein's property in theory belonged not to the villein but to his lord, who could appropriate it if he wished. (Later, this aspect of villein status allowed avoidance of actions for **debt**.)

In medieval England, royal justice did not extend to the villein, who had instead to pursue his claims in the manor court of his lord. But such manor courts were expected to apply the law according to the customs of the manor, and although the villein could be physically punished by the lord, royal justice would protect him from severe ill-treatment at his lord's hands. Although theory held that all the villein's property belonged to his lord, in practice villeins made wills (correctly, **testaments**) of personal property, and **inherited** rights to their real property.

Villein status was inherited, and could only be altered in a limited number of ways. This could be by manumission (a grant of freedom by the lord), or by marriage to a free person, or by living undisturbed in a royal borough or in London as a free person for a year and a day. A **bastard** did not inherit villein status from either parent, which led many villeins to claim bastard status.

By the sixteenth century some ecclesiastical courts, in particular the one at Norwich, would overlook residence requirements, and certify bastardy on request to meet such demands. By then villein status had lost much of its significance and was falling into disuse (for detail see MacCulloch, 1988, pp 91–100). But villein tenure remained important and became known as copyhold tenure (see **copy**), which was to last until the Law of Property Act 1925.

By the late sixteenth century the most significant difference between freehold and copyhold tenure was that title to copyhold still depended on the procedure of surrender to the manor court and readmittance. Villein status was no longer tied to villein tenure; free men often acquired copyhold land, while villeins could acquire freeholds. Legally villein status was therefore largely irrelevant, and the term was largely significant because it connoted a servile condition.

(B) The word 'villain', derived from the same root as 'villein', appears in nearly every play of Shakespeare (all but AIT), and many times it appears very frequently (as in *King Lear*). It generally indicates a person reviled for their low social and/or moral stature. Yet it is several times used playfully or affectionately, as by Sir Toby Belch of Maria in TN 2.5.12–13: 'Here comes the little villain. How now, my metal of India?'

Ambiguities between two meanings, concerning low social status and concerning despised moral stature, easily arise because 'villain' is a variant spelling of 'villein', and the two terms can be read interchangeably in the spelling 'villaine' used in Shakespeare's First Folio. Such ambiguity is deployed in AYL in a context bridging derogation of status with opprobrium. The Oxford edition modernizes the elder brother Olivier's protests and the younger brother Orlando's reply in a way that unravels an implicit pun in the single spelling, 'villaine', which is used throughout the passage in the Folio (tln 56–62):

OLIVIER Wilt thou lay hands on me, villain?

ORLANDO I am no villein. I am the youngest son of Sir Rowland de Bois. He was my father, and he is thrice a villain that says such a father begot villeins. Wert thou not my brother, I would not take this hand from thy throat till this other had pulled out thy tongue for saying so. Thou hast railed on thyself.

(AYL 1.1.52–8)

This usage corresponds with Orlando's protest that he has not been given the upbringing due his birth, but one suited to a 'peasant' (1.1.64); his implication is that in doing this his brother has disparaged (see **ward**) their mutually inherited status to villeinage.

In other Shakespearian passages 'villaine' also may imply alternately 'villain' or 'villein'. Just before blinding the high-born Gloucester, Cornwall calls him a **traitor**, and then 'Villaine' (tln 2099). This use of the word in is modernised in the Oxford edition LRF 3.7.32 (also in parallel passages LRF 3.7.85 and 3.7.94) as 'villain'. Then the heroic servant who intervenes against the blinding of Gloucester, saying to Cornwall 'I have served you ever since I was a child' (3.7.71), is called by him 'My Villaine' (tln 2152). Here again the Oxford editors choose one of two possible modernisations of the Folio spelling, supplying 'My villein!' (LRF 3.7.76). When this servant is stabbed from behind by Regan, she exclaims scornfully, 'A peasant stand up thus!' (3.7.78).

This 'villaine . . . pezant' (tln 2152, 2154), who disrupts hierarchy, kills his master without committing petty **treason**, for the master is guilty of a greater treason (as in CYL; see under **lists**). Such circumstances conform with numerous images of inversions of the social order in the play. Varied connections of similar inversions with a theme of law in *King Lear* are discussed in Sisson, 1963, Merchant, 1964, and Eure, 1975, pp 427–32.

(C) See: Baker, 1978, pp 187–92; Baker, 1990b, pp 347–50,532–37; Clarkson and Warren, 1942, pp 37–48; Pollock and Maitland, 1898, vol 1, pp 358–75, 412–32; Holdsworth, 1903, vol 3, pp 491–510. For a detailed account of the use of a fiction of bastardy to dispose of villein status, see MacCulloch, 1988, pp 101–9.

voucher (A) A voucher was a warranty of title used as part of the legal fiction employed in the method of **conveyancing** known as **fine and recovery**. Briefly, this fiction was used collusively by a vendor and **purchaser** of **land**, usually with the purpose of breaking an **entail**. The vendor chose a man of straw to act as a vouchee for the title to the land. The purchaser put up a claim to the same land on the basis of a fictitious title. The vouchee then disappeared leaving the court to award judgment and the land to the purchaser.

By the sixteenth century the vouchee was a landless, humble court official paid a sum of money who always defaulted and never satisfied the judgment made against him for warranting the title. The **heirs** were then barred from claiming against the purchaser, and although in theory they could claim against the vouchee for their loss, in practice they did not as there was no point. See under **fine and recovery** on the added refinement achieved by the **double voucher**, which barred every kind of putative successor in title.

(B) The quibbling list of legal technicalities in Hamlet's *momento mori* speech concerning a dead lawyer includes: 'Will his vouchers vouch him no more of his purchases, and double ones too, than the length and breadth of a pair of indentures?' (HAM 5.1.105–7 – see under **fine and recovery**). The legal assurance in a voucher, or even a double voucher, was not safe against death.

To 'vouch' or 'avouch' appears frequently in Shakespeare's plays and often in the environs of legal imagery or diction. To vouch in such contexts meant to declare or affirm, and some of these uses may take a shade of meaning from the fictional conveyancing practice.

Richard of Gloucester's says 'I will avouch 't in presence of the King' (R3 1.3.115). A 'vouch against' could mean an allegation, as in Angelo's, 'My unsoiled name, th' austereness of my life, / My vouch against you, and my place i' th' state, / Will so your accusation over-weigh / That you shall stifle in your own report' (MM 2.4.155–8). Both of these uses are in the claims of hypocrites, and perhaps may be inflected by the deliberate fictionality of land law vouchers.

There is no insincerity, but there is a foreshadowing of her future cunning, when Helena tells Bertram that she: 'like a timorous thief most fain would steal / What law does vouch mine own' (AWW 2.5.81–2). The fabulous complexity of her ensuing schemes to claim a legal marriage (on which see under **impediments**) might even be seen to approach that of the more fantastical fictional methods of conveyancing.

Brabantio assurance, 'I therefore vouch . . . ' (OTH 1.3.103), alleging that Othello must have used drugs to influence Desdemona, is a merely impassioned claim, and the Duke trying the case replies 'To vouch this is no proof' (OTH 1.3.106). Yet during the same trial, Othello's personal sincerity is the only possible evidence when he affirms, saying 'Vouch with me heaven' (1.3.261), that his own lust is not the cause of his wish that Desdemona accompany him to Cyprus.

An apparent 'voucher / Stronger than ever law could make' actually gives false witness in Iachimo's scheme to prove Imogen's infidelity. To cause the 'madding of her lord' Iachimo notes:

> On her left breast
> A mole, cinque-spotted, like the crimson drops
> I' th' bottom of a cowslip. Here's a voucher
> Stronger than ever law could make. This secret
> Will force him think I have picked the lock and ta'en
> The treasure of her honour.
> (CYM 2.2.37–42)

voucher

Here a 'voucher' overpowers truth with a purpose of deliberate falsification.

(C) See Clarkson and Warren, 1942, p 130, and under **fine and recovery**.

ward (A) Wardship was one of a number of feudal rights which belonged to a lord as an incident of **tenure**. The right arose when the lord's tenant died leaving an infant heir (see **land, heir**) who was unable to hold the estate until he or she came of age. Infancy lasted until 21 for male heirs and 16 for female heirs, but this was reduced to 14 if the female ward married. The lord was entitled to take all the ward's land under his control and in military tenure retained all the profit from the land for the duration of the wardship, but he was liable for any **waste**, or damage to the land. In socage tenure the lord was supposed to account to the heir when he came of age (hand over profits made from the land during the wardship), and was similarly liable for waste (see **land** for the doctrine of tenures).

In all kinds of tenure the lord also had control of the ward's person and was supposed to see to his everyday needs, education and training. In socage tenure the heir's relatives were usually appointed 'guardians', a position that was more like that of trustees. Guardians too had to account to the heir for profit made from the land during the wardship.

Wardship was very profitable feudal incident, particularly in military tenure. In addition to a right to retain all the profits from the lands of both heirs and heiresses, the lord was entitled to a fine of half a year's profit from the land from the ward who reached majority and applied formally to obtain possession of his lands. This procedure was known as **sue his livery** for those who held land from the king as tenant in chief (**in capite**), and otherwise as '*ouster le main*'.

403

The lord was also entitled to arrange the ward's **marriage**, up to the age of 21 for males or 16 for females. The ward could refuse the proposed marriage but if they did so the lord was compensated for financial loss. If the ward married without the lord's license then the lord was entitled to compensation of double the value of the marriage to the lord, and he was entitled to continue to take the profit of the land until he received such payment.

There was some safeguard for wards in the common law. Magna Carta had dealt with the law of waste and also prohibited a lord from 'disparaging' a ward by arranging a marriage with someone of an inferior status.

Because it was so valuable to lords, wardship of heirs was treated as an investment; rights of wardship, or rights to arrange the marriage of the ward, were bought and sold. But without any doubt the king was the greatest beneficiary from wardship because lordships over time had become concentrated in the hands of the king. Also the king benefited from a special right of wardship, known as 'prerogative wardship'. This arose if an infant was heir to several estates, and one of these was held of the king; then the king would have the wardship of all the heir's lands, irrespective of the rights of any other lord.

Because wardship was so important to royal revenues, the medieval kings appointed officials known as escheators to oversee the administration of wardships, and in 1540 Henry VIII set up the Court of Wards to deal with the collection of his revenue from wardship (see under **sue his livery**). The court oversaw the administration of the estates of wards and of lunatics in royal custody, and additionally could grant licence to a royal widow to remarry.

By the second half of the sixteenth century wardship was regarded as an anachronistic feudal relic. The Court of Wards became increasingly unpopular with landowners, whose representatives in the House of Commons objected strenuously to bills introduced by Burghly, Master of the Wards, to end evasions which depleted the Queen's revenues. In 1598 a proposal was made in the Commons that the Court be abolished in return for an annual payment to the crown, but nothing resulted from the plan. Then in 1603 James I's ministers themselves raised proposals to end wardship. Various alternate schemes to raise royal revenues were set out, such as the sale of freeholds to all royal copyholders and the payment of a fee to end feudal duties of homage. Again opponents of the Court of Wards proposed adding to the list the abolition of the Court of Wards in return for an annual payment to the crown. These plans too failed. Another proposal discussed at the time allowed for every landowner to draw up a **will** arranging on his death for a fee to be paid exempting his child from wardship. A Commons committee was set up to draw up a petition, and counter-petitions circulated pointing out the considerable sum of money needed in compensation if wardship were to be abolished. In the end all plans to abolish wardship failed in the face of strong opposition from officials of the Court of Wards, from the Lords, and because of royal needs to raise revenues from fiscal feudalism.

Eventually the prerogative Court of Wards and Liveries was abolished in the Civil War.

(B) Recalling the interval since their last dancing times, old Capulet's cousin reckons 'thirty years' but Capulet says he remembers 'the nuptial of Lucentio', only 'Some five-and-twenty years' past. The cousin replies that the son of that marriage is now thirty years old, but Capulet demurs 'Will you tell me that? / His son was but a ward two years ago' (ROM 1.5.39–40). The implications are that the date of Lucentio's death has moved hazily forward by at least ten years in the old man's recollection, and his past pleasures loom closer to the present than the calendar actually warrants (just as they do for Shallow and Silence in 2H4 – see under **Inns of Court**).

Crucial to AWW is the wardship of Bertram, for this determines the King's power to demand his **marriage** to Helena. The play opens with:

COUNTESS In delivering my son from me I bury a second husband.
BERTRAM And I in going, madam, weep o'er my father's death anew; but I must attend his majesty's command, to whom I am now in ward, evermore in subjection.
LAFEU You shall find of the King a husband, madam; you, sir, a father. He that so generally is at all times good must of necessity hold his virtue to you, whose worthiness would stir it up where it wanted rather than lack it where there is such abundance.

(AWW 1.1.1–10)

Does rewarding penniless Helena for her virtue rather than her birth, in effect giving up the money he could receive on Bertram's marriage

405

but not the power he has over Bertram, make the King a good father to him?

There is a question over Helena's status, and the consequent possibility that the King is illicitly 'disparaging' his ward Bertram by demanding that he marry her. This may be complicated because a king could ennoble a commoner; Ranald, 1979, p 80, asserts that 'the King outwits [Bertram] by granting Helena a title of nobility'. Yet, after the King shows his fury at Bertram's refusal to marry (the vindictive anger of thwarted authority?), Bertram submits with:

> Pardon, my gracious lord, for I submit
> My fancy to your eyes. When I consider
> What great creation and what dole of honour
> Flies where you bid it, I find that she, which late
> Was in my nobler thoughts most base, is now
> The praised of the King; who, so ennobled,
> Is as 'twere born so.
>
> (AWW 2.3.168–74)

The phrase 'as 'twere' suggests Helena is not actually ennobled for services or merit (such ennoblement is treated with rich irony or whimsy in WT 5.2.125–43). In the succeeding lines the King promises Bertram only that he will supply a marriage **portion** for Helena constituting 'A counterpoise, if not to thy estate / A balance more replete' (AWW 2.3.176). Thus it does not seem that he raises Helena to Bertram's full social or economic level (see **dowry**).

From the start then, wardship, including the submission of his 'fancy', is seen by young Count Bertram as potential 'subjection', and when it forces him to marry it becomes a highly emotive issue. Just the naming of the same concept stirs old Gloucester to hot wrath when Edmund alleges 'I have heard [Edgar] oft maintain it to be fit that, sons at perfect age and fathers declined, the father should be as ward to the son, and the son manage his revenue' (LRF 1.2.73–6).

Orlando's bitter complaints in AYL 1.1 about his poor 'breeding' or education at the hands of his elder brother Oliver motivate his removal to the forest of Arden. These complaints recall that the duties of guardians appointed by will were often selfishly stinted. A similarly poor standard of official care is indicated in Parolles' calumny that Dumaine: 'was a botcher's prentice in Paris, from whence he was whipped for getting the sheriff's fool with child – a dumb innocent that could not say him nay' (AWW 4.3.190–3), and in Salibury's inclusion in a list of unholy deeds: 'To reave the orphan of his patrimony' (CYL 5.1.185). Yet in Elizabethan times legal protection was offered to 'idiots and natural fools in royal custody' by the Court of Wards (Jones, W. J., 1967, p 383), and to children generally, and particularly orphans, by Chancery (ibid., p 385). In some urban communities the interests of private wards (not royal ones), and orphans, were supervised by borough courts; the City of London had a specialised Court of Orphans (ibid.).

The orphaned Posthumus Leonatus seems to have been the ward as well as favourite of King Cymbeline (CYM 1.1.28–50); perhaps his clandestine marriage '**contract**' to Imogen (discussed under **divorce**) outrages the King for reasons of violations of wardship as well as of a king's and a father's presumed prerogatives.

(C) For an account of wardship as a feudal incident see Simpson, 1986, p 18–19 and Holdsworth, 1903, vol 3, pp 61–5. On wardship contemporary with Shakespeare see especially Hurstfield, 1958 and Croft, 1983. See also Bean, 1968, pp 9–11, 14–20.

On the Court of Wards see Bell, 1953, and on the its increased revenues in the Jacobean period pp 46–66. On the Elizabethan Court of Wards and the City of London's Court of Orphans, see Jones, W. J., 1967, pp 383–9.

Swinburne, 1590, leaves 98–9, gives a harrowing account of the hardships of some wards, especially those married forcibly by greedy 'gardiens' in such a way that 'thou couldest wishe him no greater torment . . . hell excepted'.

Campbell, J., 1859, p 58n, points out that since Helena was not of noble birth Bertram in AWW probably could have refused to marry her, or pay any compensation, despite the powers of wardship. For comment on disparaging an heir by arranging a marriage with with someone of inferior status see Bean, 1968, p 13.

Ranald, 1963 discusses the betrothal of the King's ward in AWW. This essay suggests that a *de praesenti* **spousal** required consummation to make a **marriage** (this seems mistaken, see under **pre-contract**). The same position recurs in Ranald, 1987, pp 33–49, especially pp 37, 38, 43. Ranald, 1979 discusses disparagement in AWW.

Clarkson and Warren, 1942, pp 26–31, discuss wardship in relation to Elizabethan drama.

waste (A) The legal action of 'waste' prohibits a limited owner of an estate in land (for instance, one with a life interest) from causing damage which would affect those interested in **remainder** or **reversion** (see under **land** and **entails** for explanation of these terms). So a life tenant, or a **widow** entitled to her deceased husband's lands in **dower**, or a widower entitled to his deceased wife's land in 'curtesty', were liable for waste. Another example of 'waste' was the prohibition on lords committing waste of the lands they held when the tenant was a **ward**. Here the lord was entitled to the income of the land during the infancy of the ward, but prohibited by Magna Carta from committing waste which would destroy the value of the land.

By the Statute of Gloucester 1278, tenants for life were made liable for waste in terms of treble damages and loss of the estate. The notion of damage and depredation of land could extend to the people living on the land, so the Statute of Marlborough 1276 listed 'exile of men' as a form of waste. This meant treating **villeins** (unfree tenants) on the land so badly that they ran away (Baker, 1990b, p 534n). This Statute also mentions as 'permissive waste' the 'sale or exile' of house, woods or anything else belonging to the tenement. Permissive waste also includes failing to keep in repair. Other forms of waste are 'ameliorating waste' where the limited owner has improved the land but altered its nature, and 'voluntary waste', where the limited owner actively damages the property, for example by cutting down and selling trees.

In Shakespeare's time Chancery occasionally intervened to consider 'equitable waste' (*Brown v Lord Bridges* (1589) Tothill 51), which went further than voluntary waste and meant 'wantonly' damaging the land.

(B) The legal meaning (OED noun II.7) of this common Shakespearian word is only one of many (there are 38 OED sub-headings for the noun, verb and adjective 'waste').

The legal meaning's one indubitable appearance in Shakespeare is in WIV 4.2.195–8, where Mistress Page says of Falstaff: 'The spirit of wantonness is sure scared out of him. If the devil have him not in fee-simple, with fine and recovery, he will never, I think, in the way of waste attempt us again' (see under **fee-simple** on the context). Here multiple legal jokes culminate with an allusion to 'wanton' (equitable) waste, also combining a jest on absurdly offered 'wantonness' with a characteristic punning reference to Falstaff's 'waist' or girth.

Indeed 'waste' may have a treble import at WIV 1.3.36–9, in

Falstaff's: 'No quips now, Pistol. Indeed, I am in the waist two yards about. But I am now about no waste; I am about thrift. Briefly, I do mean to make love to Ford's wife'. For Falstaff, while referring to his own girth, also suggests he intends to lay waste Ford's estate, his money (so he says 'I am about thrift'), and that he intends as well as to ransack Ford's wife's body or waist, thus intending wantoness. There therefore may be an allusion to 'wanton waste'.

To 'waste' or 'make waste' may possibly take on **land** law connotations in:

BENVOLIO   Then she hath sworn that she will still live chaste?
ROMEO   She hath, and in that sparing makes huge waste
                                    (ROM 1.1.214–15)

or, more likely, in,

> you do me now more wrong
> In making question of my uttermost
> Than if you had made waste of all I have.
>   (MV 1.1.155–7)

In a context concerning uses of land, the dying John of Gaunt warns Richard II that *he* has become moribund, by allowing 'thy land', by which Gaunt means the realm, to be equivalent in extent to 'the waste':

> Thy deathbed is no lesser than thy land,
> Wherein thou liest in reputation sick;
> And thou, too careless patient as thou art,
> Committ'st thy anointed body to the cure
> Of those physicians that first wounded thee.
> A thousand flatterers sit within thy crown,
> Whose compass is no bigger than thy head,
> And yet, encaged in so small a verge,
> The waste is no whit lesser than thy land.
>   (R2 2.1.95–103)

See under **lease** for another land law allusion in this same passage. Yet more important than a possible allusion to land law 'waste' here is the alternate meaning of 'waste' as wastefulness; in that sense 'waste' is a repeated key-word of the play.

(C) See under **land** and **felony**, and on R2 2.1.103 Bolton, 1988, and Gohn, 1982, p 957n.

widow See under **dowager/widow** on the social and legal position of widows. Briefly, after 1536 the inheritance rights of a widow may have been either to **dower** or to a **jointure**.

When her husband died, the legal limitations on a *feme covert* ended (on these see under **marriage**). If he had committed **felony** or **treason**, or had abjured the realm (see under **sanctuary**), the same was true, but special conditions applied as described in those entries.

Until 1547 a widower who remarried or a man who married a widow was not allowed to claim benefit of clergy (see under **branded**).

Shakespeare used 'to widow' not only, as we do currently, to mean to deprive of a husband, as in COR 5.6.152. In ANT 1.2.23 it means to become the widow of someone, and in MM 5.1.421 it means to grant a widow rights to her late husband's property: 'We do enstate and widow you'.

will/testament (A) The law of wills, together with the law of intestate **inheritance**, forms the law of succession. The term 'will', properly used, refers to the devise (leaving) of real property, or **land**, while **testament** refers to the bequest of **chattels**. However, Shakespeare and contemporary playwrights frequently used the terms 'will', 'testament' and 'bequeath' without much care (for examples of Shakespearian distinctions or conflation of the terms see **testament**).

The legalities of both wills and testaments will be treated here, and to avoid confusions concerning Shakespearian texts we will use 'will' as the comprehensive term, except where particular aspects of testaments are in question.

Provided the testator was sound in mind, a valid will could be made orally or in writing (writing was required for wills of land after 1540). There was no requirement for a will to be written or signed by the testator in person, although in practice testators did sometimes sign, mark or seal their wills. Wills were drafted by local literate people,

410

notaries, or often the local priest. An oral, or nuncupative, will could be made by someone very ill; although not in writing it still had to specify **executors**. Because a nuncupative will could be made in a last illness, by Shakespeare's time superstitious people associated wills with imminent death.

Once the will was executed, any land devised was ascertained from the date of the will, and not the date of death. The 'ambulatory will', which spoke from the date of death, was not available for land until 1837, although after-acquired personal property could be bequeathed in early modern England. As today, a will once executed could still be revoked any time up to the date of death, so explaining the descriptions 'last will and testament'.

Gifts in wills were often expressed to be conditional in seventeenth century England, particularly gifts to wives which were conditional on their remaining unmarried. The church had always supported freedom to marry for **widows**, and so opposed restrictions, which nevertheless remained valid in law. But a condition preventing marriage at all would have been void in both Church courts and common law courts.

The law relating to wills has been said to be 'intimately concerned . . . with the law of property' (Jones, W. J., 1967, p 402, n. 2), but there was also a spiritual dimension to final giving. The church's involvement stemmed from the religious importance attached to the gifts of alms made by the dying. When secular and religious legal causes were separated after the Norman Conquest, the Church courts obtained **jurisdiction** over wills, and this remained unchanged by the English Reformation. Therefore wills in Shakespeare's England were governed by the church law common to Christendom; this was developed by medieval canon lawyers who adapted procedure and substance from Roman law.

However the English Church courts had no jurisdiction over any questions concerning real property, including devise of land. In fact it had not been possible to devise land at all by will in common law in early medieval England, with limited exceptions (for example in some boroughs, under burgage tenure). Probably this rule existed initially to prevent the **disinheritance** of the future **heir**, and to prevent evasion of feudal dues (on these see **land**). Simpson, 1986, p 139, suggests that to have allowed devise by will would have interfered with the feudal framework of relations within the family (see **primogeniture**) and between lord and vassal.

411

Another technical problem preventing devise of land by will was caused by the need to transfer land by 'livery of seisin' (see **land**). This was originally a public ceremony with a symbolic transfer of the land, which obviously could not take place after the death of the tenant.

Before 1536, **conveyancers** made arrangements so that the **use** would circumvent the restriction on devising land by will. It was arranged that land was conveyed to feoffees in use for the benefit of the tenant, and after the tenant's death the feoffees would pass it to the heir, so there was no need for livery of seisin. Such a scheme was impeded after *Lord Dacre of the South's Case* 1535 (B. and M. 105), which held that 'uses of wills' were not valid. In the following year the Statute of Uses 'executed' most uses (see under **use**), completely ending the employment of uses as a method of devising land. However by 1540 a compromise was reached between Henry VIII and parliament, which led to the Statute of Wills. This allowed the devise of all lands held in socage tenure and two thirds of that held in knight service (on **tenures** see **land**). So, by Shakespeare's time, devises of land by will were possible at common law. Many wills of land of the period are extant, including Shakespeare's.

The Statute of Wills required all wills of land to be in writing, but the Act made no provision for the Church courts to require probate for such wills as they did for wills of chattels. The Court of Chancery had a general jurisdiction over wills from the late fourteenth century, because it heard **bills** of complaint about contested legacies, and claimed a jurisdiction over executors. However the circumstances which would cause Chancery to intervene and hear a complaint were not settled.

Writs of prohibition were used by common law courts against Church courts which exceeded their jurisdiction. But the number of such writs against Church courts for dealing with wills of land was not as great as might be expected.

The bequest of chattels by testament, which had always been allowed at common law, was administered by the Church courts. These recognized the custom which allowed a testator freedom to dispose as he wished of one-third of his property (the remaining two-thirds was reserved for the use of his wife and children). The children's customary right to one-third of a parent's property was developed from Roman law, and was known as a *legitim*. The *legitim* was in decline in Shakespeare's time, when in general a will could override any customary division of movables between family members (but in some parts of

England free testation was not possible until 1724). The decline of the customary division has sometimes been explained as the consequence of the growth of testamentary freedom in the late middle ages and early modern England provided by the possibility of barring **entails**, and the popularity of the use. However Helmholz, 1987h, claims that the non-enforcement of the *legitim* in English Church courts even before the Reformation shows that the English church did not treat all Papal decrees as binding law; local Church courts were allowed considerable latitude in applying or modifying the custom, and freedom of testation was not entirely a post medieval phenomenon in England.

The canon lawyers were less interested in the will as a means of appointing an heir (which was the main purpose of the Roman testament), and more interested in it as the vehicle for gifts of alms, beneficial to the immortal soul. Such gifts included what are now recognized as charitable purposes, such as funding of hospitals or care of the poor or sick (see **poverty**), or building bridges and roads. But the common law had long sought to limit gifts of alms. Gifts of land to religious houses were prohibited by the Mortmain statutes from 1279, and after the Reformation the bequest of money for the saying of masses for the deceased's soul was prohibited because it was said to be for a superstitious purpose. The Charitable Uses Act 1601 was passed to distinguish pious from superstitious giving. Indeed the (repealed) preamble of this Act remains the only statutory definition of 'charity' in England.

Because the church recognised the religious motive for making a will, it upheld rights to make a testamentary bequest for those who were denied such rights at common law. So the church encouraged and administered the wills of **married** women and **villeins**. But Helmholz, 1993, p 175, claims that by 1450 married women's wills become rare.

(B) Ubiquitous concern with inheritance in his age is reflected in very frequent figurative as well as literal uses of the language of testation and/or descent in virtually all of Shakespeare's poetry and plays. Such reference is so wide that it is possible to discuss only a few particularly arresting instances.

In one King Richard II laments his pitiful state:

> Of comfort no man speak.

413

> Let's talk of graves, of worms and epitaphs,
> Make dust our paper, and with rainy eyes
> Write sorrow on the bosom of the earth.
> Let's choose executors and talk of wills –
> And yet not so, for what can we bequeath
> Save our deposed bodies to the ground?
> Our lands, our lives, and all are Bolingbroke's;
> And nothing can we call our own but death,
> And that small model of the barren earth
> Which serves as paste and cover to our bones.
>
> (R2 3.2.140–50)

The self-pathos mounting here toward its climax in the figuring of human flesh as a 'small model' of the 'barren earth' may include an implication that only a dead body, not great lands, are left to Richard to bequeath by will.

Portia's father's conditional will, making her 'a lady richly left' (MV 1.1.161), yet requiring obedience to the casket test, premises the Belmont plot of MV. The restriction it places on her marriage choices causes her to cry out at any thought of 'the word 'choose'!'. She explains:

> I may neither choose who I would nor refuse who I dislike; so is the will of a living daughter curbed by the will of a dead father. Is it not hard, Nerissa, that I cannot choose one nor refuse none?
>
> (MV 1.2.22–6).

Moreover the will places a restriction on any of her suitors, that if unsuccessful they must 'Never to speak to lady afterward/ In way of marriage' (MV 2.1.41–2). Both these provisions restricting rights to marry would have been legally unenforcable (although conditional wills requiring particular marriages might have been upheld – see Clarkson and Warren, 1942, pp 277–80).

The complication that Portia's father's crucial will is legally void may have been presented deliberately, rather than on account of indifference to or ignorance of legality (Clarkson and Warren, 1942, p 278, makes a rather typical comment that Shakespeare 'was not at all interested' in the validity of this will). The recognition of a deformity in the will may add to an uncomfortable sense that the fantastic Belmont of

414

Shakespeare's fabululation is not quite a place apart from worldly cares. It is rather a dangerous as well as a mythic place, actually outdoing mercantile Venice in manipulative legalisms.

The trial concerning a will conducted by Shakespeare's King John bears an interesting degree of legal and historical accuracy. His father's deathbed will described by Robert Faulconbridge, a second son, attempts to **disinherit** the supposedly illegitimate elder son Philip Faulconbridge. So Robert, claiming the estate as the actual elder son, says of his father:

> Upon his deathbed he by will bequeathed
> His lands to me, and took it on his death
> That this my mother's son was none of his;
> And if he were, he came into the world
> Full fourteen weeks before the course of time.
> Then, good my liege, let me have what is mine,
> My father's land, as was my father's will.
>   (JN 1.1.109–15)

Leaving for a discussion under **bastard** the question raised by this passage of the legitimacy of the child of the wife of a married man, we may consider if making such a will was valid in a historical context before the 1540 Statute of Wills. Before then a simple devise of lands by will was nearly impossible, while the customary rule of **primogeniture** prevented the disinheritance of an elder son of family lands. Yet, just before hearing as a judge the Faulconbridge family quarrel, Shakespeare's King John is revealed to have unjustly seized by force the crown from his nephew Arthur Plantagenet, the rightful child heir by the canon of descent (JN 1.1.40–3). In fact the play's implicit evaluation of these circumstances differs from the chronicles (and the issue of the succession of the throne was questionable in general – see under **election**). Thanks to Shakespeare's scenic structuring, it is made ironic that John himself, judging as King in council, endorses the canon of descent in telling the claimant Robert that the elder brother Philip must inherit: 'Your father's heir must have your father's land' (JN 1.1.129). Here Shakespeare portrays an historically legally correct judgment in a wry dramatic context.

Shakespeare was often anachronistic in inserting Elizabethan legal concerns into narratives of diverse times and places (even the classical

415

will / testament

world). This tendency may be seen in a long-noted seeming analogy between the main plot of *King Lear*, set in ancient Briton, and an Elizabethan legal conflict concerning the will of the Kentish landowner Brian Annesley, who like Lear suffered a mental breakdown, and had no living son for heir. Annesley's will favoured the youngest of his three daughters, who nursed him, who was named Cordell or Cordelia. Wilson, R., 1993, pp 215–29, suggests this analogy is connected with how Tudor 'unfettered testation' following the Statute of Wills, 1540, overcame traditional Kentish 'gavelkind'. However, on intestacy where there were no living sons, neither gavelkind nor **primogeniture** were in issue; traditionally co-parceny applied among daughters generally in England, not only, or particularly, in Kent (see under **co-heir**). The customs of Kent were the same as elsewhere in England when several daughters inherited (as in Annesley's case; however, co-parceny would not apply in a royal succession). Wilson further suggests that Lear's actions in dividing the kingdom signal a transition 'into the capitalist land market'; whether or not they do this, they do not resemble a 'nuncupative (or oral) testament', even, as claimed, 'technically' (ibid., p 233).

The practice of making a deathbed will is reflected in Nerissa's reassurance to Portia: 'Your father was ever virtuous, and holy men at their death have good inspirations' (MV 1.2.27–8). It reflects also in the foolish Slender's response to Anne Page's polite 'What is your will?'. He says in reply, 'My will? 'Od's heartlings, that's a pretty jest indeed! I ne'er made my will yet, I thank God; I am not such a sickly creature' (WIV 3.4.54–7). The same notion appears in the Painter's cynical remarks in TIM 5.1.26–9: 'To promise is most courtly and fashionable. Performance is a kind of will or testament which argues a great sickness in his judgement that makes it' (similar instances in ROM 1.1.199–200 and PER S.1.90–8 are noted in Clarkson and Warren, 1942, p 236).

(C) For a general introduction to the problems of devising land at common law see Baker, 1990b, pp 284–5, 288, 290–1.

For a discussion of the role of Chancery in supervising the administration of estates see Jones, W. J., 1967, pp 400–17.

On wills see also: Plucknett, 1956, pp 616–17, 735–46; Holdsworth vol 3, pp 556–7; Pollock and Maitland vol 2, p 333; Houlbrooke, 1979, pp 89–116; Helmholz, 1979; Helmholz, 1987h; Helmholz, 1987f; Helmholz, 1990, pp 79–89; Helmholz, 1993; Sheehan, 1996, pp 3–7, 199–210, 311–23.

416

Wills in Elizabethan drama are treated in Clarkson and Warren, 1942, pp 231–84. Shakespearian contexts reflecting the language of testaments or wills are noted in Rushton, 1869. Shakespeare's varied presentations of deathbed declarations are very interestingly treated in Frazier, 1985.

wise woman/wise man (A) During Shakespeare's time there was a widespread and generally tolerated English folk reliance on beneficent village 'cunning folk', also called 'wise men or 'wise women'. They were often employed to find lost things, cure the physically ill or mentally distressed, or to deliver children safely. But, although 'generally speaking, the cunning folk and maleficent witches were believed to be two separate species their categories did sometimes overlap, and there are many recorded examples of village wizards and charmers who found themselves accused of maleficent witchcraft' (Thomas, K., 1978, p 520; see also **witch**).

Some contemporary English writers identified all cunning folk, whether healers, finders of lost objects, midwives, etc., as 'White Witches' and condemned their powers as coming from 'sathan' (Pocton, 17c). The resulting ambiguous standing of beneficent wise or cunning folk penetrated into English ecclesiastical and civil legislation, so that:

> In 1571 Bishop Sandys asked for the presentment [at the ecclesiastical courts] of 'any that useth sorcery, witchcraft, enchantments, incantations, charms, unlawful prayers, or invocations in Latin'. This was repeated, word for word, in 1577 and 1586, with the addition of 'and namely midwyves in the time of womens travayle of childe. And whether any do resort to any such for helpe or cousayle, and what be their names.' Such wording suggests that the authorities were especially interested in white witchcraft.
>
> (Macfarlane, 1970b, p 67)

It has been noted that the civil Witchcraft Statutes also:

> distinguished between different ends. The punishments for attempting to find lost goods, for instance, were different from those for trying to kill someone by witchcraft. Yet the Statutes, by including both offences, blurred the differences.
>
> (ibid., pp 311–12)

417

Thus Alan Macfarlane holds that underlying the apparent 'immense confusion' within which 'opinions of witchcraft changed between 1560 and 1680 [and] attitudes differed between social and religious groups' probably lay a 'constant struggle' between those who would allow white witchcraft to be separate from black and those who would not,

> between those who wished to differentiate and those who wished to amalgamate. On the one hand, there were those who wished to punish equally all who used 'magical' power, irrespective of their ends . . . . For them all 'superstition', especially that emanating from Rome, was 'witchcraft' [e. g. William Perkins, *A Discourse of the Damned Art of Witchcraft*, 1608] . . . . On the other hand, there were those who wished to differentiate 'good' and 'bad' witches by their effects, and 'witches' and 'conjurers' by their degree of control over their power
>
> (ibid., pp 310–12)

Confusion over such distinctions were rife. Reginald Scot, who had witnessed false accusations of witches, claimed in 1584 that the 'vulgar people' did not distinguish between different types of witchcraft. But in the seventeenth century just such a popular tendency to distinguish between the acceptable white and the diabolical black witch infuriated commentators like John Gaule, who wrote that:

> according to the vulgar conceit, distinction is usually made betwixt the White and Blacke Witch: the Good and the Bad Witch. The Bad Witch, they are wont to call him or her, that works Malefice or Mischiefe to the Bodies of Men or Beasts: the good Witch they count him or her that helps to reveale, prevent or remove the same.
>
> (quoted ibid.)

It may be that professional jealousy inspired Edward Pocton of Petworth, a seventeenth century physician, to decry with vehemence

> it is not to be held a thing to be either new or strange, that white witches shoulde finde so many friends and favourers (as now the doe) in this last corrupt age of the world, in the which moste men minde earthly thinges (f162v) . . . the white witches they are admired, applauded, yea well nigh adored (by some of the sottish sorte). And by to many, countenanced, pleaded for and protected (f163r) . . . .

418

The common people do much respect white witches and are ready to make apologies for them.

(Pocton, 17c, f166r).

So great is the difficulty of distinguishing varieties of English witch-craft that a complex grid of categories is developed by Alan Macfarlane as a necessary preliminary to his analysis of actual witch trials in seven-teenth century Essex (Macfarlane, 1970b, pp 3–4).

(B) The complicated issue of moderate and zealot views of white ver-sus black witchcraft touches on the Renaissance topic of belief or otherwise in acceptable kinds of magic.

In some places Shakespeare treats belief in cunning folk farcically. Doctor Pinch, a local amateur, is employed as a 'conjurer' to treat 'possession' in ERR 4.4.41–131. The Folio stage direction identifies Pinch as 'a Schoolemaster' (tln 1321–2), and he might therefore might know some Latin, but he is heard attempting exorcism only in English (4.4.55–8). Pinch receives first a box on the ear, and then sees that his two victims are 'bound and laid in some dark room' (4.4.95). We later hear that his patients have chewed through their bonds, his 'beard they have singed off with brands of fire':

> And ever as it blazed they threw on him
> Great pails of puddled mire to quench the hair.
> My master preaches patience to him, and the while
> His man with scissors nicks him like a fool;
> And sure – unless you send some present help –
> Between them they will kill the conjurer.
>
> (5.1.172–8)

The gulling of Malvolio also involves dark imprisonment as a 'cure' for mental distraction; the conspirator Maria exclaims with mock-concern: 'Pray God he be not bewitched'. As cunning persons were supposed to be able to cure bewitching, the accomplice Fabian adds: 'Carry his water to th' wise woman' (TN 3.4.100 and 3.4.101).

With a similarity of farcical treatment, but also implying a deeper ambiguity, WIV reflects an uneasiness concerning the renown of a 'wise woman'. Contrasting views are illustrated in the difference between Frank Ford who 'cannot abide the old woman of Brentford' because 'he

419

swears she's a witch' (WIV 4.2.77–8), and his wife who blandly presents her as a legitimate visitor, 'my maid's Aunt of Brentford' (WIV 4.2.157). Moreover, a sense of transgression as well as ridiculousness informs the would-be seducer Falstaff's forced sudden camouflaging as this fat old woman. Farcical absurdity is emphasized when parson Evans remarks: 'I think the 'oman is a witch indeed. I like not when a 'oman has a great peard' (4.2.179–80). Yet, despite the comedy, Falstaff's unlawful cross-dressing and trespassing of gender boundaries draws to itself retribution (as does Viola/Cesario's cross-dressing in TN, which forces her to contemplate a duel). Thus Falstaff's preposterous pretence incites Ford's spluttering misogynistic fury against the 'old woman':

> A witch, a quean, an old, cozening quean! Have I not forbid her my house? She comes of errands, does she? We are simple men; we do not know what's brought to pass under the profession of fortune-telling. She works by charms, by spells, by th' figure, and such daubery as this is, beyond our element. We know nothing. – Come down, you witch, you hag, you! Come down, I say!
>
> (WIV 4.2.158–65)

And, defenceless, Falstaff is beaten.

Yet attitudes clearly vary, for slightly later the albeit witless Slender sends for the 'wise woman of Brentford' to help him locate a lost chain and to predict his marital fortune (4.5.24–50). These benign activities, typical of a popularly tolerated cunning woman, are confronted with another view again, however, when Falstaff admits that when dressed as the 'fat woman of Brentford' he was not only beaten 'into all the colours of the rainbow' but also nearly 'set . . . 'i' th' stocks, i' th' common stocks, for a witch' (4.5.107–13) by a local **constable**.

There is no levity in the portrayals of benign and charitable Cermion of CYM, or of the magus Prospero in TMP, when they use near or actual magical means to redeem lives. Yet there may be considerable ambiguity concerning Prospero's entire benignity (Sokol, 1993, 1994b), and there certainly is ambiguity concerning the bawd, midwife, necro-mancer and witch images frequently environing Paulina of WT (Sokol, 1994a, pp 150–66).

(C) See **witch**: the English witchcraft statutes, and some discussion, are conveniently gathered in Rosen, 1969.

The classic studies Macfarlane, 1970b and Thomas, K., 1978 are very helpful about ambiguous attitudes to wise men or women.

A treatise in ms. at the British Library, (Pocton, 17c) is outraged by white witches. The competition between physicians (like Pocton) and itinerant healers is discussed in Beier, 1985, pp 99–102. Ibid., pp 103–4, points out that some white magicians were itinerant; however most cunning folk were locals.

witch/witchcraft (A) In both statutory provisions and judicial practice the persecution of witches in England during Shakespeare's lifetime was much milder than in many other parts of contemporary Europe. The 1604 Act of Parliament against witchcraft, 1 Jac. I, c.12, replaced 5 Eliz., c.16, and stood until repealed in 1736. Although this act was more severe than the earlier statutes of 1542 and 1563, its severity still fell far short of many early modern continental laws.

The 1604 Act divided witchcraft offences into two categories. The more serious offences, which included conjurations of evil spirits, grave-robbing and causing death or physical harm to people by sorcery, were classified as **felonies**, punishable by death. The grave-robbing offence had not appeared in earlier Acts. Not only the witch, but also his or her 'Ayders, Abettors and Councellors' were to be treated as felons. Wherever the death penalty was imposed by the 1604 Act it was to be carried out by hanging, not by burning, unless treason had also been committed. Neither male nor female witches were burnt in Shakespeare's England, although this remained the fate for female witches convicted of being traitors to the sovereign. In theory married women traitorous to their 'sovereign' husbands, could also be burnt (see **treason**).

The lesser witchcraft offences, which included provoking 'unlawful love' and destroying cattle and goods, were punished with one year's imprisonment and a public pillory to last six hours every quarter in a market square or fair, accompanied by open confession of the offence. Imprisonment, however, was often fatal due to unhealthful conditions. Those convicted a second time of a lesser witchcraft offence were to suffer 'Pains of Death as a Felon or Felons'.

Witchcraft was tried as a felony at the twice-yearly assize by visiting **justices** and the trial **jury**. The accused person could also be brought before the **Justice of the Peace** at the Quarter Sessions (although it was customary to reserve felonies to the assize judges), or before the

421

Bishop's Consistory Court. In the Consistory Court a successful prosecution for witchcraft by a churchwarden would require the convicted witch to do penance, usually in church in a white sheet, but the Court could also demand the payment of a fine, or, for a severe offence, excommunicate the witch.

Actual prosecutions for witchcraft in English courts in Shakespeare's time were relatively infrequent, and there was a high rate of acquittal. 'Confessions' were not extracted by torture (although they were in Scotland). There was a brief spate of increased prosecutions in England in the 1640s, but there was never a great witch-hunt like those in early modern Germany, France, or Italy. Possibly this was because the English statutes of 1542 and 1604 both specifically disallowed forfeiture of the property of executed witches, so eliminating the economic motive of some professional witch-hunters as seen on the continent; the death sentence in most cases included a proviso: 'saving to the Wife of such Person as shall offend in any Thing contrary to this Act her Title of Dower; and also the Heir and Sucessor of such Person, his or their titles of Inheritance, Sucession or other Rights as though no such Attainder of the Ancestor or Predecessor had been made'.

In Shakespeare's era the opinions of the educated probably divided as to whether the diabolical phenomena of witchcraft were even plausible. Explicit expressions of doubt were very rare however, for these could have attracted the label 'Sadducee' to anyone suggesting an heretical disbelief in the spirit world. Nearly all early modern English witchcraft prosecutions abstained from allegations of diabolical compacts or of gatherings for sacrilegious purposes. By contrast, in contemporary Scotland, France and Germany, heretical compacts with the devil, gathering for sabbaths, membership in covens, and similar notions of heretical diabolism were regarded as the defining aspects of witchcraft. In particular, accusations of witches flying over long distances to join in obscene sacrilegious ceremonies, crucial in prosecutions during the early modern European 'great witch hunt', were virtually unheard of in England (this topic is pursued in Cohn, 1975, which finds, p 111, only a single 1664 Somerset case). It is also significant that the *Malleus Maleficarum*, the standard text on diabolical practices, was 'slow to impinge upon England . . . the total absence of an English edition is striking by the side of the thirteen editions on the Continent by 1520' (Thomas, K., 1978, pp 522–3).

Analysis of the legal records of English witchcraft accusations indicate that they usually concerned (often longstanding) disputes between near neighbours in which only *maleficium* was alleged, that is that adults, children, domestic animals or material goods had been harmed by supernatural means. Sometimes sexual function was also alleged to have been affected by bewitching. It has been argued that the English witch's motive for harm was typically a desire to exact revenge on those who had earlier refused his or her request for help or charity. (This model, proposed in Thomas, K., 1978, is supported in detail in relation to Essex in Macfarlane, 1970b, and has since been repeatedly applied and often confirmed.) Hence the poor and elderly were frequently the accused.

The probable reasons for differences between English and continental treatment of witchcraft are multiple and complex. For example, the King's courts may have reacted against a religio-political situation in which both Roman Catholic and extreme Protestant rivals of the Established Church promoted belief in diabolical phenomena (and in their own unique powers of exorcism). Although in his 1597 book *Daemonologie* King James condemned all forms of magic, he apparently changed his views after he arrived on the English throne in 1603. He turned from a fascination with Scottish witches to the pursuit of English witchcraft impostors and false accusers. For instance, in *Daemonologie* (James the First, 1924, pp xi-xii), James contradicted the bold witchcraft sceptics Johannes Weyer and Reginald Scot, and argued firmly that melancholy delusions could not explain witch phenomena. Yet, it has been persuasively argued that, following the 1602 Mary Glover witchcraft case in London, James approved (or even inspired) Edward Jordan's thesis that possession by witchcraft could be a medically explainable mental delusion (Macdonald, 1991, pp xlvii-liv).

Another likely reason for the moderate legal treatment of witchcraft in Shakespeare's England was the prevalence in towns and villages of very often positively valued individuals known as 'cunning folk', or 'wise' men or women. Widespread approval of their useful benignity existed, although there were also some who ridiculed, or even violently opposed, the activities of these demi-magicians or 'white' witches (see **wise woman**).

Finally, when reading Shakespeare, we should recognize that witchcraft was no doubt remembered in his time as the religious offence of **heresy** which had often been punished by public burning at the stake until recent times. Elizabethans would also have known that witchcraft was still widely attended by torture and burning in other parts of Europe.

423

(B) The words 'witch' or 'witchcraft' appear in more than half of Shakespeare's plays, with derivatives such as 'bewitched' appearing in several more. They appear most often in relation to accusations of illicit means used for persuasion or allurement. These uses may be in accord with provisions of the 1603 statute, but the terms 'witchcraft' or 'bewitching' are also often used figuratively apropos persons who are irresistibly compelling or attractive, as in, 'for beauty is a witch / Against whose charms faith melteth into blood' (ADO 2.1.169–70).

By Shakespeare's time some brave writers had openly expressed a dangerous dubiety concerning the validity and/or honesty of witch-craft accusations (see Scot, 1973; West, R. H., 1984; Macdonald, 1991; Weyer, 1991). Perhaps in accord with scepticism, in ERR bizarre events having actual natural causes that produce stark bewilderment are repeatedly attributed to witches, Lapland sorcerers, sprites, goblins, Satan, or devils (ERR 1.2.99–100, 2.2.191–5, 3.2.149–52, 3.2.162, 4.3.10–11, 4.3.48–79, 4.4.148–57).

Again suggesting a doubt about the occult, Antipholus of Ephesus becomes wild with frustration when he and his Dromio are turned over to the foolish 'conjurer' Doctor Pinch (ERR 4.4.48–108; see **wise woman**). Pinch's amateur interpretations of man or master housed in by 'Satan' (4.4.55), 'possessed' (4.4.55–8, 93–5), or having 'the fiend strong within him' (4.4.108) wholly lack the logic and insight of Emilia's far-from-occult diagnosis of the real causes of Antipholus' distraction (5.1.44–87).

Moreover, in a number of Shakespearian contexts false witchcraft accusations arise palpably from the deluded wishes or other misguided emotions of accusers, as in MND 1.1.27–45, OTH 1.2.63–75 and 1.3.60–4, PER S.9.49, WT 2.3.67–115 and 4.4.422–4. These accusa-tions are thus given psychologically plausible motives, excluding the supernatural. Yet the exposure of twisted motivations is always unem-phasised, leaving the error of the false accusers implicit; this may sug-gest that Shakespeare exercised some caution to avoid the label 'Sadducee'.

Felonious *maleficium* by witchcraft causing birth defect is feared in ERR 1.2.100, and is maliciously imputed in R3 3.4.59–76. In the latter case the accused, Lord Hastings, is summarily executed because the alleged victim is the Royal Protector, Richard. Involvement with conjur-ing involving royalty may also be judged to be treason, and is the down-fall of ambitious Eleanor Cobham, the Duchess of Gloucester (CYL

2.3.9–13). The female witch employed is sentenced to be burnt, and the witch's male assistants to be strangled (2.3.7–8; in Hall, Shakespeare's source, the men are drawn and quartered), while the Duke of Gloucester is ruined politically (for legal historical details see under **treason**).

Although not a current punishment, the burning of witches was certainly remembered by Shakespeare's audience. The accused medieval witches Joan la Pucelle and Margaret Jourdain are condemned to be burnt in 1H4 and CYL. Bawdry and witchcraft are alleged against Paulina in WT 2.3.68–9, and burning threatened 2.3.114–16 (this threat is explicitly linked by Paulina to a false accusation of heresy). Memories of medieval witch burning also serve metaphors in ROM 1.2.93 and LRF 3.2.84.

Old age and envy are the salient characteristics of Sycorax, the witch mother of Caliban described in TMP 1.2.258–84. Although Sycorax is far more 'potent' than typical English village witches, her malefic rage at being denied her requests or 'hests' aligns her predicament with many of theirs. Prospero, conversely, seems a magus or white witch who is perhaps tempted to necromancy or worse (see **wise woman/wise man**).

Both erotic and necromantic witchcraft are implicit in the statue-animation ruse of WT. At the stratagem's start the perpetrator Paulina warns:

> then you'll think –
> Which I protest against – am assisted
> By wicked powers.
>
> (WT 5.3.89–91)

This reference to the 'learned' continental doctrine of diabolical aid may seem odd in an English play of 1610, although by then continental influence had been absorbed (in part through Marlowe's theatre), and as Christine Larner put it 'popular beliefs became educated' (Larner, 1984, pp 86–7). Although the 1604 Witchcraft Act for the first time outlawed diabolical compacts, there was 'no reference in [an English] trial to an oral compact with the Devil . . . recorded before 1612' and none to a written compact before the 1640s (Thomas, K., 1978, p 528). Likewise, although accusations of witches flying were vanishingly rare in England, even after her apparent necromancy is exposed as theatrical

425

artifice Paulina ominously speaks of witch-like flying, imaging herself as an old lonely creature who will 'wing me to some wither'd bough' (WT 5.3.133–4) (see under **wise woman**).

The most complex Shakespearian passages concerning witches are in MAC. This play's chief source, Holinshed's *Chronicles of Scotland*, does not specify that Macbeth and Banquo come upon ugly old witches, but rather that they encounter dubiously prophetic 'nymphes or feiries'. Shakespeare's substitution of androgynous witches for these, and his deployment in MAC of widely diverse witchcraft conceptions and traditions, reflect a cunning artistic negotiation with contemporary tensions. Historians have shown that witchcraft accusations multiplied in regions and times suffering extreme and seemingly irremediable social disruption (as in Macbeth's Scotland). To represent witchcraft as an expression of a powerful unconscious social dynamic required delicate prudence, and this very likely motivated the self-contradictory presentation of the three wierd sisters in MAC.

These three witches of MAC are first seen meeting on a 'blasted heath', and arranging a next meeting, thereby giving a possible hint of membership in an un-English coven. But this hint is undermined because they are not summoned by Satan or a sub-devil to meet in large numbers, nor in groups of thirteen. Nor do they descend to famous pranks such as kissing diabolical posteriors in a blasphemous parody of church ritual. (These latter antics are described in a sensational 1591 pamphlet, ('Newes from Scotland,' 1924), which concerned a famous Scottish coven that was investigated by King James in connection with an alleged treason). The weird sisters in MAC engage in far more mundane activities, most of which accord with the image described by Barbara Rosen of the witches who, 'in English courts and English superstition . . . turned out to be stubbornly independent and anti-social — one might almost say, irreligious' (Rosen, 1969, p 190). When the three do next meet as planned, in MAC 1.3, they do not caper or blaspheme, but rather converse about their doings like mischievous village gossips, sociably addressing each other as 'sister'. (This term of address *may* imply a zealous association, but perhaps not, for accusations of malefic witchcraft often extended to multiple members of one family.) They compare or plan malefic exploits, such as swine-killing and spell-casting, and harken to pet animals as 'familiars'. These actions accord with the most common accusations made against supposed 'real' English witches. Moreover, the First Witch explicitly states that her motive for *maleficium* is a denial of a request to share chestnuts (MAC 1.3.3–5), just the sort of resentment of a refusal to meet a request often alleged as the witch's motive in many English witchcraft trials.

In these ways, the weird sisters of MAC closely resemble 'actual' English witches of Shakespeare's time. However they do not accord with another typical characteristic wherein early modern English witches were hardly ever strangers, but rather were nearly always well-known long-standing neighbours of less than five miles distance, and were met in familiar places. In these ways 'real' English witches were not like the apparitions that amazed Macbeth and Banquo within Holinshed's 'laund' (forest clearing), or on Shakespeare's 'blasted heath'. In fact the leading expert, Christina Larner, tells us that even in Scotland, where persecutions of diabolical witchcraft were much more frequent and severe than in England, we can 'forget about thundering torrents, impenetrable mists and high mountains . . . the places where the accused [witches] confessed to having met with the Devil were crossroads, barns, mills and churches' (Larner, 1984, p 73.)

Thus the witches of MAC combine some indigenous, some exotic, and some imaginary characteristics Some of these may be hard to distinguish. For instance *Newes from Scotland* relates that following the horrible tortures and mutilations used in the investigation of a Scottish coven, a 'confession' was obtained concerning sailing in a sieve, a feat also vaunted in MAC 1.3.7; however many routine and mundane English witchcraft accusations also mention odd uses of domestic sieves or scissors.

The interpretive problems concerning witchcraft in MAC are exacerbated because the segments containing the highly melodramatic witchcraft activities of a coven led by Hecate are usually judged to be non-Shakespearian interpolations. But even if the potion-brewing, singing, and dancing activities of this coven are excluded from consideration, still the First Witch says she can (in a way characteristic of continental diabolical, but not English witches) traverse great distances magically (MAC 1.3.7). And yet again there seems to be an English-style limitation to *maleficium* of the harm even she can direct toward the master of the Tiger: 'Though his bark cannot be lost, / Yet it shall be tempest-tossed . . . '(1.3.23–4). This still may exceed however a limitation, to psychological influence, of the riddling deceptions subsequently practised by her sisters upon the credulity of Macbeth.

427

Thus, defying the brevity of their stage appearances, the 'weird sisters' of MAC presented themselves as creatures of tremendous ambiguity, combining conflicting features of witch lore found in English, continental, folkloric, 'learned', legal, popular, and possibly even psychopathological understanding.

Shakespeare's plays generally reflect diverse contemporary social, intellectual and legal aspects of witchcraft, as well as prevailing fantasies and myths, and probably some of the subterranean swell of scepticism that by degrees led first to the practical abandonment of, and finally the repeal of, the English witchcraft laws.

(C) Rosen, 1969 collects the statutes and other information on English witchcraft. Keeton, 1930, pp 193–201, contains a somewhat dated survey of witchcraft in Shakespeare's plays.

Sensational early texts such as James the First, 1924, and 'Newes from Scotland,' 1924, often referred to in relation to MAC and other Shakespeare plays, should be viewed in broader legal, political, and social contexts. Studies such as Sharpe, C. K., 1884; West, R. H., 1939; Butler, 1948; Forbes, 1966; Notestein, 1968; Kittridge, 1972, are often helpful, but should be compared with newer works including Macfarlane, 1970b; Larner, 1973, 1984; Cohn, 1975; Kieckhefer, 1976; Thomas, K., 1978; Clark, 1984. Recent illuminating comparative and local studies include: Midlefort, 1972; Henningsen, 1980; Demos, 1982; Kunze, 1982; Ginzburg, 1983; Briggs, 1984; Weisman, 1984; Muchembled, 1985; Quaife, 1987; Tedeschi, 1987; Martin, R., 1989; Burke, 1990; Rowland, 1990; Gregory, 1991; Macdonald, 1991; Sharpe, J. A., 1991, 1992; Swain, 1994.

The many treatments of witchcraft in MAC include Jorgensen, 1971; Clark, 1980; Harris, 1980; Callagan, 1992; Sokol, 1995b.

Witchcraft in WT is treated in Pearson, 1979; Schalkwyk, 1992; Sokol, 1994a. It is considered in relation to the mock- trial in LRF in Gulstad, 1994.

Cheadle, 1994, interprets Othello's trial for witchcraft as subsequent to another effective trial: the insistent questioning of him at Brabantio's house, where he was treated as a 'fascinating prodigy'. Thus 'Such was my process' (OTH 1.3.141) is seen as referring to a quasi-legal 'process' or examination, driven by prejudice against an exotic moor who is only able to gain Desdemona's love by using sorcery.

428

Bibliography: Sources Cited

Adams, J., 'Nullius filius,' *University of Toronto Law Journal* 6 (1946): 361–84.

Ainsworth, Henry, *Counter-Poyson*, Amsterdam, 1608.

Alexander, Peter, 'Measure for Measure: a case for the Scottish Solomon,' *Modern Language Quarterly* 28 (1967): 478–88.

Altman, Joel, *The Tudor Play of Mind*, Berkeley: University of California Press, 1978.

Andrews, Mark Edwin, *Law versus Equity in the Merchant of Venice*, Boulder: University of Colorado Press, 1965.

Archer, Rowena E., 'Rich old ladies: the problem of late medieval dowagers,' *Property and Politics: Essays in Later Medieval English History*, ed. Tony Pollard, Gloucester: Alan Sutton, 1984, 13–31.

Armstrong, Walter P., Jr, 'Shakespeare and the law,' *Tennessee Bar Journal* 27 (1991): 26–31.

Ashe, Thomas, *Epiekeia*, London, 1609.

Bacon, Francis, *Works*, ed. James Spedding, Robert Leslie Ellis and Douglas Denon Heath, London: Longman, 1872.

——, *Essays (1625)*, ed. Michael J. Hawkins, London: J. M. Dent, 1994.

Baker, J. H. 'The common lawyers and the chancery: 1616,' *Irish Jurist* 4 (1969): 368–92.

——, 'The use upon use in equity,' *Law Quarterly Review* 93 (1977): 33–8.

——, ed. *The Reports of Sir John Spellman*, vol 94, London: Selden Society, 1978.

——, *An Introduction to English Legal History*, 2nd edn. London: Butterworths, 1979.

——, *The Order of Serjeants at Law*, London: Selden Society, 1984.

——, 'Law and legal institutions,' *William Shakespeare: His World, His Work, His Influence*, ed. John F. Andrews, New York: Scribner's, 1985, 41–54.

——, 'Counsellors and barristers,' *The Legal Profession and the Common Law*, London: Hambledon, 1986a, 99–124.

——, 'Criminal courts and procedure, 1550–1800,' *The Legal Profession and the Common Law*, London: Hambledon, 1986b, 259–301.

——, 'The dark age of English legal history, 1500–1700,' *The Legal Profession and the Common Law*, London: Hambledon, 1986c, 435–60.

——, 'English law and the Renaissance,' *The Legal Profession and the Common Law*, London: Hambledon, 1986d, 461–76.

429

——, 'The English legal profession, 1450–1550,' *The Legal Profession and the Common Law*, London: Hambledon, 1986e, 75–98.

——, 'The law merchant and the common law before 1700.' *The Legal Profession and the Common Law*, London: Hambledon, 1986f, 341–69.

——, 'New light on *Slade's Case*,' *The Legal Profession and the Common Law*, London: Hambledon, 1986g, 393–432.

——, 'Origins of the "doctrine" of consideration, 1535–1585,' *The Legal Profession and the Common Law*, London: Hambledon, 1986h, 367–91.

——, 'The refinement of English criminal jurisprudence, 1500–1848,' *The Legal Profession and the Common Law*, London: Hambledon, 1986i, 303–24.

——, 'Solicitors and the law of maintenance 1590–1640,' *The Legal Profession and the Common Law*, London: Hambledon, 1986j, 125–50.

——, 'The English law of sanctuary,' *Ecclesiastical Law Journal* 2 (1990a): 8–13.

——, *An Introduction to English Legal History*, 3rd edn, London: Butterworth, 1990b.

——, 'Famous English canon lawyers: Henry Swinburne,' *Ecclesiastical Law Journal* 3 (1993): 5–9.

Baker, J. H. and Milsom, S. F. C. *Sources of English Legal History: Private Law to 1750*, London: Butterworth, 1986.

Barker, Francis, and Hulme, Peter, 'Nymphs and reapers heavily vanish: the discursive con-texts of The Tempest,' *Alternative Shakespeares*, ed. John Drakakis, London: Methuen, 1985, 191–205.

Barnes, Thomas G. 'Star Chamber and the sophistication of the criminal law,' *Criminal Law Review* (1977): 316–26.

Barrett, D. S. 'Plautus, *Mostellaria* 630–32 and *The Merchant of Venice*,' *Classical Bulletin* 59 (1983): 60–2.

Barton, Anne, *Essays, Mainly Shakespearean*, Cambridge and New York: Cambridge University Press, 1994.

Barton, J. L. 'The medieval use,' *Law Quarterly Review* 81 (1965): 562–77.

——, 'The statute of uses and trusts of freeholds,' *Law Quarterly Review* 82 (1966): 215–25.

——, 'The rise of the fee simple,' *Law Quarterly Review* 92 (1976): 108–21.

Barton, J. L. and Plucknett, T. F. T. eds, *St German's Doctor and Student*, vol 91, London: Selden Society, 1975.

Barton, Sir Dunbar Plunket, *Links Between Shakespeare and the Law*, London: Faber & Gwyer, 1929.

Bate, Jonathan, ed. *Shakespeare, Titus Andronicus*, 3rd Arden edn, London: Routledge, 1995.

Bateson, Mary, ed. *Borough Customs II*, vol 21, London: The Selden Society, 1906.

Bawcutt, N. W. ' "He who the sword of heaven will bear": The Duke versus Angelo in *Measure for Measure*,' *Shakespeare Survey* 37 (1984): 89–97.

Bean, J. M. W. *The Decline of English Feudalism*, Manchester: Manchester University Press, 1968.

Bedwell, C. E. A. *A Brief History of the Middle Temple*, London: Butterworth, 1909.

Beier, A. L. 'Vagrants and the social order in Elizabethan England,' *Past & Present* 64 (1974): 2–29.

——, *Masterless Men: The Vagrancy Problem in England 1560–1640*, London: Methuen, 1985.

Bell, H. E. *An Introduction to the History and Records of the Court of Wards and Liveries*, Cambridge: Cambridge University Press, 1953.

Bellamy, John, *The Law of Treason in England in the Later Middle Ages*, Cambridge: Cambridge University Press, 1970.

——, *Crime and Public Order in England in the Later Middle Ages*, London: Routledge & Keegan Paul, 1973.

——, *The Tudor Law of Treason*, London: Routledge & Keegan Paul, 1979.

Belsheim, Edmund O. 'The old action of account,' *Harvard Law Review* 45 (1931): 466–500.

Bemiss, Samuel M. ed. *Three Charters of the Virginia Company of London with Seven Related Documents*, Williamsburg: Virginia 350th Anniversary Celebration Corporation, 1957.

Bennett, Robert B. 'The law enforces itself: Richard Hooker and the law against fornication in *Measure for Measure*,' *Shakespeare and Renaissance Association of West Virginia: Selected Papers* 16 (1993): 43–51.

Berger, Harry, Jr., 'Marriage and mercifixation in The Merchant of Venice: the casket scene revisited,' *Shakespeare Quarterly* 22 (1981): 155–62.

Berman, Harold J, 'The origins of historical jurisprudence: Coke, Selden, Hale,' *Yale Law Review* 103 (1994): 1651–738.

Bernthal, Craig A, 'Treason in the family: the trial of Thumpe v. Horner,' *Shakespeare Quarterly* 42 (1991): 44–54.

——, "Staging justice: James I and the trial scenes of *Measure for Measure*,' *SEL: Studies in English Literature, 1500–1900* 32 (1992): 247–69.

Berry, Herbert, 'Shylock, Robert Miles, and events at the Theatre,' *Shakespeare Quarterly* 44 (1993): 183–201.

Berry, Ralph, *Shakespeare and Social Class*, Atlantic Highlands: Humanities Press International, 1988.

Biancalana, Joseph, 'Widows at common law: the development of common law dower,' *Irish Jurist* 23 (1988): 255–329.

Bland, D. S. 'Shakespeare's legal language,' *Verbatim* 14 (1988): 11–13.

Blatcher, Marjorie, *The Court of King's Bench 1450–1550*, London: Athlone Press, 1978.

Boehrer, Bruce Thomas, 'Bestial buggery in A Midsummer Night's Dream,' *The Production of English Renaissance Culture*, ed. David Lee

Miller, Sharon O'Dair, and Harold Weber, Ithaca: Cornell University Press, 1994, 123–50.

Bolton, W. F. 'Ricardian Law Reports and *Richard II*,' *Shakespeare Studies* 20 (1988): 53–65.

Bonfield, Lloyd, *Marriage Settlements, 1601–1740: The Adoption of the Strict Settlement*, Cambridge: Cambridge University Press, 1983.

Boose, Lynda E. 'The father and the bride in Shakespeare,' *PMLA* 97 (1982): 325–47.

——, 'The comic contract and Portia's golden ring,' *Shakespeare Studies* 20 (1988): 241–54.

Bornstein, Diane, 'Trial by combat and official irresponsibility in *Richard II*,' *Shakespeare Studies* 8 (1976): 131–41.

Bowen, Catherine Drinker, *The Lion and the Throne: The Life and Times of Sir Edward Coke 1552–1634*, London: Hamish Hamilton, 1957.

Boyarsky, Saul, '"Let's kill all the lawyers": what did Shakespeare mean?' *Journal of Legal Medicine* 12 (1991): 571–4.

Bracton, *On the Laws and Customs of England*, trans, Samuel E. Thorne, ed. George E. Woodbine, Cambridge, MA: Harvard University Press, 1968.

Brand, Paul, 'The origins of the English legal profession,' *Law and History Review* 5 (1987): 31–50.

——, *The Origins of the English Legal Profession*, Oxford: Blackwell, 1992.

Braunmuller, A. R. '"Second means": agent and accessory in Elizabethan drama,' *The Elizabethan Theatre XI*, ed. A. L. Magnusson and C. E. McGee, Port Credit, Ontario: Meany, 1990, 177–203.

Breen, John, 'Gloucester's proclamation,' *Notes and Queries* 41 (1994): 493–4.

Brennan, Michael G. '"Now gods, stand up for bastards" (*King Lear*, I.II.22) and the Epistle to the Hebrews 12:5–8," *Notes and Queries* 37 (1990): 186–8.

Briggs, Robin, 'Witchcraft and popular mentality in Lorraine, 1580–1630,' *Occult and Scientific Mentalities in the Renaissance*, ed. Brian Vickers, Cambridge: Cambridge University Press, 1984, 337–49.

Britton, ed. Francis Morgan Nichols, Oxford: Clarendon Press, 1865.

Brodsky, Vivien, 'Widows in late Elizabethan London: remarriage, economic opportunity and family orientation,' *The World We Have Gained*, ed. Lloyd Bonfield, Richard M. Smith, and Keith Wrightson, Oxford: Basil Blackwell, 1986, 43–99.

Brooke, Christopher N. L. 'Marriage and society in the central middle ages,' *Marriage and Society: Studies in the Social History of Marriage*, ed. R. B. Outhwaite, London: Europa, 1981, 17–34.

Brooks, C. W. *Pettyfoggers and Vipers of the Commonwealth: The 'Lower Branch' of the Legal Profession in Early Modern England*, Cambridge: Cambridge University Press, 1986.

Brown, Paul R. '"This thing of darkness I acknowledge mine": The Tempest and the discourse of colonialism,' *Political Shakespeare*, ed. J. Dollimore and A. Sinfield, Manchester: Manchester University Press, 1985, 48–71.

Brundage, James A. *Law, Sex, and Christian Society in Medieval Europe*, Chicago: University of Chicago Press, 1987.

——, 'Widows as disadvantaged persons in medieval canon law,' *Upon my Husband's Death: Widows in the Literature and Histories of Medieval Europe*, ed. Louise Mirrer, Ann Arbor: University of Michigan Press, 1992, 193–206.

——, *Sex, Law and Marriage in the Middle Ages*, Aldershot: Variorum, 1993.

Bryson, W. H. 'Law reporting in England 1603–1660,' *Law Reporting in England*, ed. Chantal Stebbings, London: Hambledon, 1995, 113–22.

Buck, Andrew, 'Rhetoric and the law of property in early sixteenth century England,' *The Happy Couple: Law and Literature*, ed. J. Neville, Annadale NSW: the Federation Press, 1994, 14–24.

Bullard, J. V., ed. *Constitutions and Canons Ecclesiastical 1604: Latin and English*, London: The Faith Press, 1934.

Bullough, G., ed. *Narrative and Dramatic Sources of Shakespeare*, 8 vols, London: Routledge & Kegan Paul, 1975.

Burke, Peter, 'The comparative approach to European witchcraft,' *Early Modern European Witchcraft: Centers and Peripheries*, ed. Bengt Ankarloo and Guster Henningsen, Oxford: Clarendon Press, 1990, 434–41.

Butler, E. M. *The Myth of the Magus*, Cambridge: Cambridge University Press, 1948.

Cacicedo, Alberto, ' "She is fast my wife": sex, marriage, and ducal authority in *Measure for Measure*,' *Shakespeare Studies* 23 (1995): 187–209.

Caenegem, R. C. van, *The Birth of the English Common Law*, Cambridge: Cambridge University Press, 1973.

Callagan, Dympna, 'Wicked women in Macbeth: a study of power, ideology, and the production of motherhood,' *Reconsidering the Renaissance*, ed. Mario Di Cesare, Bingingham, New York: Medieval and Renaissance Texts and Studies, 1992, 355–69.

Campbell, John Lord, *Shakespeare's Legal Acquirements Considered*, London: John Murray, 1859.

Campbell, Ruth, 'Sentence of death by burning for women,' *The Journal of Legal History* 5 (1985): 44–59.

Campbell, Susie, ' "Is that the law?": Shakespeare's political cynicism in *The Merchant of Venice*,' *The Merchant of Venice*, ed. Linda Cookson and Bryan Loughrey, Harlow, Essex: Longman, 1992, 65–73.

Carlson, Cindy, 'Trials of marriage in *Measure for Measure*,' *Shakespeare Yearbook* 6 (1996): 355–81.

Carlson, Eric Josef, *Marriage and the English Reformation*, Oxford: Blackwell, 1994.

Carroll, William C. 'Language, politics, and poverty in Shakespearian drama,' *Shakespeare Survey* 44 (1991): 17–24.

——, ' "The Form of Law": ritual and succession in *Richard III*,' *True Rites and Maimed Rites: Ritual and Anti-Ritual in Shakespeare and his Age*, ed. Linda Woodbridge and Edward Berry, Urbana: University of Illinois Press, 1992, 203–19.

Cerasano, S. P. ' "Half a dozen dangerous words" ' *Gloriana's Face: Women, Public and Private, in the English Renaissance*, ed. Marion Wynne-Davies and S. P. Cerasano, Detroit: Wayne State University Press, 1992, 167–83.

Chambers, E. K. *William Shakespeare: A Study of Facts and Problems*, 2 vols, Oxford: Clarendon Press, 1930.

Cheadle, Brian, 'The "Process" of prejudice: *Othello* I.iii.128–45,' *Notes and Queries* 41 (1994): 491–3.

Chermely, Cynthia, 'Madness in Shakespearean England: an historical perspective,' *Shakespeare and Renaissance Association of West Virginia: Selected Papers* 12 (1987): 6–10.

Chesterman, Michael, *Charities, Trusts and Social Welfare*, London: Weidenfeld and Nicholson, 1979.

Clark, Stuart, 'Inversion, misrule and the meaning of witchcraft,' *Past & Present* 87 (1980): 98–127.

——, 'The scientific status of demonology,' *Occult and Scientific Mentalities in the Renaissance*, ed. Brian Vickers, Cambridge: Cambridge University Press, 1984, 351–74.

Clarkson, Paul S. and Warren, Clyde T. 'Copyhold tenure and Macbeth,' *Modern Language Notes* 55 (1940): 483–93.

——, *The Law of Property in Shakespeare and the Elizabethan Drama*, Baltimore: Johns Hopkins Press, 1942.

Cobbett, *Parliamentary History of England*, London: R. Bagshaw, 1806.

Cockburn, J. S. *A History of English Assizes*, Cambridge: Cambridge University Press, 1972.

——, 'Twelve silly men? the trial at assizes, 1560–1670,' *Twelve Good Men and True: The Criminal Trial in England, 1200–1800*, ed. J. S. Cockburn and Thomas A. Green, Princeton: Princeton University Press, 1988, 158–81.

Cohen, Derek, 'The politics of wealth: *Timon of Athens*,' *Neophilologus* 77 (1993): 149–60.

Cohen, Stephen A. ' "The quality of mercy": law, equity, and ideology in *The Merchant of Venice*,' *Mosaic* 27 (1994): 35–54.

Cohen, Walter, '*The Merchant of Venice* and the Possibilities of historical criticism,' *ELH* 49 (1982): 765–89.

Cohn, Norman, *Europe's Inner Demons: An Enquiry Inspired by the Great Witch-Hunt*, London: Sussex University Press, 1975.

Coke, Edward, *A Commentarie Upon Littleton (The First Part of the Institutes of the Lawes of England)*, London, 1628.

——, 'A reading on 27 Edward the First [or 27] reading[s] on fines,' *Three Law Tracts*, London: his Majesty's Law-Printer, 1764, 211–78.

——, *Second, Third, and Fourth Parts of the Institutes of the Laws of England*, 3 vols, London: E. and R. Brooke, 1797.

——, *The Reports*, 6 vols, London: Joseph Butterworth and Son, 1826.

Cook, Ann Jennalie, *The Privileged Playgoers of Shakespeare's London, 1576–1642*, Princeton: Princeton University Press, 1981.

——, *Making a Match: Courtship in Shakespeare and his Society*, Princeton: Princeton University Press, 1991.

Cornish, W. R. and Clark, G. de N. *Law and Society in England, 1750–1950*, London: Sweet and Maxwell, 1989.

Cowell, John, *The Interpreter*, Cambridge, 1607.

Crashawe, William, *A New-yeeres Gift to Virginia: A Sermon Preached in London before the Right Honourable the Lord Lawarre, Lord Gouernor and Captaine Generall of Virginia*, London, 1610a.

——, *A Sermon Preached in London before the Lord Lewarre, Lord Gouernor and Captaine Generall of Virginia Febr 21 1609*, London, 1610b.

Croft, Pauline, 'Wardship in the parliament of 1604,' *Parliamentary History* 2 (1983): 39–48.

Cummings, Brian, 'Swearing in public: More and Shakespeare,' *English Literary Renaissance* 27 (1997): 197–232.

Cunningham, Karen, 'Female fidelities on trial,' *Renaissance Drama* 25 (1994): 1–31.

Dawson, John P. 'Coke and Ellesmere disinterred: the attack on the Chancery in 1616,' *Illinois Law Review* 36 (1941): 127–52.

Day, Gillian, '"Determined to prove a villain": theatricality in *Richard III*,' *Critical Survey* 3 (1991): 149–56.

Demos, John Putnam, *Entertaining Satan: Witchcraft and the Culture of Early New England*, New York: Oxford University Press, 1982.

Denning, Alfred Thompson, *Leaves From my Library: An English Anthology*, London: Butterworth, 1986.

Denvir, John, 'William Shakespeare and the jurisprudence of comedy,' *Stanford Law Review* 39 (1987): 825–49.

Derrett, J. Duncan M. *Henry Swinburne (?1551–1624) Civil Lawyer of York*, Borthwick Papers no. 44, York: University of York Borthwick Institute of Historical Research, 1973.

DeVine, Stephen, 'Francisan friars, the feoffment to, uses, and canonical theories of property enjoyment before 1535,' *The Journal of Legal History* 10 (1989): 1–22.

Dickinson, John W. 'Renaissance equity in *Measure for Measure*,' *Shakespeare Quarterly* 13 (1962): 287–97.

Dolan, Frances E. 'Home rebels and house-traitors: murderous wives in early modern England,' *Yale Journal of Law and the Humanities* 4 (1992a): 1–31.

——, 'The subordinate('s) plot: petty treason and the forms of domestic rebellion,' *Shakespeare Quarterly* 43 (1992b): 317–40.

——, *Dangerous Familiars: Representations of Domestic Crime in England 1500–1700*, Ithaca: Cornell University Press, 1994.

Donaghue, Charles, 'The Canon Law on the formation of marriage and social practice in the later middle ages,' *Journal of Family History* 8 (1983): 144–58.

Draper, J. W. 'Shakespeare's rustic servants,' *Shakespeare Jahrbuch* 69 (1933): 87–101.

——, 'The theme of *Timon of Athens*,' *The Modern Language Review* 29 (1934): 20–31.

——, 'Usury in *The Merchant of Venice*,' *Modern Philology* 33 (1935): 37–47.

——, 'Ophelia's crime of felo de se,' *West Virginia Law Quarterly* 42 (1936): 228–34.

——, 'Robert Shallow, esq. J. P.' *Neuphilologische Mitteilungen* 38 (1937): 257–69.

——, 'Bastardy in Shakespeare's plays', *Shakespeare Jahrbuch* 74 (1938): 123–36.

——, 'Dogberry's due process of law,' *Journal of English and Germanic Philology* 42 (1943): 563–76.

Dummett, Ann and Nicol, Andrew, *Subjects, Citizens, Aliens and Others: Nationality and Immigration Law*, London: Weidenfeld and Nicolson, 1990.

Dunkel, Wilbur, 'Law and equity in *Measure for Measure*,' *Shakespeare Quarterly* 13 (1962): 275–85.

——, *William Lambard, Elizabethan Jurist*, New Brunswick, NJ: Rutgers University Press, 1965.

Edelman, Charles, *Brawl Ridiculous*, Manchester: Manchester University Press, 1992.

Elliott, Vivien Brodsky, 'Single women in the London marriage market: age, status and mobility, 1598–1619,' *Marriage and Society: Studies in the Social History of Marriage*, ed. R. B. Outhwaite, London: Europa, 1981, 81–100.

Elton, G. R. *England under the Tudors*, 2nd edn, London: Methuen, 1974.

Elton, William R. *King Lear and the Gods*, San Marino CA: The Huntington Library, 1966.

Empson, William, *The Structure of Complex Words*, London: Chatto & Windus, 1952.

Erickson, Amy Loiuse, *Women and Property in Early Modern England*, London: Routledge, 1993.

Ernst, D. R. 'The moribund appeal of death,' *American Journal of Legal History* 28 (1984): 164–88.

Eure, John D. 'Shakespeare and the legal process: four essays,' *Virginia Law Review* 61 (1975): 390–433.

Farrer, F. E. 'The bastard eigne,' *Law Quarterly Review* 33 (1917): 135–53.

Finch, Andrew J. 'Parental authority and the problem of clandestine marriage in the later middle ages,' *Law and History Review* 8 (1990): 189–204.

Findlay, Alison, *Illegitimate Power: Bastardy in English Renaissance Drama*, Manchester: Manchester University Press, 1994.

Flandrin, Jean-Louis, *Families in Former Times*, trans, Richard Southern, London: Cambridge University Press, 1979.

Fletcher, G. P. 'The metamorphosis of larceny,' *Harvard Law Review* 89 (1976): 469–530.

Floyd, John, *The Overthrow of the Protestant Pulpit-Babels, Particularly Confuting W. Crashaws Sermon*, St Omer, 1612.

Forbes, Thomas Roger, *The Midwife and the Witch*, New Haven: Yale University Press, 1966.

Fortescue, Sir John, *De Laudibus Legum Angliae*, ed. S. B. Chrimes, Cambridge: Cambridge University Press, 1949.

Frasure, Louise D. 'Shakespeare's rustic constables,' *Anglia* 46 (1934): 384–91.

Frazier, Harriet C. ' "Like a Liar Gone to Burning Hell": Shakespeare and dying declarations,' *Comparative Drama* 19 (1985): 166–80.

Gabel, Leona C. *Benefit of Clergy in England in the Later Middle Ages*, New York: Octagon Books, 1969.

Gillis, John R. *For Better, For Worse: British Marriages 1600 to the Present*, Oxford: Oxford University Press, 1985.

Ginzburg, Carlo, *The Night Battles: Witch and Agrarian Cults in the Sixteenth and Seventeenth Centuries*, trans John and Anne Tedeschi, 2nd edn, 1st edn 1966, London: Routledge & Kegan Paul, 1983.

Glanvill, *The Treatise on the Laws and Customs of the Realm of England Commonly Called Glanvill*, ed. G. D. G. Hall, Oxford: Clarendon Press, 1993.

Gleason, J. H. *The Justices of the Peace in England 1558–1640: A Later Eirenarcha*, Oxford: Clarendon Press, 1969.

Gohn, Jack Benoit, '*Richard II*: Shakespeare's legal brief on the royal prerogative and the succession to the throne,' *Georgetown Law Journal* 70 (1982): 943–73.

Gowing, Laura, *Domestic Dangers: Women, Words, and Sex in Early Modern London*, Oxford: Clarendon Press, 1996.

Gray, Charles, 'The boundaries of equitable function,' *American Journal of Legal History* 20 (1976): 192–226.

——, 'Reason, authority and imagination: the jurisprudence of Sir Edward Coke,' *Culture and Politics from Puritanism to the Enlightenment*, ed. Perez Zagorin, Berkeley: University of California Press, 1980, 25–66.

Gray, Robert, *A Good Speed to Virginia*, rpt of London, 1609, in *Early English*

Popular Literature, vol 2, ed. J. Payne Collier, London: privately published, 1864.

Green, Janet M. 'Earthly doom and heavenly thunder: judgment in *King Lear*,' *University of Dayton Review* 23 (1995): 63–73.

Green, Thomas, 'The jury and the English law of homicide 1200–1600,' *Michigan Law Review* 74 (1976): 414–99.

Green, Thomas A. *Verdict According to Conscience*, Chicago: University of Chicago Press, 1985.

——, 'A retrospective: on the criminal trial jury, 1200–1800,' *Twelve Good Men and True: The Criminal Trial in England, 1200–1800*, ed. J. S. Cockburn and Thomas A. Green, Princeton: Princeton University Press, 1988, 358–99.

Greenblatt, Stephen, 'Invisible bullets,' *Shakespearean Negotiations*, Oxford: Clarendon Press, 1988, 21–56.

Gregory, Annabel, 'Witchcraft, politics and good neighborhood in early 17th-century Rye,' *Past & Present* (1991): 31–66.

Grene, David, '*Measure for Measure*: Mythological history, reality, and the stage,' *Law and Philosophy: The Practice of Theory: Essays in Honor of George Anastaplo*, ed. John A. Murley, Robert L. Stone and William T. Brathwaite, vol 2, Athens: Ohio University Press, 1992, 871–85.

Groot, Roger D. 'The crime of rape temp. Richard 1 and John,' *The Journal of Legal History* 9 (1988a): 324–34.

——, 'The early thirteenth century criminal jury,' *Twelve Good Men and True: The Criminal Trial Jury in England, 1200–1800*, ed. J. S. Cockburn and Thomas A. Green, Princeton: Princeton University Press, 1988b, 3–35.

Gulley, Ervene, ' "Dressed in a little brief authority": law as theater in *Measure for Measure*,' *Law and Literature Perspectives*, ed. Bruce L. Rockwood, New York: Lang, 1996, 53–80.

Gulstad, William, 'Mock-trial or witch-trial in *King Lear*?' *Notes and Queries* 41 (1994): 494–7.

Guy, J. A. 'The early Tudor Star Chamber,' *Legal History Studies, 1972*, ed. Defydd Jenkins, Cardiff: University of Wales Press, 1975, 122–8.

——, 'The development of equitable jurisdictions, 1450–1550,' *Law, Litigants and the Legal Profession*, ed. E. W. Ives and A. H. Manchester, London: Royal Historical Society, 1983, 80–6.

Hake, Edward, *Epiekeia: A Dialogue on Equity in Three Parts*, ed. D. E. C. Yale, preface S. E. Thorne, from B. L. Add. 35362, c. 1603, London: Yale University Press, 1953.

Halio, Jay L. 'Portia: Shakespeare's Matlock?' *Cardozo Studies in Law and Literature* 5 (1993): 57–64.

Hamilton, Donna B. 'The state of law in *Richard II*,' *Shakespeare Quarterly* 34 (1983): 5–17.

——, *Shakespeare and the Politics of Protestant England,* Lousiville: University of Kentucky Press, 1992.

Hamilton, Marci A. 'The end of law,' *Cardozo Studies in Law and Literature* 5 (1993): 125–36.

Hammond, Paul, 'The argument of *Measure for Measure,*' *English Literary Renaissance* 16 (1986): 496–519.

Hanford, James Holly, 'Suicide in the plays of Shakespeare,' *PMLA* 27 (1912): 380–97.

Harding, A. *The Law Courts of Medieval England,* London: George Allen & Unwin Ltd., 1973.

Harding, Davis P. 'Elizabethan betrothal and Measure for Measure,' *Journal of English and Germanic Philology* 49 (1950): 139–58.

Harris, Anthony, *Night's Black Agents: Witchcraft and Magic in Seventeenth-Century English Drama,* Manchester: Manchester University Press, 1980.

Haskins, G. L. 'Extending the grasp of the dead hand: reflections on the origins of the rule against perpetuities,' *University of Pennsylvania Law Review* 126 (1977): 19–46.

Hayne, Victoria, 'Performing social practice: the example of *Measure for Measure,*' *Shakespeare Quarterly* 44 (1993): 1–29.

Heard, Franklin Fiske, *Shakespeare as a Lawyer,* Boston: Little Brown, 1883.

Helmholz, R. H. 'Bastary litigation in medieval England,' *American Journal of Legal History* 12 (1969): 360–83.

——, *Marriage Litigation in Medieval England,* Cambridge: Cambridge University Press, 1974.

——, 'Support orders, church courts, and the role of *filius nullius*: a reassessment of the common law,' *University of Virginia Law Review* 63 (1977): 431–48.

——, 'The early enforcement of uses,' *Columbia Law Review* 79 (1979): 1503–13.

——, 'Assumpsit and *fidei laesio,*' *Canon Law and the Law of England,* London: Hambledon, 1987a, 263–90.

——, 'Canon law and English common law,' *Canon Law and the Law of England,* London: Hambledon, 1987b, 1–19.

——, *Canon Law and the Law of England,* London: Hambledon, 1987c.

——, 'Canonists and standards of impartiality for papal judges delegate,' *Canon Law and the Law of England,* London: Hambledon, 1987d, 21–40.

——, 'Damages in actions for slander at common law,' *Law Quarterly Review* 103 (1987e): 624–38.

——, 'Debt claims and probate jurisdiction in historical perspective,' *Canon Law and the Law of England,* London: Hambledon, 1987f, 307–21.

——, 'Infantacide in the province of Canterbury during the fifteenth century,' *Canon Law and the Law of England,* London: Hambledon, 1987g, 157–68.

——, '*Legitim* in English legal history,' *Canon Law and the Law of England,*

London: Hambledon, 1987h, 247–62.

——, 'Usury and the medieval English Church Courts,' *Canon Law and the Law of England*, London: Hambledon, 1987i, 323–39.

——, *Roman Canon Law in Reformation England*, Cambridge: Cambridge University Press, 1990.

——, 'Married women's wills in later Medieval England,' *Wife and Widow in Medieval England*, ed. Sue Sheridan Walker, Ann Arbor: University of Michigan Press, 1993, 165–82.

Henderson, Edith G. 'Relief from bonds in English Chancery,' *American Journal of Legal History* 18 (1974): 298–306.

Henningsen, Gustav, *The Witches Advocate: Basque Witchcraft and the Spanish Inquisition 1609–1614*, Reno, NV: University of Nevada Press, 1980.

Herrup, Cynthia B. 'Law and morality in seventeenth century England,' *Past & Present* 106 (1985): 102–23.

——, *The Common Peace: Participation and the Criminal Law in Sevententh-Century England*, Cambridge: Cambridge University Press, 1987.

Hexter, J. H. 'Property, monopoly and Shakespeare's *Richard II*,' *Culture and Politics from Puritanism to the Enlightenment*, ed. Perez Zagorin, Berkeley: University of California Press, 1980, 1–24.

Higgons, Theophilus, *The Apology of Theophilus Higgons, Lately Minister, Now Catholique, Wherein The Letter of Sir Edward Hoby Knight Directed unto the Said T. H. and in Answer of his First Motive, is Modestly Examined and Clearly Rejected*, Roan, 1609a.

——, *The First Motive of T. H. Maister of Arts, and Lately Minister, to Suspect the Integrity of his Religion*, Douai, 1609b.

Hill, L. M. *Bench and Bureaucracy: the Public Career of Sir Julius Caesar 1580–1636*, Stanford: Stanford University Press, 1988.

Hinely, Jan Lawson, 'Bond priories in *The Merchant of Venice*,' *SEL: Studies in English Literature, 1500–1900* 20 (1980): 217–39.

Hinman, Charlton, *The First Folio of Shakespeare*, New York: W. W. Norton, 1968.

Hirshfield, Julius, 'Portia's judgment and German jurisprudence,' *Law Quarterly Review* 30 (1914): 167–74.

Hoby, Sir Edward, *A Letter to Mr. T. H. Late Minister: Now Fugitive*, London, 1609.

Holdsworth, Sir William, *A History of English Law*, 14 vols, London: Methuen, 1903– .

Holleran, James V. 'Maimed funeral rites in *Hamlet*,' *English Literary Renaissance* 19 (1989): 65–93.

Holmer, Joan Ozark, The Merchant of Venice*: Choice, Hazard, and Consequence*, Houndsmill: Macmillan, 1995.

Hotine, Margaret, 'Treason in *The Winter's Tale*,' *Notes and Queries* 30 (1983): 127–30.

——, '*Measure for Measure*: further contemporary notes,' *Notes and Queries* 37 (1990): 186–8.

Hotson, Leslie, *I, William Shakespeare*, London: Jonathan Cape, 1937.

Houlbrooke, Ralph A. *Church Courts and the People during the English Reformation*, Oxford: Oxford University Press, 1979.

——, *The English Family 1450–1700*, Harlow, Essex: Longman, 1984.

——, 'The making of marriage in mid-Tudor England: evidence from the records of matrimonial contract litigation,' *Journal of Family History* 10 (1985): 339–52.

Hudson, John, *The Formation of the English Common Law*, London: Longman, 1996.

Hunt, Maurice, 'Slavery, English servitude and *The Comedy of Errors*,' *English Literary Renaissance* 27 (1997): 29–56.

Hurstfield, Joel, *The Queen's Wards: Wardship and Marriage under Elizabeth I*, London: Longman's Green and Co., 1958.

Hutson, Lorna, *The Usurer's Daughter: Male Friendship and Fictions of Women in Sixteenth-Century England*, London: Routledge & Kegan Paul, 1994.

——, ' "Our old storehouse": Plowden's *Commentaries* and political conscious-ness in Shakespeare,' *Shakespeare Yearbook 7*, ed. Peter Davidhazi and Holger Klein, In Special Theme Section, The Law and Shakespeare, ed. B. J. Sokol, pp. 249–380, Lewistown, NY: Edwin Mellen Press, 1996, 249–73.

Ibbetson, David, 'Assumpsit and debt in the early sixteenth century: the origins of the indebitatus count,' *Cambridge Law Journal* 41 (1982): 42–61.

——, 'Law reporting in the 1590s,' *Law Reporting in England*, ed. Chantal Stebbings, London: Hambledon, 1995, 73–88.

Ingram, Martin, 'Spousals litigation in the English ecclesiastical courts, c.1350–c.1640,' *Marriage and Society: Studies in the Social History of Marriage*, ed. R. B. Outhwaite, London: Europa, 1981, 35–57.

——, 'The reform of popular culture?: Sex and marriage in early modern England,' *Popular Culture in Seventeenth-Century England*, ed. Barry Reay, Beckenham: Croom Helm, 1985, 129–65.

——, *Church Courts, Sex and Marriage in England, 1570–1640*, Cambridge: Cambridge University Press, 1987.

Ives, E. W. 'The law and the lawyers,' *Shakespeare Survey* 17 (1964): 73–86.

——, 'Shakespeare and history: divergencies and agreements,' *Shakespeare Survey* 38 (1985): 19–35.

James the First, *Daemonologie*, ed. G. B. Harrison, rpt of 1597, London: Bodley Head, 1924.

Jardine, Lisa, 'Cultural confusion and Shakespeare's learned heroines: "these are old paradoxes",' *Shakespeare Quarterly* 38 (1987): 1–18.

——, ' "No offence i' th' world": *Hamlet* and unlawful marriage,' *Uses of History: Marxism, Postmodernism, and the Renaissance*, ed. Francis Barker, Peter Hulme, and Margaret Iversen, Manchester and New York: Manchester University Press, 1991, 123–39.

Jenkins, Harold, ed. *Shakespeare, Hamlet*, 2nd Arden edn, London: Methuen, 1982.

Johnson, Robert, *Nova Britannia, Offering most Excellent fruites by Planting in Virginia*, London, 1609.

Jones, Eldred, *Othello's Countrymen: the African in English Renaissance Drama*, London: Oxford University Press, 1965.

Jones, Gareth, *History of the Law of Charity 1532–1827*, Cambridge: Cambridge University Press, 1969.

Jones, N. G. 'Uses, trusts and the path to privity,' *Cambridge Law Journal* 56 (1997): 175–200.

Jones, W. J. *The Elizabethan Court of Chancery*, Oxford: Clarendon Press, 1967.

Jordan, Constance, 'Contract and conscience in *Cymbeline*,' *Renaissance Drama* 25 (1994): 33–58.

Jordan, William Chester, 'Approaches to the court scene in the bond story: equity and mercy or reason and nature,' *Shakespeare Quarterly* 33 (1982): 49–59.

Jorgensen, Paul A. *Our Naked Frailties: Sensational Art and Meaning in Macbeth*, Berkeley: University of California Press, 1971.

Kantorowicz, Ernst H. *The King's Two Bodies: A Study in Medieval Political Theology*, Princeton: Princeton University Press, 1957.

Kaplan, M. Lindsay, 'Slander for slander in *Measure for Measure*,' *Renaissance Drama* 21 (1990): 23–54.

Kaplan, M. Lindsay and Eggert, Katherine, ' "Good queen, my lord, good queen": sexual slander and the trials of female authority in *The Winter's Tale*,' *Renaissance Drama* 25 (1994): 89–118.

Katz, David S. *The Jews in the History of England 1485–1850*, Oxford: Clarendon Press, 1994.

Kaye, J. M. 'Early history of murder and manslaughter,' *Law Quarterly Review* 83 (1967): 365–95; 569–601.

——, 'The making of English criminal law,' *Criminal Law Review* (1977): 4–13.

——, 'A note on the statute of enrollments,' *Law Quarterly Review* 104 (1988): 617–33.

Keeton, George W. *Shakespeare and his Legal Problems*, London: A. & C. Black, 1930.

——, *Shakespeare's Legal and Political Background*, London: Pitman, 1967.

Kelley, Donald R. 'History, English law and the Renaissance,' *Past & Present* 65 (1974): 24–51.

Kent, Joan, 'Attitudes of members of the House of Commons to regulation of personal conduct,' *University of London Bulletin of the Institute of Historical Research* 46 (1973): 41–71.

Kent, Joan R. *The English Village Constable 1580–1642: A Social and Administrative Study*, Oxford: Clarendon Press, 1986.

Kernan, Alvin B. *Shakespeare, the King's Playwright: Theater in the Stuart Court, 1603–1613*, New Haven and London: Yale University Press, 1995.

Kerr, Heather, 'Aaron's letter and acts of reading: the text as evidence in *Titus Andronicus*,' *AUMLA: Journal of the Australasian Universities Language and Literature Association* 77 (1992): 1–19.

Keymis, Lawrence, *A Relation of the Second Voyage to Guiana*, London, 1596.

Khanna, Urmilla, 'The use of proverbial phrases by Paulina in The Winter's Tale,' *Yearly Review* 2 (1988): 76–9.

Kieckhefer, Richard, *European Witch Trials: Their Foundations in Popular and Learned Culture, 1300–1500*, London: Routledge & Keegan Paul, 1976.

Kiralfy, A. K. *The Action on the Case*, London: Sweet & Maxwell, 1951.

Kiralfy, Albert, 'Taking the will for the deed: the medieval criminal attempt,' *The Journal of Legal History* 13 (1992): 95–9.

Kittridge, George Lyman, *Witchcraft in Old and New England*, reprint of 1929 Harvard University Press edn, New York: Atheneum, 1972.

Kliman, Bernice W. 'Isabella in *Measure for Measure*,' *Shakespeare Studies* 15 (1982): 137–148.

Knafla, Louis A., ed. *Law and Politics in Jacobean England: The Tracts of Lord Chancellor Ellesmere*, Cambridge: Cambridge University Press, 1977.

——, ' "Sin of all Sorts Swarmeth": criminal litigation in an English county in the early seventeenth century,' *Law, Litigants and the Legal Profession*, ed. E. W. Ives and A. H. Manchester, London: Royal Historical Society, 1983, 50–67.

Knight, W. Nicholas, 'Equity, *The Merchant of Venice* and William Lambarde,' *Shakespeare Survey* 27 (1974): 93–104.

——, 'Shakespeare before King James: betrayal and revelation,' *Iowa State Journal of Research* 62 (1988): 387–95.

Kornstein, Daniel J. 'Fie upon your law!' *Cardozo Studies in Law and Literature* 5 (1993): 35–56.

——, *Kill All the Lawyers: Shakespeare's Legal Appeal*, Princeton: Princeton University Press, 1994.

Kunze, Michael, *Highroad to the Stake: A Tale of Witchcraft*, Chicago: University of Chicago Press, 1982.

Lambard, William, *Eirenarcha: or the Offices of the Justices of the Peace*, London, 1582.

——, *The Duties of Constables Borsholders, Tithingmen and such other low Ministers of the Peace*, Facsimile, De Capo Press, Amsterdam, 1969, London, 1583.

——, *Archeion*, London, 1635.

Lander, J. R. *English Justices of the Peace 1461–1509*, Gloucester: Alan Sutton, 1989.

Langbein, John H. *Prosecuting Crime in the Renaissance*, Cambridge, MA: Harvard University Press, 1974.

——, *Torture and the Law of Proof*, Chicago: University of Chicago Press, 1977.

——, 'The criminal trial before the lawyers,' *University of Chicago Law Review* 45 (1978): 263–318.

Larkin, J. F., and Hughes, P. L. eds. *Stuart Royal Proclamations*, 2 vols, Oxford: Clarendon Press, 1973.

Larner, Christina, 'James the VI and I and witchcraft,' *The Reign of James the VI and I*, ed. Alan G. R. Smith, London: Macmillan, 1973, 74–90.

——, *Witchcraft and Religion: The Politics of Popular Belief*, Oxford: Basil Blackwell, 1984.

Laslett, Peter, *Family Life and Illicit Love in Earlier Generations: Essays in Historical Sociology*, Cambridge: Cambridge University Press, 1977.

——, *The World We Have Lost: Further Explored*, Revised, 1st edn 1965, London: Methuen, 1983.

Lathem, Agnes, ed. *Shakespeare, As You Like It*, 2nd Arden edn, London: Methuen & Co., 1975.

Laurence, Anne, *Women in England 1500–1760*, London: Weidenfeld and Nicolson, 1994.

Lawson, Peter, 'Property, crime and hard times in England 1559–1624,' *Law and History Review* 4 (1986): 95–127.

Lawson, P. G. 'Lawless juries? The composition and behavior of Hertfordshire juries, 1573–1624,' *Twelve Good Men and True: The Criminal Trial In England, 1200–1800*, ed. J. S. Cockburn and Thomas A. Green, Princeton: Princeton University Press, 1988, 117–57.

Lester, V. Markham, *Victorian Insolvency*, Oxford: Clarendon Press, 1995.

Levack, Brian P. *The Civil Lawyers in England 1603–1641*, Oxford: Clarendon Press, 1973.

——, 'The English civilians, 1500–1750,' *Lawyers in Early Modern Europe and America*, ed. Wilfred Prest, London: Croom Helm, 1981, 108–28.

Levin, Joel, 'The measure of law and equity: tolerance in Shakespeare's Vienna,' *Law and Literature Perspectives*, ed. Bruce L. Rockwood, New York: Lang, 1996, 193–207.

Levine, David and Wrightson, Keith, 'The social context of illegitimacy in early modern England,' *Bastardy and its Comparative History*, ed. Peter Laslett, Karla Oosterveen, and Richard M. Smith, London: Edward Arnold, 1980, 158–75.

Levine, Nina, 'Lawful symmetry: the politics of treason in *2 Henry VI*,' *Renaissance Drama* 25 (1994): 197–218.

Lindley, David, 'The stubborness of Barnadine: justice and mercy in *Measure for Measure,' Shakespeare Yearbook 7*, ed. Holger Klein and Peter Davidhazi, In Special Theme Section, The Law and Shakespeare, ed. B. J. Sokol, pp 249–380, Lewistown, NY: Edwin Mellen Press, 1996, 333–52.

Loengard, Janet Senderowitz, ' "Of the Gift of her Husband": English dower and its consequences in the year 1200,' *Women of the Medieval World*, ed. Julius Kirshner and Suzanne F. Wemple, Oxford: Basil Blackwell, 1985, 215–55.

——, '*Rationabilis dos*: Magna Carta and the widow's "fair share" in the earlier thirteenth century,' *Wife and Widow in Medieval England*, ed. Sue Sheridan Walker, Ann Arbor: University of Michigan Press, 1993, 59–80.

Lowenthal, David, 'The portrait of Athens in *A Midsummer Night's Dream*,' *Shakespeare's Political Pageant: Essays in Literature and Politics*, ed. Joseph Alulis and Vickie Sullivan, Lanham, MD: Rowman and Littlefield, 1996, 77–88.

McCabe, Richard A. *Incest, Drama and Nature's Law 1500–1700*, Cambridge: Cambridge University Press, 1993.

MacCulloch, Diarmaid, 'Bondmen under the Tudors,' *Law and Government Under the Tudors*, ed. Claire Cross, David Loades, and J. J. Scarisbrick, Cambridge: Cambridge University Press, 1988, 91–109.

McCune, Pat, 'Order and justice in early Tudor drama,' *Renaissance Drama* 25 (1994): 171–96.

McDonald, Marcia, 'The Elizabethan poor laws and the stage in the late 1590s,' *Medieval and Renaissance Drama in England* 7 (1995): 121–44.

Macdonald, Michael, 'Ophelia's maimed rites,' *Shakespeare Quarterly* 37 (1986): 309–17.

——, ed. *Witchcraft and Hysteria in Elizabethan London: Edward Jordan and the Mary Glover Case*, London: Tavistock Routledge, 1991.

Macfarlane, Alan, *The Family Life of Ralph Josselin: A Seventeenth Century Clergyman*, Cambridge: Cambridge University Press, 1970a.

——, *Witchcraft in Tudor and Stuart England*, London: Routledge & Kegan Paul, 1970b.

——, 'Review of *The Family, Sex and Marriage in England 1500–1800* by Lawrence Stone,' *History and Theory* 18 (1979): 103–26.

——, *Marriage and Love in England: Modes of Reproduction 1300–1840*, Oxford: Blackwell, 1986.

McFeely, Maureen Connolly, ' "This day my sister should the cloister enter": the convent as refuge in *Measure for Measure*,' *Subjects on the World Stage: Essays on British Literature of the Middle Ages and the Renaissance*, ed. David G. Allen and Robert A. White, Newark: University of Delaware Press, 1995, 200–16.

McGuire, Philip C. 'Egeus and the implications of silence,' *Shakespeare and the Sense of Performance: Essays in the Tradition of Performance Criticism in Honor of Bernard Beckerman*, ed. Ruth Thompson and Marvin Thompson, Newark: University of Delaware Press, 1989, 103–15.

445

McIlwain, Charles H., ed. *The Political Works of James I*, Cambridge MA: Harvard University Press, 1918.

McIlwain, Charles H. and Ward, Paul L., eds. *Lambarde's Archeion*, Cambridge MA: Harvard University Press, 1957.

MacKay, M. '*The Merchant of Venice*: a reflection of the early conflict between courts of law and courts of equity,' *Shakespeare Quarterly* 15 (1964): 371–375.

Maclean, Ian, *Interpretation and Meaning in the Renaissance: The Case of Law*, Cambridge: Cambridge University Press, 1992.

Maitland, F. W. *English Law and the Renaissance*, Cambridge: Cambridge University Press, 1901.

——, 'The deacon and the jewess; or, apostacy at common law,' *Collected Papers*, 3 vols, ed. H. A. L. Fisher, vol 1, Cambridge: Cambridge University Press, 1911a, 385–406.

——, 'The Shallows and Silences of real life,' *Collected Papers*, ed. H. A. L. Fisher, 3 vols, vol 1, Cambridge: Cambridge University Press, 1911b, 467–79.

——, *Equity, A Course of Lectures*, eds A. H. Chayton and W. J. Whittaker, rpt of 1909, Cambridge: Cambridge University Press, 1936.

Manning, Roger B. *Poachers and Hunters: a Cultural and Social History of Unlawful Hunting in England 1485–1640*, Oxford: Oxford University Press, 1993.

Marcus, Leah S. 'Cymbeline and the unease of topicality,' *The Historical Renaissance*, ed. Heather Dubrow and Richard Strier, Chicago: University of Chicago Press, 1988, 134–68.

Martin, Jill E. *Hanbury and Martin: Modern Equity*, London: Sweet & Maxwell, 1997.

Martin, Ruth, *Witchcraft and the Inquisition in Venice, 1550–1650*, Oxford: Basil Blackwell, 1989.

Merchant, W. Moelwyn, 'Lawyer and actor: process of law in Elizabethan drama,' *English Studies Today* 3 (1964): 107–24.

Meron, Theodor, 'Shakespeare's *Henry the Fifth* and the law of war,' *American Journal of International Law* 86 (1992): 1–45.

——, *Henry's Wars and Shakespeare's Laws: Perspectives on the Law of War in the Later Middle Ages*, Oxford: Clarendon Press, 1993.

Midlefort, H. C. Erik, *Witch Hunting in Southwestern Germany 1562–1684: The Social and Intellectual Foundations*, Stanford: Stanford University Press, 1972.

Milsom, S. F. C. *The Legal Framework of English Feudalism*, Cambridge: Cambridge University Press, 1976.

——, *Historical Foundations of the Common Law*, 2nd edn, London: Butterworths, 1981.

Mischo, John B. ' "That use is not forbidden usury": Shakespeare's procreation sonnets and the problem of usury,' *Subjects on the World Stage: Essays on British*

Literature of the Middle Ages and the Renaissance, ed. David G. Allen and Robert A. White, Newark: University of Delaware Press, 1995, 262–79.

Morgan, Victor, 'Whose prerogative in late sixteenth and early seventeenth century England?' *The Journal of Legal History* 5 (1984): 38–64.

Mowat, Barbara, 'Rogues, shepherds, and the counterfeit distressed: texts and infracontexts of The Winter's Tale 4.3,' *Shakespeare Studies* 22 (1994): 58–76.

Muchembled, Robert, *Popular Culture and Elite Culture in France, 1400–1750*, transl Linda Cochrane, from 1978 edn, Baton Rouge: Louisiana State University Press, 1985.

Muir, Kenneth, *The Sources of Shakespeare's Plays*, London: Methuen, 1972.

——, ed. *Macbeth*, The Arden Shakespeare, London: Methuen, 1977.

Mukherji, Subha, ' "Lawful deed': consummation, custom and law in *All's Well that Ends Well*,' *Shakespeare Survey* 49 (1996): 181–200.

Nagarajan, S. '*Measure for Measure* and Elizabethan betrothals,' *Shakespeare Quarterly* 14 (1963): 115–19.

Nass, Barry, 'The law and politics of treason in Shakespeare's *Lucrece*,' *Shakespeare Yearbook 7*, ed. Holger Klein and Peter Davidhazi, In Special Theme Section, The Law and Shakespeare, ed. B. J. Sokol, pp 249–380, Lewistown, NY: Edwin Mellen Press, 1996, 291–311.

Neale, J. E. *Queen Elizabeth*, London: Jonathan Cape, 1934.

——, *The Elizabethan House of Commons*, London: Fontana, 1976.

Neill, Michael, ' "In Everything Illegitimate": imagining the bastard in Renaissance drama,' *Yearbook of English Studies* 23 (1993): 270–92.

Nelson, T. G. A. ' "Impediments' in Shakespeare's sonnet 116,' *Parergon* 2 (1984): 185–9.

Newes from Scotland, ed. G. B. Harrison, rpt of 1591, London: Bodley Head, 1924.

Notestein, Wallace, *The History of Witchcraft in England from 1558 to 1718*, Reprint of Washington, 1911 edn, New York: Thomas Y. Crowell, 1968.

Oldrieve, Susan, 'Marginalized voices in "The Merchant of Venice".' *Cardozo Studies in Law and Literature* 5 (1993): 87–113.

Osborne, Bertram, *Justices of the Peace 1361–1848*, Shaftsbury Dorset: The Sedgehill Press, 1960.

Outhwaite, R. B. 'Introduction,' *Marriage and Society: Studies in the Social History of Marriage*, ed. R. B. Outhwaite, London: Europa, 1981, 1–16.

——, *Clandestine Marriage in England, 1500–1850*, London: Hambledon, 1995.

Parker, Patricia, 'Shakespeare and rhetoric: "dilation" and "delation" in *Othello*,' *Shakespeare and the Question of Theory*, ed. Patricia Parker and Geoffrey H. Hartman, New York and London: Methuen, 1985, 54–74.

447

Patterson, Annabel, *Censorship and Interpretation: The Conditions of Writing and Reading in Early Modern England*, Madison: University of Wisconsin Press, 1984.

——, *Shakespeare and the Popular Voice*, Oxford: Basil Blackwell, 1989.

——, ' "For Words only": from treason trial to liberal legend in early modern England,' *Yale Journal of Law and the Humanities* 5 (1993): 389–416.

Pearson, D'Orsay W. 'Witchcraft in The Winter's Tale: Paulina as "Alcahueta y un Poquito hechizera".' *Shakespeare Studies* 12 (1979): 195–210.

Pettet, E. C. '*The Merchant of Venice* and the problem of usury,' *Essays and Studies* 31 (1945): 19–33.

Phelps, Charles E. *Falstaff and Equity: An Interpretation*, Cambridge, MA: Houghton, Mifflin and Company, 1901.

Phillips, O. Hood, 'The law relating to Shakespeare 1564–1964,' *Law Quarterly Review* 80 (1967): 172–202.

——, *Shakespeare and the Lawyers*, London: Methuen, 1972.

Phillips, Roderick, *Putting Asunder: A History of Divorce in Western Society*, Cambridge: Cambridge University Press, 1988.

Plucknett, T. F. T. *A Concise History of the Common Law*, 5th edn, London: Butterworth, 1956.

Pocton, Edward, *The Winnowing of White Witchcraft*, British Library Sloan MS 1954: ff 161–93.

Pollock, Sir Frederick, 'A note on Shylock v. Antonio,' *Law Quarterly Review* 30 (1914): 175–7.

Pollock, Sir Frederick and Maitland, F. W., *The History of English Law Before the Reign of Edward I*, 2nd edn, reissued 1968, 2 vols, Cambridge: Cambridge University Press, 1898.

Poos, L. R. 'The heavy-handed marriage counsellor: regulating marriage in some later-medieval ecclesiastical-court jurisdictions,' *American Journal of Legal History* 39 (1995): 291–309.

Posner, Richard A. *Law and Literature: A Misunderstood Relation*, Cambridge MA and London: Harvard University Press, 1988.

Post, J. B. 'Ravishment of women and the statutes of Westminster,' *Legal Records and the Historian*, ed. J. H. Baker, London: Royal Historical Society, 1978, 150–60.

——, 'Equitable resorts before 1450,' *Law, Litigants and the Legal Profession*, ed. E. W. Ives and A. H. Manchester, London: Royal Historical Society, 1983, 68–79.

Powers, Alan, '*Measure for Measure* and law reform in 1604,' *The Upstart Crow* 15 (1996): 35–47.

Prest, Wilfred R. 'Legal education of the gentry 1560–1640,' *Past & Present* 38 (1967): 20–39.

——, *The Inns of Court under Elizabeth I and the Early Stuarts 1590–1640*, London: Longmans, 1972.

——, *The Rise of the Barristers: A Social History of the English Bar 1590–1640*, Oxford: Clarendon Press, 1986.

Quaife, G. R. *Wanton Wenches and Wayward Wives: Peasants and Illicit Sex in Early Seventeenth Century England*, London: Croom Helm, 1979.
——, *Godly Zeal and Furious Rage: The Witch in Early Modern Europe*, New York: St Martin's Press, 1987.

Ranald, Margaret Loftus, 'The betrothals of *Alls Well that Ends Well*,' *Huntington Library Quarterly* 26 (1963): 179–92.
——, 'As marriage binds and blood breaks: English marriage and Shakespeare,' *Shakespeare Quarterly* 30 (1979): 68–81.
——, *Shakespeare and His Social Context: Essays in Osmotic Knowledge and Literary Interpretation*, New York: AMS Press, 1987.
Rauchut, E. A. '"Guilty in Defence": a note on *Henry V*, 3.3.123,' *Shakespeare Quarterly* 42 (1991): 55–7.
——, 'Hotspur's prisoners and the laws of war in *1 Henry IV*,' *Shakespeare Quarterly* 45 (1994): 96–7.
Read, Conyers, *William Lambarde and Local Government*, Ithaca NY: Folger Shakespeare Library and Cornell University Press, 1962.
'Reasons against publishing the King's title to Virginia: a justification for planting Virginia,' *The Records of the Virginia Company of London*, ed. Susan Myra Kingsbury, Manuscript Bodleian Tanner XCIII, fol. 200, before 1609, vol 3, Washington: Library of Congress, 1906–35, 1–3.
Reynolds, Simon, 'The lawful name of marrying: contracts and stratagems in *The Merry Wives of Windsor*,' *Shakespeare Yearbook 7*, ed. Holger Klein and Peter Davidhazi. In Special Theme Section, The Law and Shakespeare, ed. B. J. Sokol, pp 249–380, Lewistown, NY: Edwin Mellen Press, 1996, 313–31.
Rockwood, Bruce L. 'Shylock the stranger: looking around for justice or, more than meets the eye,' *The Eyes of Justice: Seventh Round Table on Law and Semiotics*, ed. Roberta Kevelson, New York: Lang, 1994, 251–66.
Roscelli, William John, 'Isabella, sin and civil law,' *University of Kansas City Review* 28 (1962): 215–27.
Rose, Mary Beth, *The Expense of Spirit: Love and Sexuality in English Drama*, Ithaca: Cornell University Press, 1988.
Rosen, Barbara, *Witchcraft*, London: Edward Arnold, 1969.
Ross, Charles Stanley, 'Shakespeare's *Merry Wives* and the law of fraudulent conveyance,' *Renaissance Drama* 25 (1994): 145–69.
Routledge, R. A. 'The legal status of the Jews in England, 1190–1790,' *The Journal of Legal History* 3 (1982): 91–124.
Rowland, Robert, '"Fantasticall and Devilishe Persons": European witch-

beliefs in comparative perspective,' *Early Modern European Witchcraft: Centers and Peripheries*, ed. Bengt Ankarloo and Guster Henningsen, Oxford: Clarendon Press, 1990, 161–90.

Rudden, Bernard, 'For the first gravedigger,' *Law Quarterly Review* 100 (1984): 540–4.

Rushton, William Lowes, *Shakespeare's Testamentary Language*, London: Longman, Green and Co., 1869.

——, *Shakespeare's Legal Maxims*, Liverpool: Henry Young & Sons, 1907.

Russell, M. J. '1 Trial by battle and the writ of right,' *The Journal of Legal History* 1 (1980a): 111–33.

——, '2 Trial by battle and the appeals of felony,' *The Journal of Legal History* 1 (1980b): 135–64.

——, 'The champion's master in trial by battle,' *The Journal of Legal History* 5 (1985): 76–8.

St German, Christopher, *Doctor and Student*, 1523, first English editions c.1532, ed. T. F. T. Plucknett and J. L. Barton, vol 91, London: Selden Society, 1975.

Saunders, Henry, 'Staple courts in *The Merchant of Venice*,' *Notes and Queries* 31 (1984): 190–1.

Sayre, Francis Bowes, '*Mens rea*,' *Harvard Law Review* 45 (1932): 974–1026.

Scarisbrick, J. J. *Henry VIII*, Harmondsworth: Penguin Books, 1974.

Schalkwyk, David, ' "A lady's 'verily' is as potent as a lord's" – women, word and witchcraft in The Winters Tale,' *English Literary Renaissance* 22 (1992): 242–72.

Schanzer, Ernest, 'Marriage contracts in Measure for Measure,' *Shakespeare Survey* 13 (1960): 81–9.

Schoenbaum, S. *William Shakespeare: A Compact Documentary Life*, rpt of Oxford University Press edn, 1977, New York: New American Library, 1986.

Schotz, Amiel, 'The law that never was: a note on *The Merchant of Venice*,' *Theatre Research International* 16 (1991): 249–52.

Schreiber-McGee, F. ' "The view of earthly glory": visual strategies and the issue of royal prerogative in *Henry VIII*,' *Shakespeare Studies* 20 (1988): 191–200.

Scot, Reginald, *The Discovery of Witchcraft*, 1584, ed. Brinsley Nicholson, rpt of 1886, London: E. Stock, Wakefield, Yorkshire: E. P. Publishing, 1973.

Scott, Margaret, ' "Our city's institutions': some further reflections on the marriage contracts in *Measure for Measure*,' *ELH* 49 (1982): 790–804.

Scouten, Arthur, 'An historical approach to *Measure for Measure*,' *Philological Quarterly* 54 (1975): 68–84.

Selden Society, *A Centenary Guide to the Publications of the Selden Society*, London: The Selden Society, 1987.

450

Sharpe, C. K. *A Historical Account of the Belief in Witchcraft in Scotland*, Glasgow: Thomas D. Morrison, 1884.

Sharpe, J. A. *Defamation and Sexual Slander in Early Modern England: The Church Courts at York*, Borthwick Papers No. 58, York: University of York Borthwick Institute of Historical Research, 1980.

——, 'Witchcraft and women in seventeenth century England: some northern evidence,' *Continuity and Change* 6 (1991): 179–99.

——, *Witchcraft in Seventeenth Century Yorkshire: Accusations and Counter Measures*, York: University of York, 1992.

Sharpe, Kevin and Brooks, Christopher, 'History, English law and the Renaissance,' *Past & Present* 72 (1976): 133–42.

Sheehan, Michael M. *Marriage, Family, and Law in Medieval Europe: Collected Studies*, Toronto: University of Toronto Press, 1996.

Shorter, Edward, *The Making of the Modern Family*, London: Collins, 1976.

Simon, Sir Jocelyn, 'Dr. Cowell,' *Cambridge Law Journal* 26 (1968a): 260–72.

——, 'Shakespeare's legal and political background,' *Law Quarterly Review* 84 (1968b): 33–47.

Simpson, A. W. B. 'The penal bond with conditional defeasance,' *Law Quarterly Review* 82 (1966): 392–422.

——, 'The early constitution of the Inns of Court,' *Cambridge Law Journal* 28 (1970): 241–56.

——, *A History of the Common Law of Contract*, Oxford: Clarendon Press, 1975.

——, *A History of the Land Law*, 2nd edn, Oxford: Clarendon Press, 1986.

——, 'The common law and legal theory,' *Legal Theory and Legal History*, London: Hambledon, 1987a, 359–82.

——, 'Entails and perpetuities,' *Legal Theory and Legal History*, London: Hambledon, 1987b, 143–62.

——, 'The introduction of the action on the case for conversion,' *Legal Theory and Legal History*, London: Hambledon, 1987c, 93–109.

——, 'The rise and fall of the legal treatise: legal principles and the forms of legal literature,' *Legal Theory and Legal History*, London: Hambledon, 1987d, 273–320.

——, 'The survival of the common law system,' *Legal Theory and Legal History*, London: Hambledon, 1987e, 383–402.

Sisson, C. J. *Shakespeare's Tragic Justice*, London: Methuen & Co., 1963.

Slack, Paul, *Poverty and Policy in Tudor and Stuart England*, London: Longman, 1988.

——, *The English Poor Law 1531–1782*, London: Macmillan, 1990.

Slights, Camille Wells, 'In defense of Jessica: the runaway daughter in *The Merchant of Venice*,' *Shakespeare Quarterly* 31 (1980): 357–68.

——, 'Slaves and subjects in *Othello*,' *Shakespeare Quarterly* 48 (1997): 377–90.

451

Smith, Bruce R. *Homosexual Desire in Shakespeare's England: A Cultural Poetics,* Chicago: University of Chicago Press, 1991.

Smith, Lacey Baldwin, 'English treason trials and confessions in the sixteenth century,' *The Journal of the History of Ideas* 15 (1954): 471–98.

Smith, Richard M. 'Marriage processes in the English past: some continuities,' *The World We Have Gained,* ed. Lloyd Bonfield, Richard M. Smith, and Keith Wrightson, Oxford: Basil Blackwell, 1986, 43–99.

Sokol, B. J. 'A Spenserian idea in The Taming of the Shrew,' *English Studies* 66 (1985): 310–16.

——, 'Figures of repetition in Sidney's Astrophil and Stella and in the scenic form of Measure for Measure,' *Rhetorica* 9 (1991): 131–46.

——, 'The Merchant of Venice and the law merchant,' *Renaissance Studies* 6 (1992): 60–7.

——, 'The Tempest, "all torment trouble, wonder and amazement": a Kleinian reading,' *The Undiscover'd Country,* ed. B. J. Sokol, London: Free Association Books, 1993, 179–216.

——, *Art and Illusion in The Winter's Tale,* Manchester: Manchester University Press, 1994a.

——, 'Numerology in the time scheme of The Tempest,' *Notes and Queries* 41 (1994b): 53–5.

——, 'The problem of assessing Thomas Harriot's a briefe and true report of his discoveries in North America,' *Annals of Science* 51 (1994c): 1–15.

——, 'Constitutive signifiers or fetishes in *The Merchant of Venice?'* *International Journal of Psycho-Analysis,* 76 (1995a): 373–87.

——, 'Macbeth and the social history of witchcraft,' *Shakespeare and History,* ed. Holger Klein and Roland Wymer, *Shakespeare Yearbook 6,* Lewistown NY: Edwin Mellen Press, 1995b, 245–74.

——, 'Prejudice and law in The Merchant of Venice,' *Shakespeare Survey 51,* ed. Stanley Wells, Cambridge: Cambridge University Press, 1998, 159–73.

Sokol, B. J. and Sokol, Mary, 'The Tempest and legal justification of plantation in Virginia,' *Shakespeare Yearbook 7,* ed. Holger Klein and Peter Davidhazi. In Special Theme Section, The Law and Shakespeare, ed. B. J. Sokol, pp 249–380, Lewistown, NY: Edwin Mellen Press, 1996, 353–80.

——, 'Legal terms implying extended meanings in *As You Like It* III.ii.331–2 and *Troilus and Cressida* III.ii.89–91,' *Notes and Queries* 46 (1999a): 236–8.

——, 'Shakespeare and the English equity jurisdiction: *The Merchant of Venice* and the two texts of *King Lear,'* *Review of English Studies* 50 (1999b): 427–49.

Spencer, Janet M. 'Princes, pirates, and pigs: criminalizing wars of conquest in *Henry V,'* *Shakespeare Quarterly* 47 (1996): 160–77.

Spenser, Edmund, *Minor Poems,* ed. E. de Selincourt, 1910, Oxford: Clarendon Press, 1966.

Spinosa, Charles D. 'Shylock and debt and contract in "The Merchant of Venice".' *Cardozo Studies in Law and Literature* 5 (1993): 65–85.

——, 'The transformation of intentionality: debt and contract in *The Merchant of Venice*,' *English Literary Renaissance* 24 (1994): 370–409.

——, '"The name and all th' addition": *King Lear*'s opening scene and the common-law use,' *Shakespeare Studies* 23 (1995): 146–86.

Spinrad, Phoebe S. 'Dogberry hero: Shakespeare's comic constables in their communal context,' *Studies in Philology* 89 (1992): 161–78.

Spring, Eileen, *Law, Land and Family: Aristocratic Inheritance in England 1300–1800*, Chapel Hill and London: The University of North Carolina Press, 1993.

Squibb, G. D. *Doctor's Commons: A History of Advocates and Doctors of Law*, Oxford: Clarendon Press, 1977.

Srigley, Michael, 'Hamlet, "the law of writ," and the universities,' *Studia Neophilologica* 66 (1994): 35–46.

Stephen, Sir James Fitzjames, *A History of the Criminal Law of England*, vol 3, London: Macmillan, 1883.

Stewart, J. I. M. *Character and Motive in Shakespeare*, London: Longman Green, 1949.

Stone, Lawrence, *The Crisis of the Aristocracy, 1558–1641*, revised, originally 1965, Oxford: Clarendon Press, 1979a.

——, *The Family, Sex and Marriage in England 1500–1800*, London: Weidenfeld and Nicolson, 1979b.

——, *Road to Divorce: England 1530–1987*, Oxford: Oxford University Press, 1990.

——, *Broken Lives: Separation and Divorce in England 1660–1857*, Oxford: Oxford University Press, 1993.

Strachey, William, 'Lawes divine, morall and martiall, &c, for the colony Virginea Britannia,' *Tracts and Other Papers*, ed. Peter Force, rpt of London, 1612, vol 3 no. 2, Washington: Wm Q. Force, 1844, 1–68.

——, *The History of Travell into Virginia Britania*, ms. presented to the Earl of Northumberland, written 1609–12, ed. Louis B. Wright and Virginia Freund, London: Hakluyt Society, 1953.

Summerson, H. R. T. 'The early development of *peine fort et dure*,' *Law, Litigants and the Legal Profession*, ed. E. W. Ives and A. H. Manchester, London: Royal Historical Society, 1983, 116–25.

Sutton, Teresa, 'The deodand,' *The Journal of Legal History* 18 (1997): 44–55.

Swain, J. T. 'The Lancashire witch trials of 1612 and 1634 and the economics of witchcraft,' *Northern History* 30 (1994): 64–85.

Swinburne, Henry, *A Briefe Treatise of Testaments and Last Willes*, London, 1590.

——, *A Treatise on Spousals or Matrimonial Contracts*, London, 1686.

Taft, Edmund M. 'The failure of accommodation in *2 Henry 4*,' *Shakespeare and Renaissance Association of West Virginia: Selected Papers* 18 (1995): 90–103.

Tawney, R. H., ed. *Thomas Wilson, A Discorse Upon Usury (1572)*, London: G. Bell, 1925.

Taylor, Mark, *Shakespeare's Darker Purpose: A Question of Incest*, New York: AMS Press, 1982.

Tedeschi, J. 'The question of magic and witchcraft in two unpublished inquisitorial manuals of the seventeenth century,' *Proceedings of the American Philosophical Society* 131 (1987): 92–111.

Thomas, G. W. 'James I, equity and Lord Keeper John Williams,' *English Historical Review* 91 (1976): 506–28.

Thomas, Keith, *Religion and the Decline of Magic*, rpt of 1971 Weidenfeld & Nicolson edn, Harmondsworth: Penguin, 1978.

——, *Man and the Natural World: Changing Attitudes in England 1500–1800*, London: Allen Lane, 1983.

Thompson, Ann, 'Shakespeare and sexuality,' *Shakespeare Survey* 46 (1994): 1–8.

Thorne, S. E., ed. *A Discourse upon the Exposicio & Understanding of Statutes With Sir Thomas Egerton's Additions*, San Marino CA: Huntington Library, 1942.

——, 'English feudalism and estates in land,' *Cambridge Law Journal* 17 (1959): 193–209.

——, 'Courts of record and Sir Edward Coke,' *Essays in English Legal History*, London: Hambledon, 1985a, 243–68.

——, 'Dr. Bonham's case,' *Essays in English Legal History*, London: Hambledon, 1985b, 269–78.

——, 'The early history of the Inns of Court with special reference to Gray's Inn,' *Essays in English Legal History*, ed. S. E. Thorne, London: The Hambledon Press, 1985c, 137–54.

——, 'English law and the Renaissance,' *Essays in English Legal History*, London: Hambledon, 1985d, 187–95.

——, 'The equity of statute and Heydon's case,' *Essays in English Legal History*, London: Hambledon, 1985e, 155–70.

——, 'Praemunire and Sir Edward Coke,' *Essays in English Legal History*, London: Hambledon, 1985f, 239–42.

——, 'Sir Edward Coke 1552–1952,' *Essays in English Legal History*, London: Hambledon, 1985g, 223–38.

——, 'Sovereignty and the conflict of laws,' *Essays in English Legal History*, London: Hambledon, 1985h, 171–85.

——, 'Tudor social transformation and legal change,' *Essays in English Legal History*, London: Hambledon, 1985i, 197–210.

Thurston, Herbert, 'The canon law of the divorce,' *English Historical Review* 19 (1904): 632–45.

A True and Sincere Declaration of the Purpose and Ends of the Plantation begun in Virginia, London, 1610.

'A true declaration of the estate of the colony of Virginia,' *Tracts and Other*

Papers, ed. Peter Force, rpt London, 1610, vol 3, no. 1, Washington: Wm Q. Force, 1844, 1–27.

Tucker, E. F. J. 'The letter of the law in *The Merchant of Venice*,' *Shakespeare Studies* 29 (1976): 93–101.

Usher, R. G. 'James I and Sir Edward Coke,' *English Historical Review* 18 (1903): 664–75.

Van Patten, Jonathan K. 'Magic, prophesy, and the law of treason in Reformation England,' *American Journal of Legal History* 27 (1983): 1–32.

Virginia Council, 'Instructions orders and constitutions to Sir Thomas Gates Knight Governor of Virginia,' *The Records of the Virginia Company of London*, ed. Susan Myra Kingsbury, Ashmolian Manuscript 1147, fol. 175–90a, May 1609, vol 3, Washington: Library of Congress, 1906–35a, 12–24.

——, 'Instructions orders and constitutions to Sir Thomas West Knight Lo: La Warr,' *The Records of the Virginia Company of London*, ed. Susan Myra Kingsbury, Ashmolian Manuscript 1147, fol. 191–205a, 1609/10 (?). vol 3, Washington: Library of Congress, 1906–35b, 24–9.

Walker, Sue Sheridan, 'Wrongdoing and compensation: the pleas of wardship in thirteenth and fourteenth century England,' *The Journal of Legal History* 9 (1988): 267–307.

——, 'Litigation as personal quest: suing for dower in the royal courts, circa 1272–1350,' *Wife and Widow in Medieval England*, ed. Sue Sheridan Walker, Ann Arbor: University of Michigan Press, 1993, 81–108.

Ward, Ian, *Law and Literature: Possibilities and Perspectives*, Cambridge and New York: Cambridge University Press, 1995.

——, 'The political context of Shakespeare's constitutionalism,' *Shakespeare Yearbook 7*, ed. Holger Klein and Peter Davidhazi. In Special Theme Section, The Law and Shakespeare, ed. B. J. Sokol, pp 249–380, Lewistown, NY: Edwin Mellen Press, 1996, 275–90.

——, 'Issues of kingship and governance in *Richard II*, *Richard III* and *King John*,' *Shakespeare Yearbook 8*, ed. Holger Klein and Dimiter Daphinoff, Lewistown, NY: Edwin Mellen Press, 1997, 403–29.

Ward, Jennifer, *Women of the English Nobility and Gentry, 1066–1500*, Manchester: Manchester University Press, 1995.

Watkin, Thomas Glyn, 'Feudal theory, social needs and the rise of the heritable fee,' *Cambrian Law Review* 10 (1979): 39–62.

——, 'Hamlet and the law of homicide,' *Law Quarterly Review* 100 (1984): 282–310.

Weisberg, Richard, *Poethics and Other Strategies of Law and Literature*, New York: Columbia University Press, 1992.

Weisman, Richard, *Witchcraft, Magic and Religion in 17th-Century Massachusetts*, Amherst: University of Massachusetts Press, 1984.

Wells, Stanley and Taylor, Gary, eds. *William Shakespeare: The Complete Works*, Electronic edition, Oxford: Oxford University Press, 1989.

Wenterdorf, Karl, 'The marriage contracts in *Measure for Measure*: a reconsideration,' *Shakespeare Survey* 32 (1979): 129–44.

West, Robert Hunter, *The Invisible World: A Study of Pneumatology in Elizabethan Drama*, Athens: University of Georgia Press, 1939.

——, *Reginald Scot and Renaissance Writings on Witchcraft*, Boston: Twayne, 1984.

West, William, *The Second Part of Symboleography . . . Whereunto is annexed another Treatise of Equitie*, London, 1601.

Weyer, Johann, *De praestigiis daemonum*, 1583 edn, trans, John Shea, Bingingham, NY: Medieval and Renaissance Texts and Studies, 1991.

White, Edward J. *Commentaries on the Law in Shakespeare: With Explanations of the Legal Terms Used in the Plays, Poems, and Sonnets and a Consideration of the Criminal Types Presented, Also a Full Discussion of the Bacon-Shakespeare Controversy*, Littleton, CO: Rothman, 1987.

White, R. S. *Natural Law in English Renaissance Literature*, Cambridge: Cambridge University Press, 1996.

White, Stephen D. 'English feudalism and its origins,' *American Journal of Legal History* 19 (1975): 138–55.

Whittick, Christopher, 'The role of the criminal appeal in the fifteenth century,' *Law and Social Change* (1984): 55–72.

Widmayer, Martha, 'Mistress Overdone's house,' *Subjects on the World Stage: Essays on British Literature of the Middle Ages and the Renaissance*, ed. David G. Allen and Robert A. White, Newark: University of Delaware Press, 1995, 181–99.

Wiggins, Martin, '*Macbeth* and premeditation,' *The Arts, Literature, and Society*, ed. Arthur Marwick, London and New York: Routledge, 1990, 23–47.

Williamson, Marilyn L. *The Patriarchy of Shakespeare's Comedies*, Detroit: Wayne State University Press, 1986.

Wilson, Luke, '*Hamlet*: equity, intention, performance,' *Studies in the Literary Imagination* 24 (1991): 91–113.

——, '*Hamlet*, Hales v. Petit, and the hysteresis of action,' *ELH* 60 (1993): 17–55.

——, 'Promissory performances,' *Renaissance Drama* 25 (1994): 59–87.

Wilson, Richard, 'The quality of mercy: discipline and punishment in Shakespeare,' *The Seventeenth Century* 5 (1990): 1–42.

——, *Will Power: Essays on Shakespearean Authority*, London: Harvester Wheatsheaf, 1993.

Windolph, F. Lyman, *Reflections of the Law in Literature*, Philadelphia: University of Pennsylvania Press, 1956.

Wrightson, Keith, 'The nadir of English illegitimacy in the seventeenth century,' *Bastardy and its Comparative History*, ed. Peter Laslett, Karla Oosterveen and Richard M. Smith, London: Edward Arnold, 1980, 176–91.

——, *English Society 1500–1680*, London: Hutchinson, 1982.

——, 'Two concepts of order: justices, constables and jurymen in seventeenth-century England,' *An Ungovernable People: The English and their Law in the Seventeenth and Eighteenth Centuries*, ed. John Brewer and John Styles, London: Hutchinson, 1983, 21–46.

Wymer, Rowland, *Suicide and Despair in Jacobean Drama*, New York: St Martin's Press, 1986.

Yaffe, Martin D. *Shylock and the Jewish Question*, London: Johns Hopkins University Press, 1997.

Yale, D. E. C. 'Equitable estates in the seventeenth century: an explanation by Lord Nottingham,' *Cambridge Law Journal* 15 (1957): 72–86.

——, ed. *Lord Nottingham's 'Manual of Chancery Practice' and 'Prolegomena of Chancery and Equity'*, Cambridge: Cambridge University Press, 1965.

Young, R. V. '*King Lear* and natural law,' *Vera Lex* 13 (1990): 9–11.

INDEX

SHAKESPEARE PASSAGES, SCENES, WORKS

459

460

LEGAL TERMS AND CONCEPTS

abjuration — Outlawry/Banishment/Exile, discussed in Approve, Branded, Murder/Homicide, Pardon/Clemency, Press[Ing] to Death, Sanctuary

[to] account — Audit/Account, *see under* **debt** discussed in Executors

action of account — Audit/Account

actions on the case — On the Case, Trespass

alms — discussed in Poverty/Beggary

appeal of felony — discussed in Appeal, Approve, Felon/Felony, Murder/Homicide, Pardon/Clemency, Rape, Sanctuary, Treason, *see also under* **High Constable**

appeal of treason — discussed in Bills, Lists, Treason, *see also under* **High Constable**

apprentice — Apprenticehood, Prentice, discussed in Indenture, Lists, Treason, Usury/Interest

apprentice-at-law — Lawyers

assize — discussed in Justices/Justicers

assault — discussed in Battery

assumpsit — discussed in On the Case and Debt, *see under* **Contract**

attainture — discussed in Inheritance, Subcontracted, Treason

attorney — Attorney, discussed in Lawyers, *see under* **Lawyers**

audit — Audit/Account, *see under* **debt** discussed in Executors

bar — Bar, Inns of Court, Lawyers

bargain and sale — Bargain And Sale, *see under* **conveyancing**

bastard — Bastard/Bastardy, discussed in Impediments, Leet, Lists, Rape, Villein

battery — Battery

489

493